Chicago Sociology

Chicago Sociology

Jean-Michel Chapoulie

Foreword by William Kornblum

Translated by Caroline Wazer

Columbia University Press

New York

Columbia University Press gratefully acknowledges the generous support for this book
provided by Publisher's Circle member Harriet Zuckerman.

Columbia University Press
Publishers Since 1893
New York   Chichester, West Sussex
cup.columbia.edu
First published in French as *La tradition sociologique de Chicago, 1892–1961*
by Jean-Michel Chapoulie
© 2001 Editions du Seuil
English translation copyright © 2020 Columbia University Press
All rights reserved
Library of Congress Cataloging-in-Publication Data
Names: Chapoulie, Jean-Michel, author. | Wazer, Caroline, translator.
Title: Chicago sociology / Jean-Michel Chapoulie; foreword
by William Kornblum; translated by Caroline Wazer.
Other titles: Tradition sociologique de Chicago. English
Description: 1 Edition. | New York City : Columbia University Press, 2020. |
Includes bibliographical references and index.
Identifiers: LCCN 2019054948 | ISBN 9780231182508 (hardback) |
ISBN 9780231182515 (trade paperback) | ISBN 9780231544207 (ebook)
Subjects: LCSH: Chicago school of sociology.
Classification: LCC HM463 .C4313 2020 | DDC 301.0977/311—dc23
LC record available at https://lccn.loc.gov/2019054948

Cover image: Magnum Photos © Henri Cartier-Bresson, Chicago,
Illinois, USA, 1947
Cover design: Chang Jae Lee

Contents

PART II
Paths of Research

Foreword

WILLIAM KORNBLUM, EMERITUS PROFESSOR OF SOCIOLOGY
GRADUATE CENTER, CITY UNIVERSITY OF NEW YORK

I n the French-speaking world, Jean-Michel Chapoulie's analysis of the Chicago sociological tradition has been essential reading since it first appeared in 1998. The fascination among French and other European social scientists for the "Chicago School" has a history that begins with Maurice Halbwachs in the thirties and continues to the present day. Until publication of this welcome translation, however, few English readers had the opportunity to understand how that fascination emerges from the work of the Chicago sociologists themselves.

In the 1980s, Chapoulie was one of a few French sociologists who traveled to Chicago and elsewhere in North America. They wanted to see for themselves what the dominant departments of sociology might have to offer in their efforts to develop the discipline in France. The insistence on empirical research in replicable urban situations, the essential core of the Chicago sociological tradition, promised to liberate French sociology from the constraints of philosophy and armchair speculation. They met with Howard Becker, Everett Hughes, Morris Janowitz, Lyn Lofland, Sherri Cavan, Herb Gans, Erving Goffman, Anselm Strauss, and other living bearers of the Chicago tradition, including myself. In Chicago, Chapoulie formed an enduring friendship with Howie Becker that he gratefully acknowledges, along with his thanks to Arlene Kaplan Daniels, who mentored him during his stay in Chicago. The messages and examples Chapoulie and others brought back from Chicago have had lasting positive effects on French empirical sociology, and the pragmatic underpinnings of the Chicago tradition are a lively subject in contemporary French social scientific thought.

Chapoulie's immensely scholarly reading of the Chicago sociologists between 1920 and 1960 should take its place with seminal works on the Chicago tradition, notably by Martin Bulmer, Mary Jo Deegan, and Andrew Abbott. Perhaps Chapoulie's most important contribution is his critical review of many of the classics of the Chicago urban literature and particularly his questioning of the term "Chicago School," which he would rather classify as a tradition. "It is . . . not a single, clearly identifiable 'Chicago School' " that emerges from this inquiry, he writes, "but works that exist within networks of exchanges and borrowings between researchers." These networks and borrowings are carefully traced out in chapters on the original contribution of W. I. Thomas, on the race relations research sponsored by Park, by in-depth commentaries on the work of the pioneering African American sociologists, especially Charles Johnson and E. Franklin Frazier, and on the less central but enlightening research and careers of Donald Roy and Nels Anderson. Chapoulie's keen understanding of Chicago's place in American sociology and social thought clearly guide the substantive choices that structure the book.

Chapoulie traces the guiding idea of the city as a social laboratory, usually attributed to Robert Park, to an article written by Albion Small in 1896. He shows that the idea and practice of "going into the city" becomes a central tenet of the methodological approach by 1904, later much reinforced by Park and Burgess, and remained so through the second period of field research into the sixties. In consequence, through much of the twentieth century, Chicago was, as Richard Wright said, "the known city," where social scientific research was consumed by a wider public, including politicians and policy makers. Their work influenced writers outside academia like Jane Addams, Nelson Algren, Horace Cayton, James T. Farrell, Saul Bellow, Studs Terkel, Lorraine Hansberry, Carolyn Rogers, and of course Wright himself. For them the "school" in the term Chicago School was that incomparable social lab, the city itself.

Chicago was, as Gerald Suttles has termed it, the "shock city" of the early twentieth century. No city struck the imagination of artists and intellectuals around the world as did 1920s Chicago. To offer a personal example, on a visit in 2004 to Moscow with Chicago trade unionist Edward Sadlowski, we were taken to the original flat of Sergei Eisenstein, the foremost pioneer of Russian (and Soviet) cinema. The apartment was not open to the public and was preserved as it was at the time of Eisenstein's death in 1948. On his bookshelves we found almost a complete set of the first edition Chicago sociological classics. I leafed through his copy of Thrasher's *The Gang* and found copious notes that Eisenstein had made in the margins.

No doubt, as Chapoulie recognizes, his treatment of research on race relations under Park's leadership will be the most controversial aspect of this volume, as it appears for the first time to an American audience. Since the publication of Aldon Morris's *The Scholar Denied: W. E. B Du Bois and the Birth of Modern Sociology* (2015), Robert Park's stature as a founding leader of American sociology is challenged for his failure to appreciate and incorporate Du Bois's research on the African American experience in the Chicago curriculum. This is part of a broader critique of the failure of American sociology to put research by black scholars, like Du Bois and Oliver Cox, in the foreground of their writing about what they primarily thought of as "the Negro Problem."

As a sociology graduate student at the University of Chicago in the sixties, it was evident to me that on issues of race especially, the Chicago researchers of the classic period had failed to admit the importance of political mobilization, or of cultural identity politics, that gave rise to the civil rights movement, the demand for "Black Power," the slogan "Black is Beautiful," and much more of what was creating profound social change in Chicago and the nation. In the Chicago Department of Sociology, some of the old biases remained as obstacles. When we discussed Du Bois, if we ever did, it was often in connection with his early research, which was often categorized as belonging to a valuable, but prescientific, "social survey" tradition. Du Bois's *Black Reconstruction* was never required reading; perhaps, for our mentors, it was too dependent on a Marxian analytical framework. Thus students lost the opportunity to understand in detail the systematic terror and heroic black struggles of the post–civil war period. And we missed the opportunity to get to know Du Bois as a true sociological innovator and founder of our field. Elijah Anderson, (also a Chicagoan of the sixties), has succinctly described in his introduction to *The Philadelphia Negro* the sociological role model we missed as graduate students while we were learning in what, he would agree, was a sociological "white space." Anderson writes that Du Bois

> walked the streets of the old Seventh Ward—and one can just imagine this stiff and proper Victorian gentleman in his suit and starched shirt moving through the hurly-burly of the noisy, congested neighborhood—and talked to people, listened to people, mapped the area, made ethnographic observations, and collected descriptive statistics.

Written earlier than the Morris critique, Chapoulie does not directly address the issue of Du Bois's effective exclusion as a founder of American sociology.

But his readers will understand the dispositions that lead to his marginalization by the Chicago sociologists under Park's leadership. He shows that Park and most of his generation of white sociologists were committed to life in the slow lane of racial equality. Many were never persuaded that black americans could fully measure up. There were 80 lynchings of black men in 1920, but most sociologists did not want to look squarely in the eye of American racism and racial terror, or to study the "White Question."

Yet despite their failures, Chapoulie offers ample evidence for why the questions they posed and the methods the Chicago sociologists developed, continue to inspire empirical research in the United States and throughout the world. Workplace research still draws on Donald Roy's early examples. New approaches to polling and survey research always cite Blumer's original critique. Wirth's writing on the ghetto and Saint Claire Drake and Horace Cayton's monumental *Black Metropolis* continue to inform new research about segregation. Ecological models of urbanization, the study of deviance, crime, juvenile delinquency, community studies, and, yes, studies of race and ethnicity, will inevitably draw on comparisons to empirical research in the Chicago tradition. It is also true that when younger sociologists from France or other parts of the world come to study in American universities, they will likely be mentored by faculty who practice one or another of the living traditions of Chicago-style research. We have Jean-Michel Chapoulie to thank for ransacking the archives to create so thorough a scholarly analysis of the Chicago tradition's evolution over five decades, and for offering us so many new insights into how and why the work was originally produced.

Acknowledgments

I probably never would have undertaken this study had it not been for my acquaintance with Howard Becker. The possibilities and mores of the United States were still a new world to me that morning in March 1986, when Howard Becker informed me that the archives of Everett Hughes had been deposited at the Joseph Regenstein Library at the University of Chicago. He suggested that I go there to consult them, and, in the field, made the task easy by introducing me to the archivist. However, my debt toward Howard Becker goes much further than this: over the course of the following years, and over the completion of this book, he generously procured various documents, offered his recollections, encouraged my research, and ensured the assistance of a network of prudent and efficacious friends who were his equals in helpfulness. In addition to my debt to Howard Becker are the ones I owe to Anselm Strauss—who in the 1970s critiqued my first article on the works of the Chicago sociologists and thus contributed to the intellectual orientation of which this book is the culmination—and to Arlene Kaplan Daniels, my mentor at Chicago and in the United States in 1986.

I have benefited from the generosity of many other colleagues who have provided me with documents, testimonies, and promising leads, particularly Allan McDonell and Murray Wax, as well as Fred Davis, Irving Deutscher, Eliot Freidson, Joseph Gusfield, Julius Roth, Robert Weiss, Paule Verdet, Helena Znaniecka Lopata, Edward Shils, and Edward Tiryakian. I would also like to express my gratitude to Helen McGill Hughes, Everett Hughes's wife, who sent me some of his personal papers in 1985, as well as to their daughters, Elisabeth Schneewind-Hughes and Helen Brock-Hughes.

A significant portion of the printed documentation was obtained thanks to the perseverance of Josée Tertrais, research engineer at the (now defunct) center of sociological and historical research on education that I founded at the École Normale Supérieure Fontenay-Saint-Cloud. I also thank Josée Tertrais for her many suggestions regarding sources and their interpretation, from which I have benefitted. Jean Peneff sent me various documents in his possession and an interview of Everett Hughes that he had conducted around 1982. Other difficult-to-access documents were procured for me by Cécile Desmazières-Berlie and Izabela Wagner-Saffray. Hélène Fouquet conducted an interview with a former president of Fisk University for me. I have had many discussions with Jean-Pierre Briand, Jean Peneff, and Henri Peretz, and more recently with Marc Suteau, that certainly generated some of the ideas developed in this book. Henri Peretz and Jean-Pierre Briand read the final version of this text, and I benefitted from a great number of Jean-Pierre Briand's editorial suggestions.

Documents from the archives of Everett C. Hughes, Louis Wirth, Ernest W. Burgess, Robert Park, Buford Junker, W. Lloyd Warner, W. I. Thomas, and F. Matthews and the interviews conducted by J. T. Carey are reproduced with the kind permission of the Department of Special Collections at the Joseph Regenstein Library at the University of Chicago.

Quotations from the Donald Roy archives are reproduced with the kind permission of the Duke University Archives.

Chicago Sociology

Introduction

*We say "How did sociology start?" instead of asking what were those men
doing, those particular men in that historic setting in the world they had
inherited, but which they were also creating by interaction with one another.*
—Everett C. Hughes[1]

*There was, to be true, a considerable unity of thought between such figures
as Thomas, Park, Burgess, Faris and, later, Wirth, Hughes, and myself.
But there were many, many threads of difference that are ignored by those
scholars who are seeking to develop the idea of a Chicago sociology.*
—Herbert Blumer[2]

Who were the sociologists collectively referred to as the "Chicago tradition" (or "school")? What did they discover, and how did they work? How were their analyses linked to the social, political, and intellectual environments in which they carried out their research? What do they have in common with successive generations of researchers in a tradition that proclaims a degree of continuity between the end of the previous century and the beginning of the 1960s? And, more generally, what can we learn about the achievements of social science, and about its knowledge, by examining more than half a century of one of the great traditions in empirical research?

These are the questions to which this work attempts to offer some degree of response.

They were not, per se, the questions that I had in mind when I began this book. Convinced that contemporary readers would have difficulty understanding the spirit of the studies conducted by the Chicago sociologists, I initially intended to offer an historically informed general presentation of them. Of the dozen or so works dedicated to this subject, some were excellent—notably the biography of Robert Park by Fred Matthews[3] and the book by Martin Bulmer on the institutional conditions of the development of sociological research at the University of Chicago.[4] But it seemed to me that a presentation of this strain of research would benefit from expanding more broadly than Martin Bulmer's work does upon the fieldwork that lies at the heart of Chicago sociology (and that was much less well-known in France at the time, fifteen years ago, than it was in Great Britain). It also seemed to me that the importance of the Chicago sociologists' legacy through the 1960s, as well as the advantages of a broader temporal perspective, demanded the inclusion of the research generated over the course of the 1940s and 1950s by the group led by Everett Hughes and Herbert Blumer.

Like any research project, this one has metamorphosed over the course of its execution. One reason for this has been the extent of accessible documentary resources. In effect, I rapidly discovered the richness of available works on the history of the social sciences in the United States, as well as the works on social history that use the city of Chicago as their setting, or one of their settings.

Since the beginning of the 1970s, the history of the social sciences has ceased to be a domain reserved only for researchers linked to their specific fields. Researchers with the objective of neither identifying their own predecessors within the discipline, nor passing judgment as to whether specific research was "good"—i.e., achieved posterity or ought to have done so—or "bad," have collected evidence about the recent past of the social sciences. Following a historical approach, they have exploited the archives of academic institutions and foundations. Among other merits that they owe to the diversity of the available archives, these works draw attention to the diverse dimensions of the contexts in which social science research has been generated. They also expand, by means of the comparisons that they suggest, the list of questions that can be posed regarding a group of researchers. Certain works deal with aspects that interest me directly: for example, the reaction against Darwinism in the social sciences at the beginning of the twentieth century, the politics of foundation funding, the relations between the University of Chicago and the city, and the extensions of research carried out at General Electric's Hawthorne factory. Because they approach these questions from a different line of inquiry than mine, including these works could help to prevent the errors of perspective to which the exclusive focus on a particular object inevitably gives rise.

In addition to these works on the history of the social sciences, we can add another precious documentary source: a wealth of autobiographies and biographies about the researchers, even those who achieved only moderate name recognition. This reflects the breadth of the audience for English-language publishing as much as it does the relative success of the disciplines of the social sciences. Thanks to these biographies and the personal archives of scholars that have been preserved in diverse repositories, it is frequently possible to complement testimonies with the activities of the different researchers that I have studied, and sometimes even to gain access to the subjective dimension of their own perspectives on their activities.

Works of social history about Chicago offer, among other things, resources that can help us to understand the contexts in which these researchers worked. For the period from 1880 to 1960, certainly, no other city served as the setting for so many studies on such a large range of subjects: the labor movement; interethnic relationships; local political life and municipal associations; philanthropic foundations and cultural institutions; the university; and the biographies of philanthropist-businessmen, eminent women, or other actors in local life. Not all studies likely to be illuminating for the analysis of sociology were centered around Chicago, but the importance of this city in the United States between 1880 and 1960 has given it an essential place in the history of the innovations and transformations that affected American society. There are certainly also more material explanations for the large number of works set at least partially in Chicago, including the importance of the city's universities and cultural institutions and the richness of its archives (linked here to financial wealth), as well as the political dynamic of the publishing activity carried out by the University of Chicago Press over the course of sixty years.

Curiously, the resources offered by historical studies of Chicago have been used only rarely in previous work on the sociologists of this city.[5] Nobody has, for example, sought to integrate the work of sociologists of past eras with the later work of historians studying the same subjects (using their own documentary resources and their own methods). This approach, however, shines an exterior light on sociological works, which can help us to understand the researchers' methods. One such discovery that surprised me (which, in retrospective, seems naive), regarding W. I. Thomas and Florian Znaniecki's *The Polish Peasant*, was that the lasting success of a sociological study can be completely independent from the merits of its starting point.

The possibility of relatively quickly achieving a precise understanding of the different dimensions of the social environment of the sociologists of Chicago has, surely, contributed to drawing my attention toward evaluations of sociological research from outside the discipline. For an observer who is not from North

American culture and who has the advantage of a half-century's remove, the similarities and differences between the sociological analyses and public debates of the same epoch, or from the period in which their intellectual formation was carried out, are certainly more apparent than they would be for an observer from the same culture and era. I was also driven to consider the nature of intellectual accomplishments in the social sciences, or, rather, the relationship between practical investigations that take place in a historical moment and scholarly analyses. In order to explore this question, a diversified ensemble of studies certainly constitutes a more appropriate corpus than does the body of work of a single author.

In order to connect the content of social science works with the context of their production, limiting the history of Chicago sociology to the narrow framework within which it is generally inscribed—that of the establishment of sociology as a discipline—seems insufficient. Moreover, due to the absence of the critical spirit that is part of the historical profession, this type of history can lead to numerous factual errors repeated in book after book. To give only a few examples, the University of Chicago was not the first in the United States to open a sociology department; Thomas was not a sociologist in terms of his intellectual references (or his training), but rather an anthropologist; the idea of a collective undertaking of research on the city was not an original idea of Park's, but the adaptation to a favorable climate of an idea regarding the rural world tested elsewhere; the intellectual differences among sociologists, social reformers, and social workers were not large in 1920, but grew between 1900 and the mid-1930s, the result of an effort among sociologists to distance themselves from their rivals; the decline of the Chicago Department of Sociology following Park's retirement *was not* a sign of the triumph of quantitative sociology over more qualitative approaches, nor the simple result of a "conspiracy" of opponents of the political dominance Chicago held over the American Sociological Association; and so on.

To be sure, most inaccuracies in the history of sociology concern minor points.[6] Their accumulation, however, leads to a sort of garbled history, the barely concealed objective of which is to celebrate the hero-founders of sociology or part thereof, to restore glorious ancestors who have been supplanted by usurpers, to discover disciples or deserving successors. This was also, in a less academic form, one of the objectives of the Chicago Irregulars, the group of young researchers, trained for the most part at Berkeley, who were devoted to fieldwork—which is to say an ethnographic approach—in reaction to what seemed to them, at the beginning of the 1970s, the orthodoxy of American sociology (see chapter 6).

Its predetermined finality, however, is not the only failing of the type of internal history through which Chicago sociology is, in part, known today. By resorting, fundamentally, to native categories currently in use in the discipline—for example, the opposition between qualitative and quantitative methods and to rifts that have manifested between intellectual orientations, such as interactionism and functionalism—this type of history omits an essential factor: the critical explanation of the categories of thought, judgment, and action that structured the activities of social science researchers during the period in which they worked. One must recall that an appreciable part of intellectual work is writing *against* "adversaries"—some work of the previous era, or some trendy mode of thought—who, while they are not always designated as such, are crucial elements that structure the generation of new work. Rendering these adversaries visible, and more generally reconstituting the different elements of the intellectual, institutional, and socio-political context in which these works were generated, constitutes a necessary stage in approaching an exact and nuanced understanding of all social science research endeavors.

This type of understanding necessitates the adoption of a properly historical approach, which is to say, crucially, not only the establishment of institutional or biographical facts, but also the rendering explicit of categories of thought in action, and the connotations of actions, in their historical contexts. We should, however, set aside, if only temporarily, value judgments of research based on the standards of today's social sciences, since these judgments can only render unknowable the meaning that these works held in their own time. Similarly, we should not pay attention only to successful works, but also to those that did not make it past a draft or hypothetical stage, and we should take note of the apparent inconsistencies of practice of research and intellectual positions, of individual idiosyncrasies, and of the particular circumstances in which they produced research. In brief, we must pay attention to the full array of social arrangements, even relatively contingent ones, into which were inscribed the collective actions that produced the research in question. Finally, and perhaps most difficult, we must reveal not only the characteristics positively possessed by intellectual works or actions, but also those characteristics that they lacked but *could* have had in other times or places.

Supported by this approach, this book aims to offer a history of the development of sociological research at the University of Chicago centered around its relationships with diverse environments—a history with an aim toward understanding the uniqueness of this research rather than the designation and the celebration of its posterity (or rather, in this case, one of its posterities) in current-day sociology. I shall now present some of the initial choices that determined the orientation of the book.

First of all, it is necessary to observe that the limits that have come to define the appellation "Chicago sociologists" result from a lengthy initiative undertaken by their would-be successors, their adversaries, and observers who were more or less detached but reliant upon the intellectual interests established in the period in which they themselves worked. Any a priori definition of the subject—whether it was based on previous work or on the application of an objective criterion, such as the nature of one's affiliation with the Chicago sociology department or some aspect of the intellectual content of one's work—largely predetermines the results of the investigation. The a priori adoption of such a definition relies inevitably on a univocal characterization based on a small number of attributes of Chicago sociologists that are explicitly or tacitly considered essential (some aspect of their intellectual orientation, some documentary method used, some relationship with the founders, etc.). To the contrary, it is as a concrete group—or, more exactly, as a series of concrete groups—that I here consider the Chicago sociologists. I have therefore used many different definitions of these groups, according to the issue under discussion.

The activities of these concrete groups constitute the center of this study, along with their relationships with other groups through analogous activities, sometimes outside the academic world or in the context of other social science disciplines. Among these activities, a central—but not exclusive—place has been accorded to those which gave rise to texts in the social sciences. The functions of teaching have not been neglected, as they could contribute to the common orientation of a group of contemporary works of research. The activities of these concrete groups have been positioned in relation with their antecedents (rather than their successors), as have the texts that frequently resulted from these activities. At least in part, these antecedents—other texts and perspectives—are implicit, and a reconstruction of the universe in which this intellectual work originated often retains a somewhat hypothetical character.

The prominence of works and their ultimate diffusion within an area of study have not been considered here as anything more than one characteristic among others, and a place has been accorded to unpublished texts and works that never had more than a private audience, as long as their examination elucidates an important aspect of this collective enterprise.

In a general sense, the production of scholarship is subject to a certain number of constraints that contribute to determining its shape. The simplest of these are, of course, material constraints (which always have an intellectual counterpart), especially those that pertain to financing possibilities and access to the field of inquiry. Another group of constraints corresponds to the institutional conditions of the production of scholarship, which involve both interdisciplinary conflicts over fields of study and internal power structures. (A typical example in this case is the production of dissertations in a department in which prevails an antagonism between or among those in charge of directing them—an antagonism that often tends to have a character that is at once methodological and theoretical, both personal and political.)

Next, we must consider the more concrete aspects of scholarly production: documentary resources and ways of handling resources that were practical in the places and times considered. Employing the methodological transformations of research in sociology as an analytical guideline allows us to free ourselves from part of the ordinary and considerably vague reasoning that drives the history of ideas in its traditional form that has until recently constituted what passed for the history of sociology, as Martin Bulmer and Jennifer Platt have already shown.[7]

The analysis of the intellectual constraints that conditioned the production of scholarship, such as we see in the history of ideas in its traditional sense, in fact suffers from serious failings. We cannot accept without critical examination the patterns of reasoning used in this analysis, now or in the past, to qualify the affiliations between scholarly works or between researchers. The borrowing of one author's ideas by another is never an immediately obvious operation, even for the individuals implicated. Proclaimed or denied relationships between "master" and student, citations (or the absence thereof) in publications, and avowed intentions are all essentially ambiguous, since they are used strategically by the interested parties: the claiming and denying of affiliations constitute, as we know, instruments of acquisition of scientific credit in the field here considered.

Finally, we must pay attention to the constraints on scholarly production that result from argumentative rhetoric and writing styles permissible within a given period and group. These relate to documentary sources as well as to the patterns of reasoning admitted into the group, but are not limited to these.

Some of the main features of the description of the Chicago tradition found in this book follow from this quick characterization of the line of questioning that I have adopted. The limitation of the subject in fact draws more attention to its heterogeneity than to its homogeneity. The devotees (and the detractors) of the Chicago School will undoubtedly be chagrined not to find in these works the intellectual unity that they expect. I can only defend this as the price of restricting the corpus of works taken into account, when historical comprehension would instead necessitate that we expand that corpus. The role of contingencies in the production of intellectual work that concrete study inevitably makes apparent will do similar damage to the convictions of those who always hope to reduce things to a formula or paradigm, condensed to a small number of principles. One could justly consider that the emphasis placed on the heterogeneity of works is the inevitable consequence of the adoption of a true historical approach, which is to say comparable to that which is implemented, or should be, in studying education, religion, or work.

This point of view also leads to a detachment from the studied case that is perhaps greater than would be expected when dealing with works that have gained and maintained substantial reputations. I certainly never would have decided to write this book if I did not feel a sympathy for at least part of this intellectual enterprise. This sympathy aroused my initial interest, but, after this preliminary stage, the historical investigation was inevitably caught up in a dialectic between the familiar and the strange—the position of the researcher to his object oscillated between that of a Martian and that of a convert, to paraphrase Fred Davis, one of the heirs of the tradition considered here.[8] In a historical approach, it is the comprehension of the "facts" most alien to the observer that most deserves his attention and requires his best efforts, and it is also here that the researcher can expect a widening of his perspective. The same applies, I believe, for the reader, and I have therefore frequently emphasized those characteristics of the intellectual works which are no longer part of the common culture of researchers in the social sciences.

Detailed familiarity with the relevant currents in research—especially those of the final generation whose works are examined here—implies, however, that my adopted approach is probably not very different from that which these researchers themselves would certainly have employed had they studied the same subject. Parts of the epigraphs at the beginning of this chapter underline this similarity, which we should not hide.

This book is composed of two parts. The first outlines the history of the development of researchers situated around the Department of Sociology at the University of Chicago chronologically, from the foundation of the university to the beginning of the 1960s. The emphasis here is placed on institutional aspects as well as the layers of sociopolitical and intellectual background that, for this period, prove relevant. The second part consists of three essays, partially independent from each other, that are dedicated to domains of research—work, delinquency, and the relationships between race and culture—and one further essay on the careers and research of two sociologists who found themselves at the frontiers of the Chicago tradition and the academic world. Throughout, brief supplementary discourses are set in a visually distinct style, indented from the left margin, in order not to distract the reader from the main argument.

For this second edition, I have substantially revised chapter 2 on W. I. Thomas, which suffered from insufficient interpretive rigor, and added discussions in chapters 1 and 3, sometimes to account for analyses published after the first edition, and sometimes to specify what I have uncovered through later investigations. Certain justifications for these critical additions are presented in an appendix, *Remarks on Research Methods*. I have also corrected, in all chapters, reference errors and some clumsy phrasing. Not having conducted new archival research, I have preserved the references that correspond to the state in which I consulted them, which sometimes differs from their current state in cases where they have been supplemented and their classifications modified.

PART I

Sociological Research in Its Institutional Context

I

The Initial Development of Sociology at the University of Chicago, 1892–1914

Sociology was a social movement before it was part of the academic establishment.[1]
—Robert Hughes

The latest god in the world's pantheon is science.[2]
—Albion Small

The method of credible sociology must be the method of observation and induction.[3]
—Albion Small

In a letter he wrote while visiting Chicago during his first trip to the United States in 1904, Max Weber provided an arresting description of the city from the point of view of a European observer.[4]

Chicago is one of the most incredible cities. By the lake there are a few comfortable and beautiful residential districts, mostly with stone houses of a very heavy and cumbersome style, and right behind them there are little old wooden houses such as one finds in Helgoland. Then come the *"tenements"* of the workingmen and absurdly dirty streets which are unpaved, or there is miserable macadamization outside the better residential districts. In the *"city,"* among the *"skyscrapers,"* the condition of the streets is utterly hair-raising. . . .

It is an endless human desert. From the city one travels on Halsted Street—which, I believe, is twenty English miles long—into the endless distance, past blocks with Greek inscriptions—Xenodocheion [Hotel], etc.—and then past others with Chinese taverns, Polish advertisements, German beer parlors, until one gets to the "*stockyards*." For as far as one can see from the clock tower of the firm Armour & Co. there is nothing but herds of cattle, lowing, bleating, endless filth. But on the horizon all around—for the city continues for miles and miles, until it melts into the multitude of suburbs—there are churches and chapels, grain elevators, smoking chimneys (every big hotel here has his steaming elevator) and house of every size. They are usually small houses, for at most two families each (hence the enormous dimensions of the city), and they are graded in cleanliness according to nationality.

All hell had broken loose in the "*stockyards*": an unsuccessful strike, masses of Italians and Negroes as strikebreakers; daily shootings with dozens of dead on both sides; a streetcar was overturned and a dozen women were squashed because a "*non-union man*" had sat in it; dynamite threats against the "*Elevated Railway*," and one of its cars was actually derailed and plunged into the river. Right near our hotel a cigar dealer was murdered in broad daylight; a few streets away three Negroes attacked and robbed a streetcar at dusk, etc.—all in all, a strange flowering of culture.

There is a mad pell-mell of nationalities: up and down the streets the Greeks shine the Yankees' shoes for 5 cents. The Germans are their waiters, the Irish take care of their politics, and the Italians of their dirtiest ditch digging. With the exception of the better residential districts, the whole tremendous city—more extensive than London!—is like a man whose skin has been peeled off and whose intestines are seen at work. For one can see everything—in the evening, for example, on a side street in the "*city*" the prostitutes are placed in a show window with electric light and the prices are displayed! A characteristic thing here as in New York is the maintenance of a specific Jewish-German culture. Theaters present in Yiddish [*Judendeutsch*] *The Merchant of Venice* (with Shylock prevailing, however) and their own Jewish plays, which we are planning to see in New York. . . .

Everywhere one is struck by the tremendous intensity of work—most of all in the "*stockyards*" with their "ocean of blood", where several thousand cattle and pigs are slaughtered every day. From the moment when the unsuspecting bovine enters the slaughtering area, is hit by a hammer and collapses, whereupon it immediately gripped by an iron clamp, is hoisted up, and starts on its journey, it is in constant motion—past ever-new workers who eviscerate and skin it, etc., but are always (in the rhythm of work) tied to the machine that pulls the animal past them. One sees an absolutely incredible output in this atmosphere of steam, muck, blood, and hides in which I teetered about together with a *"boy"* who was giving me a guided tour for fifty cents, trying to keep from being buried in the filth. There one can follow a pig from the sty to the sausage and the can.

When they finish work at five o'clock, people often must travel for hours to get home. The streetcar company is bankrupt; as usual it has been administered by a *"receiver"* for years, and he is not interested in expediting the liquidation and hence does not purchase any new cars. The old ones break down every few moments. Around 400 people are killed or crippled in accidents every year. According to law, each death costs the company 5,000 dollars (to the widow or the heirs), an injury costs it 10,000 dollars (to the injured party, if the company does not take certain precautionary measures). The company has now calculated that those 400 indemnities cost it less than the required precautions, so it does not bother to introduce them.

Twelve years earlier, in 1892, around the time preparations for the World's Columbian Exposition brought Chicago to the attention of the Old World, a private university had opened in the city. It had a Department of Sociology, where this new academic discipline focused on the observation and analysis of the contemporary world was born. This chapter offers an overview of the first phase of sociology's evolution—not only its social and intellectual contexts, but also the finer points of its institutional arrangements as well as the characteristics and actions of those who contributed to it. I elucidate the complexity of historical factors and contingencies that gave rise to the development of sociology, which is too often considered to have been a unilinear, natural process.

Max Weber's description conveys most of the traits that made Chicago a singular city, in which the rapid development of big industry and its consequences were immediately apparent. Chicago was, in fact, the American city that saw the fastest growth in the second half of the nineteenth century. A small town of 4,500 residents in 1840, Chicago reached a population of three hundred thousand in 1870, five hundred thousand in 1880, 1.7 million in 1900, and 2.7 million in 1920. Multiple factors contributed to this growth: the city was a natural location for industries linked to the agriculture of the Midwestern plains, such as slaughterhouses and manufacturers of agricultural implements like McCormick. It was the home base for the construction of railroads to the West—one of the principal manufacturers of railcars, the Pullman Company, was based in Chicago. It was also the seat of important iron- and steel-working industries, printing works, textile factories, and tanneries: the commercial center for a market that extended over the entire Midwest. The particularly rapid growth of industries and commerce in Chicago was accompanied by the introduction of numerous business innovations. Because of its local employment opportunities as well as its role as the home base of westward expansion, the city attracted successive waves of immigration from all parts of Europe: Germany, Ireland, Sweden, Poland, Russia, Bohemia, Slovakia, Italy, and elsewhere. By 1900, about half the residents of the city were foreign-born. After 1914, along with the other great northern cities of the United States, Chicago received a new influx of migrants: African Americans from the rural states of the South.

Over the course of its growth, the city was periodically roiled by ethnic conflicts that pitted the most recently arrived immigrants against those who had preceded them, especially in the context of employment—which is to say the conditions of work and remuneration. A sort of hierarchy of immigrants can be observed in any period, partly reflecting seniority by order of arrival. In the 1860s, it was the Irish who found themselves at the bottom of the social ladder, where they were soon joined by the Germans, the Czechs, and the Scandinavians. In the 1890s, the base of this hierarchy was formed by immigrants from eastern and southern Europe, who were themselves replaced a little later by African Americans. Chicago was also, at the end of July 1919, the location of one of the most severe anti-black race riots to occur in a northern city.

Chicago was also a city plagued by what the middle classes and, later, the social sciences deemed "urban problems": the chronic poverty of a significant portion of the population, vast slums, various forms of delinquency (especially juvenile delinquency), ethnic conflicts intertwined with class conflicts, and so on. Before 1914, the economic elites of Chicago, like those of the other large cities of the United States, also worried that the administration of city government seemed, starting in the late nineteenth century, to be corrupt and ineffective.[5]

The definitions of these urban problems had a dialectical relationship with the growth of different social movements, especially the labor movement and the reform movement known as the Progressive movement. The city was, in fact, one of the principal centers in which the labor movement developed, at first mainly among immigrants of English, German, and northern European origins. Anarchist and socialist ideas circulated in these groups, as did attempts to create labor unions. Clashes between employers and workers, as well as strikes, were commonplace in Chicago starting in the 1870s.[6]

Rising tensions led to two events that would symbolically mark the American labor movement. In 1886, six policemen were killed in a bombing at Haymarket Square during a demonstration in support of a strike for an eight-hour workday; four leaders of the movement were hanged the following year. Eight years later, during the severe economic recession of 1893–1894, salary cuts provoked a long strike on the part of laborers from the Pullman plant, which manufactured railway material and was based in the south of the city. The strike took on a national dimension when railroad employees came out in support of the laborers by refusing to route trains containing cars constructed by Pullman. The intervention of federal authorities put an end to a boycott, demonstrating that the federal authorities were willing to get involved in labor disputes in favor of employers.[7]

Periodical law and order campaigns were one reaction to labor agitation. In a more diffuse way, however, another solution to the ensemble of "urban problems" was sought in the moral improvement of the working class, namely by instilling in it the values of piety, frugality, temperance, and education. The reform movement of the period preceding the First World War (known as the Progressive Era) was particularly active in Chicago.[8] Its principal actors were recruited from the economic elite of the city, but also from the middle-class "knowledge" professions—lawyers, doctors, Protestant pastors, and university professors. Also common were young women with university degrees—especially in the social sciences—who, following the partial success of the reform movement, gained access to work as administrators, university professors, researchers, and, especially, social workers. Professors in the social sciences—notably sociologists, economists, and political scientists—and in philosophy occupied an important place in this movement, the history of which is closely linked to the initial development of these disciplines in the United States.[9] The Progressive movement was also connected to a secularization of the evangelical movement, with offers of education and social services increasingly taking the place of Gospel preaching.

The subset of the reform movement of the Progressive Era that maintained the closest relationship with the social sciences, constituting a sort of avant-garde, contributed to the foundation of establishments in working-class neighborhoods known as *settlements*, which offered a place of residence for middle-class men and women as well as various services to the surrounding working-class residents.[10] The model had been set by the young British intellectuals who in 1884 installed themselves in an apartment building in an East London working-class neighborhood and established Toynbee Hall, "an outpost of education and culture" (to borrow the expression of the historian Allen Davis). Following their example, a group of young, male college graduates set themselves up in a working-class neighborhood in New York, soon to be joined by their female counterparts. Similar attempts took place, for the most part independently, in other large cities across the United States, notably Boston and Chicago, where the most famous establishment of this sort was founded.

In 1889, three years prior to the opening of the University of Chicago, Jane Addams (1860–1935), the daughter of a Quaker senator and an 1881 graduate of the Rockford Female Seminary, established Hull House in a poor neighborhood in South Chicago, along with a former classmate. The two associates, who had previously lived at Toynbee Hall, intended to offer a range of social and cultural services (such as a kindergarten, library, art museum, night courses, etc.), as well as a meeting space, to the crowded immigrant neighborhood in which they had installed themselves. The project undertaken by Jane Addams and her associates was somewhat less elitist than that of their British predecessors, who sought to bring what they themselves considered to be "culture" to the working classes. By contrast, Hull House had religious motivation and claimed, in effect, to help the target populations acquire control over their own existence. Addams also wished to promote direct interaction between populations from different class and ethnic origins. Over the following years, Hull House housed many young women pursuing studies at the University of Chicago. It also became the center of various cultural activities, as well as activities focused on reform and activism, hosting meetings of labor groups, unions, and the like.

Other analogous establishments were also set up in Chicago. In 1892, Charles Zueblin (1866–1924), a future University of Chicago sociology professor, founded the Northwestern University Settlement House, associated with Northwestern University itself, an elite Chicago Methodist institution. In 1894, Graham Taylor, a Protestant pastor who also later became a University of Chicago sociology professor, founded an independent settlement, Chicago Commons. That same year, some University of Chicago students founded a settlement in the slaughter-house district nearby, which quickly came under the control of the university and assumed its name.

A group of Hull House residents led by Jane Addams and Florence Kelley, the latter a resident with socialist sympathies who had helped to translate the works of Friedrich Engels into English, began conducting surveys among the populations of their neighborhoods, asking them about living conditions, salaries, hygiene, and so on. This model of study was also imported from England, following the research on London working classes that had been sponsored and partly conducted by the ship-owner Charles Booth, which was held in high regard by the residents of Toynbee Hall.[11] Kelley and other residents published their findings in 1895 under the title *Hull House Maps and Papers*, offering a description of Hull House's neighborhood that later served as a model for sociologists.[12] Over the course of the next thirty years, numerous similar investigations (into housing and living conditions, health, salaries, etc.) were conducted by the residents of various settlements in Chicago as well as other large cities of the East Coast and the Midwest.

Hull House and Jane Addams constituted one node of a vast network found in 1900s Chicago, which included members of the city's philanthropic elite, members of the liberal professions, journalists, social workers, and several organizers of the labor movement, in addition to numerous academics.[13] This last group occupied a particularly important role in the city, perhaps because it lacked a cultivated and sophisticated patrician elite as could be found, for example, in Boston. The academics, and in particular the professors of the University of Chicago, played the role of experts regarding cultural and social activities in the city.[14] They sat on the boards of directors for the city's philanthropic and cultural institutions (museums, orchestras, etc.), and were consulted in matters of justice, assistance, and urban politics.

Between 1890 and 1920 in Chicago, diverse associations and organizations dedicated to various social objectives proliferated, campaigning in favor of different foundations with scientific or cultural goals,[15] in favor of various reforms to the city's public education system,[16] in favor of the creation of a welfare system and labor laws,[17] in favor of justice system reform and a dedicated organization for the treatment of juvenile delinquency,[18] and in favor of a reorganization of municipal powers.[19]

The member lists of these different associations offer a preliminary idea of the close links they had with the university. The same is true for the Association of Commerce, which represented most of the prominent businessmen of the city, one of whom was the first president of the University of Chicago, William Rainey Harper (1856–1906). Harper was also a member of the Board of Education, the administrative council for city schools. Among the founders of the Civic Federation—an association with broad objectives that sought to support workers who had been made destitute during the 1893 depression—can be found the first chair of the university's Department of Sociology, Albion Small. One of the first presidents of the City Club, founded in 1903, was the philosopher George Herbert Mead, also a professor at the university. One of the advocates for the creation of the United Charities—an office dedicated to coordinating Chicago's charitable activities, founded in 1909 by the merger of two associations—was Charles Henderson, a professor of sociology and chaplain at the university. A professor of political science and an unsuccessful candidate for mayor of Chicago in 1911, Charles Merriam was one of the leaders of the reform movement in favor of the reorganization of municipal powers.[20] The founder of the university's philosophy department, James Tufts, was, like Henderson, a member of various commissions that urged the state of Illinois to vote on labor legislation.

A small group of people participated in many of these associations and found themselves at the heart of the network that made up the reform movement. Of the roughly 2,500 people appearing on the membership lists of these associations between 1890 and 1925, 215 participated in three or more of them.[21] To be sure, we must not exaggerate the unity of the objectives and opinions among those who participated at some level in a movement that consisted of people with a wide variety of origins, interests, cultures, and political orientations. Reformers disagreed on the relative importance of different social problems and on numerous other points, but they were at least close to agreement on the necessity of developing public education; supporting adult educational and technical vocational programs; and sustaining libraries, museums, and other cultural institutions. They also agreed on the necessity of reforming city government by eliminating corruption and reorienting it to its primary objective of serving the general interest. Finally, they agreed on the necessity of improving living conditions and public health, combatting prostitution and criminality, and reforming the justice and prison systems.[22]

After 1900, the reform movement—aided by a confluence of various forces, and at least partially through meeting the interests of the business elite—succeeded creating different social service agencies and transforming the judiciary system. Some of the reformers then found employment in these organizations themselves or in training programs for social workers.[23]

In the years 1890–1914, the city of Chicago and the state of Illinois were thus the sites of very diverse movements, vivid descriptions of which can be found in history books.[24] Chicago was the location of the development of union agitation and class struggles, growing out of the ideas introduced by the European labor, socialist, and anarchist movements. It was a location of political experimentation following the election of a Progressive governor, John Peter Atgelt, an anomaly in the state of Illinois. Atgelt, who served from 1893 to 1897, pardoned some of the anarchists convicted after the Haymarket attack and appointed a Hull House resident, Florence Kelley, to the role of inspecting factories for the state. Although many Chicago mayors were known for their close ties to crime, Chicago was also a site of social experimentation. For example, it saw the creation of the first juvenile court as well as the University of Chicago Laboratory Schools, a group of schools affiliated with the university that had been inspired by John Dewey. Chicago was a city in which the owners of large financial, industrial, and commercial enterprises funded the instruments of an elite culture, and in some cases were involved in reform activities. And it was also a site where echoes could be found of the investigative journalism published in the weekly magazine *McClure's*, such as that of Ida Tarbell, who waged a campaign against Standard Oil and John D. Rockefeller; that of Lincoln Steffens, a critic of the corruption of municipal administrations; and that of Ray Stannard Baker, a critic of the United States Steel Corporation.[25] Chicago was a place where numerous East Coast intellectuals settled, or at least spent time. Hull House and Jane Addams were at the center of this universe in which new ideas developed and intellectual careers began. Sociology occupied a position on the periphery of this universe.

THE BIRTH OF THE UNIVERSITY OF CHICAGO AND
THE CREATION OF THE DEPARTMENT OF SOCIOLOGY

The creation of the University of Chicago was contemporaneous with the beginnings of the reform movement. The university took over a bankrupt Baptist college, and at first the project was guided by both an association that supported Baptist educational establishments, as well as John D. Rockefeller (the owner of Standard Oil), who hoped to contribute to the foundation of a new institution of higher education.[26] After a long negotiation, Rockefeller offered a contribution of $1 million, with the condition that the project seek support from other donors. It thus became necessary to appeal to the entire Midwestern Baptist community, and then more broadly to the Chicago business community. Among the first donors to the university was Marshall Field, the owner of one of the large department stores in the city, who gave a parcel of land. A group of Jews of German origin were also some of the earliest donors.[27] It should be noted that a large portion of the donors, including Rockefeller himself, had never pursued higher education themselves. The new university, which opened its doors in October 1892, did not impose religious conditions for the admission of students nor for the recruitment of personnel, but its administrative council was dominated by Baptists.

This religious origin shaped the new university to a lesser degree than did its dependence on donors, especially Rockefeller, whose adversaries used to derisively call it "Standard Oil University." Rockefeller contributed to mitigating financial deficiencies under the university's first president, William Rainey Harper, previously a professor of Semitic languages at Yale, who continuously expanded the scope of the university's activities. He led the project of organizing the university, and would ultimately create an institution capable of competing with the major universities of the East Coast, but with an original orientation and organization. After twenty-five years, Rockefeller's contribution had increased to $35 million.[28]

The relationship between the university and its environment was marked by a certain ambiguity regarding the independence of its instructors. This manifested clearly during the Pullman strike, when Edward Bemis, a professor of political economy who had publicly taken the side of the strikers, was quickly compelled to resign.[29]

The period 1880–1890 in the United States saw a reconsideration of the function of universities, partly stemming from comparison with those in Germany. The first example of a university inspired by the German model, and thus providing a standard of comparison, was Johns Hopkins, founded in 1876 in Baltimore with the support of a sponsor. In 1880, Columbia University in New York City created a center for graduate study in political science, a formula followed ten years later by Harvard with the creation of its Graduate School of Arts and Sciences. The preceding year in Massachusetts, with the support of a sponsor who quickly separated himself from it, Clark University had been founded as a university entirely devoted to graduate study, offering MA and PhD degrees. The institution declined quickly, and the president of the University of Chicago was able to recruit some of its first professors. Others, like Albion Small, the founder of the University of Chicago's Department of Sociology, and the philosopher John Dewey, were recruited from among the graduates of Johns Hopkins.

Borrowed from the model of the German university in these early stages was the idea of the laboratory for experimental disciplines, as well as the idea of the research seminar—namely, the form of instruction in which students present their own research and reading progress, collectively examine sources, and discuss the research that they have presented to each other.[30]

In addition to undergraduate studies, Harper also undertook the creation of a center for graduate studies as well as an ensemble of affiliated institutions, including the future University of Chicago Press, which was charged with publishing academic literature. Harper also established a system of off-campus courses and lectures. (The *university extension* was inspired by and modeled after the London experiments, and one of the London movement's leaders was occasionally involved.) Harper also added a system of correspondence courses, which were modeled after Chautauqua, a social movement of Methodist origin, which began in 1874 in New York State by offering correspondence courses complemented by short sessions of in-person instruction. Harper himself had been a leader in this earlier movement.[31] It is clear that Harper did not seek to establish a university reserved only for the elite (unlike the East Coast universities), but rather one open to its surrounding environment. Also unlike the East Coast universities, the University of Chicago was coeducational, and women quickly came to represent about 40 percent of the student body. In order to promote enrollment and reinforce ties with the local community, the university installed a system of affiliation with various colleges and academies and otherwise sought to establish links with certain preexisting educational institutions.[32] In the following years, the university would absorb some of these, including what would become the university's medical school.

Harper's plans and first decisions show that his primary point of reference was biblical studies, his own specialty.[33] Neither the list of the liberal arts departments, which were established first, nor the order of creation of the following departments suggests that Harper accorded much importance to scientific study or to the applied disciplines; the faculties of medicine and technology were founded a dozen years after the creation of the university.

The importance accorded to research, however, appears clearly in the requirements for receiving a doctoral degree.[34] In a first report to the Board of Directors, which was never finished or revised, Harper explicitly insists upon the necessity of firsthand experience in training students, and proposes that each department publish its own academic journal. He maintains that professors should reserve their teaching for the graduate level, and that promotions on the academic career track should depend above all on the progress of their investigations. He also evokes the possibility of releasing academics from their teaching commitments in order to allow them to focus entirely on research.[35]

Harper turned out to be an energetic and skillful administrator. He constantly negotiated with Rockefeller in order to obtain supplementary subsidies for a budget that his initiatives had put into permanent disequilibrium. He did not seem to have a strategic plan laying out which fields and areas of study the university should develop; instead, Harper tended to seize opportunities that presented themselves, as he did regarding the recruitment of the university's first instructors. From the start, the University of Chicago consisted of separate schools, which themselves were composed of departments. For example, the Faculty of Arts, Literature, and Social Sciences was composed of a Department of Sociology, along with departments of political economy, history, political science, philosophy, comparative religion, English, German, and six other departments corresponding to classical or religious disciplines of study.[36]

Contrary to an enduring legend, the first department to use the term "sociology" in its name was not part of the University of Chicago, but rather part of the University of Kansas in Lawrence. Its original name, given in 1889, was the department of "history and sociology."[37] The question of what to call the new department merits more attention than it has generally been accorded, since it shows that the term "sociology" was one of several used at the time to designate a poorly defined group of activities. According to the 1892–1893 *Quarterly Calendar of the University of Chicago*, the new department was dedicated to "social science and anthropology" for its first year, and Albion Small, its first chair, bore the title of Professor of Social Science. The following year, the term "social science" was replaced by "sociology" in both the name of the department and the title of Small's position.[38]

The term "sociology" had been used for two decades by certain professors offer-ing instruction under this appellation at certain universities: Graham Sumner had done so at Yale since 1876,[39] and Franklin Giddings at Bryn Mawr and then Columbia University in New York since 1890.[40] The term "sociological move-ment" also popularly designated the application of "scientific knowledge" to the solution of social problems. Even if they did not have a precise idea of the objective of this new discipline, Protestant intellectual elites saw in sociology the means of furnishing a scientific base for the Social Gospel that had constituted the previous generation's secular version of proselytizing.[41]

A survey conducted in 1894 by a University of Chicago sociology student illus-trates the diversity of ideas among academics who cared enough about associ-ating themselves with the discipline to respond to the questionnaire.[42] Asked whether they preferred the term "sociology" to "social sciences," a quarter of the respondents were unsure whether they considered the field to be a science. The majority, however, thought that the discipline should be organized in autono-mous departments.

The conceptions defended by the leaders of the new discipline in the 1890s United States were diverse in detail, but had intellectual origins rooted in the work of Auguste Comte (1798–1857) and Herbert Spencer (1820–1903). In the programmatic exposés that constituted the hearts of their contributions, these first-generation sociologists proclaimed sociology to be the general social science, a synthetic discipline that synthesized discoveries from its specific branches—political economy, history, political science, and anthropology—and used those discoveries to deduce evolutionary laws.[43] This imperialist pretension contrasts starkly with the minor status of sociology when it became a formal dis-cipline, especially in relation to the field of political economy, which in 1890 had its own department at several universities.[44] Many of the first professors of sociol-ogy, such as the Yale sociologist Graham Sumner and Albion Small, had degrees in political economy; transitions from one discipline to another remained com-mon until 1914. The American Sociological Society (ASS) was founded only in 1905, as an offshoot of an economists' association that had itself been created in 1885.[45] The relationship between the fields of history and sociology was distant for a long time, perhaps because the audience for the new discipline was at that point largely based outside universities.

Nothing indicates that Harper had a clear idea about what a sociology department should be in 1892, and the form that it took was the product of circumstances. First, Harper recruited the future chairmen of the social science departments.[46] His top choice for sociology was the economist Richard Ely, who declined the offer after an arrangement had been suggested that he be the chair of a Department of Political and Social Sciences. Harper then recruited as chair of the sociology department Albion Small (1854–1926), pastor and then president of the small, Baptist Colby College in Maine. Small was first considered for a position as a professor of history, but Harper judged his qualifications insufficient and also thought that he might have a conflicting relationship with his preferred candidate for the chair of the history department.[47] Like a number of scholars of his generation interested in the social sciences, Small had received training in history and political economy in Germany. He then received his doctorate in constitutional history in 1889 at Johns Hopkins. Drafting a program of study in sociology for the students of Colby College essentially constituted the entirety of Small's previous experience in this field. The proposal for the new sociology department that he sent to Harper reveals that he only had a confused idea of the discipline into which he had been recruited:

> The academic work which I would do for the rest of my life, if perfectly free myself, would be to organize such a department of Sociology as does not exist to my knowledge. It should include a collegiate foundation in history, and economics, more thorough and comprehensive than any required for entrance upon graduate study in the United States.... It should then, on the historic side, contain courses for three years, first in English and American institutional history, second in English and American economic history; on the economic side, upon a required basis of familiarity with the substance of all that may be called contemporary economic doctrine, original studies of the actual conditions of American economic problems with a view to comprehension of the status of these questions in their concrete relations, rather than to a doctrine about them in the abstract; on the sociological side, first, courses filling one year in exposition of the philosophies of history. Second, courses filling the last year in Sociology proper—a synthesis of the facts of social physiology, as derived from the tributary biological, psychological, historical and economic sciences—being an inductive substitute for the antiquated metaphysical philosophies of history, and a clinical preparation for practical diagnosis of specific social developments.... I would never grant the doctorate to men of the microscope alone, but would insist that they shall have acquired a sharp sense of the relation of what their microscope discovers to the laws of society as a whole.[48]

These somewhat nebulous statements offer a weak estimation of the orientation of the new department and the recruitment of its first instructors. Harper's initiatives played a leading role in this matter in regards to the conceptions of Small, who accommodated Harper's wishes and adopted a conciliatory attitude. As he had done while hiring Small, Harper concerned himself more with recruiting certain instructors than with precisely defining the orientation of any department.

At almost the same time as hiring Small, Harper had recruited the anthropologist Frederick Starr (1858–1933), then employed by the Museum of Natural History. Small agreed to integrate him into the future Department of Sociology, and Starr accepted this arrangement on the condition that his discipline be recognized as distinct from sociology and would ultimately form its own autonomous department. For the position of university chaplain Harper recruited a Baptist pastor, Charles Henderson (1848–1915). Since Henderson demanded that his duties be equally split between teaching and research, and that Harper recruit an expert in the administration of charitable organizations, he was assigned to the Department of Sociology with Small's approval. Finally, Harper recruited as dean of students and professor of history Alice Freeman Palmer, who insisted that her assistant Marion Talbot be hired as well. In addition to staying on as Palmer's assistant, Talbot was also assigned to the Department of Sociology as a specialist in home economics. Her course of instruction—which went by the name *sanitary science*—was also included in the sociology department until the creation of a Department of Household Administration in 1903.[49]

These four instructors initially constituted the permanent faculty of the Department of Sociology. Neither Frederick Starr nor Marion Talbot were involved with sociology as an academic discipline. Starr, a geologist by training whose interests leaned toward physical anthropology, did not succeed in securing the creation of an autonomous Department of Anthropology during the following years, possibly due to his awkwardness or lack of interest in administration; the university directory mentioned each year simply that the inclusion of anthropology within the Department of Sociology was provisional.

Starr saw a degree of success on the Chicago campus, but only as a lecturer and in terms of undergraduate students. Starting in 1900, he went on missions in Mexico and Japan, and was frequently absent from Chicago. Anthropology remained stagnant as a field focused on the study of "primitive" societies until his retirement in 1923. Some training in anthropology was provided by a graduate of the university who had been quickly hired as an instructor, William Thomas. In 1905, however, the Department of Sociology did recruit an anthropologist, George Dorsey (1868–1931), who was also the director of a museum dedicated to the physical and natural sciences, the Field Museum of Chicago.

He did not establish a solid base of instruction in anthropology either, however, perhaps because of his many activities outside academia. He resigned in 1915 and became a journalist, but undoubtedly played a part in introducing Fay-Cooper Cole, who would be at the center of the creation of an autonomous anthropology department, to Chicago.

Henderson, who also played an important role in the Chicago movements for social service reform was, however, involved in his new discipline, in his own way. He benefited from his participation in a large number of steering committees of associations and national commissions gathering data on diverse social problems—notably delinquency, orphans, labor conditions, and so on. He published some of this data in the review founded by the Department of Sociology in 1895, the *American Journal of Sociology*, thus establishing one of the links between social work and sociology. Even if it proved difficult to collect firsthand data himself, Henderson was convinced of the necessity of an intimate knowledge of the objects of study and the importance of observation. William Thomas noted that Henderson asked him once to collect information in bars in his stead, telling him that he himself had never entered a bar or drank a beer.[50] Through his interest in concrete data, Henderson surely contributed to the direction of empirical research in the Department of Sociology at Chicago to a greater degree than he is generally attributed.[51] He also established the link between sociology and the Divinity School, which was affiliated with the Department of Sociology until his death in 1915.

In 1894, Henderson published a small book with a title testifying to the close association of sociological and religious interests: *Catechism for Social Observation and Analyses of Social Phenomena*. The introduction is framed as an observational guide for students as well as travelers, settlement residents, and the like. It begins with a comparison of the observation of social data with data collected by naturalists, and it refers in particular to Frédéric Le Play and Charles Booth. One book by Henderson on crime, published in 1914, mentions fieldwork and contains a remark on methods of approaching social reality with which, as we shall see, his successors would not have disagreed: "The only way to know at first hand the nature of criminals is to live with them. But for most persons this is neither agreeable nor practical. Next to personal acquaintance come the life stories of offenders."[52]

Though not identical, Albion Small's intellectual orientation was compatible with that of Henderson. Over the course of his career, Small contributed more to developing and diffusing a conception of the discipline than to providing a living example of it. But in his publications appear impulses and conceptions that are frequently found in the works of sociologists of the following generation.

In 1894, Small published (in collaboration with one of his first students, George Vincent) a manual for sociology students, *An Introduction to the Study of Society*, which describes itself as a "laboratory guide" intended to prepare beginners for the study of concrete subjects.[53] It includes a long, hypothetical example of the "natural history of a society," describing the development of a fictional American city starting from the settlement of the first farmers.[54] In an 1896 article, Small compared the city of Chicago to a "sociological laboratory," a remark frequently attributed to Robert Park, a sociologist of the following generation: "The most impressive lesson which I have learned in the vast sociological laboratory which the city of Chicago constitutes is that action, not speculation, is the supreme teacher."[55] The expression also appeared in the 1904–1905 directory of the University of Chicago, listed as a resource of the Department of Sociology (probably written by Small): "The city of Chicago is one of the most complete social laboratories in the world. . . . While the elements of sociology may be studied in smaller communities, and while it may be an advantage to beginners in the method of positive sociology to deal at first with more simple social combinations, the most serious problems of modern society are presented by the great cities and must be studied as they are encountered in concrete form in large populations. No city in the world presents a wider variety of typical social problems than Chicago."

In some articles, Small pleads in favor of observational method, an inductive approach, and against the deductive method advocated by some sociologists of the same period. He defends with equal conviction the necessity of using abstract analytical frameworks, as well as of collecting firsthand documentation through contact with the phenomena being studied. His introductory article in the first issue of the *American Journal of Sociology* in 1895 notes, "Analytic and microscopic scholarship is abortive without the complementary work of the synthetic scholar who builds minute details into comprehensive structures."[56]

Over the course of a career that stretched until 1926, Small's conception of sociology varied some, as did his political inclinations.[57] These variations can be partially understood as reactions to evolutions in the intellectual atmosphere of sociology, in the context of neighboring and rival disciplines, as well as in the context of the political and academic zeitgeist. Small's conceptions of sociology were successively influenced by the analogy of society to a biological organism, by behaviorism, and by the pragmatic philosophers of the neighboring department, John Dewey and George Mead. As an administrator—he remained chair of the department until 1924—Small was prudent, eclectic, and skillful, and he knew how to safeguard the development of the discipline at Chicago (in contrast to many of his rivals, like Franklin Giddings, his counterpart at Columbia, who failed to provide a solid institutional base to his enterprise).[58] He remained close to the Chicago reform movement and maintained that sociology should surpass class interests. Small also knew to obtain support for his discipline from the first president of the university and not to alienate either donors or local elites.

Small's influence over future generations of Chicago sociologists was certainly more indirect than direct. His publications essentially consisted of manuals—the first, as we have seen, in 1894, the second in 1905—book reviews, and articles of a speculative or methodological nature. He described himself, at the end of his career, as a generalist sociologist and a methodologist.[59] His teaching contributed toward maintaining contact between American sociology and German social sciences. In particular, he dedicated a non-negligible place in his courses to the exposition—and, according to him, the refutation—of Marxian analysis. Ernest Burgess, who took his courses, recalled that he laid out the evils of capitalism "to the astonishment of students entering a university whose chief benefaction had come from the largest fortune of that time."[60] Small evoked the failures of capitalism "with such vigour that his style sometimes became almost lively," one student from the last generation he taught remarked.[61] He furthermore systematically encouraged his students to undertake their own empirical research. Thus, Small's intellectual career is representative of those of a number of founders of sociology and anthropology departments who, lacking the ability—and the expertise—to pursue concrete research themselves, at least encouraged the subsequent generations to undertake it.

From the 1910s, a certain distance separated Small's conception of sociology from that adopted by his students. In 1913, some of them, including the future criminologist Edwin Sutherland, complained not only about his weak ability to find employment for his former students, but also about the research topics toward which he directed them. Small claimed that they emphasized "concrete problems" such as salary negotiations, employment agreements, and living conditions more than they did unionism, feminism, and socialism.[62] The judgment passed on Small's teaching by students of the following generations was no more favorable: testimonies evoke almost unanimously the tedious character of his courses.[63] Perhaps one of the better aspects of his limited reach was found in the remaining traces of his courses dedicated to Marx.

Over the following years, several new recruits were added to the initial core of the four instructors hired when the department opened. In 1894, Harper hired one of his former students at Yale, Charles Zueblin, who had begun his studies in theology. The founder, as previously mentioned, of the Northwestern University settlement, a successful lecturer, and the leader of a movement for the reform of municipal administration that was sometimes recalled Fabian socialism, Zueblin joined the Department of Sociology in 1908 and contributed to reinforcing the links between sociology and the reform movement. After he was pushed to resign due to turmoil that some of his lectures allegedly incited among the business community that sustained the university, he became a journalist.[64]

Two of the first four students to obtain a PhD in sociology at Chicago were also recruited as instructors by the university before they even finished their doctorates. George Vincent (1864–1941) completed his PhD in 1896 under the dual supervision of Albion Small and John Dewey, the latter then a professor in the Department of Philosophy. Dewey collaborated with Small, as we have seen, in editing a manual of sociology. Vincent quickly turned toward administration and left his position in 1911 in order to take the presidency of the University of Minnesota, and then that of the Rockefeller Foundation. On the other hand, the other new graduate recruited, William Thomas (1863–1947; PhD in 1896), would exert significant influence over the later Development of Sociology, as will be seen in the following chapter. Many other students at or just after the dissertation stage were also recruited on a temporary basis, generally for the system of outside lectures organized by the university.

Other instructors were recruited for the Department of Sociology by Harper and Small but did not play a notable intellectual role in the new discipline. One of the leaders of the settlement movement, Graham Taylor, taught in the department from 1902 to 1906, evidence for the proximity of sociology and the reform movement.[65] In 1913, hoping to replace George Vincent, Small tried in vain to recruit Jane Addams, envisioning developing the department toward the "applied" dimension of the discipline.[66] The same year, Small recruited as a part-time instructor a former resident of Hull House, Edith Abbott, who in 1905 had received a doctorate in economics at the University of Chicago and passed through the London School of Economics. Starting in 1908, Edith Abbott was deputy director of research at the Chicago School of Civics and Philanthropy, a school (independent from the university) for training social workers that was created under the patronage of Graham Taylor in the same year. Until this school became part of the university in 1920, Edith Abbott remained in the Department of Sociology.

Although anthropology had not yet separated from sociology, this was not the case for household administration, which emerged in 1903 as an autonomous department led by Marion Talbot and Sophonisba Breckinridge, a collaborator with Edith Abbot. Henderson, Thomas, and Vincent collaborated with this department, as did diverse instructors from around the university, including chemists.[67] Other permanent instructors recruited to sociology do not seem to have had notable impact on the evolution of the department: Jerome Raymond (1869–1928), who in 1895 had received one of the first two PhDs awarded by the department, taught there from 1901 to 1909 before leaving to become president of another university, but he published almost nothing and left hardly any trace in the discipline. The same is true for Scott Bedford, who was recruited in 1911 and remained for more than ten years.[68]

From an institutional point of view, the early days of the Chicago Department of Sociology seem to have been rather difficult. The number of students was not very large—an average of twenty-three enrollments per year for the first decade[69]—which Small occasionally attributed to prejudices against the discipline and to the lack of career opportunities. Between 1895 and 1919 (inclusive), forty-two PhDs in sociology were awarded (a little less than two per year), as well as forty-eight MAs.[70] Regarding the production of PhDs in sociology—in which the University of Chicago was by far the leader—even 40 percent of the sociology PhDs awarded by University of Chicago between 1985 and 1915 would outstrip the number produced by any other university.[71] Almost a third of those who obtained a Master's degree were women, and the presence of several African Americans enrolled in postgraduate courses testifies to the relative openness of the University (compared with similar institutions of the same era).[72] Among those who obtained PhDs were several pastors of various denominations—and the children of pastors—as well as high school and college instructors who were on average thirty-five years old at the time they received their diplomas. (The youngest laureates were at least twenty-four years old.)[73]

The sociology coursework offered at the University of Chicago before 1920 was organized in the program under a few main headings. But aside from introductory courses, which seem to have been established by Small to a somewhat greater degree, the courses reflected the proposals submitted by the instructors, and redundancies were numerous. Students also pursued instruction in neighboring departments, where diverse intellectual orientations prevailed, but where behaviorism was very influential. One pre-1914 student, Emory Bogardus, described the training he had received as the juxtaposition of the study of processes of association, of which Small was an advocate, with Thomas's insistence on the collection of biographies, Mead's theory of role-playing, and two other approaches inspired by behaviorism.[74]

Small or Henderson made at least two unsuccessful attempts to expand the instruction of statistics in the sociology department, and possibly also attempted to end their dependence in this matter on courses in the Department of Political Economy.[75] The first attempt, in 1894, at Small's initiative (much like the second, in 1908, at the instigation of Henderson),[76] was cut short. However, it showed that the specific orientation toward fieldwork (or, to use the term that would come to be preferred, the "ethnographic approach") that would be affirmed later was nowhere written in the department's original orientation. By contrast, the orientation toward a resolutely empirical approach seems to have manifested immediately, as is suggested by the previously mentioned description of the department in the university directory.

The students' research subjects show a wide diversity, as well as the nature of the work required for the completion of a thesis. Some of these were published in the *American Journal of Sociology*, sometimes in the form of one short article and sometimes as a set of multiple articles, reflecting the diversity of requirements. The University of Chicago Press published several theses, sometimes after a delay of years. Their subjects evoke in many cases the research topics of the following period (relativizing the influence exercised by Park in this matter): one of them covers, for example, "the social significance of the physical development of cities" (1907), another "the influence of newspaper presentation upon the growth of crime and other antisocial activities" (1910). Theses focusing on labor were rare—that of Emory Bogardus in 1911, on the relationship between fatigue and workplace accidents, constitutes an exception. The theme of labor belonged in effect to the economists at the University of Chicago. An appreciable number of theses focused on "theoretical" subjects: centered on a concept or on a group of authors, these could be based exclusively on documentary research in the library. None of the theses undertaken during this period seemed to have given rise to any work that acquired, even in a narrow sense, any renown—this would not be the case later on.

In a general manner, one could remark that the publications of the members—both instructors and students—of the Department of Sociology at the University of Chicago before 1917 had little impact. Certainly, they had less impact than did certain publications on similar subjects written by journalists and social workers. No important intellectual innovation, it seems, can be found from that period. At Chicago, as elsewhere, sociology obtained only limited recognition in academic spheres. In a 1908 letter, Albion Small, the founder of the Department of Sociology, remarked, "The chief obstacle which specialists of my sort encounter is the inveterate opinion that Sociology is merely a convenient label for leftovers within the range of human knowledge that cannot be classified under any other head."[77] Nevertheless, sociology graduates soon came to occupy relatively high positions in universities or the administrations of city school systems.

Certain students who, for one reason or another, never finished their theses, went on to teach sociology, and they directed some of the students of the following generation toward the University of Chicago.[78]

> Of the 103 MA and PhD students whom Diner found evidence of having graduated from the Department of Sociology between 1892 and 1920, around a third would become sociology professors; somewhat fewer would go on to work in primary, secondary, or higher education as instructors or administrators; 7 percent would move into social work; 7 percent would become civil servants or politicians, and 5 percent would become clergy.[79] The proportion of those who became social science professors is even higher among PhDs alone: of the forty who graduated between 1895 and 1919 and for whom some information is available regarding their later career, thirty-six were at one point or another professors in the social sciences at universities: five taught primarily in economics, three in education, four in social work, two in anthropology, and the rest in sociology.[80] Sometimes, having experience in a discipline other than sociology was considered a more favorable solution in terms of employment: Jesse Steiner thus reports that in 1915, when he received his doctorate, Small "expressed such great doubts regarding the future development of the domain of social science that he seriously considered the possibility of studying economics, which was then extremely popular." Finally, he adds, "incapable of finding a stable job in my discipline, I reluctantly turned to social work as a temporary means of subsistence."[81]

The Reform Movement, Social Research, Social Work and Sociology

Two aspects of the connections between the nascent sociology movement and the reform movement merit more precise examination, because they are relevant for the interpretation of research from this period and the one immediately following it: first, the growth of a job market for sociologists and social workers that accompanied the institutionalization of their training, and second, the movement of research on the working class that had sprung up around the settlements.

The diffusion of ideas of the Progressive movement through the Midwest fostered the creation of university sociology departments: these then recruited instructors and, by introducing them to sociology as undergraduates, prepared future graduate students for the Department of Sociology at the University of Chicago. At the same time, the application of certain reforms, especially in instruction and social work, contributed to the creation of jobs to be filled by sociology graduates.

At the University of Chicago and its satellite institutions, sociologists largely participated in the training of social workers, an ensemble of professions that coalesced around 1900 and occupied space previously held by volunteers. After 1903, at the instigation of Graham Taylor and Charles Henderson, but with the participation of Small and the support of Harper, the University founded a Social Science Institute. As part of the university extension, this institute offered training to social workers employed by charitable organizations and municipal social services. The program grew rapidly, but after the death of Harper in 1906 his successor neglected it, and in 1908 Taylor founded, as we have seen, the School of Civics and Philanthropy, which was independent from the university. Four other professors from the Department of Sociology taught there: Grace Abbott, George Vincent, William Thomas, and Charles Henderson. However, the creation of the School of Civics and Philanthropy was not accompanied by a lack of interest among sociologists for social work, as evidenced by the 1913 attempt to hire Jane Addams part-time to reinforce the curriculum in social service offered by the department.[82]

Institutional and biographical factors, however, would give rise to another issue. The school founded by Graham Taylor was in a financially precarious situation, and ultimately was integrated into the university in 1920, forming within it the School of Social Service Administration. This resulted in Grace Abbott's departure from the Department of Sociology, accentuating the institutional separation of social work from sociology that had been ongoing since Henderson's death in 1915. Very active in the city's charitable organizations and associations, Henderson in essence served as a link between the two spheres of activity, and his courses were widely attended. Small did not succeed in recruiting a replacement who was as involved in this sector, and it was ultimately Ernest Burgess, a former student in the department recruited in 1916, who took over some of the courses Henderson had previously taught.[83] His loss also damaged the ties between sociology and the university's School of Divinity. In 1902, Henderson became chair of a new department in this faculty called "practical sociology", notably signifying that the instruction of sociology could be pursued by students in this discipline.

Though omitted from all histories of the growth of sociology at the University of Chicago, the durable (at least formally) link between the Department of Sociology and the settlement founded by university students in a working-class neighborhood near campus should also be mentioned. Until 1924–1925, its head resident, Mary McDowell, a former resident of Hull House, appeared under the heading concerning the Department of Sociology in the university registrar; it appears that she was not given a teaching position.[84]

The Social Survey Movement constitutes another link between the reform movement and sociology. The idea of more or less systematically collecting data before proposing solutions to social problems that presented themselves was common to all Protestant reformers of the era. Charles Booth's vast survey of London, conducted starting in 1886 and published starting in 1889, served as the model on which, as previously mentioned, Jane Addams and her associates based their research.[85]

Although there exist several examples of this type of research between 1895 and 1907,[86] the Social Survey Movement grew significantly and became more visible after this date, with the creation of publications like the magazine *Survey*, which presented the results of these surveys, and especially with the contribution of the Russell Sage Foundation, which financed a vast survey in Pittsburgh, the Pittsburgh Survey, between 1909 and 1914. In 1912, the Foundation created a department specially charged with providing subventions for surveys.

In the majority of these social surveys, data were collected by volunteers who visited the populations in question. Institutional archives and local organizations were generally utilized, as well as relationships with social workers, and testimonies were collected from various informants. The style of the reports was journalistic, with emphasis placed on presenting the results to a broad public (essentially, the middle classes), which the surveys sought to convince of the nature of the problem studied, and of the urgent necessity of a solution. The proximity between the Social Survey Movement and sociology—and the social sciences more broadly—is a striking fact that, until recently, was left in the shadows when most American sociologists reflected back on their own history.

Some of the survey reports were, however, published in the *American Journal of Sociology*, as well as numerous articles by the participants in the survey movement. For example, one of the organizers of the Pittsburgh Survey, the journalist and professor of social economy at Columbia University Edward Devine, published an article on his survey results at Columbia in 1909; in 1910 and 1911, three articles by Sophonisba Breckinridge and Edith Abbott described the living conditions of immigrants in a Chicago neighborhood.[87] Those authors who were not academics occasionally emphasized the proximity of their activities to those of the sociologists. One example is a resident of Chicago Commons, Hegner, who in an 1897 article described the approach of the settlement surveys as "scientific" because it was "empirical, reciprocal, mediatory, and positive along the lines of social evolution," and affirmed that these establishments were "social science laboratories."[88] The American Sociological Society's 1914 creation of a committee headed by Charles Henderson and charged with proposing a sample plan for social surveys also illustrates the attention paid by the community of sociologists to social surveys.[89]

Many sociologists and philosophers at the University of Chicago participated in surveys of this type without implying a transformation in their methodology or objectives. Even before he was recruited as a sociologist by the university, Charles Zueblin wrote the chapter on the ghetto in *Hull House Maps and Papers*. In 1909, two professors of the University of Chicago, the philosopher George Herbert Mead and the sociologist Charles Henderson, worked with the university settlement to direct a survey, published 1912–1914, on the salaries, living and working conditions of slaughterhouse workers, as well as the education of their children.[90] George Mead and John Dewey also worked on a survey inspired by the Pittsburgh Survey between 1910 and 1916. It should be added that participation in social surveys was not limited to sociologists, nor to scholars at Chicago: many social science professors at Columbia University were engaged in surveys of this type in New York, and among the board members of the Pittsburgh Survey figured a professor of political economy from the University of Wisconsin, John Commons.

Thus, before 1914, sociology, and in particular sociology as it existed at the University of Chicago, was firmly integrated into a much vaster social movement; two other elements were the Social Survey Movement and the movement that would lead to the establishment of social work as a profession. As with its institutional relationships with the Divinity School and the Department of Household Administration, there was no clear division between sociological studies and certain studies conducted for "practical" purposes, and sociology could not be characterized by the absence of such aims. This point would not merit such emphasis if sociologists' later interpretations of their own written history had not almost unanimously accentuated the isolation and the autonomy of the new discipline, in which their predecessors considered practical outcomes as much as they were motivated by "science" and "objective knowledge." Thus, in terms of being an academic research discipline, sociology before 1920 was only very vaguely defined. This vagueness extended to its relationships with other disciplines, whether already established or in the course of institutionalization, such as psychology, anthropology, and philosophy, or even with the domain of training activities that constituted social work, a field of study which was itself in the process of institutionalization. It is by reference to this context, and not that of sociology as it was more precisely defined after 1920, that we must read and interpret the publications that appeared as its foundation in the United States, notably those of W. I. Thomas and Robert E. Park.

I have also emphasized that certain components of the future development of sociology at the University of Chicago appeared in the first years after its creation, but that the university's sociology department did not yet have a well-defined intellectual orientation: the creation of an autonomous Department of Sociology was due to circumstance rather than the formulation and execution of a distinct project on the part of the university founders or the first instructors in the department itself. The only clear orientation that was present from the start was an insistence on using empirical knowledge of the contemporary world, as opposed to the speculation of social philosophy.

We shall see that the generation educated between the end of the First World War and the 1930s displays a degree of homogeneity in terms of intellectual orientation, which can largely be attributed to the instruction of Robert Park and, more broadly, to the intellectual environment of Pragmatism. This interpretation is corroborated by the greater heterogeneity of orientations evident in the generation examined above, whose members finished their degrees before 1919. It is difficult to identify any common intellectual orientation among those who later occupied prominent positions in sociology—who founded or directed sociology departments, who published textbooks for the new discipline, and especially the ten who went on to become presidents of the American Sociological Society (ASS). A few sociologists like Ernest Burgess or Edwin Sutherland—both of whom were recruited by the University of Chicago in the following period—number among these prominent figures, but also in this cohort can be found Charles Elwood (one of the proponents for maintaining a Protestant-inspired sociology); those who, like Luther Bernard, espoused a scientific orientation within sociology; and, finally, the group of sociologists that included Stuart Queen, whose interests overlapped with social work.

Two important elements for the evolution of sociology—aside from its institutional and sociopolitical contexts, to which we shall return—distinguish this first period from the one that starts with the end of the First World War. The first is the publication of William Thomas's research on Polish immigration to the United States and the diffusion of the model at the heart of his research; the second is the new intellectual atmosphere within which research in the Department of Sociology was conducted following the recruitment of Robert Park.

2

William Isaac Thomas, *The Polish Peasant in Europe and America,* and the Beginnings of Empirical Academic Sociology

I attempted to reach an understanding of the present through the study of the most primitive forms of society, through the so-called savage. But a number of years ago I concluded that the only proper way to understand the present was to study the present, and that the proper way to study behavior (which is the ultimate basis of social control) was to study the individual.[1]

—W. I. Thomas

If I wanted to write a life-history I would write it myself and give it the context.[2]

—W. I. Thomas

Although their beliefs oriented them toward empirical research, the first generation of Chicago sociologists experienced some difficulty in terms of making contact with the subjects they sought to study, as previously mentioned. In large part, contacts were established through the intermediation of social workers, as well as that of different charitable and social control organizations. A parallel could be drawn with the first anthropologists, who also gained initial access to their research subjects through different intermediaries, such as missionaries. In sociology, a significant step toward the alignment of researchers and their subjects was made, at the beginning of the century in Chicago, in the form of a work by William Isaac Thomas and Florian Znaniecki, *The Polish Peasant in Europe and America.*[3]

Having been considered a model of sociological research in the United States for two decades, starting in 1945 this work developed into a sort of classic that attracted no more than nominal recognition: the portions of textbooks dedicated to it often give only a cursory sense of its contents, the objectives of its authors, and the approach that they invented. As is typically the case in this sort of treatment, the commentary focuses on re-translating the book's intentions and analyses into more contemporary language, often ignoring anything not relevant to the concerns of the present day.

A haze of legends has surrounded the production of this book, and even more so the biography of one of its authors, William Isaac Thomas (1863–1947), who was later enshrined as a founder of the University of Chicago's sociological tradition.[4] Thomas's behaviors and tastes essentially ran contrary to those of most academics of his generation, and his reputation—deliciously lurid in the eyes of the following generation—introduced a hint of adventure into a discipline heretofore represented by austere Protestants. The documentary sources concerning Thomas's activities are, furthermore, rather scarce and scattered.[5] Thus, starting in the 1960s, it became possible to find evocations of Thomas's career, personality, and scholarly contribution in research on delinquency, women's liberation, the use of autobiographies, or the development of sociology. All of these, on close examination, reveal themselves to be rather loose interpretations based on thin sources, selected with a priori aims in mind, and employing dangerous inductions. The second author of *The Polish Peasant*, Florian Znaniecki, a Polish philosopher, only participated in the research from the end of 1914, and he returned to Poland in 1920. Without implying that his contribution was secondary, it was because of the book's connection to the American context and to Thomas's career that the work was read in the years following its publication. Therefore, Thomas is the central focus here.

The Polish Peasant was the first work of research to simultaneously implement two separate forms of activity that were both covered by the poorly defined term "sociology" in 1910, as articles published in the *American Journal of Sociology* make clear: first, the construction of general conceptual schemes for the analysis of the social world, the speciality of the scholars occupying chairs in sociology; and second, the collection of firsthand data, which had since the 1890s been practiced by the Anglo-American Social Survey Movement, but not scholars (at least not in terms of producing books).[6]

The execution of *The Polish Peasant* presented significant differences from these two antecedents. One original aspect is the financing of the work: the research it interprets was the object of a contract with one of the patrons of the University of Chicago and Hull House, Helen Culver—a practice that had scarcely any precedent in the social sciences.

In 1938, eighteen years after the publication of the final volumes of *The Polish Peasant*, Thomas described the development of the research project that gave rise to it:[7]

> at that time, immigration was a burning question. About a million immigrants were coming here annually, and this was mainly the newer immigration, from southern and eastern Europe. The larger groups were Poles, Italians, Jews. . . . Eventually, I decided to study an immigrant group in Europe and America to determine as far as possible what relation their homes, mores and norms had to their adjustment and maladjustment in America. . . . I expected to find in the numerous journals of folklore rich material on the peasant, but I soon found that these materials were of no value. They dealt with such things as the coloring of Easter eggs, figures in weaving. . . . After a year's exploration, I decided to study the Poles, largely because I found there abundant materials. . . . Another reason for my choice of Poles was their behavior in America. They were the most incomprehensible and perhaps the most disorganized of all the immigrant groups. This may be illustrated by what the American police call "Polish warfare." A policeman might enter a saloon where there was a noisy crowd of Poles and say, "You men be quiet," and they might subside immediately or one of them might draw a gun and kill him. This was due to the fact that the Pole in America has two attitudes toward authority. One of these reflects the old peasant subordination to authority. . . . The other attitude reflects the conception that there are no limits to the boasted American "freedom."[8]

This account is silent regarding the trial and error that marked the development of the project that led to the book, and omits mention of the gap between the intellectual universe in which the research that became *The Polish Peasant* was embedded and in which the work was interpreted after 1920, when it was enshrined as a model of empirical sociological research. It also ignores the aspects of *The Polish Peasant* that signify a rupture in Thomas's intellectual career. He was fifty-four years old and moderately well known when the first two volumes of the book were published in 1918, and had previously published two books that did not rely on empirical research, focus on immigration, or even fall within the category of sociology according to the definition it took on after 1920. It is to this intellectual journey, combined with biographical elements that shed light on the genesis of the work, that I hope to draw attention. I shall highlight the context in which Thomas's analyses developed by pointing out, often in notes, the activities and publications of two particular groups with close ties to sociologists: investigative journalists and the Protestant reformers of the settlement movement.

Born in 1863, William Thomas was the son of a Virginia farmer and lay Methodist preacher.[9] His family included a great number of pastors and professors at Emory and Henry College, a Virginia university frequented by the local Methodist elite, from which Thomas's father had graduated in 1853. According to his autobiography, Thomas spent his first years in an environment out of the eighteenth century, spending long days hunting alone. This detail is not compatible with the chronology of his places of residence, but it is significant in terms of Thomas's interest in the "backward" (to use the term Thomas employed in 1912) cultural world of peasants.[10] Moving to Knoxville, then a small city, in 1873, Thomas later undertook classical studies at the University of Tennessee, where he also, according to his autobiography, studied zoology and geology from a disciple of Darwin and Ancient Greek from a Yale graduate.[11] In 1886 he obtained the first PhD bestowed by the University of Tennessee, which had already hired him as an adjunct professor to teach Greek and natural history—one might expect that his understanding of at least one of the subjects had to have been limited.

On the occasion of a voyage to Berlin and Göttingen in 1888–1889, his first opportunity to satisfy his taste for traveling, according to his testimony, Thomas studied philosophy, Old French, Old English, and Old German. Thomas also discovered the *Völkerpsychologie* (folk psychology) of philosopher Moritz Lazarus, philologist Heymann Steinthal, and psychologist Wilhelm Wundt—a method that sought to explain the genesis and development of cultural forms like language and religion.[12] Before returning from Germany, Thomas was hired as a professor of English and literature at Oberlin College, a new university in Ohio founded in 1833 by two Presbyterian pastors.

Oberlin was the first establishment of its type in the United States to admit, in 1834 and 1837 respectively, African Americans and women as students.[13] There, Thomas principally taught English literature, with special attention in his courses to the historical contextualization of the novels he taught. During his final year, he secured a teaching assignment under the title of "sociology."[14] During the years Thomas spent at Oberlin, he claimed to have attentively read Herbert Spencer's *Principles of Sociology*, published between 1874 and 1885. In 1892, he went to Chicago to pursue a doctorate in the recently opened Department of Sociology and Anthropology, and in 1896 was hired as an instructor there before he even submitted his dissertation, titled "On a Difference of the Metabolism of the Sexes."[15]

In his brief autobiographical account, Thomas did not recall his studies in sociology as having any importance in his intellectual formation. A notable portion of the concepts that he studied in order to obtain his PhD, and that he cited

in his autobiography, was in effect biological—such as the physiological teach-
ings of Jacques Loeb (1859–1924)—or neurological—such as the work of one
of the founders of psychiatry in the United States, Adolf Meyer (1866–1950),
whom Thomas eventually met. Scarcely older than Thomas, Loeb and Meyer
were also assistants at the University of Chicago and at the beginning of careers
that would assure them great reputations in their specialties.

Over the following ten years, Thomas published a series of articles on the differences and the relationship between the sexes, which he published, along with his
dissertation, in a book titled *Sex and Society* (1907), which had non-negligible
impact.[16] A chronological reading of these articles reveals the evolution (described
as slow by the author himself) of Thomas's convictions regarding the relative
importance of biological determinants on a subject in relation to those resulting from the social environment.[17] This evolution in his thinking was fostered by
Thomas's broad reading in the university library, where he kept himself occupied
in addition to his teaching requirements. Without a doubt, the most significant
work he read was that of the anthropologist Franz Boas (1858–1942), then an
influential analytical critic, very widely cited in the social sciences, of those who
cited "racial" differences as the explanation for behavioral differences among the
populations present in the United States.[18]

The evolution of Thomas's beliefs was also influenced by his life in Chicago
and his contacts with Hull House and its adherents: one of their shared fundamental convictions, as the historian Gary Gerstle has written, was that men
are not autonomous creatures in control of their own lives, but rather that their
opportunities and desires are profoundly influenced by their environment, both
physical and historical.[19] By virtue of its subject, *Sex and Society* is a work that was
not only concerned with the world of the Progressive reformers at Hull House
and the young women with graduate degrees who sought to emancipate themselves from the "feminine" roles assigned to them. Since 1896, magazine articles
had focused on the "New Woman," an ideal of which the first female recipients of
doctorates from the University of Chicago were examples, though not the only
ones.[20] Ten years later, changes in mores, especially in cities, were the subject of
constant discussion. The question of women's place in the social world was then
a debate over their access to the electoral body, and the educated women of Hull
House were on the front lines of the campaigns in favor of women's suffrage.[21] In
Chicago and other large cities, there was also the question of prostitution and its
regulation, which at the beginning of the century was associated with the problem of corruption in municipal administrations and among the police, with the
spread of venereal disease, with juvenile crime, and with the changing moral values of young immigrant women.[22]

Sex and Society was not based on the systematic collection of firsthand evidence, but contained references to the publications of biologists and, especially, of anthropologists and psychologists. Among these, special attention was paid to a thesis in experimental psychology submitted in 1900 by a young woman, Helen Bradford Thompson, then a student in the psychology laboratory associated with the Department of Philosophy at the University of Chicago.[23] Read in chronological order, the articles Thomas collects in *Sex and Society* reveal the progressive substitution of the environment and social experiences in place of biological factors as behavioral determinants. Thus, while Thomas sustains in an article from 1897 that differences in sex between men and women are based on biological differences, he affirms in a later article, published in the same year as the collection, that "there is also no ground for the assumption that the brain of woman is inferior to that of man."[24]

Sex and Society also reveals Thomas's growing skepticism with regards to anthropological publications: in a text written in 1907 to serve as a transition between two articles published in 1897 and 1898, Thomas emphasizes the caution necessary for evaluating their observations.[25] The penultimate chapter of *Sex and Society*, originally an article from 1906, contains remarks that seem to refer to Thomas's personal experience, and he ends with a plea in favor of the education of women and their integration into an existence that is not limited to the familial dimension: "Normal life without normal stimulation is not possible, and the stimulations answering to the nature of the nervous organization seem best supplied by interesting forms of work."[26] The book, which still accepts the model of a unilinear evolution of society, possesses a remarkably speculative character, especially in the way it advances without reference discussions of the behaviors of women in the United States, which therefore rely upon diffuse personal observations. Neither Thomas's general character nor his imprecise relationship with documentation were very far removed from the typical intellectual production of the period, as Thomas's successor at the University of Chicago, Ellsworth Faris (1874–1953), noted in his obituary for the scholar in 1948.

Even if the social science disciplines were poorly defined in this period, Thomas's interrogations, as well as his methodology, placed him clearly within the realm of anthropologists, and not that of the sociologists of his time. The names of the courses he taught also suggest this, as do the references in his articles and what is known of his activity within the university. For example, a letter to the president of the university, W. R. Harper, makes it seem that Thomas in 1896 was considering affiliating himself with anthropology.[27] Likewise, in 1907 he attempted to recruit Franz Boas for the Department of Sociology and anthropology at Chicago, and in 1908 he sought to recruit a new instructor for the same department.[28] He also maintained a durable, and certainly close, relationship with George Dorsey, assistant and then associate professor at the University of Chicago from 1906 to 1915.[29] Thomas nevertheless avoided the American Association of Anthropologists, founded in 1901, which surely can partially explain the fact that his work was little cited by anthropologists. Thomas's intellectual attachment to anthropology must be highlighted because the two disciplines were distinct in terms of their queries and their culture, even if anthropology happened to be in the same department as sociology at the University of Chicago. With regards to sociology, such as it was then represented at the University of Chicago, Thomas expressed only reticence, remarking in his brief autobiography that he was equally removed from the "methodological approach of Professor Small" and the "remedial and the correctional interests" of Charles Henderson.[30]

Beyond his proximity to anthropology and his distance from sociology, Thomas's relationship with the Progressive reformers before 1920 has frequently been poorly understood by following generations. Some attribute to him a complete indifference with regard to reform; others, an active participation with the reform movement.[31] Examined without a priori beliefs, Thomas's activism seems to have been limited, according to the available archival sources, but his intellectual proximity to the reformers is indisputable.

In effect, Thomas maintained close and, in some cases, lasting relationships with certain activists in the Progressive sphere of Chicago, to which his wife, Harriet Thomas, clearly belonged after 1910.[32] Harriet Thomas, who was associated with Hull House starting in 1895, was active as a volunteer at the Juvenile Protective Association (JPA), founded in order to supply the juvenile court in Chicago with people assigned to follow up on delinquents after their sentences.[33] She was also active in the movement for female suffrage and, after 1915, the pacifist movement, and she collaborated closely with Jane Addams (1860–1935). Harriet and William Thomas frequently visited the philosopher George Herbert Mead (1863–1931) and his wife, who also belonged to the entourage of Jane Addams and was very active in the reform movement. Thomas himself participated in conferences and wrote magazine articles to diffuse his beliefs, heterodoxical after 1906, on sexuality, marriage, and the place of women in social life. He also figured among the sociology instructors who collaborated with the founders of social work, Sophonisba Breckinridge (1866–1948) and Edith Abbott (1876–1957), at the School of Civics and Philanthropy directed by Graham Taylor, then a member of the sociology department. Thomas additionally found himself among the participants in a campaign opposing the expulsion of a Russian anarchist refugee from Chicago.[34]

The character of Thomas's participation in 1910 in the Vice Commission of the City of Chicago, which was responsible for a report on prostitution in the city titled *Social Evil in Chicago*, is very uncertain.[35] Between 1907 and 1917, prostitution was a highly debated topic in Chicago. In 1910, the Church Federation, which represented the different Protestant churches, asked the mayor of the city to nominate an investigative committee. Thomas was selected, along with Graham Taylor, Charles Henderson, and other academics, as a member of this commission charged with studying and making recommendations about the regulation of prostitution. The conclusions of the commission do not express the most conservative positions of the epoch—the report highlights, for example, the nefarious consequences of very low salaries for young workers. Nevertheless, Thomas later characterized the approach of the commission as "extremely conservative," noting that he had not participated in writing the report as he was in Europe at the time. His criticism pertained to the conditions in which the commission had worked. Thomas, however, cites the introduction of the report, in which the commission notes that it accepted the moral norms of the period and took for its goal the formulation of recommendations that were "reasonable and practical," that were "possible under the Constitutional powers of our Courts," and that would "square with the public conscience of the American people." Thus, Thomas observed, the commission ignored the moral evolutions then taking place.[36]

The range of positions held on all subjects within the Progressive movement, and particularly within the entourage of Jane Addams at Hull House, is evidently broad.[37] The critical remarks about Progressive reformers that came from Thomas's pen seem aimed at some of them, but these did not threaten the maintenance of lasting relationships with Jane Addams or others who advocated a close relationship between research into the social world and reform activities.[38]

The principal targets of Thomas's critical remarks correspond to simplistic reasoning inspired by the search for "solutions" to social problems of the moment, and to certain reformers' imposing upon immigrants their own social norms—those of the Protestant, Anglo-Saxon middle classes. This type of reasoning could be found in certain analyses of the Pittsburgh Survey, and particularly in the work of Edward T. Devine, secretary of the New York Charity Organization Society, professor of social economy at Columbia University, and author of numerous books.[39] Charles Henderson, who collected presidencies of charitable organizations, could doubtlessly be associated with this conception, but Thomas never personalized the targets of his remarks.

In 1902, Charles Henderson (1848–1915) published a pamphlet titled *Practical Sociology in the Service of Social Ethics*, which constitutes a plea in favor of putting social science knowledge to use for social progress.[40] Adopting an interrogative rhetorical style, Henderson sustains that sociology can respond "more fully and distinctly" to these questions: "(1) What ought we to seek as ends of community conduct and co-operation? (2) By what methods can society most successfully work for these ends?" It is impossible to prove that Thomas's criticisms explicitly targeted Henderson, whose positions cannot be characterized as simply conservative in the context of the period. In his autobiography, he refers to Henderson only in the two remarks mentioned in this chapter and the preceding one. A section in one of Henderson's books, *The Cause and Cure of Crime*, titled "The causes of crime," illustrates the intellectual difference separating himself from Thomas: Henderson distinguishes exterior causes, including seasons, storms, and inherited defects like weakness of spirit, from causes pertaining to the person of the criminal himself, such as bad habits acquired during youth, moral depravity, poor judgment, physical and spiritual defects, and will.[41] Thomas does not seem to have ever cited Henderson, but the remark mentioned above suggests that their personal relationship was not necessary one of conflict. In a later comment, Robert Park explains the subtext of Thomas's critique: his target is the reduction of the study of social problems, to a "science" of social reform and welfare.[42]

The summary of a conference held at Oberlin in 1894, in which Thomas set himself in opposition to Swift Holbrook, a businessman and academic lecturer who was one of the promoters of "Christian sociology," shows that his position with regard to the "practical sociology" of Progressive reformers predated his arrival to Chicago.[43] However, Thomas's criticism of research that pursues immediate practical objectives, found in many of his other texts, is put aside, perhaps for diplomatic reasons, in a 1911 letter in which he presents his research projects to Helen Culver, who financed the research for *The Polish Peasant*. In the letter Thomas states, "It would be part of my business to meet and talk with scholars, to see what knowledge they have, and to stimulate them to formulate it and give it a direct value for social reform."[44]

After his departure from Chicago in 1918, no trace of activity in favor of any cause can be found in Thomas's actions. The preceding year, in a letter to Ethel Dummer, a banker's wife who was very active in the reform movement and hoped to involve Thomas in a campaign concerning abortion, Thomas declined her proposition, stating he would refuse any role directing a reform campaign and that she should consider him "an investigator before anything else."[45]

From 1906, Thomas wrote articles remarking upon the consequences of ongoing social changes on the behavior of women. One might wonder whether these were influenced by the personal experiences of William and Harriet Thomas, who had moved from the Protestantism of the rural or semi-rural elites of the South to the secularism and rapid urban development of Chicago. Moreover, it is likely that Thomas's standpoint in his articles was fostered by the couple's observations about the city as well as the reformers of Hull House.[46]

In 1907, Thomas noted in passing that some American women "stand at the very top in their university studies and examinations" but that they were "swept away and engulfed by the modern system of marriage" and found "no career open to their talents."[47] Published the prior year, another article remarked that the young women who moved to the city alone, separated from family and neighbors, found themselves socially isolated and ready to accept anything that might stimulate them in order to break up a routine existence. This drove them to temporarily abandon a conformist existence for a more irregular life (implying liberal sexual relations), then swing back to the inverse—a much more frequent occurrence than ordinarily supposed, Thomas remarked.[48]

An acute awareness of the relativity of moral norms, particularly in terms of familial behavior and sexuality, began to separate Thomas from his contemporaries in sociology during this period. The series of articles that he published in *American Magazine* in 1908 and 1909 surely offer only a subdued version of his ideas.[49] Thomas's readings in anthropology were one source of his moral relativism and of his beliefs concerning societal variations in social norms, just as they had contributed to establishing his conviction that the social environment was the basis of differences between men and women. However, his own personal experience was certainly no less important. In his autobiography, Thomas dates to this period the deepening of his thought, which became at this point, according to him, "thoughtful," adding that he had abandoned blind trust in doctoral dissertations, including those written in German. Thomas also affirms in his autobiography that he had "explored the city"—but I have found no evidence supporting this claim, aside from a remark in a 1918 journal article in which he states that his methodology involves "association with normal and moral persons, indeed, but also association with prostitutes, thieves and bums," as well as "the possibility of being seen in places and with persons in which and with whom you are not supposed to belong."[50]

The second book published by Thomas in 1909, *Source Book for Social Origins*, gives an idea of his readings in anthropology. The book resulted from a course of the same title, which transparently referred to the *Völkerpsychologie* approach of Lazarus and Steinthal.[51] It is a collection of texts that thematically organizes the contributions of different anglophone and German anthropologists, including those of Franz Boas, Graham Sumner, Herbert Spencer, and John Dewey—this last case being a critique of Spencer. Thomas himself wrote only an introduction and brief comments at the end of each part. The book, he warns, is aimed at those who wish to acquire "a sound and comprehensive knowledge of biology, an even more particular knowledge of psychology and a very intimate knowledge of anthropology," rather than those who study sociology.[52]

Source Book for Social Origins was read widely over the following quarter of a century, and was used as a textbook for sociology students at Chicago.[53] Central themes of the book include criticism of Herbert Spencer's theses (also criticized by Albion Small around the same time) and the total refusal, following Dewey, to explain the genesis of social institutions by means of instinct, innate, or inherited tendencies. The argument rests on documents relating to diverse forms of art, morality, the family, sexuality, religion, and the relationships between societies and their geographical and economic environments. The introduction, which borrows its terminology more from contemporary psychology than from sociology, retains as unit of analysis the individual and his relationship to society, as Thomas did in all his research.[54] It emphasizes the importance of the notions of control of the environment and attention—"control is the end to be secured and attention is the means of securing it."[55]

According to Kimball Young (1893–1972), *Source Book for Social Origins* was important for sociologists of the generation following Thomas's on account of its empirical orientation.[56] This is confirmed by Thomas's successor at the University of Chicago. Ellsworth Faris, who took over from Thomas the course that gave rise to the book, sustained that "I know of no better way to break through the provincialism and ethnocentric narrowness of the undergraduate student than to expose him to this material."[57] From the point of view of his predecessors, who considered society to be "a body of legal conventions or moral ideas" that sociologists took as their mission to critique, *Source Book for Social Origins* substituted, according to Robert Park, a conception of society as a "natural phenomenon, the results of purely natural processes"—in other words, the product of interactions between populations that are neither foreseen nor desired.[58]

A comparison of *Source Book for Social Origins* with Thomas's publications on sexual differences reveals the constancy of comparative intention underlying his interest in primitive societies. This dimension seems to have been more explicit in Thomas's teaching around 1910 than in his publications, according to the recollections of his former student Emory Bogardus.[59] The introduction to *Source Book for Social Origins* also reveals Thomas's mistrust of history and the historical approach, to which he never explicitly accords credit.

In an article published in 1905, Thomas outlined the program of the new specialization of social psychology, then still in the process of definition, the domain "of the interaction of individual consciousness and society and the effect of the interaction on individual consciousness on the one hand and on society on the other," and, more simply, the study of the subjective dimension of behaviors.[60] In this article, which by a contemporary reading seems rather confused, Thomas sustains that "there is no . . . social psychology apart from . . . individual psychology."

Among the subjects presented, Thomas evokes the consequences of crisis and certain other problems on the conscience of a social group, as well as contact with another population that foreshadow a change in habits. These examples are borrowed from anthropology. Thomas also evokes the comparison of states of consciousness according to race and social class as permitting the determination of which differences distinguish them, and in what measure these differences depend on biological or social factors. The article also foreshadows the attention Thomas would pay in following years to "social change," the article marking one of the first times Thomas uses this term.

In the same period one can find several remarks by Thomas regarding class difference: "We have freed our slaves, recognizing in this that no man is an alien, to be treated as an economic value, as we treat inanimate things. But psychologically speaking our population is still divided into alien classes and the negro is not only still in virtual slavery, but the capitalistic manipulator treats the laborer and the public as inanimate things, possessing only economic value—or is only just beginning not to do so."[61] In an article in *American Magazine*, Thomas also criticizes the treatment of young women working in industry,[62] a viewpoint also found in the writing of Charles Henderson, such as his *Social Evil in Chicago*. Such criticism of the consequences of the development of capitalism concerned an important portion of Protestant reformers at the time: in 1907, the platform of the Federal Council of Churches of Christ in America, an association made up of the principal Protestant churches, condemned capitalist exploitation and proclaimed the workers' right to a decent quality of life.[63]

Thomas seems to have been a valued teacher at the beginning of the century. His audience especially consisted of young women in the course of doctoral studies, not necessarily in sociology, some of them possibly in the process of emancipating themselves from their environments of origin.[64] But around 1916, he seemed very critical of his colleagues to Kimball Young, then his research assistant: he seemed to consider Small a philosopher and an old fuddy-duddy, "even though he denied it."[65] Luther Bernard, who was his student at Chicago from 1907 to 1910, remarked that Thomas seemed at that time to have been uninterested in his students and especially preoccupied with non-academic activities—he remembers, like others, Thomas's elegant clothing, his regular golf practice, and his taste for cards and drink.[66] Bernard also described the astonishment of Charles Ellwood, an austere Protestant who had taken Thomas's course a dozen years earlier, when he heard what Thomas was teaching about women, sexuality, and morality: ten years earlier, according to Ellwood, Thomas had been a strong defender of conventional ideas in all these areas.[67] Bernard also evokes Thomas's taste, which Thomas sometimes also mentioned himself, for travel and the contacts it permitted him to make, and his yen for a less routine existence than that of academic life. This was not unconnected to Thomas's 1910 research project, which would permit him to be away from Chicago for part of the academic year in order to travel to Europe.

So far, I have shown how Thomas's intellectual convictions, and their evolution, are comprehensible when placed into the contexts of his biographical trajectory and the spheres he frequented. Occurring later than that of the philosopher John Dewey (1859–1952), his colleague at Chicago until 1904, this evolution of ideas led Thomas to replace biological determinations for behavior and the instinctual development of institutions with determinants stemming from the social environment. It also led him to a relativist point of view on the mores of his era and his surroundings that can be found in only a few academics of his generation: from this stemmed his conviction that research should be independent from all practical objectives, and disengaged from the social norms in use. In 1910, when he undertook the writing of *The Polish Peasant*, Thomas had no further research experience than the disparate observations that, according to his former students, he made use of in his teaching. His inquiries were formulated in terms that were drawn more from the studies of anthropology and psychology of the beginning of the century than from sociology.

THE DESIGN AND EXECUTION OF *THE POLISH PEASANT*

The research reported in *The Polish Peasant* is the culmination of a series of circumstances that contributed to shaping a project that was, at its start, only very vaguely defined. The chronology is not what Thomas indicates: if he had formed the intention in 1896, as he wrote in 1935, to study a group of peasants on both sides of the Atlantic, then he waited quite a long time before acting on it.[68] It was in 1910, and not in 1908 as he wrote in 1935, that Thomas obtained a grant of $35,000 from Helen Culver for a study intended to focus on "racial psychology."[69] As elsewhere, Thomas here uses the term "race" without biological connotation, in the sense of a group of European nationalities. The amount of funding obtained was important, since the majority of the Pittsburgh Survey was conducted during the same period with a budget of $27,000 from the Russell Sage Foundation (according to the first volume of the report). This grant would permit Thomas to engage collaborators for collecting, copying, and translating the documentary material, and would also pay for a replacement to teach Thomas's courses during his European travels—seemingly an uncommon practice at the University of Chicago at that time.

The project saw some delay in taking shape. Thomas began by traveling to Europe, where he made contact with researchers interested in Eastern European peasants. An article in the *American Journal of Sociology*, "Race Psychology: Standpoint and Questionnaires, with Particular Reference to the Immigrant and the Negro," which Thomas described in a letter to Helen Culver as a "book of instruction for field workers," appeared in 1912 and offered a sketch of the program as an investigation into the mental capacities of African Americans and European immigrants to the United States.[70] Although the term "social change" appears only discreetly in the article, among the questions raised in it can be found behavioral changes resulting from ruptures in customs and mores in rural societies. Shortly before the publication of this article, Thomas had met Robert Park, then the secretary of leading African American author and educator Booker T. Washington, who had invited him to an "International Conference on Negroes" dedicated to "The Education of Primitive Man."[71] Park's approach toward and understanding of the situation of African Americans enthused Thomas, who invited Park to teach at the University of Chicago. Thomas himself compared the situation of African Americans to that of European peasants, which had so far been the focus of his nascent research project.

In his article on race psychology, Thomas made references to sociologists for the first time, citing in particular two recent work: *Folkways* (1906) by William Graham Sumner and *Social Organization* by Charles Horton Cooley (1909). That same year, Thomas sent a letter, accompanied by his 1912 article, to many European colleagues, signaling to them that he was collecting documentary material with the aim of publishing volumes on seven types of immigrant peasants, and that he envisaged an eighth volume on Eastern European Jews.[72] The planned publication sought, according to this letter, to "make accessible to the scientific worker in the field of immigrant problems data concerning the life of the immigrant class . . . My ultimate purpose is to get together a comprehensive collection of documents, to which each one who interests himself scientifically in the problems of human society can attach his own theories and interpretations." The projected method of composition was that of the *Source Book for*

Social Origins—the term "source book" was also used by Thomas to designate the forthcoming volumes. It also suggests the vagueness of the objective of an investigation into the mental capacities of different populations.

In 1912 or 1913, Thomas discovered that the populations of the former territories of Poland offered abundant and relatively accessible documentation. The existence of this documentation resulted in part from the situation in Poland: a national independence movement had developed in formerly Polish territories that had been divided among Prussia, Austria, and Russia since 1815. Polish intellectuals, Znaniecki later wrote, had a particular interest in "peasants' problems, since they knew that the survival of the Polish nationality depended mainly on the peasants."[73] Thus, a weekly newspaper geared toward peasants, founded in 1863, published readers' letters on all sorts of subjects.[74] Thomas purchased a collection of issues from the last years of this publication, which would furnish a large part of the documentation for *The Polish Peasant*.

Thomas studied Polish so he could filter through these documents, but after several unsuccessful attempts he ultimately hired a translator. In 1913, he entered into a contract with Florian Znaniecki (1882–1958), the manager of an administrative division officially responsible for the protection of peasants. (Informally, it was also intended to promote the emigration of undesirables.)[75] Znaniecki had received a philosophical education in Geneva, Zurich, and Krakow, and he had some contact in Paris with Durkheim, Lévy-Bruhl, and Bergson.[76] He arrived in Chicago in September 1914 and remained there through the duration of the First World War. Thomas hired him as a collaborator, and in particular to translate a group of documents from Polish. In the free time his work for Thomas left him, Znaniecki pursued the elaboration of his philosophical system, to use a phrase from his biography.[77] It was he who collected a large part of the documentary evidence concerning Polish emigrants to America, which is to say familial correspondence. These letters—a source so far ignored by sociologists, but which Thomas affirmed in his 1912 article would "reveal life and mind in a very intimate way"—were purchased by means of short notices placed in publications addressed to Polish immigrants.

The first months of work in Chicago following the hiring of Znaniecki resulted in the investigation being narrowed to the Polish case alone, the war in Europe having rendered the collection of complementary evidence impossible. Thomas and Znaniecki decided that a general historical and ethnographic introduction to Polish peasant culture was indispensable, and the outline of it, drafted by Znaniecki probably at the beginning of 1916, was, according to him, the basis of the proposal that led Thomas to consider him as co-author.[78] Znaniecki had also written the first draft of the piece titled "Methodological note" that opens the book. When the first two volumes were finished, it became evident to the authors that it would take many years to study this one group of immigrants. Thomas thus abandoned—provisionally, as we will see—the project of studying other immigrant groups, and in 1916 the first two volumes of *The Polish Peasant* were submitted for publication at the University of Chicago Press, with Thomas and Znaniecki as co-authors. The submitted project proposed a series of nineteen volumes, eight of which were described in the proposal, under the title *The Poles: Monograph of a Society*: among these volumes figure another autobiography than that which appears in *The Polish Peasant*, two volumes on the Polish nobility and bourgeoisie, and a "synthesis of Polish culture."[79] However, only some of the volumes concerning the Polish were ultimately sketched out.

The collaboration between Thomas and Znaniecki was the object of repeated speculation. An initially frequent underestimation of Znaniecki's contribution was later replaced by a probable underestimation of Thomas's.[80] Here one must take into account the intellectual background of each, but also their linguistic competencies, which conditioned the division of duties: Thomas read Polish, but could not easily translate correspondence; Znaniecki's English was never excellent, and the work of editing the final manuscript was at least partially done by Thomas.[81] Anyone with some experience in collaborative research knows that the intellectual contribution of each cannot be reduced to the question of writing the final draft, and often cannot be clearly defined. The testimonies of the two authors, to which I refer below, are also not contradictory, and can be complemented by the examination of various parts of the work, as well as both the authors' previous and later publications.

During the period in which he prepared *The Polish Peasant*, Thomas published an article adopting an approach very different from his habitual preoccupations. He proposed in it a global historical perspective on the politics of the formerly Polish territory then part of Germany, and on reactions to these politics. In 1915, he also published a short pedagogical book on the origin of society and the state, illustrated with extracts from ethnographic analyses, which suggested that Thomas had not yet abandoned some degree of evolutionism.[82]

THE POLISH PEASANT IN EUROPE AND THE UNITED STATES

It should be remembered, first, that the period starting in 1890 was characterized by mass emigration from Europe to the United States. As opposed to the wave of immigrants from majority Anglo-Saxon, German, and Nordic origins, as the previous period had seen, starting in the mid-1870s immigrants came from eastern and southern Europe. The increased flow of immigrants from these zones was a consequence of their economic situation, as well as religious and political persecution and, sometimes, legislative provisions facilitating their departures. The utilization of steamships on transatlantic lines also increased the number of available tickets, thus lowering their cost. These new immigrants to the United States were considered by those of Anglo-Saxon origins to be different—and inferior—from themselves on account of their religion, their political and moral qualities, and their "race."[83]

Between 1899 and 1910, the Polish alone represented around a quarter of all immigrants entering the United States.[84] They established themselves principally in a few large cities (Chicago, New York, Pittsburgh, Buffalo, Detroit). In Chicago, the number of Polish immigrants and their children grew from 150,000 in 1900 to 300,000 in 1914. Like other immigrants from rural origins, the Polish took unskilled jobs in different industries, particularly ironworking, coal mines, textile mills, and, in Chicago, slaughterhouses. In the cities, the behavior of Polish immigrants constituted, in the eyes of the Protestant middle classes, a "social problem" because of the perceived frequency of interfamilial conflicts and high juvenile delinquency. This characterization was, as we have seen, one of the justifications set forth by Thomas for his decision to study Polish immigration.

The Polish Peasant begins with the long "Methodological note" written at Znaniecki's initiative, which is without doubt the part of the book read the most by the following generation of sociologists. A section of it consists of a critique of the "practical" or "common-sense" sociology—both terms are used—of social reformers.[85] The opening "Methodological note" declares the principles upon which so-called practical sociology is based to be erroneous, recalling remarks found elsewhere in Thomas's work and in his critique of the approach taken by the Vice Commission.

According to the first of these erroneous principles, the knowledge permitted by direct contact with one's target study population suffices as the basis of scientific knowledge and thus authorizes generalizations. The dependence of investigations on practical objectives that state in advance what is or is not desirable is the second erroneous principle, as a norm should not constitute the starting point for research. The implicit hypothesis that all social facts can be studied in arbitrary isolation from other aspects of the society in question is the third erroneous principle. Finally, although according to Thomas and Znaniecki practical sociology claims to reject the beliefs that people react in the same manner to the same stimuli, and that they spontaneously develop dispositions permitting them to react in the same manner to the conditions in which they find themselves, in practice the school of thought uses this reasoning, with certain social reformers according an excessive importance to modifications of the material environment.[86] These shortcomings of practical sociology are attributed to the "necessity of meeting actual situations at once."[87] A passing remark adds another critique: "persons of merely good will are permitted to try out on society indefinitely and irresponsibly their vague and perhaps sentimental ideas."[88] The affirmation that an inductive approach should be adopted, another idea previously advanced by Thomas, is also presented in the "Methodological note." Another section evokes laws the social sciences ought to establish, an element that is certainly attributable to Znaniecki and that Thomas characterized, in 1935, as "deplorable," regretting that he had not modified it while re-editing the book in 1920.[89]

The "Methodological note" is followed by an introduction dedicated to the familial organization of Polish peasants in their traditional society and to the social changes with which they had been confronted over three decades. Migration to cities, to Germany, the United States, and Brazil, and a "proletarization"—a term that is never more precisely defined—led to the end of the previous isolation of peasant communities.[90] The boundaries of these communities were defined by the existence of a social opinion influencing the family and the individual. The links of solidarity within extended families also characterized the traditional state of peasant society: behaviors were governed by collective and not individual interests, and did not take rational efficacy into consideration. The declining isolation of peasant communities resulted in familial and intergenerational conflicts, and families tended to redefine themselves on a narrower basis. This section also includes an overall picture of social class in Poland, as well as descriptions of the economic, religious, and intellectual life of Polish peasants. Behavioral norms in different domains of social life—those that regulated marital relationships, the use of different types of property, or religious practices—emerge, as well as the significance that the peasants attributed to these norms. Peremptory in style, some of these sections are not supported by the production of elements that could qualify as evidence. The book contains few references to previous work, and it includes almost no statistical data: only two statistical tables are provided, one of which is part of a document. Znaniecki noted in 1938 that he regretted this oversight.[91]

A brief discussion of the functions fulfilled by familial correspondence precedes the reproduction of two series of letters exchanged between members, both immigrant and not, of fifty families of Polish peasants based in the three formerly Polish territories. The first series corresponds to the traditional state of family relations, while the second has letters showing the dissolutions of family ties. These letters stand as evidence for the analyses of the significance the peasants attributed to these norms and their evolution.

The second part of *The Polish Peasant*, titled "Disorganization and Reorganization in Poland," examines the upheaval of the social order in traditional peasant society over the course of the thirty years preceding its incorporation into Polish society and modern civilization. Thomas and Znaniecki examined the consequences of these changes among families and communities, the struggles for the preservation of the old system, and revolutionary social or religious attitudes, as well as the emergence of new forms of social organization, such as production and other cooperatives, cooperation at the village level, and the development of a national conscience. The second chapter, focused on the disorganization of the family, presents in some detail the method of interpretation applied to the correspondence, using letters to exemplify the aspects deemed significant in familial disorganization. The reproduced documentary evidence comes principally from a periodical, *Gazeta Swiateczna*, and concerns the population under Russian dominion.

The third part—"Organization and Disorganization in America"—is dedicated to the different forms of Polish emigration (and especially to those relevant to the United States), to the settling-down of immigrants, and to the development of local Polish American communities, as well as associations and organizations with a local or national implementation in the United States. The reproduced documents principally came from commemorative books of parishes established in Chicago, or from associations in contact with immigrants. The following chapters of *The Polish Peasant* focus on the disorganization of immigrants, which is to say the consequences of the weakening influence of the norms of their original social milieu from which they were cut off, as well as the emerging norms of the United States. The authors do not concern themselves with the frequency of any particular behaviors, but rather focus on their significance for the population in question.

The fourth part (located in the middle of the first edition) consists of the long autobiography of a young Polish immigrant, commissioned by Thomas and Znaniecki. According to them, this individual's existence was affected by a process of change, but he never found an acceptable place in his new environment because his attitudes still corresponded to the old type of social organization, even though it no longer applied to him. He could, therefore, adapt only partially and imperfectly to the new conditions he found himself facing. His autobiography is preceded by a long introduction that presents itself as "the application of the methods of social psychology of an evolving human personality" and introduces categories of interpretation in order to construct a theory of individuals as social personalities.

Contrary to what its title might suggest, *The Polish Peasant* does not focus exclusively on immigrant peasants, nor even on their children: the correspondence and the personal documents were, in part, written by members of the lower levels of the middle classes. The authors were not concerned with their materials' representativeness of a population of Polish emigrants that evidently consisted of a substantial number of illiterates. The book is not focused on the objective aspects of the transformations of Polish peasant society or of immigration to the United States, but rather the reactions of peasants, their families, and communities to the changes with which they were confronted: as the "Methodological note" indicates, the work pertains to social psychology.

The introduction of the notion of "attitude," which occupies a central place in the conceptual schema of *The Polish Peasant*, constitutes one of the innovations that contributed to ensuring the book's posterity in sociology. This concept partially replaced the notion of "habit" that was widely used by Thomas's predecessors in sociology, and marked the final stage of his abandonment of a biological explanation for behavior.[92] The following definition is offered at the beginning of the book: "By attitude we understand a process of individual consciousness which determines real or possible activity of the individual in the social world." Shortly thereafter appears the expression "tendency to action."[93] This notion is connected to that of social value—introduced by Znaniecki, but used by Thomas in his subsequent work—by which is meant "any datum having an empirical content accessible to the members of some social group and a meaning with regard to which it is or may be an object of activity" or, according to a somewhat clearer articulation, "social elements of social reality which impose themselves upon the individual as given and provoke his reaction." Thomas and Znaniecki cite as examples a tool, a myth, a university, and a scientific theory.[94] In the authors' terminology, attitude is the individual counterpart of social value, and activity constitutes the link between the two. Znaniecki specifies that it was difficult for him to synthesize Thomas's theory of attitudes and his own theory of social values, and that his attempt to do so was "without great success."[95]

Thomas and Znaniecki rejected any immediate determination of attitudes by social values (and vice versa). They sustained that "The cause of a value or of an attitude is never an attitude or a value alone, but always a combination of an attitude and a value," which is to say, in more contemporary terms, in the relationship between objective factors and subjective dispositions.[96] Thomas and Znaniecki also introduce an interpretation of the situation catalyzed by social actors as being between objective factors and individual activities. The diversity of behaviors and modes of adaptation of immigrants to the United States can only be understood through the definition that they themselves conferred upon their situation: hence the importance accorded to the documentary evidence of personal documents—letters or autobiographies—that permit access to the population's interpretation of the situations and norms with which they were confronted. With the definition of these two fundamental notions—attitude and social value—and the documentary evidence of personal documents, *The Polish Peasant* opened a vast new domain to empirical investigation. This is what explains the success in the following years of the expression "definition of the situation," which has remained strongly associated with Thomas.

The emergence of new attitudes that precipitated the decline in the influence of certain norms regulating behavior and the decay of certain institutions, followed by the development of new norms and institutions better fitted to the behaviors of the population, constitutes the explanatory model of social change proposed by *The Polish Peasant*. Attitudes are analyzed in the book using a typology of wishes, "which can be satisfied only by [one's] incorporation in a society"—the desire for new experiences, the desire for recognition (which includes sexual attraction), the desire for domination and the desire for security.[97] These motivations are the foundation of the development of new attitudes as social conditions change and the norms to which behavior previously conformed weaken. Other classifications of fundamental motivations can be found, in slightly different form, in the work of Albion Small or the social psychologist William McDougall—which is to say sociologists from the generation prior to Thomas.

It is possible to see there an echo of the debates about the relationship between innate and acquired behavior: as Bogardus suggested, Thomas's objective was to replace the notion of instinct, which is charged with biological connotations, with a concept intended to grasp the ways in which individuals react to changing stimuli in their surroundings.[98] Thomas did not devote himself to this typology for long, and used many variants: Everett Hughes reports that Thomas seemed to distance himself from this classification, which he elsewhere attributed to Znaniecki's concern for presenting systematic analyses during a meeting in the late 1920s with a group of dissertation-stage students at University of Chicago, in which he stated that he no longer recalled the exact formulation used in *The Polish Peasant*.[99]

The concept of the social disorganization of a group, defined as "a decrease of the influence of existing social rules of behavior upon individual members of the group," would remain influential for a long time, and can be found in American sociological analyses for at least the following thirty years.[100] The notion was derived from that of social organization, introduced by Charles H. Cooley in order to designate the ensemble of institutions that can exist in a social group—which is to say all norms of conduct and behaviors, whether or not they conform to these norms.[101]

Thomas and Znaniecki principally examined two forms of social disorganization in Poland: that which concerned the family and that which pertained to communities. Familial disorganization was a consequence of the emergence of individualist attitudes (in contrast to attitudes relating to the familial group as an entity). Affected by these new hedonist attitudes and desire for social acknowledgment based on the behavior or possessions of the individual, and not those of the family, familial solidarity tended to rupture: intergenerational conflicts broke out inside families when some members, especially those who had emigrated, did not fulfill their social obligations.[102] The disorganization of a community is marked for younger generations by the decline of submission to a "social opinion": no longer subject to the imperative of being acknowledged by the entire community, individuals set themselves to determining—and pursuing—their economic, religious, intellectual, and hedonic interests, leading to a decline in solidarity within the community.[103] The concept of social disorganization covers, as we shall see, a large range of behaviors.

The authors also introduce the concept of personal disorganization (or demoralization), which they define as "The decay of the personal life-organization of an individual member of a social group," insisting that this does not have a regular and distinctive relationship to social disorganization.[104] The concept is doubtlessly one of the most difficult to grasp for the contemporary reader, since it makes reference to a normative conception of the relationship between individuals and society that the authors shared with readers of their own era. Thomas and Znaniecki in effect positioned an individual's conscious and rational command of actions as an ideal, remarking for example that "it is desirable to develop in the individuals the ability to control spontaneously their own activities by conscious reflection"—a remark that Thomas had made already in 1909.[105]

The concept of demoralization was used to interpret the behavior of some immigrants in the United States. Thomas and Znaniecki developed an assessment of the situation of economic dependence on charitable organizations, toward which certain immigrants of peasant origins turned when transitioning from the situation in Poland, where work was stable and the future relatively predictable, to precarious and unattractive employment in the United States. The concept of demoralization is also applied to ruptures in conjugal links in America (as distinguished from the rupture of extended families, which characterized social disorganization in Poland) and to different forms of juvenile delinquency among the children of immigrants (vagrancy, sexual activity among young women). Demoralization is a phenomenon even more pertinent for the second generation than for the first—Thomas and Znaniecki point this out but do not explain it.[106]

The introduction to the second part of the 1927 edition of the book, the autobiography of the Polish immigrant, proposes some concepts for the study of the formation of social personalities through experiences with which individuals are confronted. It introduces a distinction between the "temperamental attitudes" that individuals initially possess and the "character attitudes" into which they are transformed over the course of a process that depends on external conditions. Three principal types of organization of the social personality of immigrants—the philistine, the bohemian, and the creative—are characterized, according to their method of adaptation to new situations. Potentially conflicting relationships between society and the individual are associated with these types of personality.

The philistine, who is a conformist and whose character is determined by his temperamental attitudes, presents a high degree of fixity and is only affected by the most permanent influences of his social milieu, is set in opposition to the bohemian, whose potential evolution is, by contrast, unlimited because his character remains unformed. These two opposing types are distinguished from the third, that of the creative individual, whose organized character implies the possibility, and even the necessity, of evolution, and who remains open to influences likely to be consistent with opportunities for growth. Thomas, over the following years, seems to have been a sort of precursor to the development of the lines of questioning of the current "Culture and Personality" of cultural anthropology.[107]

THE POLISH PEASANT: ITS ORIGINALITY AND ITS LIMITS

Although it is immediately apparent that *The Polish Peasant* is an innovative book, numerous elements associated with it were not absolutely novel when it was published. This is the case for the writing style of the book, which is similar to that of *Source Book for Social Origins*. Similarly, in terms of the attention paid to the subjective dimension of social experiences, a book published in 1901, *Varieties of Religious Experiences: A Study in Human Nature* by William James, presented the diversity of religious experiences, offering examples in the form of testimonies excerpted or solicited by the author, and also adopted the same writing style as *The Polish Peasant*.

The Polish Peasant was associated reputationally with the introduction to a new type of documentation: correspondence, personal journals, and autobiographies. In his 1912 article, Thomas also cited newspapers and the dossiers of various institutions (courts, charitable organizations, etc.) as useful documentary sources. These documents were utilized in case studies, which included the presentation and interpretation of an ensemble of documents focused on one or more individuals, groups, or institutions. With the exception of the correspondence, the use of these different documentary sources are is an innovation of *The Polish Peasant*, but can be found in the work of the same era by journalists and researchers of different specialities who belonged to the sphere of Progressive reformers, some of whom had spent time at Hull House.

In 1903, the journalist Hutchins Hapgood, who was connected to William James and his family, published the autobiography of a thief.[108] William James had also contributed to the publication of the autobiography of a person who was mentally ill (manic-depressive, according to later terminology), Clifford Beers, *A Mind That Found Itself* (1908). It is not certain that Thomas knew these books, although they were widely read, but in 1906 he did write a critical note on a book, written by the journalist Hamilton Holt, that presented the autobiographies of immigrants, one of whom was a young, female laborer of Polish origin.[109] Thomas occasionally cited James, with whom he had corresponded around 1909, and he also maintained close relationships with William Healy, one of James's protégés, and George H. Mead, one of his former students.

Case studies are presented in *Friendly Visiting Among the Poor: A Handbook for Charity Workers*, a book published in 1899 by Mary Richmond, one of the founders of social work in the United States, as well as in a book published in 1912 by Sophonisba Breckinridge and Edith Abbott on juvenile delinquency which made use of the archives of the Juvenile Protective Association charged with post-trial probation for minors in Chicago.[110] Richmond's book develops the idea of an overall understanding of the whole life history, an idea sometimes referred to as an innovation of Thomas's.[111]

Two psychiatric physicians, Adolf Meyer and William Healey, with whom Thomas had been in contact, also collected and made use of autobiographies as documentary resources for their analyses and treatments. Meyer, who used a similar terminology to that of Thomas in his interpretations around 1909 (including the terms standpoint, attitudes, disorganization, and situation), was in contact with William James. He introduced a conception of mental illness that takes into account biological, psychological, and social symptoms and factors, characterizing mental illness as the product of a dysfunctional personality rather than a brain pathology. Starting in 1904, Meyer argued for the necessity of observing patients over the course of their lives.[112] His ideas were diffused fairly widely, particularly by the publication of the aforementioned autobiography of Clifford Beers, in which he was the principal reference.

Unlike his predecessors, around 1909 William Healey, who directed the psychiatric clinic associated with the Chicago juvenile court and financed (like of Thomas's studies after 1918) by Ethel Dummer, was not interested solely in the anatomical and psychological characteristics of young delinquents. Rather, Healey took into account their social experiences, which drove him to collect the autobiographical narratives of young delinquents. His correspondence around that year (cited in Tannenhaus [2004]: 111–137) shows his hesitancy over adopting an approach and his uncertainty about the possible use of autobiographies as resource, making it appear that he found his model in the dossiers furnished by social workers linked to the juvenile court.

Thomas regularly visited Meyer and Healey, including after 1918, but rather than concluding that Meyer or Healy influenced—an imprecise term—Thomas as Abbott and Egloff did, it seems to me that we must acknowledge, as Kimball Young already has, that the idea of utilizing case studies and autobiographies as evidence in order to gain access to subjective experiences was present in Thomas's intellectual milieu.[113] If one were to identify one originator for this idea, which can be found in the work of journalists and researchers belonging to the generations born between 1860 and 1875, the leading candidate would have to be William James (1842–1910), a philosopher who became extremely famous by the end of his career.

The collection and utilization of familial correspondence is, as far as documentation is concerned, the only truly novel element introduced by *The Polish Peasant*. Thomas explains in one or two anecdotes how he had discovered the value of these as documentary sources, picking up in the street some letters from a young Polish woman to her family.[114] This documentary source was later used only scarcely by sociologists at Chicago, in contrast to biographies and case studies.[115]

Some elements associated with the Chicago tradition are absent from *The Polish Peasant*, or play only a minor role. The notion of interaction, which would occupy a central place shortly thereafter in the conception of the social world in the Chicago tradition thanks to Park's work, is present only in an indirect manner, represented by the concept of the primary group. The source of evidence that frequently complements it—direct observation—is only barely mentioned by Thomas, even though he used personal observations in the classroom.[116] The study guide produced by Thomas in 1912 certainly advances personal observation, by recommending an approach that may have been inspired by Le Play, translated in the *American Journal of Sociology*: living with the family being studied.[117] Thomas does not seem to have put this methodology into use, and one might think that the use of informers, in the manner of anthropologists of the same generation, seemed to him to be a satisfactory—and perhaps equivalent—substitute for observation. Thomas occasionally invited lecturers who had direct knowledge of a sector of social life to speak at the University of Chicago. He had marked reservations about the use of interviews, which he characterized in 1912 as "a body of error to be used for purposes of comparison in future observation."[118] Thomas also never displayed more than a weak interest in methodological questions. In a somewhat paradoxical manner, *The Polish Peasant* presents only one example of autobiography characterized as "typical"—although it is known from an early outline of the book that a second, very different example had been planned.

The Polish Peasant offers no precise justification concerning the institutional facts, mores, and social norms presumed to have existed in villages or cities—in other words, it neglects the questions of interpretation that would become very important for the conception of the social world of following generations. Its writing style is quite similar to those of Sumner's *Folkways* and Cooley's *Social Organization*, as well as the social theory works of the previous generation, despite the fact that Thomas did not particularly appreciate them. Thomas and Znaniecki also neglected interpretive questions about the documents they made use of that were produced by social workers and official administrations: these documents seemed to be descriptions of facts. The method of analyzing the personal documents was that of textual commentary, which Thomas practiced when he taught literature at Oberlin College.[119] On the other hand, nothing indicates that Thomas sought to acquire the most intimate knowledge possible of Polish immigrants. In this research, Thomas thus adopted a position closer to that of an anthropologist of the previous era than of a sociologist studying a relatively familiar world, as the researchers of the Chicago tradition would later do.

Two other points merit attention, not as critiques of the book but because they influenced the intellectual legacy of *The Polish Peasant*. Developed by two authors with very different referents and intellectual backgrounds, the conceptual scheme presented in *The Polish Peasant* has a composite character: the terminology, which was a little outdated in the 1930s, was often particular to the book, which is unsurprising for a book that had no precedent. According to his own statements, Thomas was not concerned with presenting a systematic analysis— he indicated that he had, with Znaniecki, incorporated "any and everything that we found ourselves able to say"[120] into the book. Znaniecki also recalled in 1939 that his effort at clarification remained unfinished. Taking into consideration the full body of research Thomas conducted over the course of his career, it seems that his scientific convictions were less consistent than the themes of his intellectual interests. Thomas had not always been, for example, so reserved with respect to Freudian analyses as his later statements indicate.[121] The same holds for the hostility toward the use of a statistical approach attributed to Thomas by Faris in 1948, who characterized the absence of statistical data in the methodology of *The Polish Peasant* as a defect in 1938.[122] This lacuna doubtlessly reflects Thomas and Znaniecki's lack of competency in the matter, as well as the fact that statistical analysis was not yet understood to be a sign of "scientificity."

Thomas's adoption of a position in favor of a science detached from any immediate practical objective—which, according to Park, marked a decisive step in the evolution of sociology toward a "scientific" discipline[123]—should not mask the dependence of the analyses of *The Polish Peasant* on value judgments regarding ideas of how immigrants should behave, and how their futures should look. The concept of individual disorganization, as we have seen, was closely associated with moral judgment. The analysis of the future of immigrants implicitly presupposes that the self-organization of immigrant communities is an intermediate stop on the path to a final goal, assimilation into American society as defined by Anglo-Saxon Protestants.[124] *The Polish Peasant* also contains judgments underpinned by norms that are not defined, with an example being the "average moral level" of Polish immigrants or peasants in Poland. It is unsurprising that Thomas and Znaniecki were only partially able to emancipate themselves from the point of view of middle-class social reformers and were rather far removed from their espoused ideal: investigation detached from practical ends and free from the value judgments of one sector of social life. The book, like all others, belongs to its era, and what merits special attention is the absence of this critique among sociologists of the following period, who would adopt a similar point of view.

Sociological readers before 1938 were also little concerned with the empirical pertinence of the work. It does not touch much on the differences among the three ex-Polish territories from which the emigrants came, even though the introduction of the part of the book focused on the changing situation in Poland contains notes on the differences among these territories and indicates that the majority of the documentation came from the zone under Russian domination.[125] Moreover, Thomas and Znaniecki's documentation did not reflect on the widespread illiteracy in certain regions.

> The situation of peasants, and the way in which it evolved, was not the same in the three formerly Polish territories.[126] These were unevenly distant (geographically and socially) from the zones of industrial development toward which they sent a large portion of emigrants. The political situation in each of these territories was unique, as well as their religious backgrounds. The area under Prussian, later German, domination tended to be Germanized: elementary education was

strong there around 1900, although it was conducted in German.[127] There was considerable migration toward industrial centers and German cities. In the realm governed by Russia, congressional politics dictated that an alliance between peasants and an aristocracy generally inclined toward nationalism must be avoided; education was also used as a means of Russification, but in 1897 only around 40 percent of the population could write.[128] Galicia, under Austrian control, did not submit to attempts at linguistic assimilation; in 1890, complete illiteracy affected around 67 percent of the population over seven years old.[129] The first wave of Polish immigrants to the United States came from the part under Prussian dominion. After 1890, emigration to the United States came more from the territories under Russian control, and then, after 1900, from Galicia. One could conclude that a significant portion of Polish immigrants to the United States in 1910 were unable to correspond with their families.

Neither Thomas, who, as we have seen, published an article in 1914 on the politics of assimilation in the region under German control, nor, evidently, Znaniecki were ignorant of the differences among the three formerly Polish territories, but they did not accord them much importance in their book. They were also aware of the question of education, but the section about it focuses principally on the reactions of peasants with regard to education, and not to its intrinsic relationship to the reproduced documents. The question of education in Polish territories was politically rather important in 1918, and as one of its first measures the new state made instruction in the Polish language mandatory.

A portion of the Polish emigrant population therefore happened to lie outside the scope of Thomas and Znaniecki's inquiry—a point that is never raised by those who commented on the book. Another point that the authors left in the shadows: the connection of the emigrants to peasantry. The peasant families in question were only imperfectly described as such—only Madge seems to have noted this.[130] The emigrant who provided an autobiography was also the former apprentice of a family that is imprecisely described in terms of its position in the lower levels of the middle class. The families whose correspondence is reproduced in the book present a striking diversity of situation: according to the terms of the book, some of them belonged to the rural petty nobility, while others seem to have been laborers or petty urban bourgeoisie, or descendants of peasants rather than peasants themselves; certainly, the hints present in the letters are not sufficient to determine their subjects' social categorization. Groups that appear underrepresented in the sample categories are the poorest migrants and agricultural workers deprived of land, who were often illiterate.[131] Thus, the cross-section of society represented Polish families that included emigrants who had diverse relationships with peasantry, more so than actual peasants in a strict sense.

The geographical origin of these subjects is not always fully known—and some families settled in different parts of the Russian territory. The reproduced letters illustrate well one of the features found elsewhere: over the course of at least fourteen years, the rural population of the three territories had begun to move to the interior of what had formerly been Poland, to the zones close to Germany and Russia, and to emigrate to Brazil and the United States (and elsewhere). The letters depict both emigration to industrial cities and seasonal migration linked to agricultural work. Some of these migrations seem to have been families' attempts to gain enough money to purchase land, while others were the result of acute economic difficulties. It is not easy to precisely characterize the condition of these populations based on their correspondence, but Thomas and Znaniecki do not seem to have been concerned with this question. This lack of interest proves consistent with the background of each, and also with the fact that their object was not emigration itself, but rather the attitudes of immigrants.

The analyses of *The Polish Peasant* do not completely neglect the class structure in which the Polish in Poland were immersed: one chapter, as we have seen, is dedicated to this topic, but it has a conventional character and is not based on any empirical material. Thomas and Znaniecki did not study integration into the professional structure of the United States, labor conditions, or Polish immigrants' relationship with work, nor did they study union activities and participation in the labor movement, which appear only fleetingly in the section focused on the supra-regional organizations of the Polish community. Another lacuna in the analysis concerns the associations that structured the Polish American community: the objectives and the organizations of the two principal movements that sought to organize immigrants to the United States—the secular nationalists of the National Polish Alliance, founded by political emigrants belonging to the educated elite, and the Catholics of the Polish Roman Catholic Union—are presented before 1914, but the conflict between them is not.[132]

Finally, it is doubtful, to say the least, that Polish immigration to the United States possessed the characteristics—high delinquency and ruptures in family ties—which Thomas used to justify his choice of population. The data available for the period concerning divorces, separations, and delinquency are certainly too rudimentary to allow precise discussion. The question is examined only in an article by Norbert Wiley.[133] Forty years later, Helena Lopata, the daughter of Znaniecki, proposed, after conducting her own research, an interpretation of the process of restructuring the Polish community in the United States that differed from that of Thomas and Znaniecki, as well as a completely different picture of the behaviors of these immigrants. Her research, initially a dissertation completed in 1954 at the University of Chicago, which sought to explain why the Polish American community in Chicago had not ceased to exist, foregrounded the importance of internal competition for status within the emigrant community.[134] In this interpretation, immigrants utilized resources external to their community, engendering what previously had been interpreted as a sign of disorganization. Lopata makes note of the low importance accorded by immigrants to the status of their communities, as well as an underestimation on Thomas and Znaniecki's part of nationalist sentiments.[135]

A closer look at *The Polish Peasant* concerning the methodology and the relationship between documentary resources and their interpretation was the theme of a seminar that, in 1938, brought Thomas together with social science researchers of the following generation.[136] *The Polish Peasant* had been selected as the most significant work produced in the field of sociology thus far. A specialist in social psychology and methodological questions as well as a next-generation sociologist at the University of Chicago, Herbert Blumer—a protégé of Ellsworth Faris, Thomas's successor at the University of Chicago—was responsible for a methodological report on the book. His contribution, which makes up the greater part of the publication of the seminar's proceedings, notes the lack of clarity of analytical distinctions proposed by Thomas and Znaniecki, an incoherence in the usage of conceptual terms (particularly regarding the distinction between attitude and social object), and the absence of a precise relationship between the documentary material and the general formulations set forth.[137]

W. I. THOMAS AFTER *THE POLISH PEASANT*

Thomas's influence over American sociology after the publication of *The Polish Peasant* was more indirect than direct. In April 1918, Thomas was in effect forced to resign from his position at the University of Chicago, though only two of five volumes of the book had been published. If *The Polish Peasant* became a model, it was through other means than the authors' roles as teachers, and particularly through that of Robert Park in the sociology department at the University of Chicago.

Unrelated to the publication of *The Polish Peasant*, Thomas's resignation from his position on April 16, 1918 has retained much interest for those who have written about him. He had been discovered in a hotel room in the company of the wife of a military officer who was at the time in France, and was liable for prosecution for violation of the Mann Act—a federal law passed in 1910 which prohibited bringing a woman across state lines "with the goal of prostitution, debauchery, or any other immoral objective"—and for declaring a false identity in a hotel.[138] Prostitution was at that time a hot topic in Chicago, the subject of many newspaper articles between 1917 and October 1918. An assistant federal prosecutor had been very active in enforcing the Mann Act, doubtlessly due to the presence of many soldiers in Chicago. An article in the *Chicago Tribune* (March 5, 1918) put hotels on guard after a police raid led to the arrest of thirty "irregular" couples, among whom figured several officers. This assistant federal prosecutor took charge at the beginning of the Thomas scandal, but it was turned over to a local judge who made the decision to abandon the prosecution, finding that the charges—including those later considered for "immoral conduct"—were baseless, remarking in passing his judgment that the charge of adultery could not be sustained. The assistant prosecutor tried in vain to continue the proceedings concerning the violation of the Mann Act. The affair was avidly reported and commented upon by the press (especially the *New York Times* and the *Chicago Tribune*), and Thomas was forced to resign his position, like other academics in similar situations both before and after him (such as Thorstein Veblen previously, and J. B. Watson somewhat later). Although no charges were ultimately brought against Thomas, for more than ten years his name was banned from the University of Chicago, and the University Press abandoned the ongoing publication of *The Polish Peasant*, the rights to which were ceded to a small publisher in Boston. Some testimonies claim that Park and Small sought to defend Thomas before university authorities, but the former's status was still precarious in 1918.[139] The university's president at the time, Henry Pratt Judson, a highly conservative former professor of political science, was probably hostile to Thomas, as Kimball Young claims.

Janowitz and others wondered whether the scandal had ultimately targeted Harriet Thomas, who was then very active alongside Jane Addams in the pacifist movement. Harriet Thomas also led a campaign against police brutality toward pacifist students (including their son). Articles in the *Chicago Tribune* (April 12, 13, 14, 16, 18, 20, and 22, 1918) include many indications that could lend credence to the suspicion that Thomas's being caught in the act was not just due to a random check at the initiative of a hotel employee: even before Thomas was formally identified as a professor of sociology at the university, a journalist had mentioned that Harriet Thomas was president of the Chicago Peace Society, and that Thomas had "advanced" opinions regarding sexuality. He also noted the presence of Thomas's son in the room during Thomas's appearance before the judges who were to rule on the prosecution (without explaining the reason for this remark). The affair was thus exploited by the newspaper to Thomas's detriment. It is possible that the police were pulling the journalist's strings, having judged it necessary to verify the identities of the guests, whose only notable characteristics had been their difference in age, at the request of the manager of a "respectable" hotel. Evan Thomas, however, later found that there had been no file on either Harriet or William Thomas at the Department of Justice.[140] Robert Throop and Lloyd Gordon Ward thus concluded that Harriet Thomas had not been an important enough pacifist to draw any attention, or that she would have benefited from protection in Washington. Harriet Thomas, who welcomed into her home and protected the young woman implicated in the scandal, kept her distance from journalists and defended her husband in court, undoubtedly minimizing the growth of the case, during which Thomas was represented by Clarence Darrow, a high-profile lawyer. The context of the campaign conducted by the assistant federal prosecutor seems, finally, to offer the most plausible explanation.

Kimball Young suggests that Thomas let people believe that the police had targeted his wife more so than himself,[141] and posits that the court case contributed to the university president H. P. Judson's hostility toward Thomas, a detail which I have been unable to verify. Around 1916, he contributed a report to the Chicago Committee of Fifteen, composed of a group of pastors and rabbis and established after the 1910 commission on prostitution. In this report, titled *Crime in Chicago*, he critiqued as ineffective the prohibition of prostitution: hence the hostility toward Thomas, whose objective had likely been this very prohibition, on the part of the committee, as well as Judson.

After Thomas's forced resignation from the university, the *Chicago Tribune* published, on April 22, 1918, a text by him (previously cited), which seemingly makes no concession to his adversaries: he criticizes the university conformists who make research into sensible subjects hazardous, arguing that research should be free from all practical goals. In this piece, Thomas stated that he bore no prejudice toward anyone according to his own principles, noting in passing that he was not a "radical" in terms of political views, and that in this matter he was even "rather conservative."[142]

Robert Park presided over the symbolic rehabilitation of Thomas among sociologists by supporting his election as president of the American Sociological Society in 1927. Some of Thomas's former students, including Luther Bernard and Kimball Young, who credit themselves with the deed, contributed to this election, as did next-generation sociologists in the course of writing their theses at University of Chicago.[143]

After his removal, Thomas never again held a permanent teaching position in a university, although he did secure teaching work between 1920 and 1925 at the New School for Social Research, where he also attended the seminar of the behavioral psychologist J. B. Watson, and in 1936 at Harvard.[144] Luther Bernard recalled a night in December 1925 spent in Thomas's company in New York, during which he gave the impression that at certain periods he had only modest resources at his disposal.[145] One might wonder whether some of Thomas's later research activity had been dictated by financial necessities.

Before leaving the University of Chicago, Thomas had signed a contract with the Carnegie Foundation to conduct research on the experience of immigrants in the United States, a subject of major concern during the First World War on account of public fears regarding the connection some immigrants felt for their countries of origin.[146] This research was included in a publication project under the direction of a sociology professor at Oberlin College, Herbert Miller, who sought to support organizations engaged in the "Americanization" of immigrants.[147] After Thomas's resignation from the University of Chicago, the Carnegie Foundation suppressed his name as author of the commissioned work, *Old World Traits Transplanted*, which was published in 1921 under the names of Robert Park and Herbert Miller.[148] One might recognize in the book, as Znaniecki did, a sort of condensation of the preliminary draft of the 1916 publications out of which *The Polish Peasant* came. The fact that Thomas had authored at least part of the book was not fully recognized until forty years later.

Old World Traits Transplanted is based on the same type of documentation as *The Polish Peasant*, but the study is extended to other groups of immigrants (eight different cases are examined in the chapter on communities, and the illustrations are borrowed from an even larger sample). The interpretive categories are those of *The Polish Peasant*, but the analysis focuses only on the behavior of immigrants in the United States. The writing style is similar, with synthetic discussions illustrated by immigrants' letters, autobiographical fragments, and excerpts from newspapers. The a priori conviction that the endpoint of evolution is the assimilation of different communities underpins the analysis, even more so than in *The Polish Peasant*. The final paragraph of the conclusion reads: "Assimilation is thus as inevitable as it is desirable; it is impossible for the immigrants we receive to remain permanently in separate groups."[149]

Ethel Dummer, who frequently associated with sociologists and participated during the 1920s in meetings of the American Sociological Society, financed Thomas's later research, which resulted in the publication of *The Unadjusted Girl* in 1923.[150] The title refers to young women desocialized as a result of the collapse of the old social order, although the analysis focuses not only on those thought to be delinquents, but more broadly on changes in the morals and behaviors of young women, particularly in terms of sexuality, and on the institutions with which they were in contact. The writing style resembles that of *The Polish Peasant*, and the classification of fundamental motivations articulated in *The Unadjusted Girl* is here used to interpret the behaviors of young women, presented in autobiographies and case studies.

Thomas's interpretation clearly distinguishes itself from those proposed by physicians and criminologists in the same period, which focused on attributing liberal morals and entry into prostitution among young women to personal characteristics like "mental retardation" or "weakness of spirit," often associated with heredity or some physical characteristic.[151] It is also distinguished from the interpretation of reformers of the Progressive movement, who evoked, as we have seen, the low salaries of women in industrial jobs, as well as the lack of opportunities for morally "safe" recreation. Thomas's analysis is subtler, and takes into account other motivations than those caused by economic constraints, including, for example, the desire for new experiences and the fact that the routine activities of labor are unsatisfying. Thomas thus remarks that "The beginning of delinquency in girls is usually an impulse to get amusement, adventure, pretty clothes, favorable notice, distinction, freedom in the larger world which presents so many allurements and comparisons."[152]

Thomas refers to a process of individualization of behavior, resulting from technological inventions, easier means of communication, urban development, capitalism, and so on, that had profoundly transformed the influence exerted over individuals by families and local communities. In these new conditions, an individual's adjustment relied upon his or her own personality more than community and family relationships, and this was the case for European peasants and rural Americans alike: hence the appearance of new behaviors in terms of interactions between the sexes, as illustrated in the examples. Some of these forms of adaptation contradicted the moral norms of traditional society. Thomas notes that the changing of morals blurred the boundaries of prostitution. Replacing the two earlier categories of "good" women and those who were "radically bad" was a wide spectrum, including "the occasional prostitute, the charity girl, the demi-virgin, the equivocal flapper, and in addition girls with new but social behavior norms who have adapted themselves to all kinds of work," as well as young women who adopted new norms and behaviors in all sorts of work, including intellectual work. "All of them represent the same movement, which is a desire to realize their wishes under the changing social conditions."[153] The final chapter resumes the argument Thomas put forth in 1918 to justify the necessity of an approach that was detached from any practical objective and flexible in terms of moral norms that, in a period of rapid changes, were inevitably those of the past.

Less voluminous than *The Polish Peasant*, *The Unadjusted Girl* was read and cited by sociologists at Chicago interested in the analysis of delinquency. The biographical documents and the case studies presented came principally from the archives of the Cook County juvenile court, from a Jewish weekly publication with a socialist orientation named *Forward*, and from earlier research into Polish immigration.

> To assess Thomas's contribution to an approach that was simpler than that which prevailed among his contemporaries, it is possible to compare his analyses of delinquency as handled by juvenile court to the analyses of Breckinridge and Abbott in their 1912 book, and to those of Jane Addams regarding female prostitution, published in a series of articles in *McClure's* magazine and collected in a book in 1912. Breckinridge and Abbott limited themselves to noting simple relationships between situational characteristics, living conditions, and delinquency, and offering commonsense interpretations, whereas Thomas interpreted varied behaviors using the concepts that he had introduced. Not without similarity to that of Thomas, Jane Addams's interpretation does not neglect, for example, that it is not always poverty and low industry wages that lead to prostitution, invoking other factors that could be subsumed into the fundamental motivational categories described by Thomas. But Jane Addams's analysis principally offers descriptions of a variety of typical situations—conditions specific to different jobs, places of entertainment, the transition from country to city, family relationships, and so on—while Thomas's presents a more coherent point of view that takes into account the biographies considered collectively.

The first and last documents reproduced in *The Unadjusted Girl* were written by J. B. Watson, one of the founders of behaviorist psychology and a former student of John Dewey at the University of Chicago.[154] Over the course of the 1920s, Thomas occasionally made reference to Watson, his colleague at the New School for Social Research. According to Stephen Murray, his later research reveals a "conversion to behaviorism."[155] In Thomas's interest in Watson's analyses, it is also possible to see an attempt to connect the analysis of observable behaviors with that of their subjective dimension.

The book published by Thomas in 1928, *The Child in America: Behavior Problems and Programs*, is the final result of a research contract (1926–1928) with the Laura Spelman Rockefeller Foundation. The book, written in collaboration with Dorothy Swaine Thomas, a sociologist, statistician, and former student of

Ogburn recruited for the project because of her statistical competency, reports an inquest into the different studies and treatment programs focused on the "maladjustment" of children (delinquency; failure to adapt at school) in the United States and Canada.[156] It presents the different approaches to these maladjustments in existence at the time: those of physiologists, psychometricians, psychiatrists, sociologists (here including the work of Watson, Pavlov, and their successors; as well as that of Healey; and briefly that of Burgess, Thrasher, and the Chicago sociologists). The book was little cited by sociologists.

From 1928 to 1932, Thomas chaired a committee of the Social Science Research Council (SSRC), an association that brought together representatives of the American societies for sociology, political science, and statistics along with observers from the American Economic Association, and that provided subventions for research. At that time, the SSRC's financing was assured principally by the Rockefeller foundations.[157] Luther Bernard affirms that Thomas had a degree of power in this committee and in the SSRC more generally. In this context, he organized interdisciplinary meetings for psychiatrists, notably Harry Stack Sullivan, and anthropologists, the latter of which contributed to the development of research in the ongoing interdisciplinary "Culture and Personality" group. Thomas's last book, *Primitive Behavior*, published in 1937, constitutes a return to his early interests, and serves as a sort of update to *Source Book for Social Origins*. The influence of Boas is central, and that of *Völkerpsychologie* has almost vanished.

> The beginning of the first chapter of *Primitive Behavior* offers an articulation of the conception that Thomas had always held regarding the social world, and also makes it possible to identify what retained Thomas's interest in the behaviorist approach: "The social sciences are fundamentally concerned with relationships between individuals and individuals, individuals and groups, and groups and other groups. Language, gossip, customs, codes . . . institutions, organizations, governments, professions, etc., are concerned with the mediations of these relationships. The central problem in the general life process is one of adjustment, and the forms of adjustive effort are 'behavior.' In a human as distinguished from an animal society the problem of the adjustment of individuals and groups is related to a cultural situation, that is, one in which a body of values has been accumulated and preserved (mainly through the instrumentality of language) in the form of institutions, mores and codes, together with a reinforcing set of attitudes to act in conformity with prescribed behavior patterns or norms."[158]

After 1930, Thomas returned to his research project on emigration. On the occasion of his travels in Sweden, he collected documentation regarding emigration to the United States in collaboration with Dorothy Swaine Thomas as well as Gunnar and Alva Myrdal.[159] He again gathered personal documents, particularly those originating from the periodical on Jewish immigration to the United States, which had furnished some of the documents in *Old World Traits Transplanted*. This research was unfinished at the time of Thomas's death in 1947, but some of the material was published posthumously.[160] It is clear that a notable part of Thomas's research fits into the project he described in 1916, of which the published volumes of *The Polish Peasant* were only the first phase.

Thomas's intellectual journey includes both continuities—an interest in the differences and relationships between the sexes and crime, as well as modes of adaptation to social change—and discontinuities—the slow abandonment of biological determinants for behavior and evolutionism, a rather late object of study of the contemporary world, and a half-conversion to behaviorism, which seems to me rather a degree of sensitivity to the limits of the approach of social psychology.

THE POLISH PEASANT, ITS POSTERITY IN SOCIOLOGY AND ITS PARADOXES

Over the two decades following its publication, *The Polish Peasant* was the principal point of reference for empirical research in sociology as it was practiced at the University of Chicago, even if, in terms of individual copies, the diffusion of the book remained modest. Only three thousand copies were printed for the two editions of 1920 and 1927, far fewer than the print runs of the two books that were successful in the following period: *Introduction to the Science of Sociology* (1921) by R. Park and E. Burgess, and *Jack-Roller* (1930) by Clifford Shaw.[161] Thomas's influence is found in domains subject to investigation (defined by his basic concepts), in the use of personal documents as documentary sources, and in a writing style that alternates between case studies and commentary, the relationship of which with the accompanying general propositions remains imprecise.[162]

The concept of attitude, with the resource of personal documents, has provided the starting point for investigations into the subjective dimension of behavior. It saw a durable posterity with significant developments, offering a vocabulary for interpreting the results of experiments in social psychology, as well as the processing of surveys based on questionnaires in terms of tendencies toward one type of action or another, when these two types of research were still in the process of developing.[163] The posterity of other concepts introduced in *The Polish Peasant* was less durable, but researchers passing through the University of Chicago did, in the 1920s and the early 1930s, make reference to the typology of four wishes.[164] The diffusion of the types of personality presented in the book was less wide.

After being nearly forgotten by sociologists, the legacy of the analyses of *The Polish Peasant* also drew the attention of historians of immigration, with an increased awareness of the book resulting from its acknowledgment in Oscar Handlin's *The Uprooted: The Epic Story of the Great Migrations That Made the American People* (1951).[165]

Considered in perspective, the analyses of *The Polish Peasant* constitute the culmination of a reaction against the ideas regarding the social world that were commonly accepted by the American social sciences at the end of the nineteenth century. *The Polish Peasant* introduced the concept of the "social environment" and the diversity of subjective experiences, replacing the thereafter rejected concept of biological determinants. Starting in the middle of the 1930s, an era which focused on different questions in profoundly different sociopolitical and cultural conditions, changes in terminology rendered Thomas's work difficult to understand and fundamentally out of style: it was both devoid of answers to contemporary problems and reliant on argumentation that had ceased to seem convincing.

Neither the rigor of the intellectual organization of *The Polish Peasant*, nor its empirical pertinence, nor the coherence of Thomas's publications when considered collectively can sufficiently explain the position the book occupies in the development of sociology between 1920 and 1940. It is ironic that, for *The Polish Peasant*, which founded a tradition of research particularly concerned with the empirical approach, the pertinence of the original problem—the high delinquency of Polish immigrants and their children—was ultimately not examined. This, along with other cases, illustrates that the diffusion of a book in the social sciences can have a loose relationship with its relevance, as well as with the soundness of its argument. The starting point of the book was nothing more than a prejudice of the era that its authors did not seek to validate and that, a century later, is no longer well established among sociologists—facts that should provoke reflection upon the nature of what the social sciences have accomplished.[166]

3

Park, Burgess, Faris, and Sociology at Chicago, 1914–1933

*Robert Park was a reformer. All his life he was deeply moved to improve
this world. If he became emancipated from his belief in one particular
reform after another and finally even gave up trying to reform reformers, it
was that his observing eye came to see each social problem in an ever wider
web of human relations and that his spirit felt the pull of the ties that bind
each passing trouble to the eternal impulses of man.*

—Everett C. Hughes[1]

*[We have] in sociology much theory but no working concepts. When a student
proposed a topic for a thesis, I invariably found myself asking the question:
what is this thing you want to study? What is a gang? What is a public?
What is nationality? What is a race in the sociological sense? What is graft?
etc. I did not see how we could have anything like scientific research unless we
had a system of classification and a frame of reference into which we could sort
out and describe in general terms the thing we were attempting to investigate.*

—Robert E. Park[2]

Stretching between Thomas's removal from the University of Chicago
and the retirement of Robert Park, who had rapidly proved himself the intellectual leader of the Department of Sociology, is the
period that would later be associated with the term "Chicago School." Over the
course of this period, research into diverse aspects of "urban life" was published
in the form of monographs and sometimes articles, constituting what has been

thought to have been the first collective research enterprise in sociology conducted in a university setting while engaging with the contemporary social world of the researchers.

Firsthand accounts are unanimous: Robert Park provided a large part of the intellectual inspiration for this enterprise, the direct agents of which were sociology students at Chicago. But many other elements of the setting clearly had significant influence over the production of sociological studies that took place within Park's circle. This and the following chapter present several elements that contributed to the production of these studies: the analytical framework proposed by Park, which must be supplemented by the contributions of other instructors at the University of Chicago; the ways in which sociologists, and academics more generally, integrated themselves into the city and into society, notably the conditions of funding and publishing research; and finally the sociopolitical context of the period.

ROBERT EZRA PARK: FROM PHILOSOPHY TO JOURNALISM; FROM JOURNALISM TO SOCIOLOGY

In an institutional sense, and in terms of his written production, Park became a sociologist rather late in a life that he considered marked by failure before his recruitment by the University of Chicago.[3] Park was forty-eight years old in 1912 when, as previously mentioned, he met Thomas at a conference organized by the most prominent leader of the African American community in this period, Booker T. Washington. Park made a strong impression on Thomas due to his familiarity with the African American community, as well as his perspective on society, and Thomas took the initiative of recommending to the Department of Sociology at Chicago that Park be hired.[4] This was a temporary position, justified, as far as Park could tell, by his expertise with the "Negro Problem"—and in particular the situation of African Americans in the South.[5] Park moved to Chicago with the precarious status of "professional lecturer" and receiving a small salary. His acceptance of this position does not seem to have been due to any need for an income, as after the death of his father in 1911, Park enjoyed some financial security. Park thus secured his first position at the University of Chicago, teaching "Negroes in America" in the autumn of 1913. His appointment was renewed trimester by trimester and then, after 1919, year by year, until he received tenure as a full professor in 1923.[6] Before this date, Park had become the most influential sociologist with respect to the students in the University of Chicago Department of Sociology. In a 1915 article in the *American Journal of Sociology*, he proposed a program of sociological research on the city. Six years later, in 1921, along with his young colleague Ernest Burgess (1886–1966), Park published a sort of textbook, *Introduction to the Science of Sociology*, which presents the fundamental categories of a research program that would inspire the work of Chicago sociology students over the following years.[7] The book, which sold thirty thousand copies between 1921 and 1943, was nicknamed the "Green Bible" by sociology students at Chicago, as the cover of the first edition was green.

These two foundational texts of the Chicago tradition in sociology do not only offer a novel formulation of the themes developed by sociologists of the preceding period. They also present an obviously original character, even if the *Introduction* adopts a similar form to that of *Source Book for Social Origins*, the earlier textbook published by Thomas. Taking into account the brief amount of time separating Park's recruitment as a sociologist and the publication of his texts, it is clear that the sociology of Park—who was certainly the author principally responsible for the innovations proposed in the *Introduction*[8]—should be contextualized by Park's singular social experience from before he was hired by the University of Chicago.

Born in Pennsylvania in 1864, a year after Thomas, Robert Park was the son of a grocer who settled in the Midwest and became wealthy later on. His situation permitted the future sociologist, according to Burgess, to observe "the behavior of the town's 'best families' with the detachment of the outsider and with the interest in the motive springs of human action rather than the obligation of conformity to the social code."[9] A biographical document adds some specifics to this global interpretation: Park spent his childhood in a neighborhood "invaded by Scandinavian immigrants" in a small Minnesota city, and it was among this population that he spent his first eighteen years, learning to understand the world of Norwegian peasants.[10]

Park studied philosophy, with a minor in German, at the University of Michigan, then one of the most reputable in the United States in addition to being one of the most open to the outside world. There, he notably studied with the philosopher John Dewey, who introduced him to Kant, Darwin, and Spencer. Having obtained the degree of bachelor of philosophy, indicating a relative lack of success in the liberal arts, after 1887 Park turned toward investigative journalism, which he pursued in Minneapolis, Detroit, and then New York, giving him the opportunity to interact with diverse contacts with a wide variety of aspects of urban life. He later evoked the opium dens and clandestine casinos that he visited as a journalist in Minneapolis, where, according to a later remark, he became a "reformer."[11] During a diphtheria epidemic, Park reported that he had the idea of placing recorded cases on a map, thus pinpointing an open sewer responsible for the contagion.[12] In New York, Park was at one point assigned to follow breaking news within the precinct of one police station. However, no biographical documents written by Park, nor any accounts that I have consulted, give a precise sense of his familiarity with the world of crime and delinquency, although it is clear that, like Thomas, his knowledge of the social world outside the university was wider than that of most academics of the period.

It is clearly significant that Park drew attention to these contacts. This journalistic experience drove him, according to his own expression, to gain a "conception of the city not as a geographical phenomenon merely but as a kind of social organism."[13] After a few months, Park returned to Detroit, then passed through Chicago in 1897–1898, spending a total of eleven years as a journalist (the median amount of time spent in this profession during the period). Unsatisfied by his activities, Park then resumed his studies in philosophy and psychology at Harvard—where George Santayana, Josiah Royce, and William James all taught—with the intention, in his own words, of studying "the philosophical aspects of the effects of the printed facts on the public."[14] His relationship with James, in particular, had the effect of turning him away from scholarly speculation and arguably discouraged him from pursuing a career as a professor of philosophy.[15]

In 1899, after a year at Harvard, Park left for Germany, the country to which American intellectuals of the period traveled to complete their higher education, particularly those studying the area of philosophical reflection on history and society. Successively at Berlin, Strasbourg, and Heidelberg, Park was in contact with Georg Simmel, Wilhelm Windelband, and a geographer named Alfred Hettner (whose conception of his specialty was for Park a "revelation"), as well as an economist, Georg Friedrich Knapp, whose ability to make his students understand in depth the world of German peasants captured Park's attention: "I gained from his lectures a knowledge of peasant life so complete and intimate as I would never have believed possible to have of any people with whom one had not lived. These lectures were delightfully anecdotal, and at the same time amazingly informing."[16] Park remarked elsewhere that Hettner's courses gave him "The best possible introduction to an understanding of the plantation Negro."[17] Upon his return in 1903 to the United States, Park temporarily held a precarious position as an instructor in philosophy at Harvard while writing a dissertation that he defended the following year at Heidelberg: *Masse und Publikum: Eine methodologische und soziologische Untersuchung.*[18] The same year, Park declined an offer from Albion Small to teach sociology at Chicago for one semester, beginning a second detour away from academic life.[19] According to him, he was "disgusted with what I had done in the University and had come to the conclusion that I couldn't do anything first rate on my own account."[20] He then became the secretary and public relations agent for an association connected to the Baptist congregation—the Congo Reform Association—that lobbied Congress against Belgian colonization. Park wrote many articles over the following years denouncing Belgium's policies, but he also became critical of the goals of the association that employed him, considering, according to a later account, that "the Congo, like some other parts of Africa, was suffering from a kind of political disease which . . . seems to have been endemic everywhere the Europeans have intended to uplift and civilize the peoples they call natives by incorporating them in the growing world economy which the expansion of the European peoples has created."[21] This contact with the Congo led him to discover a new angle on racial relations: from observing the rapidly evolving situation in the Congo, he seems to have drawn the conclusion that inequalities between races are not based on innate traits, but on political domination and exploitation by Europeans.[22]

In 1905, Park became the secretary of the moderate African American leader Booker T. Washington, one of the directors of the Congo Reform Association. Then at the height of his influence due to his relationship with Theodore Roosevelt, US president between the years 1901 and 1909, Washington led a movement advocating the education—especially the "industrial" training—of African Americans and directed a school offering such, the Tuskegee Institute.[23] Park's duties consisted notably of writing articles and books for Washington. Among other things, he contributed to writing and gathering sources for a book published under Washington's name, *The Story of the Negro*, which focused particularly on racial conflicts in the South and African American agricultural communities in remote areas, which were, according to Washington, an example of the relationship between moral qualities and their populations. Park's notes suggest adherence to this model, as well as his reinterpretation of it within the framework of the opposition of community and society constructed by the German social sciences.[24] Park also went on different research trips at the behest, and sometimes in the company, of Washington. On one of these in 1910, Washington and Park visited urban working-class neighborhoods and rural areas of Europe in order to compare the conditions of the European working classes to those of African Americans in the United States.[25] Immersing himself in the orbit of Booker T. Washington made Park, according to Thomas in the months after they first met, an authority on African Americans; in Park's words, he became "for all intents and purposes, for the time, a Negro myself."[26]

When he arrived at the University of Chicago, Park possessed important experience in various forms of investigation into the three principal, and partly connected, domains within which he developed analyses over the following years: behavior in cities, race relations, and collective behavior, of which the diffusion of mass media serves as a particular example.[27]

The interpretation, now frequently maintained, that Thomas exerted a major influence over Park and fashioned him into a sort of disciple must be challenged.[28] This theory does not withstand a comparative examination of the intellectual experiences of the two men, almost the same age when they met, and their publications. Their correspondence (reproduced in Raushenbush 1979: 68) shows that it was Thomas who expressed the greater enthusiasm for this encounter with an interlocutor whose orientation, knowledge, and interests resembled his own. They effectively shared the same type of knowledge of the rural societies of North America and Europe, and of emigration to cities, which they had acquired principally as travelers who observed varied situations. Both had interviewed people they encountered, and both had had conversations with intellectuals and leaders of diverse movements who were potential informants on the subject. A mistrust of the perspective of reformers brought them together. Even before their meeting, both expressed reservations regarding the close association between activism and analysis: one can find a trace of this in Park's correspondence before his marriage in 1894,[29] and then again regarding the campaign of the Congo Reform Association. Park expressed this mistrust more bluntly than did Thomas, as we shall see below.

The intellectual culture of Thomas and Park, which constituted the foundation of their perspectives on the social world, partially overlapped. They both had contact with William James and John Dewey, and both had a precocious interest in the analyses of Cooley and the psychologists Münsterberg and Wundt, who figure among the references in Park's first contributions to sociological publications. Park's dissertation gives an idea of which scholars he read before 1904, among whom figure not only the philosophers with whom he studied but also the psychologist Mark Baldwin, Herbert Spencer, the French philosopher Alfred Fouillée, as well as, on the theme of his dissertation, Gabriel Tarde, Gustave Le Bon, and Scipio Sighele, who were mobilized in an inquiry focusing on, among other things, the definition of conceptual categories appropriated for an approach to collective phenomena such as crowds and the mass diffusion of the media.[30] While Park was certainly less familiar than Thomas with anthropological literature, his philosophical acculturation was broader, and he was more focused on abstract formulations, as their later respective publications confirm.

Thomas and Park also share one last, rarely noted characteristic: their works were deemed valuable contributions to the development of sociology much later in their careers than would have been normal. When they met, Thomas had a more solid institutional position than Park, but had certainly not achieved a great intellectual reputation, and sociology was at that point a poorly defined and little valorized discipline. Thomas found himself only at the beginning of his discovery of the vast field of analysis of subjective experiences—a domain also discovered by Park by way of both William James (whose essay "On a Certain Blindness in Human Beings" Park quoted relentlessly) and his activities at the side of Booker T. Washington. The first article published by Park in the *American Journal of Sociology*, in 1913, "Racial Assimilation in Secondary Groups With Particular Reference to the Negro," is a continuation of Park's previous reflections, as is what he would write in the following years on race relations.

Park read Thomas's publications, borrowed concepts from *The Polish Peasant* (which, it must be remembered, was only published in 1918–1920), and treated the book as a model research report. However, the elements that constituted his approach to the social world derived primarily from his previous reading, and secondarily from *Folkways* by W. G. Sumner. The perspective on the social world that Park developed in the following years is notably broader than that of Thomas, including, as we shall see, elements that reveal an approach to the objective dimension of social phenomena absent from Thomas's work. Park thereby embodied that which he would later cite as his reason for resuming philosophical studies in 1899: "I wanted to gain a fundamental point of view from which I could describe the behavior of society, under the influence of news, in the precise and universal language of science."[31]

After being recruited by the University of Chicago, Park dedicated part of his time to reading texts connected to his growing teaching duties. It is possible to reconstitute these from his first publications: a textbook in a collection edited by Thomas in 1915, *The Principles of Human Behavior*,[32] and an essay published the same year, "The City: Propositions for Research into Human Behavior in an Urban Context,"[33] which proposes a research program that was partially followed by Park's students. The 1915 textbook seems to have baffled later readers who qualified its orientation as "psychological," but it includes, after an inquiry into human nature and its social dimension, a formulation of Park's interrogations into the approach of collective behavior as well as references that also appear in his dissertation.[34] Thomas had suggested that Park formulate a research program on cities, an unsurprising extension to research on rural emigration into cities.[35]

The subject figured elsewhere at the same time among of-the-moment questions, constituting a sort of counterpart to the post-1908 development of a sociological research program focusing on the rural areas of the United States, in which "social problems" had newly been imputed. These were evoked in a textbook by J. M. Gillette that was published in the same series as the one written by Park in 1915. Without citing them in his essay "The City"—although he later specified this—Park relied on the example of applied research in rural sociology that had been developed some years earlier at the University of Wisconsin in the circle of C. J. Galpin.[36]

As a result of his experience in journalism and his dissertation in philosophy, Park always paid considerable attention to phenomena of opinion, as noted in this remark from the preface to *Introduction to the Science of Sociology*, which he published with Burgess: "The most important facts that sociologists have to deal with are opinions (attitudes and sentiments), but until students learn to deal with opinions as biologists deal with organisms, that is, to dissect them—reduce them to their composant elements, describe them, and define the situation (environment) to which they are a response—we must not expect very great progress in social science."[37]

It seems that neither their previous publications and intellectual experiences nor the publications that immediately followed their meeting render plausible a relationship characterized by Park's strong intellectual dependence on Thomas: Park certainly owed his recruitment in sociology at Chicago to Thomas, and also the model of methodology and research that constituted *The Polish Peasant*, but not the essential intellectual inspiration of his type of sociology, which, as we shall see, was incomparably broader than that of Thomas.[38]

Starting in 1919, Park became involved in different collective research projects in the domain of "race relations." He inspired the investigations of the Chicago Commission's inquiry into the race riot of 1919. Established by the governor of Illinois, this commission had been called for by different associations, including the Chicago section of the Urban League, which had been created the preceding year and which Park had presided over during its first year.[39] Composed of white representatives of the reformist Chicago elite along with some notable African Americans (a newspaper editor, a lawyer, and a physician), this commission was charged with establishing how the riot had progressed and analyzing its causes. Its funding was secured in large part by Julius Rosenwald, the president of the mail-order company Sears Roebuck. Charles S. Johnson, one of the (rare) African American students of sociology at the University of Chicago, particularly appreciated by Park, was the lead author of the voluminous report (672 pages) produced by the commission in 1922 under the title *The Negro in Chicago: A Study of Race Relations and a Race Riot in 1919*.[40]

It is difficult to overstate the importance of the commission's work in the development of Park's sociology. It focused not only on the progress of the riots themselves, but also on the migration of rural, southern African Americans to the cities of the North—history remembers this as the Great Migration, a new social phenomenon on account of its enormous scale, and which had lasting consequences (see chapter 8).[41] The report also examined the problems of housing and employment for the migrants, and the contribution of newspapers to constituting African American and white opinions on their mutual relationships. Park participated in gathering data, but above all he provided the general inspiration for the investigations. The arrival of black migrants to Chicago en masse had begun in 1916, and starting in that year Park, as president of the local section of the Urban League, like other association leaders was concerned about the intensification of racial conflicts in the city.[42] Park's 1918 correspondence collected by Johnson regarding migrants' letters confirms the precocity of his interest in the Great Migration.[43] The report of the commission contains the first precise data concerning it. The report was followed by no political plan of action—a point of comparison with the important work of researchers studying race relations thirty years later, as they built a case against segregation (see chapter 8).

After the end of the war, as mentioned in the previous chapter, Park participated in research funded by the Carnegie Foundation on the "Americanization" of immigrants, along with W. I. Thomas. In this context, Park published in 1922, in addition to the book on which he collaborated with Thomas, a book about media addressed to immigrants.[44] Between 1923 and 1926, Park was also directly involved with a collective investigation into racial relations on the Pacific coast: with funding from the Institute of Social and Religious Research, a religious foundation supported by the Rockefeller Foundation, and the collaboration of a relatively large team, Park directed the collection of various documents, notably autobiographies, as Thomas had done for *The Polish Peasant*.[45] Some of the results of this investigation were published in a special issue of *Survey*, the magazine of the Social Survey Movement.[46]

In the other domain of research that Park would contribute to organizing—urban studies—he himself did not directly undertake research. According to Everett Hughes, "Park really did nothing more on the study of cities except to visit them."[47] This point merits special attention, since Park's framework of analyzing urban phenomena was much less developed than his framework for analyzing interethnic relations. It is also necessary to highlight that, as has already been mentioned, the study of urban phenomena was of the moment during this period, both for members of the Social Survey Movement and for sociologists. In 1915, for example, the journalist Graham R. Taylor published a book reprinting excerpts from articles published in *Survey* about cities in which large industries had been established.[48] Some years later, with funding from the Institute for Social and Religious Research, Paul Harlan Douglass completed a study of developing neighborhoods in the United States.[49] In the 1920s, Scott Bedford also prepared a collection of texts on urban sociology, finally published in 1927 after his departure from the University of Chicago.

In the following years, Park continued to be involved in movements of immigration to the Pacific region, and made study trips to Hawaii, southeast Asia, Japan, and, in 1932, China. In 1923—somewhat significantly after the departure of the second president of the University of Chicago, Henry Pratt Judson, who seems not to have favored Park any more than he did Thomas[50]—Park was named full professor. After his retirement in 1933, he did not remain in Chicago long; in 1936, he settled in Nashville, Tennessee, on the invitation of Charles Johnson, who had become chair of the Department of Social Sciences at Fisk University, one of the best universities in the nation devoted to educating African Americans.[51] In the years after his departure from Chicago, Park remained in contact with some of his former students, participated in various conferences and seminars, and published articles in sociology journals until the end of his life.

As these biographical notes suggest, the principal contribution to Park's sociology is not a single study that would then serve as a model (for example, that of Thomas and Znaniecki), but rather the book that served as a framework for the research of Park's students, *Introduction to the Science of Sociology*, as well as various essays with a programmatic or research-guide character. These essays can especially be found in prefaces to books in the series that Park coedited with Ernest Burgess and Ellsworth Faris for the University of Chicago Press. Performing beyond the functions of a researcher, Park essentially acted as the director of a research project, defining the orientation of investigations, proposing an overall framework, and ultimately suggesting the appropriate documentation and drawing conclusions from the finished research. The work under his direction accomplished a research program that he would not have been able to complete otherwise on account of the constraints of his institutional position. The near absence of a systematic research report among his publications cannot be imputed as a difficulty that he would have encountered in fieldwork, as was the case for Albion Small and most of the sociologists and anthropologists of the previous generation.

The students and associates of Park described in detail Park's active contribution to different phases of their research, which were not always his direct responsibility, since Park was involved in research but not in establishing the limits of an academic field.[52] Park accompanied some of his students in their fieldwork, taking advantage of his knowledge of the urban underworld and his certain detachment with regard to the ordinary canons of the morality of his period and class. In his teaching, as in the course of individual discussions, Park excelled, by his students' reckoning, in formulating a relatively abstract and general theoretical framework that could make sense of individual observations made in the field. As Pauline Young writes,

Once, as a graduate student, I had rushed into print with an article on occupational attitudes of a sectarian group of laborers.[53] I proudly sent a copy of this article to Dr. Park hoping to please him with my "conceptual thinking." His reply put ashes in my mouth. "You have ruined meticulously gathered data by couching them in concepts that sound like the grips and passes of a secret society. Come to my office, I think I can teach you something." He started by taking the concept competition apart, and showed how a number of events are condensed under one general heading. I grasped that a concept is in reality a definition of a social situation in shorthand, an analysis of a class or group of facts isolated from other classes on the basis of definite classification systems.[54]

As this quote suggests, the principal concepts of the general framework Park proposed are those that appear in *Introduction to the Science of Sociology*.[55] But Park also widely used the concepts introduced in *The Polish Peasant*. He offered students practical advice that often proved useful in organizing their documentation and facilitating their writing. Some of them published practically nothing after their dissertations, but the important point here is undoubtedly the creation of a collection of sociology books at the University of Chicago Press. This gave Park the opportunity to fill a role as editor of a collection, for which his previous experience in journalism had prepared him.

A particular relationship between Park's essays and the empirical research he inspired stems from his involvement in supervising research. The research program proposed by certain of Park's essays was at least partially achievable with the documentary sources available to researchers of the period. The connections between the results of completed research and the general framework of Park's sociology remain rather loose: the categories of his sociology were sketched out rather than well defined, and the relationships between the empirical material and the conceptual categories were often imprecise. It was a conception of empirical research and its objectives, as well as the focusing of attention on certain social phenomena—and not a corpus of propositions that could be tested by empirical research—that constituted the core of what the sociologists of the following generation borrowed from Park.

THE TWO DIMENSIONS OF PARK'S SOCIOLOGY

Park's sociology can be characterized by the following elements: an abstract frame of analysis, certain elements of which were inspired by the social theories developed by the essayists of the preceding generation (Spencer on the one hand;

and Gumplowitz, Simmel, and the German social scientists of the beginning of the century on the other); an insistent attention to the spatial dimension of social facts, associated with the usage of cartography; and a particular affinity for the approach that would later be characterized as ethnography—that is, first-hand knowledge of the studied phenomena—which, for Park, more reflects his journalistic experience and the diffuse influence of pragmatic philosophy.[56] One should also note that, in order to be understood, Park's profoundly ambivalent relationship with the Progressive reform movement should be taken in the context of his statement.

I seek here to make apparent the diversity of elements that compose Park's sociology, insisting upon the traits that today seem the least easily comprehensible, and without presupposing the existence of a necessary connection among these diverse elements. One of the difficulties in interpreting Park's sociology relates to the form it took—that of essays whose developments are frequently linked by free association. Neither precision nor consistency in defining and applying concepts were major concerns for Park—the concept of process was, for example, too frequently used to have a univocal sense. Park showed no more concern for a systematic administration of proof for the assertions that he advanced than Thomas or the other American sociologists of his generation. For Park, as for some of those who claimed to be his intellectual heirs, like Everett Hughes or Howard S. Becker, the finished product of a sociological analysis was not a corpus of verified general propositions, but the articulation of a group of categories that defined a point of view (or a perspective) on the field in question.[57]

While Park's essays do contain propositions based on evidence, these do not necessarily have to be interpreted as theories firmly held by the author, as has often been done regarding the inevitability of the "race relations circle" (see chapter 8). Over the course of the years, Park did not stop himself from using modified definitions of his concepts, and he significantly changed many analyses over time. The absence of a systematic demonstration of explicitly formulated general propositions arguably contributed more than any other factor to the discrediting of his essays when, starting in the 1930s, concern for demonstrating explicitly formulated propositions began to hold a place in an American sociology obsessed with the recognition of the scientific character of its methods.

One distinction—the opposition between ecological order and moral order—and two concepts—interaction and social control—occupy central positions in Park's sociology. The distinction between ecological and moral order is only implicit in Park's programmatic essay from 1915 on the city, but becomes explicit in *Introduction to the Science of Sociology*:[58] "As a matter of fact, man and society present themselves in a double aspect. They are at the same time products of nature and of human artifice. . . . So far it is true, the conflict between Hobbes and Aristotle is not absolute. Society is a product both of nature and of design, of instinct and of reason."[59] The first term in this list, ecological order—which today seems to have been one of Park's innovations—designates as a field of study the competition of individuals and groups for the occupation of the same territory. Spencer's sociology, as well as diverse books in zoology and botany Park read around 1915, are the sources that inspired it.[60] The second term on the list, moral order, designates the realm of communication between individuals, and Park's study continues and expands upon the preoccupations of Thomas's sociology.

The idea of human ecology is based on a sort of intuition that is related to the position of an outside observer who considers the development of a large city like Chicago. This is what the formulation proposed by Park in the 1925 version of "The City" suggests: "There are forces at work within the limits of the urban community . . . which tends to bring about an orderly and typical grouping of its population and institutions. The science which seeks to isolate these factors and to describe the typical constellations of persons and institutions which the cooperation of these forces produce, is what we call human, as distinguished from plant and animal, ecology. Transportation and communications, tramways and telephones, newspapers and advertising . . . are primary factors in the ecological organization of the city."[61] Later in the same text, Park notes that ecological order is irreducible to individual will: "Personal tastes and convenience, vocational and economic interests, infallibly tend to segregate and thus to classify the populations of great cities. In this way the city acquires an organization and distribution of population which is neither designed nor controlled."[62]

The autonomization of this order of phenomena tends toward a biological analogy, which is itself partly borrowed by classical political science, and also to the perspective that drove Park to adopt the map as a heuristic for social reality, making apparent patterns exterior to individual consciences. The use of maps was not, we must recall, novel: the instrument had been in use in social survey reports at least since Charles Booth. *Hull House Maps and Papers* (1895) contains two maps of a Chicago neighborhood, with, notably, the localization of different types of immigrants displayed.[63] Charles Zueblin also seems to have used maps at the beginning of the century in a course placed in the category of "municipal sociology."[64] But at least in the two first cases, these maps served to present results of surveys. For Park—although we know that it was Burgess here who gave the decisive push—the use of maps permitted him to discover phenomena starting from their objective properties, and to explore that aspects that eluded individual consciences.

Ways of occupying space—by diverse populations, by different institutions and activities—constitute the first area toward which Park's sociology called attention. Nearly half of *Introduction* is essentially dedicated to an examination of that which Park and Burgess designate as "interaction between different populations" and characterize as a "fundamental social process."[65] The interest in spatial determinations should clearly be interpreted as a challenge to biological determinants in favor of the influence of the social environment. This conviction, which Park shared with Thomas and social science researchers influenced by Boas, led him to demonstrate that phenomena, including delinquency, suicide, divorce, and the establishment of a particular type of institution, are specific to certain urban zones, and not to the ethnic origin of a particular population. The illustration of this claim is one of the principal themes of the monographs produced under Park's influence.

The concept of interaction necessitates close examination, since one of the main ambiguities of the interpretation of the posterity of the pragmatic tradition in sociology since the 1950s results from the diversity of usages of this term. In the chapter dedicated to it, Park and Burgess insist upon the fact that interaction is not a "notion of common sense."[66] The point of departure is a sort of mechanical analogy whose partial obscurity stems, undoubtedly, as much from their uncertain mastery of Newtonian mechanics as it does from a less than rigorous use of vocabulary. In the same way that mechanical interaction (i.e., forces) is what links elements in the material world, interaction in society is what links institutions, ideas, human beings, and so on. Communication is presented as the intermediary principal of interaction in society, which explains why some discussions use the term "interaction" in a more restricted sense. Park and Burgess's concept of interaction seems equivocal from their first allusion to it in *Introduction to the Science of Sociology*: "Communication, if not identical with, is at least a form of, what has been referred to here as social interaction. . . . Communication is a process by which we 'transmit' an experience from an individual to another but it is also a process by which these same individuals get a common experience."[67]

A later article by Park is more precise: it distinguishes two fundamental types of interaction: competition (which characterizes the ecological order) and communication.[68] The principal references for the discussion on interaction in *Introduction* are Ludwig Gumplowicz and Georg Simmel.[69] In a text translated into English in *Introduction*, Gumplowicz develops the example of the ethnic or social group that "strives to subjugate and make serviceable to its purposes every weaker element which exists or may come within the field of its influence."[70] The concept is identified with that of reciprocal action used by Simmel in another text reproduced in *Introduction*. In it, Simmel suggests that a society exists when individuals maintain reciprocal relationships, and he outlines the major features of a program of the science of society conceived as the study of these reciprocal influences and forms of socialization. Park expands upon this idea, claiming that the limits of a society are defined by the interaction of its elements. "Society as interaction" is a phrase that some of Park's students would repeat after him.

Although this consequence is not explicitly developed, this formula implies also that the objects studied by sociology—notably social groups—exist in a permanent state of evolution: "Social process is the name for all changes which can be regarded as changes in the life of the group," claims the *Introduction* before expanding upon the distinctions between historical, cultural, political, and economic processes.[71] This conception of a social reality subject to permanent changes corresponds to a perception and formulation that were banal at the beginning of the century—Small and the social reformers also frequently invoked the concept of social processes.

Park and Burgess devote a lengthy section in *Introduction* to developing distinctions among "four great types of interaction": competition, conflict, accommodation, and assimilation. This is a sort of typology of the processes that influence relationships between populations present in the same space or in neighboring spaces. The idea of competition, also present in the work of Cooley, especially *Social Organization* (1909), is linked to the biological analogy of the interspecies struggle for life, as well as to the analyses of economists such as Adam Smith and Frédéric Bastiat.[72] Competition puts populations into relation with each other and corresponds to a form of interaction without contact, which is to say without communication, but can also be accompanied by a form of cooperation. The authors themselves note the paradoxical side of this type of interaction, which was not included as such in their initial definition. *Introduction* suggests that competition determines the distribution of the population in a territory—the ecological organization of society—as well as the distribution of different activities.[73]

The three other types of interaction relate to the moral order, which is to say the area in which communication between different groups and people takes place. Although Park and Burgess do not make this point explicit, the study of these forms of interaction requires the use of documentary sources that take into account the subjective experiences of agents. Conflict constitutes the form of interaction that, in contrast with competition, supposes contact between people or groups and, consequently, a form of communication (which can be mediated, as in the case evoked by the authors, by newspapers and radio). Conflict possesses a conscious character and can provoke intense feelings. The form of struggle between parties in each other's presence is not, as with the case of competition, continuous and impersonal, but rather intermittent and personal.

The idea of accommodation is borrowed from that of Darwinian adaptation. It corresponds to a case in which conflict between different elements is regular and "disappears as overt action, although it remains latent as a potential force."[74] There is therefore "an organization of social relations and attitudes to prevent or to reduce conflict, to control competition, and to maintain a basis of security in the social order for persons and groups of divergent interests and types to carry on together their varied life-activities."[75]

The fourth type of interaction, assimilation, is defined as the "process of interpenetration and fusion in which persons and groups acquire the memories, sentiments and attitudes of other persons and groups, and, by sharing their experience and history, are incorporated with them in a common cultural life."[76] More so than the previously distinguished types—as Park and Burgess note—this concept directly concerns the examination of problems with relationships between different populations. The authors concern themselves above all with the case of the United States, where the First World War gave rise, as we have seen, to a movement in favor of the "Americanization" of immigrants.[77] The definition of the concept of assimilation found in *Introduction* is ambiguous, and in the following years Park would return to this question many times (see chapter 8).

The presentation of these different types of interaction leads to a proposition that is explicitly formulated not in *Introduction*, in which the authors content themselves with remarking that social contact constitutes the origin of interaction and that assimilation is its finished product, but rather in a 1926 article by Park: relationships between ethnic groups, in the United States and elsewhere, evolve according to a "progressive and irreversible" process termed the "race relations circle," which moves from competition, through conflict and accommodation, to assimilation.[78] The diffusion of this proposition is unrivaled in importance in Park's sociology, as we shall see in chapter 8.

Like Thomas's sociology, that of Park gave a central place to the concept of social control—"social control is the central fact and the central problem of society," he claims in *Introduction*.[79] Park used the term in an encompassing sense to designate the ensemble of mechanisms that organize and channel collective behavior. The distinction among types of interaction is closely linked to the process of establishing forms of social control: "Social control and the mutual subordination of individual members to the community have their origin in conflict, assume definite organized forms in the process of accommodation, and are consolidate and fixed in assimilation."[80] *Introduction* does not propose a particular elaboration of the concept of social control (a term which belongs to the vocabulary common to social reformers and sociologists of the previous period, such as Sumner, Small, and Cooley). The book offers only a preliminary inventory of its mechanisms, among which figure public opinion and religious and political institutions, along with the spontaneous elementary forms that can be found in crowds or ceremonies.

One could remark that two concepts, though closely linked to that of social control and very present in monographs written by Park's students, are not objects of particular elaboration in *Introduction*. The concept of social disorganization appears little and is defined only by reference to Cooley and to *The Polish Peasant*. Similarly, the concept of community is not an object of deep discussion. This concept, however, occupied an important position in Park's sociology, since Park, like social reformers, advocates the organization of ethnic communities as an instrument of social control as a solution for urban "social problems" like crime (see chapter 7): "The social problem is fundamentally a city problem. It is the problem of achieving in the freedom of the city a social order and a social control equivalent to that which grew up naturally in the family, the clan, and the tribe."[81] One might observe, however, that Park's assessment of urban facts differs from that of most social reformers of his generation and the preceding one, and from that of middle-class Protestants who often came (like Park) from small Midwest cities, for whom the integrated rural community remained their model of reference. Park made many statements testifying, to the contrary, to a fascination with cities and their diversity, even if his writing sometimes evoked nostalgia for the way of life and social control typical to the preindustrial period.

Another concept that organizes certain monographs from the years 1919–1933 is that of "natural history." This once again emphasizes the central place afforded to analyses of process in Park's sociology. Relying on logic similar to the Weberian ideal type, it seeks to isolate—as opposed to providing individual histories of each social object—the ordered and irreversible series of events that constitute the evolutionary stages through which they pass. The concept was applied to extremely varied objects, ranging from religious sects to newspapers, strikes, and revolutions, and passing through the development of what Park terms the marginal personality.[82]

Intended for use as a textbook for novice researchers, *Introduction* offers discussions, including those dealing with the concepts that have just been described, on themes familiar to Park—such as collective behavior, public opinion, and the press—and on questions routinely considered by sociologists of the period. Here I shall note only the weak elaboration of the concept of social class. The discussions of it present in *Introduction* are limited to a few diffuse remarks and a short bibliography, whose principal references comment on a typology of social groups proposed by Gustave Le Bon, who vaguely defines the concept as a group linked by common interests.[83] Class differences and conflicts (which were, it should be recalled, examined in an article by Small, published just before 1914, that constituted a theme that was often present in his courses and Cooley's sociology),[84] are invoked from time to time, as evidence, in Park's essays. The concept never, however, takes a defined place in the program for investigating cities proposed by Park.

The discussion in *Introduction* that, according to the book's index, corresponds to the definition of the concept can be found in an 1898 text by Scipio Sighele: "the class represents the veritable crowd in a dynamic state, which can in a moment's time descend from that place and become statistically a crowd. And it is from the sociological standpoint the most terrible kind of crowd; it is that which today has taken a bellicose attitude, and which by its attitude and precepts prepare the brutal blows of mob."[85] Behind the antipathy toward the idea of social class suggested by the text can be found Park's refusal to admit that American society presented long-lasting class differences. His essays contain diverse remarks on the subject—for example: "It may strike the disinterested observer as a little strange that in America where, humanly speaking, there are no class distinctions, there is still so much race prejudice."[86] He elaborates on this statement in an observation found in *Introduction*: "In a free society, competition tends to destroy classes and castes."[87]

The concept of class does, along with the concept of status (which is connected to the idea of prestige, but of which Park fails to give a more precise definition), sometimes appear in Park's essays on race relations, including in the first essays on the subject: a research report published by Park in 1913 on the living conditions of African Americans in the South reveals a sustained attention to class differences.[88] Also, in 1939, one of Park's first essays to examine the evolution of race relations concludes with the remark that, in the long term, "race conflicts in the modern world, which already or presently will be a single great society, will be more and more in the future confused with, and eventually superseded by, the conflicts of classes."[89]

If Park had a conception of social classes that was neither clear nor precise, he was not alone: until the end of the 1920s, the concept was not used by sociologists who conducted empirical research, at least partially because the term itself was politically suspect. For example, E. E. Hunt, appointed by President Herbert Hoover as liaison to the Committee on Recent Social Trends (see chapter 5), wondered aloud in front of William Ogburn (1886–1959), Park's colleague at the University of Chicago, "Are they a part of the accepted terminology of American sociologists?" Ogburn responded, "In general items like 'the masses,' the 'upper class,' etc. are much more applicable to Europeans than they are to Americans, and these terms are not generally used."[90] At the time, almost all of those who performed empirical research barely recognized the existence of class differences in American society. Among the first to reintroduce the concept in empirical analysis were Robert and Helen Lynd (who borrowed the idea from Veblen). In their study of a small American city, called Middletown in their books, the Lynds distinguish from the start two classes based on their role in production, categorizing the working class as opposed to a business class. The Lynds grouped the individuals whose activities were "oriented toward people," in terms of sales and the promotion of services or ideas, although in their second book on Middletown they honed their conception, identifying six distinct emerging classes.[91]

If one pays attention to the principal traits of Park's sociology that correspond to the central concepts of his approach, one cannot help but be struck by their affinity with the perspective on American society at the beginning of the century that can be found, in a diffuse manner and in a less abstract form, in the sector of elite, intellectual Anglo-Saxons that included social reformers.[92] This inspiration is apparent in the common themes of interest, like the city and immigration, that already served as chapter titles in the 1885 bestseller *Our Country*, authored by the minister Josiah Strong (1847–1916), one of the principal leaders of the Protestant reform movement.[93] For example, in a book, published in 1913, Strong wrote:[94]

> The new city is the microcosm of the new civilization. It is in the city that the new industrial problem must be solved, for the city id the center of industrial civilization. It is in the city that the new problem of wealth must be solved, for there is wealth massed. It is in the city that the new race problem must be solved, because it is there that the races are forced into the closest competitive relations. It is in the city that the new problems of relations of the individuals and society must be solved, because there is the social organism most complex.[95]

At the heart of the perspective of these Protestant reformers was a focus on a historical phenomenon: rapidly growing cities with slum areas; the development of diverse forms of delinquency; and the influx of successive waves of immigrants who were mobile in terms of employment and habitat, whose arrival did not result in a political program expressly driven by the federal government, and who consequently took on the appearance of a sort of natural phenomenon. Publicly defined social problems, like immigrants' adaptation to their new society, conflicts among races and ethnic groups, and delinquency, constitute the immediately visible phenomena around which this perception took shape. To the contrary, the regularity of labor conflicts and the existence of recurrent class antagonisms, though not totally ignored, were left in the shadows to a degree, and were considered as phenomena typical of European societies in the same period.

Certainly, multiple factors contributed to this focalization on phenomena that could be placed under the heading of urban phenomena. One of them corresponds to the attention paid to the changing character, and not the stability, of the social positions and institutions occupied by most observers of American social reality at the beginning of the century. As for the challenging of biological determinants of behaviors—which is to say the criticism of racist explanations that began only at the start of the century—for Park this became an instrument in the quest for environmental determinants, meaning the emphasis on urban zones that were successively occupied by ethnically different populations and in which the same type of social phenomenon (crime, divorce, etc.) took place.

It must also be noted that among the singular aspects of Park's perception of social reality was the near neglect of the political dimension of social phenomena: the development of cities and the spatial distribution of populations within them are treated as "natural" facts resulting from population movements, and the involvement of local political elites and other categories of actors in these phenomena is left completely in the shadows. The same applies for the interventions of the federal state in the development of cities, emigration, or relationships between ethnic groups—which reflects the American situation before 1914 rather well, but no longer fully applies, as we have seen, to the situation after 1918. This perspective is also consistent with other political penchants held by Park, a Jeffersonian Republican (according to his own expression)—which is to say opposed to the strengthening and interventional capacity of the federal state—and with his skepticism regarding the actions of social reformers and their effects in improving municipal administrations. On this point, Park, who gladly quotes *Folkways*, resembles William Graham Sumner, a pessimistic witness of the waves of immigration at the end of the nineteenth century, who emphasized the slowness of changes in mores and the inefficacy of laws or the activities of the state in modifying them.

Thus reduced to its principal elements, Park's sociology appears to be a mix of those aspects that relate to singular aspects of his biography—starting with his intellectual training and his biographical experiences—and those that relate to a perception of American society of his time that was characteristic to the social world to which he belonged. As an abstract elaboration of a perception of this society, the frame of reference that serves as background to Park's sociology corresponds more to the state of society before 1914, with public debates about immigration, than to that which followed the First World War. More precisely, it corresponds more to the perceptions of American society held by cultivated middle-class Protestants during the time of Park's education than to those of the period in which he filled the role of research director.

PARK AND FIELDWORK

One of Park's contributions emphasized in the accounts of his former students concerns research methods—a subject almost absent from his essays, with one exception. Cartography appears to be the principal instrument for investigating the ecological order, but it was Burgess, and not Park, who contributed to assuring and perfecting its utilization.[96] The case study is the principal method of investigating the moral order, along with the use of documents such as were used in *The Polish Peasant*—notably biographies and autobiographies. In an article presenting the documentation that he sought to gather for a study he led about race relations on the Pacific coast, Park thus emphasizes biographies and formulates some judicious and (for the period) unusual remarks on the collection and interpretation of interviews.[97] Park's teaching activity also emphasizes the collection of what can be seen or understood in the places where the studied phenomena take place. Park therefore contributed to introducing interviews and observation as research instruments (albeit neither evoking nor discussing in his essays the distinction between what can be observed and what can be gathered through statements). Park's model is, as we have seen, the method used by investigative journalists, which he invoked expressly in his advice to Nels Anderson (see chapter 9). Park does not cite anthropology as a model until somewhat later.[98] Park's insistence on the value of understanding a symbolic world—a term that does not belong in the vocabulary used by Park and his contemporaries—of those whose behaviors are under study appears in several of his essays. In a 1924 article presenting the research project on race relations on the Pacific coast, Park, like Thomas in his post-1915 research, locates this aspect of empirical investigation at the heart of sociology: "The sociologist is not primarily concerned with the event itself. He rather takes that for granted. What he is more particularly concerned about are the attitudes of the persons involved, as they are reflected in their differing accounts of the same historical event. He is interested in anything, in fact, that will throw light upon these attitudes and make them intelligible."[99]

> Several statements made by those who were his students during the 1920s evoke Park's insistent recommendations that they acquire firsthand knowledge of the phenomena that they studied, and his apparent predilection for what would later be termed "fieldwork."[100] One of these statements perfectly captures what had become a fundamental principle for some of those claiming to be Park's heirs: "You have been told to go grubbing in the library, thereby accumulating a mass of notes and a liberal coating of grime. You have been told to choose problems wherever you can find musty stacks of routine records based on trivial schedules prepared by tired bureaucrats and filled out by reluctant applicants for aid or fussy do-gooders or indifferent clerks. That is called 'getting your hands dirty in real research.' Those who thus counsel you are wise and honorable; the reasons they offer are of great value. But one thing more is needful: firsthand observation. Go and sit in the lounges of the luxury hotels and on the doorsteps of the flophouses; sit on the Gold Coast and on the slum shakedowns;[101] sit in Orchestra Hall and in the Star and Garter Burlesk. In short, gentlemen, go to the seat of your pants dirty in *real* research."[102]

Park's endorsement of firsthand knowledge of objects of study does not, however, need to be reduced to his past familiarity with investigative journalism. Park's interest in knowledge of the meaning social actors invested in their activities is also in line with the pragmatism of William James. One of James's lectures, "On a Certain Blindness in Human Beings," featured among Park's favorite references in his courses.[103] This lecture develops the theme of the lack of communication between the worldviews of categories of people who regularly spend time together. Park claims that "this address, in preference to anything else that James or anyone else has written, should be required reading for sociologists and for teachers."[104] This theme, which is simple but proves fruitful, is found not only in the conceptual construction that underlies the definitions of the concepts central to the analysis of contacts between populations but also, as we shall see, in the research program of a large part of monographs from the years 1919–1933. One could maintain that it is, in fact, the central and eternal theme of a large portion of research in the Pragmatic tradition—from the sociology of work inspired by Everett Hughes in the 1940s and 1950s (see chapter 6) to the sociology of race relations, of which the brilliant book by Elijah Anderson on cross-racial street contact is one more recent achievement.[105]

PARK, THE SOCIOLOGICAL ENTERPRISE, THE REFORM
MOVEMENT, AND SOCIAL WORK

More so than that of Thomas, Park's relationship with the Progressive movement, and in particular with the Social Survey Movement and the field of social work, has been the object of divergent and frequently unilateral interpretations in recent years. Some are based on the hypothesis of a misogynistic refusal on Park's part to accept competition from women for academic jobs, and thus to take their research publications into account. Although not unfounded, such interpretations are incomplete, and contribute to concealing the similarities driving both sociology and reflections from the Protestant wing of the Progressive movement, as previously mentioned with the example of the books of Josiah Strong.

Like Thomas, Park defined anew the relationship between researcher and object, and challenged the previous definition of sociology as the "science of social problems" by insisting upon a dispassionate approach to the subjects under study. Various frequently cited accounts report Park's invectives against certain social reformers—"the greatest damage done to the city of Chicago was not the product of corrupt politicians or criminals but of women reformers."[106] His hostility and the distance that he maintained from those who, in Chicago, figured among the founders of university programs for training in social work, like Edith Abbott and Sophonisba Breckinridge, are also frequently mentioned.[107] An article by Marie-Jo Deegan suggests the existence of a personal background to the peremptory remarks Park made about the activism of reform-minded women: his wife, Clara Cahill Park, was very active around 1910 in this world of middle-class women, leading a campaign in favor of a stipend for the widows with children in the state of Massachusetts.[108] Precisely what this background means, however, is difficult to establish, and Deegan's interpretation—which makes a parallel between the "failure" of Park in his professional life before 1913 and the "success" of his wife as a leader of the reform movement—seems a little simplistic. It is also necessary to consider the known activities Park engaged in, being involved until the end of his life in activism for different causes.

Along with many leaders of social work and activist reformers including Edith Abbott and Sophonisba Breckinridge, Louise de Koven Bowen, Graham Taylor, Mary McDowell, and Jane Addams, Park was one of the founders of the Chicago Urban League, the local section of the National Urban League, the previously mentioned movement that provided aid to African American migrants who had moved to cities. In addition to serving as the first president for the Chicago branch of this organization, Park also wrote its statutes. These statutes invoke "all kinds of work for improving the industrial, economic, and social condition among Negroes," and mention the improvement of children's playgrounds, the creation of sponsorships for boys and girls, and aid for convicts and the indigent.[109]

Park also frequently presented papers at the annual meeting of the National Conference of Social Work (previously named the National Conference of Charities and Correction), the national organization coordinating assistance associations.[110] He also later actively participated in the activities of a Protestant parish led by a University of Chicago philosophy professor,[111] and, between 1933 and 1936, in those of a youth recreation center in the city.[112] His associate, Ernest Burgess, was equally active in the Chicago reform movement, and as long as he lived he participated in committees and associations that focused on address-ing the city's social problems. Many sociology students with whom Park was involved—like Frederic Thrasher and Louis Wirth—were themselves social workers at one point, and they sometimes conducted their research thanks to funding that was justified by immediately practical ends. Park himself was directly involved in research of this type. Park's relationship with the reform move-ment is thus more complex and ambivalent than is suggested by out-of-context anecdotes that recount brutally disparaging remarks about the positions of reformers, and especially certain female ones.

One significant element for interpreting Park's position is the increasing distance, following the First World War, between sociology and the declining Progressive reform movement, on the margins of which the new discipline had been born. This separation was marked by an insistence upon the "scientific" character of sociology, to which Park paid homage with the title of the textbook he cowrote with Burgess. It is also marked by the increasing distance sociolo-gists as a group kept from social surveys in the style of the Pittsburgh Survey—although the University of Chicago Settlement is mentioned until 1924–1925 in the section of the university directory that presents the activities of the sociology department. According to Ernest Mowrer, who was a sociology student at the University of Chicago during this period, "In other words 'reform' or anything of that sort was a dirty word in those days . . . the idea was to get first hand data. . . . If you happened to perform some functions as a social worker or juvenile officer, that was incidental."[113] The context of the course should also be taken into account when interpreting Park's exhortations regarding the necessity of separating sur-vey activity from that of social action: as Helen MacGill Hughes recalled, many students of the period came from social work or were the children of Protestant ministers, and they always thought normatively ("in the hortatory mood").[114]

Park's ambivalence toward the social movement from which sociology arose can be interpreted from his later use of social surveys. One of the first courses added to Park's teaching load after 1915 essentially focused on these surveys. Park offered this course almost every year of the following decade, and his essays also contained many allusions to the publications of Charles Booth and, with more reserved assessments, to the Pittsburgh Survey. At the start of the 1920s, the Social Survey Movement was still in existence, and these surveys always had a place in the culture shared by sociologists, as shown by the publication of books and articles in sociology journals.[115] Park's lesson plans and notes that touch on social surveys demonstrate his deep knowledge of these surveys as well as a critical distance from them: he examines the surveys more so as objects to be studied in themselves than documentary sources or models to follow in the sense of research methods.[116] Park's teaching focused principally on the social movement that had culminated in the production of these surveys: in particular, Park examined the relationship between these investigations and social problems, and their impact on public opinion in the communities on which they focused. This orientation toward the public opinion of the middle classes is one of the principal particularities of American surveys in relation to earlier English ones.

Park nevertheless drew significantly from the approaches and research findings provided by certain social surveys, and he did not always keep away from them. Ernest Burgess himself had been the organizer of one such survey in Lawrence, Kansas in 1916, and, in an article published the same year, he showed no reservation in principle as to the "scientific" character of these surveys.[117] Around 1920, Park and Burgess envisaged conducting a survey of this type in the neighborhood in which the University of Chicago had been established.[118] The work, supervised by Park, of the investigative commission into the July 1919 Chicago race riots followed the methodology of these surveys, notably in terms of interviews with business leaders and with African American families regarding their living conditions. The use of investigative surveys was also compatible with the social survey model. Some years later, in 1926, the distance between Park's research and the survey movement was not so great that he was unwilling to present the result of his research on relations between ethnic groups on the Pacific coast in *Survey Graphic*—a journal edited by Paul Kellogg, the lead investigator of the Pittsburgh Survey—whose readership largely consisted of participants in the Social Survey Movement.

Park's preface to a 1926 book by Burgess insists, however, on the difference in objectives between the two types of surveys: social surveys were the purview of politicians interested in developing programs and promoting initiatives. In the preface, Park also advances a principle of distinction between properly sociological surveys and those of the Social Survey Movement: the first implied the explicit formulation and verification of hypotheses, while social surveys were limited to an exploratory purpose. Neither Park's essays nor the research that he directed conformed, however, to this model as it was defined. A non-negligible portion of the analyses formulated by Park are just as far from showing the dispassionate character for which he argued.[119]

The particularities of Park's personal political and social opinions arguably also contributed, to a degree, to the ambivalence of his conceptions. Park was politically a conservative—or even a reactionary, according to one of his former students, Horace Clayton, although one of his daughters claimed he had anarchist sympathies in his youth. Park occasionally affirmed his hostility toward the state intervention that was called for by reformers of the Progressive movement. He sometimes manifested a certain confidence in what he considered the natural movement of social events. On the other hand, Park converged with a group of Progressive reformers in one aspect: he did not consider the goal of social science research to be providing leaders with decision-making instruments, but rather the mission of enlightening public opinion. He also sometimes presents sociology as an elaborated form of journalism that seeks to identify long-term developments ("big news") rather than limit itself to reporting current events ("news"): hence the type of writing Park favored, as he explained in advice given to Pauline Young, the author of one of the monographs of the 1920s: "You are not writing for professors, train yourself to write for the general public."[120] Here again Park's conception is not very far removed from that of the social reformers, who were also confident in the sociopolitical efficacy of the description of "facts" and in the consequences of the diffusion of knowledge.[121]

Considered in its context, Park's sociology seems rather less marked by a rupture with that of Albion Small's earlier generation than as one stage in a slow process of autonomization of sociology with regard to the Protestant-inspired reform movement from which it had issued. Park's professions of faith certainly indicated the direction that the discipline would take for a more complete emancipation with regard to the social problems of the moment, but they did not describe the state of sociology in his time, nor the work that he directed or inspired. These factors remained largely dependent on the social problems that provided a good part of Park's students with their research topics, and that sometimes justified the funding that they obtained.

One could note that the perspectives on the social sciences and their methods formulated by Park are only partially coherent.[122] One example is the exclusive focus on the subjective dimension of race relations in the Pacific coast study, which contrasts with Park's interest in the ecological order and his interest in the processes he designates as "natural history." His changing positions on the value of statistical inquiries are another example. *Introduction to the*

Science of Sociology contains formulations on the general laws that belong to an ordinary representation of the science that, though they can frequently be found in the same period, including in work by Thomas, fit poorly with other elements of Park's sociology.

THE CHICAGO DEPARTMENT OF SOCIOLOGY AS BASE OF A COLLECTIVE RESEARCH ENTERPRISE

During the period that stretches from 1918 to 1933, over the course of which most of the monographs associated with the Chicago School label were written, five other professors, aside from Park, taught on a permanent basis at the University of Chicago:[123] Albion Small, the chair of the department from its inception, who retired in 1925 and was replaced as a professor two years later by William Ogburn; Ernest Burgess; Ellsworth Faris, who was recruited to replace Thomas in 1919 and became chair of the department in 1925; and Scott Bedford, who resigned in 1925 and never exerted any appreciable influence.[124] If Small's audience among sociology students was, as has been suggested, weak following the war—his method of instruction seemed antiquated—we must recall that his conception of sociology was not in conflict with that of Park, with which it shared an insistence on empirical work and references to the German social sciences (especially Simmel). I shall examine in the following chapter what William Ogburn, who came from the rival tradition of Columbia University in New York, introduced in the research he conducted in Chicago. Ernest Burgess and Ellsworth Faris had, unlike Ogburn, an intellectual orientation similar in certain regards to Park's, and the impact of their teaching on the development of research conducted during the 1920s is inseparable from that of Park.

A non-negligible portion of the studies and the dissertations that would give rise to monographs associated with the Chicago School were also successively or simultaneously supervised by Park and Burgess. Some other research, such as the theses of Pauline V. Young and Ruth Shonle Cavan, supervised by Faris, also bore the mark of Park and Burgess thematically and methodologically.[125] For a substantial portion of the sociologists who passed through the Chicago Department of Sociology over the course of the period, the critical dimension of Faris's teaching—notably his polemics against other intellectual orientations—constituted a significant part of the training that they would later describe having received.

The collaboration between Park and Burgess relied as much on the way their interests and competencies complemented each other as it did on the similarities of their orientations. In a schematic manner, one could consider that Park preferred an interest in investigating a wide variety of subjects and diffused the general scheme of analysis proposed in *Introduction to the Science of Sociology*. Burgess, on the other hand, was attentive to the methodological rigor of investigations and the technical developments that transformed the idea of the ecological order into a field of investigation based on cartography. He also later advocated somewhat for the use of statistics. Through his relationships with organizations linked to the city, Burgess also contributed to the success of research projects.

In terms of his biographical characteristics, Ernest Burgess (1886–1966) was situated between the first and second generations of Chicago sociologists.[126] Son of an Anglican minister who had settled in Canada and later became a professor in the United States, Ernest Burgess spent his first years in various small cities in the Midwest and Oklahoma. Probably on the advice of one of his teachers who had studied at the Chicago Department of Sociology, Burgess went there in 1908 to write a thesis. Titled "Function and Socialization in Social Evolution," it followed the thesis model of the nineteenth century. After 1913, Burgess taught sociology, notably at the University of Kansas, where he participated, as previously mentioned, in a social survey that conformed to the model of the period: relying on the cooperation of local elites and leaning toward the examination of "social problems" in the community being studied. In 1916, Burgess was recruited by the University of Chicago to take on some of the teaching duties previously filled by Charles Henderson.[127] As previously mentioned, Burgess quickly joined forces with Park for the purposes of writing a textbook of sociology, a task assigned to him by Small, and shared with Park both an office and the advising duties of several PhD students.

In many accounts, Burgess seems almost the opposite of Park: in terms of his quiet demeanor as a Protestant bachelor—his friends joked on occasion about his personal lack of experience in the three subjects on which his research focused: crime, marriage, and family—in terms of his teaching, which was more methodical but less inspired than that of Park, and in terms of the more peaceful relationships he maintained with students. In terms of research methods, Burgess displayed a certain eclecticism, becoming interested from the early 1920s in the use of statistics, about which, as we have seen, Park was ambivalent.[128] Burgess was also concerned about demonstrating with statistical tools the sociological propositions that he formulated. In the 1920s, his research was oriented toward the statistically based prediction of the "success" of parole for prisoners, then the "success" of marriage—a type of research far removed from the topics with which Park was preoccupied.

The fruitfulness of sociology research conducted at Chicago in the 1920s was due in part to Burgess's institutional knowledge, which facilitated access for researchers to documentation held by different organizations, both public and not. He also knew how to optimize his students' chances of obtaining research funding. Burgess can therefore be found in the background of many monographs—such as that of Nels Anderson on migrant workers, and that of Clifford Shaw and Henry McKay on juvenile delinquency—illustrating how he played the role of academic sponsor as well as that of intermediary with funders.[129] This role accorded well with Burgess's academic respectability and integration into social service associations and committees, as he performed work linked to the city of Chicago. Burgess represented the Department of Sociology at the Local Community Research Committee, which was founded by the University of Chicago in 1923 to promote historical and sociological research into local communities (see the following chapter).

Burgess's intellectual impulse principally concerned three domains—urban development, marriage and divorce, and crime—and one method, the use of census data and cartography. At the beginning of the 1920s, Burgess contributed to completing the organization, by neighborhood, of the Chicago city census. From 1923, he presided over the process of dividing the city into neighborhoods. This division served as a retrospective utilization of the 1910 and 1920 censuses, and was used as the foundation of later censuses.[130]

It was principally Burgess who promulgated the use of cartography among sociologists, adding a concrete formulation that could easily be used in tandem with Park's concept of urban ecology.[131] As one of his former students, Ernest Mowrer, later remarked, it was difficult to obtain a PhD at Chicago without having used a map to localize the phenomena one studied, and without having compared the result with maps corresponding to other phenomena. The division of the city into neighborhoods, set in place through the census, was used for the manipulation of various statistics—on juvenile delinquency, suicide, divorce, and the like—gathered by different official or semi-official administrations. Relying on the example of the city of Chicago, in 1925 Burgess formulated a theory of the development of cities—widely diffused and continually discussed, especially by geographers—starting from a social characterization of different uses of territory according to concentric zones.[132]

An article by Burgess that was reprinted the following year in *The City* provides the framework for a large portion of the investigations of the 1920s that focused on the city of Chicago.[133] Presented as the introduction to a research project, this article formulates a theory of the process of the expansion of cities and its consequences, illustrated by the example of Chicago. Burgess describes the ideal model, realized to a greater or lesser degree in modern cities, as a series of concentric circles around a central business and commercial district (see map 1). Around this can be found the "transitional zone," where housing degrades in anticipation of the expansion of the center, and where one will find the most recent arrivals to the city, the bohemians, illegal activities, red-light districts, and so on. This is also the zone in which light industry and new businesses become established. Around this zone can be found the one in which educated and relatively well-off workers reside. Further from the center can be found a residential zone, and then that of the upper-class suburbs.

The first place where new immigrants settle is in the so-called transitional zone, which is thus also the place where the phenomena related to social disorganization develop, because it is where the controls associated with primary relationships disappear. The transitional zone is where a portion of the phenomena studied by monographs of the period can be found with a greater intensity than elsewhere: juvenile delinquency, youth gangs, familial desertion, poverty, suicide, and so on. This model of concentric distribution proposed by Burgess was made use of, as we shall see, in studies of crime by Thrasher and Shaw (chapter 7) and the analysis of the transformations of African American families by Frazier (chapter 8).

The use of cartography, associated with simple statistical tools (rates and averages), thus permitted a focus on the existence of relationships between different orders of phenomena, such as juvenile delinquency, divorce, suicide, and so on, and a more specific concept of social disorganization.[134] The cartographic technique here constitutes a cursory tool for resolving a problem that Lazarsfeld would treat in a more systematic manner after 1940 by using the calculation of correlations. These cartographic techniques essentially constituted a preliminary attempt to isolate the influence of an explanatory variable from other different variables. Cartography also allowed the use of "facts" that were unknown to the audience addressed by sociologists—particularly the funders of research. Finally, it made visible the influence of the environment on behavior, to the detriment of the biologically based theories preferred by sociologists at the beginning of the century: the comparison of the frequency of a phenomenon (like suicide or youth gangs) in different periods showed that it depended on the type of neighborhood and not ethnic characteristics, which varied from one period to another, of the present population living in the neighborhood.

Map 1: Plan of Chicago

▨	Railroad
—	
▨	Major public parks
▨	Major industrial areas

(A) Gold Coast
(B) Ghetto
(C) Grant Park
(D) Stockyards
(E) University of Chicago

Neighborhoods

1. Uptown
2. North Center
3. Lake View
4. Logan Square
5. Lincoln Park
6. West Town
7. Near North Side
8. East Garfield Park
9. Near West Side
10. Loop
11. Lower West Side
12. Near South Side
13. Bridgeport
14. Armour Square
15. Douglas
16. Oakland
17. New City
18. Fuller Park
19. Grand Boulevard
20. Kenwood
21. Hyde Park
22. Woodlawn
23. Washington Park
24. Englewood
25. Roseland
26. Calumet Heights
27. South Chicago

Loop: commercial center.
Hobohemia: central Near North Side, with an extension to the south.
Gold Coast: on the lakefront in the Near North Side.

Source: Local Community Research Commitee, *Social Base Map of Chicago.*

Map 2: Diagram of the concentric zones of the city of Chicago, according to Burgess

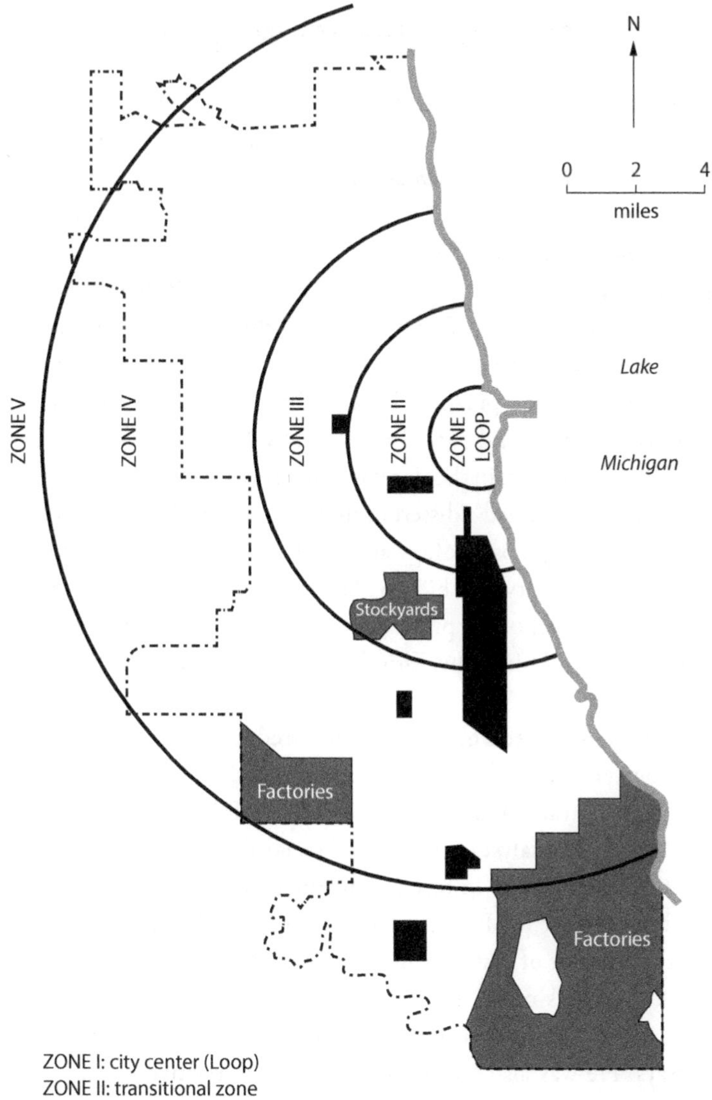

N

0   2   4
miles

Lake

Michigan

ZONE V

ZONE IV

ZONE III

ZONE II

ZONE I LOOP

Stockyards

Factories

Factories

ZONE I: city center (Loop)
ZONE II: transitional zone
ZONE III: working-class neighborhoods
ZONE IV: residential zone
ZONE V: suburbs
■ Neighborhoods with at least 50% black residents in 1940
Sources: Drake, Cayton (1945) : 16 ; Park, Burgess, McKenzie [1925] : 55.

The influence of Ellsworth Faris's (1874–1953) instruction on the research under-taken during the period has attracted less attention than that of Burgess. The form of Faris's contribution to sociology explains his later obscurity: Faris pub-lished relatively little—and almost exclusively articles—and he was not himself involved in research of an empirical character, although he presented himself as a partisan convinced of its value.[135]

Although Faris had spent several years as a Protestant minister, his experience before being recruited as a sociologist distinguishes him from previous pastors who had entered sociology (such as Small and Henderson). After a childhood spent in a rural area of the South, Faris began engineering studies. Influenced by an evangelist, he became a missionary and spent seven years in the Belgian Congo—an experience from which he drew some of his pedagogy, and which gave him a lasting curiosity about what were then seen as primitive societies. Returning to the United States, Faris taught theology and philosophy in a small Texas university before pursuing philosophical studies at the University of Chicago between 1910 and 1914. Influenced by Mead and Dewey, Faris devel-oped from his foundation in theology an interest in psychology, and it was in this discipline that he defended a dissertation in 1914. Over the course of the follow-ing five years, he taught psychology at several universities before being recruited in 1919 by the University of Chicago Department of Sociology to take over the courses in social psychology previously taught by Thomas. Rapidly promoted through the academic hierarchy, Faris filled the duties of chair of the Department of Sociology until 1939.

It was through his teaching, at the intersection of social psychology and anthropology, more so than his publications that Faris exerted influence over sociologists trained at Chicago after 1920. Like Thomas, Faris resumed Boas's critiques of analyses in terms of racial differences. Faris was also an opponent of explanations in terms of instincts (of which McDougall was the most visible proponent). In 1921, one of his first articles thus develops a chal-lenge of the concept of instinct, and more broadly of attempts to discover the irreducible elements of the personality.[136] Faris also relied on his experience in the Congo to critique various forms of ethnocentrism—a target in many of his essays. He was also an intermediary in the relatively slow diffusion of Mead's conceptions among sociologists or, rather, in presenting the framework within which social psychology would develop somewhat later, constituting one of the legacies of the Chicago tradition in sociology. Faris also exercised his talents as a polemicist against behaviorism. He manifested a precocious skepticism with regard to the development of attitude scales based on ques-tionnaire responses—the specialty of Thurstone, a psychologist recruited by the University of Chicago in 1927, in whose courses some students from the Department of Sociology were enrolled.

The courses taught by Park, Burgess, and Faris were obviously not the only ones taken by sociology students at the University of Chicago over the course of the period 1919–1934. However, their partial similarity of orientation—at least in the eyes of their students—justifies grouping them together. In the following chapter, I shall examine other elements to the context of the period.

4

Research at the University of Chicago, 1918–1933

You couldn't be at the University of Chicago at that time (1925)
without being a pragmatist.
—Everett C. Hughes[1]

T he end of the First World War marked a point of rupture for certain aspects of American society that were—or could have been—objects of study for sociologists of the period, as well as in the sociopolitical circumstances within which they had evolved.

This rupture is particularly clear regarding immigration, the question at the center of the sociologies of Thomas and Park. The war marked a rupture both in terms of the public definition of problems and in the relative importance accorded to them. American engagement in the conflict revealed the diversity of attachments among different sectors of the population. Over the course of it, all immigrant groups, except those of Anglo-Saxon origins, at one point or another positioned themselves against the policies of President Wilson. As backlash, the war gave rise among Anglo-Saxon elites to a public interrogation into the loyalty, in terms of national politics, of groups of immigrants who, as we have seen, were already under suspicion of not showing adequate attachment to republican traditions of government. The "Americanization" of these immigrant groups—which the research program, financed by the Carnegie Corporation after 1918 (with which, as we have seen, Park and Thomas collaborated), designated as "the uniting of the new with native-born Americans in fuller common understanding and appreciation"—would be the solution recommended by the

Anglo-Saxon elites for limiting the consequences of the heterogeneity of origin of this population.[2]

Two events also influenced, whether indirectly or directly, the policies taken in the matter of immigration: the Russian Revolution and the massive migration, after 1916, of African Americans from the South to the large cities of the North. In reaction to these two events, the nativist Anglo-Saxon movement that had developed since the beginning of the century reached a new height. Its representatives flaunted a fanatical patriotism and an active hostility toward recent groups of immigrants, African Americans, and the labor movement, as well as an antipathy toward cities. The period 1917–1920, marked by several violent incidents, including the 1920 bombing of Wall Street, saw the energetic repression of activists with real or imagined ties to the labor movement—as shown by the condemnation of Sacco and Vanzetti in 1921 and the deportation of Emma Goldman to the Soviet Union for "crimes" dating back two decades. Simultaneously, the labor movement weakened and, with the exception of one or two particular sectors such as mining, strikes were rare until 1929.[3]

Campaigns in favor of stopping immigration, which had begun at the beginning of the century, led to a first series of restrictive measures in 1917. In 1920 and 1924, increasingly limited quotas rendered difficult the entrance of new immigrants from southern and eastern Europe and, especially, from Asia.[4] The migration of African Americans from the South to northern cities was in part a consequence of this restriction on immigration, which led to a relative lack of workers. The city of Chicago was one of the most involved in encouraging this migration, and some of its businesses carried out recruitment campaigns in the South. Chicago's African American population, which numbered around 30,000 people in 1900 and had grown to 110,000 in 1920 and 277,000 in 1940, was, in proportion to the total population of the city, 1.9 percent in 1900, 4.1 percent in 1920, and 8.2 percent in 1940.[5] By this time, Chicago had the second-most prominent African American community, after that of New York. From 1917 onward, the large cities of the North and Midwest saw riots in which African Americans were lynched, marking the emergence of a "Negro Problem" in these cities. One of the deadliest race riots took place in Chicago between July 27 and August 8, 1919, causing the deaths of thirty-eight people (thirty-three of whom were African Americans); it led to the creation of an investigative commission whose work was, as we have seen, inspired by Park.

With several strong but short recessions, the first ten years of the postwar period corresponded with a period of economic prosperity and rapid technological changes. Over its course, there developed in the United States the chemical industry, electrical production, and the automobile industry, which all became enormous businesses. The movement of workers from the agricultural sector to urban jobs was massive. But it was jobs in the service industry and offices that increased rather than industrial ones, and unemployment remained elevated. Rapid urbanization across the United States accompanied these evolutions in employment: in 1920, the population residing in centers of more than 2,500 inhabitants surpassed for the first time that of rural areas, reaching close to 57 percent of the total population by the end of the decade.

The years between 1920 and 1930 also saw the diffusion of the automobile, the telephone, and the radio, and the development of mass publicity. The changes in employment were accompanied by the emergence of a vast middle class that tended to settle in suburban neighborhoods, thus inventing a specific lifestyle. Also taking place in this period were attempts to organize and defend the categories of a large number of professions pursued by the middle class, appropriating the mode of organization, and the privileges, of the established professions—namely medicine and law. Attached to this evolution—both a cause and a consequence—was the wide diffusion of higher education.

Chicago was directly affected by these evolutions. The period before the crisis of 1929 was marked by unprecedented prosperity. Although the population of the city, which grew from 2.7 million inhabitants in 1920 to 3.3 million in 1930, expanded less quickly than in previous years, there was a great deal of construction of new housing. The inner city and the area that borders Lake Michigan were partly restructured, with the construction of many railway stations, the opening of public parks, and the widening of roads following the spread of the automobile. This and the development of urban transportation promoted the migration of the middle class to a vast suburb—20.3 percent of the population of the metropolitan area lived in suburban neighborhoods in 1930.[6] Simultaneously, the populations of many neighborhoods in the city changed more or less completely. The most spectacular of these was the rapid expansion of the African American ghetto—in 1918 a long and narrow strip stretching from the center to the south of the city—which was accompanied by multiple violent incidents.

The political context after the end of the First World War was profoundly different from that of the previous period. The war promoted the establishment of national policies in sectors that, previously, were the domain of local community initiatives. The Progressive movement that had since the beginning of the century been waging campaigns in favor of reforms and an increased level of federal intervention, and to which, as we have seen, a portion of the Chicago scholars were connected, dispersed at the end of the First World War: its spokespeople had taken discrepant positions over the years with regard to issues such as immigration, the United States entering the war, and the Russian Revolution.

Over the course of the 1920s, the social forces that had sustained the Progressive movement became committed to divergent paths that did not allow the possibility of political alliances.[7] One can find in public debates, however, many of the themes concerning urban life that had been introduced by the Progressive movement in the previous period, such as the question of relations between ethnic groups or those of different forms of crime.

As before the war, the antagonism between city and countryside, partially overlapping with the antagonism between Anglo-Saxon Protestants and the descendants of Catholic and Jewish immigrants—and, at least to a degree, the antagonism between the middle and working classes—lay in the background of some debates: it found expression during elections and on the occasion of debates on public morality, such as the one that gave rise to the amendment establishing Prohibition in 1919.

The period was also marked by the spectacular growth of organized crime in large cities. This question tended to occupy an important place in public preoccupations, especially in Chicago, which was one of the cities most affected by this phenomenon: from 1923 to 1926, more than a thousand murders were recorded each year. Under the supervision of the Illinois Bar and the business elite of Chicago, an investigatory commission—with which sociologists were associated—into criminality was created in 1926 to study organized crime. In this period, social workers, which had formed as a profession at the beginning of the century, constituted a large category. Partially due to the influence of social workers, juvenile delinquency ceased to be a fringe issue and became a public problem.

STUDENTS AND STUDIES IN SOCIOLOGY AT THE UNIVERSITY OF CHICAGO

While the war from 1914–1918 thinned the ranks of sociology students at the University of Chicago, its completion, by contrast, led to the arrival of a new generation that was larger than the previous ones: the average number of MAs and PhDs awarded in sociology consistently rose over the following years, and during the period of 1919–1934 reached on average a little less than five PhDs per year and a little less than eight MAs.[8] This new generation of students looked rather different from their predecessors: they were more diverse in terms of social origins and previous experiences.[9] The new generation certainly still included sons of pastors from rural areas of the Midwest—this was the case for Paul G. Cressey and Everett Hughes—but students who came from urban areas were no longer the exception, although those with backgrounds in the lower levels of the working class remained rare. Women were relatively well represented (around 10 percent of those who obtained a PhD, and 30 percent of those who obtained an MA). Some graduates were ethnically Asian and others were African Americans, the University of Chicago being somewhat less closed off to them than other schools. An appreciable portion of African American sociologists from this generation who made major contributions to the study of race relations—Charles Johnson, Franklin Frazier, Bertram Doyle, Horace Cayton, Olivier Cox, and briefly Ira De Augustine Reid—spent time at the University of Chicago (although only Frazier, Doyle, and Cox obtained PhDs there).

Since the beginning of the century, sociology was taught in an increasing number of universities, especially in the Midwest. Until 1929, holders of PhDs in sociology found university jobs with relative ease.[10] The department of sociology at the University of Chicago remained the most respected producer of sociology dissertations.[11] Before 1930, an important portion of students trained at Chicago over the course of the period found teaching positions or jobs in research organizations, sometimes even before completing their doctorates. Others, like Nels Anderson and the majority of the women, did not find academic jobs and pursued activities on the margins of the discipline.

Almost all accounts of students of this period—born for the most part between 1889 (like Nels Anderson) and 1903 (like Helen Hughes) mention the sentiment of having participated in a sort of intellectual adventure that took place off the beaten path. Among the elements that contributed to nourishing this sentiment figure Park's encouragement of the collection of primary source evidence and the partially collective character of research. Some courses required students to personally undertake investigations in the city, which sometimes grew into doctoral dissertations or Master's theses. After 1924, a PhD student in the department, Vivien Palmer, was charged, under the supervision of Burgess, with organizing an apprenticeship in research methods and with coordinating student work on the city and ethnic groups. The participation of a group of these students in research projects funded by contracts and in small-scale editing work for the *American Journal of Sociology*, as well as the establishment of a collection of books in sociology at the University of Chicago Press, which at one point constituted a natural outlet for the publication of dissertations, contributed to fostering engagement in research activities.

The accounts gathered by James Carey offered numerous indices of high morale among a group of sociology students of the period. For example, one of them, Edgar Thompson, remarks: "We talked sociology from morning to night.

We interrupted a conversation to go to class, and then come back and continue with it after class. Or we continued that class after the bell rang. We went to coffee, we went to lunch, full of this stuff, the excitement of the place. . . . "[12] Another witness from the same period, Herbert Blumer, insists for his part upon small group work and the proximity between the social sciences: "The intellectual atmosphere in that period of the twenties and thirties in the department and the division of social sciences was very, very stimulating and invigorating. A great deal of discussion going on all the time. [There was] the recognition of the fact that the discipline of sociology there at Chicago in those days was embedded in this wider context of social sciences. There was a considerable amount of crossing over from one discipline to another by both faculty people and students."[13]

Among the most compelling pieces of evidence that these accounts do not reflect only retrospective wonder are undoubtedly the active participation of students in activities that were not required for obtaining their degrees, as well as the frequency of returns to the university campus after graduation, on the occasion of lectures and colloquia on work in progress. These were organized particularly by a sort of local academic society, founded by Park in 1920, which brought together advanced students and faculty members: the Society for Social Research. It also invited lecturers from outside the discipline and sociologists from other universities.[14]

As highlighted by the rather eclectic program of the Society for Social Research, as well as the diversity of sociologists invited to Chicago for the summer semester, the intellectual environment in which the research of this period was conducted was not at all limited to the courses offered by Park, Burgess, and Faris. Graduate studies in sociology required the completion of other courses offered in the sociology department and related departments. Some of the most influential and frequently taken were those of William Fielding Ogburn, who was recruited as a professor of sociology in 1927.

Ogburn (1886–1959) was himself a product of the tradition, rivaling that of the University of Chicago, that had developed at Columbia University in New York. Franklin Giddings, a sociologist of the same generation as Albion Small, contributed at Columbia to training students in the applications of statistics. Some of Giddings's students—including Ogburn, but also Stuart Chapin, John Gillin, Frank Hankins, and Howard Odum—would continue to develop this orientation after 1920. The department of sociology at Chicago recruited Ogburn as a specialist in the use of statistical techniques, with the aim of strengthening what seemed to his future colleagues to be the principal weakness of their department.

A native Southerner from Butler, Georgia, William Ogburn obtained his PhD in 1911 with a statistical study of legislation on child labor.[15] After spending one year working in the federal government's Bureau of Statistics, Ogburn returned to Columbia University as a professor of sociology from 1919 to 1927; during that time he also filled the duties of editor in chief of the *Journal of the American Statistical Association* from 1920 to 1926.

The use of partial correlation coefficients to isolate explanatory factors in the analysis of votes cast in the 1928 presidential election is one of Ogburn's principal contributions to the development of quantitative methods in sociology. At the time of his recruitment by the University of Chicago, his reputation among sociologists was also bolstered by a book, *Social Change with Respect to Culture and Original Nature* (1922), that formulated a general theory of four factors of social change and shifting rhythms (technical invention, accumulation, diffusion, and adaptation of populations).

At the start of the 1920s, along with other sociologists of the same generation, Ogburn's ideas fit within a conception of sociology (and the social sciences more generally) that was becoming increasingly common and that would find, as we shall see later on, support from institutions and financial sponsors. The model from which these sociologists drew inspiration was that of the physical sciences: sociology should follow the path toward scientific legitimacy forged by behavioral psychology.[16] Sociological analysis should thus prioritize understanding behaviors by means of their external aspects, putting emphasis on the rigor of survey methods and, in the interest of doing so, using statistical techniques, whose usage had become the measure of scientific rigor. "The sine qua non of scientific publication will be verification and evidence," Ogburn thus claimed in 1930 in his presidential address to the American Sociological Society (ASS), later adding: "In this future state everyone will be a statistician, that is nearly everyone."[17] According to these sociologists, research should be neutral from an ethical and political point of view in order that all possible audiences might be convinced of the validity of the results obtained: Ogburn congratulated himself when the results of his analyses were deemed acceptable equally by conservatives and communists.

While Ogburn's conception of sociological research here differs from those of Park, Faris, and Burgess, there are however some points of convergence between them. They (especially Faris) shared with Ogburn a longtime familiarity with the work of Boas, who, as we have seen, had been a principal critic of analyses that explained differences in behavior by biological differences between populations. Ogburn sometimes taught courses in anthropology, and remained in contact with anthropologists.[18] As we have seen, Burgess showed an active interest in Ogburn's statistical techniques and audited his first courses; Burgess would later use the same statistical techniques to estimate the chances of marital success and the parole of criminals.

Psychoanalysis was another enduring interest for Ogburn, who was one of the founders of the Chicago Psychoanalytical Society. However, this interest rather separated him from his colleagues at Chicago, whose appreciation of psychoanalysis was limited.

At the end of the 1920s, Ogburn was a visible sociologist whose principal research subject, the different rhythms of social changes in different areas of contemporary society, resonated with current events and interests. From 1927 to 1935, he was charged with organizing an annual special issue of the *American Journal of Sociology* composed of articles focused on the evolutions of certain behaviors or institutions in American society as a whole. From 1929, Ogburn led the research program on evolutions of American society commissioned by the administration of President Hoover and funded principally by one of the Rockefeller foundations.[19] Ogburn worked to provide the administration with facts concerning the ongoing evolutions of a large number of social aspects, for which he attempted to offer a "scientific" interpretation, but did not make recommendations or define a policy.

Ogburn himself contributed to this program by establishing time series datasets relating demographic or economic variables to variables concerning employment and technological innovations. These series were sometimes established on a national level, constituting a new type of data for sociologists who studied the United States. Ogburn constructed indices for measuring different variables such as living conditions or social status, performed calculations on the correlations between these variables, and sometimes compared annual variation curves. On the other hand, Ogburn was not interested in questions of the statistical use of surveys that interrogated populations through questionnaires or interviews—a type of data that would be at the heart of the work of the next-generation sociologists, who would turn toward the use of statistical methods.

Ogburn's teaching in statistics seems to have retained the attention of most Chicago sociology students to a greater degree than his analyses on social changes. Like Park and Faris, Ogburn would rapidly become surrounded by a small group of protégés. Among these, Samuel Stouffer, Frederick Stephan, Clark Tibbitts, and Philip Hauser participated over the following years in the development of statistical techniques for analyzing questionnaire surveys (see chapter 5). The emphasis placed by Ogburn on the development of statistical techniques would thus contribute to a sort of separation in the orientations of researchers trained during the 1920s and 1930s: some pursued ecological analyses using statistical methods, while others abandoned the study of the ecological order and turned, as we shall see, toward the ethnographic approach and the investigation of what Park designated the "moral order."

Instruction in sociology at the University of Chicago during the 1920s and 1930s maintained the multidisciplinary character of previous years (to which the very small number of instructors in the department evidently contributed). Retrospective accounts of former students insist upon this point, which went hand in hand with a mode of funding research in which disciplinary boundaries mattered little.[20] This situation was also a consequence of the complex network of relationships, both personal and institutional, among different departments.

Until 1929, anthropologists belonged to the same department as sociologists. But from the years 1919 through 1923, the only anthropologist in the department was Frederick Starr, who had limited contact with MA and PhD students.[21] When he retired in 1923, he was replaced by Fay-Cooper Cole, who—despite specializing in archaeology, a field that did not facilitate close contacts with sociologists—gave the anthropology curriculum an orientation that was more compatible with that of the sociologists. Cole sought, like Starr around 1895, to secure the creation of an autonomous department of anthropology.[22] Thanks to funding from the Laura Spelman Rockefeller Memorial Fund, in 1925 Cole was able to recruit Edward Sapir, who remained at Chicago until 1931, and undertake fieldwork involving PhD students. In 1927, Robert Redfield, a young instructor and Park's son-in-law, who had completed his PhD in the department, joined the University of Chicago's group of anthropologists. In 1929, the separation of anthropology and sociology into two departments was realized, but for at least an appreciable portion of students this did not result in an appreciable loosening of ties insofar as coursework.[23]

Among the courses offered in other departments, that of the philosopher George Herbert Mead, called Advanced Social Psychology, was one of the most frequently taken, with 72 percent of sociology students who completed a dissertation between 1910 and 1924 having enrolled in this course.[24] Mead was not very well known outside the University of Chicago—his later reputation was based on work published after his death in 1931—and his performance as an instructor was not free from criticism, on account of a lack of interaction with his audience that was paradoxical in relation to his own research.[25] The influence of Mead's advanced social psychology course on the sociology research conducted at Chicago over the course of the period is not obvious: almost no trace is found of his favorite concepts. In contrast, one might think of Mead's teaching as reinforcing Park's ideas in terms of its insistence on and sophisticated approach to the subjective dimension of social facts.

The question of the actual diffusion of Mead's analyses in sociological research at the University of Chicago has been an object of controversy. Anselm Strauss, who studied at Chicago in the following period before contributing to introducing Mead's concepts to sociologists, as Herbert Blumer had done, puts forward as evidence the fact that this diffusion happened after Mead's death, and that it was done through the efforts of Ellsworth Faris and, later, Blumer; this is confirmed by an examination of the research conducted (and not of statements of principle) and different accounts.[26] In a more general sense, the similarities between certain themes of Pragmatic philosophy and Chicago sociology undoubtedly owe more to their common origin than to any direct influence of philosophers on sociologists.

Mead's social psychology, like Park's sociology, presents a sort of affinity with the situation in the United States in that period, with its juxtaposition of culturally diverse populations, among which there was no general consensus in terms of behavior: hence individual uncertainty and the weakening of attachment to symbols of collective life. Individualism and social uncertainty seem to be the two faces of the problematic choices imposed by a complex and disorganized society. In such a society, individual personality must develop through interaction and include a capacity of self-control that permits the individual to follow a relatively consistent model of conduct.

Before Ogburn's arrival in the department of sociology in 1927, students enrolled in statistics courses taught by one of the economics professors, James Field. They also sometimes took other courses offered by the same department: Everett Hughes, who was a sociology student in this period, mentions courses centered on work relationships.[27] Contact was made just as often with the department of political science, where the first studies of electoral behavior that used questionnaire surveys on a sample were taking place, on the initiative of Charles Merriam.[28] The department of psychology, where advocates of a statistical approach were well represented, was also frequented by some sociology students. Louis Thurstone, having performed experimental research on army tests, after 1927 completed research there on measuring attitudes based on responses to questionnaires:[29] this orientation had more in common with the research conducted by certain sociologists at the end of the 1930s than with the research inspired by Park and Faris.

The frequency of contact sociology students had with these various departments contrasts with the rarity of contact with the courses offered by the School of Social Service Administration, a body that trained social workers and became part of the university in 1920. Few students seem to have taken courses offered by this department, due in part to the contentious relationships between Park and

Burgess on the one hand, and the principal leaders of this school on the other: Sophonisba Breckinridge and Edith Abbott (who had, as we have seen, taught in sociology part-time until 1920). But the growing distance between sociology and social work also certainly corresponds to sociology's orientation toward a quest for the recognition of a scientific status, while the second sought for its graduates the status of an established profession (according to the model of medicine).

THE INSTITUTIONAL AND FINANCIAL CONTEXT OF SOCIOLOGY RESEARCH

In the United States, the 1920s marked the beginning of a long evolution in the social sciences, including the model of intellectual organization that served as their reference, their funding, and their relationships with their audiences. The organizational model that had been increasingly imposed on the social sciences was that of the natural sciences, with its insistence on the explicit formulation of a corpus of propositions, the systematic administration of proofs of their compatibility with actual data, and its tendency to measure studied phenomena (which here implies the use of statistics).

Symbolizing this orientation at the University of Chicago was a quotation by Lord Kelvin, inscribed on the facade of the new building constructed in 1929 to house the social science departments (donated by one of the foundations in the Rockefeller empire): "When you cannot measure your knowledge is meagre and unsatisfactory."[30] The orientation summarized here concerns not only sociology, but also related disciplines like psychology, economics, and political science. At Chicago, the diffuse influence of Pragmatism over its sociologists, especially Park and Faris, certainly contributed to counteracting the adoption of some of the supposed characteristics of the model of natural sciences as reference for sociologists. With the exception of Ogburn, none of the most active proponents of this latter conception in sociology—such as Stuart Chapin, George Lundberg, and Luther Bernard—would teach at the University of Chicago for a long time.[31]

Two factors, however, facilitated the evolution of sociology by reference to the model of the natural sciences: the method of funding research that was established at the beginning of the 1920s, and an intellectual and political context that was both a condition of this type of integration of the social sciences into society and, partially, its consequence.

An inventory of sociology publications makes apparent an essential difference between the sociological research published at the University of Chicago before the beginning of the 1920s and that which was published after: in this second period, the publications that correspond to reports of empirical research became much more numerous and focused on a greater diversity of subjects. This broader fruitfulness is not mysterious, even if its material base remained somewhat shadowy for a long time: from 1923 onward, social science research in the United States benefited for the first time from important funding sources. The existence of these sources of funding—which were of a scale and duration that far exceeded those that Thomas or the researchers of the Pittsburgh Survey were accustomed to—did not only lead to an increase in research and publication. These sources of funding also influenced, if in an indirect manner, the conceptions of research, the themes and methods of investigation, and, to a lesser degree, the relationships between different disciplines in the social sciences.

With the exception of William Ogburn, the Chicago sociologists were not central actors in this evolution, but they did take advantage of it when the occasion presented itself, thanks to their proximity to some of those who, like William Ogburn and Charles Merriam, were at the center of this policy.

The funding of social science research by large private foundations—the most important being the Laura Spelman Rockefeller Memorial Fund, the Carnegie Corporation, and the Russell Sage Foundation—[32] was the culmination of a process of widening the field of their interventions that took place after 1920. Initially focused on charitable activities and assistance, these foundations turned toward funding research in the natural sciences and medicine. Administrated by businessmen and academics (or former academics), these foundations sought to apply the perspective of the business world—defined in terms of rationality, organization, and efficiency—to "rationalize" philanthropic activities through the "scientific investigation of social and physical well-being."[33]

The start of massive research grants in the social sciences corresponds to the reorientation of the Laura Spelman Rockefeller Memorial Fund, a foundation which upon its creation in 1918 was intended to maintain activities in the favorite domains of the late wife of John D. Rockefeller: public health, education, and childcare. In 1922, Beardsley Ruml, who had completed a PhD in applied psychology at the University of Chicago in 1917, became the director of the foundation at age twenty-eight.[34] He acted to conduct a global policy of funding research in the social sciences, in which Ruml would choose both the scope of activities and the awarding of funds.

A justification of Ruml's policy is presented in a memorandum that he wrote some months after taking the position: "All who work toward the general end of social welfare are embarrassed by the lack of that knowledge which the social sciences must provide. It is as though engineers were at work without an adequate development in the sciences of physics and chemistry.... An examination of the operations of organizations in the field of social welfare shows as a primary need the development of the social sciences and the production of a body of substantiated and widely accepted generalisations as to human capacities and motives and as to the behaviour of human beings as individuals and groups."[35] Elsewhere, Ruml insisted upon the necessarily multidisciplinary nature of the research to be supported, and upon its applied character.

Following an unfortunate experience that shined a light on a confusion between the goals of another Rockefeller foundation and the business interests of the donating family, the Laura Spelman Rockefeller Memorial Fund defined a policy of funding that disbursed funds to be distributed to a committee of academics. These funds were intended to allow the collection and exploitation of primary source evidence, to subsidize the infrastructures of research—secretarial expenses, publication costs, and the like—to provide stipends for young researchers, and to temporarily release some academics from their teaching duties. In short, the policy that was announced and then carried out by the Laura Spelman Rockefeller Memorial Fund was nearly, in its form and its justifications, identical to the guiding policies of foundations that supported research in medicine or the exact sciences.

In 1923, as seen in chapter 2, the academic societies that brought together researchers in political science (the American Political Science Association) and sociologists (the American Sociological Society) created a common committee, the Social Science Research Council (SSRC), in which also figured observers from the societies of economists (American Economic Association) and statisticians (American Statistical Association). The SSRC was intended to coordinate research efforts and promote the development of scientific methods in these disciplines.[36] Notably, it cooperated with the National Research Council—another committee in which different disciplines of the natural sciences were represented, and which maintained contacts with various private foundations—for a research project on migrations. Charles Merriam was the principal architect of the creation of the Social Science Research Council and served as its liaision with the Laura Spelman Rockefeller Memorial Fund, as well as the chair of the department of political science at the University of Chicago. In collaboration with the Laura Spelman Rockefeller Memorial Fund, the Social Science Research Council (SSRC) defined a research policy and in 1925 charged four committees with putting it in action in their defined areas.

In the same year as the creation of the SSRC, the Local Community Research Committee, an equally interdisciplinary committee, was established at the

University of Chicago under the leadership of Albion Small, then dean of the Graduate School of Arts. This committee was intended to coordinate research on urban problems: at a 1923 meeting, the president of the university announced a gift of $21,000 to the departments of sociology, political science, and economics, to be used toward making experimental studies "for the purpose of examining the possibilities of social research, using the city of Chicago as a laboratory"—an expression in use for thirty years, as we have seen.[37] Like the SSRC, the Local Community Research Committee gathered several disciplines: sociology was represented by Small and then Burgess, political science by Merriam; representatives of economics, history, and anthropology also took part.

The policy advocated for by Ruml was put into action during the following years. Between 1923 and 1929, the year in which the Laura Spelman Rockefeller Memorial Fund was reorganized and integrated into the Rockefeller Foundation, the foundation distributed more than $20 million for the social sciences alone, an unprecedented scale of funding.[38] The University of Chicago was the primary beneficiary of this funding: between 1924 and 1928, it received almost $3.4 million, more than twice the amount received by Columbia University in New York, which received the next highest amount. The Social Science Research Council received, for its part, around $4.1 million to fund stipends and distribute research funds.

Some of the funds allocated to the University of Chicago were invested in the construction of a building to house social science research, and in the acquisition of equipment for processing statistical data. Another portion was dispensed to fund research and provide facilities to instructors, to support the work of advanced students, and to publish books. Between 1923–1924 and 1929–1930, the Local Community Research Committee spent toward these ends a grant of about $431,000, disbursed by the Laura Spelman Rockefeller Memorial Fund, to which was added about $120,000 from other funding sources.[39] Among these other sponsors figured, generally for relatively small sums, a wide variety of charitable associations, associations with civic goals, and even businessmen (although the subventions from this last group most often went to the economists). Among the research funders, one can also find associations whose goal was the struggle against one form or another of criminality, such as the Illinois Council for Criminal Justice, which was composed of judges, lawyers, and policemen. On the other hand, the list of sponsors included neither labor organizations nor political organizations, and the contribution from the city of the Chicago toward financing research was very limited.[40]

Both directly, through the Local Community Research Committee, and indirectly, through stipends and research support, the Chicago sociologists were among the beneficiaries of the funding provided by these various organizations. The funds were dispersed among a large number of studies rather than concentrated on a small number of projects that needed significant funding (as was the case in political science). In fact, a portion of the projects that resulted in published books were at one time or another supported by these funds: this was notably the case for Frederic Thrasher's research on youth gangs, that of Landesco on organized crime, that of Walter Reckless on prostitution—which received the support of the Illinois Association for Criminal Justice—[41]that of Harvey Zorbaugh on the north side of Chicago, and that of Paul G. Cressey on dance halls.[42] Some research projects also benefited from subventions from individual donors (see the case of Nels Anderson in chapter 9), but others had no sponsor, such as Everett Hughes's study on real estate agents. Some students received stipends or financial support justified by short-term editing work for the *American Journal of Sociology*.[43]

Grants were also used for the creation of evidentiary resources, the core of what some of these works had in common. This is how the collection of demographic statistics, under Burgess's direction, for different neighborhoods in Chicago was financed, as well as the establishment of maps from these data. Later work on diverse subjects—crime, suicide, divorce, and so on—would adopt the same spatial division and use some of these data. In the framework of his teaching, Vivien Palmer assured the coordination of the collection of data concerning the city of Chicago.

The majority of research conducted by sociology students at the University of Chicago can be connected to two of the four areas selected in 1926 by the SSRC because of their relationships with the social problems of the period: criminality and race relations, the two other being agricultural economy and industrial relationships.[44] It should be noted that, in this last case, the existence of potential funding was not enough to assure the development of research in sociology of work—perhaps because, in the established division of scientific work, that particular topic belonged to the economists, who also occupied positions of influence in the committee. The committee on race relations, placed under the direction of Howard Odum, largely financed his research at the University of North Carolina, but also contributed to the development of research by the sociologists at Chicago (see chapter 8). The committee on criminality financed the research of Frederic Thrasher on youth gangs,[45] that of Ernest Mowrer on the family,[46] as well as that conducted at the Chicago-based Institute for Juvenile Research by Shaw and McKay (see chapter 7).

We must conclude that the themes of research in sociology reflected a compromise among the subjects of public concern of the period, potential funding (which itself expressed the interests of the various providers of funds), the established division of work according to specializations, and the interests of the researchers performing it, which, in the 1930s, led to the sentiment that research could inspire policies of reform.[47] We should not, however, underestimate the autonomy of some researchers—or their financial independence (sometimes brought about simply by having a job)—which permitted them to follow an original orientation: Everett Hughes neglected the study on land prices in Chicago that Park had advocated in favor of one on real estate agents, who at that time were seeking a new level of professional respectability.[48] The development of work on crime certainly owed less to Park's intellectual impulses than to the social context of the city of Chicago and the related availability of funding, which also existed in the later period. As for the development of studies on interethnic and race relations, it resulted from the meeting between Park's intellectual impulse in this field on one hand, and, on the other, the presence at Chicago of students—African Americans and whites from the South—for whom this question had particular interest.

THE MONOGRAPHS OF THE CHICAGO SCHOOL

The term "Chicago School" has been used so frequently since the 1950s that one might expect the list of publications connected to it to be clearly defined. There certainly exists a small canon of always-cited books: *The Hobo* by Nels Anderson (1923), *The Gang* by Frederic Thrasher (1927), *Suicide* by Ruth Cavan (1928), *The Ghetto* by Louis Wirth (1928), *The Gold Coast and the Slum* by Harvey Zorbaugh (1929), and *The Taxi-Dance Hall* by Paul Cressey (1932). Autobiographies written at the request of researchers and commented on by them, such as *The Jack-Roller* by Clifford Shaw (1930) and *The Professional Thief* by Edwin Sutherland (1937), are often included in this list. Other books are frequently cited, such as *The Pilgrims of the Russian Town* by Pauline Young (1932), *Social Factors in Juvenile Delinquency* by Clifford Shaw and Henry McKay (1931), *Vice in Chicago* by Walter Reckless (1933), *Organized Crime in Chicago* by John Landesco (1929), and *The Marginal Man* by Everett Stonequist (1937). On the other hand, other books are generally neglected, such as *Hotel Life* by Norman Hayner (1936), and especially *Small-Town Stuff* by Albert Blumenthal (1932) or *The Negro Family in Chicago* by Franklin Frazier (1932). Comparing an inventory of all works that can possibly be connected to the department of sociology at Chicago with a list of those that are always mentioned as representatives of the "Chicago School" would immediately cast doubt on the conclusions that might be drawn from examining only those books included in an arbitrarily established list.

Three concurrent definitions are used, depending on the case, to delimit these works: research on cities or, more specifically, on Chicago; PhDs and sometimes MAs inspired by Park, Burgess, and Faris (or even Ogburn); books from the series edited by Park, Burgess, and Faris at the University of Chicago Press. None of these definitions fully encapsulates the ensemble of cases that should obviously be considered in an overall survey of the research produced in the entourage of Park, Burgess, and Faris over the course of this period, if one wants to avoid the arbitrariness of blind choice. Some works focusing on cities are missing from this list, even though their subject matter would suggest that they should be included: this is the case for Everett Hughes's dissertation (1928) on real estate agents and that of Ernest Schideler (1928) on chain stores, which was never published. Bertram Doyle's 1937 book on the etiquette of relationships between whites and blacks in the South, as well as that of Andrew Lind (1938) on contacts between populations in the Hawaiian Islands—both of which originated as dissertations in which Park took a great interest—are not obviously related to urban sociology. The list of dissertations inspired by Park, Burgess, and Faris is also much longer than that of the monographs published in their series: some dissertations were only published much later, and by different publishers than the University of Chicago Press.[49] This was the case for Norman Hayner's dissertation on hotel residents, that of Everett Hughes, and that of Paul Siu on Chinese launderers, which was later published at the initiative of historians.[50] On the other hand, one book published in the sociology series of the University of Chicago Press originated as a dissertation completed at another university;[51] some reflected subjects that, although they may have caught Park's interest, like the study of the press, owed little to his thematic program;[52] others were certainly inspired by Park but were not based on primary source research;[53] finally, at least one other book was not based on scholarly work.[54]

The line separating dissertations and published books relied on an ensemble of fortuitous circumstances. Commercial considerations were evidently not absent from the decision-making process of the University of Chicago Press. The effects of the difficulties of the early 1930s on the rhythms of production are also clear; following the publication of *Hobo* in 1923, there seem to have been no manuscripts until 1926. In that year, two books were published in the series edited by Park, Burgess, and Faris; four books were published in 1927, four in 1928, one in 1929, and then, after a complete interruption, five in 1932. The financial difficulties of the university around 1929 demanded that University of Chicago Press authors partially fund their own books. Hughes's dissertation was consequently published by an academic society and not by the University of Chicago Press.

One could continue demonstrating the arbitrariness to which any restrictive definition inevitably leads. Accepting such a definition leads to a truncated perspective on the entire research enterprise that took place at the University of Chicago over the course of this period. I have sought, to the contrary, to here draw attention to the variety of research and publications that could be connected to the university, and to the diversity of their relationships with the central authors in this tradition. I shall limit myself subsequently to examining in a more precise manner the publications that are based at least partially on primary source evidence, and that are presented as analyses—leaving to the side those that principally have the character of simple "documents," as well as those that have an essentially general character and are based on secondary sources. I have treated the form of publication as a secondary characteristic. Thus delineated, the corpus includes PhD dissertations and MA theses, as well as the books and articles that sometimes resulted from them. I shall successively examine the themes on which these publications focused, referring to the program of research developed by Park and Burgess, the methods of documentation and the principal concepts that they made use of, and their style of argumentation and writing.

The choice of research subjects, especially for dissertations, obviously cannot be credited solely to Park, Burgess, or Faris, but must be acknowledged as having stemmed from a mixture of circumstances in which intellectual interests mingled with investigative facilities and funding possibilities. One could, however, draw some conclusions from the comparison of research conducted and work published, whether as a monograph or an article in the journal of the department of sociology, the *American Journal of Sociology*, which served as an outlet for these works.

When one compares the themes of conducted research and those of published books, one is struck first of all by the absence of publications on certain subjects corresponding to major changes specifically concerning cities in the course of the period—one of Park's top themes of interest.[55] Although there were MA theses focusing on the radio (Woolbert, 1930), the telephone (Stephan, 1926), and the cinema (Halley, 1924), no publication in the form of an article or a book resulted from these. Moreover, one does not find publications on the development of suburbs, on which subject at least two MA theses were written (Glick, 1928; Beckmire, 1932), nor on the transformations of the lifestyles of the middle classes. Only one dissertation focused on the diffusion of the automobile (Mueller, 1928), and it does not seem to have ever been cited; an almost identical situation characterizes the dissertation written by Shideler (1927) on major retail chains, although it did result in an article. Aside from the two books by Wirth and Zorbaugh, some articles on the ecological dimension of urban life were published, most notably an article by Paul F. Cressey (1938) on the succession of different immigrations into the territory of Chicago.[56]

Although not completely neglected, the aspects of urban life most specific to the United States in that period were thus not the subjects of completed work. By comparison, the importance of research on the press—the most important is the dissertation of Helen Hughes (1940)—suggests that aspects that had been "new" to society at the turn of the century were favored as objects of investigation over those that were characteristic of the interwar period. Indeed, the first article in the *American Journal of Sociology* to focus on the development of suburbs was written not by a sociologist but by a geographer in the neighboring department, Chauncy Harris (1943). Another field, work, would seem to have commanded the attention of researchers. However, analyses completely or partially focusing on groups of workers—whether laborers or white-collar workers—were rare, even though evolutions in the division of labor and the phenomena of professional mobility are evoked in *The City*.

> Among the seventy-one dissertations defended in sociology at the University of Chicago in the years 1919–1933, only seven focused on subjects that directly involved the analysis of activities of a category of workers. The dissertation of Mollie Caroll (1920) focuses on the attitude of the American Federation of Labor toward legislation and policy; the next two dissertations, by Ernest Hiller (1924) and Floyd House (1924), focus on strikes and industrial morale respectively. The next, those of Ernest Shideler (1927) and Everett Hughes (1928), focus, as previously mentioned, on retail chains and real estate agents. The dissertation of Tadao Kawamura (1928) focuses on the consequences of the expansion of Japanese industry and commerce on class conflicts, and that of Walter Watson (1930) focused on satisfaction at work.

Three factors contributed to inhibiting the development of studies on work during this period: the interests of Park and his colleagues, practical conditions of accessing basic data, and the division of established subjects among the social science disciplines and the likely consequences of this on funding.

The essays published by Park from 1915 to 1925 contain almost no developed analysis of questions relating to work, with the exception of the general evocation of the division of work in *The City*. The only reference in the index of *Introduction* refers to workers as an example of a group in a situation of conflict. Somewhat later, Park wrote the preface for Hiller's monograph on strikes—but this is considered from the angle of collective behavior and not in its relationship with the conditions and the experiences of work. Park also published a long read-er's note on *The Human Problems of an Industrial Civilization* by Elton Mayo.[57] Notwithstanding this essay, Park's personal curiosity did not particularly bear on the investigation of work, and it seems that he did not encourage students to approach their subjects from this angle, as Hughes, to the contrary, later would.

The rarity of studies on work undoubtedly resulted in even more difficulties in terms of accessing workers and businesses for academic ends (see chapter 6). The established division of labor among social science specializations also did not encourage the development of sociological studies on work at Chicago: the sub-ject belonged to the domain of economists during this period, who conducted numerous studies on this theme.[58] A similar explanation holds for the study of political behavior, which sociologists ceded to the neighboring department of political science where, over the course of this period, the first studies on forms of political participation were carried out.

Taking into account only published monographs that saw a certain degree of diffusion (table 4.1), the theme common to some of them—or, rather, the central notion around which they are organized—is certainly that of social disorganiza-tion, which can be found regarding divorce (Mowrer), youth gangs (Thrasher), suicide (Cavan), prostitution (Reckless), juvenile delinquency (Shaw and McKay), a type of commercial recreational establishment (Paul G. Cressey), and in studies focusing on certain neighborhoods or populations (Zorbaugh, Wirth, Frazier). The central quality of this concept, which played, as we have seen, only a limited role in Park and Burgess's *Introduction to the Science of Sociology*, renders visible a certain discrepancy between the program of study outlined by this book and its concrete execution.

This certainly is partly due to Burgess's influence over the selection of disserta-tion topics. It was, for example, in the framework of his course that the first study of taxi-dance halls (the official objective of which was learning to dance, but which, according to social workers, were one of the paths that led young women into prostitution) was conducted, before these dance halls became the subject of Paul G. Cressey's MA thesis.[59] Studies on crime were also generally supervised by Burgess, who knew how to secure small grants and assure useful points of access to the social services that kept some of the databases. From a more general point of view, one could also suggest that this discrepancy reflects both the influence of the possibilities of empirical research and the pervasiveness of the public prob-lems in the eyes of the middle classes of the period.

Alongside research whose central theme falls under the heading of social dis-organization, two other groups of monographs can be distinguished. The first, mostly published slightly after the studies on social disorganization, includes the

TABLE 4.1 Characteristics of Selected Monographs[i]

	Series[ii]	MA/PhD[iii]	Funding[iv]	Urban[v]	Chicago[vi]	Disorganization[vii]	Biographies[viii]	Maps	Observation[ix]
Anderson (1923)	yes[x]	no[xi]	yes	yes	yes	yes	yes	no	some
Thrasher (1927)	yes	PhD	some	yes	yes	yes	yes	yes	yes
Mowrer (1924/1927)[xii]	yes	PhD	some	yes	yes	yes	yes	yes	no
L. Edwards (1927)	yes	PhD[xiii]	?	no	no	no	no	no	no
Wirth (1928)	yes	PhD	sch.	yes	yes	yes	yes	no	some
Cavan (1928)	yes	PhD	pub.[xiv]	yes	yes	yes	yes	yes	no
Hiller (1924/1928)	yes	PhD	no	no	no	no	no	no	no
Zorbaugh (1929)	yes	PhD	yes	yes	yes	yes	yes	yes	yes
Donovan (1929)	yes	no	no?	yes	no	no	yes	no	yes
Landesco (1929)	no	no	yes	yes	yes	no	yes	no	some
Shaw, McKay (1931)	no	no	yes	yes	yes	yes	yes	yes	no
Hughes (1931)	no	PhD	no	yes	yes	no	yes	yes	some
P. Young (1932)[xv]	yes	PhD	no	yes	no	yes	yes	no	no
P. G. Cressey (1932)	yes	MA	yes	yes	yes	yes	yes	yes	yes
Frazier (1932)	yes	PhD	sch.	yes	yes	yes	yes	yes	no
Blumenthal (1932)	yes	PhD	?	no	no	no	some	no	some
Reckless (1933)	yes	PhD	yes	yes	yes	yes	yes	yes	no
C. Johnson (1934)	yes	no	yes	no	no	yes	yes	no	yes
Hayner (1923/1936)	no	PhD	no	yes	no	no	yes	no	no

Doyle (1937)	yes	PhD	sch.	no	yes	no	no	yes
Stonequist (1937)	no	PhD	sch.	no	yes	yes	no	no
Lind (1938)	yes	PhD	yes	no	yes	no	yes	no
Faris, Dunham (1939)	yes	no[xvi]	yes	yes	yes	no	yes	no
McGill Hughes (1940)	yes	PhD	no	no	no	no	no	no
Pierson (1942)	yes	PhD	yes	no	no	yes	no	yes
Siu (1953/1987)	no	PhD	?	yes	yes	yes	yes	yes
Total "yes" (of 27)	20	20	13	15	18	20	13	7

[i] I have not included the books on the study of the media published in the University of Chicago Press sociology series (with the exception of H. Hughes [1940]) in this table, as they present almost none of the properties examined here (with the exception of having developed out of a dissertation).

[ii] Publication in the series edited by Faris, Park, and Burgess.

[iii] Academic status of the research from which the book originated.

[iv] "Yes" signifies that the study benefited from a grant; "sch." signifies that the author benefited from a scholarship during at least part of the research. The evidence that I make use of here is diffuse because of the existence of many origins and different levels of funds that could be secured. A certain number of cases are more uncertain: for example, when there are mentions in the book's preface or the lists that can be found throughout; see especially AEWB, folder 127; Smith, White (1929), IJTC.

[v] "Yes" signifies that the subject studied is specifically urban.

[vi] "Yes" indicates that some of the analysis focuses on the city of Chicago.

[vii] "Yes" signifies that the book develops an analysis in terms of social disorganization.

[viii] "Yes" indicates that the book presents biographies reconstructed by the researchers or autobiographical accounts.

[ix] Presence of analyses or documents suggesting that the author performed observations.

[x] This book was probably included in the series retroactively.

[xi] MA thesis defended two years after the publication of the book.

[xii] When two dates appear in this column, the first indicates the date of the PhD or MA defense.

[xiii] PhD (church history) at the Divinity School. Funding seems very unlikely to me.

[xiv] According to Cavan in IJTC, it seems that only the publication was supported by a grant.

[xv] PhD, University of Southern California.

[xvi] Issued from the PhD dissertation of Faris and the MA thesis of Dunham.

monographs on interethnic relationships, and in particular the different aspects of relations between whites, blacks, and people of other races (Doyle, 1937; Lind, 1938; Pierson, 1942, and also a dissertation by Edgar Thompson, 1932). These monographs certainly owe much to Park in terms of inspiration, but their diffusion was limited to those specializing in the study of race relations—a field that was partially isolated from the rest of sociology from the middle of the 1930s. I shall return in chapter 8 to the themes of these monographs, which share their type of sources and writing style with the preceding ones. Finally, a third heterogeneous group of monographs—that of Kisaburo Kawabe (1921) and Helen MacGill Hughes (1940)—bears the mark of another of Park's interests: the study of the press through the lens of collective behavior. These books were read, if at all, only by researchers in this particular subfield.

Setting aside this last group, there are striking resemblances among these monographs, even if they do not all conform to one single model. But the resemblances do not principally lie in the conceptual apparatus or the frame of discussion—which is generally poorly clarified. Instead, they are for the most part found in the types of sources and their approaches, as well as their styles of writing and argumentation: these characteristics define what one might call a research formula.[60] The model of reference is *The Polish Peasant*, or perhaps rather *Old World Traits Transplanted* (1921) by Park and Miller (and Thomas), whose format is more comparable to those of these monographs.

Like this book, the monographs essentially alternate between the analyses of the author; frequently simple descriptions of "facts" (places, behaviors, etc.); general assertions defining a general framework; and the reproduction, by way of illustration or evidence (their status is never well defined), of documents of diverse origin. In proportions that vary by monograph, these documents include press clippings and quotations from other books; statistics of administrative origin, sometimes calculated by the researcher from raw data; maps constructed from these statistics; documents extracted from the files of various administrations, such as courts, police, schools, charitable associations, social workers; observation notes taken by the researcher or other witnesses; extracts from conversations and fragments of autobiographical narratives produced at the instigation of the researcher himself (or sometimes by his assistants, since students were affiliated with certain research projects).

As can be seen when comparing the monographs with contemporary books on similar subjects produced during this period (particularly by social workers), two elements of the sources are relatively specific to sociological works of the period: maps and evidence pulled from notes researchers took during fieldwork.

The utilization of maps is hardly found outside books focusing on Chicago: these maps were essentially based on the databases that, as we have seen, were the fruit of Burgess's contribution to the exploitation of the city census. Many accounts suggest that, at the end of the 1920s, focusing on maps was a sort of technique routinely used by sociology students at the University of Chicago. There are two different ways in which the maps were used: some maps served to display the environment's influence on a type of behavior, seeking to show that a particular phenomenon (suicide, divorce, youth gangs, etc.) was concentrated in one of the city's zones as defined by Burgess's model of urban development; other maps served to show similarities in the spatial distributions of various phenomena, and thus constituted a sort of substitute for the multivariate analysis that Lazarsfeld would develop thereafter, which is to say a method for analyzing the relationships between variables.

The usage of observation by the researchers through their contacts with the populations under study was framed in the 1960s as an important element of the heritage of research of this period. The sources reproduced in monographs do not suggest, however, that observation occupied a large place in the collection of evidence. These sources certainly sometimes included observations about places, people, and, more rarely, actions, but much more frequently they offered biographies summarized by the researcher and, above all, reports of conversations. The distinction between the information gathered through observation and statements is never made explicit, and a more precise examination shows that in all these monographs the categories of observation used are not well articulated. One of the rare monographs in which the researcher reports situational behavior by citing his observational notes is that of Paul G. Cressey on the taxi-dance halls. Even in this case, however, the author does not seem to have systematically defined his categories of observation any more explicitly and narrowly than a passing visitor would.

Finally, the researchers did not publish reports explaining and discussing the conditions in which they collected their documentary sources. A concern for justifying the quality of the collected data through an analysis of the observer's position would develop only after 1945, clearly on the model of anthropologists, with reflections on participant observation (the first traces of which can be found in a 1937 article by Joseph Lohman). Previously, the conditions of conducting research were left in the shadows—even though they seem sometimes to have constituted a condition of the success of collecting sources: Thrasher's talents as a street artist or Anderson's past experience as a migrant worker are hardly mentioned in the final publications that they influenced. The reflection on the collection of data for *Taxi-Dance Hall* in which Cressey was engaged was never published, and the article that he wrote was published only much later, and only because it had taken on a completely different meaning fifty years later.[61]

The comparison that has been made among these monographs suggests—and we shall see in chapter 9 that the more specific analysis of the case of Nels Anderson's *Hobo* confirms this interpretation—that the type of evidence collected and its mode of treatment, as well as the writing style and method of using this evidence in argumentation, constitute characteristics in the perception of research as much or more important than the abstract analytical schemes that are the instrument of analysis in terms of a history of ideas.

Another characteristic of these monographs that strikes a present-day reader is the frequency of their conclusions that have a practical character. This should lead one to wonder more than we have about the meaning of Park's professed detachment from practical goals. These conclusions certainly sometimes proceeded from the priorities of the monographs' funders, who would themselves justify the grants dispensed as a contribution to the solution of social problems linked to whichever subject was under study: many studies that did not benefit from financial support—for example, Hughes (1931), Stonequist (1937), Doyle (1937), MacGill Hughes (1940)—do not contain this type of conclusion. Furthermore, the different domains of research did not lend themselves equally to the evocation of practical solutions to the problems in question; the fields of crime and the behavior of particular populations are assuredly more amenable than that of race relations.

We can, however, dismiss the possibility that these discussions were contradictory to the convictions of their authors, since a number of them went on to work in similar conditions and maintained an interest in social problems, such as the splitting up of families, unemployed workers, and different forms of crime. We must therefore consider that the sociological monographs of this period correspond to a stage in the evolution of the equilibrium between a concern for affirming the scientific character of sociology and the constraints of articulating how each study is justified (including perhaps in the eyes of the authors themselves) and put to good use. In the following chapter, we shall see also that the evolutions that would permit the creation of these monographs correspond only to the beginning of a process, evoked here regarding Ogburn's career, that would lead to the adoption of a new definition of the objectives of the social science disciplines.

5

American Sociology, the Sociology Department, and the Chicago Tradition, 1934–1961

Under the impetus which the social agencies have given to social investigation and social research, sociology is ceasing to be a mere philosophy and is assuming more and more the character of an empirical, if not an exact, science.

—Robert E. Park, Ernest W. Burgess[1]

Park said to all of us one day, "Now sociology is getting to be statistics. We need it, but we also need more anthropology and social psychology; let the rest go."

—Everett Hughes[2]

When Robert Park retired at the end of the summer of 1933, American sociology was no longer the same as it had been in 1919. The position of the Department of Sociology at the University of Chicago was also profoundly different from that which it had occupied twenty years earlier. To be sure, for many years this department remained the premier center for the production of dissertations (ahead of the Department of Sociology at Columbia University), but it was no longer the principal reference in terms of research in the discipline.[3] The position of social science research in American society from the 1930s onward saw a rapid evolution that partly determined the transformation of research subjects and methods. Finally, the objectives and themes of sociology as defined by Park were no longer in agreement with the sociopolitical and intellectual contexts of the crisis period of the 1930s.

Along with other elements, these frequently led to general assertions of the decline of the Chicago Department of Sociology. This conclusion, however, is not confirmed by an examination of certain objective indices, such as publications in major journals or the election of presidents of the American Sociological Society.[4] It also has the disadvantage of being based on a simplistic model of the development of sociology in the United States, conceiving it as a succession of approaches or theories that obtained the recognition of the community of sociologists. But, on account of the scale of this conclusion, it was equally marked, at least starting in the 1930s, by the more or less troublesome coexistence of approaches adopted by groups of researchers, some of which have withstood the test of time. These approaches passed through alternating periods of success and relative discredit, during which research was conducted that would sometimes later become very famous. This was true for the years 1930–1950 and even more so for the years 1950–1960, in terms of the tradition issuing from the sociology of Thomas and Park: these were periods whose research was for the most part relatively discredited, but they also, particularly the decade following 1950, produced work that would later be recognized as important.

I have chosen for the "institutional" end of this history the 1961 departure for Brandeis (in Massachusetts) of Everett Hughes, the last of Park's former students to teach in the Department of Sociology at the University of Chicago. This choice is in part arbitrary, even though Hughes's departure was already at that time considered to mark the end of an era. Some of the publications examined in the following pages postdate this moment, and there was no notable rupture between the research published in the 1950s and that of the 1960s and 1970s. But the relationship of the Chicago tradition in the sense in which it continued to exist—which is to say in a definition privileging fieldwork and a "constructivist" approach to social phenomena—with the department that had been its home base was interrupted at the beginning of the 1960s. It was at other universities, at Berkeley, San Diego, Brandeis (close to Boston), or Northwestern University (at Evanston, near Chicago) that certain research was conducted and that elements of this tradition were transmitted to a new generation of researchers. The position occupied by the intellectual tradition that issued from Thomas and Park became less and less important at the University of Chicago, and the 1950s were a period of transition.

SOCIOPOLITICAL CONTEXT, RESEARCH FUNDING, AND THE EVOLUTION OF SOCIOLOGY IN THE UNITED STATES

One important aspect of the changing state of sociology in the United States around 1935 resulted from the increase over the course of the 1920s of the number of teaching positions in this discipline. Sociology, which forty years earlier in the Midwest had the connotation of being the study of a multitude of "social problems" linked to urbanization and immigration, by 1935 was a half-recognized academic discipline in which universities increasingly invested. In a certain number of cases, the creation of a small department at a university led to the recruitment of other sociology instructors, then sometimes to the creation of MA and PhD programs and to the development of research: the University of Chicago and Columbia University (which went through a difficult period of transition with the 1928 retirement of its founder, Franklin Giddings) were thus no longer practically the only ones to produce MAs and PhDs. The Universities of Michigan, Minnesota, and Wisconsin, as well as the University of North Carolina (which had, around Odum, an active center of research focusing on race relations) and the University of Washington at Seattle—among others—produced empirical research and trained future professors.[5] Starting in the early 1920s, some of these universities began to develop research orientations different from the one that predominated at Chicago—particularly a "scientistic" orientation that focused on the use of statistical methods. The development of sociology in the elite Anglo-Saxon universities of the East Coast occurred rather later and was more difficult: however, in 1931, Harvard transformed its Department of Social Ethics into a Department of Sociology.[6]

The situation after 1930 was difficult for new PhDs in sociology, since open positions were few, salaries were reduced due to the financial difficulties that most universities were experiencing, and promotions were slow. After 1935, however, sociologists belonging to the generation born around 1900 began to gain entry to influential positions—at Chicago as well as at Columbia and Harvard. In these two latter universities there developed new conceptions of the discipline.

These internal changes in the discipline lay in the background of what has sometimes been interpreted as a revolt against the Chicago sociologists: the American Sociological Society's decision in 1935 to publish an official journal, the *American Sociological Review*. By supplanting the *American Journal of Sociology*, which had been the leading publication in the field since 1905, this act served as the first institutional marker of the decline of the Chicago sociologists. An examination of the process that led to this decision shows, however, that it was less a reaction against an intellectual orientation and more a conflict over the control of the American Sociological Society.

The publication of the *American Sociological Review* was essentially the outcome of a "conspiracy" masterminded by Luther Bernard, a sociologist who had obtained a doctorate in sociology at the University of Chicago in 1910;

he sought above all to diminish the influence of the Chicago sociologists over the ASS, and especially to prevent them from monopolizing positions of influence within this association.

What has been interpreted as signaling the declining influence of the Chicago sociologists does not, however, have a simple intellectual background. The sociologists on the faculty of the University of Chicago (such as Herbert Blumer or Ernest Burgess) were, in this conflict, the allies of sociologists whose intellectual orientations were completely different, such as Stuart Rice or George Lundberg, two partisans of the use of statistical methods and the application of the model of the natural sciences to the social sciences. Ogburn, then a professor at Chicago and, as we have seen, one of the proponents of a "scientistic" approach in sociology, was one of the links between the two groups.[7] The opposing, and temporarily victorious, coalition was also heterogeneous, including (among others) proponents of the Protestant-inspired reformist definition of the discipline, such as Charles Ellwood (who had obtained a doctorate in sociology at Chicago in 1899); partisans of an "interpretive" sociology, such as Howard P. Becker (another recipient of a doctorate bestowed by the University of Chicago in 1930); believers in applied sociology, as well as sociologists whose point of commonality was teaching in second-tier institutions, and as a consequence taught undergraduate students who did not specialize in sociology.[8]

The evolution of sociology over the course of the years 1930–1950 toward a greater degree of academic recognition corresponds more to an a posteriori finding than to sentiments experienced by sociologists of the period. Around 1930, sociology in the academic world still seemed to be mostly a coming together of social reformers with a spirit more missionary than scientific. Still, in an intellectual atmosphere marked by the success of the physical and natural sciences, some sociologists born around 1900 were moved to demonstrate to their colleagues, as well as to university administrators and sources of research funding, that their activities merited the label "scientific."

The usage of statistical techniques—correlation coefficients, then, a bit later, sampling techniques and tests of significance—was one of the principal arguments used by sociologists to obtain this recognition of sociology as a scientific field. This is reflected in a statement by Richard LaPiere in a letter to Irwin Deutscher:

What you may not know, or at least fully appreciate, is that in the 1930s the status of sociology and hence of sociologists was abominable, both within and outside the academic community. The public image of the sociologist was that of a blue-nosed reformer, ever ready to pronounce moral judgments, and against all pleasurable forms of social conduct. In the universities, sociology was generally thought of as an uneasy mixture of social philosophy and social work. . . . The men who were to shape sociology during the 1930s were, for the most part, products of one or two departments (e.g. Columbia) of low status within their universities. They were therefore to a considerable degree self-trained and without a doctrinaire viewpoint, and they were exceedingly conscious of the low esteem in which sociology was held.

Such men, and I was among them, were determined to prove—at least to themselves—that sociology deserves recognition and support comparable to that being given psychology and economics. It was, I think, to this end that toward the end of the '20s scientific sociology came to be identified with quantitative methods in sociology, and the later in turn with reliance upon the questionnaire as the one valid tool of investigation.[9]

Two essential points are not mentioned in this account: the sociopolitical context and the mode of research funding that contributed to redefining the intellectual orientations of the development of sociology, as it did for political science and economics. We have already seen the beginning of this evolution, with the creation of the Social Science Research Council and the Laura Spelman Rockefeller Memorial Fund, which partially funded the monographs of Chicago sociologists in the years 1923–1935. We have also seen the Hoover administration's commission of a report of ongoing evolutions in American society—*Recent Social Trends*—by a group of social-science specialists under the direction of Ogburn. Funding for the report was secured by the Rockefeller Foundation, within which the Laura Spelman Rockefeller Foundation would be founded.[10] According to the terms used by the assistant to President Hoover who was responsible for this commission, it was to "produce a rounded and explicit picture of the whole American social scene, with such a wealth of facts and statistics and conclusions as to form a new and unique basis of thought and action for social scientists, social workers, and those officers of government who, like himself, have a special responsibility in relation to such problems."[11] In its conclusion, the report advocated the intervention of the federal state for resolving social problems.[12] It is clear that there was no immediate follow-up, and by the time the report was completed, the Hoover administration had been replaced by that of Franklin D. Roosevelt. It did, however, reflect a lasting orientation of the policies of the federal government and the place of the social sciences in American society.

In the context of the Great Depression, areas of federal intervention saw a significant expansion: matters previously thought to depend on local authorities alone were considered, after this point, to be problems deserving of treatment on the national level, which is to say federal policy. Thus, unemployment and poverty ceased to be exclusively the purview of local communities, and instead entered the national stage. Administrations were created to implement different projects, such as the Federal Housing Administration, created in 1934, and the Works Progress Administration, created in 1935 to sustain the unemployed.[13] Provisions were set in place concerning the development of land. In agriculture, the federal policy that had existed for twenty years was expanded. Planning was a predominant theme in the debates of the period, even if the sense of the word ranged, according to the phrasing of one historian, from "the application of rationality and available scientific knowledge to the course of human events" to "the imposition of goals and methods of a managerial elite committed to its own identification of social purposes."[14]

The theme of planning also appears among sociologists, for example, in the papers presented at the conference of the American Sociological Society (ASS) in December 1935. On this occasion, sociologists kept a distance from the Soviet connotations associated with planning by claiming that they possessed instruments permitting them to play the role of experts for the benefit of federal or state governments. In the first issue of the new official journal of the association, the *American Sociological Review*, which collected the papers from this conference, the newly elected president of the association, Stuart Chapin, develops in his address titled "Social Theory and Social Action" an operationalist perspective similar to that of Lundberg, emphasizing quantification and prediction, and concluding that sociologists could play the role of experts; the second article, written by a Russian émigré, Pitirim Sorokin, expands upon the necessary precautions for avoiding any politically unfortunate interpretations of the term "planning."

A corollary to the intervention of the federal government was an increased interest in an understanding of the social situation of the country as a whole. The administrations that managed federal programs were fundamentally concerned with making use of statistical data on the areas in question. The bureau charged with the census was reformed between 1933 and 1935—in collaboration with statisticians, including Stuart Rice—and the Central Statistical Board was established in Washington in 1933 in order to reform statistical systems. At the Department of Agriculture, the census division and the Farm Population and Rural Welfare at the Bureau of Agricultural Economy, created in 1921, employed sociologists. Some of the personnel who administered federal programs came from elsewhere in the social sciences: one estimate puts forth the number of 2,500 economists and statisticians employed by the Roosevelt administration in 1939.[15] The 1940 census considerably widened the field of areas subject to investigation by seeking to determine the consequences of the Great Depression of the 1930s on people's lives, and by including a study on housing. To reduce the cost of collecting this information, as well as information on unemployment, methods of statistical sampling were studied.[16] Three sociologists trained in Ogburn's circle at the University of Chicago over the course of the period participated on the front lines of resolving these questions: in 1933–1934, Samuel Stouffer and Frederick Stephan organized the first studies intended to determine the best sampling unit for obtaining a measure of unemployment on the federal level; Philip Hauser was assistant to the director of the 1940 census.[17]

Over the course of this period, there existed a sort of dialectical relationship between this element of the sociopolitical context and the partial reorientation of the social sciences, to which the policy of research funding contributed. After 1930, this encouraged the production of knowledge related to the problems of the period according to their national definition. Between 1930 and 1933, the Social Science Research Council, which was the principal intermediary between researchers and the foundations that provided them funding, thus defined a policy that prioritized the concentration of efforts on a small number of areas connected to social problems of the moment. The Social Science Research Council held that it should ally itself with the government in order to contribute to policies, and that the knowledge accumulated by the research that it funded should lead to practical applications. In 1935, the Rockefeller Foundation, until that point one of the principal providers of funding to the Social Science Research Council, also developed a new policy. This shift was marked by the abandonment of its efforts in favor of the promotion of fundamental research in the social sciences, and the concentration of its resources on funding three areas linked to subjects of governmental concern: international relations, economic security, and public administration. Thus, the Social Science Research Council, via the Central Statistical Board of the Roosevelt administration, led by Stuart Rice, funded Stouffer's previously mentioned research on measuring unemployment.[18]

Starting in the 1930s, sociologists' increasing interest in statistical techniques was also connected to the development of a new specialty, social psychology, focused on the concept of attitude. One of the first signs of interest in this concept among was sociologists was found, as we have seen, in *The Polish Peasant*: its introduction, as Charles Camic has shown, is partly a reaction against the biological or physical explanations for behavior that been popular in the field of behaviorist psychology since the First World War.[19] The concept of attitude thus served to eliminate any physiological dimension from the approach to behaviors.

But the success of the concept is also connected to the diversity of meanings that it can take: in 1935, a survey of previous research found sixteen different definitions of this concept.[20] Starting in the 1920s, some psychologists used the concept to interpret responses to questionnaires and allow them a quantitative approach to what was excluded by the behaviorist model: the subjective sense and psychic life.[21] The first examples of attitude scales were published in 1924 by the psychologist Gordon Allport and by Emory Bogardus, a researcher associated with Park. Some years later, statistical techniques led to the definition of attitudes as one type of variable that lent itself to be measured through scales based on responses to questionnaire surveys.[22]

But the diffusion of the use of the concept of attitude was also connected to the development, on the borders of psychology, economy, and sociology, of a new sector of activity: studies of markets and opinions. It was for these that techniques for gathering questionnaires were developed, along with their exploitation for the purpose of "measuring" attitudes—in this context, propensities for action.[23] The adoption of these approaches in sociology was relatively slow—slower, for example, than in political science, where the first empirical studies on political behaviors, conducted in the Department of Political Science at Chicago under the direction of Charles Merriam, took place at the beginning of the 1920s.[24] Some of the research used the techniques developed by psychologists like Thurstone and Allport, and sought to measure attitudes based on opinions gathered through questionnaires, dealing principally with themes touching on public behaviors and policy.[25]

Shortly thereafter, in 1935, Paul Lazarsfeld (1901–1976), a Viennese émigré trained in psychology who knew specialists in market research, established a research center in the small University of Newark. Thanks to a funding contract, he studied people who listened to the radio and the technology's effects on its audience—a subject that had acquired new importance with the recent utilization of the radio by Hitler in Germany and by Roosevelt in the United States. Lazarsfeld's approach was that of a panel survey, based on multiple interviews with the same sample of people. Over the course of the years 1935–1940, in publications based on a collaboration with Stouffer, Lazarsfeld developed different procedures permitting the exploitation of this type of data. Associating with a social psychologist at Princeton, Hadley Cantril, and benefiting from the financial support of the Rockefeller Foundation, Lazarsfeld transferred his research center to Princeton. In 1939, he was hired by Columbia University, so he again moved his research center, the funding of which was essentially secured by contracts. Lazarsfeld's center also saw a new expansion under the name Bureau of Applied Research. It was in this context that a novel conception of empirical research in sociology was developed, within which were trained a group of sociologists later hired by major universities, in particular, after 1950, the University of Chicago.

From the end of the 1930s, the type of data produced by questionnaire surveys—which provided information to public and private administrators concerned with understanding the reactions of the populations to whom they administered or addressed themselves—seemed capable of leading to promising results for sociology. The approach of questionnaire surveys also allowed sociologists to conform to a standard of evidence that those working in the social sciences at that period believed approached that of the natural sciences.

The entry of the United States into the Second World War meant the offer of significant military funding for the social sciences, leading to a new expansion of the field of use for these surveys and, relatedly, to the reinforcement of this orientation in sociology. In the context of the research department of the US Army, research dedicated to the morale of military personnel was based on the statistical exploitation of a series of interviews. Other research focused on populations subject to bombardment: in all these cases the approach utilized was that of a survey of a sample population, and the interviews focused on predispositions toward certain reactions. Samuel Stouffer, then a professor of sociology at the University of Chicago who was on a secondary posting in a department of the army from 1941 to 1945,[26] led some of this research, which would shortly thereafter be published. Lazarsfeld and some Columbia researchers also participated.[27]

Interest in this type of research was not extinguished with the end of the war: in 1945, a commission under the direction of Stouffer that brought together representatives of the federal National Research Council and the Social Science Research Council obtained funding from the Rockefeller Foundation for refining methods for measuring the opinions, attitudes, and desires of consumers.[28]

After the war, the research themes in social sciences for which there was funding available changed. But there existed a greater continuity than suggested by the debates and changes in orientation affirmed by funding bodies, which is to say the federal government and the large private foundations—Rockefeller, Carnegie, and Russell Sage, taken over by the Ford Foundation—which were the principal source of social science research funds starting in the 1950s. The policies of these foundations always emphasize the necessity of collaboration between diverse social science disciplines, although this would always remain more formal than actual. The research on themes deemed important by the federal government were always given precedence over the development of fundamental research (according to its definition in each discipline). Finally, the insistence on the usage of the scientific method—which always meant making uses of statistical tools—rather tended to reinforce itself.

An analogous policy was followed by the federal agency created in 1950 to support research in the context of the Cold War, the National Science Foundation. The manifestations of the extent of its interventions in the domain of the social sciences (which did not figure explicitly in its original field of intervention, but was gradually introduced) made this orientation clear.[29] In a presentation of the policy of the agency intended for sociologists and published in the *American Sociological Review*, Harry Alpert (1912–1977), a sociologist trained at Columbia and the first specialist in social sciences recruited by the administration of the National Science Foundation in 1952 to develop financial support for this area, insisted upon the necessity for the social sciences to conform to a model that he characterized by the following traits: "the formulation of hypotheses that can be tested and verified by experiments or systematic observations; the removal of a gradually growing body of knowledge from the realm of speculation and subjective opinion to the realm of demonstrated fact; and the effort to make predictions, at least about a few social phenomena, within approximately measurable limits of confidence."[30] Alpert also reiterated that any relationship between the social sciences and reform movements should be avoided, and noted the regrettable phonetic similarity of "sociology" and "socialism."

In this context, studies that at the time seemed innovative to the community of sociologists were above all those that made use of, and contributed to developing, statistical tools. These sorts of studies were conducted in research centers that dealt with large surveys, such as the Bureau of Applied Research at Columbia University, the Institute of Social Research at the University of Michigan, and, a little later, the National Opinion Research Center associated with the University of Chicago.

> Much evidence suggests that research based on surveys occupied a position of growing prominence from the middle of the 1930s: for example, among the articles published by the *American Sociological Review*, the portion of them that are based on this type of evidence grew from 1935, as did the portion of those that adopted a quantitative approach.[31] One might wonder about the significance of this type of evidence, but the essential point is the conviction, later adopted by researchers using fieldwork in the 1950s, that the quantitative approach, and in particular survey research, would become increasingly important in the discipline of sociology.

In these transformations of the social sciences and of the place that was accorded to them in society, sociologists had, especially in the first period, a less central role than did economists and psychologists, and even specialists in political science.

With the exception of Ogburn, the sociologists at Chicago did not play a leading role in defining the policies of the Social Science Research Council, even if
some of them, such as Louis Wirth, were longtime members of this committee
(although in 1937 Wirth wrote a report critical of the policy it implemented, and
of its dependence on funding bodies).[32] The Chicago sociologists did, however,
as in previous years, benefit from substantial funding from the Social Science
Research Council.

THE LEGACY OF PARK'S SOCIOLOGY IN THE
SOCIOLOGY OF THE 1930S AND 1940S

The interest of sociologists, following the lead of their sponsors, in new themes
and new approaches to research was complemented by an increasing discrepancy
between the immediate perceptions of the social environment following the crisis of the 1930s and the themes for which Park's vision of sociology offered a
program of research.[33]

　　We have seen that, for many aspects, the sociology of Park had an affinity with
the state of American society at the beginning of the twentieth century. In the
era of the Great Depression, the distance Park's sociology kept from the questions of public debate was, by contrast, striking: the problems of urban life—the
behavior of immigrants, interethnic relationships, crime—essentially faded into
the background, a distant second behind the problems of unemployment and
the impoverishment of some social categories, or, in terms of academic specializations, behind the problems of work and those of social inequalities. Further,
the objectives Park associated with social science research differed from those of
funding bodies, but also from those of the academics who played a leading role
among the "experts" of governmental entities (like Ogburn or even Merriam).
Park's research objectives were also distant from the conceptions of the sociologists of the following generation.

　　Park's sociology was centered on two levels of analysis: on one hand, the process of long-term evolution on a global scale; on the other hand, the spatial units
of rather limited size that a researcher can study using an ethnographic approach.
It omitted, on the contrary, the study of phenomena that figured on a national
level. For Park, research should lead above all, as we have seen, to improved
information and to the comprehension of social problems by the cultivated elites
likely to influence ongoing changes: actions that lead to social changes should
occur at the level of local collectives, cities, and above all communities—and

not the federal level. From the perspective of the application of sociology to the definition of a national policy, the use of statistical tools was an essential instrument for an overall knowledge of the American population, although the precise knowledge offered by cases—extracts from a little-known world of more or less similar phenomena—seems to have been little used. Finally, the implementation of federal policy in different areas, especially that of housing, also contributed to drawing attention to elements that Park's sociology left to the side: in the case of urban development, this meant the political dimension, as well as a lack of understanding of the city as an organism that developed naturally on its own.

Although Park's sociology was far removed from the problems of the period, some sociologists who had studied under him—notably among those who were not entirely absorbed by teaching responsibilities—adapted themselves more or less completely to the new subjects and methods of research that developed over the course of the period. A large proportion of authors of monographs published in the years 1920–1933 seem to have adhered to a reformist vision of the use of research (already presented in the recommendations that concluded most published monographs). They were no less influenced than their peers in other disciplines and universities by the atmosphere of the New Deal: some of them would later, as we have seen, conduct research on the newly current themes, such as work.[34] They probably had never embraced the conception, shared by Park and a group of the intellectuals of the same generation, of the contribution of sociology to social change: various anecdotes mention the political divergences between Park and some researchers of the 1930s. It is even less surprising that some of these intellectuals adopted the new approaches and research topics than that Park and, especially, Burgess were not inclined to consider research in the discipline to be impossible to define, as it had been in the 1920s.

Starting in the 1930s, the cultural environment in which the American social sciences developed found itself rapidly and profoundly changed by the introduction of many perspectives and currents of ideas that were completely foreign to the intellectual world in which Chicago sociology had developed. It is necessary to mention, first of all, the diffusion of the work of Freud starting in the 1920s. With the arrival of many immigrants fleeing Germany and central Europe, some of the intellectual debates—surrounding the philosophy of science, the Vienna Circle, Marxism, and psychoanalysis—previously developed in Europe took root in the United States. This is what introduced the fundamental ideas of small-group studies, which after 1945 would hold an important place in the interests of sociologists and seemed for a time capable of leading to practical applications. Neither Kurt Lewin, nor Jacob Moreno (the "inventor" of sociometry), nor Erich Fromm—who figured among the references of an appreciable portion of sociologists who had completed their studies starting in the middle of the 1930s—offered perspectives on research that were easily compatible with Park's sociology. We must also recall the importance, from the end of the 1930s, of studies on propaganda, prejudices, and the behaviors of crowds—which were in part reactions to the political success of Nazism and authoritarian movements—and that of the role played in this area by certain immigrants, such as Lazarsfeld and Adorno.

The evolutions concerning sociology and research in the social sciences that took place at Harvard after 1930 allow us to clearly perceive another factor in the decline of interest in the program of sociology as defined by Park. A Department of Sociology had been created, as we have seen, at Harvard in 1931, following the recruitment of Sorokin in the previous year. He clearly imposed there a definition of the discipline different from the one that had developed in the Midwest or even in New York at Columbia University. Harvard's choice of an émigré of European origin as a professor of sociology, rather than a sociologist trained in the United States, was significant. The president of the university insinuated to Sorokin that the intention of creating such a department had been dead in the water for eight years because of the absence of an acceptable candidate: the president did not find the discipline "respectable" as it then existed, and his initial goal had been to establish a very selective department.[35] Sorokin did not succeed in solidly establishing Harvard as the leader of a new conception of sociology, and it was a well-known physiologist and biochemist, Lawrence Henderson, a member of Harvard's board of trustees, who is found behind the two intellectual enterprises based at Harvard that would mark American sociology during the following years: the research of Elton Mayo on industrial labor and the work of Talcott Parsons.

In the contexts of the 1930s and of an elite Anglo-Saxon Protestant university, sociology kept its distance from what had marked its birth in the Midwest: the ideas previously associated with the Progressive reform movement, social work, and any suspicion of collusion with socialism. Lawrence Henderson (1878–1942), an avowed conservative, offered all guarantees in this respect. It was he who sponsored, in 1926, the recruitment to Harvard Business School of Elton Mayo (1880–1949)—an Australian professor of philosophy who was oriented toward the application of psychology to the problems of industrial labor—as well as Mayo's research at Hawthorne after 1928.[36] A passionate reader of Pareto—whose work was the subject of a seminar that he organized between 1932 and 1934, gathering people who would become allies in his quest to establish sociology at Harvard—Henderson was, in an initial period, closely intertwined in the life of the new Department of Sociology. Henderson also mentored Talcott Parsons

(1902–1979), an obscure instructor in the economics department, and facilitated his transfer into the sociology department.

Parsons was far removed from the native conceptions of sociology, and the intellectual references that he proposed reveal a clear concern for keeping at a distance the approaches that were previously fashionable. Parsons's strategic vision of the manner in which he would establish his own enterprise in the context of the social sciences of the period manifests itself in a 1948 article on the effects of the war on sociology, in which he presents a sort of inventory of notable undertakings.[37] An important characteristic of Parsons's sociology is his silence regarding the conceptions of sociology that had developed since the beginning of the century in the United States, and his almost exclusive attention to European intellectual traditions.[38] The themes that he borrowed from the European sociology of the beginning of the century, with its central image of society as a system in equilibrium with a structure—and not as an ensemble of interdependent processes—accorded both with the context of an elite university and with American intellectual and political circumstances of the moment. Parsons's insistence on the general theory presented in the form of a list of abstract concepts, guaranteed by means of their being based on work belonging to the great intellectual traditions of Europe, was certainly more favorable to the recognition of the legitimacy of the discipline than what the sociology of Park and his students seemed to offer: the uncertain integration of a disparate ensemble of studies on tightly circumscribed subjects in a poorly organized corpus of very general propositions.

Other elements of this intellectual conjuncture could also be mentioned, including the influence of Marxism among Harvard students of the period, to which Pareto seemed to be an antidote.[39] In the background of Parsons' preoccupations can also be found the reflections of philosophers of science in the tradition of the Vienna Circle, who were very present at Harvard and whose debates about operationalism fueled criticism of the state of the social sciences.

Finally, although the sociology of Park was focalized on phenomena linked to the social problems of the moment and was addressed to an enlightened audience that covered a wide range of the middle classes likely to take charge of community affairs, sociology such as it was practiced at Harvard—more generally than that of Parsons—was more focused on large organizations and addressed to an audience from a higher level of society, including in particular the elite of the established professions.[40] The augmentation of funding of the social sciences at Harvard led to the integration, in 1945, of the Harvard sociology department into a new multidisciplinary department, the Department of Social Relations, which gathered, under the direction of Parsons, social psychologists, sociologists, and anthropologists. This organization, which also partially took on the conflicts internal to the original departments, was in harmony with the funding policies of the foundations, which were always favorable toward interdisciplinary research.[41]

It was only after the end of the war, and especially at the end of the 1940s, that sociology at Harvard constituted an important element of the context pertinent for understanding the evolutions of Chicago sociology. Until 1947, Harvard sociologists held only a weak position in the debates that filled the columns of the *American Journal of Sociology*, and the book that assured Parsons's reputation as a theoretician was only published in 1951. The principal subject of controversy in the journal, of which Blumer was then editor in chief, was the merits of the operationalist point of view and sociology's adoption of a model based on the physical sciences.

> Before 1940, however, the Chicago sociologists maintained direct and indirect relationships with the promoters of sociology and empirical research at Harvard. Lloyd Warner, an associate of Mayo, was recruited, as we have seen, by the Department of Sociology at Chicago. Lawrence Henderson was a friend of Park, whom he had met, it seems, at the beginning of the century at the University of Strasbourg. In an article dedicated to Park, Hughes evokes a visit that the two of them made to Henderson: "In the late 1930s, I spent a lively day with Park and Henderson in northern Vermont. Henderson, a tremendous talker, allowed that his old friend Park was a good sociologist mainly because he had learned it for himself rather than from professionals, but maintained that all future good sociology would be done by scholars trained in the physical and biological sciences. Park, as usual, talked in his quiet, speculative—sometimes profane—way about ideas, ignoring Henderson's outrageous condescension."[42]

An essay on American sociology published in 1948 by Edward Shils (1910–1995), who belonged to the last generation of Chicago students who took courses taught by Park at Chicago—and who some years later, in 1951, was one of Parsons's associates in a seminar on theory held at Harvard—developed an interpretation, certainly an influential one among sociologists of the period, of the past approaches and accomplishments of sociologists in Park's circle and the state of the discipline at the end of the 1940s.

> As a result of his life circumstances, Shils was a sort of intermediary between Harvard and Chicago. Of German origin, and a one-time social worker during his sociology studies, he was the research assistant of Wirth—with whom he seems to have maintained a contentious relationship—and one of the experts in

German sociology. He was not consistently engaged in empirical research, and his intellectual production essentially consists of essays. Mentored after 1945 by Hutchins, the president of the University of Chicago, Shils was a member of one of the interdisciplinary research committees the former had created before being integrated into the Department of Sociology at Chicago. In a reversal, he was over the course of the last fifteen years that preceded his 1994 death a convinced admirer of the sociology of Park. Over the course of an interview, some months previously, he described to me with insistence the support that he had given to research based on fieldwork, such as that of Mitchell Duneier.

Shils's 1948 critical assessment, initially intended for English readers, is underpinned by the idea that the analyses of the previous period were lacking both because of the lack of either a prior hypothesis or systematic verification, and because of the insufficient precision of its theoretical framework.

Shils reviewed the work conducted over the course of the preceding twenty years, applying their norms of judgment to the research approaches and theoretical consistency of postwar sociologists. The studies of urban sociology conducted under the auspices of Park, then those of his successors at Chicago, were examined in terms of their relationships with two criteria:

> In the course of time the original vision vanished and there was left behind a tendency towards the repetition of disconnected investigations. From the standpoint of a mind like Park's these little studies of 'press while you wait' tailors in the Loop, dwellers in rented rooms, etc., were microphotographic illustrations of some significant aspect of modern life—something fundamental about human relations in modern society was documented by them. Even under the direct inspiration of the living teacher, they were however still not science. . . . From the point of view of their *direct* contribution to a systematic theory of human behavior and social organization, there is no value in them.[43]

Among post-1935 research projects, Shils emphasized those that focused on social stratification (which partly issued from studies of communities), research on race relations (in which Shils introduced a line of questioning into the relationship with class structure), research on communication and publication (in which he recognized the merit of having introduced a concern for sampling problems and technical questions posed by the collection of data through interviews), research on small groups (among which he counts those who continued the Hawthorne surveys and distinguishes, by virtue of their greater rigor, the research of Lewin and his associates).

In the conclusion to his critical assessment, Shils again pleads in favor of greater rigor in the collection of data and the formulation of general theories, echoing the two obsessions of the period that were emblematic of the development of the use of statistics and Parsonian theory. On the observations provided by direct contact with the subjects of study, Shils wrote, "Observations must be transformed into quantitative values, since it is only on this basis that relationships of degree can be established,"[44] but that to "contribute to our understanding and improvement of our present-day society. . . . Observations are made to test hypotheses and if hypotheses are fitted into a general system of propositions, internally consistent with one another."[45] Shils cites as a model the attempts to move in this direction represented by the research of the new Department of Social Relations at Harvard, which also included Stouffer and Parsons, and of the Institute of Human Relations at Yale.[46]

CHICAGO SOCIOLOGISTS, THE UNIVERSITY, AND THE LOCAL CONTEXT

We have seen that, during the period before 1935, the research conducted at the University of Chicago had benefited from a constellation of favorable institutional factors: the possibility of research funding, the emphasis placed on research by the university, the intellectual environment of Pragmatism and the Progressive reform movement, singularities of recruitment of students, and so on. After 1935, the environment was less favorable to the development of research in the tradition that issued from Thomas and Park.

The ongoing changes in the intellectual situation in the United States were foreshadowed by the intellectual orientation that Robert Maynard Hutchins (1899–1977), a young lawyer trained at Yale and the new president of the University of Chicago, attempted to impose starting in 1929.[47] Enterprising and inventive in terms of institutional arrangements, but also somewhat capricious, Hutchins became one of the educators with a national profile over the course of the following years, notably due to the changes that he introduced or tried to introduce at the University of Chicago, particularly in terms of his conception of undergraduate studies.

For Hutchins, the course of study offered by colleges, which led to a bachelor's degree that preceded the graduate MA and PhD degrees, ought to provide a general education that especially touched on the "Great Books"—the works deemed most important for Western culture. Some partisans of this reform explicitly referred to the *trivium* of medieval education. Mortimer Adler, a close friend whom Hutchins hired as a philosophy professor for the university, argued in favor of the adoption of a Thomist version of Aristotelian philosophy as the unofficial philosophy of academic policy at the University of Chicago. This orientation directly concerned the social sciences. Over the course of the years 1930 and 1931, Adler publicly developed a critique of their orientation: "without the principles and logic of true, that is, Aristotelian philosophy, 'raw empiricism' becomes 'bad science,' " he claimed.[48] A 1936 book by Hutchins developed a similar conception of knowledge and the role of the university, which was placed in opposition to Pragmatism due to its focus on principles rather than experience, and its overt disdain for social science research.[49]

An article published by Ernest Burgess in 1955, four years after Hutchins's departure from Chicago, gives a sense of the antagonism between the Hutchins's positions and what had been the previous trajectory of sociology at Chicago: Burgess criticizes the "great book illusion" (the pet subject of Hutchins) which made the writing of the past, ranging from Aristotle to Marx and Freud, a guide for the present, despite their having "little or nothing to contribute to an understanding of a society that has merged since the great book were written."[50] Burgess also recommended that "sociologists should not be misled to adopt biological and psychological theoretical conceptual systems for an understanding of society," and simultaneously developed an implicit critique of Parsons's intellectual enterprise.[51]

The effects of Hutchins's policy were felt more directly in the college—the curriculum of which he reformed by diminishing the role of disciplinary specialization—than in the departments that hosted graduate students. Without taking the view of the latter, Hutchins recruited for the college instructors intended to provide general courses of introduction to the "great authors": this is how David Riesman, a young lawyer educated at Harvard, was hired as a professor of social sciences in 1946. With the recruitment of certain students and young researchers of diverse disciplinary membership and intellectual training, the college became a locus of dynamic intellectual contact—in the opinion of those who studied there—completely autonomous from the departments.[52]

Hutchins also implemented a policy unfavorable to the autonomy of departments in terms of research and graduate studies, notably in terms of the recruitment of professors. In line with the policy of financing research through foundations, Hutchins favored the creation of interdisciplinary committees charged with administrating different programs: starting in 1942, to mention only those that affected sociologists, we also find a Committee on Human Relations in Industry (see chapter 6) and a Committee on Social Thought. After 1943 a Committee on Human Development was established, as well as another that focused on interethnic relations: the Committee on Education, Teaching and Research in Race Relations. From 1946 to 1957 there existed a Committee on Industrial Relations, and from 1948 to 1954 yet another Committee on Communication. Finally, after 1949, another committee, brief in existence, was dedicated to problems in planning: the Program of Education and Research in Planning.[53] Some professors—like Edward Shils in 1946—were specially recruited by one of these committees and not by a particular department. Some of these committees, such as the Committee on Human Development and the Committee on Social Thought, would develop multidisciplinary programs of graduate study, which further contributed to diminishing the role of the departments.

The Chicago sociologists (like a large portion of other social science instructors) were almost constantly reserved or hostile with regard to the innovations introduced by Hutchins, and Louis Wirth frequently appears among the avowed opponents to his policies.

The importance of departments as places of intellectual exchange also declined with the creation of specialized research centers, in which some students pursued graduate degrees, especially in cases when the use of computational resources was necessary.

From 1935 to 1952, the stability of the faculty and the largely internal character of recruitment was one of the obvious characteristics of the sociology department. One of the reasons, which held until the war, was material: from the beginning of the Great Depression of the 1930s, the University of Chicago experienced financial difficulties that were especially severe because its privileged connection to the Rockefeller Foundation weakened a bit.[54] Thus, until 1940 the university granted tenure to only a very small number of instructors. The recruitment of Louis Wirth and Herbert Blumer as assistant professors in 1930–1931, before Park's retirement, guaranteed a certain degree of continuity in the orientation of the sociology department at Chicago.[55] Samuel Stouffer (1900–1960; PhD in 1930), whose contribution to the refinement of statistical sampling techniques has been previously mentioned, was recruited on a permanent basis in 1935. He did not have the time to notably influence instruction, because his responsibilities in army research quickly took him away from the university, and, in 1946, he joined the new department of social relations at Harvard. In 1938, another graduate of the department, Everett Hughes, was also hired by the University of Chicago as an assistant professor (i.e., for three years) in order to teach the

introductory sociology course and strengthen the coverage of social organization, which had been controlled by the anthropologists.[56] The Department of
Anthropology, in which a good number of sociology students continued to take
courses, housed another graduate of the department from the same generation as
Wirth, Blumer, Hughes, and Stouffer: Robert Redfield, the son-in-law of Park,
who had been recruited in 1927.[57]

> The differences in orientation that separated the intellectual heirs of Park—who
> were Wirth, Blumer, and Hughes—are one of the keys to comprehending the
> manner in which was effected the transmission of some elements of the tradi-
> tion, and also that of the dissensions internal to the Department of Sociology
> over the following years. I shall here briefly note the relevant benchmarks.
>
> Louis Wirth (1897–1952; PhD in 1926),[58] of German origin, was employed
> between 1917 and 1922 as a social worker by a charity organization, Jewish
> Charities, which allowed him to pay for his doctoral studies. His dissertation
> in sociology, on Jewish urban ghettos, was sponsored by Park. Wirth seems to
> have been, as we have seen, one of the rare students who studied under Small to
> have drawn an interest in Marxism from his instruction. The first sociology pro-
> fessor of Jewish origin to be recruited by the University of Chicago, as well as,
> in 1947, be elected president of the American Sociological Society (ASS), Wirth
> undoubtedly encountered some difficulties in being accepted in the academic
> world—where his agnosticism, his "radical" opinions,[59] and his somewhat pro-
> letarian allure contrasted sharply with the positions of some of his classmates.
>
> After 1935, Wirth distanced himself from research in favor of activities pro-
> moting various causes: frequently consulted by associations involved in urban
> problems, he was also engaged in activist associations working for civil rights
> and racial equality. He also became one of the founders and the first president
> of the International Association of Sociology in 1950. His interest in reforms,
> including legislative ones; his activism on the level of the city of Chicago, the
> state of Illinois, and the United States as a whole; and his advocacy for devel-
> oping an "urban planning" obviously contrasted with Park's distrust of state
> intervention.[60] In 1948, Wirth's action in a Supreme Court case that ultimately
> found unconstitutional the discriminatory clauses included in residential sales
> deeds seems to have strengthened a distrust in the university administration in
> his mind: on several occasions, the university refused to make him chair of the
> Department of Sociology. Outside his participation in numerous committees
> organizing or financing research in the social sciences, Wirth filled an inter-
> mediary role, and sometimes that of translator of the works of German sociol-
> ogists and philosophers.[61] The judgments made on Wirth's teaching by those

who studied under him are contrasting: some recalled his talents as a lecturer and his virtuosity in debates, while others remembered his lack of investment in teaching activities.

One of Wirth's influential publications is a 1938 article that sketches out the characteristic traits of urban phenomena. He insists upon the substitution in the cities of secondary contacts for the primary contacts typical of small rural communities: the participation in voluntary groups thus substitutes for family and neighborhoods, with the juxtaposition of "highly differentiated modes of life between which there often is only the faintest communication, the greatest indifference and the broadest tolerance."[62] This representation of the urban way of life inspired later research, but, as Hughes sarcastically remarked, Wirth's way of life at Chicago, "surrounded by kin and a group of friends," represented a sort of refutation of the "impersonal" character of the style of relationships found in cities.[63]

Herbert Blumer (1900–1987; PhD in 1928), a descendant of German immigrants, arrived at Chicago after having to abruptly leave the small Southern college where he had been teaching, following a lecture that had provoked a Ku Klux Klan protest.[64] In the interview conducted by James Carey, Blumer imputes his orientation toward sociology to his interest in "socialism." A semi-professional football player in order to fund his doctoral studies, he became the protégé of Ellsworth Faris, under whose direction he wrote a dissertation, of critical inspiration, on the methods of social psychology.[65] When George Mead fell ill, Blumer took over one of his courses intended for sociologists. Over the following years, he began to interpret the social psychology of Mead for sociologists. In a few impactful articles, Blumer conveyed an incisive criticism of operationalism, then of the orientation of American sociology toward survey questionnaires and the study of attitudes.

It was upon this critical methodological activity that he established his reputation (see chapter 6). He himself conducted little empirical research—principally a survey on the relationship between the cinema and crime.[66] His publications often included essays, of an equally critical character, on research dedicated to race relations and on the analysis of relationships in industry.[67] Another of Blumer's areas of interest, on which he focused some of his courses, was the study of collective behavior—notably fashion, which he began to research in the 1930s, and social problems, for which he proposed a then-original approach that was promised wide diffusion, emphasizing the processes that conferred on them a public character.[68]

At the University of Chicago in the 1940s, Blumer was, according to concurring testimonies, a valued teacher, even if his "methodological nihilism" generated concerns in some students. Fred Davis, one of his former students, thus evokes the intellectual paradox of Blumer: "There was, on the one hand, I would say: his broad vision, his felicitous insight, his unerring critical facility and a sociological imagination of exceptional subtlety. Yet, on the other hand, there was also a kind of nagging skepticism about the ability of 'mere mortals' to ever fully apprehend the mysteries and complexities of social life, a distrust of classification and formula—a renunciation of method, if you will, although I do not mean to imply by this either carelessness, indifference or some vulgar epistemology of truth-through-intuition."[69]

Blumer, who does not seem to have been much appreciated by the administration of the University of Chicago, left in 1952 for the University of California at Berkeley. Charged with creating a new Department of Sociology, he succeeded in putting together a department that would rapidly become one of the most prominent representatives of the principal orientations of American sociology of the period.

Everett Hughes (1897–1983; PhD in 1928), a pastor's son from the Midwest, had written, as we have seen, his dissertation on the professionalization of the real estate agents of Chicago under the supervision of Park.[70] Contrary to the majority of Park's students, Hughes seems to have conducted research for his dissertation almost on his own. Just before his defense, with Park as an intermediary, Hughes was hired by the elite Anglophone McGill University in Montreal, where with another slightly older former student of Park, Carl Dawson, he created one of the first sociology courses to be offered in a Canadian university. In the 1930s, he conducted, with funding from the Rockefeller Foundation, a community study on an industrial city close to Montreal (see chapter 8). Returning to the University of Chicago as an instructor in 1938, Hughes undertook research on race relations in industry within the framework of the Committee on Human Relations in Industry. A little later, he contributed to the orientation of dissertations on occupations of various status (see chapter 6). A step back from Wirth in terms of activist engagement, Hughes was much more inclined than average toward empirical research in the fields of work, institutions and race relationships. Through introductory courses on fieldwork and through his connections with anthropology, he contributed, as we have seen, to promoting one of the orientations previously favored by Park: research based on an ethnographic approach.

Another graduate of the University of Chicago, Edwin Sutherland (1883–1950; PhD in 1913), also occupied a position there for some years and influenced certain dissertations. Recruited in 1930 as a research professor, Edwin Sutherland had only reduced teaching obligations and was charged with implementing a research program in criminology.[71] Over the course of the five years he spent at Chicago, he undertook numerous research projects—notably those that led to the publication in 1937 of the autobiography of a criminal, *The Professional Thief*.[72] Sutherland encouraged several students toward the study of diverse forms of crime—especially Alfred Lindesmith, who went on to study opium addiction.[73] In 1935, when he was denied tenure—according to him, because of the hostility of Ellsworth Faris—Sutherland left the University of Chicago for the University of Indiana.

In the period of budgetary restriction that began in 1930 at the University of Chicago, the only lasting hire in the Department of Sociology was that of an anthropologist from Harvard, Lloyd Warner. Hired in 1935, Warner was jointly appointed to the Departments of Sociology and Anthropology, and he contributed to tightening the bonds between the two disciplines.[74]

Trained in Boasian anthropology at Berkeley, Lloyd Warner (1898–1970) had come into contact with Malinowski and Radcliffe-Brown (who replaced Sapir at Chicago in 1931, remaining there until 1937). It was under the influence of the latter, with whom he shared a Durkheimian orientation, that Warner conducted a study on an Australian population, the Murngin, published in 1937, two years following his arrival at Chicago.[75] Recruited by Harvard in 1929 as an instructor in anthropology, Warner came into contact with Elton Mayo, who was then engaged in research on Western Electric. In this period, Warner encouraged Mayo's ambition of applying anthropological methods to a study of American communities. He rapidly abandoned his project of studying Cicero, a suburb of Chicago, arguably because this city seemed too far from an integrated community.[76] With Mayo's support, Warner finally obtained significant funding from the Rockfeller Foundation to study Newburyport (a small city in Massachusetts, which appeared under the pseudonym "Yankee City" in the publications of Warner and his associates). The fieldwork concerning this research was conducted essentially before 1934, but the publication of the different volumes that ensured Warner's reputation stretched from 1941 to 1959.[77]

From the middle of the 1930s, Warner found himself at the center of a vast program of studies focusing on diverse communities that was conducted by a group of collaborators, for the most part his former students at Harvard. Burleigh Gardner and Allison and Mary Davis studied the black and white communities of the city of Natchez, Mississippi, starting in 1934, thanks to funding from the Works Progress Administration. After 1941, another team studied a small Illinois city, Morris (which appeared under the names

"Jonesville," "Elmtown," etc.). Horace Cayton (a former student of Park) and Saint Clair Drake (a former student of Allison Davis) led a series of studies on the black neighborhoods of Chicago.[78] One of the principal innovations introduced by the study of "Yankee City" and its extensions relates to the attention paid to the system of social classes—although the sociological studies of the immediately previous period (with the exception of those of Lynd) had paid, as we have seen, little attention to this. Warner's success among sociologists had an ambiguous form, arguably related to his institutional affiliation with anthropology: reviews of his books in the major journals were frequently reserved. But on the other hand, after 1945 sociologists accorded a much greater importance to class differences than they had previously. Other studies inspired by Warner had more immediate practical ends, such as those that focused on the effects of a middle-class environment on the education of working-class children.[79]

At the University of Chicago, Warner was less involved in the activities of the departments to which he was appointed than in those of different interdisciplinary committees, such as the Committee on Human Development and the Committee on Human Relations in Industry. He left the University of Chicago in 1959 for Michigan State University.

In 1947, the Department of Sociology recruited the demographer Philip Hauser (1909–1994; PhD in 1938), who had been the student of Ogburn and an instructor in the department between 1933 and 1937 before becoming the assistant to the director of the national census in 1940. Administratively enterprising, supported by Wirth and Blumer, Hauser gave new energy to ecological and demographic studies based on census data. Under his patronage—perhaps partially because of his tense relationships with Hughes, Warner, and Riesman—researchers interested in the ecological order and those interested in the moral order (to employ the then-antiquated terminology of Park) contributed to the separation.

From 1935 to 1952, a certain number of researchers temporarily offered a course in sociology, and some of them were mentioned in student testimonies of the period. Between 1946 and 1958, the department regularly used the services of Clifford Shaw, who led the research department of the Institute for Juvenile Research, for which some doctoral students did contract work (see chapter 7). Less regularly, between 1940 and 1956, Joseph Lohman, a former student of the department who pursued a political career while remaining on the fringes of the academic world, taught some courses in which he used his direct knowledge of municipal affairs, the police, and crime (see chapter 7).[80] The Department of Sociology provisionally had recourse to the services of several graduates from the previous period: Herbert Goldhammer (1907; PhD in 1938) between 1946 and

1948; Anselm Strauss (1916–1996; PhD in 1944) from 1954 to 1958; Tamostsu Shibutani (1920; PhD in 1948) from 1948–1951; Albert Riess (1922; PhD in 1949) from 1947 to 1952. Some graduate students also took on teaching duties in the college after 1945 or served as assistants at one or another of the tenured faculty. This was the case, at the end of the 1940s, for Donald Roy, Buford Junker, Harvey Smith, David Solomon, Louis Kriesberg, and Joseph Gusfield.[81]

To the sociologists in the Department of Sociology it is also necessary to add those who taught at the college or who, participating in one or another of the interdisciplinary committees, were later integrated into the Department of Sociology. This was the case, as we have seen, for Edward Shils, who was integrated into the department in 1957, and for David Riesman, recruited as a professor of social sciences by the college in 1946, who was integrated into the department in 1954. His relationships with the sociologists of the East Coast (and especially of Columbia) made Riesman one of the intermediaries for the department's recruitment of young sociologists trained in the entourage of Lazarsfeld at the Bureau of Applied Research.

From the middle of the 1940s, the evolutions in the orientation of American sociology were clearly felt at the University of Chicago. One of the first signs was the association with the university, in 1947, of one of the major organizations conducting opinion surveys, the National Opinion Research Center (NORC), whose research directors became increasingly associated with the Department of Sociology—though not without reticence on the part of the department professors.

NORC is a nonprofit organization whose resources principally come from contracts made with the government, as its founder did not want to compete with Gallup.[82] The official mission of NORC is to measure public opinion in the service of public interest. Founded in 1941 and initially based at the University of Denver, NORC above all worked throughout the war for the federal government. After a negotiation, it was moved in 1947 to the University of Chicago, with the support of Louis Wirth and a group of university leaders. Its director, Clyde Hart, was a former student of the University of Chicago. From the start, NORC participated in a project a university interdisciplinary program affiliated with three departments (psychology, sociology, and political science) that focused on a then-fashionable subject: the study of mass communications and public opinion. A seminar was organized in March 1949 with the participation of Bernard Berelson, a former associate of Lazarsfeld. At the beginning, NORC remained somewhat removed from the departments in its purview: in 1947–1948, it was impossible to find an academic methodologist and statistician who was inclined to divide his time between NORC and the Department of Sociology.[83] After 1955, the relationship between NORC and the department was closer, and four NORC members offered courses in the department that year. Some of the young sociologists trained by Lazarsfeld and recruited by the sociology department in this period conducted research within the framework of NORC. However, the organization also engaged PhD students belonging to the circles of Hughes and Warner, who, for their own research, sometimes used an ethnographic approach.

One decisive change to which NORC, a research organization whose activities took place on a national stage, contributed relates to the environment in which sociologists' research and professional activities occurred from then on. In various ways, the activities of Blumer, Wirth, and Hughes (who maintained regular contact with Germany and Canada), like those of Warner and the sociologists recruited by the university after 1945, fit more on a national stage, or even international, than that of the city of Chicago and its surroundings. If there were still an appreciable number of dissertations that were based on research conducted in the city, this was a result more of immediate access than it was a systematic use of Chicago as a laboratory: for example, the physicians studied in the dissertation of Oswald Hall in 1944 were from Providence and not Chicago. For some of the new objects of study, such as work and the professions, Chicago did not have the particular characteristics that would make it a privileged space, as had been the case for contacts between ethnic groups or urban development over the course of the preceding period. For the most part, the city of Chicago was no longer the field of research for students in the department. For Hughes, Riesman, and Warner, Kansas City was from 1951 a privileged field; there they found a foundation that served as a sponsor (Community Studies) and sometimes-adequate points of entry.

The transformation of the environment of the activities of sociologists was rather related to the institutionalization of sociology, which had become an academic discipline with its own internal norms of success. These had a much greater importance for careers than had been the case during the 1920s: after 1945, all of the Chicago sociologists who aspired to national recognition addressed themselves to an organized world, with its major journals, its instruments of internal recognition (such as election to official functions of the American Sociological Society), and its funding situation. Consequently, the involvement of sociologists in local affairs declined, although Wirth was an exception.

Undoubtedly, in the 1950s the relationship between the university and its neighbors was also too strained to encourage sociologists to make use of the surrounding environment as a laboratory. The African American neighborhood close to the university essentially directly abutted it. The academic community that inhabited the neighborhood (Hyde Park) felt itself to be menaced by increasing criminality and the advancement of the black ghetto. The university actively intervened to maintain favorable conditions for a middle-class lifestyle, necessary to retain academics and students.[84] With other elements coming into play, like the acceptance of black patients at the university hospital, this intervention incited conflicts in the academic community and agitation regarding the problems of race relations and the question of civil rights.[85]

1952 marked the beginning of a complete overhaul of staff in the sociology department and the beginning of the erasure of the heirs of the tradition of Thomas and Park. That year, in effect, Burgess and Ogburn retired, Wirth died suddenly, and Blumer was recruited as the chair of the Department of Sociology at Berkeley. Over several years, in the eyes of the university administrators, the Department of Sociology had lost its previous stature and appeared to be undergoing a crisis. The administrators showed scarcely any sympathy for a department that was not now as fashionable as those of Columbia and Harvard. Burgess and Ogburn were at the end of their careers, and the professors of the following generation maintained a somewhat conflictual relationship—Warner and Hughes in opposition to Wirth and Blumer. The instructors of the college kept some distance from the department, as did the NORC researchers. In this ensemble of conflicts, the situation of the youngest, untenured instructors was not comfortable: many of them were not awarded tenure at the end of their contracts, including Nelson Foote and Anselm Strauss. In order to recover its lost preeminence, the department made various attempts to recruit new professors, on the initiative of the university administration rather than that of the department itself. In 1949–1950, the Department of Sociology offered positions to Merton and Lazarsfeld, the two most prominent Columbia sociologists.[86] It was in this situation of chronic crisis and with a grant from the Ford Foundation that the department organized, over the course of the academic year 1951–1952, a seminar on the state of sociology, its instruction, and the place of the Department of Sociology at the University of Chicago.

As Abbott and Gaziano have shown through their insistence on the complexity of conceptions of the disciplines faculty held during this period, the early 1950s cannot be understood as the triumph of quantitative sociology (based on the statistical analysis of survey questionnaires) over qualitative sociology (based on fieldwork)—an interpretation that has been often maintained.[87] An analysis of the accounts of this year-long seminar, which brought together professors from the Department of Sociology for an overall assessment of the discipline, makes it seem that the principal adversary for both camps—whether they were oriented toward ethnographic methods or statistical approaches—was theory, in the sense espoused by Parsons (which had, to the contrary, been appreciated by the president of the university and a group of the professors of the college).[88]

The personal relationships between the different protagonists of this seminar seem rather bitter in this period, which should not be surprising inside a community in which one group of members shared a rather long history. For example, on the occasion of Hughes's nomination as chair of the department in 1950, Wirth wrote to Blumer: "I fear that the compromise result of the impasse will be the ultimate selection of Everett as chairman, something very unfortunate in my judgment since he is not qualified by ability, scholarship or student's respect to fill the position."[89] Various dividing lines—political orientations, differences in social origin, and manners (some were deemed rude or coarse by their colleagues)—were equally or more important than similarities in intellectual orientation.[90] In this situation of chronic conflicts, the administrators of the university found themselves frequently in the position of arbitrators. The seminar of 1951–1952 revealed the diversity of positions adopted regarding research and the range of variations with regard to the sociology of Park. These debates also illustrate the fact that, in the social sciences, the intellectual integration of a group of researchers depends on many other things besides the acceptance of a small set of principles.

Over the following years, the orientation of the department took a new direction, a result of both the advancing age of the sociologists recruited in the 1930s and the ongoing transformations in American sociology. No instructor close to the tradition of social psychology represented by Blumer or with a bent toward the ethnographic approach was tenured. In 1950, however, the department hired a statistical methodologist trained at Princeton, Leo Goodman, and, partly through the intervention of Riesman, three young researchers trained in the type of research developed at the Bureau of Applied Research at Columbia: Peter Blau (in 1954), Peter Rossi (in 1956), and James Coleman (in 1957). At the end of a process marked by the alignment of circumstances and by the interventions of the university administration, the rupture with the heirs of the Pragmatic tradition had almost died out when Hughes accepted, in 1961, the offer to found a new doctoral program at Brandeis University (near Boston). At this moment, it was the use (or lack thereof) of statistical methods that constituted the principal fault line between the sociologists of the Chicago sociology department. The ecological approach used by the demographers in Hauser's circle was henceforth completely separate from the ethnographic approach, and its practitioners consisted, with those performing survey research trained at Columbia and working at NORC, of almost the totality of sociologists on the faculty of the University of Chicago. Those utilizing an ethnographic approach thought this demoralizing and felt themselves to be in such a minority that many of the doctoral students supervised by Hughes and Warner followed them to their new universities.

Nevertheless, shortly after Hughes's departure, Morris Janowitz, who had obtained a PhD in sociology at the University of Chicago in 1948, was recruited there. Although his own work was not in line with the tradition founded by Thomas and Park, he established himself over the following years as a representative of this tradition, encouraging new editions of some of its classic texts and at one point financially supporting the production of a biography of Park by Raushenbush. He also supervised many dissertations based on thorough fieldwork.

THE STUDENTS OF THE YEARS 1945–1955

As during the First World War, the number of students in the Department of Sociology declined during the Second, but the number of dissertations completed did not, with an average of five per year between 1940 and 1944 compared with four per year in the preceding years. Some professors, like Samuel Stouffer and Herbert Blumer, were also temporarily absent from the university. At the end of the war, it again saw significant activity, with the arrival of an unprecedented influx of students. The GI Bill, which offered relatively substantial scholarships, essentially permitted a cohort of demobilized soldiers, often older than the majority of students, to begin or resume higher education. Barracks were erected close to the university to lodge them, and some veterans lived there with their families. Retrospective accounts of the students of this period describe a vibrant intellectual community in terms that are not without resemblance to those used by the sociologists of the 1920s.[91]

Many doctoral students completing degrees in sociology also taught at the same time in the university's college or different Chicago colleges. Between six and ten scholarships were awarded each year to doctoral students; other students were employed for short-term research contracts, as much by NORC as by the consulting company directed by Burleigh Gardner, an associate of Warner, Social Research Inc. (see chapter 6), and in different research centers within the university or at the Institute for Juvenile Research (see chapter 7).

The characteristics of these sociology students were rather different from those of students of the preceding generation: scarcely any were the children of Protestant pastors of the Midwest. More so than thirty years earlier, there were students with urban origins, sometimes from the East Coast. A significant proportion were Jewish—as was the case for the university as a whole, where the proportion of Jews reached around 30 percent after 1930.[92] Some were from working-class origins, such as Julius Roth or Donald Roy, while others were sons of wealthy small businessmen, such as Eliot Freidson or Louis Kriesberg. For some of those who benefited from the GI Bill, sociology was a second choice of studies, sometimes after an orientation toward the sciences or medicine. Among those who pursued doctorates figured several non-Americans and a small group of Canadians (including Oswald Hall and Erving Goffman), who frequently came to Chicago because of Hughes's connections with Canada.

The responsibility for directing studies principally fell during this period on fewer than ten permanent professors managing a number of students that rarely fell below two hundred PhD and MA candidates (around thirty MAs were awarded each year). At least during the period in which the workforce was largest, contacts between professors and doctoral students were not always close, nor, for some students, especially satisfying. In 1947, a group of students complained to Burgess about the lack of availability of professors, the rarity of discussions in courses, the lack of course preparation, and the excessive amount of work demanded only to be graded by other students.[93]

Many professors, however, left their marks on the memories and intellectual careers of some students: Wirth for his brilliance; Blumer for his critical vigor; Hughes for his introduction to fieldwork and his course on work and professions, which would produce an ensemble of dissertations and monographs (see chapter 6). For certain students, like Gusfield, participation in instruction in the college under the authority of Riesman was a more important experience than the instruction received in the Department of Sociology.[94]

Students seem to have noticed disagreements within the department more often than agreements. In an early stage, the principal division seems to have set the students in the circle of Warner and Hughes in opposition against those in the circle of Wirth and Blumer.

William Whyte, who belonged to Warner's circle, remarked regarding his dissertation defense in sociology: "In my period at the University of Chicago, students had to consider not only which professors they were working for but also which they were working *against*. If you took your main work with Warner and Hughes, as I did, you had to be prepared to fight off Wirth in your field and thesis examination."[95] The antagonism between Blumer and Hughes seems to have been more moderate. Murray Wax remarked: "While Hughes and Blumer were in the same age cohort and were rivals, they were not enemies. Most of the better students of my generation worked easily with both men. To the extent that the rivalry of Hughes and Blumer became intense, it did not affect their treatment of each other's students."[96] At the end of the 1950s, the antagonisms between partisans of quantitative studies and partisans of the ethnographic approach were undoubtedly livelier, and in 1959 a candidate supported by Hughes was reproached for trying to set sociology back to the 1920s by doing process studies.[97]

The policy implemented by Hutchins until his departure in 1950, as well as the evolution of the discipline, as we have seen, increasingly eroded the importance of the departments as locations of doctoral training. Not only did certain dissertations and theses depend on the previously mentioned interdisciplinary committees, but they were prepared in the framework of specialized research centers, centered around one or two professors, and physically scattered around the university, which reinforced the cloistering of fields and methodological specializations. Research into the family was thus localized to the Family Center, founded by Burgess; those based on survey questionnaires were based at NORC (whose tenured researchers were affiliated with the department). After 1947, some research in urban ecology was conducted at the Chicago Community Inventory (directed by Hauser) and, after 1954, at the Population Research and Training Center. This situation did not, however, always lead to definitive specialization in terms of research methods or intellectual orientation: some researchers, after a dissertation on a subject in social psychology (like Julius Roth) or based on a statistical approach, later turned toward fieldwork.

The subjects of dissertations of the years 1945–1960 focused on more diverse areas than did those of the preceding period. Dissertations on groups and ethnic relations remained numerous, however. Many dissertations demonstrating the influence of Blumer and, later, that of the former students of Lazarsfeld and of NORC, focused on collective behaviors and mass media. Dissertations on the family, crime, and elderly people testify to the prolonged involvement of Burgess in these areas. Others, on the consequences of technical progress, were clearly inspired by Ogburn. Three new areas took on importance: the study of work, almost ignored in the 1920s, now became well represented. Themes ranged from labor to management, from the liberal professions to the police, and passed through the general study of the active population, as well as of unions, which served as the subject of many dissertations; one dissertation also focused on the great industrial family, the Du Ponts of Nemours.[98] Dissertations on religious and educational institutions, two sectors represented among the subjects addressed during the previous period, were now complemented by dissertations on the army in the immediate postwar period and, a little later, on the hospital and the medical sector—an area for which research funding would become important after the beginning of the 1950s. Finally, demographic studies occupied a rising place following the recruitment of Hauser.[99]

This diversification of subjects was, however, less specific to Chicago than to American sociology as a whole in this period. A striking point is, as has been already noted, the declining importance of work focusing on the city of Chicago: it was no longer the laboratory that it had been for the previous generation. The new themes of study no longer led to the same deeply rooted territoriality of subjects any more than they encouraged new methods of data collection.

CONCLUSION

The evolution that has just been described can be interpreted as the end, by rupture, of the tradition born in the Department of Sociology at Chicago. This is what the declining visibility of the principal sociologists of the generation born around 1900 and the increasing funding that seemed to benefit other approaches, especially those based on statistical techniques, seems to suggest. The success of the book on social mobility published in 1967 by Peter Blau (one of the sociologists trained at Columbia and recruited by the University of Chicago) and Otis Duncan (a former student of Ogburn at the University of Chicago), which served as a model of this type of study, might confirm this interpretation. But one can also find between 1950 and 1970 the publication of a body of research conducted by sociologists trained during the 1940s and 1950s, despite their dispersion, who had a place (or would later have a place) within the intellectual genealogy of the Chicago sociologists under whom they had studied.

These studies, which are certainly less thematically unified than the monographs of the preceding period, resulted in dissertations and articles as well as, sometimes after a long delay and with considerable revision, books. This was the case for the books by William Westley on police, by Joseph Gusfield on the temperance movement, by Erving Goffman on the study of public relationships, by Fred Davis on the familial experience of poliomyelitis, by Tamotsu Shibutani on the propagation of rumors, and by Alfred Lindesmith on the consumption of opium, all of which acquired lasting reputations in their respective specialized areas of research.[100] Other work by researchers trained at Chicago, which did not turn into dissertations, developed the same assortment of ideas, including that of Eliot Friedson on medicine, Julius Roth and Anselm Strauss on hospital treatments, and Murray and Rosalie Wax on education on Indian reservations.[101] It is based on some of these works that, today, a Second Chicago School tends to be defined—at the cost, yet again, of a largely arbitrary selection among works and researchers.

In the two first chapters of the second part of this book, the reader will find an overview of the intellectual intermediaries between some of these works and those that preceded them.

PART II

Paths of Research

The second part of this book is dedicated to examining the contributions of sociologists connected to the Chicago tradition in different areas of research. It takes the form of essays that are partly independent from each other. By using the word "essay" to designate the chapters of this second part, I hope to draw attention to the fact that none of them covers all aspects useful for understanding the works examined, nor does any cover the entirety of the work of Chicago researchers in the area under consideration. The choice of areas, studies, and factors taken into account is consequently partly arbitrary, as are the connections between them. I am, however, convinced that other paths would lead to similar conclusions concerning the Chicago tradition as a whole.

Each of these essays penetrates inside the researchers' works, and sometimes their offices and laboratories, to probe the relationship between the substance of these studies and aspects of the contexts within which they appeared. The essays also raise questions about continuity and discontinuity in successive approaches to the same type of phenomena, as well as the transmissions of analytical schemes from one subfield to another and the transformations in the use of evidentiary methods and writing styles. The choice of topics selected, and of the works examined within them, is, as I have just said, partly arbitrary, although it became clear that certain topics were indispensable. I mention here some of the possibilities that were considered but not included.

If we were to recognize the defining characteristic of the preoccupations of Park—whose importance as a source of inspiration for the following generation appeared more and more striking to me as my investigations progressed—an examination of studies on collective behavior, and especially on the press and methods of mass communication, would have been all the more justified, as previous books about the Chicago tradition have left this theme unexplored.[1] It would have been necessary to depart here from Park and Blumer and to examine, among the studies published by the post-war generation, that of Tamotsu Shibutani, of Kurt Lang, and of Orrin Klapp, since the relative isolation of this domain with respect to the rest of American sociology, linked to market characteristics, rendered these names relatively less visible.

Although I have omitted discussion of these studies with some regret, I never, to the contrary, imagined that I would examine the debates and publications generated by the reinterpretations of the analyses of Mead, as well as by the network of studies that from the end of the 1960s were placed under the banner of symbolic interactionism. These studies were not based on a common empirical foundation, and furthermore there were many books devoted to this theme, which benefited from greater visibility after the creation of the journal *Symbolic Interaction*.[2]

The development of cities, the spatial distribution of different activities and populations, and urban ways of life are three other topics that could have been the object of deep examination. The complex threads connecting Robert Park, Ernest Burgess, and Roderick McKenzie (or even William Ogburn) to Otis Duncan on the one hand, and, on the other, those connecting Robert Park, Louis Wirth, and the now almost-forgotten Albert Blumenthal to Erving Goffman, Gregory Stone, and perhaps Herbert Gans could have been traced. The rupture in the use of Park's ecological perspective has been finely analyzed.[3] While some of these works continued to serve as references in the study of cities, they did so for social geographers much more than for sociologists. But the essential justification for the omission of studies on the city lies in the lack of unity in the field and on the correlated diversity of intellectual contacts between the different lineages that I have just mentioned.

A survey of research on the family and of the use of statistics for purposes of prediction would permit more importance to be accorded to Ernest Burgess. This could also contribute to correcting the dearth of attention paid to his work by earlier studies, as noted by others. Its embeddedness within the current that leads in a direct line to more recent approaches is partly responsible for the relative obscurity of Burgess's work: it is rendered more dated, and in some ways more obsolete, by the very fact that it sometimes had almost direct continuations.

An essay could also have been devoted to the development of inductive approaches in the construction of general analytical schemes, as well as to reflection on these approaches, by giving a more prominent position to Alfred Lindesmith and Anselm Strauss.

Organizing part II by generation would have facilitated comparing the research of the 1930s with the entire corpus of works of the generation trained at the University of Chicago after the Second World War, including Howard Becker, Eliot Friedson, Herbert Gans, Erving Goffman, Joseph Gusfield, Fred Davis, Julius Roth, Donald Roy, Gregory Stone, Murray Wax, and more, to whom it would have been necessary to add, from the preceding generation, Alfred Lindesmith, Anselm Strauss, Tamotsu Shibutani, and Kirson Weinberg.[4] Another acceptable division would have led to the collective examination of the studies on medicine and the hospital during the 1950s and 1960s, which would have permitted greater attention to be accorded to Erving Goffman and, again, to Anselm Strauss. It would also have been possible to point out the internal diversity of works from this second generation, perhaps even more striking than that of the works of the first generation, and to show its relationship with the increased diversification that resulted from the integration of the social sciences into American society.

Four of the five themes selected here—fieldwork, work and institutions, race relations, and crime—are directly justified by their importance to research in the Chicago tradition. The fifth—an examination of work situated on the margins of this tradition—illustrates an approach largely practiced by some Chicago sociologists, such as Hughes. The part of chapter 9 devoted to Nels Anderson constitutes an investigation into ways of reading minor classics in sociology; the part that focuses on Donald Roy involves an inquiry into the relationship between personal affinities and research orientation.

Each of the chapters in this part of the book is focalized on one or a few particular aspects; what is sometimes left out but appears in other chapters should not be considered secondary. However, the first essay, devoted to the sociology of work and to fieldwork, is indispensable for the comprehension of what follows: it would have been placed in the first part if I had not feared lending credence to the idea that Hughes's essays on work and institutions had occupied a position comparable to Park's essays on the city or on race relations during the previous period—which is clearly not historically accurate.

6

Hughes, Blumer, Studies on Work and Institutions, and Fieldwork

*Students in the department of Chicago in the 1950s thought of themselves
as Hughes students or Blumer students, but not both. Most people learned,
some sooner than others, that we were almost always both.*

—Howard S. Becker[1]

When Hughes left the University of Chicago for Brandeis in 1961, it would certainly have seemed preposterous to the majority of observers of American sociology to consider his contribution over the course of the twenty preceding years as constituting an important moment and a source of lasting inspiration for sociological studies; the comparison with Herbert Blumer, who at that point was even less visible than Hughes and whose publications remained scattered, would have only increased the strangeness of such a judgment. The following years would, however, see a progressive reevaluation of the contributions of Hughes and Blumer, which from the 1950s onward accompanied the rising reputations of many of their former students, notably Erving Goffman and Howard Becker, both of whom were authors of books that were widely read and highly esteemed among sociologists and beyond. Some of the stages of this resurrection—or, rather, this rewriting of the past that resulted in the idea of a Second Chicago School[2]—are evident: within the discipline were Robert Faris's book on the research of the 1920s and 1930s,[3] as well as the 1962 publication of a collection of essays and research reports edited by Arnold Rose. This collection included contributions from representatives of all then-active generations, from Ernest Burgess (born in 1886) to Howard S. Becker (born in 1928); passing through Everett Hughes, Herbert Blumer, Franklin Frazier, and Ruth Cavan for the second generation; and Anselm Strauss, Tamotsu Shibutani, Erving Goffman, Gregory Stone, Herbert Gans, Eliot Friedson, and Julius Roth for the last.[4] Outside of the discipline, the academic (and ethical) crisis in the United States at the end of the 1960s would, among other things, contribute to rendering sociology as practiced by researchers at Columbia and Harvard unfashionable, and, by contrast, to drawing attention to (among other things) the ethnographic approach. The publication of a series of books based on this approach—notably those by Erving Goffman, Howard Becker's *Outsiders*, and the monographs included in the series edited after 1964 by Becker at Aldine—could be read as extensions of the work published in the sociological series that Burgess, Faris, and Park had edited for the University of Chicago Press.[5] And, from the mid-1960s, the publication in a new series, edited by Morris Janowitz at the University of Chicago Press, of revised editions of a collection of books would render newly accessible some of the classic texts of Thomas, Mead, Park, Burgess, Wirth, Frazier, and so on.

Among other factors facilitating the reappearance of the visibility of this research tradition should be mentioned the 1951 creation of the Society for the Study of Social Problems, of which Burgess and Blumer were the first and third presidents, and in which could be found a subset of the sociologists who spent time at the University of Chicago.[6] In addition to this was the development of undergraduate instruction in sociology in the United States, which created a new audience for easily accessible books on subjects that were interesting to students. New academic centers were also created in California; these employed some researchers trained at Chicago over the preceding years, including some of those who considered themselves to some degree the students of Hughes or Blumer. A sort of intellectual movement emerged at the end of the 1960s, bringing together both advanced students and young instructors from new Californian centers to gather around a core of mid-career researchers. In 1971 it produced the journal *Urban Life and Culture*, the editorial committee of which included Blumer and Hughes, and in 1974 it produced the Society for the Study of Symbolic Interaction (SSSI), which grew up around Gregory Stone, a sociologist trained at the University of Chicago in the early 1950s.[7]

One of the events that contributed to launching this movement was the conference organized in September 1969 on the fringes of the annual meeting of the American Sociological Society by a group of young Californian sociologists, many of whom were former students of Blumer and Goffman and inclined toward research in urban ethnography. In a discussion before an audience that was already interested in the Chicago School, Hughes and Blumer evoked their memories of the 1930s through the 1950s. A transcription of this discussion was published eleven years later, suggesting that interest in this past was lasting.[8] We could also mention the collections of studies in honor of Hughes and Blumer published in 1968 and 1970, to which their former associates, both friends and students, contributed, also attesting to the clear division between these two categories.[9] Since the beginning of the 1960s, a series of essays has asserted the unity of this group of works and researchers by foregrounding a small, central nucleus of common ideas or orientations.[10] Most often, emphasis is placed on Meadian heritage and on the label "interactionist," which had been invented by Blumer in 1937 but was not in use before the beginning of the 1960s.

> With this term, Blumer hoped to designate the "view of original nature of human beings" in which "the development of the infant into childhood and adulthood is fundamentally a matter of forming organized or concerted activity in place of its previous random activity, and of channelizing its impulses and giving them goals or objectives."[11] In 1960, usage of this label was infrequent and, when Irwin Deutscher, who collaborated in the preparation of the Arnold Rose collection, asked what the label meant, "[Rose's] face flushed as he angrily shouted, 'It is what they do at Chicago!' "[12] The usage of the terms "interactionism" and "Chicago School" in textbooks such as Don Martindale's, and in the essays cited below, arguably contributed more to the identification and the visibility of this current than the works of sociologists allegedly connected to it did. We might also remark upon the variability of rankings: Martindale includes not Park but rather Cassirer under the heading "Interactionism," and describes Park as a "neo-Kantian."

I shall not further elaborate upon the analysis of this construction of a tradition, but instead examine here only some of the elements upon which it is based and to which it has given a new meaning: principally the studies on work and institutions conducted in the circle of Hughes, the development and transmission of an expertise in fieldwork, and Blumer's critical approach to the perspectives and approaches used in prominent sociological studies after 1945.

HUGHES, BLUMER, AND RESEARCH ON WORK AND INSTITUTIONS

When Hughes returned to the University of Chicago after his time at McGill University, he had not, as we have seen, achieved any particular renown. He had published only a few articles pulled from his dissertation and his ongoing research on Canada.[13] From 1942, having completed the book that resulted from these articles, he undertook a new study on a subject of contemporary importance: the problems posed by the ongoing introduction of black workers into major industry, which was also connected to one of the themes of the book that he had just completed.

> The entry of the United States into the Second World War was accompanied by a sudden reversal in the employment situation. The elevated level of unemployment that had persisted until the end of the 1930s was suddenly replaced, with the military deployment of a significant portion of men, by a relative lack of manpower in industry: the unemployment rate fell from 9.3 percent of the active population in 1940 to 1.3 percent at its lowest point in 1944. New types of workers—women and African Americans—also made their entrance into businesses that had not previously hired from these categories.
>
> Other aspects of labor relations saw significant transformations during this period. Since 1933, union activities had progressed, especially among semi-skilled workers. Starting in 1938, unions became involved in a system of collective negotiation with management and with the Roosevelt administration.[14] The year 1941 was marked by numerous strikes and the establishment of a system of arbitrage concerning war manufacturing: this rendered strikes and layoffs difficult and caused salary freezes, but sometimes ensured union membership. (Unionization was quasi-obligatory in certain factories.)
>
> In the 1940s, the problems of labor, unions, and their relations with management and the federal government thus occupied a much more central place on the public stage than they had over the course of the preceding twenty years.

By studying the integration of black workers into the workforce of big industry, Hughes found a foothold in what was not only a question of contemporary importance but also, for sociologists, a new field of research. We shall see that Hughes's research in fact developed on the margins of one of the prominent research currents of the period, patronized by certain businesses and oriented toward practical application. It is in reference to this context that we can appreciate the originality of Hughes's contribution of to the study of work.[15]

As has been indicated regarding the University of Chicago, before 1914 the study of work was an area almost completely reserved for economists. During the First World War, however, psychologists began to invest in becoming involved in the measure of aptitudes of workers. This double disciplinary origin in economics and psychology can be traced for the studies, affiliated with the Graduate

School of Business Administration at Harvard, that were conducted in Western Electric's Hawthorne factory in the Chicago suburbs.

From 1928, the principal inspiration behind these studies was Elton Mayo (1880–1949).[16] After having encountered some difficulties in finding an academic position in the United States, Mayo, an Australian philosopher, made his way, as previously mentioned, into the circle of protégés of the administrators of the Rockefeller foundations. He was finally hired by Harvard's Graduate Business School and was integrated into the laboratory for studying fatigue, directed by the biochemist Lawrence Henderson. Shortly thereafter, in 1928, Mayo was introduced by his mentors to the studies that had been ongoing for four years at the Hawthorne Western Electric factory. Although the anthropologist Lloyd Warner was associated with these studies during the 1930s, no sociologist appears among Mayo's associates. The book that made the results of these studies known to sociologists, written by Fritz Roethlisberger, a philosopher who taught at Harvard Business School, and William Dickson, an economist employed by Western Electric, was not published until 1939. One of the principal results of this research lay, we should recall, in the discovery that the behavior of workers—and especially their activities at work—is not only defined by their individual aptitudes and their personal economic interests, but also depends upon their integration into groups developing an organization unto themselves, and upon the relationships these groups had with management. This research thus cast doubt on the efficacy of aptitude tests upon hiring, which were recommended by psychologists, and of payment based on performance, which was recommended by the majority of economists.

Outside these studies, there were no more than a few scattered works whose lines of questioning could be incorporated into a sociological perspective on work: those of George Bakke at Yale or Mary Van Kleek, whose studies, a distant avatar incarnation of the Pittsburgh Survey, were funded by the Russell Sage Foundation.

The University of Chicago was the first to organize a research program in the field of work in which sociologists, anthropologists, economists, and geographers participated, with the 1943 creation of the Committee on Human Relations in Industry.[17] This establishment was followed by that of the Industrial Relations Center in 1945 and, the following year, of the Committee on Industrial Relations, with which professors from the Business School of the University and, among the sociologists, Ogburn, Wirth, Warner, and Hughes were affiliated.[18] After the end of the war, other universities—Cornell and Yale in 1945, the University of Michigan in 1947, and so on—also organized research or doctoral programs in this area, with the participation of sociologists and social psychologists.[19] In 1948, about thirty universities had set up research centers on industrial relations, a label that also covered unions.[20] The term "industrial sociology" appeared in the programs of the American Sociological Society in 1946. Papers on this theme were presented in different sessions at the first meeting of the year, in Cleveland.[21] For the second meeting of the year, in Chicago, the anthropologist Conrad Arensberg, a former student of Warner, was responsible for organizing a session that took the term as its title.[22] The term was in common usage in the following years, and many articles written by prominent sociologists, or those on the path toward becoming prominent (George Homans, Wilbert Moore, etc.), were published in the two major sociology journals. The specialization was also described as promising by Parsons and Barber in a 1948 article taking stock of advances in sociology over the years 1941–1946.[23] It is apparent that the Chicago researchers occupied an eminent position in industrial sociology and that recognition of this new specialization was rapid.

The inspiring forces behind the Committee on Human Relations in Industry established at the University of Chicago were Lloyd Warner and Burleigh Gardner, who had been associated with the second phase of research at Hawthorne.[24] Everett Hughes was the only sociologist among the founders of the Committee, but he was joined the following year by William Whyte (1917–1999), a former Harvard student and a protégé of Warner who had recently completed a study on an Italian American neighborhood in Boston, which resulted in *Street Corner Society*.

After having worked at Hawthorne for five years, Burleigh Gardner (1902–1985), a Harvard-trained anthropologist who had been one of the main authors of the study on Natchez inspired by Warner, became a business consultant and developed relationships in the executive world.[25] The Business School of the University of Chicago offered him a full-time job in 1942, after he successfully taught a night class to a mix of management-level businessmen and anthropology students.

The objective initially assigned to the Committee on Human Relations in Industry was not exclusively the study of problems of work.[26] First, it offered to conduct studies for clients found by Gardner—namely, six large companies, to which the mail-order company Sears Roebuck was soon added. Each of these companies would be offered the analysis of a problem that interested them: to respond to questions Sears Roebuck had regarding its commercial policy, for example, Warner gave a series of lectures on social class.

The initial budget of the Committee on Human Relations in Industry was thin, and it began by organizing meetings between academics and upper management in which "semi-philosophical" discussions would take place, according to a statement by Whyte. An interview study was undertaken regarding the integration of workers into their neighborhoods. The companies that funded the Committee on Human Relations in Industry did not facilitate researchers' access to their field of study: management feared that if tension was high in the factories, the arrival of researchers would exacerbate things and, if the situation was relaxed, conditions would deteriorate. Finally, the vice president of a large metallurgical company deemed that the situation had become so tense in one of his Chicago-based factories that the presence of researchers could not make things any worse. Thus, he approached Gardner, who was interested in problems encountered by hiring African Americans in the industry, to propose that he enter this factory. During the following years, members of the Committee on Human Relations in Industry and some PhD students belonging to the circles of Warner and Hughes who worked on related subjects enjoyed direct access to certain factories; some of these, including Donald Roy and Melville Dalton, were themselves employed by the companies that they studied.

Gardner, who in 1943 was secretary of the Committee on Human Relations in Industry, left his academic position in 1946 to found a research company aimed at businesses, Social Research Inc., for which Warner served as consultant.[27] Social Research Inc. provided temporary employment to a certain number of students from the circle of Warner and Hughes in the course of their doctoral studies, such as Buford Junker, Erving Goffman, and more. Even if they only secured partial research funding, the Committee on Human Relations in Industry and Social Research Inc. offered these students an environment favorable to the development of research on work and businesses.

The first sociological studies sponsored by the Committee on Human Relations in Industry—those of Whyte on the restaurant industry,[28] Warner and Low on a company in Newburyport,[29] and Hughes on the consequences of hiring African American manpower in industry—have clear, non-negligible differences from the research conducted at Hawthorne.[30] Unlike Mayo and his associates, the researchers of the Committee on Human Relations in Industry were attentive to the implications of the integration of businesses into the surrounding society, as well as to the workers' diversity of social identities and objectives pursued; they also no longer neglected unions (although it was not possible to do so in 1945).

Within the framework of the research of the Committee on Human Relations in Industry, Hughes gathered, or had gathered, biographical interviews on laborers, with a specific interest in those who, treated as black in their neighborhoods, passed for white at work.[31] He also conducted observations in workshops.

In one of the three articles that resulted from this research—his only publication to feature a research report—Hughes studied the consequences of the introduction of new types of workers into different workshops, mainly the setting forth of complex forms taken by the solidarity of ethnic groups at work.[32] At this point, Hughes's orientation was clearly influenced by that of his associates in the Committee, at least in terms of which aspects merited being studied. In a preparatory note for a course that he offered regarding race relations in industry, he refers to Burleigh Gardner, Lloyd Warner, and Allison Davis as the first formulators of the three research directions that he was planning to develop: the consequences of the existence of an informal organization of workers opposed to the organization put in place by management; the consequences of the integration of workers in a community and in unions; finally, the consequences of social and ethnic diversity, as well as of the variety of goals pursued by workers.[33] It was, according to Hughes, on the occasion of this study that he discovered the fruitfulness of paying attention to the behavior of workers on the bottom of the social hierarchy, as well as the importance of phenomena linked to status.[34]

Hughes was not, on the other hand, interested in applications of his research in the same way as some researchers, like Gardner and Whyte, who had become members of the human relations movement aimed at reforming social relations in business.[35] Hughes's perspective, according to what his articles and correspondence from the period suggest, remained essentially similar to that which Park had pursued in other areas: inclined toward the detached comprehension of a segment of social life, but little concerned with providing advice to management or unions. Hughes thus made the only goal of his study on race relations in industry "to quicken the eye of persons who have to deal with such problems, to make them see things which they might overlook."[36] Hughes no longer seems to have been concerned about the difference between his perspective and that shared by the other members of the Committee on Human Relations in Industry. Thus, his involvement in the activities of this committee seems to have corresponded principally to the opportunity to conduct research on a subject then rendered newly accessible, and to borrowing some new ideas that were only indirectly related to the practical orientations of those who had originally formulated them.

Hughes's distance from the human relations movement was probably reinforced by the atmosphere of critical reflection against the work of Mayo and his associates. The reception of these studies on the part of sociologists was initially mixed. The 1940 review in the *American Journal of Sociology* of Roethlisberger and Dickson's book was frankly hostile: it notes the almost total lack of any mention of unions—surprising in the circumstances of that period, but much less so for the period between 1927 and 1929, during which the survey was conducted—and ends with a sarcastic remark about the "new and unexpected" character of the results set forth.[37] Many of the first articles to survey industrial sociology also used a clearly critical tone with regard to studies in that area.[38] One, written by Wilbert Moore, a former student of Parsons,[39] reviews the publications of Mayo and his associates, those of Warner and the researchers of the Committee on Human Relations in Industry, and especially their collective publication, *Industry and Society*. In his article, Moore criticizes the empiricism of their approach and the absence of any theory organizing their investigations. He also underlines the ambiguity of a conception that does no more than repeat that of business executives.

But the most radical critique of research in industrial sociology came from the University of Chicago. An article by Blumer contains a direct attack on the corpus of research in this area: without referring precisely to any single publication, but by alluding to work on the behaviors of laborers in workshops, Blumer reproaches sociologists who study industrial work for committing themselves to a level on which nothing important happens—a critique based on the authority of his experience as a mediator in ironworkers' labor conflicts.[40] According to Blumer, the research neglects the complex web of established relationships and negotiations between business executives and unions. The dynamic, nebulous, and changing character of relations between workers and leadership during the period should be centered in research, according to Blumer, with an emphasis on the levels of industrial sectors and relations between businesses and national unions: "Thus labor relations became increasingly a matter of relationships between gigantic organizations of workers and management, each of which functions through central policy and executive groups."[41]

The formulations adopted by Blumer in his critiques are extremely harsh: he characterizes as a "faddish concern" the development of research in industrial sociology, the attraction of which is based on the expectation of "great and easy rewards," although "such ideas and modes of research are essentially hackneyed, unrealistic, and uninspiring."[42] Although he formulates a relatively positive assessment of the "Harvard group," whose research was conducted "carefully and conscientiously," one of his criticisms focuses on those who are very attentive to questions of status in factories—aimed at Warner and perhaps Hughes—as well as those who focus on the current of human relations in industry—namely Gardner and Whyte.[43] Blumer recommends the usage of observation based on an intimate familiarity with the phenomena studied, but sustains that the nature of the subject necessitates going beyond observation of one company, since it is necessary to understand relationships that exist on many levels:

he compares the observation of relations in one factory with what a soldier can observe on the battlefield, when what he needs to understand is the entirety of a military campaign.[44]

This perspective, which incidentally demonstrates the oversimplifications of the general understanding of Blumer's position and of the symbolic interactionism that became widespread starting in the 1970s, certainly cannot be reduced to an emotional reaction. Some years after the publication of his article, in 1969, Blumer returned to the same point during a debate with Hughes in San Francisco: "I served as chairman of the board of Arbitration for the US Steel Corporation and the Steel Workers of America[45] for some two years where I was placed almost in daily contact with Phillip Murray on one side and with top officials, particularly John Stevens, vice president of US Steel, at the other side, and I was seeing what was going on in this enormously complex relation, full of conflict, between these two groups. And, incidentally, in so doing, I came to recognize the absurdity of the dozens and dozens of schemes that were being concocted by university professors in the area of labor relations because they just didn't have any understanding of what was going on."[46]

The radicalism of Blumer's critique of studies in industrial sociology did not escape the notice of the group of researchers—Buford Junker, Harvey Smith, Melville Dalton, Donald Roy, and more—at Chicago who gathered around William Whyte and performed research on industrial workers. These researchers noted that Blumer thought that the principal factors did not relate to interaction and that questions of status and communication were futile.[47] One of them, Harvey Smith, remarked that he felt that Blumer was passing through a "nihilist phase. Last quarter a student asked him whether he knew of any kind of social research which was being accepted as good job and he said he didn't."[48]

I have found no trace of Hughes's reaction to Blumer's article. A remark Hughes made to Blumer, in the course of a discussion of the Department of Sociology seminar focusing on its orientation during the academic year 1951–1952, suggests that Hughes shared the opinion of some of the students regarding Blumer's methodological nihilism: "I think the impression is quite widely abroad, not that you say that you don't believe in research, but the net effect of what you say is against research."[49]

Hughes's publications on work that resulted from research conducted after his return to Chicago were spread out between 1945 and 1970.[50] They principally consist of essays combining, without any polemical intention, criticism of conventional perspectives with the presentation of his own analytical schemes. These essays rarely cite the empirical studies that nonetheless constitute their foundation. We can, however, easily infer which of them are the subject of Hughes's quick allusions: first of all, his own work on the entrance of African Americans into industry, and some research on ethnic relations in the context of work conducted by PhD students.[51] We also find two other types of study: those inspired by his course on the sociology of occupations at the University of Chicago, and the somewhat later research of Hughes and his associates on medical students and occupations in the medical sector.[52] To these latter ones we can add the (sometimes earlier) research on institutions—a term that Hughes employs, in a manner that is in a sense derived from Sumner, to designate all sorts of establishments with a minimum level of permanence and a more or less specialized staff.

> The unity of Hughes's research on institutions has always been less prominent than his research on occupations, despite the titles of his dissertation, the volume of contributions in his honor, and the principal collection of his essays and his preface to it. In this preface, Hughes indicates that he examines institutions as "enterprises that mobilize people into various offices and capacities."[53] The studies upon which he relies (but to which he makes only a few specific allusions) are dissertations bearing on the establishment of institutes of higher education and religious institutions.[54] The originality of Hughes's perspective in this area relates in part to the fact that the definition he adopts sidesteps the functions filled by the institution studied, thus opening up their empirical study. Alongside the study of the division of work, the study of careers is one of the principal links between studies of work and occupations and studies of institutions.[55]

The year after his return to Chicago, Hughes taught a course on what had been one of the central interests of his dissertation: the study of professions.[56] Although not completely constituting a research subject at the time, high-status professions had at that point begun to garner attention, and Hughes noted in a letter to Ogburn before his return to Chicago that Talcott Parsons had offered a course on this theme at Harvard.[57] Hughes recounted how he had adapted Parsons's course on professions by reacting against the inclinations of his audience:[58] confronted with students' desire to demonstrate that their own chosen field of work (current or future) was or would become a profession (with the positive connotation that the term possesses), Hughes substituted "sociology of work" for the title of the course in order "to overcome to some extent the constant preoccupation with upward mobility of occupations."[59] But he also encouraged his students to study, with the limited resources available to them—that is, through observation and interviews, and possibly through the analysis of archival evidence—the lines of work to which they had access.

> The testimony of Hughes here intersects with that of Julius Roth (and others): "A number of dissertations on occupational groups at the University of Chicago are based entirely or largely on information collected by students who worked at the job they studied without revealing their professional interest to their fellow workers. . . . Some of these people took their jobs mainly to make money to pay tuition and living expenses, and then decided to use the opportunity to collect data for a study of an occupation." Other research would focus not on the occupations of the students themselves but on those of their family members, or simply on occupations that the students had encountered by chance.[60] Not all of the research undertaken led to an MA or a PhD. Hughes encouraged students to choose occupations that were of lower status, or that were marginal rather than prominent, having rapidly acquired the conviction that this type of occupation offered less resistance to analysis and therefore more chances to notice interesting phenomena. However, some of the research that would be lastingly cited focused on well-known professions of middle or elevated status: physicians, lawyers, schoolteachers, nurses.[61] The degree of Hughes's involvement in this work was extremely variable: he inspired the orientation of some studies almost completely,[62] but in other cases he did not.[63]

In 1952, Hughes became editor of the *American Journal of Sociology*. In a special issue of the journal that same year, he published the results of some finished research centered on work—evidently, the publication had moved on from industry, the topic of the special issue published three years earlier.[64] According to it, Hughes had only noticed after some time that the studies on occupations that he had encouraged students to undertake constituted something of a contribution to an "American ethnology."[65]

From 1951, Hughes participated in a body of research on the occupation of nursing on behalf of the American Nurses Association. These studies gave rise to a book, half a report of empirical research and half a summary of studies by other researchers, of which the principal author was Irwin Deutscher.[66] While there were fewer cases in this study than there would be, a little later, in that of medical students, the familiarity Hughes acquired with this profession shone through in many articles. Moreover, Hughes's essays on work often used the perspective of nurses on medical work as a critical element of comparison with the perspective of doctors.

Like the study on nurses, a study on the training of medical students was conducted partly at the University of Kansas, funded by a local foundation that also secured funds for other studies undertaken by the University of Chicago. Hughes recruited Howard Becker, one of his former students, for the study, as well as Blanche Geer, who was then a psychologist, and Anselm Strauss, then an assistant professor in social psychology at the University of Chicago.[67] The study of medical institutions in their various aspects was, starting in the 1950s, a new field opening up to sociologists, owing in particular to funding from the National Institute of Mental Health.[68] Hughes's involvement with this research subject was, again, probably due to blind chance. He had set himself to studying medical school professors, but the results of this part of the study were not published. The project focused on the same theme as a study directed by Robert Merton at Columbia University: training for the high-status profession of medicine.

The Hughes archives reveal an intellectual competitiveness that was present in the background of his project. Hughes had hoped to show that both his entry point into the study of occupations and his investigative approach of choice—deep fieldwork—were more fruitful than the approach to professions employed by Parsons and Merton, which was associated with the use of survey questionnaires.[69] The final results published by Hughes and his associates as *Boys in White: Student Culture in Medical School*[70] (the principal authors of which were Becker and Geer) analyzed the experience of medical students from a perspective that was much more distant from and critical of occupations than that proposed by Parsons and Merton. The book still remains an unrivaled example of the systematic and rigorous use of observation—a characteristic that Hughes owed, in part, to the intellectual emulation of what had given rise to the Columbia study and, as we shall see below, to the contemporary critiques of the ethnographic approach. *Boys in White* was soon followed by *Making the Grade: The Academic Side of College Life*, a shorter study, conducted according to the same approach, of students beginning higher education.[71]

The writing style employed in Hughes's essays on work was relatively unusual for the period in which they were published: organized by the free association of ideas and lacking reference to the empirical research on which they were based, these essays offered elaborations of ideas that often remained associated with Hughes's sociology of work—restriction of output, dilemmas of status, errors in work, "dirty work," routine and emergency, careers, and so on. These ideas defined a frame of inquiry that was applicable to new investigations, as Hughes had also indicated in the preface to the major collection of his articles.[72] By contrast, his essays contain few propositions that could lead to systematic empirical verification: Hughes was interested much more in the range of variations in the phenomena that he studied, and in the diversity of forms that they could take, than in propositions that lent themselves to being formulated in the language of causality.[73] These essays also contain critiques, more often implicit than explicit, of the conventional approaches to professions—namely those adopted by Hughes's contemporaries, but also those frequently adopted by junior researchers.[74]

> The most significant evidence of Hughes's critical take on certain conventional approaches is perhaps the almost complete absence in his work of references to the analyses of professions (medicine, professions, lawyers, etc.) developed starting in 1939 by Talcott Parsons, which became very prominent in the 1950s and 1960s. No direct reference to these works can be found in Hughes's writing, even though his analyses consist of challenges to the self-representations put forth by the members of these professions, and hence, implicitly, Parsons. One very indirect critique can be found in a 1956 remark warning against analyzing the relationship between doctor and patient as a "social system," because this neglects all other categories of workers. Hughes cites only the article by the Harvard biochemist Lawrence Henderson, whose terms Parsons employed.[75] From 1951, however, Hughes wondered about the usage of the notion of ethical code as a category of analysis: "For as I began to give courses and seminars on occupations, I used a whole set of concepts and headings which were prejudicial to full understanding of what work behavior and relations are. One of them was that of 'code of ethics', which still tended to sort people into the good and the bad. It was not until I had occasion to undertake study of race relations in industry that I finally, I trust, got rid of this bias in the concepts which I used. . . . Now there grow up in work organizations rules of mutual protection among the persons in a given category and rank, and across ranks and categories. If one uses the term 'code of ethics' he is likely not to see the true nature of these rules. These rules are of necessity to do with mistakes, for it is in the nature of work that people make mistakes. The question of how mistakes are handled is a much more penetrating one that any question which contains the concept 'professional ethics' as ordinarily conceived."[76]

The overall characterization of Hughes's approach to work that I have set forth obviously resembles that which can be applied to Park's essays on relations between races and cultures (see chapter 8). Like them, Hughes's output is organized by the free association of ideas, based on the research work of students, and seems fundamentally intended to inspire new research. There exist significant differences, however. Hughes was less inclined to formulate general propositions than Park. Furthermore—unlike Park in his studies of race relations thirty years earlier—Hughes was not recognized by students, and even less so by his colleagues, as a sort of leader in his own time: it was only after the fact that his essays and the articles and books by his students were perceived as a group possessing a certain unity.

An examination of dissertations written at the University of Chicago in the domain of work unambiguously show the limited recognition accorded at the time to the analytical scheme proposed by Hughes. A significant portion of these dissertations barely mention his name, and we should therefore conclude that his initial influence took place through his teaching much more than through his publications. (The same could be said regarding Blumer.) Some of those whom Hughes would later claim as students or friends—like Julius Roth—had also written dissertations in other areas and with evidentiary methods other than fieldwork: it was only in their later research that their affinity with Hughes's orientation was revealed.[77] In the small, above-mentioned group that studied labor in the middle of the 1940s, which William Whyte led for a time, it was not essential to reference Hughes: the group was in search of a theoretical grounding for its ongoing fieldwork, something not offered by Hughes's work, nor that of Warner or Gardner.[78] The relationship with Hughes was even more distant for another group—Jack London, Bernard Karsh, Joel Seidman, and the like—who worked on unionism and strikes, both subjects neglected by Hughes.[79]

In 1954, one of the first critical reviews of the body of publications on the sociology of occupations did not accord any particular place to Hughes.[80] Even in 1958, during the publication of *Men and their Work*, which collected some of Hughes's essays on work, the critical reviews published in the *American Sociological Review* and in the *American Journal of Sociology*, written by two former members of the Committee on Human Relations in Industry at the University of Chicago in the post-war period, contained mixed assessments and did not name these essays as a reference. To be sure, the author of the review in the *American Sociological Review*, Harold Wilensky, made a very positive assessment of the richness of Hughes's suggestions for research, and compares reading his essays to consuming too many cocktails before dinner with the result of ruining one's appetite.[81] The author of the review in the *American Journal of Sociology*, Robert Dubin, characterizes Hughes as an "interestingly disturbing anachronism in the contemporary sociological scene," noting that "as a minimum I would like to see the data from which he derived them. I have a hunch that it does not exist in organized form."[82]

In retrospect, however, some of the ideas developed in Hughes's essays on work and institutions can be found in studies conducted over the course of the 1960s by scholars of the following generation: the work on deviance by Becker (as we shall see in chapter 7), but also the study on behavior in psychiatric hospitals by Goffman and the studies on medicine by Freidson. This thread is rather easy to uncover, since Hughes's essays introduced and developed a small number of substantive approaches and ideas that diverged from the contemporary analyses of sociologists of work to a greater degree than it was at the time understood, including by Hughes himself.

In terms of approach, Hughes first establishes a sort of skepticisim in principle, completely unusual among sociologists of his generation, in regard to the system of representations and justifications set forth by members of professions or their spokespeople in order to justify their status or demands.[83]

It was this skepticism that inspired the comparative approach between very different occupations—especially those that happen to be at opposite extremes of hierarchies of respectability, such as medicine and prostitution. Hughes frequently elaborated upon the idea that professions and high-status workers had at their disposal more effective means to impose on the social sciences their own conceptions of their activities, and to resist being objectivized, than did those of lower status.

This point is expanded upon in an article by Hughes that opens the 1952 special issue of the *American Journal of Sociology* on the sociology of work: "Now the conventional and evaluative term 'profession' carries as connotation the convention that there is no conflict of interest or perspective between professional and client—or at least that there is none between the good professional and the good client. Consequently doctors, professors, school teachers, and their like conceal the various degree from laymen generally, from naïve investigators in particular, and from themselves their feelings of antagonism and resistance toward their dear but troublesome patients, students, and pupils' parents. The janitor and the jazz musician are troubled by no such problem of public relation or anxious guilt. Basingone's study upon a conventional term, such as 'profession,' may lead one to group together and observe only those occupations which, since they cherish and publish a common stereotype of themselves, engage in a common concealment. The social scientist may become the dupe of this common concealment; the more so, since he, too, fancies himself a professional."[84]

This skepticism with regard to representations of the professions corresponds to an equal skepticism of the self-perception of institutions. One of the most explicit examples can be found in the notes (written in 1957) regarding Goffman's essay at the beginning of *Asylums* that develops the concept of total institution. Hughes claims parentage of this concept and continues:

"In the case of mental hospitals, I suppose it would be hard to say what society would be like without them. Apart from the burden on families and, I suppose, the actual danger for families and to peoples, the hospitals don't really do much. At last it seems to me that very little on the ways on therapy goes on in them, and I suppose it is an open question whether those who do get well any way. We might therefore look at the mental hospital and ask what indeed is its function. It would certainly turn out be only a very minor way that of therapy."[85]

This type of questioning, which would become more common at the end of the 1960s, was certainly not common among sociologists of Hughes's generation: it directly contrasts, for example, with the respect Parsons and Merton accorded to the field of medicine.

While he recommends a critical perspective toward the manner in which objects of study present themselves to the researcher, Hughes argues in favor of sustained attention concerning the experiences of the different categories of actors involved directly or indirectly in the system of work being studied. (Hughes's predilection for fieldwork is in turn an expression of this insistence.) The phenomena of status and diversity in the moral value of tasks completed by workers, referring both to professions or groups of workers themselves as well as to society as a whole, correspond to two essential aspects of this experience: "Our aim is to *penetrate more deeply* into the personal and social drama of work, to understand the social and social-psychological arrangements and devices by which men make their work tolerable, or even make it glorious to themselves and others."[86]

One of the principal themes of the study of work for which Hughes advocated is that of encounters between different groups of workers—as well as, potentially, the encounter between those groups and the consumers of their services—and the specific definition of the situation, interests, and logic of action developed by each of these worker groups.[87] This theme is designated by the expression "social drama of work" and various derived expressions. Behind the comparison between encounters of workers on the stage of work and the encounters of actors onstage in a theater can be found the theme of encounters between categories of social actors leading to incomplete communication—something evoked in the William James article "On a Certain Blindness in Human Beings," which Park frequently quoted. As Hughes suggests in a 1952 lecture that was published only much later, "wherever you find people at work, there is some basic difference in the situation of the people receiving the service and the situation of the person giving it. There is an essential part of what we mean by the work drama or social drama of work."[88]

Analyses of the opposition between routine (of the practitioner) and urgency (of the consumer or the client), the necessities of professional secrets, clients' ambivalence with regard to the necessity of practitioners' objectivity in work, and so on are only a few illustrations of this theme: "where people are giving and receiving services, there is a basic difference in the perspective from which they see the situation. The receiver wants skill, but he's a little afraid of the objective, detached attitude that makes skill possible. The giver is seeing this case in the perspective of his whole life career. He might do the wrong thing."[89]

The application of this methodological rule, the same one he put to use in his research on institutions and race relations, constitutes a second suggested direction of investigation for Hughes. According to him, researchers erroneously thought that the limits of the system of interactions in which the subject under study exists were immediately obvious. To the contrary, Hughes held that it is necessary to determine these limits through investigation of all relevant social contexts. Regarding work, Hughes uses the term "social matrices" to designate the context within which an occupation is performed or a work situation takes place.[90] Thus, he includes in his analysis adjacent lines of work, those that contribute directly or indirectly to defining conditions surrounding the activity of the profession under study. In an article that maintains a programmatic character, for example, Hughes shows the necessity of a study of the ongoing evolution in the addition, transformation, and abandonment of types of tasks performed by nurses, rejecting that the determinants are principally technical.[91] The general model that guides the study of occupations—including the established professions—is that of a social movement whose limits are partly defined by the collective actions of its members, who bring an essential contribution to defining the needs to be satisfied: "Professionals do not merely serve; they define the very wants which they serve,"[92] Hughes wrote in 1970.

Careers in various types of organizations constitute another group of central phenomena in Hughes's perspective, even though he devoted only a single essay specifically to this idea.[93] Hughes does not limit the usage of the concept of career to a single area of work; here, too, he expands the field of comparison by evoking careers in religious, political, and philanthropic organizations; the careers of women in the family; and the careers of people treated in medical institutions—the latter being an example that several of his former students would further develop.[94]

In his treatment of occupations, as with that of race relations, we find one of the major themes underlying Hughes's sociology: the critique of ethnocentrism.[95] By giving this term a broader sense than that attributed to it by its originator,

Graham Sumner, we can characterize Hughes's conception of sociology through its primary objective of overcoming the forms of ethnocentrism that naturally result from the social roots of the researcher. Hughes does not attempt to discuss the existence of an objective, scientific point of view to which researchers can and should seek access; however, he sustains that, even if the result can only ever be partial and provisory, researchers' efforts should aim for a lesser degree of dependence with regard to socially constituted points of view—and especially with regard to those that, stamped with the seal of legitimacy, are self-imposed. There, we find a justification for the incompleteness of Hughes's essays, which seek to offer provisional elaborations of analytical categories that new studies should aim to surpass.

This critical obsession with regard to all forms of ethnocentrism was fed by Hughes's proximity to anthropology: he applied to the study of contemporary American society the concepts that constituted a part of the research program of anthropology of the period. It is also based on a reflection regarding his own life, as presented in various unpublished or little-circulated texts, and extended by a reflection on the lives of students belonging to the generations he taught.[96]

Hughes's life trajectory resembles those of a large number of sociologists of his generation (such as Talcott Parsons) and the preceding one (such as Ernest Burgess) whose version of sociology was marked by Anglo-Saxon Protestantism. Traces of this origin are easy to find in Hughes's essays. However, his encounters in Chicago with immigrant workers from Eastern Europe and his experiences in Canada and Germany probably encouraged a critical distance from this origin and from the accepted beliefs of the period, which served to set him apart from sociologists of his generation. This distance is defined less by an emotional detachment than by a capacity to recognize and control, from the outside, an area that Hughes knew intimately: his essays on work and institutions frequently evoke the example of the ministry—and the experience of pastors' sons, held somewhat apart from the community but possessing knowledge of its secrets. The later testimony of Helen Hughes, in a letter to Anselm Strauss, insists upon this experience: "Everett was a PK, a 'preacher's kid,' and often speculated on the role. . . . On the small Ohio town where Everett grew up, the PK was always something of an outsider. From childhood Everett was disposed to look on people analytically, dispassionately. . . . He speaks of [the move] to [the sociology department at the University of Chicago] as an escape from Methodism. . . . Why did he choose sociology? Being a PK was basic to the decision. He was detached, an observer. . . . "[97] During these later years, Hughes frequently returned to his experience transitioning from the environment of a

rural ministry to the intellectual world of cities, which he treated as a particular example of the necessary emancipation from his origins a researcher must
undergo.[98] This was simply the biographical expression of a never-finished critique of ethnocentrism.

THE DIFFUSION OF FIELDWORK AND THE REFLECTION
ON THIS APPROACH

During the same period in which he was engaged in research on work and institutions, Hughes secured a teaching assignment in which a mix of beginning and
advanced students received hands-on training in fieldwork. The aim of the course
was for students to learn to gather evidence by means of direct contact with the
people involved in the phenomena under study.

> This course built upon the legacy of what Park and Burgess had offered over
> the course of the preceding period, but with significant changes. The formula
> Hughes used varied somewhat from year to year. In one of the available descrip-
> tions, each student was assigned a block of buildings whose characteristics he or
> she had to determine before outlining a feasible research project on the block.[99]
> The course sought to send students out into the field early in their training,
> thus giving them experience in the different roles that anyone practicing obser-
> vation must take on and making them consider observation itself as a social
> phenomenon. In contrast with other sociologists of the period, Hughes also
> clearly distinguished between data issuing from observation and data issuing
> from interviews. Those who took this course recalled how rarely Hughes gave
> explicit instructions, as well as his demands in terms of the acuity of observa-
> tion: when students let themselves be fooled by the appearance of building
> facades, for example, Hughes showed them the necessities of thorough observa-
> tion.[100] Some students seem to have had some difficulty in immediately under-
> standing the interest, as Ned Polsky suggests in the preface to a book that relies
> on this approach: "I took his [Hughes's] course in methods of field research
> only because it was required, hated it, suffered through it, and did not begin to
> see its enormous value or apply its lessons until years later."[101]

The approach to the acquisition of evidence through direct contact with the studied phenomena—including the direct observation of behavior and the collection

of transcriptions of speech in the field—does not correspond to any approach to sociology that was clearly identified in the 1940s and 1950s.[102]

The term "fieldwork" was (along with other expressions) rather frequently employed by anthropologists starting in the 1940s to designate the approach modeled by Malinowski.[103] But a stabilization of conceptions of the differences in approach appeared among sociologists somewhat later. In an article published in 1945 in the fiftieth issue of the *American Journal of Sociology*, Burgess uses the following headings to list the principal innovations in method that sociology had seen over the course of the fifty preceding years: statistics, personal documents and case studies, typologies, sociometry, interviews.[104] In this categorization, fieldwork is partially discussed under the heading of "case studies," and observation is not clearly distinguished from the diffuse collection of information permitted by presence in the places under study. Two years later, Merton remarked in an article that there were scarcely any reflections among sociologists on these methodological questions: "Among the most widely practiced and least codified procedures of social research are those comprised by the large-scale collection of observational and interview data in communities. A few accounts of participant-observation are available but, in general, a deep silence cloaks many of the concrete problems found in field work. . . . As a consequence, these procedures have largely remained private skills passed on through example and word-of-mouth to a limited number of apprentices."[105] In fact, the first controversial question posed by a sociologist was that regarding the participation (or lack thereof) of the researcher in the activities that he studied—following an article by Joseph Lohman, the first to use the expression "participant observation" in its current sense.[106]

Articles describing observation and approaches to fieldwork in some detail began to be published at the beginning of the 1950s. The 1955 second edition of *Street Corner Society* by William Whyte included a methodological appendix that, according to the author, contributed greatly to the success of the book and marked the appearance of a new genre. In this appendix, the researcher described the conditions of gathering his data and the incidents that occurred during this collection, as well as his reflections on his experience. The publication of this type of text indicates that the reader is invited to assess, on the basis of the author's reporting, the validity of the research results. The first articles reflecting on the problems encountered in the course of fieldwork were published in the journal *Human Organization* (especially after 1956, when Whyte became editor in chief).[107]

The emergence of fieldwork as a clearly identified model of an approach to socio-logical research is one of the visible results of how researchers who practiced this approach reacted to the critiques of those who held the statistical approach as ideal. As we have seen, starting at the beginning of the 1930s, the attention of a great part of the sociologist community became focalized on the use of sample survey questionnaires and evidentiary materials that lent themselves to statisti-cal treatment. The success of survey questionnaires with statistical techniques was accompanied by sociologists' increasing adherence to criteria for assessing research that accorded with this approach: representativeness of the sample of cases studied; independence of survey results with regard to the conditions of collection and the individual characteristics of the researchers who obtained them; and the conformity of research to the (supposed) model of the physical sciences, which is to say to a process that ranges from the prior formulation of hypotheses to their validation or rejection by an empirical procedure. Compared to these criteria, fieldwork often seemed a less rigorous approach, best used in the preliminary stage of a study in preparation for the collection of evidence that lent itself to a statistical treatment. For example, this is the objective which Barton and Lazarsfeld ascribed to fieldwork in their 1955 article.[108]

Rare were the sociologists who, over the course of the 1940s and 1950s, argued against this definition of research that was in the process of becoming established as a model. At the University of Chicago it was Blumer who, in his teaching, developed a critique of the approaches of survey questionnaires and a related challenge of the soundness of attitude and public opinion as concepts, then in vogue among sociologists practicing survey questionnaires. This criticism can also be read as a plea for fieldwork, but Blumer never explicitly developed a pos-itive argument in favor of this.

> Blumer almost never employed the term "fieldwork," nor any expression includ-ing the adjective "ethnographic." In the section of his 1928 dissertation in which he examined methods of social psychology, he omitted any examination of observation in the locations of behaviors, and even showed reticence, almost in principle, with regard to observation: "Perhaps the points raised in these para-graphs [which focus on data based on the evidence used by historians] can be taken in general as a criticism against accepting as reliable scientific observations which are made in the loose run of everyday participative experience."[109] After 1945, in place of the word "fieldwork" Blumer used alternative terms like "obser-vation based on intimate familiarity"[110]or "direct empirical observation."[111] In a 1966 preface, he used the term "participant observation," which well suited the emphasis he placed, by referring to Mead, on the experience of "role taking."[112]

The critical articles Blumer published starting in 1948 give an idea of the argumentation against questionnaire surveys that his teaching would further develop.

> An article initially presented at the end of 1947 at a meeting of the American Sociological Society challenges the adequacy of the concept of public opinion for its intended ends.[113] Blumer particularly notes the illusory character of the standardization of the collection of data obtained by questionnaires.[114] In 1955, he added to this criticism that of the concept of attitude—a central notion in the interpretation of survey questionnaires—which raised, as Deutscher later would, the uncertainty of the relationship between situational behavior and the responses gathered in the situation of a survey.[115] Elected president of the American Sociological Society in 1956, Blumer gave an address that served as a global critique of the variable-based analyses toward which the statistical exploitation of survey questionnaires led. Blumer particularly insisted upon the arbitrariness of the choice of categories established among variables, on the nongeneric (since variables were context-specific) character of relationships between these variables, and further still upon the fact that this type of survey by definition ignored the process of interpretation by individuals—a process that is, according to his perspective, central in the definition of any social action. Finally, Blumer did not recognize the pertinence of this type of analysis except in those "important areas" where there existed no process of interpretation— but he does not specify what these domains are.[116]

Blumer's critiques were echoed by a group of sociology students at Chicago, whose occasional experience conducting surveys at NORC sometimes bolstered their skepticism with regard to this type of survey.[117] It was always to Blumer (rather than Hughes, who was little inclined toward criticism) that these students attributed the origin of their reservations with regard to questionnaire surveys and attitude-based interpretations.[118] But there existed another possible defense of the ethnographic approach. Criteria of evaluation related to aspects left undeveloped in the methodology of questionnaire surveys could be brought forward, such as the validity of the meanings attributed to behaviors in their context and the discovery of properties and analytical distinctions, which relied on an inductive approach (rather than solely deduction based on a priori propositions). The rigor of data-gathering procedures could also be improved by a critical familiarity with the consequences of their conditions that did not leave the process of the production of data outside the scope of the studies. It was in this direction that Hughes was oriented starting in the 1950s.

In 1952, Hughes obtained a small grant from the Ford Foundation for both his teaching and a study on the fieldwork approach.[119] He intended to analyze the experience of those who had employed this approach—which Hughes defined in the preface to the resulting book as "observation of people in situ, finding them where they are, staying with them in some role which, while acceptable to them, will allow both intimate observation of certain parts of their behavior, and reporting it in ways useful to social science. . . ."[120] Buford Junker, an anthropologist by training who had worked with Warner on many community studies and who was at that point one of Hughes's assistants for the course on fieldwork, was affiliated with this project.[121] To broaden the amount of testimony that was available, another PhD student, Ray Gold, conducted interviews with current and former sociology students at the University of Chicago who had used the approach.[122] The initial result of this research was a mimeographed document for the use of students in the Department of Sociology, *Cases on Field Work*, followed by a book published under the sole authorship of Buford Junker in 1960, for which Hughes wrote a preface that was both a historical essay and a reflection on approaches.[123]

This book, which is based on the analysis of cases borrowed from the anthropological tradition as well as completed or in-progress works from members of the circles of Hughes and Warner, offers an analysis, bolstered by many examples, of the diversity of ways in which researchers relate to their fields and to the people they study. To those who used the fieldwork approach, therefore, the book offered means for comparing their own style of involvement in their field with the experiences of others. Without completely articulating this point, it suggests that the explanation of the conditions in which data was gathered is a means of the collective control of their validity. As Hughes indicates in his preface, the perspective that inspired this book is one of a sociology of sociology, which here means a sociology of work with regard to the work of sociologists.

Around the time this reflection on fieldwork developed, an evolution in the style of writing up research results, especially in the case of journal articles, can be observed among researchers in Hughes's circle. Instead of presenting results in a synthetic manner, briefly summarizing field notes and interview transcripts, some research reports from this point on reproduced full passages from interviews and field notes. A technical element of the 1950s—the diffusion of tape recorders—certainly facilitated this evolution in interviewing, leading to a clear articulation of the question of the fidelity of transcription in research reports.[124] Reproduced with a new concern for fidelity and attested to by research into modes of manual transcription adapted to spoken language, excerpts from interviews before the diffusion of tape recorders were used to illustrate a property or specify the meaning of a category of analysis. One of the earliest examples of this style of writing can be found in Oswald Hall's dissertation and articles on the practice of medicine, which would later serve as models for this style of writing.[125] The same type of writing can be found later, based this time on observation notes, or what passed for them.[126] The transformation that thus manifested itself in writing standards encouraged a more explicit presentation of analytical categories by which meaning was attributed to elements of the gathered material. It also permitted the reader to assess for himself the chosen interpretation of the speech or behaviors recorded in the field notes. On the other hand, it necessarily led to a greater degree of rigor and systematicity in the collection of information. In other terms, to employ terminology previously used, we might consider these studies based on fieldwork as defining a new research formula clearly different from that of the monographs of the 1920s and 1930s.

> The change in the style of composition corresponds to a change in rhetorical strategy: by putting the material he had employed and the meaning he had conferred upon select elements on display, the author of a particular work sought to guide the reader into adopting his point of view. The reader is therefore no longer asked to rely solely on the testimony of the person who collected the material, since it is the overall sufficiency of the perspective for encompassing a set of phenomena, and not a simple conclusion concerning "facts," that is the challenge of reading. Although it has never, to my knowledge, been called attention to, the importance of this change in the strategy of presenting field research should not be underestimated, since thereafter this type of composition became widespread in monographs that would become classics of fieldwork, and also in articles in the journal *Urban Life and Culture*.[127]

Alongside the reflections and reports of experiences presented in Junker's book, the research model based on systematic and intensive fieldwork that constitutes *Boys in White* also contributed to the upsurge in its reputation among sociologists at the end of the 1960s. *Boys in White* soon became the consummate example of this type of study. It was based on many years of fieldwork conducted by researchers who would, in following years, emerge among the most productive practitioners in this field. It was exacting and explicit in its production of field notes, and was accompanied by the publication of several articles reflecting on the methods of Becker and Greer, which rapidly emerged as classic references.[128] One of the indices of Hughes and his associates' success in this area is certainly the quasi-equation, toward the end of the 1960s, of fieldwork with the Chicago tradition. As Jennifer Platt has shown, it was also possible to equate fieldwork with the social anthropology of researchers trained at Harvard, such as Warner, Arensberg, Whyte, and so on.[129]

THE LEGACIES OF HUGHES AND BLUMER

As previously noted, the perspectives developed by Hughes and Blumer were frequently associated with each other starting in the 1960s, and it is easy to find, among their students and their friends, echoes of analyses developed by one or the other in research conducted between the 1940s and the 1960s. The necessities of defending one sort of argumentation against partisans of quantitative approaches obviously explain Hughes borrowing certain materials from Blumer. He also offered a frame of interrogation for the study of social problems as products of public definition, as well as for the study of collective behavior, the preferred area of research for those who participated in his *Festschrifts*, more generally.[130] On the other hand, the orientation that Blumer's essays propose for the study of work relationships in industrial settings had, it seems, no legacy; his articles on the subject were scattered and, in some cases, not easily accessible until a 1990 edition.

In the subfield of the sociology of work, while it is not easy to evaluate the importance of Hughes's essays, it is, however, clear that they were not forgotten. This is evident in the publication of a new collection in 1994 by the University of Chicago Press, the organization in 1995 and 1997 of sessions devoted to Hughes's work at meetings of regional sociological associations, the presentation of papers at the World Congress of Sociology in Montreal in 1998, and the publication of an unpublished essay and a volume of critical essays in 1997 and 2016 respectively.[131] One reason for the inequality of references to the works of Hughes and Blumer is evidently connected to the importance of the critical dimension of the essays of the latter. Some of what Blumer critiques has ceased to have a place in the culture of sociologists, while Hughes's essays, due to their programmatic character, have remained usable for research.

However, there existed an affinity in intellectual orientation between Hughes and some researchers of the following generation, who explained that the works of the group of researchers trained at the University of Chicago after 1945—who were more likely to refer to Hughes at the end of his career than the beginning— seemed to fit within the legacy of the perspective he had opened up.

As I have emphasized regarding the study of the established professions, one of Hughes's particularities compared with other sociologists of his generation is linked to his radical, though discretely formulated, skepticism of official objectives and the respectable aspects of American society of his time. Despite a social origin that was typical for a sociologist of his time and a professional career ultimately marked by the privileges and functions that then characterized distinguished academic careers, Hughes seems, partly due to his inclinations, to have been a sort of " 'outlier' with an irreverent eye" (to use an expression from Arlene Daniels). Moreover, he expressed interest in somewhat atypical students—like Donald Roy or even Howard Becker—who studied unconventional subjects at a time when the recognized value of a subject depended strongly on its social prestige.

Becker evokes the contrast between these two aspects of Hughes's leanings in an essay he presented in 1983, at a session organized in honor of Hughes by the American Association of Sociology:

> He was, symbolically, one of the several children of Park. It always seemed to me that there was a rivalry between those children (Wirth, Redfield, Blumer) as to what had inherited the mantle and that Hughes was nearest to the Park spirit in his love of complexity and confusion, in not longing for simplicity and order. That made a curious combination with his rather conventional exterior. The consequence, I sometimes thought, was that, happily for us, he wasn't always in full control of his own mind. Its sociological side, making intuitive analogical connections and reasoning from unconventional metaphors, produced results that both shocked and tickled the conventional side.[132]

The unconventional ideas presented in Hughes's essays on work and institutions are more often half-implicit than explicitly formulated.[133] It was probably through his teaching more than his essays that Hughes transmitted to the next generation something distinct from approaches that conformed to established concepts of legitimacy. But this transmission probably would not have happened if these elements had not also held meaning for some of the researchers of the following generation.

Their experience of the social world was frequently marked, as we have seen, by origins that located them somewhat outside mainstream American society— for example, as working-class Jews or from the lower levels of the middle class. It was also influenced strongly by the experience of the Great Depression, and sometimes by having spent time in the army and at war before returning to university to study a discipline other than the one they had originally chosen.

An autobiographical essay by Joseph Gusfield suggests the significance of some of these elements for the orientation of this generation of researchers: "The depression was more than a bend in the business cycle. It was a cataclysmic destruction of belief in the special providence of America and a long period of deep anxiety and frustration. Many of us who went through it continue to feel that the structure of solid institutions is a facade, always liable to sudden and unexpected tremors that undermine the foundation.... I could say that all those experiences create the aura of a world in which violence and discontinuity were palpable possibilities. They suggest a world in which rules are broken as much, if not more, than followed. I do not think that was my personal feeling about my own life, but it may well have shaped my sense of history as unpredictable and unmeasurable."[134] Gusfield elsewhere describes the perspective that he attributes to some sociologists of his generation trained at the University of Chicago: "an identification with the less respected, less established elements in the society and a notable dose of skepticism and disrespect for the well-off, the authoritative, and the official."[135]

We can therefore understand the type of affinity between the orientation that Gusfield attributes to himself and some of his friends and that of Hughes, a semi-outlier in terms of inclination, but not in terms of behavior (as Park, in a different sense, had also been). Hughes's contribution to the persistence of this current in research—and, partly, to its reestablishment—ultimately returns to a random interaction of unique individual characteristics and collective experiences determined by particular historical circumstances.

7
From Social Disorganization to the Theory of Labeling

All these factors [population change, poor housing, poverty, the proportion of immigrants and Negroes, the frequency of tuberculosis, adult crime, mental disorders], including juvenile delinquency, may be considered manifestations of some general basic factor. The common element is social disorganization or the lack of organized community effort to deal with these conditions.

—Ernest Burgess[1]

Finally, I quit Joliet and took a job with the Institute for Juvenile Research, one of those outfits that were always studying the causes of juvenile delinquency, making surveys of all the kids in cold-water tenements with rats nibbling their toes and nothing to eat—and then discovering the solution: camping trips and some shit they called character building.

—Saul Alinsky[2]

The respect recent immigrants and the working class held for the prevailing moral standards of the Anglo-Saxon middle classes was, as we have seen, one of the principal concerns of social reformers, with whom the first sociologists were fellow travelers. Before 1920, there already existed numerous publications on divorce and desertion (that is, men or women abandoning their families), on dependence on economic assistance (always suspected of being systematic), as well as on the usual forms of delinquency in adults and minors, including truancy. Some of these publications were written by prominent members of the reform movement, including the sociologist Charles Henderson and Sophonisba Breckinridge and Edith Abbott, the founders of the School of Social Service Administration at the University of Chicago who made use of data generated by a specialized court.[3] Dissertations in sociology were also devoted to juvenile delinquency: in 1906, Mabel Carter Roades completed her dissertation on young delinquents who appeared before the juvenile court in Chicago, and in 1915 Earle Eubank completed his on familial desertion. Although Eubank, like Breckinridge and Abbott, made use of data issuing from administrative statistics, his interpretation does not depart from the common-sense, middle-class perspective of the period. The audiences for the two dissertations would remain limited to sociologists.

Phenomena linked to delinquency, and especially juvenile delinquency, were at the center of the field of social work, which became autonomous after the end of the war. But research in these topics remained partly under the purview of sociologists, despite the sometimes-pointed competition between the two specialties. Numerous sociological works published after 1920 were devoted to this group of phenomena, believed to be specific products of the new urban society. The creation of the term "social disorganization"—used first by Cooley, then by Thomas and Znaniecki (but ignored by Henderson and Eubank)—signaled the new frame of questioning within which sociologists placed these phenomena after 1920. The introduction of this term allowed sociologists to suggest that their approach was specific and more objective than the previous approach, which was defined in terms of "social problems" or "social pathology"; in short, this new terminology made the field of sociology seem more scientific.

The legacy of the term "social disorganization" would greatly exceed the circle of sociologists tied to the Chicago tradition, as Stuart Queen remarked in 1957: "During the lifetime of this writer theories of social disorganization have put their appearance, taken various forms, and fallen into the background of American sociology."[4] The notion of social disorganization reached its height of popularity toward the end of the 1930s. In 1939, the annual meeting of the American Sociological Society was devoted to social disorganization, with many of the papers on that theme published the following year in an issue of the *American Sociological Review* (vol. 5, no. 4 [1940]). However, the presenter of the annual meeting remarked that he was not certain of the utility of the term. In the 1930s and 1940s, it covered material also frequently placed under the labels of "social problems," "social pathology," "applied sociology," or even "practical sociology," which had been in use during the previous period. To borrow a list found in the textbook written by Robert Faris (the son of Ellsworth Faris) bearing this term as its title, social disorganization included: poverty, criminality, delinquency, drug use, prostitution, gambling, suicide, mental illnesses, familial ruptures, political corruption, crowd disturbances, and violent riots.[5]

Starting in the 1920s, the development of research on social disorganization at the University of Chicago relied upon sources of funding that were stable but often of limited scale; upon the professional knowledge acquired by certain researchers who held positions as social workers or employees of the administrations and associations that focused on these social problems while conducting their studies; and, specifically, upon the relationships Ernest Burgess maintained with the organizations (courts, associations) that provided the basic data exploited through these studies.

It is possible to put together an extensive list of studies in this domain published by researchers in some way associated with the University of Chicago after 1920. A first group of those dissertations and studies related to diverse agencies dealing with social problems, and they focused on youth gangs,[6] suicide,[7] a type of dance hall,[8] prostitution,[9] mental illnesses,[10] and organized crime.[11] When their authors pursued research careers, they did so outside the University of Chicago and did not have much contact with the university's researchers of later generations. A second group of studies, centered on juvenile delinquency, developed around Clifford Shaw and Henry McKay at the Illinois Institute of Juvenile Research between the 1930s and the end of the 1960s.[12] These studies saw a broader diffusion among sociologists working in this area than the previous ones: Burgess thought that one of these books, the annotated autobiography of a delinquent, *The Jack-Roller* (1930), had contributed more to the diffusion of Chicago sociology than any other book.[13] A third group, comparable to the preceding in reputation, corresponds to the studies conducted by Edwin Sutherland—a sociologist trained at the University of Chicago before 1914, who returned, as we have seen, as a professor between 1930 and 1935—and his circle.[14]

I shall begin by examining studies on juvenile delinquency from the 1920s and 1930s, as well as their legacies. I shall leave to the side studies conducted in Sutherland's circle, noting only their critical dimensions.[15] Moreover, it was at the University of Chicago that, in the 1950s, the research that would contribute to formulating a new perspective on deviance (which included at this moment the domain of delinquency) was undertaken. This perspective was formulated in Howard Becker's *Outsiders* (1963), a book that would become widely read, and variations are also found in the analyses of other researchers who spent time at the University of Chicago after the Second World War. A preliminary analysis shows that there was no continuity in inspiration between the works of the 1930s and those of the new generation, even though Becker worked alongside

Shaw and McKay for a time. The second objective of this chapter will be devoted to understanding how one of the first challenges to the social disorganization approach to delinquency emerged in the same intellectual environment in which works on social disorganization had previously been developed.

JUVENILE DELINQUENCY AND SOCIAL DISORGANIZATION

We have seen the importance of the theme of social disorganization in the analyses of *The Polish Peasant*. The distinctions proposed by Thomas and Znaniecki, who used the terms "social disorganization" and "personal disorganization," are found in incomplete form in the analyses of the 1920s and 1930s. A more direct source of inspiration for the use of the concept of social disorganization in these can probably be found in three essays by Park, published in *The City* (1915): in the first chapter (a short passage of which, republished in the *Introduction to the Science of Sociology* by Park and Burgess, constitutes the essential core of the book's discussion of the notion of social disorganization); as well as in two other chapters, one devoted to juvenile delinquency and the other to the organization of communities.

Park presents the notion of social disorganization in *The City* starting with an overall interpretation of the societal changes that follow the development of large-scale industry, and the correlated transformations of forms of social control. In rural communities, social control was effectuated, Park claims, following Cooley, in the framework of primary relationships (in other words, face-to-face relationships, especially those in the family and the community), in an immediate and spontaneous manner, without necessary reference to any abstract principle. In cities, the population was mobile, primary relationships were weak, and the moral order, which relied on these factors, dissolved: "It's probably the breaking down of local attachments and the weakening of the restraints and inhibitions of the primary group, under the influence of the urban environment, which are largely responsible for the increase of vice and crime in great cities . . . it is from this point of view that we should seek to interpret all those statistics which register the disintegration of the moral order, for example, the statistics of divorce, of truancy, and of crime."[16] In cities, social relationships had a more formal and less intimate character, and the moral order was based upon traditional institutions, like churches and schools, that were called upon to fill new functions. Alternatively, social relationships were based on new institutions, like juvenile courts, parent-teacher associations, youth clubs, and so on.[17] The rapid changes during this period placed some of the population, particularly among those who had migrated toward the cities, in an environment to which they were "not able to accommodate."[18] This, according to Park, was the explanation behind the increased adult and juvenile delinquency that struck some communities. The term "disorganization" is not explicitly defined, but one phrase associates this notion with a "process by which the authority and influence of an earlier culture and system of social control is undermined and eventually destroyed,"[19] conforming to the analysis given by Thomas.

A second essay by Park, "Community Organization and Juvenile Delinquency," relies on W. I. Thomas's research as well as on that of Nels Anderson, who researched the hobo community of Chicago (see chapter 9), and on Frederic Thrasher's then-unpublished research on youth gangs in Chicago. Park formulates a sort of policy of struggle against the forms of social disorganization that involved youths, through the establishment of institutions (such as recreational clubs) intended to encourage social control of young people by offering them a new environment, "a group in which [they] can live." A third essay, "Community Organization and the Romantic Temper," argues in favor of organizing communities in cities in order to create an environment favorable to the adaptation of individuals. Park advocates the development of communities on the model of those that had been built by certain groups of immigrants; in short, as he suggests in the penultimate sentence of this essay—"Our problem is to encourage men to seek God in their own village and to see the social problem in their own neighborhood"— finding something comparable to the style of social control that existed in rural communities.

Park's remarks are not simply the expression of a utopian nostalgia for the rural communities of the previous period; they were, as we have seen, directly connected to the framework within which Clifford Shaw and Henry McKay conducted their studies on juvenile delinquency.

Studying juvenile delinquency under the label of social disorganization signified, first of all, a challenge to the accepted interpretations of the previous period. The most widespread one held that delinquency had a biological or psychological basis—that it was connected to belonging to an "inferior race," to innate tendencies presenting in certain individuals or to individual characteristics like intellectual disability.[20]

An article Burgess published in 1923 (i.e., prior to the publication of the principal study conducted in this area at Chicago) clearly identifies the intellectual adversaries against whom the sociologists of his circle argued. The study of the criminal, according to Burgess, is a study of human behavior and not the study of a particular biological variety, as Lombroso had sustained, or of a particular social category, as Tarde had claimed. Relying on examples intended to show the difference between the perspective of psychiatry and that of sociology, Burgess then develops the idea that delinquents should be studied as people, which is to say as "the product of social interaction with his fellows."[21] He also criticizes the common-sense perspective of social workers, denouncing its practical consequences: "Too often the 'blame' is placed by the social agency upon the refusal of the person or of the family to co-operate in spite of the many 'good chances' offered."[22] This claim is illustrated by a case study of a young delinquent girl, in which the treatment proposed by social workers belies their profound lack of understanding of the world and interests of young delinquents.[23]

The study of juvenile delinquency was, when Burgess wrote this article, already a semi-formed field in Chicago following the creation in 1899 of a special court for minors, the first of its kind in the United States, as well as of various establishments for the treatment of abandoned children or delinquents.[24] The creation of these institutions depended, among other things, on the conviction that juvenile delinquency led to adult criminality. The existence of such institutions made data on the relevant populations available: it was upon this data that Sophonisba Breckinridge and Edith Abbott based their two pioneering studies in 1912, as did a Chicago psychiatrist, William Healy, in 1915. The former studies proposed a sort of characterization of social situations that produce delinquency—immigrant families, poverty, the status of being an orphan or homeless, living in decrepit or overpopulated locations, and so on. Healey's book, which presents the study that led its author to renounce the theories of Lombroso and more generally any analysis assigning a single determining factor to delinquency, was the point of departure for the reflections of Park and Burgess. These latter two, as we have seen, introduced a novel idea for those interested in delinquency: delinquent behaviors were engendered by the interactions of youths with their environment.

Among psychiatrists, the success of the environmentalist theories advanced by sociologists was, at least during an early period, almost null: in 1934, the psychiatrists of the Illinois Reformatory believed that 99.5 percent of inmates enrolled in the institution between 1919 and 1929 presented mental pathologies.[25]

The first study in this area to be inspired by Park does not focus directly on juvenile delinquency, but on a connected phenomenon: gangs of young boys and adolescents in city slum neighborhoods. Undertaken in 1919 or 1920, but completed only in 1926, Frederic Thrasher's dissertation used Chicago as its principal setting, although the book that resulted from the dissertation the following year made some allusions to other cities.[26]

The book was the first in the series of monographs published by the University of Chicago Press to include a map. It located gangs geographically throughout Chicago in relation to industrial establishments, regions occupied by railroad tracks, and neighborhoods in which various groups of immigrants were concentrated. Thrasher remarks that gangs emerged in transitional zones, a concept originating from Burgess, meaning the zones at the edges of the inner city or close to the factory areas, where immigrants settled upon their arrival.

> Housing in these transitional zones was kept in poor condition because landlords, anticipating the possibility of speculation due to the expansion of the inner city, had ceased to maintain their properties. Thrasher defined youth delinquency as an interstitial phenomenon, which is to say one taking place in the spaces between the better organized zones of the city: "The most important conclusion suggested by a study of the location and distribution of the 1313 gangs discovered in Chicago is that *gangland represents a geographically and socially interstitial area in the city*."[27] We might note that Thrasher does not identify the poverty of the residents of the zones from which members of these bands came as a primary phenomenon, although he does not completely neglect it.[28]

The spontaneous formation and evolution of youth groups, which Thrasher wished to study, inspired the model of the evolution of sects outlined by Park and Burgess in *Introduction to the Science of Sociology*. Drawing on testimonies, Thrasher describes different aspects of life in gangs, including the organization of their activities and the development of forms of social control, as well as the problems that they posed for their communities through their encouragement of juvenile delinquency, which itself fed organized crime and contributed to the political organization of cities. Gangs further contributed to juvenile delinquency by dispersing of criminal techniques and attitudes, thus facilitating the perpetration of criminal acts.

This analysis was further developed over the following years by two other researchers of the same generation as Thrasher: Clifford Shaw and Henry McKay. In contrast to Thrasher, who left Chicago in 1927 to become a professor in the Department of Sociology of Education at New York University,[29] Shaw and McKay did not hold academic positions: throughout their careers they were employed by the Department of Sociology of the Institute of Juvenile Research, an institution for treatment and research dependent upon the state of Illinois.

The Institute of Juvenile Research is the name adopted in 1917 by the Juvenile Psychopathic Institute, a Chicago psycho-pedagogical research center founded in 1909. Led from the start by the psychiatrist William Healy, its objective was the study and treatment of delinquents.[30] Starting in 1914, the institute was funded by Cook County, the administrative division that included the city of Chicago. It came under the control of the state of Illinois in 1917. In 1926, a sociology department responsible for conducting research on juvenile delinquency was added onto what had until that point principally been a treatment center. On Burgess's recommendation, Clifford Shaw, who was then completing his dissertation in sociology, was named director. The following year, Shaw hired Henry McKay, with whom he undertook a lengthy collaboration.

From 1926, the financial resources provided to the Institute of Juvenile Research by the state of Illinois were supplemented by those from the Behavior Research Fund, of which Burgess was named director in 1929.[31] The administrative council of this foundation included representatives of the great fortunes of Chicago. However, its budget principally relied on contributions of limited size from a few hundred donors, as well as, more occasionally, help from the Social Science Research Council and the Rockefeller Foundation. The importance of individual contributions shows, to some degree, that in the mid-1920s, juvenile delinquency was a problem relevant to the interests of local communities. The Behavior Research Fund largely funded the work of Shaw and McKay—along with other studies relating to law, biology, or psychiatry. This funding primarily served to pay the researchers' salaries and to promote the publications of the Institute of Juvenile Research. An attempt to prolong the existence of the Behavior Research Fund by five years failed. Its dissolution was announced in 1934, and its resources were completely exhausted in 1948. Shaw and McKay were forced to seek out other sources of funding for their works, especially for their reports for investigative committees.

Testimonies consistently identify Shaw as the one who originated the perspective that would inspire the first research activities of the Institute of Juvenile Research. On the other hand, they attribute the majority of the work of developing and writing later publications, especially those based on statistical evidence, to McKay. From the 1930s onward, Shaw would primarily devote himself to directing an action plan inspired by his studies, the Chicago Area Project. Burgess's presence in the background of these works must also be emphasized. In a previously quoted article, he formulated the general outline of the research program that Shaw would pursue over the following years.[32] He added notes and prefaces to the major publications of the Institute of Juvenile Research. Burgess was also active in the administrative councils of the Institute of Juvenile Research, the Behavior Research Fund, and the Chicago Area Project.

There exists an obvious connection—which he sometimes emphasized in lectures—between Clifford Shaw's life experience and the analyses of delinquency that he would develop.[33] The son of an Indiana farmer, Shaw (1895–1957) spent his first years in a miniscule village, where he would experience the model of informal community control of children's behavior noted in the lectures he later gave as publicist for the Chicago Area Project.[34] Employed for a time on his family's farm, Shaw then undertook studies at a Methodist college intending to become a minister. He distanced himself from religion quickly, however. Abandoning this path, he enrolled at the University of Chicago in 1919, after spending two years in the army. At Chicago, Shaw lived for a time in a settlement where he came into contact with immigrants. A course taught by Burgess sparked his interest in juvenile delinquency. In order to acquire firsthand knowledge of delinquents, from 1921 Shaw worked part-time as a parole officer at an Illinois state school for juvenile delinquents, monitoring children who had been conditionally released. In 1924, he worked as a probation officer for the Cook County court. In these positions, Shaw developed relationships with a number of delinquents who came to trust him enough that he succeeded in obtaining autobiographical documents, which he later published.

After being hired as chair of the sociology department of the Institute of Juvenile Research, Shaw did not finish the PhD in sociology that he had begun: according to Snodgrass, he never passed the foreign language examination required for obtaining the degree. He remained in this position—to which, several years later, he added that of director of the Chicago Area Project—until his death in 1957. From 1941, as we have seen, Shaw regularly taught in the sociology department of the University of Chicago. Until the end of the 1950s, several dissertations and research projects were conducted within the framework of the Institute of Juvenile Research.[35]

Aspects of the life of Henry McKay (1899–1980) are comparable to those of Shaw: he was also rural and Protestant in origin, somewhat wealthier but probably less marked by religion. Arriving in Chicago in 1923, McKay undertook doctoral studies in sociology, but after being hired by the Institute of Juvenile Research he did not complete the degree, seemingly for the same reasons as Shaw. Following Shaw's death, McKay succeeded him in the position of director of the Institute of Juvenile Research.

The similarities in Shaw's and McKay's backgrounds were accompanied by a striking contrast in their personalities. According to Snodgrass's description,

"McKay was the quiet statistician, a man who stayed removed at the Institute and plotted the maps, calculated the rates, ran the correlations and described the findings which located empirically and depicted cartographically the distribution of crime and delinquency in Chicago. Shaw, on the other hand, was an activist, who 'related' to delinquents and got their life stories, and an organizer who attempted to create a community reform movement."[36]

The first publications of the sociology department of the Institute of Juvenile Research were based on two evidentiary sources typical of studies conducted at the University of Chicago Department of Sociology during this period. In these can be found statistical analyses based on official data produced by administrations—in this case, the courts—which make use of the cartographical techniques of presentation honed by Burgess.[37] We also find delinquents' autobiographical accounts written at the request of the researchers. Interpretations of these accounts are supported by corroboration from other sources: diagnoses from doctors and social workers, documents from personal files, statistics, and so on. The first book presenting such a case study (to employ the terminology of the period), *The Jack-Roller* (1930), centered on the autobiography of a young delinquent of Polish origin, written at Shaw's request.[38] The book quickly became a classic in the field of research that would become institutionalized during the following years as "criminology."

Two other books based on case studies of the same type were also published. The first presents the case of a juvenile delinquent later convicted of rape. The second presents the case of five delinquent brothers.[39] The total number of autobiographies of delinquents collected by the Institute of Juvenile Research exceeded eighty, and three other similar manuscripts were completed but ultimately not published.[40] The various editions of *The Jack-Roller* saw wide readership, with sales before 1981 reaching 23,000 copies. The second published case study had sold, by the same date, around 3,600 copies, before the release of its second edition in 1976; the third had a similar diffusion.[41]

The publications of Shaw and McKay often simultaneously presented statistical analyses, cartography, and case studies. Each of these approaches filled a function in an argumentation that had several objectives. The handling of the statistical evidence sharply refuted other accepted interpretations of delinquency. The publication of case studies, the central element of which was autobiographies, was meant to give the reader access to an understanding of the perspective of the delinquents. Following many others who collected autobiographies, Shaw thus sought to secure the support of an audience broader than just sociologists: obtaining funding from the Chicago Area Project was one of the goals of this argumentation.[42]

Although Thrasher's book illustrates the specific localization of gangs—and thereby delinquency—in a single map, Shaw and McKay constructed, for comparative purposes, several maps corresponding to correlated phenomena (juvenile delinquency of boys and girls, at different periods, etc.) and proceeded to calculate rates of juvenile delinquency by zone, making use of data collected by the juvenile court of Cook County since its creation.

Working off of statistics for the city of Chicago in the period 1900–1926 concerning the home lives of children who evaded compulsory school attendance and were referred to the juvenile court of Cook County, Shaw and McKay sought to demonstrate that these phenomena were characteristic of certain zones of the city and thus constituted indices of social disorganization. Neighborhoods with high levels of delinquency were found at the periphery of the inner city or next to industrial zones: as Thrasher had already noted, these were the neighborhoods in which new arrivals to the city settled, where the housing stock was in poor condition, and where the proportion of inhabitants benefiting from some form of charity was high.

Shaw and McKay also calculated rates of delinquency by dividing the city according to the model of concentric zones proposed by Burgess, by which method they showed that delinquency rates decreased in correspondence with distance from the inner city. Using the same data over various periods, they concluded that these rates were specific to the different zones, since they remained unaffected by changes in the ethnicity of the population following the arrivals of successive waves of immigration. Shaw and McKay also showed that the rates of juvenile delinquency among children in diverse populations of immigrants declined with the duration of their presence within the United States. Once the condition of a population of immigrants had improved enough to allow them to establish themselves in the residential zones further from the inner city, their children ceased to display elevated rates of delinquency. In sum, these results refuted the interpretations of delinquency as an expression of the biological or cultural inferiority of certain populations.

Conforming with the hypothesis previously advanced by Park and Burgess, Shaw and McKay note indices in accordance with the interpretation of delinquency as a group (and not an individual) behavior: for example, they emphasize, 82 percent of those who were monitored in 1928 did not act alone.[43] Certain zones of the city were persistently marked by delinquency, since the youths who lived there were subject to social pressure from peers, by which the youths adapted their own behavior to conform to the norms of the group. The techniques necessary for perpetrating delinquent acts were transmitted through intergenerational contacts in peer groups. The autobiographies of delinquents here offer the principal elements of justification supporting this claim. Shaw and McKay conclude that delinquent behaviors are the acts of normal individuals (and not those who are weak-willed, psychopaths, etc.), resulting from socialization through interactions between future delinquents and those with whom they were in contact.

Clearly, the interpretation that Shaw and McKay propose is the same as that proposed by Park and Burgess at the beginning of the 1920s:[44] the delinquency of youths was a consequence of the waning influence of the social control exerted by traditional institutions such as churches, the family, and local communities in the new conditions encountered in cities by immigrants of rural origin.[45] The young people who lived in these inner-city neighborhoods were exposed to diverse norms as they came into contact with the unconventional values of the delinquent world, while in other zones norms and values remained homogenous and conventional.

A large number of social workers—as well as some of the first sociologists to publish books on criminology—adopted the approach then characterized as multifactorial.[46] This corresponded to a sort of popular version of Healy's works: delinquency was explained by the combined effects of familial ruptures, alcoholism, emotional immaturity, poverty, insufficient education, weakness of spirit, and so on. Shaw and McKay made their opposition to this point of view explicit in a 1932 article, based on statistical data, that showed that the claimed correlation between the frequency of broken homes and the frequency of juvenile delinquency—advanced by the "classic" books by Breckinridge and Abbott (1912) and Healy (1915)—disappeared when controlled for zone of residence, nationality, and age of the delinquents.[47] Over the course of the 1920s, new interpretations of delinquency influenced by psychoanalysis spread among social workers, who tended to focus their attention on individual cases, with less interest in delinquents' social environment. Behind the adoption of these interpretations by social workers and their increasingly distant ties with sociologists can be found the evolution of the conditions of their activities: after 1918, social work became a full-time occupation (as opposed to it being done on a volunteer basis), and social workers justified their claims of status by their possession of specific knowledge and a specific technique, casework.[48]

The interpretation of juvenile delinquency as the consequence of social changes that accompanied the settlement into cities of each wave of immigrants arguably began to seem less convincing in the 1930s. While juvenile delinquency remained a massive phenomenon in large cities over the course of the 1930s and 1940s, neighborhoods with high rates of delinquency could no longer be easily characterized as zones in which newly arrived immigrants resided, since, aside from African Americans, there were almost no new arrivals.

African Americans originally from the South were the only newly settled population of numerical importance in Chicago around 1930. (The other new arrivals, Mexicans of rural origin, numbered scarcely more than twenty thousand.) The urban segregation to which African Americans were subjected meant that they quickly came to occupy the zones in which they settled almost exclusively.[49] The process of neighborhood transformation thus differed from that seen over the course of the preceding period. The rates of delinquency among young African Americans by zone were, for a long time, particularly high. McKay, who studied the variations in frequency of delinquency according to geographic origin, race, and nationality, was able to demonstrate in a new section in the second edition of *Juvenile Delinquency and Urban Areas*, published in 1969, that rates of delinquency were significantly lower in certain African American neighborhoods, which he interpreted as a sign of the reorganization of the communities concerned: "areas disrupted by change have high rates of delinquents, but after a while, movement toward stability can be observed as new institutional forms are developed or old institutions are modified to meet new problems."[50]

An examination of the analyses subsequently published by Shaw and McKay reveals a progressive evolution in their interpretations of juvenile delinquency.[51] Until the second edition of their last book in 1969, Shaw and McKay certainly sustained the basic outlines of their interpretation: juvenile delinquency was a consequence of the disorganization of communities, induced by changes connected with population movements. However, they did not neglect to note that, while the communities in which delinquency was most frequent were those where the most recently arrived populations lived, they were also those whose population had the lowest economic status.[52]

Starting with his last case study published in 1938—the comparative autobiographies of five brothers—Shaw's interpretation of delinquency put greater emphasis on the economic status of the population from which the delinquents came, and insisted less upon the process of change to which this population had been subjected. Or, rather, it was less centered on the characteristics of primary relationships in neighborhoods and more so on the ambient pressure of society as a whole.[53] In other words, alongside the social disorganization interpretation that emphasized value conflicts there developed an interpretation of delinquency centered on differential access to legitimate means of attaining the objectives that defined success in society. The same point is repeated in Shaw's following book, from 1942: "Despite these marked differences in the relative position of people of different communities, children and young people in all areas, both rich and poor, are exposed to the luxury values and success patterns of our culture. . . . Among children and young people residing in low-income areas, interests in acquiring material goods and enhancing personal status are developed which are often difficult to realize by legitimate means because of limited access to the necessary facilities and opportunities."[54]

Shaw's turn toward an interpretation emphasizing structural determinants— delinquent behaviors as a reaction of young people belonging to the poorest social strata faced with scant possibilities of improving their situation—led to an analysis similar to the one proposed in a 1938 article by Merton that, starting in the 1950s, constituted a central reference for works on delinquency.[55]

Some of Shaw's and McKay's analyses targeted the judicial-penitentiary system for handling delinquents. The notes on the autobiographies of young delinquents published by Shaw and McKay contained remarks and some digressions emphasizing the judicial-penitentiary system's inefficiency, and denouncing the poor treatment that it inflicted on some delinquents. These claims, already found in the first published autobiography, *The Jack-Roller*,[56] recall Shaw's first contacts within the prisons of Cook County.

Shaw was particularly critical of the formal method of treating cases that was practiced by social workers: this method, according to Shaw, resulted in a misunderstanding of the delinquent's perspective on his environment and his actions.[57] Placements of delinquents in foster families were, consequently, frequently poorly suited, as in cases when they were placed with families that conformed strictly to conventional moral norms. The second case study, published in 1931, was that of a delinquent who, in contrast with *The Jack-Roller*, started off with mild misdemeanors but soon engaged in more and more serious forms of delinquency. This suggested the inefficacy of the institutional mode of handling delinquency, although this point was developed not in Shaw and Moore's commentary, but rather in the final chapter written by a judge of the Cook County juvenile court.[58]

The last case study, published in 1938, emphasized that contact with other delinquents at a more advanced stage in their criminal career facilitated the learning of new delinquent behaviors and demonstrated that the experience of life in penitentiary institutions reinforced the hostility of delinquents toward society: "Presumably, the methods of treatment administered in juvenile institutions not only failed to deter the brothers from further delinquency but contributed rather to their continuance in careers of crime."[59]

Through what they sought to establish and through their criticism of institutional treatment, the analyses of Shaw and McKay led to the establishment of a policy on delinquency. This was put into action in a program, of which Clifford Shaw was the director from 1934: the Chicago Area Project (CAP).[60]

An experimental program aimed at the study and prevention of juvenile delinquency, CAP was partially funded by the state of Illinois. It proposed an alternate solution to the individual treatment of delinquents by social workers. Believing that youths could only be influenced by those who shared their own background—family, peers, and neighbors—this program sought to facilitate the community taking charge of delinquency problems itself, rather than having an institution do so in its stead. It emphasized primary relationships, which is to say interventions through face-to-face relationships.

In a 1937 interview, Shaw remarked: "You can't get under a kid's skin with the old probationary and social work methods. You can't come at a boy as the functionary of an institution. You've got to meet him as a person. . . . We've got to change the emphasis of our approach from organizations and institutions to face-to-face human relations."[61]

CAP's experimentation took place in the Chicago neighborhoods belonging to Burgess's transitional zone, in which rates of delinquency were high. To facilitate the reorganization of communities, the program recruited not social workers, but rather residents of the zone being studied. The staff's primary role was to aid in the organization of volunteer groups to intervene in the areas thought to be related to juvenile delinquency. In a report produced twenty-five years after CAP's establishment, one of the sociologists engaged in this project, Solomon Kobrin, grouped the interventions of the Chicago Area Project under the following headings: youth recreation organizations, especially summer camps; campaigns in favor of ameliorating conditions in the community in terms of schools, sanitation, and the like; direct interventions concerning delinquents and pre-delinquents, which include support for the police and judiciary personnel, work with youth gangs, and control of delinquents on parole.[62] In the same way that the efficacy of social work was never subject to a precise evaluation (as Shaw himself remarked at its start), there was no evaluation of the effects of the Chicago Area Project, and Kobrin was content to remark in the presentation of his results: "Such action has probably reduced delinquency in the program areas."[63] Shaw himself expressed doubts very early on regarding the efficacy of the actions undertaken.[64]

The idea of community organizing—and the program inspired by Shaw—saw a late diffusion in the 1960s. In 1961, a federal law—the Juvenile Delinquency and Youth Offenses Control Act—provided funding for youth development programs in the twenty largest urban areas of the United States.[65] Among the inspirations for this program figured the authors of a 1960 book on juvenile delinquency, Lloyd Ohlin—an old friend of Shaw—and Richard Cloward—a former student of Merton.[66] Cloward and Ohlin had recently participated in implementing an action plan in New York, adopting the ideas of mobilizing the community and recruiting native-born leaders. During this period, McKay was also one of the active members of a national commission on criminality (the President's Commission on Law Observance and Enforcement), created in 1961.

FROM CRITICISM OF SOCIAL DISORGANIZATION TO A DEVIANCE-BASED APPROACH

Even though the studies of Shaw and McKay remained among the principal references in the study of juvenile delinquency after 1945, from the end of the 1930s the social disorganization approach generated reservations among certain sociologists. One of the first criticisms was proposed by Edwin Sutherland and his circle. Sutherland participated in a synthetic contribution devoted to the subfield of delinquency commissioned by the Social Science Research Council,[67] which was published under the sole authorship of his associate, Thorsten Sellin. In it, Sutherland criticized the approaches that did not challenge criminal laws and whose definitions were "formalist, unilateral, and variable,"[68] and he was attentive to what historical and ethnographic case studies, in which foreign laws were set in place in colonized areas, might offer. Sellin proposed reinterpreting the concept of social disorganization by developing the idea that violations of legal norms should be interpreted as the expression of conflicts between norms of conduct linked to divergent cultural systems.

Sutherland's reservations with respect to the social disorganization interpretation of delinquency were honed over the course of the studies that he conducted on white-collar crime starting in 1928. In an address he gave on this theme as president of the American Sociological Society in 1939, Sutherland formulates a radical critique of the definition of the domain of criminology as the study of working-class delinquency—which is how social disorganization analysis viewed it.[69] For Sutherland, explanations of delinquency that associated it with poverty, or with characteristics attributed to it, were wrong because they were based on biased samplings. Sutherland draws attention to the frequency of violations of the law perpetrated by the leaders of large businesses and members of the established professions in the economic sphere. He emphasizes the importance of the protection guaranteed by an elevated social status and by collective actions: the repression of awareness and repercussions for criminal activities depends on the relative power of those who commit deviant acts versus that of their victims. Sutherland proposed broadening the field of inquiry to all actions that violated the law, whether they led to consequences or not. This essay did not, however, abandon the notion of social disorganization, which Sutherland invoked as one of the terms of a general theory applying to the two principal forms of criminality mentioned. A little later, another article by Sutherland recognized that the concept of social disorganization, which had been introduced in order to break with previous normative approaches, could be criticized along the same lines: its use was accompanied by hidden value judgments, since the concept treated as universal norms whose socially constructed character should be recognized.[70]

Another index of the growing lack of credence in the concept of social disorganization was the success of a 1943 article by C. Wright Mills, which would frequently be cited in the following years. Adopting the perspective of the sociology of knowledge, Mills analyzes the professional ideology underpinning around thirty sociology textbooks, published over the course of the twenty preceding years, devoted to social problems, social pathology, social progress, and social disorganization—to use the terms that appear in the titles of these books.[71] Mills did not directly have Clifford Shaw and his close associates in mind, who do not appear in the list of authors whose textbooks he examines, but rather sociologists of the same or the immediately previous generation. Mills accuses these sociologists of imposing the perspective of middle-class, small-town Protestants in their analyses, claiming that they could not perceive class structure and their approach, in terms of the individual, was similar to that used in social work: "Thus, instead of positional issues, pathologists typically see problems in terms of individuals, such as immigrant, 'adjusting to a milieu' or being 'assimilated' or Americanized."[72] Noting the implicit character of the normative conception of the social order that inspired these approaches, Mills also suggested that "the notion of disorganization is quite often merely the absence of that *type* of organization associated with the stuff of primary-group communities having Christian and Jeffersonian legitimation."[73]

At the University of Chicago, a challenge to the social disorganization approach also surfaced in an incident sparked by William Whyte's dissertation defense. Whyte had studied the youth gangs of an Italian neighborhood in Boston, in his own words, "like an anthropologist."[74] He came to Chicago in 1942 to adapt the book he had written after three years of fieldwork into a dissertation, which he would not have been able to do in the more constraining context of doctoral studies at Harvard.[75] Whyte had conceived of his study in the intellectual environment of Harvard at the end of the 1930s, particularly through contact with reflections upon the community studies of the anthropologists Elliot Chapple and Conrad Arensberg. Whyte claimed to be unfamiliar with the works produced at Chicago over the course of the preceding period, and did not discover them as resources until he had almost finished his fieldwork demonstrating that the structured organization of a neighborhood under study did not correspond with that of its surrounding society. Introduced to Lloyd Warner by Arensberg, Whyte joined Hughes and Warner's small group of associates, as we have seen, and thus, in the context of the Department of Sociology at the time, that of Wirth and Blumer's adversaries. While defending his dissertation, Whyte's analysis aroused the hostility of Wirth, who firmly asserted that slums should be defined in terms of social disorganization.

> According to Whyte's account, it was Everett Hughes who, in the absence of his doctoral supervisor, Lloyd Warner, suggested a compromise that allowed Whyte to satisfy the requirements of the department (or rather those of Louis Wirth) by supplementing his book with a literature review on the subject.[76] In the article that he wrote for this purpose, Whyte develops a reasoned criticism of Zorbaugh's analyses in terms of social disorganization; he notes that Zorbaugh argues only that the organization of slum neighborhoods in which families live differs from that of middle-class neighborhoods in terms of policy. (Whyte relies on his own data as well as an unpublished report written in the context of the Chicago Area Project, focusing on the neighborhood previously studied by Zorbaugh.)[77] Whyte notes that if Thomas and Znaniecki's analysis were applied to these neighborhoods, the children who were not subject to their parents' control would be expected to commit criminal acts according to individual impulses. This was not what was shown by Thrasher and Shaw's analyses, and the social organization interpretation testified solely to a sort of middle-class ethnocentrism (though Whyte does not use this expression): "The sociologist who dismisses racket and political organizations as deviations from

desirable standards thereby neglects some of the major elements of slum life. He fails to see the role that they play in integrating and regulating the smaller and more informal groupings of the district."[78]

It is, however, only in retrospect that *Street Corner Society* seems to mark a stage in the challenge of the social disorganization approach. The book would not have a wide readership, as has been noted, until after its 1955 second edition.[79] After Sutherland's departure from the Chicago Department of Sociology, no tenured professors in the department studied delinquency as the principal domain of research. If the incident that took place during Whyte's dissertation defense left any trace at Chicago, it was only because Whyte remained at the university over the following years, both as a researcher and to teach, and not because the interpretation of phenomena of delinquency was a central concern for Chicago sociologists. However, some dissertations were undertaken on this theme over the course of the following years at the University of Chicago, principally under the encouragement of Burgess. Several of the dissertations were centered around the prediction of the success of conditional releases, and were prepared under the auspices of the Institute of Juvenile Research, or by using its resources. Two such dissertations on delinquency were thus defended in 1948, four in 1949, two in 1950, one in 1951, and two in 1954.[80]

Beyond criticisms of the use of the concept of social disorganization, an evolution in the field of research into which studies on delinquency fit can be discerned: the transition from the concept of social disorganization to the broader concept of deviance is a sign of this evolution. The emergence of this new term is difficult to date precisely, but it spread rapidly after the mid-1950s.

A comparison of different editions of *Webster's Dictionary* suggests that the term "deviance" appeared in American English at the beginning of the 1940s. (The word, rare, existed with a completely different sense in the fifteenth century in England.) Neither it nor the term "deviant" figures in the article Robert Merton published in 1938, "Social Structure and Anomie," which would later be considered the first formulation of the approach to delinquency that would occupy a central place in the 1950s and 1960s.[81] This article utilizes the expression "deviate behavior," suggested by the usage of "deviation" in statistics. When this article was republished in a 1949 collection, Merton placed it after another essay that included the expression "deviant behavior."[82] Parsons uses the term "deviant" in a 1942 article, and the concept has a certain importance in his book *The Social System* (1951), in which, by contrast, the index does not contain the term "social disorganization." The same year, the term "deviant" appeared, probably independently from Merton and Parsons, in the writings of Edwin Lemert (an anthropologist by training), and thereafter it can be found rather frequently in articles in the *American Journal of Sociology*.[83]

Although they had adopted a more relativist perspective than sociologists regarding social norms, anthropologists do not seem to have ever used the terms "deviant" and "deviant behavior" before 1945: they are not found in the 1926 book by Bronislaw Malinowski on criminality in Trobriand society (although he is very attentive to the importance of reaction to acts labeled as delinquent, and was later quoted by Becker in *Outsiders*), nor in the major publications of the same period by Margaret Mead, Ralph Linton, or Radcliffe-Brown.

In 1960 the term "deviance" enjoyed common usage in sociology, even in textbooks. The diffusion of this new term, which was spread, as we have seen, by researchers of diverse backgrounds, reflected, at least for some, a lack of satisfaction with previous approaches.

OUTSIDERS AND THE NEW APPROACH TO DEVIANCE

At the University of Chicago, the studies that contributed to the development of a new approach that would redefine the field in the 1960s were not conducted under the supervision of Shaw and Burgess but, rather, at something of a remove.[84] The book that would offer a point of reference for this approach, Howard Becker's *Outsiders*, was not written by a researcher who specialized in delinquency.[85] Furthermore, it was not developed from a dissertation, but rather included articles pulled from a MA thesis written in the Department of Sociology at the University of Chicago. Its intellectual genesis is surprising on first glance: based specifically on a study on marijuana consumption conducted at the Institute for Juvenile Research, the book seems to adopt an orientation completely different from that of Shaw. Its connection to the Chicago tradition, then in the course of being rediscovered (or redefined), was, however, immediately accepted.[86] Finally, the book was not based on the study of a "classic" category of delinquents: clearly, neither marijuana smokers nor jazz musicians, the two populations being studied, could claim this title. These are the apparent paradoxes that I seek to examine here.

Becker's contribution was not an outlier in terms of its influence on the production of young researchers trained at the University of Chicago around 1950. While the connection was made a posteriori, other studies conducted at the University of Chicago by researchers of the same generation expanded upon different subjects from similar perspectives. The same was true for the studies conducted as dissertations in sociology (such as those of William Westley on the police and Joseph Gusfield on the American temperance movement), and, to a certain degree, for the slightly later book by Erving Goffman, *Stigma* (1963).[87] In *Outsiders*, Becker's references to the works of sociologists belonging to his same generation are another indication of the fact that this new perspective meant a change in the intellectual circumstances.

> This new perspective was a posteriori given the appellation "labeling theory" by its detractors, as Edwin Lemert, one of the perspective's originators, remarked.[88] Again, a recognition that there was something in common among these authors does not imply anything other than "an extremely loose set of themes, rather than an explicit and coherent theory," to use a statement by Gibbons.[89]

The preliminary draft of an application for funding written by Becker in December 1954 outlines a research program in the new subfield of deviance, for which *Outsiders* would provide a definition.[90] It includes few references to previous works—the only ones cited are Sutherland, Durkheim, Gouldner, and Goffman, who had still published almost nothing.[91] It is clear that the works of Shaw and McKay (although well known among sociology students at the University of Chicago at the time), and especially those of Becker, who had the previous year been employed by the Institute of Juvenile Research, did not serve as important references. In an account, Becker also evokes, as a negative reference, Merton's perspective on deviance, developed in the 1950s.[92] Like the studies of Shaw and Sutherland, Merton's work focused on the etiology of deviance in individuals, a question Becker neglected.

In this preliminary draft, Becker proposes another original theme of investigation: the contribution to the definition of deviance made by those in contact with the acts considered deviant, or, rather, their reaction to such acts. Becker insists upon the relativity of social norms, and upon the fact that deviance is only defined by reference to specific groups: "Deviance in one group may be conformity in another," he remarks. He also notes, "Some rules are attached to extremely general roles . . . such as those related to specific roles in industrial organizations, and have no meaning or importance outside of this context."[93] The outlined research project focused on the organization and the social positions of deviant groups, that is, their relations with legitimate society. Becker adds the study of deviant careers, a theme directly issuing from Hughes's studies in the sociology of work. Surveying the areas of research that could have been chosen, Becker remarked: "I would prefer to study an organization which could be localized for observation. . . . Bringing in my active interest in the sociology of work, it seems as though the logical kind of study might be one of a work organization—school, factory, store, etc.—in which rules could be discovered, non-conformity to them and its consequences noted, etc."[94] This time, it was the studies of Melville Dalton on corporate executives and those of Donald Roy on blue-collar workers that stood in the background of the project, as confirmed by their evocation some years later in *Outsiders*.[95]

In his retrospective reflections on this book, Becker always insists upon the fact that the new perspective of the study of deviance introduced by *Outsiders* resulted from the application of what then constituted the usual intellectual baggage of that generation's University of Chicago sociology students to this particular domain. To these elements could be added young researchers' experience of the social world, as well as the context of American society of the period. I shall give an overall explanation of these elements to demonstrate how *Outsiders* is situated at their convergence. I shall begin by quoting passages from several of Becker's own testimonies.

> I originally conceived *Outsiders* as a contribution to the understanding of deviance, as that term was narrowly understood by American sociologists and criminologists: the study of crime and delinquency, as defined by the official decisions of police and courts. I thought we could understand these phenomena better by treating them from the point of view of the sociology of work, by seeing that defining some activities as crimes, accusing people of committing those crimes and seeing to it that they were convicted by the courts—that all of that was, after all, someone's work, to be understood just as we understood the work of physicians, lawyers or industrial workers.[96]

In another statement, Becker remarked:

> I say that is not particularly a novel point of view because, if one did not accept the perspective of the conventional institutions, then a standard sociological perspective would be exactly to look for definition: who defines the situation in what way, how people define each other, and so on. It's only that in that case we accept the definition of the powerful institutions of society and we say "This institution after all represents the State, how can it be wrong? it must be correct" and we accept their definition, but it can't be done, the definition is political, not scientific.

I came to this change of perspective exactly from that point of view, that is I simply refused to accept the standard definition of what the problem was. I did that because I had learned in my early classes in sociology that what are studied was exactly the definitions of the situation. So I look to this case and I could see that different people define the situation differently and that, while, let's say the police or the physicians define certain of the actors as criminals or deviants, the people, defined in that way, say "No, we disagree, we are not like that, they are wrong, they in fact, are corrupt or stupid, or whatever" . . . are last two possible points of view. If you didn't give a special privilege to one point of view, you have to came to the position I took, which, in fact is the standard sociological position, current in all the historical varieties of sociology, and it's not a question of theoretical differences, you see, it's only a question of whether the theory of sociology generally is applied in a rigorous impartial way or not.

Now, I could say that in part I came to the change of perspective because of my own experience. I was marginal by virtue of being engaged in a marginal profession, that is to say, I played piano in small jazz groups, in bars, in cabarets, and so I had a lot of experience with the demi-monde. And I knew that these were people who were conventionally looked down, but who themselves looked down on the conventional world and these gave me, I think, a kind of perspective outside of the conventional way of seeing this problem which perhaps made it easier to come to this way of defining the whole question of deviance.[97]

In a previous testimony, Becker offered another indication of the intellectual origin of his study on marijuana smokers, the results of which can be found in *Outsiders*:

I started the marijuana study more or less as a technical experiment. I had read Lindesmith's book *Opiate Addiction*[98] in which he used the method of analytic induction. It really struck my fancy and I wanted to try it. I started in '51 and it was done in '53, and it was done because of Lindesmith's book. . . . I wrote the first draft of the theoretical part of the book in 1954. . . . At that time I had not read Lemert's book. . . .[99] "Labelling theory," so called, is a way of looking at deviance which actually represents a complete continuity with the rest of sociology. In other words, if a sociologist were going to study any topic, he would probably take such an approach, unless there were reasons not to. But there have been reasons not to approach criminology and the study of crime in the same way we might approach some more neutral topic. In studying most kinds of social organization, we will more likely understand that we have to study the actions of all the people involved in that organization. . . . But somehow when sociologists studied crime they didn't understand the problem that way. . . . The study of crime lost his connection with the mainstream of sociological development and became a very bizarre deformation of sociology, designed to find out why people were doing bad things instead of finding out the organization of interaction in that sphere of life. I had approached the problem differently, the way I'd learned to do in studying occupations. . . . So I approached deviance as the study of people whose occupation, one might say, was either crime, or catching criminals. . . . The theory, and it really was a pretty rudimentary theory, wasn't designed to explain why people robbed banks but rather how robbing banks came to have the quality of being deviant.[100]

It is easy to demonstrate the relationship between the different elements Becker (and others) cited and the perspective that he would develop. First of all, we recognize the elements issuing directly from Hughes's sociology of work and institutions. A course Hughes taught in 1951, published later in *Sociological Eye*, reveals an original approach to the different institutionalized forms of deviation from norms, taking the example of those that govern relations between men and women.[101] Several of the ideas Becker developed came directly from Hughes's analytical model of work and professions: the attention to the perspectives adopted by the actors themselves on the sector of activity under consideration; the focalization on the process of interaction leading to the attribution to certain actors of a label; the refusal to adopt as a research perspective either the point of view of those at the top or those who found themselves at the base of the hierarchy of legitimacy.

Another element invoked in Becker's testimonies is the pedagogy of Joseph Lohman. Situated on the margins of the academic world, he taught rather regularly, with a precarious status, in the Department of Sociology. Lohman had firsthand knowledge of police, criminal worlds, and politicians by virtue of his other activities, and his teaching drew on his familiarity with these worlds.

Joseph Lohman (1910–1968) began his study of sociology at Chicago in 1931, and from 1932 to 1939 was employed by the Institute of Juvenile Research and the Chicago Area Project.[102] According to two accounts, he began to study organized crime for his dissertation, but threats he received at the beginning of this study led indirectly to his departure from the Chicago Area Project at the end of the 1930s.[103] He abandoned his doctoral studies, but, from 1939 to 1959, he secured teaching work in the Department of Sociology of the University of Chicago. A recognized expert in race relations, urban police, and the treatment of delinquency, from 1946 Lohman participated in several federal commissions and embarked on a political career in the state of Illinois. From 1949 to 1952, he led the Department of Corrections; in 1954, he was elected police commissioner of Cook County, then, in 1958, treasurer of the state of Illinois. He was a candidate for the position of governor of Illinois in 1960, but was not elected. Abandoning politics, the following year he became a professor and dean in the School of Criminology of the University of California at Berkeley.[104]

In one account, Becker emphasizes how Lohman made use of his familiarity with the world of delinquents in his teaching: "When I was in graduate school, he used to teach a class in sociology, one night a week, it was a three hours class, on one thing, of crime. It consists almost entirely of Lohman telling stories of his experiences and it was fascinating and we became accustomed, like all graduate students, it was better than the movies."[105] He specifies elsewhere: "[Lohman] was a model of someone who had done real fieldwork with criminals, and he was contemptuous of a lot of criminological research that was going on, on the grounds that it was innocent and naive about how things worked, especially about the role of corrupt local politics in crime."[106]

The example of Frank Tannenbaum, whose 1938 book would later develop a perspective similar to that of Becker, confirms that a firsthand knowledge of delinquency *could* lead to this type of perspective. Tannenbaum (1893–1969), who was a professor of Latin American history at Columbia University from 1936 to 1961, had personal experience of prison due to his involvement in organizing a 1914 occupation of churches by homeless and unemployed people. The starting point for his 1938 book on delinquency and prison can be found in a 1925 magazine article emphasizing the importance of reactions to deviance.[107] Tannenbaum then wrote a report for the National Commission on Law Observance and Enforcement—which had also commissioned the report by Shaw and McKay (1931)—but this part of the report was probably not published. In any case, Tannenbaum's report was not as widely read as the part containing Shaw and McKay's report, although some of it was reprinted in a 1938 book. Tannenbaum's perspective is formulated at the beginning: "The process of making the criminal . . . is a process of tagging, defining, identifying, segregating, describing, emphasizing, making conscious and self-conscious; it becomes a way of stimulating, suggesting emphasizing, and evolving the very traits that are complained of."[108]

The presence of another group of significant elements in Becker's testimonies—which refer to "ideas in the air" regarding the perspective of *Outsiders*—can be confirmed by comparing them with the testimonies of sociology students of the University of Chicago who belonged to the same generation. In contrast to those who had embarked upon studies in sociology in the 1920s or 1930s and who, as Hughes phrased it, had to emancipate themselves from their Protestant and rural origins, the students who followed this same path after 1945 were, as previously noted, rarely religious Protestants with middle-class rural origins. The prior experiences of some students of this generation had brought them into contact with the diversity of norms in usage in different circles in the large cities of the period—Becker, as previously mentioned, was a jazz pianist.[109]

In a biographical essay, Freidson, who belonged to the same generation, remarked:

> As the fortunes of my father's shoe business improved my parents bought a house in Brookline, then an upper-class suburb of Boston. For me, at age ten, it was a move from a fairly homogeneous, protective neighborhood to a place in which Boston "Yankee" norms, including its politely condescending version of anti-Semitism, were dominant. Perhaps because of the minority position I found myself in when I transferred to the sixth grade of an elementary school in Brookline, I came to feel rather detached from the conventional world. By the time I was in High School I felt little identification with either Yankee or Jewish institutions and questioned the authority and virtue of both.[110]

It should be noted that one student from the same generation who did have Protestant, rural, Anglo-Saxon origins comparable to those of many sociologists of the preceding generation—James Short, the son of a small-town Illinois high school principal (PhD in 1951)—developed analyses that continued the legacies of Shaw and McKay.[111]

Finally, it is necessary to add some elements of the social context of the end of the 1950s, particularly the evolution of juvenile delinquency as a public problem. The official statistics suggest a strong increase in acts of delinquency between 1938 and 1944, then a decline until 1948, followed by a significant growth until the end of the following decade.[112] Probably more important than this increase were the progressive public discoveries of new forms of juvenile delinquency concerning the middle class, such as drug use and engagement in forms of cultural dissidence.[113]

Whether these correspond to changes in behavior or to public focalization on these changes, these phenomena are mentioned in the works of researchers at the end of the 1950s. It was, as we have seen, in the context of a study project based on this belief that Becker's study on marijuana was funded at the Institute of Juvenile Research.[114]

> The public attention paid to juvenile delinquency in the 1950s was linked to questions about the consequences of the development of mass culture.[115] Between 1953 and 1956, many articles were published about the delinquency of youths. A senatorial commission was created in 1953 and would become very active after 1955. The middle classes seemed concerned by increasing juvenile delinquency, even if there existed some doubts regarding the significance of statistics: the director of the Children's Bureau (the administration charged with publishing these data) himself remarked in 1958 that, "to some, the manner of attire—the mere wearing of blue jeans or a ducktail haircut—is sufficient to label a child a delinquent."[116]

Thus, the context of the period, the life experiences of some then-students in sociology, and the borrowing and transmission of a small number of ideas from one area of study to another that formed a sort of common knowledge for a group of researchers were all elements that *could* have led to the change in perspective with which *Outsiders* has been associated. The relationship between the analytical models used by the two groups of studies considered here is more complex than either direct descent within the same subfield or the reaction against ideas that had been accepted in the previous period, but were refuted by obvious public phenomena (of which we shall see some examples in the following chapter). We might interpret this transformation of the interrogation into juvenile delinquency that took place over the course of the 1950s as a step toward a greater detachment in the social sciences from the perspective and practical ends that were adopted, regarding these phenomena, by those who acted in this area.

But we must also recall that some remarks made in passing by Chicago sociologists of the preceding generation anticipated the perspective developed by Becker. In 1930, in a letter to Louis Wirth regarding one of his articles, Park noted, for example, the importance of the definition of delinquency: "I think the point you make that delinquency is only delinquency because of social definition of the group in which the delinquency occurs is the core of the whole thesis."[117] In the same way, in a memorandum prior to the creation of the Behavior Research Fund, Burgess remarked: "The term criminology as used here includes the whole process of defining crimes, committing crimes and reacting to crimes. Thus it includes law making, law breaking, the treatment of criminals, and the prevention of crime. As such it is closely related to more general processes of making rules, breaking rules and the reaction to the breaking of rules, and should be studied in relations to the more general processes."[118]

The elements evoked here represent only some of those that must be taken into account when analyzing the intellectual genesis of *Outsiders*. There exists a second intellectual context in which the book positions itself, that of exchanges within an informal network of researchers that took place in California at the end of the 1950s. In it can be found the exchanges of many of those—notably Edwin Lemert and two of his students, Aaron Cicourel and John Kitsune—who, over the course of the same period, would contribute to the formulation of ideas that Becker had noted were in the air in this period.[119]

8

Research in the World

The Study of Race and Intercultural Relations,
1913–1963

I was not, as I found later, interested in the Negro problem as that problem
is ordinarily conceived. I was interested in the Negro in the South and in the
curious and intricate system which had grown up to define his relations with
white folk. I was interested, most of all, in studying the details of the process
by which the Negro was making and has made his slow but steady advance.
I become convinced, finally, that I was observing the historical process by
which civilization, not merely here but elsewhere, has evolved, drawing into
the circle of its influence an ever widening circle of races and peoples.

—Robert Park[1]

It is safe to say that if the various racial groups in American society had had
harmonious and democratic relationships, no field of race relations study
would have ever emerged.

—Herbert Blumer[2]

I f the collection of books and authors assembled under the label
"Chicago School" had been the result of a planned construction
rather than a collective process that occurred over the course of the
development of sociology, emphasis would surely have had to have been placed
on the study of relations between racial and ethnic groups. This was the theme
of *The Polish Peasant* by Thomas and Znaniecki, and at the center of the analytical framework proposed in the *Introduction to the Science of Sociology* by Park
and Burgess; race and ethnic relations were also the subject of a large number of

dissertations in sociology defended at the University of Chicago through the end of the 1950s. A long list could be compiled of research works on this theme that, in one period or another, were conducted by researchers who had unquestionable intellectual ties to Thomas, Park, and the Chicago sociology department.[3] In this list would appear the books of the first black sociologists to gain national renown, such as Charles Johnson, E. Franklin Frazier, and Horace Cayton, the last of whom co-authored with anthropologist Saint Clair Drake a book on the African American neighborhoods of Chicago, *Black Metropolis* (1945). It would also include the works on the populations of the Hawaiian Islands by Romanzo Adams and Andrew Lind,[4] and those of Edward Reuter and Emory Bogardus, two sociologists trained at the University of Chicago before 1920 who maintained lasting relationships with Park.[5] The list would have the works of Edgar Thompson on the plantation system[6] and William Brown on prejudices,[7] both sociologists who studied at the University of Chicago at the beginning of the 1930s, as well as, in political science, Harold Gosnell's study on black politicians.[8] We would also find books, articles, and lectures by Park's institutional successors in the University of Chicago sociology department, Louis Wirth, Herbert Blumer, and Everett Hughes.[9] Finally, we might add some works from the 1940s and 1950s by the students of Park's successors, including Tamotsu Shibutani, Lewis Killian, or Joseph Lohman and Dietrich Reitzes.[10]

A considerable number of books that examine Chicago sociology, however, accord a somewhat limited importance to these works when compared to works centered on cities or delinquency.[11] Many factors have contributed to this relative lack of attention.

We must recall, first, that the domain of works on relations between racial and ethnic groups (I shall return to these labels further on) never fit into a strictly disciplinary framework. Sociologists, anthropologists, economists, historians, and independent researchers unaffiliated with any academic discipline participated in this same area of study, without disciplinary affiliation constituting any obstacle to the diffusion of their analyses among their colleagues in different disciplines. More so than it was a subject of scholarly research, the question of relations between races and ethnic groups was a subject of passionate public debate, initially on the position of immigrants in American society and, after 1920, on the position and the future of African Americans. As we shall see, social science researchers participated in these debates and were inevitably influenced by them, even if the effects of this influence were not always simple.

It is also necessary to remark that precisely delimiting which studies fall or do not fall within Thomas and Park's legacy of works is an enterprise destined for failure—unless we settle for a formal definition based upon the personal connections among the researchers in question. The circle of researchers in the area of relations between racial and ethnic groups was rather limited before 1950, and the intellectual and personal contacts within it were frequently manifold. Research in this area essentially took place in only a few universities: the University of Chicago; the University of North Carolina, where, with significant funding from the Rockefeller family foundations, there developed a program of research on race relations around Howard Odum;[12] the University of Hawaii, around a small number of sociologists trained at the University of Chicago; and the traditionally African American universities Fisk (in Nashville, Tennessee) and Howard (in Washington).

Some researchers who had no or few contacts with Park, or whose careers had unfolded outside the orbit of his associates, have generally not been connected to the tradition he began, although they sometimes maintained close ties with it. Thus, Guy Johnson, one of the most productive researchers in Odum's circle, obtained an MA at the University of Chicago, which he left soon afterward, recruited by the University of North Carolina. Likewise, the sociology dissertation of Ira De Augustine Reid—who spent only a few months at the University of Chicago and defended his dissertation at Columbia in 1938—is similar to the dissertations Park supervised at the University of Chicago in terms of his approach to black immigrants from the Caribbean and in terms of his types of evidence.[13]

Finally, some of Park's students who worked in this area—such as Johnson, Frazier, and Hughes—were productive over the course of long careers after having left Park's orbit. Their activities fit within sociopolitical and intellectual contexts outside of Park's, and their research was produced and read in the context of references other than their connection with his sociology.

The posterity of the Chicago tradition in the subfield of race and interethnic relations is obvious—Park remained an author of reference in this domain much longer than any other—but rather difficult to identify. By examining some of the studies that clearly relate to this tradition, I here propose to analyze how this perspective took into account events and trends that seem important in retrospect, and how the studies were shaped by elements of context, such as the internal evolutions of the social sciences and their means of funding.

Relying on historical works of the last decades, I shall present here an overall view of the evolutions, the events, and the controversies relating to the relationships between African Americans and broader American society that were behind these studies. I shall focus attention both on elements that are connected to the sociology of Park and his students, as well as those that, by contrast, have gone unnoticed in this approach. I shall then survey the ways in which studies in this domain were funded, and finally examine the analytical framework proposed by Park and the ways in which it evolved in reference to these contextual aspects, as well as the later contributions of Charles Johnson, Franklin Frazier, and Everett Hughes.

Recall that the term "race," as used by Park and almost all social science researchers since the 1920s, refers to a social and not biological definition. As Hughes wrote, "the first thing obvious to a complete outsider would be that race in this country is a linguistic invention; of course there is a lot of history behind it, a behind any linguistic invention."[14] In France, the term "race" has, on the contrary, retained a strong biological connotation, and this type of social definition is almost unknown.

I have selected here Blumer's definition, which roughly corresponds Park's usage of the term: "A race has come to mean simply a group of people who are regarded and treated in actual life as a race. The membership of the race simply consists of those individuals who are identified and classified as belonging to it."[15] The concept of "ethnic group"—defined by a combination of traits like language, religion, race, national origin, and so on—thus corresponds to a more general category than does "racial group."

The relationship between the terms "racial group" and "ethnic group" is, however, a subject of deep-rooted controversy in the United States. During Park's time, black Americans were not considered to be an ethnic group because they were not seen as having their own culture; there was also the alleged impossibility, a viewpoint espoused by many, of their assimilation into the rest of the population—which is to say, even if the question is generally left unspoken, of integration by intermarriage. Today, by contrast, any claim to the intractable distinctiveness of black Americans refers to an emphasis on the indelible character of racial differences, and to the statement that, at least in the United States, the consequences of belonging to a racial minority group cannot be compared to those of belonging to ethnic groups resulting from European emigration.[16] Despite these controversies, I have sometimes, when there is no ambiguity, used the term "ethnic group" in a broad sense, encompassing the concept of "racial group."

I use here the terms "black" or "African American," which were not in use in the 1920s, and have retained the then-current "Negro" in only a few cases for historical terms (such as "New Negro" and "the Negro problem").[17] These difficulties in terminology remind us that today, as in Park's time, the concepts used in sociology are closely tied to concepts native to the societies within which they emerged.

EVOLUTIONS OF RACIAL AND INTERETHNIC RELATIONS
AND PUBLIC CONTROVERSIES BETWEEN WHITES
AND AFRICAN AMERICANS

After the nativist reactions of Protestant Anglo-Saxons at the end of the First World War, questions of immigration from Europe or Asia lost some of their pointedness in public debates. The cessation of Asian immigration and the obstacles set up to stem new immigration after 1921 translated into a rapid decline in the proportion of foreign-born residents in the United States. They made up more than 4.7 percent of the population in 1930, and only 1.3 percent in 1940.[18] From the 1930s, public attention was less focused on the possible consequences of the cultural, religious, and so on heterogeneity of the American population than it had been before 1914.[19] Complete assimilation into the Anglo-Saxon group, that is, "Americanization," was not the only path that lay before immigrants and their descendants: the idea of an ethnic pluralism, which is to say the permanence of cultural differences between groups, found some defenders after the war, such as the philosopher Horace Kallen. Thus, the terms "melting pot" and "pluralism" acquired more varied meanings than they had during the preceding period.

In the intellectual milieu of the United States, and particularly among social science researchers, racist theories interpreting the differences between ethnic groups as biological differences continued to lose credit after 1918. Shortly thereafter, in the 1930s, reactions to the rise of anti-Semitism in Germany accentuated the discrediting of this theory, and anthropologists, principally Boas and his students, reiterated their criticisms of a biological conception of race in response to Nazi propaganda.[20]

This transformation of the conception of interethnic relations in intellectual contexts was accompanied, and partially inspired, by the evolution that took place on the political level over the course of the New Deal. While no legislative dispensation was taken in favor of immigrants to the United States, public administrations at least abandoned some measures that actively oppressed them. Public funds were used for radio broadcasts presenting, according to one Roosevelt administration official, the "rich heritages that have come to us through the many races and nationalities which make up our population," and some newspapers and films successfully condemned racism and xenophobia.[21] Aside from an interlude corresponding to the war against Japan in the Pacific, with its brutal consequences for Japanese immigrants and families of Japanese origin,[22] it was the question of African Americans more so than other groups that continually drew attention between 1920 and 1960.[23] African Americans also constituted the more numerous group by far: according to data from the 1930 census, African Americans accounted for 9.69 percent of the population, Mexicans 1.16 percent, Indians 0.27 percent, Japanese 0.11 percent, and Chinese 0.06 percent.[24] An essential contextual element of studies on relations between racial and ethnic groups thus corresponds to the vicissitudes of relations of African Americans, and it is this historical example that was at the heart of the field, at least until the mid-1960s.

The migration of African Americans from the rural South to northern cities, which had been massive during and just after the First World War, did not come to a stop in the following years.[25] In Chicago, the number of African Americans, which had grown between 1910 and 1920 by 65,300, increased by 124,000 over the course of the following decade, and by 43,800 between 1930 and 1940.[26] This influx of a population that was principally rural in origin led to a new situation: the establishment of a vast black ghetto, as existed in the other northern cities. The limited resources of the new arrivals condemned them to settle en masse in cities' transitional zones (to use Burgess's expression). They were also excluded from the majority of urban neighborhoods through both intimidation and clauses in deeds of ownership prohibiting the sale or rent of residences to African Americans.[27] Racial segregation in certain public places, such as hotels and restaurants, appeared in northern cities, where it had not existed before 1914. Boards of Education in certain cities also facilitated segregation by redrawing school districts.

The consequences of the clustering of African Americans in certain neighborhoods would become evident over time. In some sectors (banks, real estate agencies, certain businesses, etc.), black entrepreneurs succeeded in imposing a semi-monopoly on clientele in the ghettos, to their profit.[28] Doctors, lawyers, and members of the established professions also benefited from a semi-monopoly on black clients due to segregation in the institutions that employed them. The clustering of African Americans also permitted the emergence of the black politician and the black vote, which around 1945 would play a determining role in the federal government's decisions in favor of racial equality.

Employment constituted another domain in which antagonisms between the races developed. Excluded from unions, African Americans were used as strikebreakers in northern cities, as certain groups of European immigrants had previously been. The difficulty of their access to employment was a growing concern for associations defending their interests.

The interwar period was marked by the development of organizations aimed at ameliorating the African American condition, and sometimes at radically changing it. One school of thought, the so-called "gradualist" position which was part of Booker T. Washington's legacy, held that the condition of African Americans should be gradually improved by stages, through their separate development. The Urban League was a proponent of this method and attempted, without great success, to persuade employers and unions to accept black workers.[29] The influence of the Urban League declined over the course of the 1920s, giving rise to the more incisive actions of the National Association for the Advancement of Colored People (NAACP).[30] This organization secured legal defense for African Americans after race riots, waged a legal attack on certain practices of segregation, and sought the recognition of African Americans' constitutional rights, especially their political rights. Initially, however, the NAACP was little concerned with their rights as workers.

The NAACP, like the Urban League, was founded, and for a time led, by whites. The same was not true of another movement created in 1914, the Universal Negro Improvement Association. Between 1918 and 1921, it won a large audience among the poorest African Americans in cities. Built around its charismatic leader of Jamaican origin, Marcus Garvey, this movement criticized light-skinned elite African Americans who benefited from higher education and, addressing the popular masses, advocated the return of African Americans to Africa by proposing the development of a distinct racial type of civilization.[31] Shortly thereafter, in the 1930s, with an audience that was small but grew in certain circumstances, the Communist Party recruited certain intellectuals, often very provisionally, and sometimes found temporary allies in union leaders critical of the moderate positions of the Urban League and the NAACP.[32] One of these momentary allies, Philip Randolph, a journalist who had founded and led the Pullman Porters Union, also referred to Marxism and believed that capitalism was at the origin of the prejudices and discrimination to which African Americans were subjected, and that only communal action from black and white workers could ensure the improvement of the African American condition.[33]

African Americans—particularly intellectuals—began to occupy more and more positions of influence in some of these movements and were no longer merely a labor force for members of the elite and the white social workers, who figured largely among the leaders of the principal organizations defending African American interests. The Urban League thus in 1921 recruited Charles Johnson, a former student of Park, as the editor of its magazine *Opportunity*. In 1925, the NAACP hired as general secretary the poet James Weldon Johnson.

Charles Johnson's (1893–1956) career demonstrates some of the concrete links between the social sciences and the political and intellectual controversies regarding race relations. The son of a freed slave who became a Baptist pastor in Virginia, Johnson came to Chicago in 1917 to pursue studies in sociology.[34] He was, as we have seen, hired in 1919 on Park's recommendation as the secretary overseeing the studies of the investigatory commission on the Chicago riots. Before this position, he had collected evidence (particularly letters and biographical documents) for a book on the migration of African Americans to the North during the First World War.[35] Johnson did not obtain his doctorate, but in 1921 he settled in New York and became research director of the Urban League. Johnson was responsible for the organization's magazine, *Opportunity*, and it was in this capacity that he played a role in the cultural movement of the 1920s.

In 1928, Johnson became the chair of the new Department of Social Sciences at Fisk University (where Park finished his career, as we have seen). From the 1930s, he belonged to the small world of foundation administrators who funded research on race relations. Johnson developed a center of information on the condition of African Americans and the state of race relations in the South, organizing the collection and publication of statistical data and publishing several books on the subject. He performed various official missions for the League of Nations and wrote reports for the Hoover, Roosevelt, and Truman administrations, as well as UNESCO later on.[36] Johnson was also a consultant to the NAACP for the choice of strategy that would lead to the decision rendering segregation in education illegal.[37] Johnson was the first African American to be elected vice president of the American Sociological Society, as well as president in 1946 of the Southern Sociological Society (which brought together established sociologists in the South, which was composed of segregationist states). Johnson acceded the same year to the presidency of Fisk University, a position that he would hold until his death.

A new interest in African American culture appeared in the 1920s, principally in New York, where Johnson then found himself. Along with other cities, New York was marked by the blossoming of the Harlem Renaissance, a literary and artistic movement among its African American population.[38] In 1925, Charles Johnson and a young black Harvard graduate, Alain Locke, organized a special issue of *Survey Graphic*, the journal of the Social Survey Movement. It served to launch a group of writers and musicians into New York's intellectual and artistic circles.[39] Breaking with what Booker T. Washington had advocated over the course of the preceding period—African American acceptance of the inferiority of their status—the movement proposed the model of the "New Negro," to quote the title of the special issue of *Survey Graphic*: the New Negro asserted race membership, demonstrated his attachment to the black subculture, demanded his rights as a citizen, and reclaimed full participation in American society.

The mass migration of African Americans to the North was accompanied by a phenomenon less visible than the emergence of individual black intellectuals, but important due to its later consequences: an increasing number of African Americans were pursuing secondary and higher education, which was easier in the northern cities than in the South. Some students benefited from scholarships from organizations like the Rosenwald Foundation, which sought to encourage the emergence of an African American elite more so than the development of research on African Americans.[40]

Migration from the rural South to northern cities was not completely halted during the Great Depression, as shown by the previously mentioned statistics concerning Chicago. The establishment of departure assistance for workers in the agricultural sector following the agricultural crisis in the South, as well unemployment assistance for those in the cities of the North, facilitated the continued migration of African Americans northward. However, the intervention of federal authorities during the New Deal was not always favorable to African Americans. This was not the case in agriculture, or for housing, where funds were always specific to each race. However, certain social programs in the North were less discriminatory than those in the South, and African Americans were not excluded from the list of the disadvantaged upon which the authorities focused attention.

The New Deal was also marked by symbolic advances in the position accorded to African Americans in public life: they were entrusted with some public positions, with prominent individuals, notably Eleanor Roosevelt, publicly decrying behaviors discriminatory to African Americans. The black vote in the large cities of the North was an important element in African Americans' accommodation by political authorities: in 1936, they abandoned voting for Republicans in favor of voting for Democrats for the first time, thus contributing to Franklin D. Roosevelt's reelection.

From the mid-1930s, one of the principal battlegrounds for associations supporting African Americans was that of discrimination in employment. Partly under the influence of the NAACP, which maintained relationships with the CIO (Congress of Industrial Organizations), a newly founded unionist organization aimed at industrial workers,[41] some unions began to accept the membership of African Americans. The alliance of the NAACP and the CIO marked the recognition by union leaders of the impossibility of organizing workers while excluding African Americans: in 1941, during a Detroit automobile industry strike, the union of auto workers sought and obtained the intervention of the NAACP with the aim of rallying African Americans for the strike. During the following twenty years, the solidarity between unions and African Americans would become the political touchstone of the NAACP.

Over the course of the Second World War, African Americans encountered the same difficulties they had faced during the First: discrimination in the army and on the labor market, racial tension in the South as well as in the cities of the North.[42] The March on Washington Movement, which put pressure on Washington through the threat of a march of black workers on the initiative of Philip Randolph, led to Roosevelt's creation of the Fair Employment Practices Commission in June 1941, intended to encourage the hiring of African Americans. Though unable to intervene directly, this commission facilitated some advances in the employment of African Americans in the war industries.

Meanwhile, a new type of urban riot had appeared even before the beginning of the Second World War. In 1935 in Harlem, in reaction to a police intervention and the (unfounded) rumor of the death of a black adolescent in the course of this intervention, rioters attacked stores belonging to both blacks and whites.[43] During the Second World War, political leaders and specialists in race relations repeatedly expressed their fear of the appearance of riots in cities, like those that had occurred at the end of the First World War. Several riots marked the year 1943—one in Detroit, in June, resulted in thirty-four deaths, making it the deadliest since the 1919 Chicago riot. This renewal of racial tensions spurred the emergence of numerous local committees focusing on racial conflicts, which were in general run by liberal whites. Some gave rise to administrations and to a new profession, that of the specialist in "intergroup relations," the euphemistic appellation that was used over the course of this period to designate racial relations. The National Association of Intergroup Relations Officials brought together leaders of the administrations newly created by states and cities as well as those of older organizations, such as the NAACP and the Urban League.[44] Over the following years, this association served as one of the points of contact between sociologists and the liberals who defined race relations as a social problem to which rational solutions aiming for progressive social changes should be applied.

After 1945, with the mechanization of cotton agriculture in the South, the massive migration toward cities of the North and to the West Coast resumed and, by consequence, so did the expansion of black ghettos. In Chicago, the black population went from 277,700 in 1940 to 492,200 in 1950, a growth five times greater than that of the preceding decade. It was followed by a new influx of 320,300 people between 1950 and 1960.[45] Other northern cities saw similar developments, which strengthened the electoral importance of African Americans. This became clear in 1948, during the election of Harry Truman: he recognized the support African Americans provided him through the official desegregation of the armed forces and by the pressure his administration put on firms that worked for the federal government to hire black workers. But the direct effects put into place by the Truman administration were perhaps less important than the changes in norms in terms of race relations that they would sketch out.

During the 1930s the state of race relations was also influenced by international circumstances. From the New Deal, and even more so during the war, numerous liberals—middle-class whites who were partisans of an evolution toward greater racial equality—became cognizant of the contradiction between the fight against Nazis abroad and the acceptance of segregation in the South. After 1945, the Cold War—the propaganda of the Soviet Union frequently referenced the situation of African Americans in the South—and the growing importance of Africa and Asia in American politics reinforced the position of those who supported the dismantling of segregation in Southern states.

Legal advances toward equal civil rights took place during the 1950s. The NAACP successfully practiced a policy of legal harassment against segregationist practices in the South. In 1954, the Supreme Court reached a momentous milestone with their decision that rendered educational segregation illegal. During the following months, the most important development was the increasing recourse of African Americans to nonviolent, direct mass action. This movement especially sought to prohibit discrimination in public services. The victorious 1955 bus boycott in Montgomery, Alabama facilitated a success that would have immense consequences. The visibility of this new form of action relied especially on one black leader, the Reverend Martin Luther King, Jr., an advocate of nonviolent protest inspired by the example of Gandhi, and on the Congress of Racial Equality (CORE), a new organization which argued for direct action and took an interest in the problems of poor neighborhoods.

At the end of the 1950s, the success obtained by the NAACP in the legal condemnation of segregation in the South redirected African American activism toward economic and social problems in the cities. In the spring of 1960, a series of nonviolent demonstrations by students opposed to segregation in businesses marked a rupture with the earlier legal techniques of the NAACP and put an end to its preeminence over the other organizations defending African American rights. The same year, after the election of John F. Kennedy as president, the federal government included a significant number of African Americans for the first time. Discrimination in housing funds was immediately abolished, and in 1962 a committee was charged with ensuring that hiring policies in companies benefiting from contracts with the federal government were not discriminatory against African Americans.

Other developments were not so favorable to African Americans. Over the course of the 1950s, their economic situation in cities, which had since the end of the 1930s seen a significant improvement, ceased to progress—at least in comparison with that of whites—notably as a result of the declining number of non-skilled jobs. According to official statistics, the median familial income of African Americans, which was around 30 percent of that of whites in 1930, reached about 54 percent in 1953, but stagnated at that level in 1963.[46]

The exacerbation of rivalries between the different organizations defending African American rights also encouraged the radicalization of their positions. With the development of direct action—high school and college student demonstrations against school segregation in the South, demonstrations in front of businesses with discriminatory hiring policies and those practicing segregation—the rate of evolution accelerated at the beginning of the 1960s. Supported by Philip Randolph, the major Protestant churches, and some union leaders, the March on Washington of August 1963 brought together more than two hundred thousand people and marked a sort of apogee of mass mobilization in favor of action on the federal level. It led to legislation on civil rights in 1964, which expanded the possibilities of the intervention of federal authorities. The following years were marked by riots during which African Americans attacked white-owned businesses in poor urban neighborhoods. A radical fringe group of African Americans argued in favor of violent and revolutionary action against oppression by the white community, demanding not only equality, but even the separation of races. An official report emphasized that this marked a new reversal in the objectives of African Americans: "Much of their economic program, as well as their interest in Negro history, self help, racial solidarity, and separation is reminiscent of Booker Washington. The rhetoric is different, but the ideas are remarkably similar."[47]

Researchers studying African Americans in the United States—and, more generally, all those working in the domain of racial and intercultural relations—have been confronted with this turbulent history. Without expanding further, we note that many researchers in the field perceived the events and the rapid evolutions of the 1960s as signaling a sort of intellectual weakness in the collective perspectives of the social sciences, which had failed to recognize, understand, or predict them. This sentiment was notably expressed in Everett Hughes's address in his capacity of president of the American Sociological Society in August 1963, and it targeted, if not for Hughes then at least for others, the research inspired by Park.[48] We shall return later to the relationship of Park's framework with this history.

RESEARCH AND RESEARCH FUNDING IN THE DOMAIN
OF RELATIONS BETWEEN RACES AND ETHNIC GROUPS

At the beginning of its involvement in funding studies in social sciences in 1923, the Laura Spelman Rockefeller Memorial Fund included among its objectives the funding of studies on the "Negro problem."[49] Leonard Outhwaite (1892–1979), who had pursued training in anthropology, was charged with defining and organizing this program. He shared the views of Southern liberals, for whom racial segregation was a durable, or even definitive, condition. For them, it sufficed to support the development of viable institutions aimed specifically at African Americans and the emergence of an elite of leaders, particularly in the liberal and intellectual professions. One of the privileged domains of intervention was, as at the time of Booker T. Washington, providing appropriate education to African Americans. Among Outhwaite's concerns figured better recognition of the internal differentiation of the black population, supposedly a more harmonious method of managing race relations.[50]

During a 1927 meeting of the administrators of the Laura Spelman Rockefeller Memorial Fund, Outhwaite roughly formulated the practical objectives of the intervention of funds with respect to the black population:

> We are dealing with a group of people incorporated in our country for better or worse. . . . There seems to be no way of getting rid of them even if we desire so. Our objective then, probably is to bring them as early as possible to a state where they can develop their own leadership, and where they can finance their own welfare. The sooner that is done, the sooner the burden will be taken off the general welfare and public administration of the rest of the country for their support.[51]

Until 1940, this policy of supporting the separate and autonomous development of the black community would inspire the disbursement of funds not only for the Laura Spelman Rockefeller Memorial Fund, but also for other foundations intervening in this area, such as the General Education Board, another foundation funded by the Rockefeller Foundation which supported educational institutions, or the Rosenwald Foundation. This policy partially determined research possibilities in the social sciences, as well as the careers of researchers. The University of North Carolina was one of the institutions selected to develop a research program on African Americans, and the members of the circle of the sociologist Howard Odum received significant subsidies. The foundations also agreed to support programs for advanced education and research in a half-dozen historically black universities. At Fisk University (in Nashville, Tennessee), under the patronage of Outhwaite, there developed a Department of Social Sciences whose direction was entrusted, as we have seen, to Charles Johnson. The mission of this department was the study of the black populations of the South and race relations. Over the course of the following twenty years, almost all black researchers in the social sciences taught, at least for a time, at Fisk.[52] The Laura Spelman Rockefeller Memorial Fund also offered some scholarships to black PhD candidates. One of the beneficiaries was Franklin Frazier.

The action of the LSRM, and of the Rockefeller Foundation that replaced it, was tightly intertwined with that of the Rosenwald Foundation, created in 1917 by the president of the mail-order company Sears Roebuck, the most significant in the United States at the time. The Rosenwald Foundation initially had very general objectives, but, between 1917 and 1927, its funding capacities were principally used to support the construction of rural schools for African Americans in the South. Restructured in 1928, the Rosenwald Foundation was placed under the authority of Edwin Embree, previously a member of the directory council of one of the Rockefeller family foundations, who made use of his broad autonomy to define a policy. According to Embree, the collapse of the plantation economy of the South was the origin—or was at least an aggravating circumstance—of African Americans' problems and racial conflicts in the South. The policy of the Rosenwald Foundation thus fit within a perspective of support for regional development in the rural South. Its resources were devoted to interventions in different aspects of the "Negro problem"—including education, health, support for organizations in favor of interracial cooperation—and to supporting studies.[53] From 1931, many studies on workers from agricultural regions were thus intended to guide—or to justify—the federal administration's policy with regard to African Americans from the South. One study funded in this manner, which gave rise to Charles Johnson's book *Shadow of the Plantation* (1934), constituted the sociological part of a study on venereal diseases.[54] Shortly thereafter, a series of studies was undertaken on the state of agricultural populations of the South, as well as on African Americans in industry.[55]

The close links between studies on African Americans, sociopolitical circumstances, and practical goals are apparent in studies beyond those supported by the Rosenwald Foundation. The Youth Commission, a committee bringing together representatives from different educators' associations, funded a series of studies on young African Americans in different regions of the United States. Many researchers with some degree of established reputation in the field were involved in this project: these researchers included those belonging to Park's circle, like Johnson, who studied youths in the rural areas of the South,[56] and Frazier, who studied youths in cities on the border between the North and the South;[57] as well as associates of Lloyd Warner, such as John Dollard and Allison Davis, who studied relations between blacks and whites in the South.[58]

> The framework within which these studies were conducted in the area of education corresponds to a plan rather similar to that of the Social Science Research Council. At its start in 1935, we find a widespread concern among university presidents and other educators for the situation of young people struck by unemployment during the Great Depression, which drove a massive increase of high school education. In order to propose a definition and determine the different aspects of the "problems of youths," the Youth Commission organized studies and solicited funding from the General Education Board, one of the Rockefeller foundations. The investigation would determine the effects of belonging to a minority racial group on the personality development of young African Americans. The General Education Board was not long involved in the activities of the Youth Commission, which consequently disbanded in 1942.[59]

In almost the same period, the Carnegie Corporation, whose activities were mostly directed toward supporting educational work, undertook the organization of a study on "Negro education and Negro problems."[60] The direction of this study was entrusted in 1938 to a Swedish economist, Gunnar Myrdal (1898–1987), whose lack of previous knowledge of the field was considered a guarantee of objectivity. Myrdal appealed to American specialists in the field, including Charles Johnson and the anthropologist Melville Herskovits, to write a number of preliminary reports, and he solicited the opinions of Louis Wirth and Franklin Frazier on the final report.[61]

From the 1940s, the foundations became less active in supporting studies on race relations. The Rosenwald Foundation abandoned its policy of providing aid to regional development in the South after its leaders became alarmed by the "proletarian" character of movements developing among African Americans in the South at the beginning of the war.[62] Over the course of the following years, it instead directed its support to the civil rights movement.[63] The only research project of large size resulting in a publication that drew the attention of social science scholars prior to 1960, the survey directed by Adorno, focused on anti-Semitism and was no more than adjacent to this domain.[64]

Not all of the studies funded in the field of relations between racial and ethnic groups had objectives so closely linked to highly debated topics of the period. This was the case, for example, of Hughes's 1943 monograph on a city in Quebec. Although it was partially funded by the Rockefeller Foundation, it existed in the framework of support for the development of sociology in Canada and for a research program on unemployment.[65] The Works Progress Administration, an organization created by the Roosevelt administration to coordinate the actions of federal institutions offering work to the unemployed,[66] also contributed to the realization of various studies led by Horace Cayton and Lloyd Warner on the black neighborhoods of Chicago. These would many years later lead to the publication of *Black Metropolis* (1945), thus falling within the double intellectual lineage of Robert Park and Lloyd Warner. Further, the studies inspired by Hughes and Warner on race relations in work were funded, as we have seen, as studies on work and businesses in the framework of the Committee on Social Relations in Industry of the University of Chicago.[67] We should also mention that some dissertations in the field did not benefit from any funding—or at least any significant funding. Often remaining unpublished, they would, however, sometimes give rise to journal articles.

This quick inventory shows that a large portion of studies on race relations and African Americans—particularly many of those whose audiences were not limited to the social sciences—were undertaken in connection with political interrogations that insisted upon a public problem that was omnipresent in American society. As Herbert Blumer wrote in 1958 in the remark used as an epigraph to this chapter, research in this area after 1930 took place in a context ruled by an "amelioristic interest in the improvement of the relations between racial groups" and, more precisely, their slow and progressive amelioration—the opposite of the evolution that would take place in the 1960s. The choice of themes of investigation—the agricultural workers of the plantation regions, family behaviors, segregation and racial discrimination and their effects on young people, the unionization of industrial workers, black college graduates, and so on—and sometimes even the orientation of interrogation (as can be seen regarding studies on the rural South) were the direct echo of contemporary issues. The connection between studies in race relations and the areas on which they focused thus differed from that regarding studies on delinquency, whose public definition owed less to general political positions and more to professional interests invested in this sector.

THE PERSPECTIVE OF PARK ON RACE RELATIONS IN
THE CONTEXT OF THE 1930S AND 1940S

During his entire career as a researcher, Park stayed interested in questions of contacts between races and cultures, with a particular focus on this topic—as revealed by his correspondence—throughout his voyages in China, Japan, India, and the Hawaiian Islands.[68] Like the majority of Park's writings, those that concern racial relations were essays of circumstance (book prefaces, papers given at meetings of researchers, etc.). They generally took a sort of thematic organization that did not facilitate identification of the general framework of the author's reflections. These essays frequently overlap with each other, and a first reading suggests that they present variations that cannot a priori be claimed to correspond solely to differences in wording. They contain both very general peremptory assertions, which cannot be based on anything but the result of long study, and expressions of hesitation on the interpretation of some phenomena. Park's writing style, finally, does not facilitate a precise reading: addressing a broader audience than that of the social sciences, perhaps in the habit of a journalist, Park often avoided explicitly defining the terms he used.

Collectively, these characteristics make Park's essays a corpus that is relatively open to varied interpretations. I shall here outline what, in Park's sociology, served as the starting point for the empirical studies of his students—or at least some of them. It was arguably the term "perspective" as used by Karl Mannheim that served best to designate what Park's students took from him. A sort of organization of the perception of phenomena in the domain of contacts between races and cultures can be discerned in Park's essays, drawing attention toward certain phenomena, leaving others unexplored, and proposing interpretations of these relations that unite different aspects of them. Of course, Park was not concerned with separating these elements from a certain number of propositions on the ongoing evolutions of race relations, or from his interpretations of potentially unrelated historical facts: as we shall see, for example, for his entire life he claimed that after their arrival on the American continent African Americans had rapidly lost all African cultural heritage—a claim that would later seem erroneous but was unconnected to the basic elements of his perspective.

Park's perspective, like all new perspectives at the moment of their initial formulation, corresponds to a reaction to previously established conceptions in the domain. It is in relation to this context that the meaningful elements that compose the perspective must be uncovered. I have also made use of a second criterion: the principal features of Park's perspective should be sought among those that remained almost unchanged from his first sociological essays, in 1913, until the end of his career.[69] Elsewhere, the social science researchers who have referenced this perspective cite his essays as a corpus, without concern for their date of publication, and neither they nor Park himself sustain that there existed any rupture in his conception of race relations.[70]

In light of the magnitude of the changes that had occurred in race relations in the United States between Park's first publications in 1913 and his last, at the beginning of the 1940s, it is remarkable that critical discussion focuses so little attention on the changes in historical contexts of reference, even though Park made frequent allusion to later developments in racial relations in the United States. It is thus necessary to recall, first of all, that Park's first article on the subject, written in 1913, refers to the essentially peasant and folk population of African Americans in the South, who lived under the imposed regime of segregation that started in 1877. It was characterized by the physical as well as psychological separation of races, with the legal prohibition of mixed-race marriages; the absence of political rights for African Americans; an almost complete segregation of whites and blacks in the use of health facilities, transportation, and schools of all levels; as well as the respect of a ritualized code of conduct ruling face-to-face contacts between the races in public.[71] This regime of segregation was accepted at least partially by African Americans themselves: the principal black leader of the period, Booker T. Washington, did not protest against claims of the inferiority of African Americans and argued in favor of the separate development of the two races. To the contrary, Park's final articles, written at the end of the 1930s, refer to a situation in which, although segregation persisted in the South, almost half of the country's African Americans had settled in northern cities and demands for equal political rights and access to industrial employment were vigorously defended by organizations in which African Americans occupied positions of influence.

One of the two first articles Park published in 1913 in a journal specializing in the social sciences focuses on the question of African Americans' integration—specifically that of African Americans in the South—into American society.[72] Park's conception of the notion of race almost completely rejects the idea of a biological difference between races.[73]

Park's conception should be cross-checked with the belief of African Americans' inferiority to whites, which was commonly accepted before 1914, including by social science researchers. A typical example is provided by the article "Negroes" in the 1911 edition of the *Encyclopedia Britannica*:

The Negro is inferior to the white; The remark of F. Manetta, made after a long study of the negro in America, may be taken as generally true of the whole race: 'the negro children were sharp, intelligent and full of vivacity, but on approaching the adult period a gradual change set in. the intellect seem to become clouded, animation giving place to a sort of lethargy, briskness yielding to indolence. . . . For the rest, the mental constitution of the negro is very similar to that of a child, normally good-natured and cheerful, but subject to sudden fits of emotion and passion during which he is capable of performing acts of singular atrocity.[74]

The sociology dissertation of Howard Odum (1884–1954), defended at Columbia in 1910 under the supervision of Franklin Giddings, adopts a similar perspective: as suggested by its title, *Social and Mental Traits of the Negro*, it proposes a general inventory of the traits supposedly characteristic of African Americans.[75] Of course, the conviction that the assimilation of African Americans into other populations in the United States (particularly through interracial marriages) was neither possible nor desirable appears as the primary consequence of African Americans' alleged biological inferiority.

An important number of Park's analyses and the pre-1940 works inspired by his perspective developed an explicit argumentation against stereotypes defining African Americans by a collection of traits. But Park especially departs from previous approaches by taking for his subject the analysis of interracial relations, rather than of racial groups themselves. In his definition of interracial relations, Park emphasizes the immediately perceptible physical differences between populations, which had durably (or even definitively) important consequences insofar as they were accorded attention by interested parties and those with whom they were in contact. Park also emphasizes the ambiguity of the notion of assimilation: in his 1913 article, he is principally interested in the process "by which groups of individuals, originally indifferent or perhaps hostile, achieve this corporate character" that establishes segmentations in society, and not in the process by which they achieved intellectual unity and a fully developed morality.[76] The primary obstacle to the assimilation of African Americans (or Japanese Americans)—at the time unanimously deemed impossible by Southern whites, as Park notes by quoting one of them—was not owing to their mental capacities but their physical traits, their "distinctive racial hallmarks," which put between the races the "the invisible but very real gulf of self-consciousness."[77]

According to this first article, Park compares the case of African Americans to that of the populations of different European ethnicities. Like all his contemporaries, Park affirms—and he maintained this point of view for the entirety of his career—that the conditions in which African Americans arrived in the United States had erased any trace of African heritage. It is this characteristic, according to him, that distinguished the case of African Americans from that of the groups of European immigrants who had brought to the United States their own cultures of origin: the African Americans had not adapted elements of a culture from their old world, but had rather reinterpreted Anglo-Saxon culture. Apart from this characteristic, European immigrants and African Americans were, for Park, essentially rural people who encountered "adjustment to the conditions of a city environment and to modern life,"[78] as he would later write.

As described schematically by Park in 1913, interracial relations in the South after the end of slavery were characterized by the isolation of African Americans from the surrounding society. For previous generations living on plantations, a lesser degree of isolation from white society had similarly distinguished domestic slaves from field workers. The close contact between whites and their domestic slaves over the course of the period of slavery, according to Park, had engendered relationships of comprehension and sympathy that sometimes persisted into the following period. The emancipation of slaves then reinforced the separation of the two races, which was also facilitated by the relative lack of manpower that permitted black agricultural workers to move on when they were unhappy with their employers. However, in these matters newly freed African Americans were disadvantaged by their "ignorance of business matters" and "a long-established habit of submission."[79] After emancipation, African Americans acquired new habits and what can be termed a "cultural dynamic" resulting from closer contacts within their racial group, now isolated from the world of whites. Sentiments of racial solidarity and belonging developed—Park already notes the birth of an art and literature unique to the group, and, more generally, that of a specific ideal in different spheres of existence. Drawing a parallel with the model of the development of nationalities in Europe, Park claims that it was through struggles against privileges and discrimination that race consciousness was constructed and strengthened in the United States: thus, he remarks, employing a phrase of Booker T. Washington, African Americans were in the process of becoming "a nation within a nation."[80] In conclusion, Park notes the inclination to establish a biracial organization of society in the South, permitting African Americans to work toward achieving a limited autonomy, but he refuses to predict the final outcome of this movement.

The conceptual framework that defines Park's essay includes a conception of the notion of race, a sketched-out definition of assimilation and the central hypothesis of Park's sociology of interracial and intercultural contacts: face-to-face and personal contacts were the path that could lead to assimilation. In this framework, Park sketches an interpretation of the history of racial relations in the South and cautiously formulates a hypothesis concerning their future evolution. The propositions that can be drawn from this interpretation—though Park himself does not formulate them explicitly—can be subjected to systematic verifications.

Shortly thereafter, in *Introduction to the Science of Sociology*, Park and Burgess propose other distinctions for the study of race relations, defining four processes of evolution: competition, conflict, compromise, and assimilation. (In more contemporary language, one might rather think that these processes also constitute phases in relations between racial groups.) The most encompassing analysis of racial relations published by Park in 1939, at the end of his career, evokes only in passing the distinction between these four processes, but they remained in the background.[81] The concepts explored in the 1939 essay are the same that had appeared in the 1913 article, and comparison with this latter work illustrates what, in Park's perspective, remained unaltered either by changes in situation over the course of the period or by Park's own research and experience. Like the 1913 essay, the 1939 one is centered on relations between races and emphasizes the awareness of race.

Park's 1939 essay formulates the concept of race consciousness that had appeared in the 1913 article without notable alteration: "Race relations . . . are the relations existing between peoples distinguished by marks of racial descent, particularly when these racial differences enter into the consciousness of the individuals and groups so distinguished, and by so doing determine in each case the individual's conception of himself as well as his status in the community. . . . Race relations . . . are not so much the relations that exist between individuals of different races as between individuals conscious of these differences."[82] Park specifies that the term "race relations" includes "the relations which are now conscious and personal, though they have been; relations which are fixed in and enforced by the custom, convention, and the routine of an expected social order of which there may be at the moment no very lively conscience."[83]

The field of comparison invoked in 1939 is broader than that of 1913. The case of African Americans in the United States forms part of a long series of historical examples, ranging from Ancient Greece to India, to China, and to contemporary Europe, to religiously based cultural groups (like the Mormons of Utah). Park also designates—which he had not done in 1913—one of the origins of the movements that had brought into contact the populations of the world: it was "the demands for crude labor" that, in the modern period, had introduced populations that had otherwise lived isolated from each other.[84] An article published in

1944 develops this point, suggesting that it was then acquiring increasing importance in Park's conception.[85]

In 1939 Park expanded upon an idea he had outlined in a slightly different form in 1913, advancing that the particularities of race relations relied on the absence of links between groups established by marriage and procreation. These were the only means that could make differences in customs, tradition, religion, and sentiments disappear: here we find the idea that intimate relationships (especially those within the family) and communication are the factors likely to erode the barriers maintaining the integrity of racial groups.[86]

The 1939 essay does not refer only to African Americans from the South, and indeed Park devotes a substantial discussion to the situation of African Americans in the North. The migration toward the North resulted in competition between black and white Americans for employment and housing—"a niche in which negroes will enjoy relative security from competition with white competitors"—in which competition existed not only on the individual level, but also concerned entire groups.[87] Park emphasizes the new political role that resulted from this migration, the possibilities of education that it opened, and, consequently, the increasing variety of professions practiced and the appearance of a black middle class—in brief, an ensemble of phenomena identified by the research of many of Park's former students, and especially, as we shall see, by Franklin Frazier.

> The idea that race relations marked a significant change linked to the development of professional and industrial classes first appears in Park's writing in a 1928 essay about the South.[88] The point is somewhat more developed in the preface to a 1937 book by one of his students, Bertram Doyle: "Although caste still persists and serves in a way to regulate race relations, many things—education, the rise within the Negro community of a professional class . . . and of an intelligentsia, seeking to organize and direct the Negro's rising race consciousness—have conspired not merely to undermine the traditional caste system but to render it obsolete."[89] Further on, Park adds that these changes also concerned the North. In a later essay, Park (who does not cite Frazier) is still more explicit: "The most profound changes in race relations, if not in racial ideology, have come about with the rise to some sort of occupational classes within the limits of the Negro race, so that Negroes can and do rise to some sort of occupational and professional equality with other races and peoples who have not been handicapped by the segregations and institutions of a caste system."[90]

These internal evolutions within the black population disrupted the earlier caste-based organization of relationships between whites and blacks, Park claimed, since the distance that separated the two populations within the same social class tended to diminish: African Americans were thus in the course of becoming a minority in the United States. Even if this conclusion was not formulated in the terminology of *Introduction to the Science of Sociology*, Park's claim is clear: twenty years after the mass arrival of African Americans in the cities of the North, a new stage had opened up in the relations between races.

Like others of the same period, such as Warner and his associates, Park used the notion of caste to designate hierarchical groups in which marriages outside of one's group were prohibited, and where passage into a higher group was impossible.[91]

Behind the claim of a transformation of race relations from a caste model into a minority one can be read Park's reaction to the interpretations of Lloyd Warner and his associates, who conducted research on a Southern city in the middle of the 1930s.[92] The volume in which Park's 1939 article was published was one of the sites of this confrontation. In their contribution to this collection, Lloyd Warner and Allison Davis advance that there had not been progress on the essential points for African Americans in the South over the course of the twenty preceding years, and that relations between blacks and whites were those of fundamentally stable castes. Shortly thereafter, Warner also interprets the relations between races in the North in terms of castes.[93] By contrast, Park's contribution to the 1939 volume edited by Thompson insists, as we have just seen, upon the magnitude of the ongoing changes, as does Charles Johnson, who concludes the volume. Johnson emphasizes factors like the elevation of the cultural level and increased social differentiation that had accompanied urbanization, the introduction of new technologies that had modified the labor market, the changing position of women, and unionization. In sight of later evolutions, the analyses of Park and Johnson seem more penetrating than those of Warner.

Park does not venture to specifically predict African Americans' future in American society in his 1939 essay. However, while listing missing elements in his conclusion, he cites the analyses of a contemporary, Holmes, who had evoked several possibilities: different forms of disappearance through the mixture of the two populations or the lasting persistence of a biracial society. The 1939 essay concludes with an overall interpretation of the global evolution of race relations linked to the expansion of Europe, the last phase of which was marked especially by the development of large cities: "It is the essence of race relations that they are the relations of strangers; of people who are associated primarily for secular and practical purposes; for the exchanges of goods and services." Differences in race, custom, tradition, religion, and emotion mutually reinforced each other when not interrupted by intermarriages. There existed "an irrepressible conflict between society founded on kinship and a society founded on the market place; the conflict between the folk culture of the provinces and the civilization of the metropolis." Racial conflicts, Park concludes, "are the ineluctable conflicts between the 'little world' of the family in its struggle to preserve its sacred heritage against the disintegrating consequences of contact with an impersonal 'great world' of business and politics . . . race conflicts in the modern world, which is already or presently will be a single great society, will be more and more in the future confused with, and eventually superseded by, the conflicts of classes."[94]

Clearly, the comparison of Park's two essays (1913 and 1939) does not identify any notable modification in his perspective on the relations between races, but rather a reformulation of the same ideas and the addition of specific discussions of aspects initially left vague. The emphasis placed in the later essay on the importance of conflicts (absent in the first essay, but present from the 1920s in other texts) seems to reflect events marking the period since 1913, particularly the periodic urban riots in which African Americans were at first victims and, from the 1930s, sometimes active participants.

> The insistence found in some of his later essays upon identifying the development of conflicts and the mobilization of African American action as driving forces of this evolution distinguishes Park's perspective from that of the majority of researchers from the period 1930–1965. In a 1943 letter to one of his former students, Horace Cayton, Park doubles down on the opposition between his point of view and those of liberals who believed that the evolutions by necessity must be slow and progressive:

> > I think the liberals realize now that the Negro's cause must in the long run win. The only thing is they don't want it to win too soon and they don't want the change to be so rapid as to result in disorders that we have had. Personally I don't agree with these liberals. In fact I've never been a liberal. If conflicts arise as a result of the efforts to get their place it will be because the white people started them. These conflicts will probably occur and are more or less inevitable but conditions will be better after they are over.[95]

The expansion of the list of cases Park knew—whether directly through his own studies and travels, through those of his students, or simply through his reading—was, as has been suggested, considerable between 1913 and the end of his career. In contrast to the case of African Americans, whose evolution Park had followed over time, he added that of relations between black and white Brazilians, which was very different from the example of the United States,[96] as well as the example of the Hawaiian Islands, which was characterized by a relatively rapid mixture by intermarriage of the native Polynesian population and the different groups of immigrants (Japanese, Chinese, Filipino, Portuguese, Anglo-Saxon, etc.).[97] Even more so than in 1913, in 1939 Park's perspective was distinctive from that of his contemporaries, and a fortiori that of researchers from the period after 1945, due to its historical dimension and the scale of its comparative frame.

What seems to have struck Park during the period between these two essays can be integrated without difficulty into his analytical framework, particularly, after 1918, the results of his studies on the media of groups of immigrants, their modes of adaptation (with William Thomas and published under the signature of Herbert Miller), and on race relations on the Pacific Coast. As shown by the report that he published in 1923 on the books of the Harlem Renaissance,[98] and his attention to the emergence of black politicians,[99] among other things, Park took great interest in signs of race consciousness among African Americans. His studies from the beginning of the 1920s identified that the participation of immigrants in specific institutions improved their standing in the competition with other groups and facilitated a more complete integration into American institutions. The studies on the Pacific Coast revealed the crucial importance for second-generation immigrants of participation in secondary groups, as well as of contacts—at school, in recreation, by the press, and the like. To Park, this generation appeared Americanized in its attitudes and its future perspectives at the price of internal conflicts.[100]

Set in the historical context of the evolutions within race relations between 1900 and 1960, Park's interpretations seem rather clairvoyant: many phenomena to which he paid attention at the time (conflicts concerning housing, work, and status; the emergence of race consciousness among African Americans, etc.) are ones that later historical analyses have emphasized.[101] By contrast, Park paid little attention in his essays to actions organized by whites—in the South and elsewhere—in order to maintain the inferior status of African Americans or to reinforce segregation in housing and employment.[102] He never envisaged the possibility of an effective intervention by political powers or the federal state in the domain of race relations, although the ongoing developments of the 1930s could suggest the possibility and importance thereof. Park's blindness with regard to the possibilities of federal state intervention was undoubtedly strengthened by the fact that the period around 1890 had been marked by what he (like others) had interpreted as a pronounced deterioration of the situation of African Americans in the South.[103] Like Graham Sumner, Park was convinced that it was impossible to significantly alter moral evolutions through legislative dispositions. Finally, Park's description of race relations, both during slavery and during the period around 1890, when a regime of extreme segregation was established in the South, largely omitted the most violent aspects of white domination.[104] This omission—similar to omissions that can be found in historical works written in any period on any subject—did not go unnoticed by Park's readers from the 1960s onward.

An assessment of Park's analytical framework for the most visible aspects of interracial contacts over the course of the period, while paying attention to what he left out, makes it clear that the framework is a sort of abstraction of the historical experience of the United States, with emphasis on the competition between groups for work and housing. It must be pointed out that Park's framework is from the perspective of a member of a dominant group, who sees assimilation into this group (in a sense that cannot be entirely precise) as the main conceivable future for other groups of the population.

This presentation of Park's essays diverges notably from what is standard in the field of sociology. Generally, the hypothesis of a race relations cycle is accorded a central place; however, Park only explicitly formulated this theory once, in a 1926 article.[105] Although the conclusion of his 1939 article mentioned above is not totally incompatible with this interpretation, a different hypothesis concerning the future of African Americans found in the same article should prevent us from according that of the race relations cycle a central position. Park cites several historical examples—Jews in Europe and Indian castes (which, he claims, are the result of the subjection of a population by its invaders)—that disprove the theory that all evolutions conform to one such cycle. Furthermore, Park does not completely define its endpoint, assimilation, nor does he specify the temporal pace at which it would unfold.[106]

Park voices his uncertainty about the concept of assimilation in a (rarely cited) article published in 1930 in *Encyclopedia of the Social Sciences*. There, Park treats the notion as a common-sense one, remarking that it "as popularly used is a political rather than a cultural concept."[107] Park does not propose a more precise definition in the remainder of the essay, and in its conclusion he returns to the political dimension of the notion: "Assimilation becomes thus merely the most generic and abstract concept for which Americanization and the verbs Americanize, Anglicize and Germanize are more specific terms. All these words are intended to describe the process by which the generally accepted social customs and political ideas and loyalties of a community or country are transmitted to an adopted citizen."[108] The case of African Americans is not what Park principally has in mind here, but he devotes a paragraph to it in which he notes, "The Negro, during his three hundred years in this country, has not been assimilated.

This is not because he has preserved in America a foreign culture and an alien tradition, for, with the exceptions of the Indian and the Appalachian mountainer no man in America is so entirely native to the soil," and emphasizes that "this distinction which sets him apart from the rest of the population . . . is based not upon cultural traits but upon physical and racial characteristics."[109] Thus, the question of assimilation, with all the uncertainty regarding the term's definition, is one of those by which the era's sociopolitical investigation into the future of African Americans is introduced in Park's analyses.[110]

The idea of a race relations cycle appeared in Park's work in 1926, just after a voyage to the Hawaiian Islands, and he leaves no doubt that this particular example was very present in his mind. The article in question ends with this remark: "In the Hawaiian Islands, where all the races of the Pacific meet and mingle on more liberal terms than they do elsewhere, the native races are disappearing and new peoples are coming into existence."[111]

Park (also rarely) uses the race relations cycle as a sort of simplified scheme that allows examples of historical evolutions to be put into perspective, and not as a general proposition for predicting the future of race relations always and everywhere. An unpublished manuscript by Park also contains this remark: "the pages which follow are intended to review this race relations cycle in more detail; not so much for the purpose of proving it, but of checking it. This cycle is an hypothesis, and the only proper way to deal with an hypothesis, a scientific hypothesis, at any rate, is to find out when and under what circumstances it is not true."[112] In his review of *Race and Culture* in the *American Journal of Sociology*, Frazier adopts this interpretation: "Park did not regard the frame of reference as one representing necessarily chronological stages in the development of race and culture contacts."[113] We shall see that Hughes abandoned this idea (which he rightly treated as a vulgarization rather than one of Park's original ideas) very early during his research on French Canada.

If any such importance was accorded in the United States to the question of the end point of the evolution of interracial relations, it was because the studies in this area were dominated by a nagging public interrogation into the evolution of relations between blacks and whites. It was in comparison to what researchers saw as the plausible or desirable outcome that Park's essays—like other later analyses—were deemed outdated or, to the contrary, acceptable. Beyond the repeated focus on his neglect of the political factors influencing the evolution of race relations, criticisms of Park's essays evoked his lack of awareness of a specifically black culture, his overestimation of the homogeneity of their political objectives, his underestimation of the actions taken by whites in favor of maintaining status quo in race relations, and above all the fatalism inherent to his point of view—the latter being the principal criticism expressed by Myrdal.[114]

We shall note that these criticisms are based upon evidence resulting from a singular point of view in a particular period, situated on the same field as some of the claims made by Park, who relied on an overall observation of race relations and their evolution—as journalists and essayists did in the past as well as today. As James Vander Zanden noted much later and in different circumstances,[115] the vocabulary of assimilation, integration, and compromise is inadequate when one recognizes the racial and ethnic heterogeneity of the United States, because it assumes a host society in which culture and values will be noncontradictory and stable, and to which immigrants will ultimately conform. In this way, Park's analytical perspective reflects the point of view of an Anglo-Saxon Protestant.

Before turning to some of these questions regarding the studies that continue the legacy of Park's analytical framework, I shall briefly evoke his analysis of prejudice with respect to racial groups, which constitutes another important theme of his essays in this domain.[116]

Park devoted many essays to the question of racial prejudice. An initial examination of this question can be found in his introduction to the 1917 book by Jesse Steiner on prejudice against the Japanese.[117] Park challenges the then-widespread idea of there existing an instinctive antipathy between races, and argues that racial prejudices constitute a spontaneous defensive phenomenon, whose practical effect was the limitation of free competition between the races.[118] Prejudices against Asians, like those against African Americans—and the evolution of their intensity—seemed to be a byproduct of the respective racial minorities' struggles to improve their status—characterized by Park as "a struggle to preserve his personal prestige, his point of view, and his self-respect."[119] On many occasions, Park equates the struggle for work and housing with African Americans' struggle for status, to which he accords a decisive place for the ongoing period. Before 1865, the established caste organization in the South required each person to stay in his place, while assuring each racial group a monopoly over a certain domain of activity, which, by Park's reckoning, eliminated racial animosity and rendered interracial cooperation possible. For Park, the peculiarity of racial prejudices as compared with prejudices toward other immigrants relied on the "external mark" that segregation permitted, and on the isolation that was both cause and effect of racial prejudice.

Even if Park did not make multiple references to them, a mutually dependent relationship linked his essays with the empirical research on particular themes by sociologists who had been his students and friends. Examining this research, we can understand the effective functioning of and further developments to Park's proposed analytical framework. Park's research refers in equal measure to the confrontation of this framework with the evidentiary approaches introduced to sociology over the course of the following years, to reactions to later developments of race relations in the United States, and to the life experiences of different researchers. I shall first examine two studies that focus on the South.

STUDIES ON AFRICAN AMERICANS OF THE SOUTH

Paradoxically, it was only at the end of Park's career that his detailed study of modes of interracial contact and their evolution in the South would inspire a dissertation, indirectly testing one of Park's claims concerning the relationship between intimate contacts on the one hand, and interracial comprehension and sympathy on the other. The dissertation of Bertram Doyle, a black pastor from the South, then a professor at Fisk University, is centered on what Park considered to be the most elementary and persistent form of social control: the etiquette that rules face-to-face contact between members of the two races. For the publication of his dissertation three years later in the 1937 series edited by Faris, Park, and Burgess, Doyle added a preface in which, adopting the detached tone characteristic of Park, he declared himself not to be "overconcerned with solutions."

> The sociological career of Bertram Doyle (1897–1980) was relatively short. He began his doctoral studies after his ordination as minister of the Colored Methodist Episcopal Church in 1924, finished it in 1934, taught sociology at Fisk from 1927 to 1937, then continued to teach in Atlanta. He was dean of a community college in Louisville, Kentucky between 1942 and 1950, and in 1944 he published a second book. Doyle then returned to an ecclesiastic career: as a bishop in different states in the South, he maintained almost no contacts with sociologists. A 1970 letter to Everett Hughes, however, suggests that his attachment to Park's perspective remained strong. Although he hardly cared about the second edition of the book that had resulted from his dissertation, in his letter to Hughes he insisted that Park's preface would have to be retained in it.[120]

Doyle's study focuses on the period of slavery and, more briefly, its abolition, which was marked by the swift imposition of a regime of segregation in the South. The evidence Doyle used was of the variety typically used for historical studies—but his subject had thus far been neglected by historians: Doyle made use of travelers' narratives, letters, personal journals, slave narratives, and press articles relating incidents, and he examined the legal dispositions set in place after 1865. For the latter period, he invoked testimonies and, with a certain discretion, his own observations, illustrating the lack of attention paid by Park and his circle to methodological questions. Doyle's book is also more cursory regarding the post-emancipation and contemporary periods than his previous one, with a particular interest in relations between races on large plantations, perhaps because of the available evidence. As Frazier remarked in a review of the book, Doyle does not formulate a hypothesis and his writing style is essentially descriptive, with the citation of evidence serving to support the claims set forth.[121]

Doyle sought to explain how whites and blacks in the South could coexist peacefully in the framework of established inequality. Face-to-face relations between the members of the two races in domestic life and public places were subject to strictly prescribed rules of conduct. As Park articulates in his preface, the etiquette dictating contact between races was the very essence of the Southern caste system (although Doyle rarely used the term "caste"),[122] in which the separation of the races was fixed by customs and mores: this etiquette asserted the superiority of whites, minimized discord, and averted conflicts. For Doyle, complying also ensured the comfort of African Americans, since defying the caste system would strengthen white people's prejudices and engender conflicts.

From 1877, when Southern whites had reestablished political control over the old Confederate states, they passed laws imposing upon African Americans acceptance of their social inferiority, reinforcing the rules prescribing deference to all whites as well as a systematic physical separation. A biracial system was thus established within institutions and in certain occupations, notably professions such as medicine, law, and teaching. Doyle's conclusion emphasizes the slowness of change in race relations and the continuity between the period of slavery and that in which he was writing, as well as the decline of "communication and reciprocal exchange of influence."[123]

It is clear that this analysis illustrates claims previously advanced by Park more so than any systematic research. Doyle confirms and specifies these claims, but he omits what Park had also neglected: the scale and recurrence of conflicts, another aspect of relations between masters and slaves that later historical studies would identify.[124] Doyle therefore identifies a new truism that would be assimilated without difficulty into Park's interpretation: during the period of slavery, the maintenance of a formal distance between the two races was often accompanied by the development of intimacy between individuals at the cost of respecting ritual: racial prejudices were thus not instinctive, contrary to what researchers of the previous period had claimed.

In its subject as well as its analysis, Doyle's book shows the possibility, in the context of its completion and its publication, for research to remain relatively separate from the debates and interrogations of the period. The study of rules of etiquette and the subjective adaptation of African Americans to an inferior status imposed upon them had no obvious utilization in the argument in favor of equality and integration by political leaders and black intellectuals of the period. By insisting upon the slowness of changes in mores, and on the subjective comfort that obeying the rules of etiquette afforded to whites as well as African Americans, Doyle's conclusions went against the interpretation that would be proposed some years later by Myrdal, who put emphasis on the discomfort of white Americans caused by the contradiction between their racism and the democratic creed of the American nation.[125] Finally, Doyle's conclusion had no obvious implication for thought related to the regional development of the South—central, as we have seen, in research funding on this region at the time.[126] The book remained relatively obscure—probably in part because the rest of Doyle's career took place outside the social sciences—until its "rediscovery" at the end of the 1960s, with the reemergence of black nationalism.

Political questioning regarding the South does, by contrast, appear in the background of *Shadow of the Plantation*, Charles Johnson's study on African Americans on plantations that was published three years before Doyle's book. It proposes an overall picture of the lives of African Americans in the rural areas dominated by the plantation economy around 1930. The book, as Park's preface emphasizes, offers access to the interior world of this population, seeking to render intelligible its institutions, its customs, and its sentiments.

Two other objectives were added to these. In accordance with the wishes of the study's sponsors, who hoped to promote the development of the South, Johnson was to study the social conditions accompanying an elevated frequency of cases of syphilis. Johnson moreover committed himself to refuting the stereotype, then very widespread, of the happy, carefree existence of African Americans on plantations. By focusing attention on rural African Americans thought to be culturally backwards, Johnson adopted a strategy almost the opposite of that advocated by W. E. B. Du Bois for improving the white opinion of African Americans: he emphasizes not the "talented tenth," which is to say the black middle class, but rural African Americans of the working class. Johnson's project thus reflects a context and the particular position of its author within that context.

The region studied in *Shadow of the Plantation* was one of the poorest in Alabama, Macon County (home of Tuskegee University, the technical school founded by Booker T. Washington). The study's approach is not the same as the one found in urban sociology monographs of the 1920s: Johnson collected his evidence through a series of interviews with a sample of more than six hundred black families. (White sharecroppers, increasing in number in the region, were omitted.) The book includes the presentation of statistical distributions of these families' sociodemographic characteristics related to material culture, education, incomes, and so on. Numerous excerpts from his interviews are quoted, and the writing style differs from that of monographs in urban sociology of the same period.

Two shadows hovered over the lives of the black population in Macon County: the economic crisis of the cotton plantations and relations with whites, which remained in the background of analyses. Aside from some black landowners, the population under study essentially consisted of sharecroppers and agricultural day laborers. The different aspects of the existence of this population are related to the transformation of the plantation economy after the abolition of slavery, including that which occurred after the cotton crisis.

Johnson departs from the interpretation of the conservative historian Ulrich Phillips (at the time, the main reference in terms of Southern history), who sustained that the plantation system was the principal phenomenon and slavery merely a means by which this system was maintained.[127] By claiming that it was the economic system of the plantation that had left this population outside the principal current of American culture and marked it by "isolation and cultural lag,"[128] Johnson distinguishes himself from analyses imputing a sort of pathology to the behaviors of poor rural African Americans. He insists upon two factors linked to the past of this population: the existence of a "tradition of dependence on planters,"[129] with respect to whites, and the fact that families, atypical in relation to American culture, were distinguished by the composition of households and the importance of the role of mothers.

Quoting passages from interviews, Johnson describes the familial behaviors of African Americans. He notes the elevated frequency of common-law marriages, illegitimate births, and adoptions; expresses the singularity of moral norms related to sexuality, marriage, and the rights and obligations of spouses; and presents the subjective interpretations of different events and familial contexts of those interviewed. The observed variations in these matters were compared by the family units' degrees of exposure to the norms in use by the rest of American society.

The economic organization of the community also preserved traces of the previous period of slavery and corresponded to a "transitional phase of agriculture."[130] Hardly more than 10 percent of the black agricultural population owned land,

and around 20 percent earned wages. Black sharecroppers found themselves in a state of chronic debt to white landowners, who themselves were indebted to banks. Illiteracy reinforced African Americans' dependence and vulnerability, as they were forced to leave the documents establishing the state of their debts in the hands of their creditors. The economic system thus corresponded to a vicious circle of debt, in which the black sharecropper, at the bottom of the social ladder, shouldered the heaviest burden.[131]

The only two institutions that intervened in the lives of the black population were the schools and the churches. A brief chapter in *Shadow of the Plantation* on schools emphasizes ongoing changes in attitude with regard to education. (Black illiteracy had been enforced during the period of slavery.) It was through increasing literacy, and then thanks to education, that the population came out of its isolation. Johnson notes the correlation between spending time in school and changes in terms of family behaviors (such as birth rates), health-related behaviors, and interest in owning land: educated people tended to adopt stricter moral norms, which is to say ones closer to those of the American middle classes. This large expansion of the cultural horizon had the effect, however, of inciting African Americans to emigrate, thus rendering more difficult their adaptation to a world that did not welcome change.

Religion offered both a "channel of formal expression" and a means of "recreation and relaxation."[132] For a population whose places of residence were spread far apart, it was in places of worship that face-to-face social relations took place. Johnson notes that religion filled less and less a function of social control, since "there is widening gap between doctrine and behavior which leaves the traditional doctrine empty and unconvincing in relation to the normal currents of life."[133] The report of observing two religious services, which constitutes the majority of the chapter on religion, emphasizes the emotional dimension of participation in religion and the efforts of ministers to maintain it. It was, according to Johnson, a sign of the "cultural lag" of the community, since the religiosity of whites had previously presentedthis same characteristic. The examination of the simultaneous transformations of religious mores and sentiments of the faithful after the period of slavery led Johnson to conclude that "They were not converted to God, but converted God to themselves."[134]

The final chapter of *Shadow of the Plantation* notes in passing the similarity of the situation of African Americans to that of Polish peasants, who were equally trapped by a static economy. Further, it insists upon the fact that black culture, commonly perceived as different from that of Euro-Americans, was simply the product of their adaptation to the economic system of the plantation. It was this system that had fashioned the behaviors of African Americans in certain areas, inducing apathy, cultural retardation of the workforce, and, more generally, cultural isolation. A comparison of different regions of the South suggested that the abandonment of the inherited plantation system (and of sharecropping), as well as the ownership of property, facilitated the development of African Americans' individual autonomy and a transformation of mores, permitting in particular the establishment of active affectional relations between parents and children.

A research report written shortly thereafter by Johnson and two other leaders of the Rosenwald Foundation repeats this conclusion, making a plea to the Roosevelt administration in favor of transforming sharecroppers into landowners—the solution then advocated for by the liberals of the South.[135] *Shadow of the Plantation* ends with a phrase that invokes the necessity for the country, and not only for the South, to have an overall plan (which must be understood in the sense given to the term by the Roosevelt administration): "But the fate of the tenant is but an aspect of the fate of the southern farmer generally, and the plight of all of these awaits a comprehensive planning, which affects not merely the South but the nation."[136]

It is clear that *Shadow of the Plantation* is not a simple illustration of the analytical framework proposed by Park, even if an examination of the consequences of the isolation of the black population constitutes its central theme.[137] In it can be found the mark of the particular circumstances in which this study was conducted and the political position to which the author adhered: the interpretation of the South as an economically underdeveloped region.

Shadow of the Plantation only barely evokes one of the themes that would occupy a central place in studies on African Americans over the following years: social differentiation within this population. However, a later book by Johnson, *Growing Up in the Black Belt* (1941), explains the place of the "folk Negroes"— the isolated rural population studied in the previous book—within the social structure of the black population: they formed a set of the working class that stood out in terms of culture more so than in terms of economics. Funded by the Youth Commission, *Growing Up in the Black Belt* serves as Johnson's contribution to research on the development of personality of young African Americans and develops an analysis of class differences within the populations of the rural zones. These are defined by the combination of many criteria—property and income level, stability of housing, belonging to a respectable family, education level, occupation practiced, and so on.

The population is thus grouped into three broad categories: an upper class estimated at 6 percent of the population of the South, a middle class (12 percent), and an ensemble of lower classes that comprise 82 percent of the population, within which can be distinguished several groups by function of economic and cultural criteria.[138] One of the central themes in this analysis of the experience of young African Americans is their relationship with the status conferred upon them by society. The conclusion of *Growing Up in the Black Belt*, modest but premonitory, again recalls the sociopolitical backdrop of these studies on African Americans: "In general, the Negro continues to occupy a subordinate position, but the fact he is struggling against this status rather than accepting it, and that the white group is constantly redefining its own status in relation to the Negro, indicates that in the future, if one cannot safely predict progress in race relations, he can at least predict change."[139]

The evolution of survey methods and modes of argumentation is visible when *Shadow of the Plantation* is compared with *Growing Up in the Black Belt*. While *Shadow of the Plantation* already partially relied, as we have seen, on the statistical utilization of a survey by interview, *Growing Up in the Black Belt* was based on different tests constructed from responses to questions posed to more than two thousand adolescents. The two works are also based on a more qualitative survey (a term which figures in *Growing Up in the Black Belt*), which is in fact the principal source of Johnson's descriptions.[140] As in other domains of research, the statistics issuing from questionnaire surveys were decreed in the 1930s necessary instruments for the description of what populations did and thought, even though personal documents (to employ the terminology of the 1920s) remained an essential resource for argumentation.

These studies on black Southerners offered exemplified descriptions of different aspects of their condition, in the framework of the perspective defined by Park's essays. They repeatedly affirm that it is the conditions of existence under which these populations live, and not their genetic characteristics, that explain the original traits of their behaviors. They also posit that the behavior of these populations is not based on a historical, pre-slavery experience—an "African heritage." They accord particular attention to phenomena of status—to relations of institutionalized inequality—in their subjective and objective dimensions. An interrogation into the evolution of race relations and its eventual culmination in a form of black assimilation is present in the background of these studies, but more implicitly than explicitly, as that event seemed uncertain and, at the very least, far in the future.

It was Frazier's research on the adaptation of black families to an urban environment that would offer a more precise demonstration of the instruments and categories of analysis furnished by the Chicago sociology of the period. But Frazier also added a new element: a sustained attention to phenomena of social differentiation within the black population.

FRANKLIN FRAZIER AND THE DIFFERENTIATION
OF BLACK POPULATIONS IN CITIES

We have seen Park's hesitation, at the beginning of the 1920s, in using the notion of social class. The term, however, sometimes appears in his later essays on race relations, even if its meaning there is no more precise than it had been in previous ones. The study of the settling of African Americans in cities drove Park's interest in this population's internal differences. Thus, showing the effects of the environment on the adaptation of populations could easily lead to an interest in the principles of differentiation at work within them.

What were the significant differences within the black populations of cities? W. E. B. Du Bois had already posed the question before 1900, during his survey of African Americans in Philadelphia.[141] Like others of the same period, he had been more sensitive to the differentiation of behaviors in their moral dimension than in differences in income: in his characterization of what he designated an "aristocracy," Du Bois insisted upon the respectability of families and the social consideration associated with the respect accorded to moral norms. He did not describe these social norms in detail, but they were obviously those of middle-class Protestants.[142]

Researchers in the social sciences had evidently not been the first to pose the question of the essential principles of differentiation in the black population. As Du Bois's example shows, they found themselves immediately confronted with collective explanations of the perception of differences internal to the black population. Among the implicit criteria upon which these explanations were based figures the diffuse social recognition accorded to families, often linked to their status prior to emancipation—a free origin was valorized, as was, for former slaves, belonging to the world of the plantation's domestic staff rather than that of agricultural workers. The amount of time since a family's establishment, the part of the city in which it lived, the possession of land in the countryside, and the conformity of sexual and familial norms to those positioned as belonging to mainstream American society were also emphasized. Finally, the nuance of skin color was treated as an index of social status. None of these characteristics could, however, be systematically utilized in surveys of such a large population. In the research Frazier conducted on black families in Chicago can be found one of the first attempts to grasp the new differentiations internal to the black populations of cities in a systematic manner.

E. Franklin Frazier (1894–1962) was, with Charles Johnson, one of the rare black sociologists to achieve wide renown in the period 1930–1960.[143]

He was the son of a Baltimore bank courier, who, according to Cayton, had not attended school, although he was, by the criteria of the period, described as a member of the black middle class.[144] Frazier first pursued studies at one of the major black universities, Howard University in Washington, DC. From these years, Frazier displayed convictions deemed radical by the times, not only in terms of race relations—he was opposed on numerous occasions to prescriptions of the code subjecting African Americans with respect to whites—but also in social matters. He himself occasionally characterized his opinions as socialist or anti-capitalist.[145]

Having taught various subjects (mathematics, English, history, etc.) at different colleges in the South, in 1919 Frazier undertook studies in sociology at Clark University under the supervision of a former student of Giddings. He completed an MA thesis focusing on new currents in ideas among African Americans, notably the forms of radical opinions that then were developing.[146] The following year, with the financial help of the Russell Sage Foundation, he studied black dockworkers in New York. He then spent a semester in Denmark to study agricultural cooperatives and rural schools, which led him to defend, for a time, the idea that the type of education employed by such schools could be profitably imitated in the southern United States. On his return from Denmark, he attended the Second Pan-African Congress, organized in Paris by Du Bois.

Instructor in sociology at Morehouse College and director of the School of Social Work in Atlanta from 1922, Frazier published several articles in social work journals while remaining in contact with the leadership circles of activist movements for racial equality. Following a conflict and the publication of an article on racial prejudice, Frazier had to leave Atlanta suddenly, and in 1927 he resumed his studies at the University of Chicago with the intention of writing a dissertation in sociology, benefiting from a scholarship and a research grant obtained with the support of Park and Burgess.

With his dissertation completed, in 1931 Frazier was hired by Fisk University—where he showed less diplomatic moderation than Charles Johnson with respect to racial segregation. In fact, a contained rivalry set him in opposition with Johnson, and, in 1934, Frazier left Fisk to become chair of the Department of Sociology at Howard University,[147] where he would remain until the end of his career, except for the years between 1951 and 1953, when he was chief of the Division of Applied Social Sciences at UNESCO. Until the end of his life, Frazier remained a periodically engaged sociologist: in 1935, he was, as we have seen, research director of the commission charged by the mayor of New York with studying the riot occurring in Harlem. Frazier wrote his findings up into a report, which the mayor refused to make public.

Frazier always encountered more difficulties than Johnson in obtaining grants for research, particularly because of his opinions that periodically came off as pro-communist. But his publications—and particularly two of his books—won him a superior reputation in the sociological community.[148] Elected president of the Eastern Sociological Society in 1946, Frazier became the first African American elected to the presidency of the American Society of Sociology two years later. A study of a sampling of the major journals in the social sciences between 1944 and 1968 concluded that Frazier was the most-cited author in the domain of race relations, far ahead of Charles Johnson, who occupied only the sixth place.[149]

As has just been suggested, Frazier's connections were not limited to the level of individual social science researchers. On his arrival in Chicago, he had already authored several publications in journals and magazines aimed at an intellectual audience. Although only few references to Marx and socialism can be found in his publications in social science journals, this was an area he was familiar with. (Frazier was, it seems, at one point politically close to the journalist and union leader Philip Randolph.) Frazier's attention to the social differentiation of the black population certainly predated both his arrival in Chicago and his introduction to Park, and it appears in some of his magazine articles.

A 1925 article, devoted to the new middle class of entrepreneurs in Durham (North Carolina), outlines the differences separating this class from that of the old established professions, which were considered a sort of aristocracy, separate from the mass of black workers in terms of behavior and moral respectability.[150] To show that black entrepreneurs were no different from their white counterparts, Frazier describes the careers and lifestyles of some wealthy businessmen and notes with apparent satisfaction that they even shared conservative political opinions. One finds here, as already noted in Johnson's *Shadow of the Plantation*, a reminder that not all African Americans were indolent country folk, and that, placed in the same conditions as whites, they adopted identical behaviors. Another article, published in 1929 in a politico-literary magazine of opinions, brings a less favorable assessment to the black middle classes. It explains why African Americans are not inclined to adopt radical opinions and ally themselves politically with the proletariat, offering a complex and nuanced picture of class differences internal to the black population and their impact on the relations of each class with its white counterpart.[151]

These articles are based on scattered evidence, in contrast to Frazier's dissertation and his 1932 book *The Negro Family in Chicago*, in which the question of differences internal to the population was the object of a systematic treatment.

The subject of this book—through the study of families and how African Americans adapted to their new situation in large cities—is in line with Park's sociology. Frazier would come to show that the characteristics of African Americans' familial behaviors, despite the stereotypes that attributed them to "moral inferiority," varied just as much as the behaviors of other populations undergoing the process of becoming established in the city. The identification of principles of variation of familial behaviors other than race is thus, here, a means by which the case of the black family could be related back to a common one.

Frazier later explained how he had come to one of the basic ideas of his dissertation:

> My interest in the study of the Negro family began while I was the director of the Atlanta School of Social Work. Through the reading of the works of Burgess and Mowrer, I developed the idea that a more fundamental knowledge of the processes of disorganization and reorganization of Negro family life than was in existence at that time should be made available for social workers. Subsequently, when I entered the University of Chicago, I was very much impressed by the ecological approach to the study of social phenomena. One day in "The Temple," as the old social research laboratory was called, I separated the data on Negro homeownership from similar data for whites according to zones of urban expansion in order to find out if the rates for Negroes showed a gradient as did the figures for the total population. Thus I discovered the zones in the Negro community which became a frame of reference for my other data on the family.[152]

The instruments, notions, and interpretive method used by Frazier in *The Negro Family in Chicago* are essentially those utilized during the same period in statistical studies on so-called urban phenomena like delinquency or mental illness. By constructing statistical data on the different neighborhoods of Chicago, Frazier showed that the black population was distributed over the territory of the city in accordance with Burgess's hypothesis: the greater the distance from the center (with the exception of the intermediary zone in which could be found prostitutes and bohemians), the higher the portion of the population consisting of members of the commercial and liberal professions, as well as business leaders, public services workers, and skilled workers. Rates of homeownership also increased, although the proportion of women working did not decline.

The new arrivals from the South were concentrated in the zone surrounding the central city, and different indices of familial disorganization (including divorce and familial desertion, illegitimate births, dependence on social aid, and juvenile delinquency) were elevated. These different indices according to geographical zones presented the same variations as other populations, and Frazier interprets the frequency of demoralization of black families as an index of community disorganization. Over the course of the "process of selection and segregation"[153] to which the population was subjected, the African Americans who adapted to the urban lifestyle established themselves in zones further and further from the inner city. Eventually, they became integrated into communities in which the family behavioral norms of the Anglo-Saxon middle classes prevailed. Frazier notes the efforts of African Americans belonging to the privileged classes to maintain behavioral norms that threatened the arrival of rural immigrants, with whom they refused to be identified.[154]

> One of the innovations Frazier introduced to research on analogous subjects lies in the refinement and utilization of a code for exploiting census data on the occupations of the heads of families. This code brought together individual activities that were significantly related in eight categories of occupations, which were different from those used by the census.[155] In the article in which he presented this code, Frazier sought to show variations in the differentiation of the black population by city, making use of the 1920 census and relating it "to the extent that the Negro participated in the whole community," connected especially with the state of racial segregation in these cities.[156] The exploitation of the Chicago censuses by neighborhood, which he explored in his dissertation, permitted Frazier to offer an evaluation of the division of the black population in the city in 1920 into broad categories: 49 percent of black men at the time were laborers or unskilled workers, 28 percent were domestic servants, and only 1.2 percent were members of an established profession—a division obviously very different from those observed in other population groups.

A chapter in *The Negro Family in Chicago* is devoted to the history of a black family. It attributes the behavioral singularities of African American families to the experiences of slavery and the backlash to emancipation. When they found themselves liberated from traditional controls, according to Frazier's work, theft and licentiousness characterized their behaviors.[157] Frazier distinguishes several cases: the descendants of long-free black families (who were frequently of mixed race) often knew how to construct a family tradition, transmitted from generation to generation, which ensured the control of familial behaviors. These families had also arrived at "the complete assimilation of the highest ideals of family life."[158] For the immense majority of African Americans who remained on plantations (which Frazier does not examine in detail), family life was based on sympathetic relationships facilitated by the necessities of the living situation, which recalled the situation in the time of slavery.[159] Among a small minority of them, landownership reinforced the authority of fathers and overall conformity to the moral norms of American society: this minority tended to play a dominant role in communities, supporting religious and educational institutions. Frazier claims that the black family saw a degree of stabilization when migration toward cities broke down the controls that had been set in place.

Frazier's following book, *The Negro Family in the United States* (1939), is the one that established its author's reputation.[160] It focuses on black families in rural areas as well as in cities, and it overtly adopts a historical perspective. Through this perspective, as through his insistent attention to class differences, Frazier separates himself from the formula of monographs that were standard in urban sociology of the time. His book was well received by Chicago sociologists, and Burgess, in the preface, wrote that it was "the most valuable contribution to the literature of the family since the publication, twenty years ago of *The Polish Peasant in Europe and America.*"[161]

Part of *The Negro Family* is devoted to the history of a black family up to its migration toward cities. Based on evidence of the same type that Doyle used, as well as on family biographies collected by himself or his students, Frazier proposes a description of familial behaviors that is attentive to their subjective dimension, contradicting previous interpretations imputing the immorality of the familial behaviors of black slaves to race or a "culturally retarded" character. Although Frazier is attentive to the internal diversity of the population—especially by region—the data he uses (disparate testimonies, local censuses, etc.) leads him to a description of the evolutions illustrated by examples, and not to a systematic investigation of this diversity.[162]

Marked primarily, according to Frazier, by their occasional character or dictated by slaveowners in the interest of reproduction of manpower, relations between the sexes among slaves in rural zones of the South were rapidly "modified and controlled by feelings of tenderness and sympathy toward those who shared his bondage and enabled him to escape from loneliness and isolation."[163] The emergence of slaves as "human beings was facilitated by their assimilation in their masters' houses, where they borrowed ideas, attitudes, morals, and manners." But material interests and economic forces constantly threatened familial ties, and only relations between mothers and children were not broken: hence there evolved the central position in black families of the mothers and grandmothers as elements of stability. In the rural zones of the South, sometimes with a focus on their diversity, Frazier examined the instability of marital unions among rural black populations, along with the (elevated) frequency of extramarital births, separations, and illegitimate relationships over the course of the period following emancipation. Women's growing authority in family units and their decreasing subordination to men resulted from an economic situation in which they had learned to depend on none but themselves. The organization of families in the rural South was thus characterized by a matriarchy dominated by the authority of grandmothers, which was contingently maintained among migrant families in the cities.

A completely different type of organization was found among certain black families when they "developed a feeling of solidarity and some community of interest under the authority and discipline of the father."[164] The reinforcement of the father's authority over his family, often associated with the acquisition of land or homeownership, was the sign of the beginnings of the organization of the family on an institutional basis.[165] Moreover, belonging to a church reinforced men's authority through Biblical passages favoring women's subjugation to men. Coming from a different history, the families that had descended from African Americans emancipated before 1865 presented a few similar characteristics, with the accumulation of property permitting their development on an institutional base.

On two important points—the importance of African cultural heritage and the unique features of black families over the course of the period following the Civil War—these analyses were refuted by later historical analyses. First, Frazier, like Park and all sociologists and historians until the 1960s, consistently repeated that the African culture of black Americans had been completely eradicated shortly after their arrival in the United States through their dispersion across plantations: they saw African Americans as culturally identical to Anglo-Saxon Protestants. At the end of the 1950s, Frazier still claimed in one of his most frequently cited synthetic books on the subject: "As a racial or cultural minority, the Negro occupies a unique position. He has been in the United States longer than any other racial or cultural minority with the exception, of course of the American Indian. . . . Having completely lost his ancestral culture, he speaks the same language, practices the same religion, and accepts the same values and political ideals as the dominant group."[166]

The anthropologist Melville Herskovits was the first to contest this assertion in 1941, but he did not convince sociologists or historians (or anthropologists).[167] In the context of the 1920s through the 1960s, emphasizing African heritage was interpreted as an indirect way of affirming African Americans' cultural inferiority, and thus justifying their condition in the United States. Frazier had read the first works of Herskovits during his studies at Chicago.[168] In a reader's note to the 1941 book by Herskovits, Frazier concludes that if one were to establish that African Americans had a cultural past and that this cultural past still influenced behavior, it would not change their status in American society. This conclusion testifies to the political character of Frazier's hesitations. At the end of the 1960s, in a situation marked by African Americans claiming an identity specific to the black population, several historical studies insisted, to the contrary, upon the importance of the African heritage in its influence on religious and familial behaviors.[169] These studies would gain a recognition that Herskovits's argument had been denied.

Frazier's explanation of the relationship between the experience of slavery and the preeminence of women—as well as the correlated erasure of men—in many black families was later challenged by a historical study based on evidence more systematic than his own.[170] Starting with the exploitation of censuses of different zones and cities, Herbert Gutman (1928–1985) arrived at a description of the black family that starkly contrasted that of Frazier, and found an autonomy of the black population with respect to white cultural norms. According to Gutman's data, in plantation zones the families of slaves were not characterized by the general absence of men, and family behaviors were regular even under the regime of slavery. Gutman also challenges the idea that white families served as a model for black slaves, and that "the old intimacy between master and slave" had relied on "the moral order under the slave regime," as Frazier and Park had both stated.[171] Finally, Gutman established that in cities at the beginning of the century and until 1925, men had not been absent within black families. In consequence, Gutman claimed, the later decomposition of families was not linked to arrival in the cities, but to the massive unemployment that struck a significant part of the male black population starting in the 1930s.[172]

In the time that elapsed between the studies of Frazier and Gutman, there took place a transformation both in social science approaches—with greater attention paid to the question of the representativeness of samples being studied—and in sociopolitical circumstances. In the circumstances of the 1960s, marked by the discovery and, relatedly, the assertion of a "black identity," Frazier's theory of the black family tended to be confounded with the one found in a report by Daniel Moynihan intended for the administration of President Johnson, who after 1965 inspired the policy of the federal state with regard to African Americans and was largely echoed in public opinion.

Although he did not mention the economic, political, and structural determinants of racism, Moynihan acknowledged the deterioration of black families in cities, on their "matriarchal structure which . . . seriously retards the progress of the group as a whole, and imposes a crushing burden on the Negro man."[173]

Through his emphasis on the pathological character of the black family and his suggestions for how to reform it, Moynihan's report can be read as blaming African Americans for their own victimhood. By slightly truncating certain of Frazier's quotations and omitting some of their context, Moynihan notably simplified Frazier's analyses. For example, he omitted the positive elements corresponding to the reorganization of the black family in cities.[174]

Debates were no longer organized around the themes developed by Frazier, however: starting in the mid-1960s, emphasis was placed on the valorization of Afro-American culture and nationalist sentiments, as well as the sensitivity to anything that might resemble a moralist denigration of the lower classes (to reuse the expression of one of Frazier's principal critics).[175] The fate of Frazier's analyses after 1960 provided a new example of how interpretations of research results depend on circumstances in a politically sensitive domain.

Another section of *The Negro Family in the United States* examines the consequences of migration to cities on familial organization. Here, Frazier principally uses case studies (brief autobiographies borrowed from different sources) to illustrate interactions between the sexes among African Americans who had settled in cities. Without limiting himself this time to Chicago, Frazier continues the interpretations of the preceding book: the elevated rates of men abandoning their families, divorce, juvenile delinquency, and so on in zones peripheral to the inner city are held to be indices of the "lack of organized community life"[176] that went hand in hand with the absence of customary forms of social control.

The last part of the book examines trends in the reorganization of familial life in cities that accompanied the emergence of a new mode of social differentiation, based principally on employment. Frazier proposes a picture of types of families and familial behaviors that are in the process of establishing themselves in the urban environment, and more generally of the evolution of the two principal social classes into which black urban populations were grouped in the 1930s.[177]

The middle class, defined by its position in the economy, presented notable differences in its lifestyle and mode of consumption with relation to the whites who occupied a similar economic position. Frazier insists upon the conservative opinions of some of its members, partisans of the continuation of racial segregation, the disappearance of which would threaten their own status. According to Frazier, this middle class could not prosper in an economy in which segregation was imposed. Its growth depended on the increase in number of salaried workers who would assimilate—this is the term Frazier used—with white workers holding the same types of jobs once race barriers were erased.

To designate the second class that had appeared in cities starting at the end of the nineteenth century, Frazier employed the term "proletariat"—which Park used only very rarely. Frazier describes the perspective on existence that this new class had gradually acquired as it emancipated itself from the ideas and norms of the black middle class. Without neglecting internal variations, he concludes that some of the singularities of African American populations, such as men's weakness of authority and failure to support their families, were fading: by becoming industrial laborers, they adopted the modes of family behaviors and the ideas of the majority of laborers.

It is apparent that these conclusions on the class structure of the black population and the evolutions to come were not founded on the data presented by Frazier. But they do reveal a new approach at play in race relations that was subordinate to those of permanent evolution and class structure. This is one of the themes that Frazier would develop over the following years, particularly in the essay that served as his presidential address to the American Sociological Society in 1949.[178] This essay proposes, along with a reformulation of the contribution of Frazier's research, a critical assessment of the state of research on race relations. Insofar as the critiques formulated by Frazier are found, at this moment or shortly later, in the work of other students of Park's (like Blumer), this essay can be understood as evidence for these researchers' reactions to the new current in research in this domain following the publication of Myrdal's *An American Dilemma*. Frazier rebukes studies in line with this new current, centered on attitudes—particularly the racist attitudes of whites measured through tests or questionnaires—for not taking into account the social context within which contacts occurred and treating individuals like isolated atoms: in other words, for not taking into account the situation within which behaviors existed.[179] Frazier also challenges Warner's interpretation of race relations as castes, calling it overly static and inattentive to ongoing changes as well as to African Americans' new reactions to the discrimination to which they were subjected.

Also in Frazier's essay can be found the outline of an implicit criticism of some of Park's previous analyses: Frazier notes that sociologists had neglected the political dimension of race relations and again states, contrary to the explanation of population distribution in cities exclusively in terms of community mores and impersonal forces, that segregation resulted from the actions of identifiable economic and political actors, such as real estate agents and representatives of economic interests.[180]

Despite these criticisms, Frazier fit within the legacy of Park's perspective. Based on the results of his own works, Frazier insists upon the necessity of taking into account the "social organization of black and white communities," accounting for the "social universe" within which African Americans as well as cultural institutions (like churches) existed in order to understand the evolutions of contacts and race relations. Frazier also shows how certain behavioral models found in members of different classes within the black community affected contacts between races: for example, the more mobile elements tended to have a higher class status in the black world, and were surrounded by a social world with a lifestyle (characterized by conspicuous consumption and leisure activities typical of upper-class whites) that distinguished them from middle-class whites of the same levels of income and education.

The addition of a class-based analysis to an analysis based on ethnic (or racial) relations appeared, at this time, to be a normal extension of Park's perspective, as confirmed by Helena Znaniecka Lopata's dissertation on the Polish American community, cosponsored by Wirth, Blumer, and Hughes. Lopata sought to explain why the Polish community in the United States had not disappeared, contrary to the predictions of Thomas and Znaniecki. She emphasized competition in terms of status and its relationship with class structure within the Polish community.[181]

FRAZIER, WIRTH, HUGHES, AND THE QUESTION OF ASSIMILATION

The second theme of reflection that, along with the differentiation internal to the black population, is at the center of Frazier's preoccupations corresponds to a question already raised in Park's sociology: that of assimilation, or, to take the only really important case in the United States, the question of the assimilation of African Americans. We have seen Park's uncertainty regarding a notion that he considered to have multiple meanings and to dominate the future of race relations in the United States. Frazier was no less uncertain, as shown by the oscillation of his expectations regarding this latter point. Though Frazier did not completely abandon it, assimilation was not the term he used most frequently; he resorted to other concepts—for example, integration and acculturation—to more precisely characterize the complexity of evolutions corresponding to areas of behavior.[182]

In the conclusion to his book *The Negro in the United States* (1949), Frazier barely uses the term "assimilation," nor does he give it a definition. Rather, he proposes distinguishing integration into different domains of American social life, namely the various possibilities of African Americans' access to positions or activities.[183] He claims that the integration of African Americans had progressed above all in the domain corresponding to secondary relations (in the sense used by Cooley)—work, economic life, leisure, or school—and not in the domain of "sacred" relations that took place in the church and family. Regarding this, Frazier evokes a factor so often neglected in previous studies: that the "final and strongest barrier to social acceptance is, of course, the disapproval of intermarriage."[184] This impossibility of intimate association had as its counterpart the "moral isolation" affecting those African Americans who were no longer "rural folk" when they sought to conform to American norms of conduct.[185]

Frazier's conclusion invokes the different factors contributing to the "reorganization of American life"—transformation of forms of communication, the necessity for national and international motivations for respecting the democratic creed of racial equality—and seems rather optimistic. But certain later essays of his are more reserved: in 1955, when he completed a disillusioned study of the black bourgeoisie who adopted the behaviors of whites and rejected lower-class African Americans without succeeding at winning the acceptance of whites,[186] Frazier claimed that "the Negro has not found acceptance in American society, and he has not been able to identify completely with Americans."[187] His final text, a paper for the World Congress of Sociology in Washington in 1962, ends with a somber picture of the situation of the black population in cities. With a clear-sightedness exceptional for his period, Frazier notes what are now the well-known properties of urban ghettos: massive unemployment (Frazier evokes the unemployability of some of the population on account of the transformation of production); consumption of alcohol and drugs; the development of religious movements and black nationalism. He concludes with this statement: "That it is in the cities that Negroes are being subjected to the rigorous ordeal of American civilization, the outcome of which no one can predict with certainty."[188]

Frazier's uncertainties regarding the conceptualization appropriate for understanding the evolution of race relations and identifying its end point show that sociological analysis here picked up of-the-moment questions regarding a particularly burning political issue without supplementary elaboration. With reference to historical examples other than that of African Americans, Park's other intellectual heirs tended to elaborate the analytical categories necessary for a reexamination of the question of evolutionary trends in relations between racial or ethnic groups.

In an essay about the consequences of the Second World War for nation-states that would be cited frequently over the following years, which has the character of a general reflection, Louis Wirth proposes as example a typology of minorities based on the different collective goals they pursued.[189] Wirth distinguishes pluralist minorities, who sought only to obtain a tolerance of what made them different; assimilationist minorities, who laid claim to a more complete participation in society, aiming for full acceptance and seeking to merge into the broader society; secessionist minorities, who demanded political and cultural independence; and militant minorities, who tried to dominate others. This construction did not accord well with the hypothesis of the existence of a race relations cycle, and it opened up a path to an interpretation of African Americans as collectively pursuing a goal other than assimilation.[190]

It was the research on Canada conducted by Everett Hughes, another of Park's students, that would most clearly broaden its analytical perspective concerning the question of an evolutionary process of race relations. The case of Canada, with its two principal populations, Anglophone and Francophone, essentially offered a historical example, and Hughes perceived its radical difference from the case of the United States.

In the mid-1930s, Hughes, who then taught at McGill, undertook a study of the development of industry in a city in Quebec. With funding from the Rockefeller Foundation, which was interested in the topical question of unemployment and which Hughes had initially convinced to support a study on employment and interethnic relations, Hughes studied Drummondville, a city of twenty thousand inhabitants.[191] This study was intended to be part of a series in which also figured the study of a rural community (conducted by Horace Miner, a student of Robert Redfield),[192] and that of an urban metropolis, Montreal (which was never undertaken).[193] In short, this study fit within the comparative perspective then developed by Redfield based on his work on Mexico. Drummondville was located on the "ethnic frontier" within Canada (to use Park's expression), the site of textile companies with executives of Anglophone origin and a labor workforce of rural, Francophone origin that had established themselves over the course of the preceding thirty years. The study was conceived of as a community study, one of the approaches then in vogue, and did not follow the formula of the monographs in urban sociology of the 1920s.

According to his testimony, Hughes arrived in Montreal with two possible interpretations of Francophone Canadians' situation in mind, suggested by the training he had received at Chicago. The first, based on the example of the United States and adopted spontaneously by the majority of Anglophones, considered the Francophones to be a group of immigrants in the process of assimilation: the diffusion among the Francophones of certain cultural traits (like the use of the English language or the adoption of tweed jackets) had long been held to be a sign of the progress of their assimilation with Anglophone Canadians. Hughes quickly became convinced that this interpretation was erroneous. The second interpretation considered the Francophones a national minority. This seemed no more acceptable to Hughes, since the Francophones claimed neither connection to France nor (at the time) political autonomy. Deeming Anglophone culture no superior to their own, the Francophones claimed integration into a vaster ensemble, but with cultural autonomy and equal respect—which is to say representation in sought-after positions in proportion to their number.

The terminological inadequacy of this alternative analysis of the Canadian case led Hughes to study the ethnic division of work, which constituted one of the principal themes of his monograph.[194] Hughes also discovered that sharing the same culture was not a necessary condition for the existence of a nation.[195] The example of Francophone Canadians also showed the significance that racial groups could sometimes invest in their own actions, and thus their own contributions to defining their future.[196]

Returning to the University of Chicago in 1937, Hughes undertook research on the integration of the black labor force into industry over the course of the following years—particularly concerning the employment of semi-skilled workers, as we saw in chapter 6. This research did not give rise to a planned book but to several articles presenting provisional results and to a synthetic volume.[197] Although Hughes's work illustrated the potential contribution of an ethnographic approach only imperfectly, it indicated one of the directions in which Park's perspective could lead: the detailed ethnographic study of the division of labor in workshops, factories, institutions, or professions, taking into account its ethnic dimension and correlation with other dimensions.

The syllabus of a course on the study of race relations in industry offered during the summer of 1945 gives an overall idea of Hughes's project. Its originality, in comparison with contemporary studies in the sociology of work, is apparent in its Park-like regard for linking structural aspects and observable concrete behaviors.[198] Hughes remarked that modern industry was approaching a moment in its development at which it would begin to hire workers without previous industrial experience. In light of this, the case of African Americans might ultimately be compared with others in terms of their situation, the progress that they achieved, and their attitudes. The uniqueness of their case was due only to the fact that African Americans were the only group permanently relegated to an inferior social position.

Ongoing ethnographic research would, as we have seen in chapter 6, take into account the relationship between the formal structure of authority in industry and informal groupings of workers: Hughes wished to study how the interplay of these groupings affected race relations when blacks and whites worked alongside each other. This theme was developed in a research report published in 1946.[199] Its analysis would also take into account the fact that industry was always rooted in a community in which other organizations and activities could affect race relations. It would also touch upon variations in the conception of work, unionization, coworkers, and so on as social characteristics for African Americans. Over the course of the following years, other studies at least partially in line with this perspective were undertaken in Hughes's circle. Some dissertations were devoted to African Americans in education or the medical or legal professions, and they resulted in articles.[200]

Another criticism of the idea that there existed a unique and inevitable end point to the process of the evolution of race relations can be found in an essay published by Blumer in 1965, long after his departure from Chicago.[201] Sketching out a comparison of the examples of South Africa, the American South, and the new African states, Blumer challenges the idea that there is a simple and necessary relationship between the process of industrialization and the type of evolution seen in race relations. He thus challenges the hypothesis that industrialization would dissolve racial differences: "Industrialisation will continue to be an incitant to change, without providing the definition of how the change is to be met. It will contribute to the reshuffling of people without determining the racial alignments into which people will fall. Its own racial ordering, to the extent that it has any, will be set by that in its milieu or that forced on it by the authority of a superior control."[202]

Starting in the mid-1930s, however, work conducted or inspired by the Chicago sociologists represented only a small amount of research in this area: studies on relations between races and cultures were no longer organized principally according to the questions and analytical models proposed by Park and his close associates. This reflected changes both in the political situation and in prominent approaches in the social sciences, most especially in sociology.[203]

FROM THE INVESTIGATION OF RACIAL PREJUDICE AND ASSIMILATION TO THE REVOLT OF THE BLACK GHETTOS

It was the success of Gunnar Myrdal's book, the result of a commission from the Carnegie Corporation, *An American Dilemma*, that rendered this new current in research visible and provided the general framework within which a large number of post-1945 works took place. The central part of this book essentially proposed an interpretation of the "Negro problem" in the United States that was profoundly different from Park's: Myrdal emphasizes the unique situation of the South and the attitudes of members of the two racial groups, especially the prejudices of whites. He leaves in the background, however, conflicts between the races.

Unlike Park, Myrdal does not situate the case of African Americans within the global movement of contacts between races and cultures, with its accompanying conflicts. To the contrary, he emphasizes a characteristic specific to African Americans' situation: the contradiction between the principles proclaimed by American society—its democratic convictions and adherence to Christian morals—and the discriminations to which African Americans were subjected. The "Negro problem" is thus defined as a problem of ideology and irrational psychology, and not as a problem of competition for work, housing, and status. Myrdal claims that racist ideology is based on the experience of race relations in the South and that the United States is a "moral nation." Consequently, the evolution of African Americans' situation must result from white Americans perceiving the dissonance between their democratic ideals and the treatment that they inflicted upon African Americans, since this would occasion psychic discomfort and motivate them to move away from such a state of contradiction. What Park considered an ideology based on a long historical experience was thus, according to Myrdal, susceptible to rapid change, since "the whites are aware of the tremendous social costs of keeping up the present irrational and illegal caste system."[204] Also in contrast to Park, Myrdal accorded hardly any attention to the protests of African Americans and to the race consciousness that they had acquired in the timespan between the two wars. He claimed that legislative changes (the beginnings of which were seen in the period in which he was writing) were a means for the transformation of race relations. He believed that the general orientation of Park's essays, and of a large part of studies in this domain, was fatalist, and that the scientific knowledge to which his book sought to contribute should serve as a guide to public action.[205]

In retrospect it is easy to perceive an affinity between the point of view developed by Myrdal and the situation such as it was perceived in intellectual circles of the period.[206] The Second World War had given rise among the latter to fears of totalitarianism, and thus they constructed as their primary goal the weakening of racial tensions. Intellectual circles were convinced that the key to national unity lay in collective experience and the sharing of a set of ideals. The control of attitudes and prejudices conditioned by stereotypes and ideologies consequently acquired decisive importance. Myrdal's interpretation, which attributes the prejudices of whites to their ignorance, suggests that this control is possible.

There exists, by contrast, a clear discrepancy between this situation and Park's inclinations: it certainly contributed to the declining interest in his essays, which seemed somewhat outdated in the 1950s. After 1945, Blumer, like Wirth, also held that political action could transform race relations. Outlining the elements necessary to formulate a new perspective on these relations in 1958, Blumer invokes, for example, the "efficacy of institutional decree and of organized action in bringing about deliberate changes in racial relations," and characterizes as an "academic illusion" the idea that no deliberate change could be provoked.[207]

In the context of sociology over the course of this period (see chapter 5), Myrdal's perspective also accorded well with studies using a then-fashionable approach: the study of attitudes based on survey questionnaires. Myrdal's interpretation essentially led to the study prioritizing white attitudes over those of other groups. Surveys of population samples served as an appropriate and scientific method for these ends, although they accorded less directly with the study of conflicts, to which Park's perspective had drawn attention. The analysis of prejudices, stereotypes, and the ideologies reinforcing them would in fact become one of the principal themes of research in the field after 1945.[208] This search for the determinants of attitudes focused attention on individual characteristics, and by contrast led to the neglect of the characteristics of the situations in which contacts between races took place, as well as macro-institutional factors such as structures of domination. This opposition between the insistence upon attitudes and the insistence upon the situation was, as we have seen, noted early on by Frazier and developed by Blumer.[209] The studies fit within the legacy of Park's perspective, with emphasis placed on the different domains in which competition between the races took place and attention paid to middle-term evolutions. Thus, they fit less easily within the disciplinary structure of sociology and just as poorly with two of the approaches celebrated in the 1940s and 1950s: the psychological study of small groups and the statistical exploitation of sample surveys.

The credit accorded to the conclusions of studies on attitudes, however, was not very lasting. Even before the mid-1960s, the success of the Civil Rights Movement in view of dismantling segregation in the South, the mass mobilization of African Americans, and the rapid transformations of their demands shook confidence in the analyses of race relations that had taken place over the preceding twenty years. None of them had imagined the development of a mass movement led by African Americans, nor a fortiori that of a movement capable of rapidly attaining some of its objectives through overt conflicts, nor the assertion on the part of African Americans of their own cultural identity. It was, to the contrary, the hypothesis of slow changes in the situation of African Americans, by small steps and preferably without overt conflict, that those who had adopted liberal positions in this area, as well as the majority of sociologists, had chosen. The changes anticipated had to do with white attitudes, rather than the abandonment of the attitude of submission and relative passivity attributed to African Americans. Moreover, black separatism had been considered a phenomenon of the past—a bygone step in the strategy previously proposed by Booker T. Washington, or a marginal phenomenon, as suggested by the failure of Marcus Garvey's movement in the 1920s.

In the 1960s, in reaction to this new situation, some critical essays asserted the profound inadequacy—the term "failure of perspective" is sometimes employed—of the studies of the previous years.[210] One of the very first critical reactions to the ongoing evolutions can be found in the presidential address given by Hughes in August 1963 to the American Sociological Association, at the moment when the March on Washington that constituted one of the apexes of mass mobilization in favor of black civil rights took place.[211] With its meaningful title, "Race Relations and the Sociological Imagination," Hughes's essay can be read as a piece of evidence showing how Park's perspective—enriched by later research—confronts the unexpected evolutions of race relations in the United States and the state of social science research in this domain.[212]

Hughes's essay was centered on the question of the incapacity of researchers in the social sciences to "foresee the explosion of collective action of Negro Americans towards immediate full integration into American society."[213] The elements of response Hughes contributed were situated on two levels: that of the analysis of race relations and that of approaches and intellectual innovations in social science research.

On this last point, Hughes's argument in favor of the sociological imagination includes an allusive criticism of the sociological framework for thought based on survey questionnaires, adapted only for the study of average behaviors. It also includes a more explicit criticism of those who wanted sociologists to behave like members of a profession, using standardized and routine methods of collecting and handling data, with correspondingly limited creativity.[214]

Hughes agrees with the conception, previously endorsed by Park, of the relationship of the researcher to his subject, and claims for the former the right to a "great and deep detachment" from what he studies. Hughes notes the narrowness of the usual conception of sociology as the study of recurrent phenomena privileging slow evolutions:

A process may be repeatable, but it may occur in some set of circumstances which has never happened before or yet. Whenever before was there a race-caste of 20,000,000 people, literate, with the aspirations and basic skills of a modern industrial society, with money to spend and the tastes which make them want to spend it on the same things as do other people of highly industrial societies, yet limited by others in their full realization of all these things; living in a society which has preached that all men are created free and equal, and has practiced it not fully, but enough so that with every increase of education, standard of living and of middle-class achievement of the race-caste, the discrepancy between partial and full practice of equality becomes a deeper, more soul-searing wound. Why should we have thought, apart from the comfort of it, that the relations of the future could be predicted in terms of moderate trends, rather than by the model of the slow burn reaching the heat of massive explosion?[215]

Hughes's essay makes apparent a significant break from Park's analyses of race relations. An examination of the two substantial examples of evolution Hughes selected—African Americans and Francophone Canadians—is, however, explicitly situated within Park's analytical framework, and Hughes quotes long excerpts of many of his essays. Tracing in broad strokes the recent evolutions and the sudden effervescence in each case, Hughes notes the divergence of solutions put forth by the two groups: the African Americans demanding the disappearance of what made them a group, while Francophone Canadians called for the survival of their group with equal status on a social, economic, and political level. Hughes, however, notes the diversity of objectives pursued by different segments of these populations and their usage of specific rhetorics: some African Americans absolutely did not want to be assimilated with whites and desired to conquer a separate domain by force, while others wanted to enjoy particular rights in order to arrive more quickly at assimilation, and still others desired the disappearance of the perception of their differences from whites. In the same way as the French Canadians who claimed rights equal to those of Anglophones throughout Canadian territory, we find African Americans who claimed the right to establish their own state. This diversity of objectives relates, Hughes claims, to class structure and its evolutions.

Hughes also proposes a way to analyze the explosion of collective action in the 1960s. The unexpected entrance of African Americans—including the middle class—into collective action relied, he notes, on the fact that different generations did not have the same interests: the youngest did not necessarily accept the compromises made by their elders in different circumstances—an idea that Hughes borrowed from Park. Young black doctors, for example, found their futures threatened by the transformations in the organization of medicine and by the weakening of their monopoly on providing healthcare to African Americans, because "institutional time is not the time of social movements."[216] Hughes thus here proposes what is essentially a complication of the analytical model used by Frazier, adding a new principle of variation: generational differences. While Hughes did not contribute a precise explication to the new element of the participation of whites, who were not directly invested, in mass collective action in favor of civic rights, he was rather interested in the question. He presented his response five years later in a paper at another meeting of the American Sociological Association.[217]

I have at my disposal only summary indications of the reception that Hughes's address received in 1963. His criticism of methodological orthodoxy (the use of a statistical approach), then dominant in American sociology, and his argument in favor of returning to the study of contemporary problems garnered approval, anticipating the reaction that would take place over the following years against Parsonian functionalism and Lazarsfeld-style survey research (although we might think that a number of those who appreciated these critiques would have omitted the plea in favor of detachment).[218] The fact that Hughes remained so faithful to the overall perspective of Park's sociology of race relations, proposed as an acceptable framework in the new circumstances, seems not to have been remarked upon. This is perhaps because Park's sociology had long been reduced to a critical stereotype of his shortcomings and a popular version centered on the race relations cycle leading to an assimilation—unrealistic in the context of the renewed ethnic identities of the 1960s.[219] As to Hughes's response to the question of the reasons for the failure of the social sciences, it seemed in retrospect more rhetorical than substantial once criticism of the assimilationist character of the analyses of the previous period developed.[220]

CONCLUSION

By centering this chapter on some of the studies focusing on African Americans, I have selected one of the political hot topics in the United States over the course of this period, and thus one of those most exposed to judgments on a sociopolitical and individual basis (connected with the life and social experiences of each researcher). This domain is thus one of those that least conforms to the criteria of the conventional definition of a scientific domain, which separates scholarly analyses concerned with proof from sociopolitical analyses and devoid of practical aims. Consequently, it offers particularly appropriate terrain for analyzing the relationship between the knowledge of the social sciences and the context within which it is elaborated.

I have shown, first, that the research perspective proposed in Park's essays is a sort of translation of the immediately visible characteristics of the United States on the eve of the First World War into semiabstract terms, according to the particular point of view of the politically dominant group to which Park belonged. It leaves out what Anglo-Saxon Protestants could not imagine: a future for different ethnic groups other than a sort of cultural alignment with the dominant ethnic group, as well as the potential influence of ethnic minorities on the dominant group itself. It also omits the political dimension of race relations, which reflects among other things the absence of federal intervention in this domain over a long period, and a long blindness toward the actions of certain groups. A second important element of Park's perspective—the role of primary relationships in the dissolution of race relations—corresponds to the articulation of an idea found in many other social science analyses of the period. Thus, Park's perspective on race relations was a composite product, in which elements issuing from scholarly elaboration intermingled with elements based directly on aspects that were immediately obvious from a particular point of view.

This perspective cannot be reduced to a small number of propositions easily subjected to verification. Aside from the general elements that, properly speaking, constitute this perspective on race relations, we find some claims of facts, concerning, for example, the history of the black population in the United States. Some among them have been debunked by later historical studies whose results are now generally accepted by the community of historians. We also find half-articulated elements, such as the idea of assimilation borrowed from debates of the period, which is present through a sort of investigation into the future of the black population of the United States that underlies the analyses.

Later assessments of Park's perspective—and even of what has been labeled as such—have largely been determined by the sociopolitical meanings taken by different component elements, and this is probably why such a large distance between the letter of his essays and the synthetic, overall presentations of his sociology of race relations found in his later works exists.

The examination of some empirical research conducted by those who have been identified as Park's students, and the principal modifications that they introduced, serve as proof of the fruitfulness and the limits of his approach.

Some traits directly issuing from the original model from which Park had taken inspiration—the United States just before 1914—were eliminated over time. Thus, in different forms, Park's four principal intellectual heirs—Wirth, Blumer, Hughes, and Frazier—tended to criticize elements of the implicit assimilationist hypothesis in his essays. This broadening of perspective by the elimination of too-particular and outdated hypotheses resulted from taking into account examples from outside of the United States, as well as the ongoing evo-lutions from within it and the public debates to which they gave rise. In brief, the critical reflection on social science research played a role here, as did the histori-cal experience of the period.

Park's perspective was thus complemented by the introduction of supplemen-tary explicative principles. There was, first, class structure—a principle of vari-ation that some social science researchers sought to hone starting in the 1930s. Then, there were generational and temporal differences: we have seen that this new principle of variation also reflected a reaction to the ongoing evolutions concerning the behavior of African Americans at the beginning of the 1960s.

But the enrichment of Park's perspective was also influenced by evolutions internal to sociology that dealt with survey approaches, because they implied a more precise formulation of questioning concerning, for example, contacts between races in terms of class differences or the conditions and effects of the introduction of the activities of black workers into different sectors.

The domain of social science research on race relations never succeeded in ensuring a broad autonomy from public controversies. A large number of studies were also not exclusively addressed to a specialist audience: some of their argu-mentation sought to discredit opposing positions that were not always explicitly designated, but were associated with well-known sociopolitical positions of the time. What this indicates is that, in a domain so marked by public controversies, any claim of "fact" was immediately charged with political meaning. Often linked to research arguing in favor of one policy or another, the way in which research was funded strengthened its dependence on public controversies. Perhaps Park's and Hughes's plea in favor of detachment from practical aims and engagements, and the dispassionate style that characterized Doyle, Johnson, and Frazier in the majority of their studies, should be interpreted as a reaction to this situation. But we cannot consider that the manner in which researchers like Johnson, Frazier, or even Park himself worked during the period under consideration could be characterized by an entrenched separation between sociopolitical positions and positions of research.

The interpretation of previous research at any given time also reveals itself to be very dependent on controversies of the moment, determining the selection of elements considered essential. Racial conflicts, central in Park's perspective, were thus for a long time forgotten, including over the course of the period after the 1960s, when there existed a focalization on the criticism of assimilationist perspectives. In a general manner, it is rather difficult to recognize Park's analyses in their popular version that has become widespread. When one rereads Park's essays thirty years after the turning points in the public definition of questions of race—and, relatedly, in the established positions in this field of study that marked the end of the 1960s—an analytical perspective becomes visible that is both more encompassing and more subtle than what would replace it. And yet, this perspective is also incomplete, and thus susceptible to being adapted to take into account new phenomena.

Considered all together, the analyses of Park and his students certainly do not form an organized theory (although we know that these never hold up well over time in our discipline). Composed of essays proposing generalizations that were only partially subjected to tests of empirical verification, as well as fieldwork conducted in a common frame used without particular respect for its different elements, the analyses placed under the label of the Chicago tradition have a composite character, which constitutes both the weakness and the strength of this current of research.

This contribution to the study of contacts between races and cultures seems typical of what are, in most cases, the contributions of collective enterprises of research to a domain. Some of the framework proposed by Park passed imperceptibly into the common culture of researchers in the area of race relations in the United States and can thus be found in the basic principles of current studies. The emphasis placed on relationships and not on substantial groups and the concern for comparisons are only a few examples. Another part of Park's frame of reference inspired research whose results are controversial but still accepted by some social science researchers. A final part, to conclude, has been almost totally forgotten, which does not exclude the possibility of its later reintroduction as something new to the field.

9

On the Margins of the
Chicago Tradition

Nels Anderson and Donald Roy

He [Anderson] is also, paradoxically perhaps, Weber's ascetic individualist
(for whom, as he once declared in explaining why he cut short a more
deserved vacation, "the work is the boss"), but without the hard-heartedness
and elemental pessimism of the ambitious puritan.

—Noel Iverson[1]

I know of no one who has given his life over to sociology more completely than
Don Roy and no more modest about it.

—Edgar T. Thompson[2]

Alongside the researchers whose works have just been examined, others can be found who, although they worked in the same intellectual environment, are not always associated with the Chicago tradition. An examination of these cases is necessary for an understanding of the relative positions occupied by the different elements that contribute to the definition of this tradition, as well as the repercussions of this label. I have already evoked the case of Frank Tannenbaum, a professor of Latin American history at Columbia University, who seems to have had no direct contact with the sociologists of the Chicago tradition and is never associated with it. A student and protégé of the philosopher John Dewey, Tannenbaum wrote books on race relations and, as we have seen in chapter 7, delinquency, which testifies to an obvious proximity to the Chicago scholars.[3]

It is also possible to apply this label to Samuel Kincheloe (1890–1981), a Protestant minister. He was a former student of Park as well as a professor at the University of Chicago Divinity School in the 1950s.[4] The label of the Chicago tradition could even, from another perspective, be applied to Erving Goffman on account of his early research, which was closer to the post-Durkheimian tradition in anthropology (to which Lloyd Warner, under whom he had studied, was connected) than to the tradition defined by the essays of Hughes, Blumer, and Wirth. Two sociologists described by colleagues in their cohorts of University of Chicago graduates as marginal in their life trajectories, inclinations, and, to a certain degree, their central intellectual interests could also be placed under this heading: Nels Anderson belonged to the generation of students present at Chicago in the 1920s; Donald Roy, to the generation of students at the end of the 1940s. Both, despite difficult or obscure academic careers, conducted studies that would acquire lasting status as minor classics: Anderson through his book on the homeless in Chicago, *The Hobo*; Roy through several articles on factory work.

A point of similarity exists in the life paths of these two researchers: both had origins more working class than almost all sociologists of their generations.[5] Before undertaking doctoral studies, they both had direct experience in the world of the laborer, something unusual for sociologists, and this background remained present behind their research. An examination of these two examples, which were very different, as we shall see, makes visible the intellectual orientation that could accompany this type of marginality in terms of background and career. An examination of *The Hobo* and its relationship with Anderson's career also illuminates the importance of various elements in the perception of the Chicago tradition.

THE HOBO (1923) AND NELS ANDERSON

Nels Anderson (1889–1986) left no trace in the history of sociology beyond a sole book, *The Hobo*, published in 1923 as the first monograph in what would later become the series edited by Park, Burgess, and Faris.[6] *The Hobo* figures in all lists of monographs in the Chicago tradition, and is almost always given as a typical example of it.[7] A more careful reading, however, shows that it was an unusual book in several respects: the ideas that appear in it are not found in other monographs of the same period, and the subject seems elusive. I shall begin by recalling some of the neglected aspects of the circumstances in which *The Hobo* was written, as well as of Anderson's life, as known from his own essays and cross-checked with his correspondence and other evidence.[8]

Nels Anderson was born in Chicago in 1889, a few months before his family departed for Spokane, Washington.[9] He was the son of an immigrant of Scandinavian origin who performed, over the course of his peregrinations in the Midwest, a wide variety of jobs in agriculture, construction, and industry. His father pursued the goal of establishing himself as a farmer and wanted his children to do the same, and he saw no use in their education beyond the bare minimum. From a very young age, Nels Anderson performed different small jobs, and his family's poverty did not allow him to pursue studies. Before his sixteenth year, following the example of his elder brother, he left the family home and, over the course of a dozen years, lived the itinerant and economically precarious existence of a migrant worker—working successively in the construction of roads and railroads, mining, logging, and agriculture.[10] His semi-adoption by a Mormon family in Utah allowed him, at twenty-two years of age, to resume his studies in a small high school and then at the nearby university while continuing to work. After a stint in the army at the end of the First World War, he applied to the graduate program in sociology at the University of Chicago on the advice of one of his professors. Nels Anderson was then thirty-one years old. He was offered a place in the program after passing an entrance exam before the department's founder, Albion Small, who took the opportunity to discover the limits of his academic acculturation: Anderson believed that the uniqueness of his life path had earned him favorable treatment. To pay for his studies, he found work as a handyman, then as a nurse's aide in a home for the chronically ill. In his writings, he recalls his difficulties in mastering the sociological language used by his classmates, as well as the marginality of his lifestyle and mannerisms compared to the other students, whom he describes as ministers or the sons of ministers of small towns in the Midwest.

> "I can't think of a single one [student at Chicago in sociology] who had a working class background, and I had not been exposed to their kind of company before,"[11] Anderson would later remark. While ministers and ministers' sons constituted only a small portion of his classmates, none seem to have spent significant time working as a laborer.[12] Anderson's employment in a home for the chronically ill that had until that point refused to hire students from the university suggests, like other details, that he effectively distinguished himself from other students through his mores and his manners. According to the testimony of Guy Johnson, who shared an apartment with him for a time, upon arriving in Chicago in 1920, Anderson spent his first night sleeping under the open sky.[13]

He himself insisted on many occasions upon the social distance that separated him from his classmates:

> When Thrasher, for example, talked about his study of boy gangs, or Reckless talked about vice areas, it seemed to me that much which was discussed as sociological wisdom was, after all, but common sense knowledge. But if I spoke of the hobo or other men in my sector of Chicago, their ways of life and work, it was all remote from their understanding. They would respond with some sort of weary willie humor, which reminded me over and over of a sort of cultural gap between my colleagues and me. It seemed wise to talk as little as possible about my study among my middle-class fellows.[14]

By contrast, Anderson seemed to his classmates to excel at the collection of interviews with members of the working class, an activity that was often difficult for middle-class university students.[15]

The study that gave rise to *The Hobo* resulted from the 1921 meeting of Anderson and Ben Reitman, a physician familiar with many different social worlds, ranging from that of vagrants to some of the Chicago elite, passing through those of union activists, anarchists, and sociologists.

Ben Reitman (1879–1942) himself gave a suggestive description that Anderson quotes in his book: "I am an American by birth, a Jew by parentage, a Baptist by adoption, a physician and a teacher by profession, cosmopolitan by choice, a Socialist by inclination, a celebrity by accident, a tramp by twenty years' experience, and a reformer by inspiration."[16] The son of a peddler of Russian origin, Reitman had essentially lived as a vagrant before finding, like Anderson, a protector who made it possible for him to pursue his studies. After obtaining a degree in medicine, he again undertook an itinerant existence and in 1907 met James Eads How, who was then seeking to establish a charity for migrant workers. The following year, Reitman met the anarchist union activist Emma Goldman, and he participated in activities in the anarchist sphere until 1918. Even during the periods of his life in which he wandered and performed occasional jobs, Reitman never lived the life of a migrant worker, as Anderson would remark. Reitman, whose reputation in Chicago was notorious, was, from the 1920s, a sort of fellow traveler of Chicago sociologists and one of the intermediaries between them and the delinquent worlds: it was in the waiting room of the clinic where he worked as a slum doctor specializing in venereal disease that Edwin Sutherland recruited his "professional thief," who would shortly thereafter become Alfred Lindesmith's principal informer with regard to opium addicts. Nels Anderson and then Herbert Blumer were at one time friendly with Reitman, who himself attempted to document their life stories.[17]

Along with a doctor friend, the former director of health services for the city of Chicago, Ben Reitman found a small stipend of around $100 per month for Anderson. He was to spend a year studying the homeless in the area of Chicago around West Madison Street, which is referred to in the book by the pseudonym "Hobohemia."[18] This funding allowed Anderson to devote a little more time to his studies, which had been his principal goal. Provided with a laconic blessing by Robert Park—"write down only what you see, hear, and know, like a newspaper reporter"[19]—he began gathering evidence about the area in question.

For this study, Anderson set himself up in a hotel in the neighborhood where he had sold newspapers in his childhood, and he again came into contact with a population familiar to him, observing places and scenes, gathering interviews in an informal manner, holding discussions with the inhabitants of the quarter, and reconstituting elements of their lives. Ernest Burgess, who was the most directly responsible for supervising the study, seems to have lent his support primarily by reading Anderson's field notes and posing some questions to him.[20] In his biographical essays, Anderson also recalls the sporadic character of his contacts with the professors of the sociology department, including Burgess and Park. He emphasizes the deep sense he had of the shortcomings of sociological culture and observes that he had neither the time nor the stomach for these contacts: "I never got well acquainted with Park. I never was much of a student to talk with professors. . . . Until I left the university, I think I hadn't talked to Park a half an hour altogether. As for Faris, I talked even less with him. . . . My relations with Burgess was as impersonal as with the others."[21] He also indicates that he did not become familiar with Park's thinking until after he wrote *The Hobo*, something confirmed, as we shall see, by an examination of the book.

Arguably the obligation to provide a report contributed to the rapid progress of the research. Anderson submitted his report to the outside committee charged with sponsoring it, within which figured the two physicians who had orchestrated the project: the leader of the organization coordinating charity work in the city (United Charities), as well as Ernest Burgess. Subsequently, Park proposed the report's publication in the series of books in sociology planned by the University of Chicago Press.[22] The committee asked for only minor revisions.

Two points merit notice. While the book was (at least according to Park, as we have seen) the first in the series edited by Park and his colleagues, Anderson did not give the book its title, but discovered that it had been attributed that of *The Hobo* only when he received a copy.[23] Feeling that what he had studied was the vagrant population of one Chicago neighborhood, he thought that the title should have been something like *Homeless*.[24] Two years after its publication, *The Hobo* was presented as an MA thesis to strengthen Anderson's position, when he had just been hired by the University of Washington to temporarily replace Roderick McKenzie. The addition of a typewritten page, which appears in the copy of the thesis preserved by the Joseph Regenstein Library, was apparently the only revision made. A scholarly committee of professors in sociology carried out an examination of Anderson's sociological training—always insufficient in his own eyes. Here again, it was Small who concluded in favor of Anderson by proposing to confer his MA, judiciously remarking: "You know your sociology out there better than we do, but you don't know it in here."[25]

From the circumstances that gave rise to *The Hobo* there emerge three questions: who are the eponymous hobos being studied in the book, and what subject is Anderson actually dealing with? How did he gather and interpret his material? From where do the themes developed in the book come?

The term "hobo" (the first appearance of which dates to 1889, according to *Webster's Dictionary*)[26] meant, until the end of the 1920s, the migrant workers employed on a temporary basis for seasonal tasks in the West and the Midwest. They often spent the winter in the cities of the Midwest and especially in Chicago, their home base due to its being a railroad hub. While the term "hobo" was current around 1900, the category was, however, imprecisely defined. A recent history of the American labor movement between 1865 and 1925 proposes the following definition: hobos are male, white, Anglophone laborers who go from site to site, and whose prototype is the veteran railroad construction worker—the term "white laborer" is also used.[27] It must be added that they were isolated workers, unable to regularly provide for the maintenance of a family. We have no precise estimate of the headcount of these types of workers—Anderson estimates three hundred thousand who spent time in Chicago around 1920, and a half-million who traveled on freight trains around 1910. These migrant workers did not generate, and did not consistently participate in, any mass organization, which, along with the reduced size of their population, probably partly explains the lack of attention paid to them by historical studies of the labor movement.[28] At the time, hobos seemed to have occasionally captured the attention of part of the middle class, fascinated by what went on in the camps ("jungles") on the outskirts of cities: newspaper articles of the time relate journalists' visits to these camps.[29]

Between 1880 and the 1920s, the term "hobo" was associated with various connotations. It was used as a pejorative among those who were concerned about the incidence of vagrancy, and those who believed that hobos and other homeless people were immoral loafers:[30] one might recall here a particular illustration of the point of view, frequent among the elites and the middle classes of the nineteenth century, that attributed properties of the behaviors of the lower classes to moral depravity. Other uses of the term, by contrast, attributed positive connotations to it, seeing in the migrant worker the model of an individualist who was free and unattached to conventions: Ben Reitman was attached to his title, given to him by a newspaper, of "King of Hobos," as was James Eads How, the "Millionaire Hobo," who since 1905 had funded an association aimed at hobos, the International Brotherhood Welfare Association (IBWA).[31] A monthly publication run by the IBWA that addressed migrant workers was titled *Hobo News*. Thus, the definition of what hobos were lay at the heart of a conflict of which only traces appear in Anderson's book.

The ambiguity of the term "hobo" appears clearly in a conversation between Jacob Coxey and Ben Reitman, recorded by the latter: "The trouble with these movements of the unemployed is that people fail to recognize that there are men honestly seeking employment. They think they are a lot of ruffians and property destroyers. They call all out of work 'hobos.'" "A lot you know about hobos," Reitman gently shot back. "When you led your army of three thousands to the lawns of Washington to pay your respect to President Cleveland you were at the head of a mob of unemployed hobos. A hobo is a man tramping around looking for work." "That's not the way I've heard the term used," Coxley responded, "and I have been hearing the word for forty years. A hobo is a good-for-nothing fellow who would rather beg or steal than work. I never led hobos to Washington."[32]

Anderson's testimony does not allow for a definite understanding of whether or not the perspective on hobos expressed here by Reitman predated his own research. In the most developed of his autobiographical essays, Anderson claims that his first discussion with Reitman, during their introduction, focused only on the fact that, in the lecture that he had given to an audience of social workers, he had not clearly distinguished "hobos" from similar groups, "tramps," and "bums"—a category that especially consisted of alcoholics and drug addicts—who did not work.[33] By contrast, in *The Hobo*, Anderson attributes to Reitman the distinction between migrant workers and the other inhabitants of Hobohemia, which he partially confirmed in a 1972 lecture at the University of New Brunswick, in which he claimed that Reitman had once at a conference insisted upon the distinction between "hobo" and "bum."[34] Anderson's field notes show that the definition of the term "hobo" was one of the subjects upon which the intellectual hobos that he presents in his book readily wrote: some gave him presentations of their own classifications and analyses of these populations, which were sometimes later published in the press.[35]

Determining the different types of people living in the precarious conditions of Hobohemia—and especially distinguishing between migrant workers and other categories of people that had limited resources and more or less lacked stable housing—was one of the objectives of Anderson's study. Another objective was to determine what would happen to migrant workers as they aged.[36] Although Anderson proposes in *The Hobo* a definition of the different types that composed the impoverished population of the neighborhood, his analyses leave a vague impression. Neither the book as a whole nor the majority of its individual chapters chooses clearly between two possible strands of investigation: studying migrant workers or studying the populations of economically precarious status in one neighborhood of Chicago.

> Rather, Anderson continually moves from one perspective to the other. He describes, for example, the encampments of migrant workers outside cities, but is almost silent on the work of migrant workers outside Chicago; one chapter of the book presents the means whereby men with few resources procure cheap or free housing and food, and thus concerns some populations other than migrant workers who spend time in large cities.
>
> Anderson's uncertainty concerning the subject of his book was deep and lasting. In one of his field notes in 1922, he indicates that he had been frank with one of his interviewees, and that he had sought to understand the causes and effects.[37] By contrast, Anderson wrote in the preface to a new 1978 edition of the parody of *The Hobo* published in 1930 under the pseudonym of Dean Stiff:[38] "My job was to undertake a study of the 'homeless man' (to me, the hobo) in Chicago." He also recognized in his autobiography that at that time migrant workers had no longer constituted the majority of the inhabitants of the Chicago neighborhood that he was studying.[39]
>
> Park himself contributed to the equivocation concerning the subject of *The Hobo*. His preface presented the book as the study of a West Madison population of precarious status, defining it, in very general terms, as a contribution to the study of urban phenomena and the types of personalities that the city created. However, elsewhere he adopted a completely different point of view: "*The Hobo* is unique in so far as it is investigates the casual laborer in his habitat,

that is to say in the region of the city where the interests and habits of the casual laborer have been, so to speak, institutionalized."[40] This uncertainty regarding the subject of *The Hobo* reflects a type of imprecision that can be found in other monographs of the time, and thus partly characterizes the state of sociological research of this period.

The Hobo presents a clear definition of the different types of homeless people—based on the double opposition between work and lack of work, and geographical mobility and immobility. It also introduces a second distinction between those seasonal workers possessing an occupation that they exercised with regularity (as Anderson himself was for a time, a class which he occasionally designated as the "hobo elite") and those who took whatever work was available. But Anderson does not systematically examine whether these categories were clearly distinct, nor study the conditions of passing from one to the other and the concrete relationships between them. He remarks only that "the distinctions . . . are not hard and fast."[41] Arguably, the thematic division of the book (which examines, among other things, the health, sexual life, and intellectual life of hobos) also contributed to Anderson's rendering these points obscure, and neglecting the transformation, by illness or age, of migrant workers into urban beggars. The resource represented by the biographies—though collected in large number by Anderson—was little utilized on this point.

Another characteristic of Anderson's description of hobos draws attention: the importance accorded to their intellectual life and their sociopolitical interests. Anderson describes the media addressed to hobos, their newspaper-reading, their participation in discussions, principally on political subjects, and, briefly, the "hobo university" funded by James Eads How (where Reitman, Burgess, and the sociologist Edward Ross, of the University of Wisconsin, gave lectures). The intensity of the intellectual life of hobos clearly confirmed the uniqueness of this population (at a time when the United States, to curb immigration, required candidates to prove their literacy for entry into the country). But Anderson certainly accorded excessive importance to one subset of migrant workers, surely the most visible but small in number: the circle of those who established themselves, or who sought to establish themselves, as spokespeople for the category.

Several factors feed into this doubt: James Eads How, who seems to have been the principal funder of some hobo institutions, particularly the Hobo College, insists in his program upon the necessity of instruction, which shows that not all hobos had intellectual and political interests as chapters 13 through 15 in the book suggest. Anderson's approach could only encourage the overrepresentation in his sample of intellectual hobos: according to his field notes, he had met some of those he had interviewed at the Hobo College, and he does not seem to have shown any reluctance in including documents in his book given to him by the population of this neighborhood.

By attaching such importance to what was arguably a minor aspect, Anderson slid toward another definition of his subject of study—that of a social stereotype that belonged to a sort of urban folklore of the time. This definition is clearly adopted in the parody book on hobos published by Anderson under a pseudonym in 1930. It presents itself as a sort of guide for those wishing to understand the lifestyle and the singular cultural universe of hobos, defining them as the possessors of an innate, instinctive quality that leads them to permanent wandering. The description of their lifestyle prescribes strict behavioral etiquette concerning relations with other hobos.

An examination of the field notes written by Anderson suggests that his own uncertainty on the subject of *The Hobo* reflected the fact that he had let himself be guided by his approach and the empirical material that he had collected without drawing practical conclusions from an examination of the categories, especially that of the hobo. This is the approach newcomers to empirical work adopt without exception, and contrasting in principle with that advocated for by Park, who was attentive, as we have seen, to the socially constituted character of definitions of social objects.

Anderson's analyses also seem rudimentary in ways other than the definition of their object. His attempt at explaining what led to housing instability for migrant workers remains curiously vague. He makes heavy use in his report of analyses from that period on the propensity for wandering—influenced perhaps by Reitman and certainly by Anderson's own experience—[42]and he gives this the same weight that he does the other factors invoked: economic conditions, health problems linked to work accidents and alcoholism, perturbations in family life, and personality troubles. He concludes that many of these factors frequently acted simultaneously. In 1934, in an article on vagrancy written for the *Encyclopedia of the Social Sciences*, Anderson insists to the contrary, claiming an economic determination for the wandering lifestyles of hobos.

Finally, as he would indicate thereafter, in 1923 Anderson did not perceive any more than Park and Burgess, who wrote the preface, that the type of migrant worker after which his book was named was on the verge of disappearing as a mass phenomenon, with the end of the construction of the railroads, the denser population of the West permitting the local recruitment of seasonal laborers, and the technological changes in the agriculture and lumber industries.[43] The use of the term "hobo" continued during the following years, but it sometimes meant a completely different type of migrant worker. It often designated the workers set on the road by the crisis of 1929, who moved with their families, more often in a car than by hopping freight trains, seeking, unlike the hobos of the previous period, a place to settle permanently. Anderson was one of the first to perceive these changes, perhaps because of his ultimate position in the Federal Emergency Relief Administration, created by Roosevelt. *Men on the Move* (1940), a second book probably born from the project of revising a new edition of *The Hobo*,[44] begins with the death certificate of the previous type of migrant worker and describes in some detail the later incarnations of claims to the stereotype of the hobo. In particular, it explores the International Itinerant Migratory Workers' Union-Hobos of America, Inc., whose founder, Jeff Davis (who referred to himself as "King of the Hobos"), rather implausibly claimed a million members in 1937.[45]

If we place the subject of *The Hobo* back in its historical context, the book corresponds, in a sort of inversion that is not without irony, to the descriptive study of a historically singular object. The book was thus destined to become, like the last classic monograph to later be published—that of Paul Siu on launderers of Chinese origin—a sort of document of social history, much more than the analysis of one of those generic subjects that, according to Park, constitute the object of sociology itself: "History seeks to reproduce and interpret concrete events as they actually occurred in time and space. Sociology . . . seeks to arrive at natural laws and generalizations in regard to human nature and society, irrespective of time and place."[46]

Fieldwork in The Hobo

Anderson believed, as we have seen, that he had conducted the work for *The Hobo* in the manner of a journalist, and had not sought to follow a specific approach. There did not exist, at the time, a well-identified model of the ethnographic approach: *The Argonauts of the West Pacific* by Bronislaw Malinowski was published in 1922, the same year in which Anderson gathered his evidence. Moreover, as Anderson himself remarks in the preface to the 1961 edition of *The Hobo*, he did not find himself in the working situation typical of classic ethnography or participant observation after 1940, which some of his classmates, like Paul Cressey, would approximate.[47] Rather, Anderson would gather evidence about a world from which he had come, and from which he wanted to emancipate himself. The salient fact here is that, in 1923, Anderson left his direct and intimate knowledge of the world of migrant workers which underpinned his interpretations unsaid. The sole mention of his direct experience with the world of hobos is found in the book's preface—probably written by Burgess—attributed to the committee that had sponsored the book: it notes simply that the author had shared the "experiences 'on the road' and at work" of migrant workers.[48] By contrast, as has been suggested, many allusions to this experience can be found in Anderson's field notes, but Park, Burgess, or Anderson himself deleted these indications from the final work.

This erasure probably could not have gone any differently in the context of American sociology of the 1920s. Shortly after finishing his book, Anderson began to worry about being too closely associated with hobos, and more generally with the parts of society held to be the least honorable.[49] He remarked regarding the field notes that he had submitted to Burgess: "in time, I came to realize that he [Burgess] was being cautious. A university had to avoid research regarded as outside the zone of respectability."[50]

In order to write his book, Anderson relied on varied evidence, borrowing statistics and reports from different Chicago institutions related to the homeless. The major source he invokes consists of interviews he himself had conducted, which are quoted most frequently in the form of synthetic summaries, particularly for those concerning biographical narratives. Anderson's field notes reveal that he worked somewhat differently than a reading of the book alone might suggest. He generally entered into conversation with those who interested him in public places or at Hobo College gatherings, often presenting himself as a novelist or a journalist. He sometimes brought those who seemed disposed to recount some episodes of their lives to his home or to a café, frequently offering them a small amount of money or inexpensive drinks in exchange for their testimony. He then often followed them and observed their activities from afar, inquiring about them from people he knew. He reconstructed biographies from information sometimes obtained in casual conversations. His field notes reveal that he was aware of the problems posed by these reconstructions: he sometimes specifies the conditions within which he had collected the information, writing down his doubts regarding the veracity of what had been said, and he then sometimes notes corroborating information from various sources. None of this concern appeared in the published text, which reflected the norms of writing and publication of the period, privileging reconstructed facts rather than problems of interpretation.

The importance of Anderson's familiarity with the population in question with regard to the production of this study is clearly conveyed in his field notes:

he knew the rules of socializing within the context, which would have been foreign to the middle classes of the period. Some of those he interviewed were his
old acquaintances: one he had worked with, others he had met during an earlier
study conducted in Salt Lake City. Anderson also knew to demonstrate a moral
relativism sufficient for studying, without being shocked by, homosexual behaviors (a subject that he considered studying more deeply a short time later).[51]

Explicit references to observations of behaviors are rare in *The Hobo*: they are
limited to the description of some hours passed in a night shelter. Anderson's
field notes reveal one part of a much broader observation. For each, or almost
each, person he encountered, Anderson noted in detail their physical appearance
and the state of their clothing, which he interpreted as indications of the "moral
situation," the current financial situation, and the sobriety of the person in question. One note in the book very briefly summarizes a trial of a group of hobos by
a Chicago court, which showed the arbitrariness of the judicial system in handling this population: one might think that a certain caution was at the origin
of this discretion.[52] Thus, reading his field notes would suggest that Anderson's
qualities as a researcher greatly surpassed what can be determined from reading
the book in isolation.

One of the types of evidence Anderson collected is hardly mentioned in
the book. This was a survey questionnaire of four hundred migrant workers
and vagrants encountered in the region of Salt Lake City in June 1921.[53] This
survey focused particularly on movements, activities performed, and family situation. Anderson's synthetic report mentions the hesitancy of the population
to respond to these questionnaires: he ultimately gathered the information he
was interested in over the course of informal discussions. He established some
distributions sorted according to two variables. The results were rather close to
those of the survey conducted some years earlier by a Chicago social worker,
Alice Solenberger, whom Anderson cites rather heavily in his book.[54] One of
his uncertainties focused on the number of questionnaires that he had been able
to collect (four hundred, though he had hoped for one thousand) and on the
validity of the sample.

Finally, according to his testimony, Anderson constructed maps—the
technique then in vogue in the Department of Sociology at the University of
Chicago—but they were not retained for the final version of the book.

With this exception, in terms of the evidentiary sources presented in the book
and their relative importance, *The Hobo* is similar to other monographs written
by University of Chicago sociologists during the same period, showing the same
writing style and inclusion of documents in the analyses. With the alternation of
analyses and the reproduction of the often rather long documents upon which

they are based, *The Hobo* is not far removed from the model of *The Polish Peasant in Europe and America* by Thomas and Znaniecki, and *Old World Traits Transplanted* (1921). As in these books, the status of documents—pieces of evidence or simple illustrations—with relation to the analyses remains indeterminate. *The Hobo* also shares with many later monographs a concern for presenting a contribution to the solution of social problems in the area in question—showing once again that the division between social reform and sociology, for which Thomas and Park had pleaded so vigorously in their teaching and publications, was far from existing in the field. *The Hobo* thus concludes with a list of recommendations intended for the solution of the "problem of hobos," written by the committee; Anderson claims that it was written by Burgess.[55]

> These recommendations were in fact somewhat strange coming from the pen of a former migrant worker. During his interviews with sociologists of Anderson's generation, James Carey sought in vain to understand whether Anderson had been the author, inquiring also into Anderson's political beliefs, which might shed light on the meaning of these recommendations. Guy Johnson provided Carey with the following description of Anderson: "Nels was not what you call a radical, though I think he did admire Karl Marx's writing. . . . He was for the little man. It must have been sort of a semi-socialist point of view."[56] One of Anderson's biographical essays suggests that religious references were perhaps more important to him than political references. Having converted to Mormonism during his time in Utah, Anderson recounts his difficulties over the course of his first two years in Chicago in reconciling Darwinism with a religious orthodoxy that he upheld for a substantial part of his life.[57]

The Hobo is distinguished from other monographs in the Chicago tradition through the themes and notions it develops. Concepts from Park's sociology are essentially absent from the book, which makes no allusion to the distinction between the ecological and moral orders. Anderson was no more interested in the process of the evolution of the neighborhood in question. We do not find the notion of "social control," which was central in the work of sociologists of the period, nor a fortiori that of social disorganization, which would seem applicable to the populations studied in *The Hobo*. We find only a small trace of the notions introduced in *The Polish Peasant in Europe and America* by Thomas and Znaniecki, and particularly of then-fashionable interpretations based on Thomas's typology of attitudes (the "four wishes").[58] The favorite notions of George H. Mead are also absent—but the same is true for the other monographs. Anderson did not seek to study the symbolic universes of the different categories he distinguished, nor how these categories maintained in contact with each other, with charity organizations, or with conventional society.[59] Finally, as we have previously seen, Anderson was not concerned with precisely defining the subject that he studied, and he did not seek to connect what he was studying to a broader class of subjects or processes, in accordance with one of the precepts developed by Park's teaching. An examination of *The Hobo* thus completely confirms Anderson's remarks regarding his ignorance of the sociological analyses that were prominent at the time: "I did not tell him [Small] that the book contained not a single sociological concept," remarked Anderson regarding his thesis defense.[60]

Anderson after The Hobo

The Hobo saw some public success, essentially because of the exotic character of its subject, according to Anderson's testimony, with the result that, over the course of the following years, Anderson was sought-after as a lecturer to speak about this mysterious population. But this same success contributed to Anderson becoming more closely associated with the book and the population he'd studied. Despite his efforts to conceal his past as a migrant worker, he never succeeded in finding a stable position as a professor of sociology in a university, even after obtaining a PhD in Sociology in 1930,[61] and even though he had been one of the co-authors of a book reviewing new trends in sociology.[62] Anderson interpreted his difficulties in obtaining an academic job as the result of the stigma that his first research subject represented:

> As for me, the favorable reception of the book was often embarrassing. There was frequent invitations to speak to clubs, social groups, classes, a task for which I was ill-suited. I would come away each time dissatisfied with myself. Each time I have to evade personal questions. I would try to nurture the fiction that I was only a student with a curiosity about hobos and their ways. . . . *The Hobo* gave me an identity, a lasting identity, which continued to mark me as something less than a fully accepted sociologist. About two years after the book appeared, Burgess recommended me for a teaching vacancy at Rockeford College for women. I went there for an interview with several officials and faculty members. No answer came, but I learned indirectly that some professors objected to me because of my identity with hobos. They thought it meant equal familiarity with "other underworld characters." I would have rejected myself for lack of knowledge of sociology.[63]

One might think that Anderson's proletarian style and tastes strengthened prejudices with this respect.

The negative effect the success of *The Hobo* had on Anderson's career, which was accompanied, as we have seen, by a misunderstanding of the book, does not seem to have been the only reason for his ambivalent relationship with it. Anderson published a parody of it in 1930, and he himself seemed to always have been the loudest—and often best—critic of *The Hobo*. The book came to represent for him the somewhat awkward and incomplete work of a beginner: "I have never understood why *The Hobo* was never convincing to me. Perhaps it colored up too much the culture of the homeless in Chicago's Hobohemia. Perhaps I was too well aware of so much that was left unsaid."[64] Anderson's autobiographical essays, like his prefaces, were largely attempts to correct different aspects of his analyses—especially his ignorance of the looming disappearance of the hobo subculture in 1923—as well as the interpretation of *The Hobo* as a monograph typical of the Chicago tradition.

After finishing *The Hobo*, Anderson spent some months working in a social work organization, the Juvenile Protective Association of Chicago, and was then hired as an assistant at a residential program organized by the city for the rehabilitation of the homeless.[65] He secured short-term teaching positions at various universities;[66] participated in several studies in Chicago and then in New York (particularly on the homeless in Manhattan); published papers, some magazine articles, and a book on Mormons.[67] Anderson then found, as we have seen, a position in an agency created by the Roosevelt administration where he especially focused on relations with unions. After 1940 he worked in the administration in the Navy and from 1945 until 1953 he was charged with the organization of unions in Germany. He then served as the director of UNESCO in Cologne until 1963.[68] He then returned to research activities and teaching, publishing sociology books on the problems of industrialization and urbanization. Finally, in 1965, at seventy-six years of age, Anderson undertook a third career as a sociology professor: after a year at Memorial University in Newfoundland, he taught sociology at the University of New Brunswick almost up until his death in 1986. One of his biographical essays ends with the expression of the achievement that access to these positions represented for him: "The goal of my dream forty years earlier was not reached until ten years after entering active retirements. I cannot recall ever having dull jobs, or ever having a more satisfying one than in this professor's chair, which truly is a little large."[69]

An indefatigable worker, Anderson was not content merely to teach over the course of his third career. He published, between 1955 and his death in Fredericton (New Brunswick), at least seven books in sociology, some of them textbooks, especially on work, leisure, and cities.[70] In these books, Anderson does not fit within the Chicago tradition in an obvious and unequivocal way, either in terms of his references, which attest to a varied acculturation and a certain eclecticism, or by any particular inclination toward fieldwork. His identification with this tradition, so durable and widespread despite his own efforts, demonstrates the predominance of writing style over conceptual similarity in the perception of this affiliation—as well as the approximative character of readings that have been made of the book.

DONALD ROY (1911–1980) AND THE STUDY OF BLUE-COLLAR LABOR[71]

The biographical information available to me about Donald Roy is more limited and less certain than that of Nels Anderson: aside from indications given by Roy in his writings and his correspondence with Hughes, it comes from documents archived by his second wife along with an almost-completed book manuscript.[72] According to these documents, Roy was the son of a hairdresser, originally from Eastern Europe, who had settled in Spokane, Washington. Roy's mother belonged to a family of farmers established in the Spokane area. Roy demonstrated an unequivocal attachment with respect to this background, maintaining until the end of his life the desire to take over this operation.[73]

After a brilliant education in the small Spokane high school, and before beginning his undergraduate studies at the University of Washington in Seattle in 1929, Roy spent four years saving money to pay for his studies: he seems to have worked successively as an employee at a hotel and at a shop, then at a logging camp and in construction. At the time of the Great Depression, this situation was not exceptional for a student, but Roy's resources seem to have been especially precarious. There is nothing to give any indication of what oriented him toward sociology.

In 1936 Roy defended an MA thesis in Sociology, for which he had studied a Seattle neighborhood, christened "Hooverville" like others of the period, in which the homeless resided in makeshift housing. These homeless consisted of migrant workers similar to some of those described by Anderson thirteen years earlier, unattached people devoid of regular resources, and the unemployed.[74] For this study, sponsored by George Lundberg, Stuart Queen, and Norman Hayner,[75] Roy, who benefited from a grant from the Washington Emergency Relief Administration, initially proceeded through direct observation by setting himself up in makeshift housing in the neighborhood. He then distributed questionnaires, calling them a census. This double approach could be connected to the instruction Roy received from George Lundberg.

> As Roy recognized, his MA thesis was essentially a description of the neighborhood in question and its inhabitants. It does not include any reference to a sociological analysis, not even to Anderson's book. (However, Lundberg and Hayner had both been in contact with Anderson in the 1920s.) Roy's thesis was written with the same sarcastic tone and complexity of expression as his later works, as suggested by this passage from the final paragraph: "Thus has arisen Hooverville to glorify the hobo 'jungle' and carry on to new frontiers the traditional American spirit of rugged individualism. And there remains Hooverville, scrap-heap of cast-off men, junk-yard for human junk, an interesting variation of the grimace of laissez-faire."[76]

In 1931, and then from 1933 to 1937, Roy claimed to have participated in different studies and contributed, without pay, to the completion of several dissertations.[77] He secured a position teaching introductory statistics at the University of Washington, then taught for a year at the University of Oregon, where he met a student whom he would soon marry. For some of the following year, lacking funds, he lived with her in the woods in the Spokane area. Shortly thereafter, he offered correspondence courses. On the advice of Edgar Thompson, in 1941 Roy came to Chicago to begin doctoral studies, "fired up over the idea of doing research on social mobility,"[78] and became, according to Thompson, a "student of Hughes." To secure an income, he worked in a restaurant, at a mill, on an oil field in California, and in a navy yard in Portland. Roy held many more jobs over the course of these years, but frequently for very short durations: in 1950, he recounted with pride twenty-four different jobs in twenty branches of industry. Other than blue-collar jobs, he also took service jobs and sometimes intellectual work—in the summer of 1942, Roy, along with William Whyte, provided training for primary school instructors, an initiative funded by the Kellogg Foundation.[79]

Hired in 1944 as a machine operator in a metallurgical company in the Chicago suburbs, Roy claimed to have taken this job with no particular intention, but after a month he began to take notes on what went on in the workshop. In a 1956 lecture, he attributes credit to Hughes for having transformed happenstance into a research subject: "But I did not begin to 'notice things' until Professor Hughes introduced me to participant observation with its constant attentiveness to and daily recording of happenings in the factory."[80] Thus with an eye toward his dissertation, Roy commenced collecting data, which would take ten months.[81] He discovered in himself an affinity for fieldwork that until the end of his life would lead him to accumulating detailed notes on the non-academic jobs that he temporarily held, then on the unionization campaigns in which he participated.[82]

Defended in 1952 with Hughes's enthusiastic approval, Roy's dissertation was not published—like many other dissertations of the same period—and Roy did not succeed in revising it into a book, partly because after 1956 he became attached to a new subject. But he published three articles that presented some of his results. He then wrote a fourth article that was never published because (at least in part) of its excessive length, which Hughes advised him to convert into a book. Roy published an article on blue-collar work, based on field notes he took in another factory, shortly thereafter, and a final one still later, based on field-work conducted in the same period.[83] While writing his dissertation between 1946 and 1950, Roy was also associated with various projects for the Committee on Human Relations in Industry at the University of Chicago. In this context, he conducted interviews with workers holding various positions in factory hier-archies, thus discovering a wide variety of perspectives.[84] He also participated in the discussions of the small group of researchers that constituted the circle of William Whyte until Whyte's 1948 departure for Cornell.[85]

In the autumn of 1950, after having taught at both the University of Chicago and Roosevelt College—a recently opened university, intended for a broad public—Roy joined the small sociology department at Duke University in Durham, North Carolina, on Hughes's recommendation to Edgar Thompson, the head of the department, as instructor in industrial relations.[86] This position, in which Roy would remain until his retirement in 1979, did not prevent him from occasionally taking various manual jobs. During the summer of 1953, he worked as a waiter in a Spokane restaurant, keeping a field journal, perhaps with the intention of beginning a new study. A letter to Hughes indicates that Roy, along with his wife, had wanted to work in a factory again. From these different biographical details, we can conclude that Roy had an intimate knowledge of working-class labor, and that he focused on the condition of the working class an interest that was passionate and not exclusively intellectual in character, as revealed in his correspondence. Roy's entire career revolved around two subjects, both centered on the working class; he came to the second, like the first, some-what by chance.

From the start, Roy's intellectual points of reference, including those that appear in his working notes, seem somewhat different from those of other researchers of his generation at the University of Chicago, who always fore-grounded the publications of those under whom they had studied.[87] Roy seems to have found intellectual inspiration less from sociological literature than from that of the philosophers of the 1920s and 1930s—Ernst Cassirer, Suzanne Langer, Arthur Bentley, and especially John Dewey, Roy's most constant reference until the end of his life. However, a closer look at the sources Roy utilized in his teaching and research, as well as the list of sociologists with whom he maintained lasting relationships, shows the important place of references that were themselves related to references connected to the Chicago tradition.

The documents reproduced by Roy for his teaching show that he made use of classic texts like the essay "On a Certain Blindness in Human Beings" by William James, the essays of Cooley, or Hughes's preface to Junker's book on the experience of fieldwork.[88] When Roy worked on unions, he commenced by referring to a book by Gilman on unionization in the South, which resulted from a dissertation defended at the University of Chicago.[89] A note by Roy's second wife also emphasizes that the Society for the Study of Symbolic Interaction had been "the one organization he really believes in."[90]

Roy shared with some Chicago sociologists of the same generation a particular faith in deep fieldwork, a profound skepticism with regard to data produced by survey questionnaires, and an attentive interrogation of the meanings of behaviors and their subjective dimensions. Roy also kept himself somewhat removed from the academic world over the course of his life. While he sometimes participated in conferences, he was more likely to do so in ones that addressed unions and the world of work than conferences principally attended by sociologists or other social science specialists.

As stated in the abstract of his dissertation, the subject of research to which Roy devoted the first part of his career was defined by the question of how one can obtain full collaboration between laborers and management in industrial production. This question was then reformulated in the following manner: in what conditions and in what measure do industrial workers put forth effort in production?[91]

The point of departure for Roy's analysis is found in the works of Elton Mayo.[92] Roy picked up his idea that the limitation of production is an expression of the "code of manual laborers" (Mayo's phrasing) that follows from the frustration of social relations as they exist in the factory. But Roy radically departs from Mayo in his interpretation, developing what could be termed (using an expression unknown to Roy) as a criticism of the perspective of management that had implicitly inspired Mayo.[93] Roy presents his study as "exploratory," seeking to identify hypotheses "still of rude character" rather than validate them. But his results can be accepted with few reservations: Roy himself remarked elsewhere that over the five following years, during which he had observed comparable situations as employee or researcher, he found no data contradicting his observations.[94] Perhaps the best validation in this case is the fate of his articles as classics that went unchallenged by many later studies.

To designate his approach, Roy used the term "participant observation," referring to the methodological textbook by Pauline Young.[95] He distinguishes three different types of data that he collected: those coming from his own direct observation of behaviors and situations; those reported by other workers in casual interviews that offer indications of their feelings and interpretations; and those coming from Roy's own personal experience.[96] No allusion can be found to Hughes's reflections on fieldwork, even though Roy had been his assistant for the course on this subject from 1947 to 1950, and considerations on fieldwork are one of the themes of their epistolary exchanges. Instead, Roy evokes the example of Ernie Pyle, a then-famous war correspondent killed on the front in 1945, who sought to present the point of view of the second-class soldier.

Roy's analyses, in his dissertation as well as in his first three published articles, are based principally on two types of documents: statistics concerning his daily production and field notes relating behaviors, conversations, and incidents in and outside the workshop. Roy is to my knowledge the only Chicago researcher of this period to have used observation notes and statistics simultaneously. His dissertation and articles are even further distinguished from works of the same period by the unusual number and density of quoted observation notes they contain, as well as by the attention Roy accords to actions in addition to the words accompanying them.

An initial article from 1952 reveals one of the principal conclusions of Roy's dissertation: the limitation of production by the laborers of a workshop is not the homogenous phenomenon postulated by Mayo. Roy distinguished two types of limitation of production practiced by machine operators relating to the system of payment used in the workshop studied. In order to understand the distinctions that Roy introduces, it is necessary to take into account the singularities of the mode of remuneration in this workshop, as well as the state of labor relations during the period, a point Roy left somewhat unexplored.[97]

The laborers in the workshop in which Roy was situated worked on various types of drills. They were assigned to different tasks at different periods and could, in certain cases, be paid according to one of two types of remuneration: for some of the tasks to which they were assigned, workers could opt for a guaranteed hourly wage, independent from their output, or for an output-based pay according to a scale fixed by a methods office that timed tasks. The methods office would also occasionally intervene to modify the rates associated with a task. Roy describes the methods office as the feared opponent of the operators, or even a personification of the company's management. Two teams, a day team and a night team, worked successively on the same machines, which permitted the management to make comparisons. Roy belonged to the night team, which, due to the absence of the majority of managers, was the object of less strict surveillance than the day team.

The factory where Roy worked was subjected to constraints specific to wartime. The union had a monopoly on hiring, which for the workers involved a direct levy of union dues from their pay. The right to strike was restricted, and it was not easy for workers to quit the factory, but on the other hand the licensing of workers was difficult. Salary raises were also limited. Resulting from a compromise made between the bosses and the unions under the aegis of the Roosevelt administration (see chapter 6), these conditions had put distance between the unions and the workers.[98] Curiously, since this was the second theme of research to which Roy devoted the second part of his career, he does not seem to have been interested in unions, which were little present in the factory. Roy does not present these different aspects of the situation systematically and directly, and they appear in his analyses when their consequences on the behavior of workers emerge.

The worker to whom Roy was assigned on his first day immediately initiated him into one of the rules known to all workers in the shop:[99] the level of production paid by the piece beyond a certain hourly wage threshold should never be exceeded, since this would trigger the methods office to immediately recalibrate the corresponding rate of by-piece payment.[100] This first type of limitation of production (mentioned much earlier by Frederick Taylor) should be distinguished from a second type.

By distributing his work hours according to the salary that he would have earned if he had always been paid according to performance, Roy demonstrated that there existed a large span of hours in which his production was lower than what it would have been if he had been paid on an hourly basis. This second type of limitation of production was linked to the difficulty, and sometimes the impossibility, of producing enough pieces per hour that the supplementary gain represented by performance-based work justified the necessary supplementary effort in the eyes of the workers. The workers exerted themselves as little as possible whenever a work assignment required too much effort to permit them to earn much more than the base wage. When surveillance was weak, the workers also outright stopped working when they considered themselves to have completed this minimum. Roy also practiced, and observed in his coworkers, different decelerations in production during work paid according to the hourly rate, with strategic timing of new tasks or mending of defective pieces. He provided different evaluations of the production time thus lost—sometimes up to a third of it. The limitation of production seems to have been rather omnipresent in the workshop, where, to use an expression from the resulting article, "The work group was applying a heavy foot to the production brake, day in and day out."[101]

Mayo attributed the limitation of production in general to the lack of comprehension on the part of the workers of the "purely economic logic" which, according to him, corresponded to the behaviors of the management. On the contrary, Roy understood the behavior of workers to be adapted to the situation. Observations such as the statements collected during or after work suggested to him that the workers were extremely attentive to their own economic interests, since they scrupulously evaluated the effort to put forth for performance-based, per-task pay and decided whether it was justified by the supplementary gain over the base wage. The workers also sought to encourage the reevaluation of tasks paid for on a performance-based scale, and to avoid a decrease in rates. They were, as we have seen, perfectly conscious that exceeding the maximum collective norm would lead to a decreased price of labor. The workers' behavior thus seemed to be motivated by the search for maximum financial rewards in exchange for minimal effort.

Roy's later articles each slightly complicate the interpretation proposed by his preceding article. Published a year after the first, the second article explains why, how, and in what measure the system of piece-based remuneration succeeded in increasing workers' production. Roy shows that workers' behaviors do not exclusively follow the economic logic described in the first article: some of them clearly had objectives other than purely economic ones. Roy observed cases in which workers refused to surpass the threshold of production corresponding to performance-based pay, although it would have been relatively easy for them to do so; there were also cases in which they prematurely left the workshop, were absent an entire day, and so on, even though they could have earned more and their financial situations were precarious, according to statements that he had collected on other occasions. Based also upon his own example, Roy concludes that some of the effort of workers in performance-based work can be explained by performance-seeking and by a game among coworkers that represents a sort of victory over the methods office: working by the piece gave an objective to the activity, overcame the boredom of monotony, and could even attenuate the impression of fatigue. There also existed rewards linked to participating in a group of workers: while not surpassing the maximum level of production was a group norm, a group could also encourage performance-based work when there were tasks known for making an interesting reward possible. Roy also notes that the maximum enthusiasm he felt for working by the piece coincided, for him, with the period during which he felt the strongest hostility toward the company. Working by the piece, workers found themselves free from some surveillance by management and could partially use this free time for contact with their coworkers, or even for symbolically defying their supervisors. Therefore, on the whole it was an inextricable mix of financial and social rewards (play, gaining free time, group recognition by peers, and the expression of hostility toward management) that encouraged workers to work by the piece. In the conclusion to his second article, Roy surmises that per-piece work should not be attributed solely to an economic motivation on the workers' part, remarking that the economic reasons they put forth to justify their choice of performance-based work sometimes had an ambiguous meaning. Even though Roy does not explicitly note this point, this conclusion to his research is convincing only when we accept that deep and prolonged fieldwork ensures the selection of an interpretation of the meaning behind workers' actions.

Roy's third article introduces a new complication to the analysis by examining the intervention of other groups of workers and of middle management.[102] He demonstrates how the solidarity between groups of workers and machine operators who conspired to trick the management into permitting them to dispense with official norms concerning the manner of production impacted antagonism between management and machine operators.

It was an established belief among laborers in the workshop that they could not earn an attractive salary working by the piece unless they flouted the official rules concerning the manner of work and usage of tools, and resorted to some fraud with regard to the moments at which the pieces were effectively produced, their quality, and so on. In order to free themselves from the rules prescribed by the management, the operators relied on the tolerance and often the active complicity of other groups of workers present in the workshop. Roy describes in detail the diversity of practices intended to increase apparent or real production, from slowing down machines during chronometry to the usage of tools forbidden for the tasks in question, with a blind eye turned by the staff controlling the passage from one task to another as well as the warehouse keepers who provided tools. Roy again illustrates the omnipresence of an antagonism between workers and management in the life of the workshop. Thus, contrary to what Mayo and his associates had argued, it was not a failure in communication between a rational management and irrational workers that allowed for an understanding of what went on in the workshop. Roy, however, refused to completely overturn Mayo's argument and hold up workers as a group possessing the logic of efficiency on account of their calculated rates according to which production was ultimately carried out. Citing Dewey, Roy proposes going beyond these stereotyped definitions and taking into account both the goals pursued and the feelings of all present parties.

The clearest formulation of Roy's opposition to Mayo's interpretation can be found at the beginning of his dissertation, in a section where he argues for the importance of the low status within which laborers were positioned:

> The view held here is that machine operator form frustrated groups, but the "bite" that they feel is not that of the mosquito of failure to understand the economic logic of management. It is the tiger of rejection, of exclusion from participation, of degraded status that exclusion implies, that slashes at their vitals and arouses them to aggressive counter-attack. Machine operators are rejected as a group, or "en masse," by management. . . . They are "second class citizens" of the factory, and their behavior is what might be expected of any subordinate group that does not accept a degraded status. . . . But whatever the origins of the rejection relationship, it does exist; and machine operators respond to it with individual resentment and group "'norms of conflict" that include prescriptions for restriction of output.[103]

Though it remained for a long time unpublished, the fourth article Roy pulled from his dissertation focuses on the changes that affected relations between groups over time.[104] Basing the article on the observation of forms of cooperation and antagonism in work, of which the previous article had already given some examples, Roy sought to specify the notion of the informal group of workers, which, in the usual way in which it is used, is according to Roy a "free-floating entity." His article thus corresponds to a criticism of studies of small groups— prominent during the period—sarcastically remarking that researchers had turned away from the analysis of production activities only to become interested in peripheral aspects of work, which included "such striking social configurations as the car pool and the kaffee klatsch."

Roy's field notes illustrate the idea that relations between groups of workers were subject to continual transformations as a function of the context in which these interactions took place. Returning to the collaboration between various groups of workers in increasing production by violating the rules dictated by management, Roy shows, for example, how the relationship between the machine operators and the group of workers responsible for supervising the quality of production changed from overt hostility into a sort of harmonious partnership when the interests of these two categories were not in opposition. He also emphasizes that antagonism could at times develop even between two generally close and allied categories, such as the operators and those who adjusted their machinery. Within each group of workers, individual variations also affected relations with members of another group: lines of conflict between groups were variable over time, and they passed through the interior of each group. Here again, on the basis of field notes attesting to a fine perception of the meaning and diversity of behaviors, Roy diverges from the simplistic vision of a univocal opposition between groups of workers.

It was in the direction opened up by this article—and expanded in a later article from 1959 on the life of groups of workers—that Hughes advised Roy to commit himself in order to write a book. But another subject had already caught his attention, and Roy pursued the study of blue-collar labor in workshops no further. (Although he did, as mentioned, pull two further articles from the field notes he took when working in another factory.)

It is remarkable that later references to Roy's research seem largely to neglect the very particular context within which his observations were made—that is, the characteristics of the period, but also those of the company and the work-shop. Like those of Anderson, Roy's interpretations were taken out of their con-texts without particular care. I shall not further develop this point, which was highlighted by the dissertation research of another University of Chicago sociol-ogy student, Michael Burawoy, who thirty years later found himself in the same workshop, almost unchanged, where Roy had worked.[105]

As for the research for *The Hobo*, it is impossible not to draw connections between the primary characteristic of Roy's analyses—the richness of his field notes—and his own life trajectory. But this trajectory also influenced an intellec-tual objective that appears behind the objective Roy explicitly pursued: the anal-ysis of determinants of the production effort of workers. This second objective, which neither Roy nor his contemporary readers seem to have remarked upon, is present in the form of a criticism of what can be qualified as the pro-management ethnocentrism of studies on blue-collar work. Among Roy's repeated references figures an essay by Allison Davis, which presents, addressing a middle- and upper-class audience, the behavioral logic of disadvantaged workers (African Americans, Mexicans, etc.).[106] That presenting workers in a sympathetic light had implicitly been Roy's objective is also confirmed by his correspondence with Hughes as well as scattered remarks in his essays, in which Roy foregrounds his affinity with the "lower ranks" of society—to use the expression that he some-times employed.[107]

The choice of studying working-class worlds, sometimes presented by Roy as fortuitous, reflects a sort of immediate affinity, as he himself indicated in a later article: "I must admit that conversing with working stiffs is for me a matter of taking the line of least resistance. The union organizers of my acquaintance are for the most part only improved varieties of old-fashioned blue-collar drudges, and having experienced somewhat the same beatitudes and stringencies of condition, I find a pleasing measure of fellow feeling in our otherwise professional relationships and correlatively an ease in informal communication. My academic career has been, in a sense, an appendage to an earlier horizontal progression through a series of miscellaneous low-caste occupations. During my graduate student days, research in a factory gave me an opportunity to escape from my reference group to spend the afternoon observing and interviewing the machine-tending hoi polloi. In the bowels of the factory we were all dropouts; I was the dropout who went on to get a Ph.D".[108]

Roy's correspondence with Hughes in the 1950s emphasizes the critical dimension of Roy's analyses, as well as the relationship that Roy himself established between his biographical characteristics and his aptitude at understanding the world of the workshop: "So many writers have a little corner—they fuss around the edges, cutting hairs and trimming toenails—but nobody digs into the intestines, liver, heart, spleen and bumgut of the thing. These guys on role theory, like Sarbin, Newcomb, Parsons, etc.—always circling, making passes, but never moving in for the kill. I ask myself 'How can they possibly miss this?' I guess the answer is that they lack the experience with lower class behavior. And may be they have missed certain experiences in their childhood, or have forgotten about them. Survey research techniques can't possibly catch it. It can't be told. Sapir would call it 'unconscious culture.' Only observation would catch it, observation that is preceded by experience and insight."[109] A slightly earlier letter, written at a moment when Roy was despairing of the academic life and the atmosphere of the Duke sociology department, compared academics and laborers: "Why I *can't accept* academic institutions? I think it largely traces back to a year's experience I once had in a tunnel camp. . . . Those hard rock miners were not educated men, but they were *big* men, not rabbits . . . tired old women like our teachers and administration. They showed less concern for their lives than the academic man shows for some status point. . . . That atmosphere stuck with me, and every thing has been a sort of anti-climax ever since."[110]

While, as Alvin Gouldner argues that one of the traits of the sociologists of the Chicago tradition was the adoption of a point of view in affinity with the less legitimate sectors of society,[111] Roy offers a typical example of one of these studies to the extent that its analysis was developed from the point of view of one of the categories then among the least studied, for reasons relating to the division of labor between disciplines, research funding, conditions of access to this object of study, and the social trajectory of sociologists of the generations in question. At the same time, Roy's political beliefs, like those of Anderson, remained remarkably faithful to a sort of democratic and reformist option, of which one of the principal references was, for Roy, the philosopher John Dewey.[112]

A 1962 lecture by Roy offers an explanation—to my knowledge the only one in this case—for the antagonism between laborers and managements in the terms of Cooley or Park: "The endemic fear and hostility that I have observed would be, it seems to me, phases of a stereotyped reaction to the unfamiliar, to the stranger, so characteristic of man throughout his long history of in-group out-group experience. . . . The world of good guys and bad guys . . . is the world of management in its relations with labor. The monsters are still here, now in the form of blue-collar workers, not with one eye in the middle of their foreheads, but with their crude appearance, their rough language, their quick and ready postures of physical violence."[113] In 1978, in one of his last lectures, Roy maintained that the solution to the problem of antagonism between laborers and management necessitated the participation of the former in the organization of production—the same end point as his dissertation. He concludes here that only unions constituted the provisional means of realizing partial democracy by the intermediary of lobbying groups.[114]

The interpretation of the role of unions alluded to in the 1978 lecture corresponds to Roy's primary preoccupation over the course of the second part of his career. After completing his dissertation, Roy did not pursue the study of the organization of factories and the limitation of production in workshops for long: in April 1956, an organizer from the unionization campaign of the Textile Worker Union (a union affiliated with the CIO) of North Carolina made contact with him, seeking a sociology student who could distribute flyers for the union. Roy did not succeed in recruiting one of his students, but he would himself observe the union campaign. As the organizer did not mind Roy taking notes, he began to work on the subject, which would absorb him until the end of his life. Over the course of the following years, Roy followed different campaigns of union organization and some strikes, principally in the North Carolina textile industry, a sector in which unions had not fully succeeded in becoming established, despite low wages and difficult conditions of work.

As in his previous study, Roy began with a simple and practical question: how to explain the success or failure of unionization campaigns? Roy was aware that the subject was delicate in the context of Duke, and of the South in general, and one colleague had expressly warned that mention of the subject was banned. Together with one of his close associates, Roy would have many experiences demonstrating how justified this colleague was in warning him. He felt blacklisted in the industrial world and partly in the South, sometimes suspected of being a semi-communist. The progress of this new study was slow. Roy published many articles, but an attempt to write a book, during a sabbatical year spent at Cornell alongside William Whyte, fell short, with Whyte hesitant due to the insufficient integration of the material into an overall analytical framework.[115] Over the following years, Roy started new observations of unionization campaigns in the South. Shortly after his retirement and just before his death, he had almost finished a book on the difficulties of unionization in the South—its manuscript is preserved in the archives of Duke University. In it can be found the characteristics of Roy's research on blue-collar labor, which shows a variety and a precision almost unequaled in field notes. The lack of publication of this book perhaps has relegated Roy, like Nels Anderson, to the group of authors who produced one unique study recognized as a minor classic in sociology.

What have we learned from these two analyses of sociological works on the margins of the Chicago tradition?

First of all, they confirm the rudimentary character of attributions and affiliations admitted in the accepted history of the discipline. Even frequently invoked works like *The Hobo* were read summarily, the reader seeking nothing but the confirmation of stereotypes—in this case despite the almost desperate efforts of the author himself. The writing style and, here, the form of usage of and reference to the evidence are apparent as decisive elements in the comprehension of studies.

For Anderson, as for Roy, we have seen that the originality of their works cannot be dissociated from certain specific characteristics linked to their particular life stories. Both knew how to conduct particularly deep fieldwork (even if, in Anderson's case, he only partially utilized it) in worlds that were practically inaccessible for their peers—or accessible only at a high cost. Their field notes abundantly illustrate the importance of the qualities of sociability linked to their experiences prior to the execution of their studies. In the two cases, but especially in Roy's, their relationship to the world that they studied was accompanied by a sort of intellectual project aimed at explaining the meanings of behaviors in this universe, in close relationship with their sociopolitical orientations. The lasting recognition of the value of Roy's and Anderson's studies thus seems indissolubly linked to their social marginality and, in another manner, to the difficult careers of both.

The differences between Anderson and Roy are just as striking as their similarities, which should be enough, if needed, to discourage any reduction of the two works to overall characteristics of social trajectories. Despite relatively similar social backgrounds, Anderson was persistently concerned with distancing himself from his origin and from the research subject that was correlated to it. To the contrary, Roy sought to remain close to his origin, at least through his research. Another difference: one was durably connected to a research tradition which he hardly cared for and considered himself partly an outsider from, and deservedly so; while the other, who shared with the Chicago sociologists of his generation somewhat more than first glance would suggest, was not especially associated with the tradition by the legacy accorded to his research.

Conclusion

Social science appears to have a double burden laid upon it. The one is to analyze the processes of human behavior, and especially of persistence and change thereof, in terms relatively free of time and place. The other is to tell the news in such form and perspective—quantitatively and comparatively—as to give clues for the taking of those chances of which action consists. The balance between these two functions or burdens varies from man to man, from time and place to time and place.
—Everett C. Hughes[1]

A way of seeing is also a way of not seeing—a focus upon object A involves a neglect of object B.
—Kenneth Burke[2]

I can think of no better expression to characterize these similarities than "family resemblances"; for the various resemblances between members of a family: build, features, colours of eyes, gait, temperament, etc. overlap and criss-cross in the same way.
—Ludwig Wittgenstein[3]

This book has proposed, first of all, to offer an overview of a group of sociologists who were among the first to have conducted empirical research on the social world surrounding them, examining the methods of their studies, the social science texts whose production was their primary objective, and the approaches and conceptual frameworks that they developed over the course of these studies.

An initial conclusion emerges at the end of the path taken: the label "Chicago School" as it is still currently used corresponds to an arbitrary division within a much vaster set of works and researchers, groups possessing some common characteristics that give them something of a family resemblance.[4]

We have sought to discern which contextual elements of the production of these studies are necessary for understanding them. Entire swaths of the history of American society lie behind those elements that gave meaning to the terms used by researchers used and the motivations that inspired their analyses. To mention only those aspects that have been especially emphasized here, it is necessary to take into account the Protestant reform movement of the late nineteenth century; the policies of the major foundations (Rockefeller, Carnegie, etc.) and their contribution to the development of higher education and research in the social sciences; the transformation and broadening of areas of intervention of the federal state; conflicts between races and the emergence of a black autonomy movement; and even the American labor movement and the evolutions of its position on the public stage.

Another meaningful contextual element of the development of these studies had been noted by earlier research: the process of autonomization of sociology as a scholarly discipline. We have pointed out here how this was reconciled with the maintenance of the sometimes rather close relationships sociologists had with their funders and with the public controversies of each period.

The development of research in sociology at the University of Chicago over the course of the period in question could be described from the starting point of the variation of the framework of reference within which the research of these sociologists was situated. Until the beginning of the twentieth century, those who bore the uncertain title of sociologist were very close to the Protestant reform movement that emerged from the American middle classes. After the First World War, the Chicago sociologists sought to remove their social science endeavors from any immediate commitments by distancing themselves from this movement, whose unity had ruptured during the war. The group of Chicago sociologists occupied the area of empirical research in the new discipline almost alone at that point. The city of Chicago, where during this period the changes and social problems that had been at the heart of public controversies since the end of the nineteenth century were concentrated, constituted for this group both its social environment and its principal field of study. At this time, these sociologists tended to expressly refuse engagement in reform movements in favor of submitting to the criteria of the new discipline, which had a seat in a growing number of universities. Practical aims—referring to the policies of the federal government, then in the process of being defined in new areas—left their mark on research orientations, however. These practical aims were articulated within foundations, the principal source of funding for research, and they expressed a mix between the views of the federal government and those of certain economic and intellectual elites of the period.

From the mid-1930s, it was through comparison with American society as a whole, in the framework of the federal state, that American sociology tended to be organized. The Chicago sociologists who were situated more directly in the legacy of their predecessors at the same university no longer occupied the center of the development of their discipline, where new approaches and conceptions came into play that broke with those of the previous period. These new approaches and conceptions, which met the expectations of research funders, were more concerned with the United States as a whole, and with recurring facts that could be related to a stable social structure, than they were with the study of a process taking place in one part of the territory or another. The city of Chicago, or any other local entity, thus did not seem as appropriate a field for empirical investigation as it previously had.

In the 1940s and 1950s, the research of the Chicago sociologists who had maintained the orientation of previous work did, however, benefit from funding and opportunities to access new areas of study (such as work), and were certainly encouraged on these two fronts by their acquired institutional reputation. To defend their place in the environment of the discipline as it was at that point— with its new sources of evidence and modes of handling data—some sociologists of the Chicago tradition developed explications of their analytical categories and what then became their more specific evidentiary approach, fieldwork. They also defined a conception of research, with its intellectual objectives and its criteria of rigor, which constituted an alternative solution to the conceptions then in vogue.

This description, drawn in broad strokes and from outside the frame within which the Chicago tradition developed, omits two aspects to which an important part of my investigation has been devoted: the relationship between the perspectives or analytical models of a set of social phenomena and the universe within which they were conceived, and the transmission from one period to another—and from one generation of researchers to another—of these same analytical schemes and methods of handling evidence.

With more or less detail according to the case and the sources available, we have demonstrated the intelligible relationships between the finished products of research and elements of the social universe within which they were developed. Three types of elements have been more specifically examined: the perspectives proposed by previous social science research; questions of the moment, sometimes relayed by research funders; and the social positions and biographical experiences of researchers considered in their collective and individual dimensions. These same elements also intervened in the transmission, or the non-transmission, of analytical schemes and perspectives from one period to another. Here I have used the term "intelligible" to qualify these relationships, since while they sometimes take the form of a sort of homology that can be presented in a table with two columns, or that of a simple link between two elements that differ in nature, they rarely, if ever, appear in the form of necessary relationships. Putting the studies in question into perspective in the context of their positions leads only to a finer-grained understanding of them.

I shall here return to only two very different examples. We have shown that the investigative frame that constituted Park's essays on race relations was a sort of distillation of the situation in the United States before 1914, traced from the point of view of the dominant ethnic group, which evidently considered its durability legitimate, if not a foregone conclusion. Over the course of the later evolutions of race relations in American society and the studies conducted within the analytical framework outlined by Park, some of the evidence of the period that had been accepted without question began to be subjected to empirical testing. Basic notions were thus partially redefined, and the list of questions subject to investigation was broadened. It was the evolutions and the events perceived in this domain over the course of the period—or, perhaps, the collective experience of race relations—that were principally at the origin of the progress of the development of analyses, which is to say the introduction of new distinctions.

The studies conducted starting in the 1930s were thus a sort of composite amalgam of the public debates of the time and the abstract line of questioning issuing from the analytical frame proposed by Park. Even when it did not encompass the phenomena upon which the attention of the public and the elite were focused, the conceptual frame was kept alive, which is to say it was reworked, reformulated, and partially transmitted to the next generation. We acknowledge a certain autonomy of sociology as authorizing the publication and legitimation of a type of knowledge over the course of this period. This example illustrates the knowledge concerning a domain of social life produced by this research current: a set of articulated analytical categories; the formulation within this frame of questions particularly detached from the practical notions in use in the sociohistorical context of the phenomena in question; and the identification of characteristics and variables that remained implicit in this context. The deepening of knowledge in the social sciences here corresponds to the increased length of the list of questions that should be asked in every study and the progressive development of analytical notions, which is to say their separation from the context in which they were initially utilized.

Second example: the origin and conditions of the development of studies on work and occupations by researchers whose principal toolset was the approach developed by Thomas, Park, and their contemporaries in order to analyze other social phenomena. Three elements that are independent from each other, and dissimilar in nature, account for the direction taken by these studies: first, the impetus given—and the possibilities of research opened up—by the development of a contemporary social movement on the margins of which these studies were developed, aimed at the intervention of social science researchers as experts and advisors; second, an affinity between the intellectual orientation of Everett Hughes, who a posteriori appeared to be the principal organizer of these works, and those orientations which the researchers of the generation owed to their own life experiences; and third, the radical critique developed, almost independently, by Herbert Blumer of what had at the time become orthodox in the discipline, concerning both the approaches and objectives of research. The approach thus developed for the study of work, formulated in an abstract manner by Hughes, was transferred a little later to delinquency as a domain of research, which was then occupied by studies conducted according to the perspective developed by Chicago researchers of the preceding period. Hence the succession in a few years among researchers of the Chicago tradition to approaches that were very different, but all based on elements already present in the sociologies of Thomas and Park.

We have also seen, in numerous examples, that each study, not only in its execution but also in the future destiny that secured its diffusion, depended on the confluence of an ensemble of numerous and heterogeneous factors whose effects, though intelligible when examined up close, are too complex to likely be found in the same form in the development of other traditions of research in the social sciences. The development of the sociological tradition in question would certainly have been substantially different if Park or Hughes—or even Ogburn or Warner, whose contributions were linked more to reactions than to subsequent researchers directly borrowing their perspectives and know-how in terms of approaches—had refused the positions offered to them at the University of Chicago, if research funding in sociology had not been available at that precise moment, or if none of the students recruited had been led by their previously constituted interests to adopt a point of view removed from the domain that they studied.

We have seen why the transmission from one researcher or group of researchers to another of analytical schemes, acquired investigative skills, or even justifications implicit to an approach to a domain of social life is never solidly acquired in the social sciences. Interest in these elements—the subjective meanings they conceal for those who conduct research—as well as the possibility of their implementation depends on researchers' previous social experiences, but also on the intellectual, sociopolitical, and institutional circumstances. This, for example, underscores the similarity in orientation—notably the attention to the perspective of people or institutions on the margins of respectability—that exists between Hughes and some researchers of the following generation. However, it must not be forgotten that this similarity is in part an a posteriori creation produced by this same transmission.

Over the course of these analyses and following a somewhat arbitrary path among the studies of the Chicago tradition, recurrent relations between the associated books and the contextual dimensions of their production have also been demonstrated.

The relationship between funding and the development of research in the social sciences, a subject neglected by the history of social science until the 1980s, appears to be relatively simple. Significant and lasting funding was indispensable to the early days of creating a large university in terms of its aims and its organization; it was also arguably indispensable to the recruitment of instructors and researchers in a new discipline in sufficient amounts that the enterprise had durable future prospects. But the funding of research in the 1920s could have led, like other similar undertakings, to a set of soon-forgotten works and to a knowledge that was not transferrable to new domains of research. An examination of the second period, after 1935, here sheds a complementary light: the Chicago researchers whose works we have followed only barely participated in the large research undertakings of this second period. They did, however, benefit from—or knew how to take advantage of—financial returns on the reputation they had acquired during the previous period. They maintained their credibility by being content to remain on the margins of some research activities that were important at the time. It is more often funds of limited scale, in a world in which the opportunities for support—grants and so on—were relatively numerous, that can be found behind the works of the 1940s and 1950s. Even if returns on important funding in social sciences did not often appear as soon as sponsors expected, the existence of such funding was, on average, one of the conditions that enabled the development of a tradition of research, which is to say the momentary stability and transmission of previously acquired knowledge.

The existence of funding opportunities that redefined the potential functions of an autonomous department of sociology, thus opening up possibilities for the publication of research, is certainly only one element explaining the birth in Chicago of sociology in a relatively similar form to what existed at the time in other countries, especially in France after 1945—a discipline concerned about both an empirical approach to the familiar and contemporary world, and the formulation of general analytical schemes applicable to human societies. Other particularities of Chicago, a city of social innovations and confrontations, are also apparent in the background of this development. We have brought to light the existence of dense networks of individuals who, occupying prominent positions at various moments in their careers and in various domains of public life—in the intellectual world, or in the administrations of major universities and foundations, or even in the federal government—contributed to rendering possible studies in new or previously noted domains, thereby introducing novel ideas and perspectives in their research. The idea of the applicability of research results to the implementation of reforms constitutes the principal link between social science researchers and those who contributed to making it possible for them to accomplish these studies. Over the course of the years, one of the evolutionary trends in the intellectual organization of these generations of researchers corresponds to a growing distance with respect to application of research results, and even to the relevance of such an objective. This is what Goffman, a marginal heir of the Chicago tradition, formulated in his presidential address to the American Sociological Association in 1982: "We all agree, I think, that our job is to study society. If you ask why and to what end, I would answer: because it is there. Louis Wirth, whose courses I took, would have found that answer a disgrace."[5]

Contrary to the stereotype that is often associated with them—as well as one of the missions that Hughes assigned to sociology in his statement used as an epigraph to this conclusion—the Chicago sociologists only very partially took advantage of the fact that many significant events and social innovations of the first half of the twentieth century took place precisely within their city. Despite their claims, the deep analysis of new phenomena was not often a strong point for them: neither the transfer of residence of the middle class to the suburbs; nor the spread of the automobile, the telephone, and chain stores; nor the organization and the expansion of social work; nor the growth of education; nor that of the new leisure market were the subject of visible and widespread studies during the 1920s and 1930s. In the cases in which the Chicago sociologists studied some of these aspects, study results remained off the record or were esteemed for completely different reasons.[6]

Among the domains examined here, it is almost exclusively in the study of race relations that works of research were closely linked to the issues of the day. This connection was not just superficially defined by public debates, but was also shaped by the insights of well-placed first-hand witnesses of unfolding events, such as (in various functions before 1945) Robert Park, Charles Johnson, and

Franklin Frazier. The conclusion concerning the perspicacity of the Chicago sociologists in the study of new phenomena would likely be somewhat more favorable in the following period (1945–1960) if we examine from this angle the studies of executives, unions, and methods of mass communication.

One of the recurring phenomena encountered over the course of these investigations concerns the determination of the studies' content by a critical reaction to the established popular or scholarly analyses of the period immediately prior. Thomas's studies on immigration were thus, firstly, a reaction against biological determinants; Park's were a reaction against these same determinants, but furthermore against the simplistic vision of the period 1917–1920 with respect to the "Americanization" of immigrants. Studies on juvenile delinquency of the 1930s were primarily a reaction against the biological and psychological approach that interpreted delinquent acts as no more than individual behaviors. Hughes's analyses of occupations were primarily a reaction against the transfiguration in sociological theory of the system of justifications by which the established professions and the occupations looking to model themselves after these professions sought to justify their privileges and their status. The foundation of these reactions to fashionable ideas was often the collective experience of a group of researchers belonging to a single generation, and it certainly cannot be reduced to its intellectual elements alone. What we might designate by the term "influence by reaction" is always connected to the intellectual circumstances of a period, and the generation of researchers hired during the following period, consequently, had little chance of inheriting it.

The valorization of what can be presented as an innovation—a norm of assessing works of research in the social sciences directly borrowed from the natural sciences—contributed to reinforcing the differences between the research conducted by researchers of successive generations. However, in the case studied here, there existed some continuity between generations of instructors, and the phenomenon was of relatively limited scale. One might think that influences by reaction and the valorization of innovation constituted two important factors of the rupture in the orientation of successive generations of researchers in the social sciences.[7]

Some elements, like the choice of the type of evidence and the way of treating it, the style of reporting research results, or the attention paid to some class of phenomena, lent themselves well, by contrast, to being easily transmitted from one generation of researchers to another. In fact, during the entire period studied here, the Department of Sociology of the University of Chicago housed instructors coming from perspectives other than that which can a posteriori be considered the central branch of the tradition. This borrowing of different perspectives then led to a certain heterogeneity of the elements that characterized the orientation of studies during each period. The research conducted over the course of a single period always had a composite character, because it was based on varied elements whose cohesiveness was contingent. From one period to another, some of the legacy transmitted to one generation of researchers could rapidly disappear almost without a trace, notably when certain elements were replaced by elements originating elsewhere. New ideas and research methods, like those introduced by Ogburn and Warner (who had little to do with the orientation of their colleagues of the same generation), were almost imperceptibly added to the core knowledge belonging to the central branch of the tradition (Park, Faris, and Burgess for the first period; Hughes, Blumer, and Wirth for the second) that was transmitted by their colleagues.

We now understand why it is only a family resemblance that unites the studies that have been collected under the label "Chicago tradition." I have not here sought to select a corpus of works or authors in order to expose common characteristics, as (in one way or another) previous studies on the Chicago tradition have done. Taking as point of departure the institutional foundation of this research current represented by the Department of Sociology at the University of Chicago, I have, to the contrary, examined a sample of studies connected to it, whether well-known or not. I have endeavored not to allow myself to be guided by the fame of their connection to the Chicago tradition, which is itself a historical construction. Unless we are prepared to be content with a summary understanding of these studies, it is necessary to abandon the usual representation of what the groups of researchers or works in social sciences that have been placed under the heading of a "school" have in common: a small cluster of rather abstract ideas permitting various implementations, to which were sometimes added new knowledge or types of approaches to evidence.[8] Among the various works examined here, we can scarcely find more in common than a steadfast confidence in the value of empirical implementation and in a back-and-forth between the field and abstraction. It is clear that other groups of social science researchers present the same quality—especially among historians. The impression of unity of the works of the Chicago tradition suggested by previous analyses essentially depends upon taking into account the restriction of the field (limiting it to one period) to the arbitrary exclusion of some works. It also, as we have seen regarding Nels Anderson's *The Hobo*, occasionally depends on superficial readings.

It is, therefore, not a single, clearly identifiable Chicago School that emerges from this inquiry, but works that exist within networks of exchanges and borrowings between researchers—and direct borrowings are certainly not more important than critical reactions to previously developed analyses. Moreover, these networks did not unite and separate sociologists alone; they extended to groups of authors sometimes situated in other disciplines or outside the academic world. This conclusion, negative with respect to the relevance of the use of a term like "Chicago School," will discourage, I hope, the use of this book as a source to reduce to a simple formula what was a blossoming research enterprise, which mobilized considerable sums of money and a great deal of energy over many years.[9] Rather, I hope it will encourage the discovery of the diversity of analytical schemes that manifested in these studies and that, in some cases, were later forgotten—or at least were in danger of being forgotten, as is always the case in the social sciences.

If we renounce the reduction of works to a small set of abstract ideas dictating the investigation of empirical subjects, and if we bear in mind that the path I have followed is only one of those possible—since I have arbitrarily left out works or aspects that could just as well have been included—there is no longer a risk in establishing an inventory of ideas that recur frequently, but not always, and in various forms, in the examined works.

Among the principal basic elements of the perceived similarity of works put under the label "Chicago tradition" certainly figure those connected to the approach to evidence and the utilization of certain documents in the argumentation of the texts produced. This similarity reflects one of the constraints placed on researchers as well as the ease of borrowing certain elements. We have seen that the classic works of the 1920s and 1930s can be considered as examples of the execution of what I have designated a research formula—which corresponds both to a type of evidence and its treatment, as well as to a style of writing and argumentation—of which *The Polish Peasant* offers the initial model. This first research formula was practiced at least until the end of the 1930s. Conformity to this model in its most formal aspects was undoubtedly a more essential element than the identity of the analytical schemes implemented, at least in terms of the later perception of published studies. For the following period, we have demonstrated the existence of a second, somewhat different research formula: the principal evidence here comes from fieldwork, with researchers utilizing the quotation of notes and passages from interviews to give the reader an understanding of the interpretive approach that plays a role in the argumentation comparable to the role codified statistical procedures play in other types of analyses. Here as well, the justifications of the style of writing remain tacit.

I have claimed that an unwavering faith in empirical work was the only characteristic that can be found in all the researchers whose work has been examined here. This was reflected in their frequent adoption of an inductive approach and placing emphasis more on the discovery of new perspectives on a sector of social life than on the verification of propositions (as was desired in the neopositivist model of scientific practice). We might add a more external characteristic that is equally important but concerns only some studies: the audience explicitly or implicitly envisaged by their publication was an educated public, rather than being limited to specialists in the social sciences. The researchers' principal objective was the transformation of the reader's perception of the sector of social life in question. Paul Cressey in *Taxi-Dance Hall*, like Everett Hughes in his essays on work; Charles Johnson and Franklin Frazier in their studies of black populations; and Howard Becker in *Outsiders* sought to push their readers to pay attention to things they previously had neglected, such as less visible actors, their intentions, and their interests, which were less mysterious than simply absent from ordinary attention because they happened to exist outside of the legitimate awareness of the middle classes to which the sociologists belonged.

Characterized by the audience that they sought and by the objective of empirical work, the studies fall within the line that can be drawn from Robert Park to Howard Becker, passing through Everett Hughes and representing one of the conceptions of empirical research on the contemporary and familiar world that had been the principal raison d'être of sociology since the beginning of the century. This can be put into opposition with other conceptions, for example, that which led to the production of statistical models serving as instruments for politico-administrative decisions, or that which, intended for a politically defined audience, sought to bring to light to the hidden determinants of the social order.

The evidentiary resources exploited by many of the studies in the Chicago tradition that have just been distinguished were, firstly, the direct knowledge of places and people owing to researchers' presence on the scene at opportune moments—a resource also accessible to laymen. The envisaged audience was an educated public, which sometimes included the elites responsible for the administration of different domains of society. The goal pursued was, as we have seen, the transformation of this audience's perception of a segment of social life, which explains the style of writing used in these works, written in common language, but with a critical dimension to it, and marked by conceptualization through which this transformation in perception was accomplished. These works always included a descriptive dimension, because it was necessary to begin with description in order to reform common perceptions. As it worked better to persuade a reader of the pertinence of a perception than to offer proofs establishing an esoteric knowledge of the phenomena that were outside the possibilities of ordinary actors' perception, the writing style included quotations of documents (field notes, interview excerpts, and documents produced by or regarding actors in the domain in question). Compared with the practical perspectives that any type of actor develops in a situation, sociological analysis here proposes only to offer a slightly broader frame of reference, with the aim of explaining the context further than each type of actor could or would seek to do. The contribution of successive research corresponds to a sort of enrichment of the comprehension of the context, and, through it, to an expansion of the list of questions that could be asked—the same objective that Paul Veyne attributed to historical research some years ago.[10]

By placing it in a perspective of longer duration, which would include works from the 1960s and 1970s, it is possible to show that the evolution of studies within the Chicago tradition distanced their authors from the pursuit of the practical goal—enlightening the educated middle classes—that had initially justified or inspired the choice of subjects of study and the orientation of investigations. Increasingly, the narrower objective of the production of knowledge principally intended for specialists in the social sciences, and removed from any concern for defined practical goals, imposed itself. This is the point of view that, thirty years after the studies examined here, was expressed by one of the heirs of this current, Joseph Gusfield:

> A sociology that makes no pretense to instruct or lead the public, that provides no scientific rationale for the authority of practitioners, is neither likely to be sought after by a State and its agencies nor by political critics. If we search for analogies perhaps our best choices lie in self-awareness which literature, philosophy and history have made their raison d'être. . . . Such a sociology cannot offer the society a technology, a method for discovering or solving public problems, nor a science, a body of knowledge whose indisputable character resolves moral and political conflict. Its social value lies in widening our understandings of self and others and in revealing the many alternatives from which to make choices and interpret events. Its aesthetic value lies in the joy of knowledge and interpretation that is neither science or art, but yet it both.[11]

Although I have not systematically sought to present the elements that allow comprehension of the difficulties encountered by the spread of studies in the Chicago tradition in France—and arguably nearly everywhere in Europe—some of the elements emphasized over the course of the internal analysis of the evolution of this tradition in the United States can be used to explain why this diffusion was so late. It was essentially at the end of the 1980s that the appropriation of the Chicago tradition seems to have been effectuated, and only with difficulty, by French sociology.[12]

The case of the reception of the Chicago tradition in France is not an exception: the slowness of the diffusion of a research tradition in foreign contexts is a recurring phenomenon in the disciplines that it is tempting to unite under the term "sciences of culture" (with, of course, the emphasis on culture and not on science). In these disciplines, essentially, the comprehension of a group of works passes through the filter—always controlled more implicitly than reflectively— of the culture shared by those who belong to the world within which this diffusion is likely to take place. And this culture, in terms of a discipline like sociology, is also marked by national intellectual circumstances, which manifest especially in the particularities of questions developed either publicly or within the discipline. The position held by the discipline in question within the range of the sciences of culture, varying according to national history, is another characteristic that affects this diffusion.

It can be noted, a posteriori, that for a long time the circumstances were unfavorable for an assimilation of the Chicago sociological tradition into French sociology. I shall begin with the last aspect mentioned because it is well known, at least in its simplest form.

French sociology as an academic discipline remained, at least until the beginning of the 1970s, institutionally linked to philosophy. Some sociologists had been recruited among current or future high-school (*lycée*) teachers in philosophy, especially among *agrégés*. The same was true for some of the most prominent researchers and professors, from the Durkheimians to Georges Friedmann and Raymond Aron, then to Pierre Bourdieu, to mention several generations. This institutional link was accompanied by an intellectual dependence of sociology on philosophy, which in fact exercised a sort of authority over the assessment of intellectual production, and additionally over the careers of sociologists. Some of those who spent time studying philosophy preserved—often unwittingly—some of their previous conceptions and interests. They especially continued to accept the conception of abstraction and generality cultivated by French academic philosophers, and the related scale of value for intellectual products. The sociologists who were not philosophers by training—who undoubtedly always represented the majority of sociologists after 1945—compensated, with rare exception, by being perhaps even more inclined to refer to the model of intellectual accomplishment proposed by philosophy, thus giving precedence to some kind of general theory. This relationship with philosophy, which was maintained at least over the first three quarters of the century, did not encourage comprehension of the research of the Chicago tradition among French sociologists.

Pragmatism—for a long time identified with William James, rather than with Charles Peirce and John Dewey—did not receive a warm welcome from French philosophers. Indeed, it is no exaggeration to suggest that the orientation of these philosophers was generally disparaged until the 1970s.[13] A sociology similar to a philosophy that was for a long time considered unsophisticated, or even vulgar, could not garner more than weak interest in a discipline marked by the culture of French philosophers. The skepticism shared by many sociologists of the Chicago tradition was fomented by their indifference to the formulation of a clearly identifiable conception of their activities with reference to principles, and by the demarcation of other positions defined in similar terms. For example, Hughes still used minimalist terms to present his perspective on research in the introduction of his major collection of essays in 1971. That same simplicity of approach constituted a supplementary obstacle, especially among those who gave precedence to the direct knowledge of the researcher, namely fieldwork. It sometimes sparked a search for complicated interpretations and philosophical antecedents to the approaches and investigations that, as I have shown here, fit almost naturally into the various contexts within which they were developed.[14]

Additionally, one of the rare formulations in terms of principles that can be found prior to 1970 among the researchers of the Chicago tradition, proposed by Blumer in the methodological essays that punctuated his career, is almost void of philosophical references. This likely gave French readers, who were often philosophically trained, the impression of an undeveloped perspective reducible to vulgar empiricism.[15]

The importance of intellectual and political reference to Marxism among French philosophers and sociologists was another element that certainly did not contribute to facilitating among the latter an understanding of the Chicago tradition.[16] This was not only because the themes of central interest developed by this tradition did not coincide with theirs, but because the versions of Marxism that prevailed in France seemed to already have the answers to questions that, for the sociologists of the Chicago tradition, could only be obtained through empirical research. In the background of the negative assessments of the Chicago tradition should be mentioned the profoundly ambivalent relationship French researchers had with the intellectual currents and products coming from the United States, such as the empirical research methods developed after 1950.

But these characteristics, which already testify to the great distance separating French sociologists from American sociology, were undoubtedly less determining than the successive divergences between the preoccupations of researchers on both sides of the Atlantic.

If, as has been emphasized, the activities of a generation of researchers largely forms a reaction against certain ideas accepted by the previous generation and with reference to public issues, either of the moment or of the immediately previous period, we might expect that coincidences between the issues recognized as significant by researchers belonging to different cultural worlds would be rare.

Essentially nothing predisposed French sociologists undertaking new research during the interwar period to concern themselves with challenging the biological determinant explanation of behavior, nor to accord much attention to issues of contacts between ethnic groups, of increasing urbanism, or of delinquency. Between 1918 and 1940, there was no place in the French university for the development of the new discipline defined by Durkheim: his rare students who survived the war of 1914–1918, with the exceptions of Célestin Bouglé and Maurice Halbwachs, held positions on the periphery of the academic system, and in 1940 there were only two or three positions for professors in sociology.[17] But, if there had been more, it would probably have made no difference with regard to the relationship to the principal themes of Chicago sociology.

Despite the presence of a significant proportion of immigrants in France and xenophobic campaigns, the future of immigration in the country was perceived in intellectual circles as a rapid integration into the Republic. An accelerated growth in urbanization and the correlated lifestyle changes were no longer envisaged, much less considered inevitable, even at the end of the Second World War. Neither delinquency nor collective behaviors—including riots, the spread of radio, the effects of political propaganda, etc.—were topics of significant debate in France in the interwar period. Class confrontations and the emergence of the middle class—the subject of one of the rare novel sociological studies conducted in France just before 1940—were otherwise topical. But on these subjects, Chicago sociology had almost nothing to offer.

The discrepancy between the interests of sociologists in France and in the United States was just as striking after 1945, when, particularly surrounding Georges Friedmann and the CNRS, French sociology became institutionalized. The study of immigration was at that point principally conducted at the Institut national d'études démographiques, the origin of which rendered it somewhat suspect to researchers in sociology and that, anyway, found itself slightly removed from academic research. Contacts between Friedmann and his circle on the one hand and Hughes on the other were relatively close on account of their common interest in the study of work, but they did not lead to anything more than sporadic relations that were either noncommittal or had a personal rather than a scientific character.[18]

The model of fieldwork, also not very developed before 1960, was not considered by French researchers a practical method of inquiry: they were less concerned with meticulously establishing the meanings of behaviors that they studied than with imposing them through the establishment of allegedly indelible facts upon their rivals—political or otherwise—who also sought to know the social world, by means of the instrument of objectification that is statistics.

From the middle of the 1950s, the preoccupation with of the new discipline in France thus focused on the acquisition of a scientific respectability.

While some of the young, intellectually ambitious French researchers of the years 1945–1960 spent some months at the University of Chicago, more of them went to Harvard and Columbia. It was the perspective proposed by the association of Lazarsfeld and Merton, and thus the research formula elaborated by the Bureau of Applied Research at Columbia University, that principally caught their attention. Over the course of the 1960s, the development of contract research for public sponsors encouraged this same orientation, as studies on the model of the Chicago monographs of the 1930s would hardly satisfy the senior government officials and planning commissioners who were then among sociologists' principal interlocutors and funders.

It was only at the end of this period that conditions became more favorable to the comprehension of works in the Chicago tradition. Among the new elements can be mentioned a critical disposition with respect to the institutions that had developed simultaneously on both sides of the Atlantic, and the reaction within the social sciences against the neopositivist model of questionnaire surveys and its summary treatment of the symbolic dimension of social phenomena.[19] The development of studies on cities, and later on immigrant populations, drove some researchers to seek out the classic works of researchers in the Chicago tradition.[20] Later, over the course of the two decades that had just ended, some French sociologists found themselves in a market condition similar to that of the Chicago sociologists. Starting in the early 1970s, the execution of large studies on the behavior of France's population shifted almost completely into the domain of activities of large public organizations with adequate means at their disposal, such as INSEE, INED, and CREDOC. By contrast, there developed a demand for surveys on the level of cities or regions—a demand indifferent to the national stage, and thus more favorable to the development of studies with the character of a monograph. This new context alone certainly did not guarantee an immediate comprehension of studies in the Chicago tradition—and especially studies from the period 1918–1933—for French sociologists, but it removed one of the obstacles that had impeded the comprehension of the spirit of this research venture.

I shall now abandon the historical and non-normative perspective hitherto employed in order to point out some works in the Chicago tradition that seem to me to especially merit the attention of contemporary readers. I shall, obviously, skip over the work of Everett Hughes and Howard Becker that I have contributed to translating into French, and which constitute an anticipated response to this question.

Among the suggested works could certainly be placed some research based on an ethnographic approach. These frequently offer an original and organized perspective on the subjects that they study, based on substantial evidence. The best older example seems to me to be *The Taxi-Dance Hall* by Paul G. Cressey. Among the most convincing products of the following period, I would single out the articles on blue-collar labor by Donald Roy, the book by Melville Dalton on managers—which has never been equaled on this subject, especially in terms of its critical independence with respect to the perspective of corporate executives— as well as the set of articles on the sociology of work written in Hughes's circle during the same period. (I obviously leave aside publications in areas that I have not examined here—particularly those by Alfred Lindesmith, Erving Goffman, Julius Roth, Murray Wax, Joseph Gusfield, etc.) Other studies than those based on an ethnographic approach developed equally suggestive analyses: Andrew Lind's book on the Hawaiian Islands remains one of the best illustrations of an ecological approach.[21]

For their subtlety, I also place on the first rank of texts meriting attention the essays by Robert Park on relations between races and cultures. These essays reflect a vision that expanded over the years, informed by a rarely matched comprehension of the perspectives of various parties involved in the great process of contacts between disparate populations. I also place here the essays, critical or otherwise, of Herbert Blumer, the scale of which we are only beginning to perceive. They essentially offer one of the clearest and most systematic presentations of a research perspective that is, to use a term of the 1960s, antipositivist—that is, it is careful not to project the point of view of the researcher onto the social actors.

Another set of publications that can be distinguished by an attentive reading consists of the autobiographical works and studies conducted in the frequently difficult conditions experienced by the first black Americans to become researchers in the social sciences. If some of these works—which range from the autobiography of Booker T. Washington, to which Park contributed, to that of Horace Cayton, passing through the studies of W. E. B. Du Bois, Charles Johnson, and Franklin Frazier—are now partly outdated in terms of the facts or interpretations that they present, they remain essential milestones on the path toward a fine-grained comprehension of the long journey undertaken by African Americans to erase the moral and symbolic traces of slavery. The intimate mixture of engagement and an effort at objectivity to which these works testify constitute one of the most successful outcomes of what the social sciences can produce when they venture into the study of sensitive questions.

Afterword to the English Translation of
La Tradition Sociologique de Chicago

How Should the History of the
Social Sciences Be Written?

*Part of the historian's function is to help us to escape from, or at least to
loosen the hold of, those categories of thought we take so much for granted
that we become almost unaware of their existence.*

—Stefan Collini[1]

*One of our chronic temptations is to assume that the limits of the systems
of action that we study are a known instead of being, as they are, one of the
unknowns which is our business in each case to discover.*

—Everett C. Hughes[2]

The completion of a research project often leaves its author unsatisfied. In addition to regret over abandoned discursions and neglected verifications, there is also the sense of having settled on a conclusion that is insufficiently thorough with regard to the research project as a whole. An afterword therefore serves as an opportunity to extend the research, to more fully identify what has been accomplished, and possibly to offer critical reflection.[3] This afterword was written following the completion of a book more closely linked to *La tradition sociologique de Chicago* than might be suggested by its title—*Enquête sur la connaissance du monde social. Anthropologie, histoire, sociologie. France-États-Unis 1950–2000*. Its subject deals with a critical analysis of research methods and a reflection on their degrees of rigor in the fields of history, anthropology, and sociology over the course of the last fifty years in the United States and France. This latter title makes explicit and tests

the conceptions of the activities and consequences of social science that under-
pin my research into the Chicago sociologists, to which this afterword returns.
In the years following the publication of *La tradition sociologique de Chicago*,
I did not have the opportunity to conduct new archival research into the sub-
ject. However, when asked to write articles or respond to questions about it,
I have returned many times to the evidence I gathered while writing this book.
The resulting published articles have focused on, among other things, William
Isaac Thomas and the posterity of *The Polish Peasant*, the thematic similarity
between the "best-seller" published by a contemporary Protestant preacher and
Park's sociology, Burgess's research into crime, and the diffusion of Chicago
sociology in France.[4] These were all opportunities to take some distance from
the book.

As indicated in the introduction, *La tradition sociologique de Chicago* was
conceived of as a reaction against the typical manner of writing contributions
to the history of sociology as well as other social science disciplines (aside from
history), which was practically the only approach used in France at that time.[5]
This conventional history was essentially a history of ideas about the social world
insofar as they could be extracted from the "great books" or the "great authors,"
accompanied at most by a cursory historical contextualization.[6] There can also
be found, in the United States and elsewhere, disciplinary histories focusing on
a field of research, such as (in sociology) crime, labor, or race relations, which
adopted a similar program sometimes depending, like their predecessors, on
cursory historical presentations of intellectual institutions (departments, associations, journals).[7]

The authors of these studies did not always seek to make the past comprehensible in its full diversity through a body of research. But, lacking any competing
analysis, these contributions were also the only options available to those interested in a particular topic, and they were treated within each discipline as contribution to their own history.[8] The two types of contributions identified above were
considered to be a minor genre of publication, almost completely monopolized
by members of the discipline in question and only barely considered research. In
the United States, as in France, for a long time the history of sociology drew only
weak interest, as is confirmed by the fact that it was not until 1999 that a section
was devoted to it in the American Sociological Association, whose members
over the course of the past fifteen years have been primarily professors emeritus.
Journals specializing in the history of the social sciences are also a recent creation:
true, the oldest, the *Journal of the History of Behavioral Science*, was created in
1965, but by psychologists and psychiatrists who were for a long time its principal
contributors. Founded in 1978, the *Journal of the History of Sociology* went out

of publication a dozen years later. The two specialized journals, one French and one English, were much more recent creations: 1988 for *History of the Human Sciences*, and 1999 for the *Revue d'histoire des sciences humaines*.

If the lines of questioning, documentary sources, and rigor of these conventional histories are obviously insufficient for the field that inspired them, no alternative had been clearly proposed when I began work on *La tradition sociologique de Chicago*. In the United States, some research conducted by historians on the origins of the social sciences was already partly distinct from this model, but their interrogations into professionalization did not seem satisfactory to me.[9] Breaking with the established method of writing the history of a discipline to which one belongs is a task that cannot be accomplished by a simple decision on principle: recurrent obstacles, some specific to the history of cultural production and others linked to the proximity of the observer to his subject, prevent the adoption of an authentic historical perspective on the social sciences. The same was true—even if the two cases should not be equated a priori—for the natural sciences.[10] I should specify first of all that the term "social sciences" used here (with, as its semi-equivalents, the terms "human sciences" and "behavioral sciences") has no widely accepted definition: rather, it designates only the de facto units—academic disciplines—or, to use a phrase of David Hollinger's, "an academically organized branch of inquiry" delimited over time by university departments and a system of publications and conferences that became international at the end of the twentieth century.[11]

The orientation of the research organized in *La tradition sociologique de Chicago* took form very slowly and not without trial and error, first by unraveling the history of research methods that soon revealed themselves to be too restrictive.[12] In its abstract dimension and in its final form, as distinct from the completed research, this perspective—history in its own right, to reuse an expression regarding the conception of Lucien Febvre—represents no originality; it is what a historian whose work continues the legacy of (for example) the Annales school would adopt regardless of subject.[13] It could be sustained that this orientation should have been used from the beginning. But it concerns a domain—the history of the social sciences—upon which, as with the history of the natural sciences, the semi-historical perspective that I have characterized as the conventional history had been widely imposed for a long time. Moreover, this orientation fails to clarify either what separates it from a truly historical perspective or the consequences implied by the a priori conception it maintains of what the social sciences produce.

Leaving aside the path followed during the course of my research for *La tradition sociologique de Chicago*, I propose returning to the reflections that mark

the stages in the critique of the conventional story of the social sciences and the
obstacles that must be surmounted in order to adopt a truly historical perspective
of the social sciences and their products. To achieve this aim, it is also necessary
to read works about the history of social sciences that confront similar obstacles,
which are embedded in a sort of cultural subconscious that determines the ordinary conception of intellectual work. I will then identify some of the research
themes whose importance emerged over the course of my investigations into the
Chicago sociologists despite not having initially drawn my attention. They are
therefore included as such among my research findings.

THE CONVENTIONAL HISTORY OF THE SOCIAL SCIENCES AND ITS CRITIQUE

What I call the conventional history of the social sciences displays other characteristics beyond what has already been discussed. The framework of this history
is almost always disciplinary. Each discipline (sociology, anthropology, political
science, geography, etc.) is thus treated as if it constitutes a natural niche rather
than an administrative division, produced by a process that has political, institutional, and cultural dimensions specific to each national context. This implies a
considerable heterogeneity of practices and products connected with these units,
as is well known in the cases of anthropology and sociology: these disciplines are,
to complete Hollinger's characterization and to employ, with an important addition, a formulation of Richard Whitley's (1984: 25), systems of work organized and
partially controlled by means of reputation. (I have added the word "partially.")

The disciplinary framework adopted among these histories is also that of the
present moment. The general conceptions of the social world and its evolutions,
or only those of one domain reduced to a body of ideas (of concepts and relationships between concepts), as distinct from the scholarly works under consideration, constitute the principal subject. The model of the reports is based
on the history of literary and philosophical works, reducing the history of the
production of books to a history of ideas. The patterns of reasoning are those
applied to literary and philosophical works, which are also the schemes used
in practice by researchers in the social sciences. The ideas are, for example, borrowed, and the researchers are connected to each other by teacher-student relationships, subject to influences, and so on.[14]

Providing an explicit characterization of the works—which is obviously an
interpretation of them—and of their relationships with other books (or with an
intellectual context or the social experience of their author), figures among the
principal objectives of these histories. This work will develop the theme of the

relevant discipline's progress up to the endpoint the author associates with this history, which is to say his own particular conception of the discipline and what he considers to be its endpoint.[15] These engaged histories thus are based upon value judgments belonging to the present moment, but the discovery of their criteria is left at least partially to the reader. Books written prior to the institutional beginnings of the social sciences, one of the most frequent subjects of early studies of the history of sociology, are thus arbitrarily interrogated with regard to the present state of a discipline whose proto-researchers were surely not aware of its existence. Finally, the history of sociology is one that lacks archives, focalized on the only publications of research (and sometimes drafts and unpublished work) that rely on interpretive techniques ordinarily applied to philosophical or literary texts. When a historical contextualization is proposed, it is generally reduced to very general assertions—for example, what "everyone knows" about the Industrial Revolution or the New Deal. The poverty of the sources used obviously implies a strict restriction of the lines of questioning pursued: only rarely considered are the networks of relationships and collaborations behind any published work, the financial or other resources that permitted that work's execution, and the methodologies used.

Many deviations from this ideal type, which with some modifications appears in the history of other social science disciplines, can certainly be found in what for a long time have passed as contributions to the history of sociology.

Criticism of this type of publication appeared in the Anglo-Saxon world in the mid-1960s, discreetly in an essay by Robert Merton (1967) and, in a more developed manner, in a 1965 essay by George Stocking, a historian by training who during the following years instigated a reimagining of the history of anthropology toward a framework that was not national, but rather European and American.[16] Stocking's editorial, published in the third issue of the *Journal of the History of Behavioral Sciences*, distinguishes between two different manners of writing the history of the social sciences: that of history written from a "presentist" perspective (which I have characterized as conventional) "for the sake of the present" of the discipline, and history written according to a "historicist" point of view, which aimed to understand the past on its own terms. Stocking's characterization of history written from a presentist point of view is uninviting. He recognized in it the following weaknesses: "anachronism, distortion, misleading analogy, neglect of context, oversimplification of process." But Stocking also affirmed that there were "legitimate and compelling reasons" reasons that could induce one to write social-science history in a presentist manner, and he declared himself in favor of an active presentism that took into account the weaknesses of presentist approaches. This could lead, in light of the final remark in Stocking's article and his own later work, to a favorable judgment of narrative written from a historicist point of view but available for a presentist use. Stocking, who relies on Thomas Kuhn's 1962 *The Structure of Scientific Revolutions*, also notes that the history of the natural sciences, which had accepted the idea of scientific progress as dogma and, consequently, had looked to presentism as an interpretive model, had recently moved away from it.

Stocking does not expressly say as much, but this conventional history contravenes the largely accepted norms of the historical profession regarding most objects of study: for example, the refusal to interpret actions or activities through the frameworks of later periods, the research of retrospective intellectual genealogies (or "the idol of origins" to use Lucien Febvre's expression), the implementation of value judgments that implicitly rely on anachronistic criteria in the selection of evidence, and so on. In other words, this presentist approach to history is profoundly flawed according to widely accepted criteria. It can be justified by the particular qualities familiar to its objects—the enterprises producing knowledge based on supposedly rational and universally valuable approaches—and in the usage of this type of history, as Stocking has remarked.

Stocking's essay is part of a much broader movement that is critical of the method of writing the history of the natural sciences and, on its margins, the history of the social sciences.[17] It was partly a consequence of historians' conquest of new research subjects, facilitated in the United States and (in the case of the social sciences) by the importance of intellectual history. This can be seen in the first books written by trained historians to break free from the conventional perspective, such as those by Mary Furner and Thomas Haskell, or the biography of Robert Park by Fred Matthews. Another of the movement's first manifestations can be found in the 1962 publication of *The Structure of Scientific Revolutions* by Thomas Kuhn, a physician by training who turned to the history of physics. The book shook the confidence placed in representations of science and its progress.[18] Another element of this movement can be found in the rigorous program of the history of political ideas in Great Britain presented in an article by Quentin Skinner that became an immediate classic.[19] The diffuse influence of the development of "science studies" after 1970, as well as the critiques of logical empiricism by philosophers of science, simultaneously contributed to undermining the so-far accepted representations of the natural sciences and, by extension, the social sciences (although I shall not go into that here).[20]

Although the tradition of the history of science in France proceeded from a different orientation than in the Anglophone world, and although science studies saw a late diffusion into any area beyond a very narrow field, Jacques Roger (1920–1990), a historian of eighteenth-century life sciences, proposed in a 1984 essay a precise characterization of a program that would apply an authentically historical perspective to science—this he characterizes as historian's history.[21] It consists, Roger writes, of "comprehending the past on its own terms," or, rather, achieving an approximate knowledge of it. This type of history aims to "reconstruct and . . . understand the real history of scientific activity in the past, such as it was." Jacques Roger also notes that "even the emergence of the notions of 'science' and 'scientific truth' is indissolubly an epistemological, institutional, and social phenomenon."

Some differences in objective distinguish this program from that of conventional history: it is not a question of glorifying the progress accomplished according to the criteria of science recognized today (or of decrying its lack of accomplishment), nor of providing arguments in favor of the adoption of some epistemological conception. Rather, Roger's program aims to comprehend what these sciences were in their own times, and what connects (or does not connect) them to previous or later states, as well as to their environment. Because it avoids a priori hypotheses about the nature of the sciences and their products, scientific practices, and the factors likely to determine them, the list of questions under investigation for this type of history is much longer than that of conventional history, and the types of phenomena it takes into account are more diverse. It is also necessary to take stock on a case-by-case basis. This history is not blindly dependent on the state of the scientific domain in question at a particular moment, nor on the epistemological and theoretical convictions of the author.

Roger's essay develops a critical examination of different conceptions according to which the history of science had been written up to that point. What Roger proposes is distinct from what is generally written by scientists, for whom it is a secondary activity, as well as by philosophers and epistemologists. Roger does not evoke the case of the history of social sciences, but his analysis suggests that similar obstacles stand in the way of the adoption of historically acceptable perspectives on different disciplines. I was not aware of Roger's essay while writing *La tradition sociologique de Chicago*, but his criticism of the perspective of conventional history written about the social sciences was, as we have seen, in the air at the time.[22]

CHALLENGES IN THE ADOPTION OF A COMPLETE HISTORICAL PERSPECTIVE ON THE SOCIAL SCIENCES: NATIVE REPRESENTATIONS AND CULTURAL PROXIMITY

Why was a standard historical approach applicable to the study of any object—groups of individuals, human production, institutions, abstractly formulated problems—not a given requirement in the history of the social sciences? A detour through the history of science (in which, as we have just seen, it was not easily established) allows for the identification of justifications of a presentist approach.

As for any subject, the development of a historical perspective on the sciences creates conflicts with its ordinary representations, the definitions of which constitute an important element.[23] It is necessary to distinguish here between researchers' private, internalized representations—which they develop within and through their practice, including the beliefs and ways of reasoning that constitute their profession and the professional ideology associated with it—and their public representations.[24] These public representations hold a strong legitimacy in Western societies, and they are mobilized especially for the defense of collective interests—legal, financial, and otherwise—by those who establish themselves as spokespeople for a particular discipline or specialization. The central element of this representation with regard to the natural sciences over the course of the twentieth century was systematized by a logical empiricism based on the example of physics: science consists of the body of logically associated propositions regarding explicitly defined concepts that withstand empirical tests.[25] This approach continues to be accepted even by some current critics. Two other elements can be found in the idea of scientific progress through successive accumulation and the belief that the criteria of assessing the validity of theories are timeless. The first of these seems to justify the association of the status of a discipline at one moment in time with the most appropriate perspective—that reputed to be the most objective—for considering its past.

More so than other social science disciplines, sociology has adopted this representation in its long, ongoing quest for the status of a "scientific" field, sometimes moderating its most clearly contestable characteristics. For example, the objective of establishing universal laws has generally been abandoned in favor of the formulation of theories—small groups of logically related propositions—whose compatibility with empirical reality can be empirically tested through research. But the discipline's widely recognized lack of cumulativity as well as the related uncertainty regarding its progress means that any presentist perspective is deprived of the justification that knowledge accumulation provides in the case of the natural sciences. In the case of the social sciences, the justifications for the adoption of a presentist program are thus weaker than for the natural sciences: a history that is based on the present norms of a discipline can seem convincing and acceptable when these norms are widely shared, and when their variations over time are small. This is the case for the natural sciences (at least for long periods), but it is very much not so for the social sciences, and sociology in particular. A presentist history depends on conceptions that are, inevitably, particular to the author, while standards of assessment—in terms of epistemology, interest, and rigor in research—are controversial and variable.[26] These standards also retain a partly implicit character, rendering them obscure and barely applicable for purposes other than polemics regarding the resultant judgments. Presentist histories of the social sciences thus lack the essential element which justifies presentist histories of the natural sciences.

In contrast with the history of science, the history of the social sciences has been of little interest to philosophers, and was for a long time almost the sole domain of researchers who themselves belonged to the disciplines whose histories they wrote. The proximity between researchers and their object of study has therefore always been extreme in this case: those who write the history of the social sciences thus adhere to varying representations and standards of judgment concerning the field they study. Such proximity is a major obstacle to the adoption of a historical, rather than a presentist, perspective.[27] Freeing themselves from their own convictions in terms of research methods, and from expected features of the social world, is surely not an easy operation; many convictions held by researchers are based upon the knowledge they acquired in the course of their training or practice, and are therefore internalized and taken for granted.

Among the most overt of these convictions is the affirmation of the specificity of each social science discipline, an argument frequently used in situations of evaluating researchers or research. However, it neglects the previously mentioned elementary fact that disciplinary boundaries are historically determined and thus logically contingent. Emancipation from professional conventions particular to a certain era and a necessarily narrow frame of reference, as employed by any researcher with respect to his training and research-based relationships, is a long process that can be facilitated by deep reading, reflection, and attention paid to that which is not immediately comprehensible in archival documents, comparisons between international examples, and disciplines.[28] This emancipation is arguably easier for those who work on distant periods and foreign traditions than for those who work on familiar traditions (or those erroneously considered as such).[29] This is not specific to one type of research, as this difficulty can be found in the ethnographic approach when the researcher studies something close to his own field, as noted by Fred Davis and many others.[30]

The recommendations regarding this so-called reflexivity that have multiplied since the 1980s are of weak efficacy. They seem more suited to foster pretense and good conscience than to rendering objective those categories of analysis and reasoning that do not occur at distinct moments in a single study, but rather take place through frequent trial-and-error investigations, fortuitous discoveries, and analogies with other analyses whose conclusions encourage reflection on the difficulties encountered in the course of research. The necessary emancipation from the ideology of the relevant discipline requires efforts that for a long time had little chance of being employed in an area of activity as minor as the history of the social sciences, occupied by a group of elite researchers and professors inclined either to present the past of the fields to which they belong as having culminated in their own analyses or, to the contrary, to lament the field's decline if their own methods received a mixed reception.

This last remark recalls the fact that this type of engaged, conventional history has numerous reasons for existing—or, rather, end goals—that are far from disappearing so far as sociology is concerned.[31] These histories play an initiatory role in a discipline marked by differences in approaches, methods, and the like by furnishing a primary system of identification in this complex universe (hence the importance of classifications, no matter how approximate, in terms of schools and theories), as well as a sort of justification of their agglomeration under the same label, as noted by Shils (1970: 760). For a long time this type of history offered, and still offers, an alternative to research for professors not inclined toward (or lacking competence in) empirical investigation, and who established themselves as specialists in theory. Along with other means intended for the same ends, it works as a strategy whereby the author can acquire or strengthen his scientific credit: rewriting part of a discipline's history allows one to claim the symbolic support of a tradition or of poorly interpreted founding fathers, or, to the contrary, to claim radical novelty due to rectifying an error made by all the author's predecessors.[32] This type of history thus offers various elements that can legitimize and delegitimize positions in a discipline in which many conceptions of approaches, research programs, or conceptual systems coexist in quarrelsome competition, but none has established itself for long (even within a national tradition).[33] It is therefore doubtful that this genre, the presentist history of ideas about the social world, is destined to disappear, even though it is generally recognized as deficient according to the criteria of history (which are otherwise generally unknown by sociologists and anthropologists). The usual criteria of historical research are not applied here, even though this type of history has served as the history of sociology for a long time.

THE SOCIAL SCIENCES AS A COMPLEX OF ACTIVITIES

The perspective of a complete history, briefly described by Jacques Roger in the context of the history of natural sciences, can be applied without significant modification to the social sciences, simply taking into account the patent differences between natural and social sciences—including the social sciences' less acknowledged legitimacy and absence of internal consensus within their disciplines regarding research subjects, approaches, knowledge, and specific types of evidence.[34] The field of social sciences defines only a general orientation of research, since many subjects can be—and certainly have been—at the center of a historical analysis, including the publications themselves, the ensemble of practices that contribute to their production, their diffusion within and outside the social sciences, researchers and groups of researchers, academic institutions, controversies, the transformation of lines of questioning, the evolutions of a particular domain of research, the relationships between national traditions, and the relationships between and among the different subjects that have just been listed. All these choices, and others, are also acceptable, and there clearly is no one single history of a subject like Chicago sociology in the years 1920–1930 but rather multiple historical analyses focusing on different aspects and various questions. However, the state of the accessible documentation—archives, preserved books, possible testimonies from participants—determines the topics that can be studied effectively.

The appropriate scope of investigation is never, or almost never, a single discipline in the social sciences, including instead a larger assemblage of disciplines and specializations that vary according to the subject and period in question, the national tradition to which they belong, and so on. The frontiers between disciplines were always porous over the course of the twentieth century in terms of subjects, approaches, conceptualization, and research methods, even if the boundaries were, simultaneously, difficult to cross for some of their products.

The principal product of these disciplines during the twentieth century, and their reason for existing, can be found in publications in the form of articles, books, or research reports. However, the distinction between these types of publications and those intended for a wider audience (textbooks, encyclopedias, books meant for the educated middle class) is not always clear, in contrast with the case of the natural sciences from the end of the nineteenth century. Other outcomes of the activities of researchers, such as teaching, institutional foundations and involvement in academic departments, scholarly associations, journals, committees of various purposes, expert activities—this last subject has been relatively little studied—also merit further attention.[35]

The term "publications" should be understood as referring to texts—a remark also made by Jacques Roger regarding the natural sciences in the eighteenth century.[36] This conception is not held for the most part in historical research in the social sciences, notably by those characterized here as presentists, for whom the social sciences produce theories or conceptual schemes which may or may not be associated with empirically based publications. As I have already noted, the importance of this representation of the principal product of the social sciences owes its visibility to the contact between the conception of sciences based on logical empiricism and the usual way of treating controversies concerning philosophical or literary work.[37] By defining the principal product of the social sciences as theories and not texts, the singular characteristics of the field are erased, notably the inevitable ambiguity of these texts and their various interpretations, as well as the question of their rhetorical organization, which maintains a close relationship with the audience to whom the research reports are addressed.[38]

Without going into detail, one must recall that these texts make use both of concepts—and vocabulary—borrowed from the social world under investigation, and of concepts that belong to the culture of graduates of institutions of higher education. These texts also frequently include more or less elaborate social science concepts about certain domains (for example, demography and kinship systems), as well as (sometimes) concepts that are defined explicitly in the particular analysis that they implement but not part of the common language of the discipline. These social science concepts remain indexed by period and culture—they are semi-proper names, to employ the expression of Jean-Claude Passeron, and, to cite Blumer, few or none among them can be considered generic concepts.[39] Hence the impossibility of giving a clear, unambiguous translation of social science texts in a set of definitions and propositions.

A second characteristic of social science texts can be found in a system of references to elements that validate analyses, namely documentary sources and treatments thereof.[40] These validating elements allow the reader—more imagined than real in most cases—to check how the conclusions of the research are justified. One could remark that the accepted criteria for judging the elements of validation are extremely variable by discipline, period, and national traditions, just like the standards that determine the acceptability of documentary sources and the practices of handling data: this is a field of investigation that has so far been left undeveloped.[41]

Interpreting the texts produced by the social sciences is an essential research operation. This is a banal activity for the historian, who, when possible, uses other texts relating to his subject to the same end: drafts, correspondence, later testimonies, texts of the same status, and the like. This interpretation requires a practically ethnographic understanding of the universe of the text's production, which should be acquired for each period and group of producers, with frequent reference to the accessible documentation as the principal resource. In the case of *La tradition sociologique de Chicago*, the correspondence between Hughes and his former classmates and the sociologists of the following generation constitutes the base of this documentation. Confirmation is provided for the following generation through the collection of their testimonies, and for the previous generation by the testimonies collected by James Carey.[42] Interpreting the actions and the writing of W. I. Thomas, which are nearly absent from the archives and which took place during a period in which his behavioral standards were already far removed from those of my contemporaries, has proved less easy, as I have indicated in this second edition.

As for any other subject, an essential intermediate objective of investigative work is the discovery of the system of interaction (or of action) within which the activities of the group of agents in question took place—to borrow a formulation of Hughes's—or, to employ phrasing closer to that used by historians, the discovery of the pertinent contexts.[43] This system is effectively never known from the start, and the fruitfulness of empirical work lies in large part in the discovery of elements of the system that did not figure among the initial hypotheses of the study. This discovery of pertinent contexts relies, like the interpretation of texts, on diffuse work in which the examination of archival documentation (even that not closely related to the subject) and interpretation (of the available works on the field and in neighboring or even distantly related fields, and of archival documentation) occupy a prominent place alongside reflections in which analogy and comparison play a role. In the case of the Chicago sociologists, the diversity of historical research conducted on the city, especially for the period 1890–1940, has been a significant resource. Certain elements of the system of action can be almost invisible, as missionaries and, to a lesser degree, aboriginal informants were long unrecognized as contributors to classic anthropological monographs.[44] Other elements, some never mentioned in the documentation, can appear in what can be characterized as "influence by reaction," signaled for example by the efforts of producers in the social sciences to distinguish their products from those of their contemporaries. In the case of the Chicago sociologists, sociology as a discipline is only one element among others. Furthermore, it is one that is almost negligible in an early period, and the evolution of systems of action imposes a division into periods.

As previously mentioned, the concrete element at the root of these investigations can be found in a group of sociologists associated with an ensemble of produced texts, to whom the label "Chicago School" was later applied. These two groups have definitions, and therefore limits, that are blurry. An alternative, or complementary, point of departure can be found in those who contributed to a collection of essays published in 1962, the subtitle of which is an alternative label (symbolic interactionism) that encompasses three generations of sociologists, most of whom spent time at the University of Chicago.[45] Retaining a precise definition a priori is of no use, and, to the contrary, it is necessary to bring attention to the limits of applying these labels. This is illustrated in the final chapter of *La tradition sociologique de Chicago*, which focuses on Nels Anderson and Donald Roy; Anderson is always connected to the Chicago School, even though his first book deviates from the investigations of his contemporaries in everything but writing style, while Roy, on the other hand, is neglected. The elements that constitute this point of departure—the various activities of a group of researchers, the characteristics of the texts they produced, the constitution of the group, and the labels associated with it—are all subjects of investigation. The approach was in part regressive: it locates the origins of the publications of the period 1920–1940 which are the most closely associated with the Chicago School label, chiefly the publications and other activities of those who, in the preceding generations, were the organizers and catalyzers of this research in terms of contributing to their intellectual orientation and furnishing models of composition, and opening possibilities of publication. We have seen how W. I. Thomas, with his changing intellectual interests and his lack of attention to disciplinary limits, deviated from the stereotype associated with the founders of the academic discipline or school of thought.

The transformations over time of the systems of interaction in which the researchers in question were embedded led me to associate three periods with three generations.[46] The first generation, that of W. I. Thomas and R. Park, is that of the inventors of a definition of empirical inquiry in sociology, which was then a very vaguely defined discipline. This generation provided the field of sociology with a name, publication outlets, and a national association, but neither a definition nor an a fortiori model of completed research. The system of interaction taken into account for this generation includes investigative journalism, the Social Survey Movement, the domain of activities in the course of institutionalization that would a little later constitute social work, and many academic disciplines such as philosophy, psychology, and economics—history, by contrast, is practically absent.

The reference to economics, although barely mentioned in *La tradition sociologique de Chicago* for this period, is important: much better established than sociology, this discipline partially limited the domains of research in which sociology could invest—permitting investment in delinquency, for example, but not the work that falls within its own scope. Two other elements of this system are the irregular and barely institutionalized way in which research was financed by rich donors acting in isolation, and the very vaguely defined public to which publications were addressed. This audience included not only a restricted circle of specialists and future specialists in social sciences, but also the "enlightened" segments of the middle classes. A comparison with the contemporaneous context in which the founders of academic sociology in France operated can illustrate the necessity of the discovery of this system of interaction: in France, sociology did not seem to have any relationship with investigative journalism, which barely existed, nor a Social Survey Movement playing the role of competitor. (The successors of Le Play occupied a minor position in the intellectual world.) By contrast, sociology's key interactions lay with the disciplines (philosophy, law, etc.) as constituted by the State, the custodian of degrees and institutional boundaries between disciplines.

The system of interaction within which the sociologists who created the Chicago School monographs of the following period (1920–1940) operated is notably different. Social work still mattered, but with a very different role than it held during the preceding period, since sociological research had begun to distinguish itself at least symbolically. Statistics, however, took an increasingly important position after 1930, not as a discipline but as a technique. The relationships between sociology, which from then on presented itself as a full academic discipline, and research emerging from disciplines with which it previously had been close—philosophy, psychology, anthropology—were beginning to show some distance.

The Department of Sociology at the University of Chicago then occupied a generally accepted position of eminence, as shown by the list of presidents of the American Sociological Society, as well as the proportion of PhDs awarded at Chicago compared with the total number of PhDs in sociology. The financing of research depended somewhat less directly than before on sponsors: there were now some foundations linked to great fortunes, and more to the point there were committees dedicated to various social problems who ensured the majority of funding. The allocation of funds for research was frequently done by organizations like the Social Science Research Council (in which different disciplines were represented by researchers), to which a degree of discretionary power was ceded. This organization permitted a certain distance between the intentions of the financiers of the Laura Spelman Rockefeller fund, concerned with conforming to what its managers considered a scientific approach, and the practical orientation of research inspired by Park.

As shown by its writing style, and conforming to its conception, the finished research was essentially addressed to a wide middle-class audience, within which it spread a scientific perspective on social phenomena like urban juvenile delinquency and race relations—arguably with the end goal of enlightening and guiding their audience's engagements with city life. From the late 1920s, some of the research belonged to a different context, with its intended audience being the federal government administration, which then intervened in a wider range of fields. This was more true for the development of research along a statistical approach, which involved some researchers trained at the University of Chicago who do not generally fall under the label Chicago School.[47] The writing style and rhetoric of research reports are clearly not the same in the two cases, nor the expected forms of evidence.[48]

In the period 1945–1960, during which a third generation was trained, the context of production for the successors of the previous period was again profoundly transformed. From this point, these constituted only a portion of sociologists (certainly an important group but one with a controversial orientation in a rapidly growing discipline), as new training centers—notably Columbia and Harvard—defended other conceptions of research in sociology. Sociology as an academic discipline at this moment was of sufficient size that an important proportion of research was addressed primarily to fellow researchers in the field, as well as to a rapidly expanding student audience. Sociologists invested in new fields, such as the study of work and, later, financed by the National Institute of Mental Health, that of health and medical institutions. Research into work meant the introduction of new sponsors, businesses, and business associations, with their own practical goals in sight. Sociologists who published in this field found themselves confronted with new categories: business leaders, different categories of workers, union members, spokespeople of semi-professional associations—the latter not only sponsors, but also those who sought legitimacy in representations of their activities.[49]

The internal differentiation of sociology—in terms of methods and relationships with sponsors—at this point had implications for relationships with audiences and diversified neighboring disciplines. In terms of audiences and sponsors, the three examples of research on work, delinquency, and race relations are very different, and the last case is particularly dependent on political conditions. The disciplines that had to be included in literature reviews were thus specific to each group of researchers that defined a domain of activity and a research methodology. Each of these carved out a sort of niche within sociology that tended to be associated with a system of publication—an evolution that became somewhat more completely accomplished at the end of the 1970s. For those researchers who relied on an ethnographic approach, the relationship with anthropology withered but did not entirely disappear—the role of intermediary with anthropologists reverted almost exclusively to Hughes. For those who also trained in sociology at the University of Chicago in the same period but are relegated to the margins of my book, it is their relationship with the growth of applied statistics that should be examined.[50] The domain of research based on an ethnographic approach is one in which a definition of an audience analogous to that defended by Park is still maintained, with books sometimes becoming widely read, such as Elliot Liebow's *Tally's Corner*.

The division whose principles have just been discussed is certainly not novel, and various presentations of the Chicago tradition have adopted but not justified it, as if a vague sentiment of the difference between periods sufficed. A closer look shows it to be an important result of investigations, which the chronological organization of *La tradition sociologique de Chicago* arguably seems to take for granted. I now return to some of the themes that are developed, which are either neglected or discussed in too narrow a manner when one adopts the conventional approach to the history of the social sciences.

The production of social science texts is work like any other, and one can therefore make use of categories developed in the sociology of work for the study of other activities, as Everett Hughes proposed to do in the mid-1950s.[51] This leads to an interrogation into the techniques and norms of production, collective claims, professional ideologies, and career issues, all questions largely neglected by the conventional perspective on social sciences. With the characteristics thus established, we can put them into relation with the texts produced. As an example, in the two last periods studied, the division of work between early-stage researchers and those who inspired them is immediately apparent in the differences between types of publication. The former published reports of empirical research that were sometimes awkward and often uninventive; the latter, which is to say Park and then Hughes in the last period, are notable for their recovery and putting into perspective of original elements from these reports, much more so than the production of original research.

For a research current that has been granted a degree of continuity over time, the question of the relationships between successive generations is a theme worth investigating. Approaching the principal products as texts calls attention not only to the conceptual schemes that organize them, but also to their formal characteristics such as rhetorical dimension and the mode of reference to documentary sources. Each characteristic of texts is susceptible to being transmitted from one generation to the following, or, in contrast, to being abandoned. Within each generation of Chicago sociologists, a dominant writing style seems to be more widespread and noticeable than the similarity of conceptual schemes. The transmission of the latter from one generation to another is filtered by the research domain and the institutional, political, and intellectual context of the period, and therefore is always selective. Hence the impossibility of determining the precise intellectual characterization of a tradition that concerns many successive generations.

Another theme of investigation is each specific relationship between research and the different elements potentially present in its environment: public investigations and those conducted in a narrower field (as in the case of deviance), as well as orientations defined by the sponsors and previous social experiences of the researchers. These relationships are completely different in the three fields in question—work, delinquency, race relations—and there is hardly any doubt that one might find even more different relational systems in research on families or cities.

By remaining closer to the practical aspects of production and the material and intellectual dimensions of their products, the historical perspective on the social sciences leads, as we have seen, to conceptions that are profoundly different from how the conventional perspective shapes the ordinary conception of researchers (which is to say, their professional ideology). Analogous discrepancies between native representations and concepts elaborated by historical analysis can be found for any subject; clarifying contextual elements that give meaning to native representations is a permanent objective of historical analysis, as is communicating these elements in a manner comprehensible to a contemporary lay reader. Compared with the list of determinants of work maintained by conventional history, this history considerably lengthens the list of elements under investigation. Documentary sources; the treatment of documentation; lines of questioning and the conceptual and rhetorical schemes of reports; social contexts of the creation of research, including the conditions of securing financing; contexts of publication and reception; and biographical experiences of the producers all constitute elements on which the analysis can focus. Infinitely variable according to discipline and circumstances—in short, according to ordinary historical contingencies—the way these elements produce their effects constitutes one of the principal themes of the history of the social sciences.

To what degree does *La tradition sociologique de Chicago* follow the program that has just been described? Certainly imperfectly, since the program emerged gradually, and only partially in the research conducted. Furthermore, it is impossible to do away entirely with the normal schemes of reasoning to which we in the discipline have been socialized. But a more complete break from the conventional perspective on the social sciences and its terminology might, perhaps, have made it more difficult for the reader to understand certain aspects that would have required new terminology. I have therefore not, in this edition, sought to eradicate phrasing that now seems equivocal, nor added discussion to broaden the program followed for research from the years 1920–1940 and 1940–1960. Furthermore, since the publication of the book, the presentist manner of writing the history of the social sciences is no longer the only one widely represented, which undoubtedly reflects the general zeitgeist of widening the objects of history in which *La tradition sociologique de Chicago* was written, making it now less likely to be read through the filter of conventional history.

The original project included the corpus of research produced by the group of sociologists trained between 1940 and 1960 at the University of Chicago, later gathered under the title "Second Chicago School"—wisely qualified with a question mark—in a book published under the direction of G. A. Fine.[52] The increasing clarification of the research program just described, the obstacles encountered during its implementation by a group whose activities took place in extremely varied contexts, and the experience of searching through archives all led to my abandoning this part of the project. Adopting a distanced point of view was rather easy for pre-1940 research, augmented by the themes and the writing style of contemporary research, but seemed more difficult for research dating from the period 1940–1960. Some of this research, as well as the accompanying methodological reflections, provided foundational elements (though not the only ones) for my conception of the social sciences. For later studies by these sociologists, my direct and lasting relationships with many of their authors exacerbated the difficulty, by blurring the line between personal knowledge and necessary attempts at objectivization and distancing. I concluded that this familiarity would not permit me to write an expanded section on research after 1960 that was in line with an authentically historical perspective. This could, however, have been written using a point of view that was more engaged, for example by developing the aspects of this research that seemed fruitful in the context of French sociology, which at that point neglected the systematic ethnographic approach.

How *La tradition sociologique de Chicago* differs from an analysis organized according to the perspective of a research tradition turning its own instruments toward itself thus seems clearer than the introduction to the book probably suggests. The conception of the social sciences on which it is based—presented more explicitly in my book mentioned at the beginning of this afterword—cannot be identified with the one that underlies the studied research. The book is clearly not an endorsement of sociology in the style of the Chicago sociologists. The attempts of some French sociologists to attribute to it patronage of the Chicago School, a claim that coincided roughly with the book's publication, absolutely contradicts its intention. This book aims to propose a historical understanding of an undertaking that belongs to the past, in terms of a context that is not the one in which the social sciences exist today, in France or elsewhere. My avoidance of the term "Chicago School," so significant to a preeminent French publisher that they passed on publishing the book because I refused that title, serves as a warning against a superficial reading. Treated not only as a summary designation, a label like this constitutes, as I hope to have shown, an obstacle to a thorough comprehension of the research subsumed under it, and, to paraphrase Lucien Febvre, a mask imbued with a reality that belongs to none but its creators.[53]

APPENDIX

Remarks on Research Methods

ARCHIVAL WORK AND THE VERIFICATION OF SOME FACTS

When I finished this study, my sole regret was the impossibility of pursuing certain archival leads and verifications. On a correlated note, it was necessary to content myself with the conclusions of researchers who had already studied these same questions, such as the biographies of the individuals mentioned in my analyses or the activities of foundations.

The necessity of relying upon the research of other scholars is unsatisfactory here for two reasons. A significant amount of the secondary sources, which include essays and semi-autobiographical accounts written by sociologists and other researchers in the social sciences regarding some event or period in the life of an institution, are based on poorly identified and moderately reliable testimonies. Awareness of historical accuracy was, essentially, not the dominant quality of the sociologists who produced some of these secondary sources. Very critical with respect to the testimonies of others regarding what they themselves studied, they by contrast accepted freely and without verification their own memories and the testimonies of their colleagues about their own activities or disciplines—in short, their familiar world. Whoever uses their essays consequently risks mistaking for independent, overlapping testimonies what is simply the echo of a single, sometimes uncertain source. This uncertainty is stronger here because these are secondary facts, touching on generally obscure individuals and events concerning the miniscule world of the social sciences. Verification with more solid information often takes a particularly long time, since this is frequently buried in documentation that is scattered and difficult to access.

The difficulties of a historical approach were greatest concerning William Isaac Thomas. Both he and his publications are presented in some detail in several monographs focusing on various subjects—the history of ideas, especially regarding relations between the sexes, the history of the social sciences, etc. The intellectual training that Thomas gave himself, as well as the backdrop of his research activities, were for a long time known only through a small number of statements made by himself in his correspondence, and by his contemporaries in articles or prefaces. Thomas did not leave substantial archives, with the result that, in order to verify these accounts, it was necessary to refer to scattered correspondence in various archives. Over the course of fifty years, those who wrote about Thomas's sociology were primarily sociologists themselves. They contented themselves with immediately accessible sources, assuring them a wide distribution, which led their successors to treat these analyses as if they came from independent sources that confirmed each other. The ups and downs of Thomas's life, his nonconformity to the moral norms of the time, and perhaps his own relationship to his biography all provoked a priori convictions in those who wrote about his activities—some took him to be a kind of tourist in the urban underworld, others as a braggart who knew how to benefit from the labor of his collaborators, and others still as a barely converted literature professor. These convictions have inspired the selection of elements present in such analyses.

In the 1980s, however, some research in previously unexploited archives, particularly bodies of correspondence like those of Ethel Dummer or Jane Addams and the archives of the University of Chicago Press, did—including in some of the contributions that I have just criticized—begin to rectify some of the points wrongly assumed to be set in stone (see for example the articles by Haerle and Orbach). But even those who uncovered these new sources frequently could not escape the legends surrounding Thomas on other points. The criticisms that I have just set forth are relevant for the second chapter of the first edition of this book. In the material impossibility in which I found myself of revisiting all relevant primary sources during the preparation of this new edition, I have adopted as a point of departure what evidence corresponding to the most solid sources has established, especially in terms of chronology.

For each secondary source, I have sought to distinguish between what has been established directly, based on archives, and what has been borrowed from the authors of other publications. I did not do so for this chapter in the first edition, in which I placed excessive confidence in the craftsmanship of my predecessors. I failed to take into account that the majority of them were sociologists or historians of ideas, and insufficiently rigorous in their use of archival sources.

This was frequently the case in respect to the chronology of the beliefs advanced by Thomas, which were not necessarily the same in 1913 and in 1918 (for example). The most recent example of the combination of the errors I have just listed can be found in the book by Salerno (2007: 57–68) on "sociology noir" (analogous to American film noir of the 1950s), but they are also present in the analyses of Bennett (1981); Rosenberg (1982); Deegan (1988); Ross (1991); Lindner (1996). (These also, it must be emphasized, have characteristics that justify citing them as references.) In the revised chapter 2, I have noted the points that cannot be established in any certain manner, avoided overly definitive conclusions concerning Thomas's intellectual evolution, and called attention to the relevant chronological benchmarks.

The growing number of publications concerning Thomas, Park, and their contemporaries led to another difficulty in the preparation of this second edition. This increase has certainly had positive consequences insofar as the usage of the same sources by many researchers constitutes a control on the interpretation selected by each. But its drawbacks appear when the constraints of publication lead researchers to adopt interpretive hypotheses that seem above all to inspire a bias toward originality. The same sometimes applies to interpretations of the analyses of Thomas and Park, which led me to add, in chapter 3, a critical discussion of the interpretations that reduce Park to the status of Thomas's disciple— a strange idea for anyone who has closely read their respective publications.

For some of the facts I was unable to verify directly with primary sources, and as such I have been unable to eliminate all errors resulting from the usage of testimonies embedded in essays or recollections. As there still exist numerous unexplored archives, or even ones that will be established in the years to come, we may yet hope that later works will allow for the correction of errors I have not detected, and those that I myself have made.

THE STARTING POINT OF THIS STUDY: A CRITICAL REACTION AGAINST THE HISTORY OF IDEAS

As I indicate in the introduction, the initial perspective adopted by this study was formed in reaction against the history of ideas, insofar as it was then the general mindset with regard to social science. This specialization corresponds to the natural inclination of a good part of those who taught the history of sociology or sociological theories. It tends to reduce studies to a small core of abstract ideas, which it then situates in a long series of paradigms or theories to which the history of social science research (in other words, the history of a set of activities and products) is reduced.

When starting this study, it was my intention to examine the development of Chicago sociology in reference to the transformations of research methods. This perspective underpins an initial article published in 1984 which focuses on the discovery of fieldwork by sociologists. Soon, I noticed that two English colleagues, Martin Bulmer and Jennifer Platt, had adopted a similar approach to the history of sociology. Shortly thereafter, I expanded my study on Chicago sociology with the aim of incorporating an examination of the content of the studies that had been conducted. In the meantime, I had come to understand how knowledge of the historical context of their production modifies the way these works should be interpreted.

Although I have posed questions not usually studied by historians of ideas, I have been directly confronted with the insufficiency of their methodological instruments. We cannot be satisfied by analyses that characterize the relationships between works and scholars in terms of the likes of teacher-student or colleague-colleague influences and relationships. The perceptive musicologist Charles Rosen and an art historian, Michael Baxandall, seem to have discovered this long ago.[1] It was only in the 1990s that an article by Charles Camic and an essay by Maines, Bridger, and Ulmer proposed more developed approaches.[2] One of my primary resources for analyzing these weak—that is, not necessary—relationships between works, researchers, and contexts corresponds to my own experience of the social world of research and the university. It is upon this point that I will expand here.

INDIRECT SOURCES

The orientation of this study was largely determined by my professional experience, starting in the 1970s, in an environment that was not completely dissimilar to the one examined here. As a member of a small community of French sociologists, I acquired broad, direct knowledge of the mode of relations that exist within this type of community. This inspired my interpretation of the indices of the positions and both the individual and collective behaviors of academics that can be found both in the correspondence between researchers and in their testimonies.

Rather than accepting conventional and simplistic interpretations (such as the stereotyped invocation of the teacher-student relationship, the assumption of solidarity between former students of the same cohort in the same university, the apparent significance of explicit references or the absence thereof, etc.), I took for my starting point interpretations modeled upon what I observed around me, sometimes with the help of colleagues with whom I had been in contact through university activities. I was thus more attentive than my predecessors in the study of Chicago sociology to forms of competition between researchers, to the ambivalence of mutual sentiments within groups, to the occasional alliances that were one consequence thereof, to the ordinary constraints to the functioning of committees that funded research, to the complex processes which determined the career development and reputations of researchers, and so on. Making use of potential overlaps, I sought to establish the meaning of the indices available to me, at the time and place in question, in order to understand the state of relations within the community of sociologists. I also took advantage of experience in the domain of interpreting numerous but tenuous indices I acquired over the course of a previous study with Jean-Pierre Briand, in which we together conducted similar interpretive work on the behaviors of political staffs and public education administrators in France in the nineteenth and twentieth centuries.[3] Although private correspondence and informal testimonies—gathered in casual discussions—allowed numerous verifications of the soundness of the hypotheses underpinning the chosen interpretations in this book, this method involved some uncertainty regarding the mutual relationships of the people being studied; however, this was preferable to hasty certainty.[4]

My investigation into the relationships between successive generations of sociologists was also fed by a reflection on my own relationship with the studies of early-career French sociologists of the period 1945–1950 (which is to say sociologists of the generation preceding my own). It is probably not enough to say that some researchers of my generation turned their backs on these forerunners. By analyzing what they did—and I have particular gratitude to Viviane Isambert-Jamati, a rigorous eyewitness of this period—I noticed some of the same phenomena that I subsequently found among the Chicago researchers. This experience was prolonged by my discussions with a group of young researchers gravitating around the doctoral program in the field of institutions, work, and education in the contemporary world. These researchers gave up, for my benefit—despite my functions in this program—the protection ensured by the ordinary limitations of communication between generations and, here, between instructors and students.

To conclude, I would like to mention two experiences. The first was likely crucial to my comprehension of the spirit of Chicago sociology. Teaching sociology at the University of Paris-VIII in the years after 1970 was certainly an excellent opportunity for understanding the underlying potential for sociology students of self-emancipation from their backgrounds.[5] It offered them an opportunity to reflect on the relationship between personal characteristics and the capacity to conduct an empirical investigation into one situation or another. Thus, my break with the intellectual training that I myself had received (in which I still see the mark of French academic philosophy) was definitively completed. Finally, around 1990 I was asked by Claude Dubar to participate in a report on the state of academic research in sociology, commissioned by the research director of the national education ministry. This presented me with an opportunity to reflect upon the diversity and limits of studies with practical objectives, and upon the relationships between groups of researchers and their sponsors. I thank those who, generously at times, responded to questions that surpassed the immediate objectives of these investigations.

Notes

ABBREVIATIONS

ABJ: Archives of Buford H. Junker
AFM: Archives deposited by Fred Matthews after the completion of his biography of Park
AECH: Archives of Everett Hughes (A small number of references—indicated by the note "old file"—
          correspond to a provisional classification of the Hughes archives, which were reorganized in
          1997.)
AEWB: Archives of Ernest W. Burgess
ALW: Archives of Louis Wirth
AREP: Archives of Robert E. Park
AREPA: Archives of Robert E. Park, addenda
AWIT: Archives concerning William I. Thomas
AWLW: Manuscript of a collective biography of Lloyd W. Warner archived by Mildred Warner
IJTC: Transcripts of interviews conducted by James T. Carey for his 1975 book on the Chicago
          sociologists
          Note: All these documents are housed in the Department of Special Collections at Joseph
          Regenstein Library, at the University of Chicago. (These archives are often organized by file and
          sub-folders. In general, I have indicated sub-folders with a ":" followed by their number.)
ADR: Archives of Donald Roy housed at Duke University (Durham)
SE: *Sociological Eye*, major collection of the essays of Everett Hughes
          To refer to the three volumes of selected works of Robert E. Park, the beginnings of their titles
          have been used as abbreviation: *Race and Culture*, *Human Communities*, and *Society*.
AFL: American Federation of Labor
ASS: American Sociological Society (before 1960)
ASA: American Sociological Association (after 1960)
CAP: Chicago Area Project
CIO: Congress of Industrial Organizations
LCRC: Local Community Research Committee
LSRM: Laura Spelman Rockefeller Memorial Foundation
MA: Master of Arts
NAACP: National Association for the Advancement of Colored People
NORC: National Opinion Research Center
PhD: Doctor of Philosophy
SSRC: Social Science Research Council

INTRODUCTION

1. Remark suggested by Toulmin's book on Wittgenstein in AECH, unclassified.
2. Letter to Rudolf Haerle, June 29, 1984, cited in Haerle (1991): 36.
3. Matthews (1977).
4. Bulmer (1984).
5. The exception is the work of a sociologist, James Carey (1975).
6. Some of these errors are due to the poverty of sources regarding the characteristics of less well-known actions or people. We must sometimes accept a testimony without cross-checking in an area where experience quickly proves that reliability is weak. Furthermore, the sociologists who write about the history of their discipline generally have an excessive confidence in their knowledge of the part of the past that they directly witnessed: they often accept the testimonies of their colleagues and under-value cross-checking them with secondary sources that actually support the same primary source. I have attempted to exercise rather more prudence, but I certainly have not avoided all of the pitfalls that pseudo-cross-checking conceals.
7. Bulmer (1984); J. Platt (1996). This last book resumes the analyses published starting in the 1980s. I adopted an analogous point of view in an earlier article—Chapoulie (1984)—that constitutes the point of departure for the present research.
8. F. Davis (1973).

I. THE INITIAL DEVELOPMENT OF SOCIOLOGY AT THE UNIVERSITY OF CHICAGO, 1892–1914

1. Hughes (1964) (SE: 543).
2. Small (1896): 564.
3. Small, Vincent (1894): 15.
4. This description is quoted in the biography by Marianne Weber (1975): 285–287.
5. Hays (1964).
6. For a simple overall view of labor agitation during this period, see Hays (1957): 37–43; see also Montgomery (1987).
7. Dubovsky (1994): 28–31.
8. I use the term "movement" here for purposes of simplicity, but really this was more of a nebulous collection of activities with complex connections between them. Interpreting these activities is controversial, especially concerning the respective contributions to these reforms of the economic elites and the middle classes: see Hofstadter (1955), Wiebe (1967) for divergent interpretations, and Rodgers (1982) for a survey of more recent work. On the middle classes and social problems of the period, see Boyer (1978).
9. See Diner (1975) and Deegan (1988) for detailed descriptions of these relationships. I have conformed to the established usage in American historical research on the period by designating the listed categories by the term "middle classes."
10. On the settlement movement, see A. F. Davis (1967), which can be supplemented by Carson (1990).
11. Booth (1889–1891).
12. On this often neglected point, see Deegan (1988): 56–67.
13. See Diner (1908); Fish (1985); Deegan (1988). Recall that Jane Addams was also a leader of the feminist movement and, during the First World War, a pacifist leader.
14. I adopt here the interpretation suggested by Vidich, Lyman (1985): 152–153.
15. Horowitz (1976); McCarthy (1982).

16. Hogan (1985).

17. See Diner (1980): 137–153; this also analyzes other dimensions of the relationship between the reform movement and the University of Chicago.

18. A. Platt (1969); see also chapter 7.

19. Diner (1980): 154–175.

20. Charles Merriam, born in 1879, was a graduate of Columbia University, the principal center of political science teaching in this period. He was recruited in 1900 as an instructor in the department of political science at the University of Chicago. His local political career was only moderately successful, but it provided him with numerous connections with the business world and with foundations. After 1920, he became chair of the department of political science and contributed to the development of empirical research in this discipline. At the same time, he occupied a central position in the movement that led to the nationwide growth of social science research (see chapters 4 and 5).

21. Diner (1980): 56. Deegan (1988) describes in some detail Jane Addams's relationships with academics, such as philosophers John Dewey and George Mead; sociologists Albion Small, Charles Henderson, William Thomas, George Vincent, Charles Zueblin, Graham Taylor; and members of the city's economic elite, like the McCormick family and Julius Rosenwald (see note 28).

22. Diner (1980): 65–66.

23. On the institutionalization of social work, see Lubove (1965), which does not study the case of Chicago in detail.

24. See for example Ray Ginger (1986), as well as Curtis (1991) regarding the lack of satisfaction felt by Protestants of the generation born between 1860 and 1870 regarding the explicitly religiously inspired engagements of the preceding generation.

25. Published between 1902 and 1906, these articles had a large public impact, as did the book that was drawn from the articles by Lincoln Steffens on corruption in municipal administrations, *The Shame of the Cities* (1904). These journalists belonged to the same generation as William Thomas and Robert Park, the founders of the Chicago tradition in sociology.

26. On the origins of the University of Chicago, see Storr (1966), Diner (1980) and a book by one of Rockefeller's advisors, Goodspeed (1916).

27. Goodspeed (1916): 87.

28. This evaluation was given by Goodspeed (ibid.: 273), who also reproduced the list of principal donors (pp. 493–498). Among the three most important donors (aside from Rockefeller) who increased the total from a little less than $1 million to $2 million was Helen Culver, who also donated land to Hull House and was later the sponsor of William Thomas's research into Polish immigration (see chapter 2). Julius Rosenwald, a Jew of German origin and future president of the mail-order company Sears Roebuck, who would later finance some development of the study of race relations (see chapter 8), also gave an important contribution.

29. Furner (1975): 163–198.

30. On the diffusion of the research seminar in the United States, see Veysey (1965): 153–158.

31. See Gould (1961).

32. Recall that colleges are institutions of higher education offering undergraduate studies, and that during the nineteenth century academies prepared students for college.

33. Storr (1966): 64.

34. Ibid.: 154–155.

35. Goodspeed (1916): 144–146. Harper always used the term "investigation" rather than "research."

36. Storr (1966): 75.

37. The founder of the department of sociology at the University of Kansas, Frank Blackmar, had been the classmate at Johns Hopkins of Albion Small, founder of the department of sociology at the University of Chicago. According to an undated manuscript by Ernest Burgess, who had worked with Blackmar for a time around 1913 (AEWB, folder 3: 1), Blackmar had proposed the term "Sociology"

in the course of negotiations following the University of Kansas's refusal to accept the appellation "Political Science." Sica (1990) contains an analysis of the origins of sociology at the University of Kansas and a discussion of the diffusion of the false claim that the University of Chicago had the first sociology department.

38.　Earlier studies have paid little attention to the question of appellation, although the poorly defined character of the terms then used have been discussed: thus Storr (1966: 75) claims that the department was called "Social Science [Sociology] and Anthropology," while Diner (1975: 520) attributes it the name "Social Science, Anthropology and Sanitary Science." It is very possible that both these terms were used in certain official documents.

39.　Morgan (1982); Hinkle (1980): 44–45. Bernard (1909: 164–213), after a survey of universities, counted eight institutions of higher education offering instruction under the label "sociology" before 1890, to which five more were added in 1891 or 1892. The term "social gospel" seems to have been introduced in 1886, and was then used as the title of a Georgia magazine after 1898—see especially White, Hopkins (1976: 151; 167, note 13)—then later used by American historians of the period after 1940. The term "Christian sociology" had almost the same meaning.

40.　Furner (1975): 295.

41.　Fleming (1963: 123–146) gives a synthetic description of the evolution of social thought in the United States, and especially the progressive reaction against Spencer's ideas that had marked Graham Sumner's generation, the one just prior to that of the founders of the University of Chicago department of sociology.

42.　Howerth (1894).

43.　For a survey of the conception of the discipline held by sociologists of the previous generation, see Hinkle (1980): 45–50.

44.　On the conflicts between sociologists and economists, see Furner (1975): 297–305.

45.　Sociologists were interested in the concept of institutional economy as delineated by German economic historians, one of the two research orientations they shared with economists. One of the leaders of this subfield in the United States around 1890 was a Johns Hopkins professor, Richard Ely. He was an important actor in the reform movement of the Progressive Era, especially following his recruitment by the University of Wisconsin, a state whose governor, Robert M. La Follette, was one of the figures at the forefront of the Progressive movement. Recall that the other research orientation associated with American economists at this point—influenced by the English school, which focused on formal models and a deductive method and had a narrower field of interest—finally overtook its competitor, allowing sociologists to stake their claim in the territory abandoned by economists. See Furner (1975: 297–305) for an analysis of the first stages of this debate, and Ross (1991) for its later developments.

46.　The origins of the Chicago department of sociology are described in Diner (1975).

47.　Bannister (1987): 38.

48.　William Rainey Harper Collection, housed at Harper College (Palatine, Illinois), Box 15: 3.

49.　The university directory for 1892–1893 and the two following years also lists Edward Bemis among the instructors of the department of sociology, noting that he was "Professor of Political Economy" (the chair of the department of economics refused to integrate him into that department).

50.　Baker (1973): 248; Diner (1975): 525.

51.　The comparison between the development of sociology at Columbia (Wallace [1992]) and at the University of Chicago indirectly confirms Henderson's importance.

52.　Henderson (1914): 1–2.

53.　Small, Vincent (1894): 15.

54.　Ibid.: 97–166.

55.　Small (1896): 581–582.

56.　Small (1895): 8.

57. The variations in Small's scientific and political opinions are described in Bannister (1987): 47–63.
58. Wallace (1992).
59. See Small's conference in 1924, reproduced in Dibble (1975): 210.
60. Burgess (1948): 761. A conference paper (Small [1912]) gives an idea of the contents of this course: Small insisted upon the importance of Marx, whose contribution to the social sciences Small compared with that of Galileo to the physical sciences (p. 812). Small remarked (p. 815) that "we assert the universal fact of class as strongly as he [Marx] did."
61. Hughes (1964) (SE: 546).
62. Bannister (1987): 58–60.
63. See the testimonies collected by James Carey in IJTC. George Mead's opinion of Small in 1901 seems to have been equally negative (Diner [1975]: 539). One of the only positive appreciations of this course that I can find appears in a statement of Wirth's, as reported by his daughter: "In these years the University of Chicago was one of the few American academic centers where Marxism and later Leninism were the subject of intellectual scrutiny, partly due to the interests of Albion W. Small" (Wirth Marvick [1964]: 335); see also Salerno (1987): 6.
64. See Deegan (1988): 77–78; 89–92. Deegan does not mention that Zueblin was a protégé of Harper's, and that he left the university shortly after his death.
65. Harper sought to hire Taylor starting in 1896. Taylor was then recruited by Chicago Theological Seminary, a religious college connected to the University of Chicago, where he worked as a professor of "Christian sociology," charged with "observing social and labor conditions, classifying facts, and drawing conclusions" (Wade [1964]: 95).
66. Diner (1975): 536.
67. This department existed under this name until 1925, the year of Marion Talbot's retirement. It then was renamed "Home Economics and Household."
68. Howard Woodhead, who had received a PhD in 1907 for his dissertation on cities, was an instructor (the lowest rank) in the department of sociology from 1908 to 1913, at which point he disappears from the course listings, and seems to have died in 1919. His recruitment, like that of Bedford—who had a similar specialization (see chapter 3)—testifies to the department's interest in developing the study of cities before the arrival of Park.
69. Morgan (1982): 50.
70. This statistic is based on the list of graduates in sociology provided by R. Faris (1970). Harvey (1987) provides another list concerning theses: seven theses were added on the basis of two other sources. Six of these theses, as Harvey in fact hypothesizes elsewhere, were probably written under the direction of Henderson at the Divinity School.
71. According to the tally of graduates between 1895 and 1915 in Hinkle (1980), out of ninety-eight total sociology PhDs, thirty-six were bestowed by the University of Chicago, twenty-four by Columbia, thirteen by the University of Pennsylvania, and ten by Yale, with the contributions of other universities totaling less than ten. It should be noted, however, that it is risky to identify all of these graduates as sociologists: among those from Chicago figure several anthropologists, and the graduates of the other universities mentioned studied in departments that did not consist entirely, or even always principally, of sociologists.
72. Among these figures is one of the only two black sociologists (the other being W. E. B. Du Bois) to have a certain visibility in their generations: George Edmond Haynes (1880–1960). After having obtained an MA at Yale in 1903, Haynes studied at the University of Chicago during the summers of 1906 and 1907. In 1912, Haynes ultimately became the first African American to receive his PhD in economics from Columbia. Like Du Bois, Haynes did not spend his whole career in sociology: although he was chairman of the department of social sciences at Fisk University from 1910 to 1921, he then became secretary of the Federated Council of the Churches of Christ in America, a position he held until 1947.

73. The information concerning pre-1919 recipients of sociology PhDs upon which I rely comes from a biographical file based on different sources: a book by Odum (1951), the different volumes of *Who Was Who in America*, obituaries in the *American Journal of Sociology*, the catalog of the Library of Congress in Washington, D.C., and the *International Dictionary of Anthropologists* by Christopher Winters (1991).

74. Bannister (1979): 56.

75. Starting in 1894, Small entered into conflict with the economists of the neighboring department, who tried to make him accept the sociological affiliation of the economist Bemis. For more information on the reportedly difficult relationship between Small and the department of economics of the University of Chicago, see Diner (1975): 545–546.

76. Ibid.: 535.

77. Cited in Furner (1975): 292.

78. See the many examples in the interviews gathered by Carey, in IJTC.

79. Diner (1975): 548. One statistical observation regarding American universities across the board gives another estimation of the professions that holders of PhDs and MAs in sociology went on to have between 1893 and 1901: a third of them became university professors and another third became pastors or high school teachers (Morgan [1982]: 51–53).

80. Three of those who did not become social science professors went on to have business careers, and one of the PhD graduates, who was of foreign origin, pursued a career in his own country. (These evaluations are based on my own data and not those of Diner.)

81. Steiner (1956): 409.

82. Diner (1975): 548.

83. Ibid.: 536.

84. On the University of Chicago settlement and Mary McDowell, see A. F. Davis (1967): 112–122 and throughout.

85. On the Social Survey Movement and its consequences, see Bulmer, Bales, Sklar (1991); on its connections with the settlement movement, see A. F. Davis (1967): 170–174.

86. See especially the survey conducted by the residents of a settlement in Boston: Robert Woods (1898), as well as the survey conducted by W. E. B. Du Bois (1899)—a young African American who had just received a PhD in History from Harvard—on the African American community in Philadelphia, which placed him under the umbrella of sociology.

87. See Devine (1909a); Breckinridge, Abbott (1910–1911). A quantification of the contributions of Hull House residents to the *American Journal of Sociology* can be found in Deegan (1988): 47–48.

88. Hegner (1897): 176.

89. See also an article by Burgess (1916), whose title, "The Social Survey: A Field for Constructive Service by Departments of Sociology," is also representative of the conception of social surveys defended by sociologists.

90. Diner (1980): 124–127.

2. WILLIAM ISAAC THOMAS, *THE POLISH PEASANT IN EUROPE AND AMERICA*, AND THE BEGINNINGS OF EMPIRICAL ACADEMIC SOCIOLOGY

The revisions to this chapter for the second edition are based on publications and archival sources that have recently become accessible, especially as a result of the Mead Project led by Robert Throop and Lloyd Gordon Ward (https://brocku.ca/MeadProject/inventory5.html). The second edition also accounts for recent publications, as well as a more precise interpretation of Thomas's publications before 1917.

1. "Thomas in Defense Paints Self Martyr," *Chicago Daily News*, April 22, 1918: 15–16.

2. Letter to Kimball Young, May 4, 1930, Thomas Papers, Special Collections, Regenstein Library, University of Chicago (in the Thomas AWIT folder).

3. The work is widely referred to by the abbreviated title *The Polish Peasant*. As of 2017, various editions can be consulted online at https://archive.org/details/polishpeasantineo1thom. In what follows, page numbers refer to the Dover edition reproducing the 1927 edition of the book, which is itself almost identical to the 1920 Badger edition, albeit with different pagination.

4. For examples of presentations of Thomas's research accompanied, most often, by biographical elements, see House (1936): 283–290; Barnes (1948): 793–804; Locke (1948); Bogardus (1949); Madge (1962): 52–87.

5. For a long time, the principal sources for details of Thomas's biography and the conditions surrounding the book's creation were limited to the introductions to two collections of his texts, the sources of which are not cited, but which were for a long time treated as solid references: Volkart (1951); Janowitz (1966). To these have been added testimonies published by former students—Kimball Young (1948; 1962–1963), and in Lindstrom, Hardert (1988; 1995); Burgess (1948); Faris (1948); Bogardus (1949; 1959; 1962)—as well as an account by Znaniecki (1948) and comments he made along with Thomas on the occasion of a symposium focused on *The Polish Peasant* (Blumer, 1939a). More recently made accessible are an autobiographical text written by Thomas for a book on the history of sociology that was prepared by his former student Luther Bernard (Thomas, in Baker, 1973), and a letter and memo written by Thomas ("How the Polish Peasant Came About") and preserved in the archives of his second wife, Dorothy Swaine Thomas. The archives of the University of Chicago in 2000 preserved only a small folder labeled with Thomas's name (AWIT), which contained a copy of this document, but other works of correspondence by Thomas are preserved in other series and archival collections. Evan Thomas used some of these sources for his PhD (1986). Since the 1980s, archival research has furnished new information and invalidated elements present in earlier accounts: see especially E. Thomas (1986), Deegan (1988), Haerle (1991), Orbach (1993). Some archival documents concerning Thomas directly or indirectly became accessible in 2017 through the Mead Project directed by Robert Throop and Lloyd Gordon Ward, notably the chapter of an unpublished book by Luther Lee Bernard, preserved in his archives at Pennsylvania State University (Bernard, undated). It must be admitted that Thomas's memory was not always infallible and that he recounted certain anecdotes in varying ways, even if the interpretation of his own testimony, or that of his interlocuters concerning him, is done with particular prudence. There are accordingly no serious reasons to radically challenge them. The "Remarks on research methods" in the appendix returns to the question of publications concerning Thomas.

6. In the 1990s, *The Philadelphia Negro* by W. E. B. Du Bois (1899) was often considered the first empirical work of sociology. Despite its originality and empirical merits, this book fits much more directly into the trajectory of the Social Survey Movement than does *The Polish Peasant*.

7. Blumer (1939a): 103–105.

8. AWIT.

9. His mother, the daughter of a pastor of some renown, belonged to a wealthy family. By her death in 1910, she had converted to Christian Science (a Protestant sect that considers physical ailments to be illusions that should be cured through prayer). His father, who at birth was given a piece of property of around two hundred hectares by his godfather, sold it in 1873 in order to become editor in chief and co-owner, along with his brother-in-law, of the *Holston Methodist*, a Tennessee publication whose headquarters were transferred to Knoxville following a fire. Thomas's father established himself in Knoxville with his family, but sold his partial ownership of the publication in 1875 to become a marble merchant. When he died in 1884, he was described as a "hard student and critical scholar"

in a sort of obituary. Most of this information is taken, sometimes without corroboration, from Price (1913): 295–296. It contradicts claims that can be found in other biographies, but suggest for Thomas a hidden, very religious, origin, as well as an inevitable familiarity with the question of slavery. (His father owned three slaves according to the 1860 census.) Numerous comments on Thomas's family can be found in Tate (1974), which is based mostly on local archives.

10.   Abbott and Egloff (2008) challenge the chronology of this biographical essay, written at the behest of Luther Bernard (Thomas, in Baker, 1973). This interpretation seems erroneous to me. In this chapter of his still-unpublished book, Luther Bernard reports having heard Thomas give a similar account in a class "to illustrate the significance of changing environment forces on changing development." The interpretation of Abbott and Egloff, whose article nevertheless brings interesting points to bear on Thomas's intellectual career, depends on the hypothesis, which seems to me simplistic and naïve, that one must take literally the claims Thomas made on several occasions regarding his distant relationship with his intellectual work. An ambivalence on Thomas's part with regard to his research is much more plausible, and is even suggested by the existence of a memoir intended for his second wife.

11.   According to Luther Bernard, Thomas's university studies were at least partially funded by a banker impressed by his courage when, around sixteen or seventeen years old, he agreed to a public fight with an alcoholic brute of the town. This anecdote is not found elsewhere, and I have never found anything to corroborate this episode. Bernard claims here, against Thomas's own recollection, that he had been recruited by the University of Tennessee to teach "modern languages." On his education see also Thomas (1986): 10 and Abbott, Egloff (2008): 246–247.

12.   See Klautke (2013) for a precise description of this attempt to found a new discipline—occupying the place of the social sciences—on the margins of psychology, in which one will recognize the program and the a priori beliefs, especially the idea of a hierarchy of cultures, of Thomas's first two books. Klautke notes that Thomas also found in *Völkerpsychologie* a critique of the contemporary scientific conception of racism, and of the theories of Lombroso.

13.   However, while Thomas taught there, Oberlin College had implemented segregation of black and white students in cafeterias, at the initiative of the latter group. A series of incidents and controversies marked the 1880s, during which the institution began to separate from its religious origins. None of Thomas's surviving testimonies concern the time he spent at Oberlin. In his autobiographical essay, he remarks only that "I was not at that time sufficiently irreligious to be completely out of place." On the background of Oberlin College in the 1880s, see Waite (2001).

14.   On Thomas's teaching activity at Oberlin, see Abbott, Egloff (2008). Many of the English novels on which Thomas's classes focused have a biographical or autobiographical dimension and develop themes that also appear in *The Polish Peasant*.

15.   In 1892–1893, according to the directory of the University of Chicago, Thomas taught a class titled "Historical Sociologies," an "Exposition of significant classical, mediaeval and modern attempts to interpret social phenomena. Criticism of data, methods and conclusions." The following year Thomas bore the title of Fellow of Social Science, and the next year that of Instructor in Ethnic Psychology, then that of Assistant Professor of Folk Psychology. At the time, these different terms had a more precise meaning than did "sociology."

16.   Abbott, Egloff (2008): 222.

17.   See Balfe (1981) for one such interpretation. Thomas's book combines the articles and some texts serving as transitions with significant alterations, as shown by Balfe. Regarding the evolution of Thomas's ideas around 1907, see also Rosenberg (1982): 120–131.

18.   Regarding Boas's influence over American social sciences, and sociology especially, at the beginning of the twentieth century, see Cravens (1988): 124–153. Analysis of Thomas and Boas's intellectual relationship can be found in Stocking (1968: 260–264) and Murray (1988), and analysis of the

debates and reactions to the diffusion of Darwin's ideas in the intellectual context of the United States between 1870 and 1910 can be found in Bannister (1979).

19. Ginger (1986): ix.

20. A quick and partial analysis of the cultural changes of the 1890s in the United States can be found in Higham (1975). On the transformations of female behavior and the relationship between the sexes as urban phenomena, see McGovern (1968) and, for an overall view, J. V. Matthews (2004). A large portion of the participants in the Progressive movement, and especially the women, belonged to the middle classes and to the generations born between 1860 and 1875: among them were Jane Addams (born in 1860) and Thomas (born in 1863).

21. On the movement for women's suffrage, the first aspects of which emerged in the 1860s, see Kraditor (1967).

22. On the question of prostitution in Chicago, see Lubove (1962); Connelly (1980): 91–113. More generally on the context of public inquests into prostitution between 1900 and 1915, see Rosen (1982): 14–68.

23. On Helen Bradford Thompson (known for her later publications under the name of Wooley), see Rosenberg (1982): 68–72. Thompson's thesis relied on different tests, which in no way confirmed the then-accepted existence of important differences between men and women in terms of emotional process, intellectual capacity, etc. This thesis was deemed exceptional by the members of her committee.

24. Thomas (1907b): 255.

25. Ibid.: 50.

26. Ibid.: 245. In the developed version appearing in this book, this essay ends with considerations regarding what could render marriages happier. That there was a semi-autobiographical dimension to this observation seems probable: a letter from Thomas to Jane Addams dated December 27, 1909 (cited in Throop, Ward, 2007) thanks her for welcoming his wife, who had until then been entirely focused on their children, into the activities of Hull House.

27. Letter cited in Murray (1988): 388. In the university directories, the majority of Thomas's courses appear immediately after those of the anthropologist Frederick Starr, except for the year 1895–1896, when they were separated by "Folk Psychology."

28. AWIT, folder 1, letter from the papers of William Jones. Half Fox Indian through his mother, Jones was a former student of Boas who had received a PhD in Linguistics. He was killed in the Philippines in 1909 while conducting fieldwork. Thomas dedicated his second book, *Source Book for Social Origins*, to him.

29. George A. Dorsey, one of the first recipients of a PhD in Anthropology at Harvard, was always more oriented toward physical anthropology. He collected abundant documentation on diverse North American Indian tribes, and later on the populations of Australia and Southeast Asia. Dorsey was a foreign correspondent for the *Chicago Tribune* from 1909 to 1912, and during one trip he wrote a long series of articles on the Italian, Austrian, Romanian, etc. sources of immigration to the United States (see, for example, *Chicago Tribune*, August 9, 1910). Dorsey, on his return, and after having performed official duties in Lisbon, established himself in New York. Like Thomas, he taught at the New School for Social Research in the 1920s.

30. Thomas, in Baker (1973): 249. I have found only rare indications of the relationships Thomas maintained with his colleagues in the Department of Sociology. He never cites Graham Taylor, a pastor and activist in the Progressive movement, Charles Zueblin, or George Vincent, who had obtained his doctorate in the same year as Thomas, and whose beliefs regarding morality and religion were in opposition to his own.

31. The second interpretation can be found, for example, in Deegan (1988: 121), which claims that Thomas was "extremely involved in social reform," to mitigate this statement somewhat further.

32. On Harriet Thomas, see R. Throop and L. G. Ward (2007). Harriet Thomas (born probably in 1864), who married Thomas in 1888, came from a notable Tennessee family, undoubtedly rich land-owners. Her father, a Presbyterian minister and onetime principal of a seminary for young girls, attended Princeton, but I have found no indication of his daughter's education. She was perhaps the intermediary who put Thomas in contact with Ellen Culver, who financed the research of *The Polish Peasant*. Harriet Thomas seems to have spent her first years in Chicago primarily dedicated to her three sons, born in 1890, 1891, and 1893, as well as her two daughters, who were born after 1893 and died young. The little evidence available suggests her strength of character and intellectual range. She was the author of a 1910 review of a book by Addams in the *American Journal of Sociology*. In the public conferences in which she participated, she sometimes responded to her opponents, according to press accounts, with spirit, but she proved her self-restraint and judgment as we shall see in the context of the 1918 incident that caused Thomas's removal from the University of Chicago. One could reasonably suppose that Thomas's ideas about women owed a great deal to their interactions. Their marriage was not terminated after 1918, although they no longer lived together permanently. Their divorce was granted in 1934, some months before Harriet's death.

33. On the juvenile court, see Getis (2000): 28–52. On the Juvenile Protective Association, see Diner (1980): 104–106.

34. Deegan and Burger (1981) provide an inventory of Thomas's involvement in activist activities. They do not mention Thomas's lecture—noted by Ross (1991: 309)—given at Chicago in 1915 to a militant activist association focused on women's suffrage, that provoked violent incidents.

35. On the context of the Vice Commission of the City of Chicago and its report, see Connelly (1980): 91–106. The composition of the commission and its history are briefly described in Taylor (1911).

36. Thomas (1918): 15–16; (1923): 229–230. Janowitz (1966: xiv) and others have suggested that Thomas's opinions had been considered aggressive by certain members of the Vice Commission. This reaction would later have consequences during the affair that caused his resignation. I have found neither confirmation nor invalidation of this claim, nor of any other active participation in this commission on Thomas's part, which he denied.

37. Feffer (1993): 111–112.

38. See especially Jane Addams's preface to *Hull House Maps and Papers* (1895: vii–viii), and the following contribution by Agnes Sinclair Holbrook. The positions Thomas defended regarding the question of women's work, prostitution, and juvenile delinquency are not very different from those of Addams, as noted by E. Thomas (1986: 18–26), who, however, too quickly identifies Thomas's ideas in the years before and after 1918.

39. See Devine (1909b).

40. Henderson (1902). On Henderson's research activities and conceptions after 1900, see Getis (2000): 58–60. Another possible target of Thomas's remarks can perhaps be found in Carroll D. Wright's 1899 book, *Outline of Practical Sociology*; Wright was a statistician who contributed to the development of labor statistics in the United States.

41. Henderson (1914): 32–35. One might also wonder whether Thomas's critiques were aimed at Sophonisba Breckinridge and Edith Abbott, who belonged to the Hull House entourage and figured among the founders of social work. The articles that they published around 1908 in the *American Journal of Sociology*, such as Abbott (1909) on Greek immigration to Chicago, are essentially descriptive and are based on the testimonies of informers without taking into consideration the subjective dimension of behavior. One article, which focuses on work placement agencies, proposes changes to their regulation. The book by Breckinridge and Abbott (1912) on the case of delinquency referred to the Chicago juvenile court also has a very factual character, with some quick claims on the links between delinquency and family situation.

42. Park in Kurtz (1982): 337.

43. See Barnard (1969): 94–96. "Christian Sociology" may be defined as "the study of society from a Christian point of view, with an objective of Christianization"—the term is practically equivalent to "practical sociology."

44. Letter to Helen Culver, December 9, 1911, cited in Haerle (1991): 28.

45. Letter of June 6, 1915, cited in E. Thomas (1986): 58. Such a remark remains ambiguous, because it also refers to Thomas's relationship with Ethel Dummer, who financed the research for *The Polish Peasant*. Ethel Dummer (1866–1954), an old acquaintance of Harriet Thomas, maintained an intellectual correspondence with Thomas, especially during the 1920s. For more material on Ethel Dummer, see Platt (1992).

46. Thomas's silence regarding his own relationships with women—certainly unsurprising for someone of his generation in the United States—has curiously veered his commenters away from inquiring into the biographical dimension of the evolution of his ideas.

47. Thomas (1907b): 468.

48. Thomas (1906b): 42.

49. *American Magazine* was a publication founded by three very famous investigative journalists who were characterized as "muckrakers" by Theodore Roosevelt: Lincoln Steffens, Ida Tarbell, and Ray Stannard Baker, who had left another publication, *McClure's*.

50. Thomas (1918): 15–16.

51. A summary of notes taken one year in this course was published by Bogardus (1959).

52. Thomas (1909b): 13.

53. Abbott, Egloff (2008): 222.

54. As noted in Cravens (1988: 58–59; 72–74), American psychology had been influenced, as Thomas had at the start of his career, by Darwinian evolution, neurology, and European psychology. Cravens associates the perspective of the Protestant middle classes with the conviction that the individual is the focal point of explications of the social world. The difference on this point between Thomas and (for example) Durkheim is striking.

55. Thomas (1909b): 17.

56. K. Young (Lindstrom, Hardert [1988a]: 275–276) reports that Boas vigorously challenged the expression used in the title of Thomas's book, which bore the mark of *Völkerpsychologie*. Boas had followed Steinthal's teaching but abandoned the idea of a hierarchy of cultures and the resulting research program, which could explain his reaction. Kimball Young (1893–1972), a descendant of Brigham Young, founder of the Mormon sect, was a student at Chicago around 1917. Young obtained a PhD in Psychology at Stanford in 1921 and became a professor of social psychology.

57. Faris (1948): 757.

58. Park, in Kurtz (1982): 336.

59. Bogardus (1949): 36.

60. Thomas (1905): 445.

61. Thomas (1908): 736.

62. Thomas (1909a): 465.

63. Link, McCormick (1983): 23.

64. Some among them later pursued research into differences in sex and sexuality: Rosenberg (1982: 125) cites Frances Kellor, Katherine Bement Davis, and Helen Bradford Thompson Wooley. One of these, Katherine Bement Davis, conducted a questionnaire survey in 1920 on the sexual experiences and behaviors of middle-class women.

65. Lindstrom et al. (1995): 2.

66. Bernard (undated). An article by Thomas (1901) on the "gaming instinct" describes this leisure activity as "fascinating" and repeatedly mentions golf.

67. According to Bernard, around 1907 Thomas defended free sexual relationships, and sustained that in the near future women would have children outside of marriage. Charles Elwood (1873–1946),

a sociologist who wrote his thesis in sociology at Chicago between 1896 and 1899, specialized in the study of social problems with an eye toward reform, according to a worldview that was undoubtedly close to that of Henderson. Around 1925, Elwood was one of the opponents of Thomas's election to the presidency of the American Sociological Society.

68. Memorandum for Dorothy Swaine Thomas in 1935, in AWIT, folder 1. A chronology of research can be found in Haerle (1991) and in Orbach (1993).

69. These funds were the object of a contract between Helen Culver and the University of Chicago, a point established in detail by Haerle (1991).

70. Haerle (1991): 29.

71. Raushenbush (1979): 67–69.

72. See AWIT as well as Haerle (1991): 33.

73. Znaniecki (1948): 765.

74. An interest in newspapers is not very surprising for someone whose father had been the editor of a publication and, occasionally, a journalist.

75. On Znaniecki, see the intellectual biography of Dulczewski (1992) as well as the analysis of his daughter, Znaniecka Lopata (1976b), revised and completed in Lopata (1996).

76. See Dulczewski (1992): 37. Znaniecki's contacts with Durkheim and the Durkheimians were surely very limited, based on the archival document cited by Wiley (1986): 23. Znaniecki also took a course with Bergson and at one point planned to write a thesis under his supervision.

77. Dulczewski (1992): 65–70. This system relied on a "principle of relativity of values." Znaniecki published a book (in English), *Cultural Reality*, in 1919.

78. I retain here the version of Znaniecki (1948). Thomas attributed the offer he made to Znaniecki to co-write *The Polish Peasant* to his composition of the "Methodological note." On the grounds of the archives of the University of Chicago Press, Orbach (1993: 153–157) identifies the beginning of 1916 as the latest date for the start of an equal collaboration between Thomas and Znaniecki, correcting on this point Thomas's account giving a later date, which thus far has generally been preferred.

79. Orbach (1993): 156–157.

80. Barnes (1948: 797–798) and Janowitz (1966: xxv) consider Znaniecki's contribution to be secondary; by contrast, Orbach (1993) and H. Znaniecka Lopata (1996) seem to be committed to minimizing that of Thomas. E. Thomas (1986: 323–346) has made an inventory of the different interpretations of this collaboration and proposes a more balanced analysis of the respective contributions of the two authors, based especially on correspondence in the possession of Znaniecki's daughter, Helena Lopata.

81. K. Young, in Lindstrom, Hardert (1988a): 288–289.

82. This little textbook (Thomas, 1915) seems to have been overlooked by those who have written about Thomas's publications. It is the first of a series of six, with pedagogical intention, edited under Thomas's direction. All adopt the same formula: a text from the principal author, all but one of whom taught at the University of Chicago, followed by some documents. The second of these brochures, written by a professor of history, Ferdinand Schevill, focuses on the progress and development of democracy, and develops an analysis regarding social class. It is accompanied by texts by socialist theoreticians. The last textbook of the series, to which we shall return in the following chapter, was written by Robert Park.

83. A synthetic presentation of the "new immigration" of this period from the Anglo-Saxon point of view can be found in Persons (1987).

84. For an overview of Polish immigration in the period 1870–1920, see Pacyga (1991: 15–24), Greene (1975), and also Parot (1981).

85. Thomas, Znaniecki (1927): 4–14. The adversary is designated with quotation marks: "'practical' sociology."

86. This type of reasoning is essentially found among certain founders of social work, such as Julia Lathrop. Zaretsky (1984: 12) attributes it also to the researchers of the Pittsburgh Survey, and Connelly (1980: 29–30) to the reasoning of Progressive reformers regarding prostitution.

87. Thomas, Znaniecki (1927): 14.

88. Ibid.: 66. An earlier section mitigates this critique: in the absence of a social science, "Certainly social life is improved by even such a control as common-sense sociology is able to give" (p. 15).

89. Memorandum written by Thomas in 1935 for his second wife, Dorothy Swaine Thomas (in AWIT).

90. The concept of primary relationships was borrowed from Cooley (1909): 23.

91. See Blumer (1939a): 88.

92. On this point, see Fleming (1967: 322–330) and Camic (1986). Fleming remarks that introduction of the concept of attitude permitted sociologists to resist the threat of invasion of their territory by behavioral psychologists who made use of the concept of habit, and whose scientific legitimacy was better recognized. Orbach (1993), relying on notes taken during one of Thomas's classes, sustained that it is only in *The Polish Peasant* that the notion of attitude, as used by Thomas, is freed of all biological connotations.

93. Thomas, Znaniecki (1927): 22, 27.

94. Ibid.: 21; 1131. The terminology of Thomas and Znaniecki rapidly became obsolete, and Blumer (1969a) uses the term "social object" in place of social value.

95. Znaniecki (1948): 767.

96. Thomas, Znaniecki (1927): 44.

97. Ibid.: 72–73. During a 1917 conference in which he presented his typology of wishes, Thomas added that all forms of behavior can be reduced to two fundamental "appetites": food and reproduction. What's more, the idea of "desire for new experiences" seems to have a personal dimension in Thomas's writing. It occupies an important place in the interpretation of the sexually liberated behavior of young women in his following book.

98. Bogardus (1949): 37.

99. Hughes's recollection, reported in Coser (1971): 514.

100. Thomas, Znaniecki (1927): 1128.

101. Cooley is one of the influences acknowledged by Thomas in his brief autobiography, along with the anthropologist Boas and the psychologist J. B. Watson.

102. Thomas, Znaniecki (1927): 1134–1140.

103. Ibid.: 1171–1175.

104. Ibid.: 1128, 1647.

105. Ibid.: 72.

106. Ibid. (1927): 1134–1140.

107. Murray (1988).

108. Hutchins Hapgood (1869–1944) had been a student at Harvard, then in the Department of English at the University of Chicago, and he maintained an amicable relationship with a rather unconventional professor of English, Lovett, who was himself still in contact with Thomas during the 1920s. Thomas makes an appearance in Hapgood's memoirs as a dinner companion, along with Robert Morss Lovett, around 1920 (Hapgood [1939]: 542). Thomas's book *The Unadjusted Girl*, published a few years later, quotes extracts from two autobiographies that Hapgood had brought to his attention. On investigative journalists in the 1900s, and especially Hapgood, see Lindner (1996): 15–30 and *passim*.

109. Thomas (1906). Holt (1872–1951), who had published some autobiographies, had been a journalist before becoming a university president. A graduate in sociology from Columbia University, he was also active in the Progressive movement.

110. By 1918, Thomas very probably was already familiar with these archives, which he used substantially in his following book, *The Unadjusted Girl*.

111. See, for example, Richmond (1899: 59) regarding alcoholics. On Richmond, see Agnew (2003).

112. On Adolf Meyer and the similarities between his analyses and those of Thomas, see Abbott, Egloff (2008): 238–245. Meyer, who had left Chicago in 1895 for a hospital in Massachusetts, then became an associate of William James.

113. Lindstrom, Hardert (1988a): 288–289.

114. Thomas gave two different versions of this "discovery," which can be found in Baker (1973: 250), and in Burgess's testimony in Janowitz (1966): xxiv.

115. Among the exceptions figures a book by Edith Abbott (1924), characterized in her preface as a "source book" intended for the instruction of graduate-level social work students, which contains various documents on the history of immigration to the United States, as well as numerous letters, mostly those written to social workers to request help but sometimes also letters to parents. According to Raushenbush (1979: 94), Charles S. Johnson, a student of Park and perhaps also of Thomas, collected letters from migrants during the Great Migration in 1919: see Scott (1920).

116. K. Young (1962): 6; Locke (1948): 908.

117. Thomas (1912): 770–771.

118. Ibid.: 771.

119. See Ross (1991): 154–155. This point is developed upon with insistence by Abbott and Egloff (2008), who do not cite Ross.

120. Letter to Ellsworth Faris, cited in Janowitz (1966): xxiii.

121. According to Znaniecki (1948: 767), Thomas had then used the term "desire" instead of "wishes," changing his terminology because American students were using the term "Freudian wish," while Everett Hughes, in a letter to Alice Rossi (June 28, 1977), recalls Thomas's hostility toward Freud in the 1920s: "Thomas . . . was the most anti biology man you can imagine. He would not allow anyone to speak kindly about Freud and Freudian theories" (AECH, folder 53).

122. Blumer (1939a): 86–87.

123. Park, in Kurtz (1982): 337.

124. Thomas claims, however, that the goal should be the control of society itself, not the control of the established population over immigrants.

125. Thomas, Znaniecki (1927): 1119; 1124–95.

126. I also rely for the following on Kieniewicz (1969b) and Pacyga (1991). I owe a debt of gratitude to Izabela Saffray-Wagner for verifications in works published in Polish, and the translation into French of many documents from Kieniewicz (1969a), especially those cited here.

127. Kieniewicz (1969a): 484–486.

128. Ibid.: 798–802.

129. Ibid.: 806–807.

130. Madge (1962): 56.

131. Here, I rely on Kieniewicz (1969b) regarding Polish emigration.

132. For analyses of these conflicts, see Greene (1975); Parot (1981). The descriptions of Polish immigration to Chicago provided by these books do not accord well with those of Thomas and Znaniecki, who seem to have underestimated the role of religion in the lives of Polish emigrants.

133. Wiley (1986). Thomas and Znaniecki's claims concerning the instability of Polish families were also critiqued in an article by John Thomas (1950), who provides only a small amount of statistical data, which is also weak. The first relatively precise treatment of data on delinquency—controlling for age distributions in diverse immigrant populations—can be found in Taft (1936). The author, who does not cite the analyses of Thomas and Znaniecki, suggests that Polish delinquency was rather limited around 1900. Other data can be found in Shaw, McKay (1942): 152–158. In the first edition of her synthetic book on the Polish American community, Helena Lopata (1976a: 106–108) does not cite other sources on these two points and concludes as I do here.

134. Lopata (1996): 55–58.

135. Lopata (1994): 67–83.

136. This seminar was organized by the Social Science Research Council (discussed below). The proceedings were published with the addition of a contribution by Znaniecki, who had not been present: Blumer (1939a).

137. Blumer notes the non-representativity of the documentation, but only in terms of the question of personal documents; the point is expanded upon more clearly in his preface to the second edition of the book, where he observes that he did not know the solution to the problem (Blumer [1979]: xxx–xxxii). The realm of personal documents is essentially indefinable.

138. See Janowitz (1966): xiv; Deegan (1988: 178–186) provides references and specific elements of the chronology of the "events" that led to Thomas's resignation, complemented the press reports presented by Salerno (2006): 75–80. These are both accessible via the Mead Project; see also the testimony of Kimball Young (in Lindstrom, Hardert [1988]: 292–293). The young woman with whom Thomas was found was the sister of the actress who was then Dorsey's mistress—Young errs on this point by confusing her with her sister (see the later interview of Dorsey in the *Chicago Tribune*, July 5, 1922: 3).

139. The chair of the Department of Political Sscience, Charles Merriam, also supported Thomas, according to Karl (1974): 87.

140. E. Thomas (1986): 539–540, note 56; Chad Heap (2003): 462–463, note 6.

141. Young (1988a): 273.

142. Janowitz (1966: xv) interprets this text as the tragic defense of a man trapped by circumstance, which in my opinion seems baseless. Deegan (1988: 181) adopts a similar interpretation. The difficulty lies in judging what Thomas would have considered appropriate or not for the readers of the newspaper whom he addressed, a problem that also arises with the interpretation of a letter from Thomas to Albion Small regarding incidents provoked by Thomas's lecture during a meeting in support of female suffrage, which Bulmer (1984: 59) characterizes as pitiful ("in an abject manner"), while Robert Throop and Lloyd Gordon Ward interpreted it in the opposite way ("W.I. Thomas and the Suffragists," Toronto, The Mead Project, 2007).

143. The decisive moment for Thomas's "rehabilitation" in sociology was his 1925 election to the second vice presidency of the Society, a step toward his election as president (Lindstrom, Hardert, Johnson, [1995]: 22; L. Bernard [undated]). Thomas later mentioned Bernard, but not Young, as one of the young sociologists with whom he maintained contact.

144. In a 1930 letter to Kimball Young, Thomas affirms that "getting thrown out of the University turned out the most beneficial thing that ever happened to me," AWIT. His later acceptance of teaching positions at the New School and his momentary interest in a potential offer by Columbia University makes it seem unlikely that this remark can be taken at face value, as Abbott and Egloff think.

145. Bernard (undated).

146. The frequent claim that Park hired Thomas for this research following his removal from the university is erroneous, as shown by the correspondence between Thomas and E. Dummer, quoted by Abbot and Egloff (2008): 221.

147. As previously mentioned, Robert Park contributed to another volume in the series of books on Americanization. Herbert Miller (1875–1951), a sociologist sometimes recognized as an immigration activist, was later described by Thomas, like Park, as an "old friend."

148. See Donald Young's preface to the 1971 re-edition of the book by Patterson Smith. A fairly detailed account of the stages of the composition and the publication of the book can be found in Raushenbush (1979): 85–94. In his correspondence with Hughes (AREPA, folder 9: 2), Raushenbush, who in 1920 was Park's assistant, attributes him a very active role in this research, and Park includes the book among his publications (AREPA, folder 1: 3). Deegan (1988: 184) quotes a letter from Thomas that seems to confirm Park's role: "I really did the work in the place of Miller, who undertook it originally." The version of the events commonly accepted today, which places Thomas as the sole

author of the book, is thus probably no more true than the earlier official version. K. Young (in Lindstrom, Hardert [1988a]: 294) attributes to Miller the correction of the proofs of the book, which is certainly incorrect since Miller, otherwise occupied, quickly withdrew from the project. If Kimball Young affirms that Thomas was angry at Miller at least at one point, Thomas claims to the contrary that Park and Miller "were my friends, and acted friendly" (letter to Kimball Young, May 4, 1930, AWIT). I here designate the book by the names of the reported authors of the first edition.

149. Park, Miller (1921): 308.

150. Dummer's philanthropical interests leaned toward children, women, and prostitution, subjects regarding which she defended positions that were nonconformist for the period. In her preface to Thomas's book, Ethel Dummer likely made a discreet allusion to the incident that caused Thomas's removal from the University of Chicago (Thomas [1923]: xiii): "One of the surprises of the war work was the definite number of married women carrying on not commercial prostitution, but clandestine relationships. They were not vicious but immature. Their husbands being away, they seemed unable to get on without the aid of a friendly man."

151. See Mennel (1973: 78–108) on the different theories concerning the characteristics of prostitutes advanced during the period: some were influenced by Lombroso, and others by eugenicist theories. See also Rosen (1982: 22–23; 137–168) for a general analysis of the characteristics of prostitutes from sources focusing on several cities. The analysis does not contradict that of Thomas, except perhaps in terms of the relationship between immigration and prostitution, and on the fact that not many prostitutes seem to have moved to cities after a rural childhood.

152. Thomas (1923): 109.

153. Ibid.: 231.

154. The interest of J. B. Watson (1878–1958) is not as surprising as Murray seems to think. The second text by Watson quoted in the book suggests that Thomas hoped to find in his experimental techniques a way to evaluate the influence of environmental factors. Watson's analyses on the behavior of newborns foregrounds what could be interpreted as one of the "wishes" described by Thomas, the desire for recognition.

155. Murray (1988): 386; see also K. Young (1962–1963): 386–387.

156. On Dorothy Swaine Thomas (1899–1977)—Thomas was her father's surname—the first woman elected president of the American Sociological Society, see Bannister (1998). In 1935, W. I. Thomas divorced Harriet Park Thomas in order to marry her.

157. On the SSRC, see Sibley (1974), and also, for a critical analysis, Fisher (1993). The organization, in which representatives from the political science field—as well as, in an early period, Charles Merriam—played a preponderant role, contributed, starting in the 1930s, to the orientation of American social sciences toward statistical approaches. Thomas's involvement in the SSRC accords with his lack of later hostility vis-à-vis statistical approaches and could have influenced the choice in 1938 of *The Polish Peasant* as one of the most significant books in the social sciences.

158. Thomas (1937): 1.

159. On this project, see the entry by Everett S. Lee on Dorothy Swaine Thomas in the *International Encyclopedia of the Social Sciences*, vol. 18: 763–765. See also AEWB, folder 138: 9. The project would associate Ernest Burgess (who had studied familial behavior) and Edwin Sutherland, another sociologist trained at the University of Chicago before 1914 (and who studied delinquency), and mix a statistical approach with the gathering of personal documents.

160. Bressler (1952).

161. Madge (1962): 52.

162. In the conclusion to his presentation of the book that probably laid the interpretive groundwork for the following generation, Park (in *Society*: 252–266) emphasizes documentary material, the language of description, and a new perspective from which social problems might be addressed (see p. 265). This last element is more questionable than the previous two.

163. Fleming (1967): 339–357.
164. The testimonies collected by Carey corroborate this point: see IJTC. A partial inventory can be found in Colyer (2014).
165. See Zaretsky (1984): 31–35.
166. There is a certain similarity between the "weaknesses" of *The Polish Peasant* and those put in evidence by Wax (1972) regarding Malinowski's book, *The Argonauts of the Western Pacific*, which played a foundational role for anthropology that is not without analogy to the role *The Polish Peasant* played for sociology. Like Malinowski, who did not perceive the cargo cult into which he had probably been taken, Thomas did not take into account several of the simplest facts concerning the people he studied.

3. PARK, BURGESS, FARIS, AND SOCIOLOGY AT CHICAGO, 1914–1933

1. Eulogy for Robert Park on February 9, 1944, on the occasion of the memorial ceremony organized at the Joseph Bond Chapel at the University of Chicago, in AECH folder 107: 2.
2. Letter to Howard Odum in 1936, in Raushenbush (1979): 158–159.
3. Two biographies have been written about Park. Matthews (1977), who relies on numerous accounts, offers his overall view, and an often penetrating and critical analysis, of Park's intellectual orientations within their contexts. The book by Winifred Raushenbush (1979), who was Park's assistant after 1920, benefited from the assistance of Park's former student, Everett Hughes, who offers an inside perspective of the intellectual current to which Park belonged. Raushenbush relies especially on material that Hughes had saved from Park's archives, the archives of many of his associates and students, and diverse narrative accounts. To these two sources can be added first the testimonies of Charles Johnson (1944), Ernest Burgess (1945a), Erle Young (1944), Helen MacGill Hughes (1980), and Edward Shils (1991a); an account by Werner Cahnman (1978) illuminates the end of Park's career at Fisk University. Publications by Park prior to his recruitment into sociology are reprinted in Lyman (1992). Two biographical essays were written by Park himself: see Baker (1973); *Race and Culture*: v–ix. Park's archives and the documents filed by Matthews after the completion of his book at the J. Regenstein Library (in AREPA) contain, finally, biographical documents that have guided my interpretations: see AREPA folder 1: 3. Below, I quote from three volumes of selected essays by Park published under the direction of Everett Hughes et al. by their titles and pagination.
4. The correspondence between Park and Thomas, reproduced in Raushenbush (1977: 67–76), testifies to Thomas' great enthusiasm for the analyses on the condition of African Americans developed by Park.
5. Kurtz (1982: 337).
6. For many years, Park was principally affiliated with the Divinity School of the university, which was close, as we have seen, to the Department of Sociology; it was there that he met different students who would become sociologists, such as Carl Dawson, one of the founders of sociology in Canada. The first dissertations Park supervised were those of Reuter and Kawabe, defended in 1919.
7. Park, Burgess (1921). In what follows, I always refer to the lightly revised 1924 edition of this book.
8. The respective contributions of the two authors are easy to discern thanks to an account by Burgess and to the fact that certain sections of the *Introduction* repeat previously published texts by Park: see Burgess (1945a), (1961: 16—in which Burgess describes his role as that of "junior author"); Janowitz (1969). Albion Small had initially entrusted the drafting of a textbook to Burgess, who was then charged with the introductory sociology course. Failing to obtain the collaboration of Scott Bedford, he substituted Park instead, who increasingly took control of the project and imposed himself as primary author of the book.

9. Burgess (1945a): 256; Matthews (1977): 195–196.
10. AREPA, folder 1: 3.
11. Ibid. See also Matthews (1977): 9. Park's experience in journalism and its connection to his later activities as a sociologist have been analyzed in detail in Lindner (1996).
12. AREPA, folder 1: 3.
13. "Autobiographical Note," in *Race and Culture*: viii.
14. Cited in Matthews (1977): 31.
15. Statement by Hughes, in Matthews (1977: 57), noted by Park (1941); see also, regarding the intellectual relationship of Park and William James, Matthews (1977): 31–33.
16. Park (1941): 37. Park's courses are sometimes described in similar terms.
17. Baker (1973): 256.
18. It was translated into English only in 1972. Little appreciated by his dissertation committee—and, it seems, by Park himself at the moment of its completion—it went practically unread by sociologists. On Park's voyage to Germany and his preparatory reading list for his dissertation, see Raushenbush (1979: 29–35), as well as Guth (2012): 55–93.
19. Matthews (1977): 57; Shills (1991a): 125.
20. Autobiographical note quoted in Matthews (1977): 62.
21. Ibid.: 58. Some of these papers are reprinted in Lyman (1992).
22. Here I use the terminology employed by Park and contemporary American researchers, who maintained a social, rather than biological, definition of the concept. See chapter 8.
23. Tuskegee Institute in Macon County, Alabama notably included a school for the training of different artisanal professions. Booker T. Washington, unlike the other prominent African American leader of the time, W. E. B. Du Bois—the holder of a doctorate in history from Harvard who argued for the necessity of political action to solve racial inequality—believed that "the most fundamental way to solve the race problem is to encourage individuals to solve their own problems" (Park, cited in Matthews [1977]: 70); for this, Washington advocated the separate development of African Americans and the white population. One can also find in the book by Meier, Rudwick (1976: 220–226) an analysis of the positions of Washington and Du Bois. Park's position as Booker T. Washington's secretary had initially been offered to Du Bois. Drake (1983) offers complementary elements on the relationship between Park and Booker T. Washington.
24. Matthews (1977): 71–76. See Lyman (1990) for an analysis of Park's first publications on Southern African Americans. Based on a mix of journalistic style and abstract analysis, these sketched a sometimes-optimistic description of the condition of African Americans in the South, and of its evolution in the preceding years: see especially Park (1908): 1913.
25. An account of this voyage was published: Booker T. Washington (1912). Park, its primary author, is mentioned on the cover as a collaborator.
26. Autobiographical document in Baker (1973): 258. According to an anecdote reported by Jessie Bernard (Matthews [1977]: 72), an employee of a Chicago hotel for African Americans remarked to Park, with the intention of flattering him, that he could pass as white (the cherished hope of many African Americans in this period, as noted in a famous book by the African American writer John Weldon Johnson).
27. These three rubrics are used by Park in a 1936 letter, quoted by Raushenbush (1979: 158), to define his principal research interests.
28. See, for example, Murray (1988): 386; Lannoy, Ruwet (2004); Guth (2012): 166–167. The interpretations of Lannoy, Ruwet (2004) are based on the hypothesis, which accords poorly with what is known about their relationship, of Park's concealment in his publications of what he owed to Thomas. Lannoy (2004) interprets Park's 1915 essay on the city as a presentation of his conception of sociological surveys (as distinguished from those of the reformers). This interpretation does not fit well with the content of the essay, which lacks a methodological dimension, nor with

Park himself, who inspired the research of numerous students. Nowhere do the former students of the years 1914–1930 consider Park to have simply been a disciple of Thomas. For example, Helen MacGill Hughes (1980: 71) wrote that Park had "learned a great deal" from Thomas, after listing the references Park mentioned in his course, notably including notes taken during a course taught by Simmel at Berlin, of which she provides a translation.

29.   Raushenbush (1979): 23.

30.   Park made another, arguably significant, reference to a thesis on the German debate regarding social science methods written by one of his classmates in Germany, the Russian Bogdan Kistiakowski, titled *Gesellschaft und Einzelwesen. Eine Methodolische Untersuchung,* Berlin, Otto Libman, 1899.

31.   Park (s.d.: vi).

32.   This short textbook (Park [1915a]) was the last of six publications edited by Thomas mentioned in the preceding chapter. Its first thirty pages are reprinted in *Introduction to the Science of Sociology.* One of these textbooks, written by Scott Bedford, a professor of sociology at the University of Chicago, focuses on American cities; another, by John M. Gillette, a sociologist on the faculty of the University of North Dakota, focuses on rural communities. The treatment of the subjects seems conventional.

33.   This essay will be referred to by the short version of its title, "The City," to distinguish it from the collection titled *The City* in which it was republished, with some modifications, in 1925.

34.   In the United States, the foundational texts of the origins of psychology, published by philosophers by training like William James, Hugo Münsterberg, Stanley Hall, and Mark Baldwin, predated the analogous texts by sociologists and figure among the references of Park and Thomas.

35.   See Park's account in Kurtz (1982): 338.

36.   B. L. Melvin, according to C. and Z. Loomis (1967: 682–682), reports that he heard Robert Park claim that it had been C. J. Galpin who had given him the idea of studying cities, on the occasion of a 1925 conference at Purdue University. An extract of Galpin's book *The Social Anatomy of an Agricultural Community* (1915) figures in Park and Burgess's *Introduction to the Science of Sociology* (1921). Galpin proposes a long-employed approach for determining the zones of influence of commercial centers in rural areas, based on routes frequented by their inhabitants. This method was then used, with modifications, to define the zones of influence of schools, hospitals, etc.—a typically ecological, with regard to Park, approach. On the history of the development of rural sociology, see Brunner (1957).

37.   Park, Burgess (1921): vi.

38.   In an essay written in 1928 and published in 1931 in a book on social science methods, Park presents two books that, according to him, figure among the most important in the field: *Folkways* by Sumner and *The Polish Peasant.* He characterizes these as the "work of pioneers," and recognizes them for offering a vocabulary for describing empirical material. He also recognizes that the second of these books represents "a point of view, a new approach of social problems" (in *Society*: 265).

39.   The Urban League, which had been founded in 1911 by African Americans close to Booker T. Washington, members of the economic elite, and white social workers, had as its objective the acculturation of migrants to northern cities: see Strickland (1966).

40.   On the work of the commission, see Waskow (1966): 60–104; Carey (1975): 78. The other author of the report was the journalist Graham R. Taylor—the son of one of the first professors of sociology (see chapter 1)—who seems to have contributed more to the writing itself than to the collection of data (Bulmer [1984]: 75).

41.   The Great Migration, which began in 1916, followed a period of increased migration toward cities dating back to the 1890s: see Spear (1967): 129–146; Grossman (1989).

42.   Waskow (1966): 40.

43.   Raushenbush (1979): 94.

44.   See Park (1922). The question of the immigrant press was a sensitive question, and different measures for regulating or prohibiting it were proposed (Persons [1987]: 18). An account of the problems encountered in the course of this project, from which the Carnegie Foundation rapidly pulled its support, can be found in Raushenbush (1979): 86–94.

45.   One of the principal contributors to this study, Emory Bogardus, drew from this experience a 1926 textbook on survey methods. Park wrote the preface for the work, explaining how evidence was collected during the study.

46.   *Survey* (and, after 1921, *Survey Graphic*) was the title, after 1909, of the periodical (formerly *Charities and the Commons*) of the Settlement movement. The funding for the survey on the Pacific Coast was abandoned after 1925 following a conflict Park and its sponsor, but undoubtedly also because of the voting in of a 1924 law that restricted Japanese immigration. The survey project had as its objective, according to Park, "improving race relations" rather than "promoting academic studies in race relations" (Raushenbush [1979]: 117).

47.   Letter to James Short, AECH, folder 55: 19.

48.   Taylor (1915). This book is an argument in favor of a city's rights with regard to these establishments. Among the examples offered in these articles figure the city of Gary, Indiana (in the immediate proximity of Chicago), as well as the neighborhood built by Pullman in the south of Chicago.

49.   Douglass (1925). P. H. Douglass (1871–1953) shared with Park a late entry to sociology: originally from Iowa, Douglass was a Protestant pastor for a dozen years, then permanently hired by a religious organization seeking to create schools for African Americans in the South; he only became a sociologist after age fifty. He led the Institute for Social and Religious Research. See Luker (1998: 301–310) on the positions maintained by Douglass regarding African Americans in the South. Like Taylor, Douglass belonged to the same milieu as Park and, for instance, collaborated with W. Raushenbush, Park's former assistant and biographer, in documentary research.

50.   Shils (1991a): 126.

51.   No account I am familiar with completely illuminates the reasons for Park's departure from the University of Chicago, where many of his associates still taught, including Ernest Burgess, his former students Louis Wirth and Herbert Blumer, as well as his son-in-law, the anthropologist Robert Redfield. The notorious lack of affinity between Park and the most prominent professor of the 1930s, the statistician William Ogburn, a Southerner, offers perhaps one element of explanation. Fisk might have been attractive to Park since, with different financial supports, a social science research program on race relations had developed there around Charles Johnson (see chapter 8, as well as Stanfield, 1985). Park taught at Fisk for many years, sometimes, it seems, without accepting a salary.

52.   Accounts about Park's intellectual relationships with students can be found especially in the interviews conducted by James Carey: see IJTC; the journal, also kept at the Joseph Regenstein Library, of Norman Hayner, a sociology student in the 1920s; as well as various statements made by Nels Anderson (1961; 1975; 1980–81; 1982; 1983).

53.   Young (1932).

54.   Raushenbush (1979): 184.

55.   On the different interpretations of Park's sociology, see Lengermann (1988), which in my opinion remains, for the period around 1921, the best justified for a precise reading of *Introduction* (see pp. 366–367).

56.   Hughes (in Raushenbush [1979]: 83) proposes a slightly different characterization in the *Introduction*: "The basic framework of the Park and Burgess *Sociology* is that of Simmel. . . . Even in using Simmel, however, [Park] was very thoughtful and original. As I think of it, he seems to have built his system out of these basic ingredients (perhaps more): 1) the very abstract but infinitely flexible conception of interaction which he got from Simmel, and 2) the notion of collective behavior, crowd, public, social unrest, social movements) which he got in part from Windelband, Tarde and al. But he also worked a new concept of evolution into it—evolution as itself a product of interaction. This idea

is the leading one of the new school of evolutionary biologists." Recall that Simmel had been relatively well-known in the United States in 1913, notably thanks to Albion Small's translations of several of his essays in the *American Journal of Sociology*; some of these essays had issued from one of Simmel's principal expositions on sociology, *Soziologie: Untersuchungen über die Formen der Vergesellschaftung*, published in 1908, which Park had probably read.

57. The accusation of empiricism sometimes put forth regarding research conducted at Chicago influenced by Park is based on an undue separation of his essays and the work that he inspired. A judgment along the lines of that expressed by the Durkheimian French sociologist Halbwachs (1932), who characterized the monographs inspired by Park as "descriptive works rather than scientific ones, uneven, disappointing sometimes, but often very picturesque," corresponds to a lack of comprehension of the relationships of these monographs with Park's essays. For lists of past interpretations of Park's body of work, see Martindale (1960), as well as Lengermann (1988). Halbwachs's relationships with the Chicago sociologists were the object of an overall analysis by Topalov (2015).

58. The distinction is equally explicit in the revised version—usually the only one cited—of this essay that was published ten years later in Park, Burgess, McKenzie (1925).

59. Park, Burgess (1924): 29–30.

60. Among the books known by Park figure especially those of two naturalists: Eugenius Warming: *Plantesamfund* (1895)—translated from Danish to English in 1909 under the title *Oecology of Plants* and excerpted in Park and Burgess (1924); William M. Wheeler: *Ants, Their Structure, Development, Behavior*, Columbia University Press, 1910. On Park's reading activity, see Raushenbush (1979): 79.

61. Park, Burgess (1925): 1–2. The distinction between the ecological order and the moral order became more complicated in 1936, when Park substituted for it the distinction among ecological order, economic order, political order, and moral order; the hierarchy of these orders corresponds, in this new version, to the degree of liberty available to individuals in a state of competition that sets them as opponents (see Park, 1936).

62. Park, Burgess (1925): 5.

63. See Deegan (1988: 46–47, 68, note 15) on the usage of cartography by the entourage of Jane Addams. Deegan (pp. 62–65) notes the decline over time of the frequency of allusions to the work by Park and Burgess.

64. See Hunter (1973): 5.

65. Park, Burgess (1924): 280.

66. Ibid.: 339.

67. Ibid.: 36–37.

68. Park (1939a), in *Human Communities*: 240–244.

69. The importance of Gumplowicz among the sources of inspiration for Park's formulations was unmentioned by Raushenbush and Matthews, as well as Bulmer; only an essay by Shils (1980) accords to Gumplowicz a certain influence over American sociology in the 1920s. In Park's articles, however, one can find occasional references to Gumplowicz, who was also one of Small's favorite references (account of Young in Lindstrom, Hardert [1988]: 270). Starting from the concept of interaction was not the only point of commonality between Gumplowicz's sociology and that of Park: both were centered around conflicts and gave a central place to those who set ethnic groups in competition with each other, the theme of one of Gumplowicz's major books. Gumplowicz's own social experience—being a Jew of Polish origin, and a law professor at Graz—in the ethnic mosaic that constituted the Austro-Hungarian Empire at the end of the nineteenth century, is arguably the basis of the similarities of his perspective with that of Park.

70. Park, Burgess (1924): 347.

71. Ibid.: 51.

72. The idea of competition is also present in books by Cooley: *Social Organization* (1909), which constitutes one of the sources of Park's formulations, and *Social Process* (1922).

73. Park, Burgess (1924): 508.

74. Ibid.: 665.

75. Ibid.: 735.

76. Ibid.: 735.

77. The definition of "Americanization" adopted by Park is not identical to that used by certain Anglo-Saxons—such as Frances Kellor, a prominent member of the Progressive movement whose positions would at one point find an echo in the federal administration of education: "Every effort should be bent toward an Americanization which will mean that there will be no 'German-Americans,' no 'Italian quarter,' no 'East Side Jew,' no 'Up-town Ghetto,' no 'Slav movement in America,' but that we are one people in ideals, rights and privileges and in making common cause for America. We are far from that ideal citizenship today . . . " p. 24. (quoted in Hartmann [1948]: 115). The application of the idea of assimilation to the United States is based on the implicit conviction that only Anglo-Saxon culture is compatible with the democratic form of United States government—see Persons (1987): 1–27. Cahnman (1978), a German immigrant who knew Park in the 1930s, suggests that Park's reflection on this subject was constrained by his "patriotic" attachment to the United States.

78. Park (1926a).

79. Park, Burgess (1924): 42.

80. Ibid.: 785.

81. Park (1929), in *Human Communities*: 74.

82. As Cahnman (1978: 335) notes, Park tended to transform a type of regularity having a historical character within the United States into a universal truth.

83. Park, Burgess (1924: 206). I shall further discuss below the elements of a broader analysis of the use of the concept of social class over the course of the years 1920–1930: see also Chapoulie (2000a).

84. One of the sections of Cooley's book *Social Organization* (1909) focuses on social classes based on "inheritance and competition." The concept is also presented in *Social Process* (1922). It appears, evidently, in the work of Veblen, with whom Park was familiar. None of these authors, however, offered an example of the use of this concept in analyses based on empirical evidence.

85. Park, Burgess (1924): 206. A similar antipathy toward the notion of class can be found in the book *Races, Nations and Classes* (1924) by Herbert A. Miller, a friend of Park, who was at that time a sociology professor at Ohio State University. In one of the last chapters of this book (pp. 151–167), Miller curiously (with respect to the title) focuses on class conflicts. While he takes for granted the existence of the proletariat, he by contrast considers radical extremes as "the product of psychologically abnormal conditions."

86. Park (1928), in *Race and Culture*: 233.

87. Park, Burgess (1924): 230. The conviction of the potential nonexistence of class in the United States probably refers to Park's faith in the idea that "opportunity for those willing to work was a staple of American life," to borrow the expression of Lal (1990): 93.

88. Park (1913a).

89. Park (1939b), in *Race and Culture*: 116.

90. Gilkeson (1995): 331.

91. R. S. Lynd, H. M. Lynd (1929; 1937).

92. See Persons (1987): 38.

93. See Strong (1885). This book was widely read—176,000 copies were sold in 1916. On different aspects of Strong's career and positions, see Muller (1966); White, Hopkins (1976): 60–65; Luker (1998): 268–275. Strong was not ignorant of academic sociologists: he authored an article offering advice for organizing local associations with missionary aims among different Protestant sects, published in 1896 in the *American Journal of Sociology*, vol. 1, no. 2. The similarities between Park's sociology and the perspective of middle-class Protestants before 1914 have been further discussed in Chapoulie (2008).

94. Strong (1913): 282.

95. The absence, in Park's work, of the theme of industrial organization is easy to explain: at that time, work belonged to the domain of economics, and not that of sociology. Strong, of a generation prior to Park's, distinguished himself by his proclaimed adherence to the idea of the superiority of Anglo-Saxons over other ethnic groups, and more generally by his objectives of religious and imperialist proselytism.

96. See Samuel Kincheloe's statements on the respective contributions of Park and Burgess in the use of cartography in IJTC.

97. Park (1923b).

98. Anderson (1961): xii. The reference to anthropology—to Robert H. Lowie and Franz Boas, but not to Malinowski—figures in the revised version of Park's article (1915b) published in 1925 in *The City*. Recall that the book that established the ethnographic approach among anthropologists, Malinowski's *The Argonauts of the Western Pacific*, was not published until 1922.

99. Park (1924), in *Race and Culture*: 153. One of the most explicit presentations of this dimension of social phenomena is found in Park (1930a), an article that presents the book of a criminologist.

100. Some interpretations of these accounts also drew the conclusion that Park was completely hostile to the use of statistics, which seems to me excessive: the article cited above (Park [1930a]) suggests, rather, a certain skepticism, confirmed by this remark from Norman Hayner's journal (February 10, 1922), a photocopy of which is preserved at the J. Regenstein Library at the University of Chicago: "Park does not think much of census idea especially if questionnaires are sent by mail." Hughes further notes Park's incoherence in terms of the quantitative approach (AECH, folder 55: 19, letter from Hughes to J. Short). In the sources gathered by Carey, there figure students of the last cohorts to take Park's courses who report his reserved remarks on the use of statistical methods: one could perhaps see there a reaction to the increasing importance accorded by sociologists of the period to the use of statistics, as well as an expression of the chilly relationship between Park and William Ogburn, recruited as a professor of sociology by the University of Chicago in 1927 (see chapter 4).

101. This was a neighborhood in the north of Chicago, inhabited by the local elite, which was studied in the monograph by Zorbaugh (1928).

102. Statement made by Howard P. Becker, a sociology student at Chicago in the 1920s, cited without other specifics in McKinney (1966): 71.

103. James (1899).

104. Park (1941): 39.

105. E. Anderson (1990).

106. Raushenbush (1979): 96–97. The attention paid to this anecdote is probably poorly founded, as suggested by several remarks by Hughes. Accepting it as a characterization of Park's opinion is to forget the context of teaching that gave rise to it—through a student who apparently annoyed the often irascible Park.

107. According to Deegan (1988: 154), there was a general agreement among Park's former students to keep quiet about the reasons behind this antagonism, which was undoubtedly at least partially of personal character. Margaret Redfield, Park's youngest daughter, made sure that Raushenbush's biography did not mention various aspects of Park's existence, and one might suppose that the archival documents that she permitted Raushenbush to access were not preserved. Hughes suggested in a letter from March 29, 1975 (Park addenda 9: 2) that, when Park made the remark cited above, there had been a conflict between sociologists and social workers since they refused to open their archives.

108. This campaign, which encountered the hostility of Protestant assistance organizations, led to a law in the state of Massachusetts, the Mothers' Aid Act (1913) inspired not by the association to which Clara Cahill Park belonged, but by social workers in these organizations: see Traverso (2009): 27–41. The activism of Clara Cahill Park has been described in some detail in Deegan (2005). One might note the difference between the objective of the movement in which Clara Cahill participated and the conviction of Park regarding the inutility of state interventions.

109. Strickland (1966): 39; 40–43.

110. Topalov (2014): 85–86.

111. Raushenbush (1979): 169.

112. Raushenbush (1979): 145–147.

113. Statement of Ernest Mowrer, in IJTC.

114. MacGill Hughes (1980): 73.

115. Two dissertations in sociology at the University of Chicago, defended in 1914 and 1919, focused on the Social Survey Movement. The first resulted in publication. The expression "social survey" figures in the titles of three articles in the *American Journal of Sociology* in 1916, 1920, and 1928. The methodology handbook published by Vivien Palmer (1928), a PhD student charged with supervising the instruction in research methods of students in the Department of Sociology at Chicago, emphasized the differences in objectives between social surveys and sociological surveys, but what she proposes borrows largely from experience acquired by social surveyors. The same is the case for the handbook of Pauline Young (1939), another former student of the department, which presents and discusses the method of these surveys in comparison with the method characterized as "sociological."

116. See Bulmer (1988): 69–73, as well as AREPA, folder 5: 1.

117. Burgess, to the contrary, expressly manifested his adherence to the concept of the survey conducted by a community on itself, while defining it as "the scientific study of its conditions and needs for the purpose of presenting a constructive program for social advance" (Burgess [1916]: 392).

118. See AEWB, folder 52: 9. The religious personnel of different churches embedded in this community (Hyde Park), as well as social workers, would form the backbone of the collection of data. See also Bulmer (1984): 74.

119. See, for example, "Natural History of the Newspaper" (1923), in *Society*: 89–104.

120. Cited in Raushenbush (1979): 185; see also Matthews (1977): 183–84; Bulmer (1984): 68.

121. Park's conception of the process of utilizing research in the social sciences is described as follows by Burgess (1961: 16): This process supposes: 1) the understanding of a problem, in its origin and its development; 2) the establishment of significant facts concerning the problem; 3) the diffusion of this knowledge; 4) the development of a structure within which "social planning" can take place.

122. On this point, see Lengermann (1988).

123. I leave to the side here the anthropologists who figured in the same department as sociologists until 1929.

124. Scott Bedford (born in 1876) was pushed to resign by the university administration (Bulmer [1984]: 110–111). See also the account of Young (1988: 296), who does not mention Bedford's name; as well as the elliptical remarks of Blumer and Hughes in 1969, in Lofland (1980). A student at the University of Chicago from 1905 to 1907, although he never obtained a doctorate, Bedford had taught sociology at Miami University from 1908 to 1911. His specialty had been urban sociology, but his reputation as a researcher and instructor was weak—the only favorable assessment of his teaching, to my knowledge, is found in the testimony of Ernest Mowrer in IJTC. Bedford's collection of texts in urban sociology, published in 1927, contains a short text by Burgess but does not cite Small, Thomas, or Park. In the following years, Bedford was, according to *Who's Who in Chicago*, research secretary for United Charities (which federated local charitable work), then director (between 1937 and 1939) of adult education for the city of Chicago.

125. See Cavan (1928), Young (1932).

126. The available biographical evidence concerning Burgess is more succinct than that concerning Park. I have relied especially on Faris (1970: 26–27), the essay by Nancy Goldman in Cottrell, Hunter, Short (1973); Matthews (1979: 105); Bulmer (1984); and Shils (1991b).

127. Diner (1975): 536.

128. The difference in interest in statistics between Park and Burgess is illustrated by their respective behaviors after Ogburn's (whose reputation in sociology was based on his contribution to the

development of quantitative methods) arrival to Chicago: Burgess regularly assisted in Ogburn's courses, while Park increased his skeptical remarks about the statistical method.

129. See Carey (1975): 142–43; 148, note 9. The point is developed in several interviews he conducted: see especially those of Cottrell, Robert Faris, McKay, Mowrer, Reckless in IJTC.

130. See E. F. Young (1925) for a presentation of this project in the terms of the period, and Bulmer (1984: 154–162) for an analysis. According to Ogburn (1940: 69–70), Burgess perfected, and applied to the field in Chicago, an approach previously utilized in New York for the census and statistics about the city.

131. Here, I adopt the same interpretation as Shils (1991b: 10).

132. Here, it is necessary to mention Roderick McKenzie (1885–1940), one of Park's first students at Chicago who, in 1921, defended his dissertation on a small Ohio city at the University of Chicago, and contributed to developing this approach. McKenzie remained in contact with Park, and until 1936 they envisaged writing a collaborative book on the subject—a project that was never undertaken due to McKenzie's illness and Park's other activities: see on this point Raushenbush (1979): 159–163.

133. Burgess (1924).

134. See Burgess, Bogue (1964: 5–6) on the use and diffusion of cartographical methods.

135. His major articles were gathered in a collection: Faris (1937). The principal biographical information concerning Faris can be found in Gerald Suttles's preface to the 1976 abridged edition of this book, as well as in the book written by his son, Robert Faris, on the Chicago sociologists (1970: 30–32; 88–99; 158), and in various obituaries.

136. Faris (1921).

4. RESEARCH AT THE UNIVERSITY OF CHICAGO, 1918–1933

1. In John V. Murra (ed.), *American Anthropology: The Early Years* (New York: West Publishing, 1974) 139.

2. Park, Miller (1921): vii. On the movement in favor of "Americanization," see Hartmann (1948).

3. For an overview of the period, see Bernstein (1960); on antecedents to the events of 1919 and the campaigns against radicals, see Coben (1964).

4. These entry quotas by nationality were fixed in 1920 on the basis of immigrants represented in the 1910 census, and were reevaluated in 1924 using immigration numbers from the 1896 census. The result was a maximum limit to immigration from southern and eastern Europe, the population of which was mostly non-Protestant. The measure had already been envisaged in 1911 by a Congressional commission.

5. Drake, Cayton (1945); Spear (1967).

6. Mayer, Wade (1969): 283–360.

7. Link (1959): 833–851; on the changes brought by the First World War to the sector of the movement associated with social surveys, see A. F. Davis (1967): 218–245.

8. I have relied on the lists established by R. Faris (1970) and Harvey (1987). These lists include, for the end of the period, a certain number of dissertations in ethnology and archaeology. Some graduates were non-Americans, and some did not ultimately settle in the United States.

9. Here I have relied principally on Carey (1975) and interviews he conducted (IJTC), as well as on the testimonies of N. Anderson (1975) and H. Hughes (1980–1981).

10. R. and G. Hinkle (1965: 19) offer an approximate sense of the increasing number of sociologists by presenting the number of members of the American Sociological Society, which grew from 852 to 2,182 between 1919 and 1929; they also emphasize the increasing importance, over the course of this period, of sociologists based in the Midwest.

11. According to the lists of R. Faris (1970) and the national data of Sibley (1963: 45) for the periods 1926–1929 and 1930–1934, the University of Chicago awarded around 11.5 percent of doctoral degrees in sociology.

12. Carey (1975): 155.

13. Ibid.: 163.

14. Kurtz (1982); Bulmer (1983a).

15. On Ogburn, see Bannister (1987: 161–187), which relies especially on his personal journal.

16. See Ross (1991: 125–130) for an overview of this current, which she places under the label of "scientism." Ross interprets this new conception as the product of the reaction to the cultural crisis resulting from industrial development, urbanization, and the decline of rural Protestantism. She emphasizes that it had been influenced by the close contact during the war of the social sciences, biology, and psychology.

17. Ogburn (1930): 302–303.

18. Murray (1986): 246–247.

19. For a critical assessment, from a "presentist" point of view, of Ogburn's conception as evidenced by this report, see Smelser (1986).

20. See IJTC, as well as Bulmer (1984): 191–192.

21. See Hughes's statement in Raushenbush (1979): 181.

22. Some elements of the history of the Department of Anthropology at the University of Chicago can be found in Stocking (1979); see also Stocking (1985): 121–125.

23. On the curriculum in anthropology at Chicago after 1925, see the account of Fred Eggan (1974): 5–8; on the separation into two departments, see Murray (1986).

24. Kuklick (1984). In the survey Carey conducted of a sample of sociologists trained at Chicago over the course of the period, Mead is cited more than any other non-sociologist professor, including the chair of the political science department, Charles Merriam, and Edward Sapir, both of whom are more frequently cited than James Field, the economist responsible for teaching statistics, and the psychologist Louis Thurstone; see Carey (1975): 160.

25. Rucker (1969): 20–21.

26. Strauss (1964). See Harvey (1987: 156–161) for a synthetic overview of the controversies surrounding Mead's influence among sociologists, especially those who inspired the book by D. J. Lewis and R. L. Smith (1981).

27. Raushenbush (1979): 181.

28. On the Department of Political Science and its relations with sociologists, see Bulmer (1984): 176–178; 193–195.

29. Ibid.: 176–177.

30. It was Ogburn who had proposed this quotation, adroitly excerpted from a longer phrase. The reticence of Charles Merriam with regard to this sponsorship—see Karl (1974): 154—was undoubtedly shared by other academics with ties to Pragmatism.

31. On Lundberg, see J. Platt (1993); on Bernard, see Bannister (1987).

32. These foundations had begun to disburse grants at the beginning of the century, as we have seen regarding social surveys (Russell Sage), before financing studies on "Americanization" (Carnegie).

33. Karl, Katz (1981): 244.

34. See M. Bulmer, J. Bulmer (1981: 354) on the training and early career of Ruml.

35. Quoted ibid.: 362–3.

36. The institutional aspects of the funding of the social sciences in the 1920s are presented in detail in D. Fisher (1993).

37. See the note in the *American Journal of Sociology* 29, no. 1 (1923): 97. The origin of the amount is not mentioned in this note, in keeping with the policy of discretion maintained by the Laura Spelman Rockefeller Memorial Fund.

38. M. Bulmer, J. Bulmer (1981): 386.

39. Bulmer (1984): 141.

40. A list of associations that financed the Local Community Research Committee in 1929 figures in T. V. Smith, White (1929): 33–39. I have also relied on the conclusions drawn by Carey (1975: 121–149) from documents preserved in the Charles Merriam archives.

41. Ibid.: 138.

42. Bulmer (1982). In general, acknowledgments of the existence of these contributions can be found in the prefaces to published monographs. These are, however, discreet regarding the funds' origins: the policy of the Rockefeller foundations was explicitly not to draw attention to their contributors. Therefore, it is the Local Community Research Committee and the Social Science Research Council that were mentioned.

43. I have not verified whether the funding for these projects came from the University of Chicago, the Rockefeller foundations, or another source.

44. D. Fisher (1993): 50–56.

45. Thrasher (1926).

46. Mowrer (1927).

47. My interpretation diverges here from two opposing interpretations of the SSRC's policy, which are in my opinion too univocal: Bulmer (1984) emphasizes the researchers' autonomy, and D. Fisher (1993) their manipulation by foundations.

48. At the same time, Homer Hoyt (1896–1984), an economics student at the University of Chicago of the same generation as Hughes, studied the price of land in Chicago. He was almost never cited by sociologists, even though in 1941 he had published an article in the *American Journal of Sociology*.

49. For the following, I have relied on the list provided in a catalog, published in 1967, of books published by the press between 1895 and 1965. The comparison between this list and the correspondence preserved in the Burgess archives reveals inconsistencies: neither Doyle (1937) nor Pierson (1942) appear in the series according to the catalog, despite the fact that their first editions show that they had been part of it. The author of the catalog claims that the series debuted in 1926, which would imply that *The Hobo* by Anderson was included within it a posteriori (see chapter 9), although Park's preface to that book indicates that it belonged to a new series.

50. Siu (1987).

51. Margold (1926). This book resulted from a dissertation supervised by Cooley and defended at the University of Michigan; its preface was written by Edward Devine, one of the main leaders of the Social Survey Movement.

52. Kawabe (1921). This book, which resulted from a dissertation defended in 1919, was appended after the fact to the series edited by Park, Burgess, and Faris; see also Wildes (1927).

53. L. Edwards (1927); Hiller (1928).

54. See Frances Donovan (1929) on saleswomen. The author, a schoolteacher, pursued undergraduate studies for a time at the University of Chicago. She had previously published a book on schoolteachers.

55. For this analysis, my point of origin was the lists of MAs and PhDs offered by R. Faris (1970) and Harvey (1987), as well as an examination of the *American Journal of Sociology* for the years 1920–1934. Only some of the memoirs of PhD and MA students are preserved at the University of Chicago's Joseph Regenstein Library. The titles of the cited dissertations can be found in the bibliography.

56. P. F. Cressey (1938); this article (the author of which should not be confused with P. G. Cressey) came out of a dissertation defended in 1930. Neither Jakob Horak's (1920) dissertation on Czechs in Chicago nor that of Vivien Palmer (1932) on areas of initial settlement resulted in books or visible articles.

57. Park (1934).

58. A list of these studies can be found in the inventory of work funded by the University of Chicago's Local Community Research Committee, in T. V. Smith, White (1929); it mentions several studies on unions and branches of industry.

59. See Bulmer (1983b).

60. I have presented and made use of this concept elsewhere: Chapoulie (1991): 322.

61. P. G. Cressey (1983); this article was fortuitously discovered by M. Bulmer in the Burgess archives.

5. AMERICAN SOCIOLOGY, THE SOCIOLOGY DEPARTMENT, AND THE CHICAGO TRADITION, 1934–1961

1. Park, Burgess, McKenzie (1925): 110.

2. In John V. Murra, ed., *American Anthropology. The Early Years* (New York: West Publishing, 1974), 141.

3. Based on the data in Sibley (1963: 45), it is possible to estimate the portion of dissertations produced by the University of Chicago Department of Sociology in relation to the total number of dissertations in the discipline: for the period 1935–1939, the department produced 8 percent of dissertations; for the five following years, 9 percent; 19 percent for the period 1945–1949; 13 percent for the period 1950–1954; 6 percent for the period 1954–1958. The decline at the end of the period reflects the creation of doctoral programs at numerous universities.

4. See Evans (1986–1987).

5. Around 1920, a sociologist of the period, Stuart Chapin, counted 130 "interesting" positions in sociology—which is to say positions that included research possibilities; see Bannister (1987): 189.

6. The implantation of sociology occurred even later at Princeton. At Yale, where it had been established by Sumner, it survived by remaining for a long time somewhat removed from other currents in the discipline.

7. See Lengermann (1979); Bannister (1987): 188–214. In order to avoid an overly simplistic view of these alliances, one might recall that Ogburn also, from his start at Chicago, was on cold terms with Park and had even more distant relationships with Blumer and Wirth.

8. See notably Bannister (1987): 190, 200. On the interests of the professors who taught sociology to undergraduate students, see S. Turner and J. Turner (1990): 62–63.

9. See Deutscher (1973): 36–37. This description appears in a letter addressed to Irwin Deutscher by Richard LaPiere, a sociologist born in 1899 who obtained his PhD at Stanford in 1930.

10. See D. Fisher ([1993]: 96–111) for an analysis of the contents of this report, which makes the continuity with the preoccupations of the following period apparent.

11. Quoted in ibid.: 101.

12. Ibid.: 108–109.

13. See Karl ([1983]: 135–136, 129–130) for an overall analysis of this policy; Converse ([1987]: 45–53) offers a list of projects involving researchers in the social sciences.

14. Karl (1983): 120–121.

15. Wirth (1940): 6.

16. M. Anderson (1988): 170–178.

17. Ibid.: 182–190.

18. Converse (1987): 47.

19. Camic (1986).

20. Allport (1935).

21. Converse (1987): 57.

22. See Camic (1986; 1994).

23. For an overall analysis of the development of the sector of studies using survey research, see Converse (1987). The history of the concept of attitude among psychologists and sociologists was traced by Fleming (1967).

24. See Gosnell, Merriam (1924); Gosnell (1927).

25. Converse (1987): 54–86.

26. Ibid.: 163.

27. Stouffer, Suchman, De Vinney, Williams (1949).

28. Converse (1987): 229.

29. On the creation of the National Science Foundation and its political difficulties in including the social sciences in its mission, see Larsen (1992): 38–46.

30. Alpert (1954): 210.

31. According to the assessment of Wilner (1985), the portion of articles in this journal that used a quantitative approach went from 40.6 percent in the period 1936–1941, to 68.4 percent in the period 1957–1975.

32. This report is analyzed in D. Fisher (1993): 172–176.

33. This analysis of the decline of interest accorded to Park's sociology builds on elements evoked by Kucklick (1973), Matthews (1977; 1989), Wiley (1979), and Farber (1988). My interpretation agrees with that of Matthews (1989): he insists upon the rupture in social science approaches that, in the 1930s, led to the abandonment of analyses in terms of process in favor of analyses in terms of structure.

34. Carey (1975).

35. See Sorokin (1963: 238), as well as the account of Homans (1984): 129.

36. Gillespie (1991): 96–100, 118, 258. Gillespie notes the social conservatism of Mayo.

37. Parsons, Barber (1948). See also Camic (1992), who shows how Parsons was committed to eliminating from his references the institutional economists whose reputations were then in decline.

38. Even after 1946, the members of the Department of Social Relations at Harvard (which took over the Department of Sociology) continued to neglect the American sociological tradition, as noted by B. and M. Johnson (in Klausner, Lidz [1986]: 134), who specify that only Cooley, Mead, and Thomas were treated with respect.

39. Heyl (1968).

40. Buxton, Turner (1992).

41. Homans (1984): 293–296.

42. Hughes (1964) (in SE: 544).

43. Shils (1948): 11.

44. Ibid.: 54.

45. Ibid.: 55.

46. The Institute of Human Relations at Yale included psychologists, historians, and anthropologists—notably George Murdock and John Dollard.

47. On Hutchins, see the biography by Dzuback (1991); his influence on the University of Chicago is examined by McNeill (1991).

48. McNeill (1991): 36–40.

49. Hutchins (1936). On the reception of the book by the Chicago scholars, see Dzuback (1991): 186–189.

50. Burgess (1955) (in Burgess [1974]: 356).

51. The testimony of Shils (1990: 222), which is probably based more on his contacts over the course of the period after 1945, claims that Hutchins did not like sociology and despised studies that used a statistical approach.

52. See MacAloon (1992), and especially the testimony of Gusfield (1992): 167–177.

53. In the background of the creation of these committees, one sometimes finds funding possibilities: for example, the Committee on Industrial Relations would receive funding from large businesses; the Committee on Social Thought relied on the resources of the wife of its director, John Nef; see McNeill (1991): 120–124.

54. Geiger (1988): 199.

55. According to Salerno (1987: 15), Wirth, who had previously been an instructor at the University of Chicago for two years, was hired during the summer of 1930, while Park replaced Faris as chair of the department.

56. Here, I take on the interpretation of Hughes, which seems plausible. See notably his interview with Robert Weiss (AECH, folder 1: 13), where he says that he does not think he was expected to become important, and that Wirth and Blumer hired him because he was suited for the job and a hard worker. (He taught an introductory course taken by a significant number of students.) Hughes's correspondence also suggests that he served to strengthen research on institutions.

57. Robert Redfield (1897–1958; PhD in 1928) was the son of a lawyer and a Danish woman of aristo- cratic background. He seems clearly distinguished from the majority of sociology graduates of the same generation in terms of his elevated social origin, his appeal, and his manners. His rise in the administrative hierarchy of the University was much more rapid than that of Wirth, Blumer, or Hughes: Hutchins named him Dean of the Division of Social Sciences in 1934. His book *The Folk Culture of Yucatan* made him a prominent anthropologist after 1941. Hughes named Redfield as his closest friend in the 1930s, and it is possible that he contributed to Hughes's return to Chicago, although I have not found anything to definitively confirm this in the archives I have made use of.

58. On Wirth, and especially his sociopolitical activities, see Salerno (1987): 25–37. Complementary evidence can be found in the biographical essay later written by one of his daughters, Elizabeth Wirth Marvick (1964).

59. Wirth was at one point suspected of having been a communist propagandist in the 1930s.

60. According to the critical assessment of Hughes, Wirth was always marked by having the perspective of a social worker—a profession that his wife also exercised for a long time.

61. Wirth notably translated into English a book by Mannheim (1929). Wirth's role as intermediary between German and American sociologists probably reinforced his antagonism toward to Parsons (which was also fed by their differences in political orientation): one anecdote recalls the presence of Wirth, ostensibly occupied by his mail, in the front row of the auditorium during a lecture given by Parsons at Chicago; see Gusfield (1992): 170.

62. Wirth (1938).

63. Letter to James Short (1970) (in AECH, folder 55: 19).

64. See the semi-biographical interview by Carey (in IJTC), as well as Wiseman (1987) and Wiley (2014); I have also made use of the testimony of Arlene Kaplan Daniels and various statements by Chicago students of the 1940s and 1950s, which incidentally also touch on Wirth, Redfield, Warner, and Hughes, in Verhoeven (1995): 14–30.

65. Blumer (1928). This dissertation is almost the only evidence that provides a sense of Blumer's intel- lectual cultivation; he is otherwise silent regarding his philosophical references. The majority is dedicated to an examination of American sociology from the 1900s to 1925, from J. Baldwin to E. Faris and C. Ellwood, by way of J. B. Watson and A. L. Kroeber.

66. Two books resulted from this research: Blumer, Hauser (1933); Blumer (1933). The distance between the approach taken in the first book, which seeks to analyze the influence of cinema attendance on crime, and the requirements of rigor he later defended in his essays is utterly striking.

67. The majority of known articles are reprinted in Blumer (1969a) or in Lyman, Vidich (1988), which also include some articles from rather inaccessible publications that are never cited. Some of Blumer's essays remained for a long time unpublished: see Blumer (1990) for his critique of theories of industrialization, and Blumer (2004).

68. Some of Blumer's essays in this area, of a programmatic character, were also later published: see Blumer (1969b; 1971). Examples of the legacy of Blumer's approach in this domain can be found in the Festschrift edited by Shibutani (1970).

69. F. Davis (1991): 3. See also Strauss (1996b).

70. Hughes (1928).

71. See Gaylord, Galliher (1988): 101–122.

72. Sutherland (1937).

73. See Lindesmith's preface in Gaylord, Galliher (1988).

74. Stocking (1979): 25.

75. Only a few accounts and analyses exist regarding Lloyd Warner. The principal sources are the manuscript written by his associates, filed as the Warner Archives (AWLW) in the special collections of the Joseph Regenstein Library at the University of Chicago (chapter 8, written by Havighurst, focuses on Warner's activities at Chicago), as well as the book that seems to have been put together by his wife, Mildred Warner, in 1988.

76. During the same period, Ernest Burgess had also proposed a study of Cicero, and Warner had given Elton Mayo a negative assessment of this proposal.

77. M. Warner (1988): 101–102; Gillespie (1991): 155–158.

78. Drake, Cayton (1945). This monograph was unorthodox in comparison to Warner's approach. The program inspired by Warner also included studies of communities in Ireland, conducted by Conrad Arensberg and Solon Kimball.

79. Havighurst, Loeb, Warner (1944).

80. Another of Park's students during the 1920s, Samuel Kincheloe (1898–1981), was recruited as a professor by the Divinity School of the University of Chicago, but enrollment in his courses among sociology students of the years 1945–1960 is only mentioned by Killian (1994).

81. I have relied here on the annual directories of the university, as well as the biographical entries in *American Men of Science (Social Sciences)*, and additionally the lists reproduced by Harvey (1987) and Fine (1995) (in this case, with the correction of some errors).

82. Converse (1987).

83. Ibid.: 324, 525.

84. McNeill (1991): 167.

85. Ibid.: 133–138.

86. On this recruitment project, see ALW, folder 1: 3; AEWB, folder 3.1. Intended for the hiring of a specialist in social psychology, it was Merton whose recruitment was particularly desired.

87. Abbott, Gaziano (1995). The fundamental documents can be found in AEWB, folder 33.

88. Blumer's reservations with regard to the sociology of Parsons were exposed in an article published much later, in 1975.

89. ALW, folder 1: 3.

90. The correspondence between Hughes and Riesman contains numerous judgments of this type, regarding their colleagues as often as candidates under consideration for a position in the department.

91. See Gusfield (1990): 114; (1992); (1995): xv–xvi; Friedson (1977); Becker, Debro (1970); Lopata (1995): 372; Killian (1994): 42–49; Farber (1988). I have also made use of the testimonies of Goffman (Verhoeven, 1993), Rainwater (1969), Short (1969), and Gans (1990), as well as various accounts quoted in Fine (1995) and the analyses of Winkin (1988): 13–92.

92. McNeill (1991): 52.

93. AECH, folder 66: 7. The representative of the students was Gregory Stone.

94. Burgess and Ogburn seem to have lost, in this period, some of the audience that they previously had—but Short (1969) mentions their courses favorably. The themes studied by the former, such as the elderly, were not very attractive to young students. The research themes that interested Ogburn were removed from popular subjects of the period. Otherwise, Ogburn's having sided with Germany

during the war and a certain anti-Semitism on his part (on this point, see Bannister [1992]: 188–190 and 196–197) certainly did not help to expand his audience.

95. Whyte (1969): 44. Another former student of the same period, Bernard Farber, confirms this account with a pithy statement: "Woe to the foolish doctoral candidate who has both Wirth and Warner on his dissertation committee" (Farber [1988]: 342); see also Rainwater (1969): 96.

96. Wax (1997).

97. Letter to C. Bolton of July 11, 1959, in AECH, folder 9: 3.

98. Lawton (1955). Lawton's correspondence with Hughes (AECH, folder 35: 5) makes it clear that he did not succeed in finding a publisher for a revised version of his dissertation, probably on account of reasons relating to the delicate nature of the subject. Hughes's assessment of the dissertation was—deservedly—very laudatory.

99. Dissertations that do not fit into this list can also be found: for example, various dissertations on art and one on lifestyles (probably inspired by Warner).

100. Dalton (1959/1949); Westley (1970/1951); Gusfield (1963/1954); Goffman (1959/1953); F. Davis (1963/1958); Shibutani (1966/1948); Lindesmith (1947/1937) (the second date is that of the defense of the corresponding dissertation). The list of books resulting from these dissertations is obviously much longer; for less well-known examples, see: Gilman (1956/1955); Carter (1962/1959). In other cases—for example, those of H. S. Becker, D. Roy, and O. Hall—articles issuing from dissertations became classics.

101. Friedson (1970); Roth (1963); Strauss, Schatzman, Butcher, Ehrlich, Sabshin (1964); Glaser, Strauss (1965); M. Wax, R. Wax, Dumont (1964).

PART II: PATHS OF RESEARCH

1. Turner (1988) and Snow, Davis (1995), which focus on post-1940 studies in this area, are almost the only two exceptions.

2. See especially Meltzer, Petras, Reynolds (1975) and Rock (1979).

3. Maines, Bridger, Ulmer (1996).

4. See Fine, Ducharme (1995) for an analysis of the ethnographic works of this second generation (which they compare to those of a third generation trained at the beginning of the 1960s).

6. HUGHES, BLUMER, STUDIES ON WORK AND INSTITUTIONS, AND FIELDWORK

1. Becker (1988): 19.

2. Edited by Fine (1995), the book *A Second Chicago School?: The Development of a Postwar American Society* perhaps marks the last stage of the institutionalization of the posthumous association of Hughes and Blumer—even if it contains, in an ultimate irony, a contribution by Abbott and Gaziano that describes the rather tendentious relationship between Hughes and Blumer at the beginning of the 1950s.

3. A. Rose (1962). Published shortly after was the volume of articles by Manis, Meltzer (1967), explicitly characterized as symbolic interactionism.

4. R. Faris (1970).

5. A letter from Becker to Hughes (February 7, 1964) also claims that the series of books he was planning "will be very much like the old Chicago series" and would include "books based on fieldwork" (AECH, file 8: 1).

6. On the Society for the Study of Social Problems, see the October 1976 special issue (vol. 24, no. 1) of *Social Problems*.

7. On the origins of the SSSI, see the twentieth anniversary issue of the journal published by this association, *Symbolic Interaction* 20, no. 2 (1997).

8. In the proceedings of this conference, Lyn Lofland (1980) cites the initial nucleus of this interest in the Chicago School—in fact, in works in urban ethnography—to have consisted of John Lofland, Sheldon Messinger, Sherri Cavan, John Irwin, Jacqueline Wiseman, and herself. The respondents to the discussion between Hughes and Blumer include, aside from this group, former students of Blumer at Berkeley (Arlene Daniels, Fred Goldner) or of Blumer and Hughes at the University of Chicago (Howard Becker, Ned Polsky), as well as Carl Couch, who inspired another group of researchers that claimed heritage from Mead, the Iowa School. Blumer and Hughes both kept their distance from the idea of a "school," Blumer bluntly remarking that "It seems to me that the work that was being done at Chicago is very, very much in order *as a point of departure*" (Lofland [1980]: 275). For his part, Hughes asserted, "I don't like the idea of talking about a Chicago School or any other kind of school," claiming that those who participated in a *Festschrift* in his honor "weren't trying to preserve a tradition. I'm not in favor of trying to preserve a tradition" (Lofland [1980]: 276).

9. Only Anselm Straus and two Canadian sociologists, David Solomon and Leo Zakuta, contributed to the volumes of both Becker et al. (1968) and Shibutani (1970).

10. See, among the major examples, Martindale (1960); Gouldner (1962; 1970); Matza (1969); Meltzer, Petras, Reynolds (1975); Rock (1979).

11. Blumer (1937): 153.

12. Deutscher (1984): 71.

13. The copies of the 1931 abridged version of Hughes's dissertation were accidentally lost. According to Robert Redfield, whom he then considered his closest friend, Hughes's research domain was the "study of social organization with special reference to social institutions" (Letter to Hughes, February 7, 1938, in AECH file 66).

14. See Lichtenstein (1982; 1989); Lipsitz (1981): 14–134; H. Harris (1982): 44–60.

15. Discussions of different aspects of Hughes's sociology can be found in Chapoulie (1973; 1984; 1996; 1997a; 1997b); see also Helm-Hayes, Santoro (2016).

16. Gillespie (1991): 96–126.

17. The hiring of Warner in 1935 broadcasted this orientation, since his relationship with Mayo had factored into the positive assessment of his candidacy, according to a letter from Redfield reproduced in chapter 8 of the manuscript of the biography of Lloyd Warner written by Havighurst (in AWLW).

18. I rely here on the series of *Registrar's Reports* from the University of Chicago.

19. See Converse (1987): 356–360; Kaufman (1993): 63.

20. An association bringing together researchers in this field was also founded in 1947. Labor economists held the primary position in it. See Gillespie (1991): 252–253.

21. One of them, presented at a general session by Mary Van Kleek, was published the same year in the *American Sociological Review*. It claimed to define the field: two other papers were presented at a session titled "Social Research" by Chicago researchers—Hughes on the one hand, and Gardner and Whyte on the other—and were published in the same issue of the *American Sociological Review*.

22. Arensberg was, with Chapple, one of the major partisans of the application of the ethnographic study of interactions within groups to relationships inside companies; see M. Rose ([1976]: 148–152) for a characterization of his operationalism-influenced intellectual orientation.

23. Parsons, Barber (1948).

24. Gillespie (1991): 184.

25. See chapter 9 of the manuscript of Lloyd Warner's biography in AWLW, as well as the accounts of Whyte ([1994]: 141–149) and Gardner (1977).

26. Gardner, Whyte (1946): 507.

27. Gardner (1977); Rainwater (1969): 92–93.

28. Whyte (1948).

29. Warner, Low (1947). This was one of the volumes of the Yankee City series whose research was already almost complete at the time of the creation of the Committee on Human Relations in Industry, but that was (probably formally) integrated into its program.

30. See the volume edited by Whyte (1946)—which includes Hughes (1946b)—for the Committee's first presentation of research.

31. AECH, file 98.

32. Hughes (1946a). At the time, Hughes envisaged writing a book on race relations in industry, a project that he abandoned after 1950, having complained in his correspondence of not having enough time for research. Some of the material for the planned book appears in a condensed form in E. Hughes, H. Hughes (1952); see also Hughes, Hill (1946). This theme of research was pursued by many students around 1945; see especially Collins (1945) and the 1947 MA thesis of Harvey Smith.

33. See AECH, file 98: 10. Hughes specifically attributes one of his ideas to each of these authors—the last, which seems all the more original in light of the time period, was owing to Allison Davis, an anthropologist in Warner's circle. Davis's contribution to the volume edited by Whyte (1946) is a criticism of middle-class ethnocentrism in the study of disadvantaged workers.

34. See Hughes (1951a) (SE: 338–339), as well as Hughes (1970b), see especially in SE: 418. This essay, written at the instigation of Edward Gross, one of his former students of the 1940s, constitutes both a testimony and a sort of assessment of Hughes's research on work.

35. On the human relations movement, of which Whyte and Gardner were the main spokespeople, see Kaufman (1993): 76–99. The intervention of researchers of the human relations movement sometimes had direct consequences on relations within companies. One example is Whyte and Gardner's study on a chemical business (to which is devoted an entire issue of *Applied Anthropology* 5, no. 4 (1946). In this scenario, the researchers managed to convince the president of the firm to accept unions in the company; see Whyte (1994): 159–163; Chapple (1953). The human relations movement practically disappeared at the end of the 1950s.

36. AECH, file 98.

37. *American Journal of Sociology* 46, no. 1 (1940: 98–101). The eight-line report published by the *American Sociological Review* (6, no. 2 [1941]: 304–305) is more favorable. Park had in 1934, as we have seen, written in the *American Journal of Sociology* a very favorable review of Mayo (1933), which accounted for some of the Hawthorne study (*Society*: 293–300).

38. Aside from the two cited here, articles critical of this domain were numerous from 1947 to 1949, written by prominent or soon-to-be prominent sociologists (including Daniel Bell, C. Wright Mills, Robert Merton, Reinhard Bendix, etc.), but they were not published in sociology journals; see Gillespie (1991): 257–261.

39. Moore (1947).

40. Blumer (1947). The fact that three years later Blumer published in the *American Journal of Sociology*, of which he was editor in chief, a special issue on industrial sociology illustrates the mixture of radical intellectual opinions and extreme liberalism he demonstrated at different moments in his career.

41. Ibid.: 273.

42. Ibid.: 272.

43. His assessment is still more reserved with respect to those who studied the behavior of workers by means of attitude scales—evidently the University of Michigan group and the disciples of Kurt Lewin.

44. A 1949 paper Blumer gave before the association of researchers in the field of industrial relations—republished in Lyman, Vidich (1988)—specifies his point of view: he developed a critique of the

means proposed by the social sciences for reducing conflicts in groups of interests (economic, union, professional) and suggested that the real issue was the relationships between these groups and the state.

45. This was a union affiliated with the CIO. Philip Murray, cited below, was president of the CIO.

46. Lofland (1980): 275.

47. The expression one of them employed in the report of the 1947 meeting at which they discussed this point is as follows: "the main social issues, he feels, are not involved in the business of interaction" (ABJ, file 4).

48. ABJ, file 4.

49. Meeting on November 8, 1951, in AEWB, file 33: 4.

50. A final article in this field, published in 1976, is the text of a 1952 lecture.

51. Collins (1945); Killian (1952). See also the dissertation of Josephine Williams (1954) on female doctors and that of William Hale (1949) on young African American lawyers, as well as the article adapted from it: Hale (1952).

52. In my notes for the French translation of Hughes essays can be found an explanation of some of the allusions made to works on occupations.

53. Hughes (1971): viii. See Hughes (1962) (SE: 52–64) for the major essay on this theme that had originally appeared (at least) in 1957.

54. The rare references given by Hughes correspond to the MA thesis and PhD dissertation of Leona Nelson (1953). One might add the dissertations of Lawson (1955) and Carey (1958).

55. See Hughes (1937).

56. Recall that in the United States at this time, the term "profession" meant those occupations— initially physician, lawyer, university professor, and minister—to which significant prestige was attributed. The 1940s and 1950s were marked by numerous occupations also claiming the status and privileges of professions: see Chapoulie (1973).

57. Letter to Ogburn of March 4, 1938, in AECH, file 66: 6–8. In 1939, Parsons also published one of the presentations of his perspective on professions.

58. Hughes (1970b) (SE: 417–427).

59. Ibid. (in SE): 418.

60. An example of the first case is offered by the detailed study of Kriesberg (1952) on fur vendors; an example of the second, by Habenstein's research on funeral directors; see Habenstein (1968): 208; Habenstein (1962).

61. On doctors, see the dissertation of Oswald Hall (1944)—as well as the articles adapted from it (1946; 1948; 1949)—and the dissertation of David Solomon (1952). On lawyers, see the dissertation of William Hale (1949); that of Dan Lortie (1958); and that of Jerome Carlin (1959)—see also Carlin (1962). On business executives, see the dissertation of Melville Dalton (1949)—and Dalton (1959). On city administrators, see the dissertation of George Floro (1954)—and Floro (1955). On school-teachers, see the dissertation of Howard Becker (1951), which resulted from a research contract sponsored by Hughes—as well as Becker (1952a; 1952b; 1953a); on school principals, see the dissertation of Harold McDowell (1954). On nurses, see the dissertation of Rhoda Goldstein (1954).

62. See the study of janitors by Gold (1952) and the statement on it: Gold (1964), note 8.

63. See the testimony of F. Davis ([1974]: 314–315) regarding his study on taxi drivers (F. Davis [1959]).

64. This special issue on work (vol. 57, no. 5 [1952]) includes, particularly, four articles by researchers supervised by Hughes—Roy, Becker, Kriesberg, and Gold—and two written by sociologists more in contact with Blumer—Weinberg and Arond, Kornhauser.

65. Hughes (1951a) (SE: 343).

66. E. Hughes, H. Hughes, Deutscher (1958).

67. It was initially to Goffman and then to Fred Davis that Becker and Hughes offered the job that would finally go to Geer; see AECH, file 124: 8.

68. Hughes and his associates received for this study a subvention from the National Institute of Mental Health. The same organization funded, after 1954, the research by Goffman that would lead to Asylums. The similarly inspired studies of Friedson, on medical practices, and Strauss were somewhat later.

69. See passim, in AECH, file 66: 11; file 124: 8, 9, 11.

70. Becker, Geer, Hughes, Strauss (1961).

71. Becker, Geer, Hughes (1968).

72. Hughes (1971): viii. Hughes also wrote an *Outline for the Study of an Occupation* intended for students in his course on the sociology of occupations.

73. Becker ([1998]: 67–108) is almost the only one to note this essential point.

74. Hughes was a little more explicit in his references in the essay in which he formulated his approach to institutions; see Hughes (1962).

75. Hughes (1956) (SE: 309). A memorandum (February 13, 1964) advances another argument: Parsons's point of view led to the supposition that professions filled an objective defined a priori, while his own experience of his father, a minister admired by his congregants but without influence over their conceptions on education and racial differences, suggested the a priori indetermination of attained objects (AECH, file 8: 1). In a later report—Hughes, Thorne, De Baggis, Gurin, Williams (1973)—on training in various professions, funded by the Carnegie Corporation, no reference can be found to Parsons's essays on professions.

76. Hughes (1951a) (in *SE*: 338–347; *RS*: 77–78 [© Éditions de l'ÉHESS, Paris, 1996]). It was only in the 1960s that criticism of Parsons's position on professions became more explicit in American sociology, with the articles of Freidson (1960); Bucher, Strauss (1961); Becker (1962); and Habenstein (1963).

77. Hughes himself was little moved to attribute the role of leader to himself: in a 1976 memorandum intended for the chair of the Chicago sociology department, he gives a list of those who, according to him, considered themselves his students: among them figured Oswald Hall, Howard Becker, Harvey Smith, Edward Gross, and Julius Roth. Hughes deliberately excluded Anselm Strauss, S. Kirson Weinberg, William Kornhauser, and Harold Wilensky (AECH, file 66: 7). Goffman is not mentioned in this list, and it was Goffman himself who, after 1960, claimed affiliation with Hughes. In a 1980 interview he claimed, for example, "If I had to be labeled, it would have been as a Hughesien urban ethnographer" (Verhoeven [1993]: 318). Hughes's correspondence also shows on many occasions his reticence to consider Goffman one of his students, although he did refer to him as such in a 1969 letter to an editor (AECH, not cataloged).

78. See the minutes of meetings of this group in 1946 and 1947 in ABJ, file 4.

79. The dissertation of Bernard Karsh (1955) on strikes was inspired by the book by Hiller on the same subject, resulting from a dissertation supervised by Park. It contains only a few references to Hughes and Blumer. However, Karsh contributed to a volume of homages to Hughes, by whom he claimed to have been trained (Karsh [1968]: 35).

80. Smigel (1954).

81. *American Sociological Review* 24, no. 3 (1959): 414–415.

82. *American Journal of Sociology* 55, no. 1 (1959): 115–117.

83. A letter by Hughes suggests that his mistrust with respect to medicine had a biographical basis.

84. Hughes (1952) [© Transaction Books, New Brunswick, NJ, 1984].

85. AECH, file 15.

86. Hughes (1951a) (SE: 342). One of the examples most frequently cited by Hughes is that of the work of janitors (studied in Ray Gold's MA thesis). But, as we have seen, it was outside the study of black workers that Hughes was struck by this type of phenomena.

87. In his autobiography, Killian ([1994]: 44–45) indicates that it was Hughes's teaching that drew his attention to the points of view of all parties present in racial conflicts, and particularly to the point of view of those who are prejudiced.

88. Hughes (1976).

89. Ibid.: 5.

90. In the text assessing his research (Hughes 1970b), Hughes criticizes some of his previous work for its insufficiency at taking into account the system of interactions within which activities of work were performed.

91. Hughes (1951b) (SE: 311–315). The idea of systematically studying the division of labor remained unexploited (at least in a systematic form) in later empirical research.

92. Hughes (1970b) (SE: 424).

93. Hughes (1937) (SE: 136–140). A second essay, first published in French translation, was used by Hughes in his teaching from the end of the 1950s. It was recently published in English (Hughes 1997).

94. See the studies of Becker (1963) on marijuana smokers; of Becker, Carper (1956) on the careers of students; of Goffman (1961), F. Davis (1963), Roth (1963), and Strauss, Schatzman, Bucher, Ehrlich, and Sabshin (1964) on hospital patients.

95. Hughes himself rarely used the term "ethnocentrism" except to designate what he also called the "methodological ethnocentrism" of American sociology of his time—which is to say the common practice of ignoring the fact that surveys by standardized questionnaires were not adapted to anything but the study of relatively culturally homogenous populations, corresponding, in the United States, only to the middle and upper classes. An essay by Strauss (1996a) emphasizes the importance of the criticism of ethnocentrism in Hughes.

96. Hughes (1970a).

97. Quoted in Strauss (1996a): 283.

98. See the interview conducted by Robert Weiss, in AECH, file 1, as well as Weiss (1997).

99. See the interview with Hughes conducted by Robert Weiss in 1981 (in AECH, file 1), as well as the description of the goals of this course in a memorandum titled "Introduction to Field Studies," and in the instructions given to students in 1947 (in AECH, file 79: 6); see also the introduction to Gold's dissertation (1954), which is based on interviews with students who took this course.

100. See the testimonies of Verdet (1996): 62–64; Gans (1968): 301; Becker (1983).

101. Polsky (1969): xiii. Gold ([1954]: 13) notes the (middle-class) origin and the ambitions of students who had this often-painful experience.

102. On the transformations of distinctions in approaches to the field between 1930 and 1960, see J. Platt (1983).

103. Malinowski ([1922]: 4) already used this term, which he styled "field-work."

104. Burgess (1945b). The methodology textbook by Pauline Young (a former University of Chicago student), published in 1939, used comparable categories.

105. Merton (1947): 304.

106. Lohman (1937).

107. *Human Organization* is the journal published by the Society for Applied Anthropology, which then brought together a large number of those who studied, using fieldwork, "non-primitive" societies, and especially American society. The Society for Applied Anthropology was founded in 1942 by a small group in which figured historians, anthropologists, and sociologists; see Hughes (1974) on the founders. The majority of articles on fieldwork published in this journal over the course of the ten previous years were republished in Adams, Preiss (1960).

108. Barton, Lazarsfeld (1955).

109. Blumer (1928): 427.

110. Blumer (1947): 278.

111. Blumer (1948), in Lyman, Vidich (1988): 149.

112. Blumer (1966). Goffman also notes—Verhoeven (1993): 331—that Blumer "was never interested in ethnography."

113. Blumer (1948).

114. The article does not name any one study, but the reactions of some involved were lively; see Theodore Newcomb's report of the discussion inspired by the presentation of the 1948 article by Blumer at a meeting of the American Sociological Society. A little later, his criticism of *American Soldier* made Stouffer describe Blumer as "the gravedigger of American sociology" (Becker [1988]: 15).

115. Deutscher (1973). This book, of an explicitly Blumerian inspiration, republishes analyses published in the form of articles starting in the mid-1960s.

116. Blumer (1969a): 139. In one of Strauss's final essays can be found a fine analysis of Blumer's position: Strauss (1996b); see also the special issue (11, no. 1) of *Symbolic Interaction* and most especially Becker (1988). Hammersley (1989) offers a general discussion of Blumer's contribution to the development of qualitative methods.

117. See Roth (1965) for a retrospectively analyzed example of this type of experience.

118. See the testimonies of Goffman (in Verhoeven [1993]: 332), Verdet ([1997]: 63), and Wax (1997). The critical role of Blumer was not without resemblance to that filled by Ellsworth Faris for the previous generation.

119. For a detailed analysis of the development of this project, see Cefaï (2002).

120. Hughes (1960): iii (SE: 496; RS: 267).

121. Buford Junker (1911–1978), who had followed Warner from Harvard to the University of Chicago, obtained a PhD in sociology in 1954. He was the first permanent researcher of Social Research Inc.

122. Hughes's importance in the project surpassed the writing of its preface alone; for example, Gold then dedicated his 1958 article to Hughes "with compliments of the plagiarizer" (AECH, file 26: 9). See also in AECH (file 77: 5) the summaries of Hughes's discussions with advanced students about this project.

123. Hughes (1960). See also Gold (1958), an article adapted from the dissertation of the same author.

124. The first (to my knowledge) article on the usage of tape recorders for collecting interviews was, notably, written by a student of Hughes (Rue Bucher) and a student of Blumer (Quarantelli): Bucher, Fritz, Quarantelli (1956). The situation referenced is that of a NORC study (and not the field research of an individual researcher). The article particularly notes the importance of material lost from unrecorded interviews and the elimination of the inevitable distortions in interviews whose reportage is based on memory; it mentions only at the end the greater specificity of data.

125. Hall (1944; 1946; 1948; 1949). The majority of previously cited articles in the sociology of work resulting from MA theses and dissertations are at least partially based on interviews and reproduce excerpts from them.

126. The first examples of citations of field notes introduced into articles can be found in those of Becker (1951b) and Roy (1952b).

127. Not all researchers in Hughes's circle presented their field notes in an explicit manner: this was not the case for Strauss or Goffman. Recall that the question of writing reports was later at the center of controversies over the use of the ethnographic approach.

128. See Becker (1958)—an article that is an implicit response to that of Barton and Lazarsfeld, which Becker characterized as important; Becker, Geer (1957; 1960).

129. J. Platt (1997). An analysis of Hughes's conception with respect to the later evolutions of the practices and the point of view of field researchers can be found in an article by one of his former students at Brandeis, Emerson (1997).

130. Shibutani (1970).

131. Helm-Hayes and Santoro (2016).

132. Becker (1983).

133. R. S. Weiss ([1997]: 80–83) describes in detail how in his course Hughes abstained from formulating interpretations explicitly and in a general manner.

134. Gusfield (1990): 106.

135. Gusfield (1995): xiii.

7. FROM SOCIAL DISORGANIZATION TO THE THEORY OF LABELING

1. "Preface," in Shaw, McKay (1942): xi.
2. "Candid Conversation," *Playboy* (March 1972): 68.
3. See Henderson (1893; 1914) (the second book is based on secondary sources); Breckinridge, Abbott (1912).
4. Queen (1957): 167. The first article in the *American Journal of Sociology* to have a title containing the expression "social disorganization" was published in September 1930 (vol. 36, no. 2) by a student of Park, Andrew Lind. A 1941 article by a former Burgess student, Mowrer, proposes a classification of different usages of the term.
5. R. Faris (1948).
6. Thrasher (1927).
7. Cavan (1928).
8. P. G. Cressey (1932).
9. Reckless (1933).
10. R. Faris, Dunham (1939).
11. Landesco (1929). This study, conducted by a survey commission, was for a long time the only one devoted to a subject whose particular topical nature, in the case of Chicago in the 1920s, cannot be ignored. Landesco (seemingly) abandoned his dissertation after a marriage that freed him from the necessity of paid work. Two other sociology students of the same period sought to study aspects of serious crime: Joseph Lohman and Saul Alinsky, who began but never completed a study of a murderer (see AEWB, file 2: 12). On these studies and especially that of Landesco, see Reynolds (1995).
12. Shaw, F. Zorbaugh, McKay, Cottrell (1929); Shaw (1930); Shaw, McKay (1931; 1942).
13. Supporting evidence for the importance of the diffusion of the works of Shaw and McKay in sociology can be found in Cole (1975), Laub (1983).
14. The researchers in the circle of Edwin Sutherland—Donald Cressey, Daniel Glaser, Albert Cohen—had not been trained at the University of Chicago but at the University of Indiana, where Sutherland taught after 1935. Alone among those who collaborated with Sutherland, Alfred Lindesmith obtained a PhD in sociology at the University of Chicago in 1937 and conducted research in an adjacent field. But all these researchers considered themselves participants in the Chicago tradition, and they maintained numerous contacts with the researchers at University of Chicago; see Laub (1983): 188–189. On Sutherland, see Snodgrass (1976); Gaylord, Galliher (1988).
15. The lack of prominent position accorded here to Sutherland's work results from an arbitrary choice: they have as much a claim to be associated with the Chicago tradition as the ones taken into account here.
16. Park in Park, Burgess, McKenzie (1925): 25.
17. Ibid.: 109.
18. Ibid.: 108.
19. Ibid.: 107.
20. This point of view was held by Charles Henderson in 1899; see A. Platt (1969): 30–31.
21. Burgess (1923): 662–663. See Chapoulie (2003) for a more detailed examination of this article.
22. Burgess (1923): 674.
23. Ibid.: 674–675.
24. The creation of these institutions was one of the successes of the social reformers in Jane Addams's entourage. See Mennel ([1973]: 102–157), Finestone ([1976]: 38–53) for a history motivated by a critical assessment, A. Platt (1969).
25. Sutherland (1934): 894.

26. See Thrasher (1927). The book was intended to inaugurate the series edited by Faris, Park, and Burgess, but the author took two or three years longer than expected to finish his PhD. Frederic Thrasher (1892–1962) does not seem to have enjoyed much intellectual esteem among students of his generation.

27. Ibid.: 22; the italicized passage is Thrasher's.

28. Ibid.: 23, 37.

29. Thrasher was hired at the same time as Harvey Zorbaugh by the department, where he conducted new research into juvenile delinquency and remained until the end of his career.

30. On William Healey, see Mennel (1973): 161–168. Bennett ([1981]: 111–112) especially analyzes Healey's collection and use of autobiographies of delinquents, resources made particularly valuable due to the fact that Healey used this type of evidence before the sociologists did.

31. AEWB, file 2: 11.

32. Burgess (1923). Park was also involved in the Chicago Area Project; see the testimony of Hughes in AECH, file 55: 19.

33. Snodgrass (1976): 12–13. This point is made in many testimonies, including those of Shaw's friends; see the interview of McKay in IJTC; that of Sorrentino in Laub (1983): 241. The most specific biographical evidence concerning Shaw and McKay can be found in Snodgrass (1976), which is based especially on an unpublished autobiographical essay of the latter. The article by Rice (1931) is based on an interview with Shaw from the 1930s and offers some supplementary evidence. See also Finestone (1976), Bennett (1981). On Shaw's activities, see also James Carey's interviews with Leonard Cottrell and Walter Reckless in IJTC.

34. An excerpt from one of these is quoted in Snodgrass (1976): 12–13.

35. Among the researchers who had either brief or prolonged contact with the Institute of Juvenile Research figure Solomon Kobrin, Leonard Cottrell, Harold Finestone—who specialized, at least for a time, in the study of delinquency—and Joseph Lohman and Saul Alinsky, whose careers would unfold partially or completely outside of sociology. Some years later, Lloyd Ohlin, James Short, and Howard Becker also became involved with the Institute.

36. Snodgrass (1976): 2–3.

37. Shaw, F. Zorbaugh, McKay, Cottrell (1929); Shaw, McKay (1931); Shaw, McKay (1942).

38. Fifty years later, tracked down by another sociologist, the "Jack-Roller" gave a follow-up to his autobiography: Snodgrass (1982).

39. Shaw, Moore (1931); Shaw, McKay, McDonald (1938).

40. Bennett (1981): 184.

41. Ibid.: 317.

42. For a detailed analysis of the functions of the usage of delinquent autobiographies by Shaw and his predecessors, see ibid.: 179–210.

43. Shaw, McKay (1931): 194. They also remark that this point had already been advanced in Breckinridge, Abbott (1912): 35. With less precise data, a similar remark can be found in Shaw, F. Zorbaugh, McKay, Cottrell (1929): 8.

44. As noted by Finestone ([1976]: 89), who refers only to Shaw and McKay, this interpretation is slightly different from that found in *The Polish Peasant*. Thomas and Znaniecki argue that juvenile delinquency resulted from the inadequate socialization of the second generation of immigrants, while Shaw and McKay, probably on the basis of their direct experience with delinquents, sustained that it was grounded in an alternative mode of socialization.

45. This interpretation is evoked by the title of the 1976 book devoted to juvenile delinquency—*Victims of Change*—by Harold Finestone, one of the last associates of Shaw and McKay.

46. Of the first three sociology textbooks on the subject—Parmelee (1918), Gillin (1926), Sutherland (1934)—only Sutherland's does not adopt a multifactorial interpretation, but rather an interpretation similar to that of Shaw.

47. Shaw, McKay (1932).

48. Lubove (1965): 86–114.

49. On the specifics of the segregation that affected black settlement in Chicago, see Philpott (1978): 116–146.

50. Shaw, McKay (1969): 387.

51. I rely here on the comparison of Shaw, F. Zorbaugh, McKay, Cottrell (1929); Shaw, McKay (1931); Shaw, McKay, McDonald (1938); Shaw, McKay (1942; 1969).

52. This is the term used by Shaw and McKay ([1931]: 74), who remark that these neighborhoods were also those in which rents were lowest, the frequency of reliance on forms of charity were the most elevated, etc.

53. Shaw, McKay, McDonald (1938): 99. Here, I partially take up the analysis of Finestone (1976): 92.

54. Shaw, McKay (1942): 438. For an analysis that emphasizes the consequences of contacts with the delinquent world, see Shaw, McKay (1969): 170–173.

55. Merton (1938). Shaw and McKay ([1969]: 387) also remark that there was no contradiction between their analyses and those constituting the legacy of Merton's theory.

56. Shaw (1930): 11–13.

57. Ibid.: 18.

58. Shaw, Moore (1931). The authors' point of view is made clear in the notes commenting upon each chapter of the biography.

59. Shaw, McKay, McDonald (1938): 347.

60. On the Chicago Area Project, see Kobrin (1959), Finestone ([1976]: 116–150), and Sorrentino (1972), as well as the testimony of Sorrentino in Laub (1983).

61. Quoted in Carr (1941): 224–225.

62. Kobrin (1959).

63. Ibid.: 19; see also Finestone (1976): 133–149. The evaluation of a similar project based in Boston in the 1950s did not lead to a positive conclusion insofar as a reduction in delinquency: see W. Miller (1962).

64. See Snodgrass ([1976]: 16), which notably reproduces excerpts of conversations between Shaw and Sutherland starting in 1936.

65. Piven, Cloward (1971): 256–276.

66. Cloward, Ohlin (1960). Ohlin explicitly borrowed ideas on the organization of communities from CAP: see the testimony of Ohlin in Laub (1983): 210–217.

67. See Sellin (1938a); for a summary and excerpts, Sellin (1938b). At the origin of this commission can be found the radical criticism of the entire criminological approach as nonscientific, made by Michael, Adler (1933). The second author, Mortimer Adler, was the philosopher opposed to pragmatism recruited to the University of Chicago by Hutchins—see chapter 5.

68. Sellin (1938b): 98.

69. Sutherland (1940). Regarding Sutherland's research on white-collar crime, see Gaylor, Galliher (1988): 101–109.

70. Sutherland (1945): 431–432.

71. The list of books selected by Mills is not homogenous: alongside textbooks, it includes two books by Cooley and *Races, Nations and Classes* by Herbert Miller (1924). Only some of the authors of these books spent time at the University of Chicago.

72. Mills (1973): 171.

73. Ibid.: 175.

74. See the autobiography of Whyte (1994), which can be corroborated by Hughes and Warner's correspondence. A presentation of the historical context of Whyte's research can be found in Henri Peretz's introduction to the French translation of *Street Corner Society*.

75. Whyte (1943a).

76. Whyte (1994): 108–115.
77. Whyte (1943b).
78. Ibid.: 38.
79. The book initially attracted hardly any attention. The rather favorable review by Edwin Sutherland in the *American Journal of Sociology* treats it as a community study, among other things.
80. Three of those who completed dissertations then—Albert Reiss, James Short, and Lloyd Ohlin—would specialize in this area over the course of the following years.
81. Merton (1938). Two of the major books on juvenile delinquency of the period 1940–1960—Cohen (1955); Cloward, Ohlin (1960)—follow in the footsteps of Merton's article, even if the relationship is complicated, as shown by Besnard (1987).
82. Later, Merton (1969) sought to distinguish between the domains of social disorganization and deviant behavior. His attempt left no lasting mark on research or the usage of these notions.
83. Lemert (1951)—the conventional title of this book, *Social Pathology*, does not give an exact idea of its orientation. The term "deviant" is found in an article by a Norwegian criminologist, Vilhelm Aubert, in the *American Journal of Sociology* (1952) and, the following year, in an article by Howard S. Becker.
84. A largely similar interpretation of research on delinquency in this second period at the University of Chicago can be found in Galliher (1995).
85. On the diffusion of *Outsiders*, see Cole (1975): Becker is the most frequently cited author between 1970 and 1973 in the sample of publications selected by Cole; he ranks ninth for the period 1965–1969.
86. Chapter 4 of *Outsiders*, initially published in *Social Problems* in 1955, figures in the collection edited by A. Rose (1962), which contributed to the "resurrection" of the Chicago tradition.
87. See Westley (1951; 1953; 1956; 1970); Gusfield (1954; 1955; 1963); Goffman (1963)—a book in which Goffman ostensibly takes a certain distance from deviance-based approaches and, it seems to me, from Becker's analyses.
88. Lemert (1976): 244.
89. Gibbons (1979): 146.
90. Becker (1954)—a copy of the text currently in my possession comes from the personal archives of Everett Hughes.
91. In an interview that I conducted in 1997, Becker indicated that he had discussed this subject with Goffman and had attentively read the essay, published as the third part of *Asylums* (Goffman [1961]).
92. In the same interview, Becker recalls that "Merton was the target of this text."
93. Becker (1954): 2–3.
94. Ibid.: 5.
95. See Dalton (1949; 1950a; 1950b; 1959); Roy (1952a; 1952b; 1953; 1954).
96. Becker (1985): 238–239.
97. Becker (1996): 65.
98. Lindesmith (1947). This book was adapted from a dissertation supervised by Blumer at the University of Chicago, which was defended in 1937.
99. This was *Social Pathology* (1951).
100. Becker, Debro (1970) (in Becker [1986]: 29–34 [© H. S. Becker]).
101. *SE*: 98–105. The moral relativism noted by some of Hughes's former students is more evident in this essay than in Hughes's other articles.
102. On Lohman, see Blumer (1968); as well as the interview of Hans Mattick in Laub (1983): 33–67.
103. Testimonies on Solomon Kobrin and Daniel Glaser reported in Reynolds (1995): 149.
104. In the obituary he wrote for Lohman, Blumer ([1968]: 255) remarked that he "was the progenitor of the pregnant view that the delinquent became a delinquent in make-up and action through the labeling process in society." An article for the general public by Lohman (1958) confirms this interpretation.

105. Testimony of Becker (1997).
106. Letter from Becker in 1991, quoted in Galliher (1995): 167; see also p. 166 for the summary of a statement by Habenstein on Lohman.
107. Tannenbaum (1969): 303–319. The author of the preface to the volume indicates (p. x) that Tannenbaum had been brought up in a rural community "and ever since he has tended to see the world in terms of the experience of a face-to-face community."
108. Tannenbaum (1938): 19. According to the testimony of Mattick in Laub ([1983]: 35), Lohman contributed to spreading the works of Tannenbaum. Intellectual reasons for the affinity between the perspectives of Tannenbaum and Becker can also be found: Tannenbaum was a friend and former student of Dewey.
109. See also Gusfield (1990); Lopata (1995): 375.
110. Freidson (1977): 116.
111. Short (1969).
112. Haskell, Yablonsky (1974): 16–19.
113. At the time Becker gathered his interviews on the consumption of marijuana, he conducted a long biographical interview with a middle-class heroin addict—a case that seemed rare at the time, but not for much longer. After long negotiations reported by Bennett ([1981]: 217–234), the document was published: H. Hughes (1961).
114. Regarding the emergence of questioning regarding the consumption of drugs, see the interview of Kobrin in Laub (1983): 96; AEWB, file 3: 7.
115. Gilbert (1986): 63–78.
116. Ibid.: 140. For a plausible interpretation of the growth in delinquency over this period, see Perlman (1959). One of the first analyses that took the existence of significant delinquency among middle-class youths for granted was published by England (1960).
117. Letter from Park to Wirth from August 1930, quoted in Raushenbush ([1979]: 123), regarding Wirth.
118. AEWB, file 2: 12. See also the analysis of Burgess in Shaw, Moore (1931): 244. Remarks suggesting a similar point of view for Shaw and McKay can be found—see especially the interview of the later in IJTC—or Sutherland. I am, by contrast, less tempted to consider an article by Mead (1918) as an earlier formulation of the same point of view, contrary to an interpretation sometimes advanced.
119. On this point, see the report of the discussion organized by Troy Duster (1983) between Lemert, Cicourel, Kitsuse, Matza, Messinger, and Becker.

8. RESEARCH IN THE WORLD: THE STUDY OF RACE AND INTERCULTURAL RELATIONS, 1913–1963

1. Park (undated [after 1934]) (in *Race and Culture*: vii–viii).
2. Blumer (1958): 405.
3. For an overall view of Park's perspective in this area, see the four volumes that resulted from bringing together the colloquia of major researchers in the field: Reuter (1934); Thompson (1939); Lind (1955); Masouka, Valien (1961); which brings together the contributions to the homage to Park organized in 1954 at Fisk University.
4. R. Adams (1937); Lind (1938).
5. Reuter (1926); Bogardus (1928).
6. The principal articles by Edgar Thompson on the plantation system have been brought together in Thompson (1975); see also his dissertation (1932).
7. Brown (1930; 1931).

8. Gosnell (1935).

9. After defending his dissertation, *The Ghetto*, in 1928, and even though he had devoted courses to the subject, Wirth published no more on this theme until a 1944 magazine article, which was an outgrowth of his activism in this domain. Blumer's publications—his articles from 1939 and 1955—were relatively late and were not based on original evidence. As we have seen, however, Hughes devoted some of his empirical research to this area.

10. Shibutani, Kwan (1964); Killian (1952); Lohman, Reitzes (1952; 1954).

11. The bibliographical study of Kurtz (1984) omits, for example, some of the references most visible in the field, among them the majority of the publications of Frazier and Johnson and the book by Pierson (1942) on Brazil. Furthermore, Kurtz cites no publication by Thompson, etc. Bulmer (1984) takes into account the works of Charles Johnson for the survey commission on the 1919 Chicago race riots, but leaves out the works of Frazier, as well as the other continuations of Park's analyses in this domain. The subject is, however, covered by the biography of Matthews (1977). Books specifically devoted to the sociology of relations between ethnic and racial groups always accord an important position to Park, as well as to Frazier: see Lal (1990); Persons (1987), the only book specifically devoted to research conducted in Chicago; Lyman (1972); Steinberg (1993). The diversity of interpretations of Park's sociology, its merits and its limits, should be emphasized. In their quasi-totality, these analyses pertain to the history of ideas and leave to the side the empirical dimension of the studies.

12. See G. B. Johnson, G. G. Johnson (1980) for a description of this research.

13. Reid (1939).

14. Hughes, "Race and Language," lecture at Florida State University, January 19, 1967, in AECH, file 109: 16. Perhaps the best illustration of this point resides in the variability of definitions used in quantifying the population. An analysis of the meanings invested in the different appellations of non-white populations in the United States can be found in Hare (1962).

15. Blumer (1955): 4.

16. One of the first to emphasize this point was Robert Blauner (1972). Blauner insists upon the differences between the historical experience of black Americans and that of European immigrants: African Americans had been relegated to outside the centers of advanced industrial development and found themselves confronted with structural mechanisms maintaining a division of work on a racial basis.

17. We must also recall that, particularly after 1920, there was an influx of immigrants from the Antilles, whose behaviors differed from those of the populations resident at the time in the United States. Park never refers to this case, which was numerically very small.

18. Weiss (1979): 568.

19. Thus it was possible to write (Bodnar [1985]) a history of European immigration to the United States almost void of allusions to events and legal decisions; such a task would be impossible for the history of African Americans over the course of the same period.

20. Barkan (1992): 281–285, 310–318.

21. Weiss (1979). He also mentions a greater tolerance of some educators, concerned about the treatment of the children of immigrants.

22. Around 120,000 Japanese immigrants and American citizens of Japanese origin were interned in camps according to Archdeacon (1983): 194–196.

23. The case of Mexican immigrants also drew attention for a time. Many were killed over the course of a riot in Los Angeles in 1943 (ibid.: 196, 176–177). It was only in the 1960s that the case of Indians became a subject of public interrogation.

24. Hill (1936).

25. For an overall view of the situation of African Americans over the course of the period 1920–1960, see Meier, Rudwick (1976): 232–270.

26. Hirsch (1983): 17.

27. Meier, Rudwick (1976): 236–237.

28. The situation and the evolution of commerce and services are described, for the city of Chicago, in Drake, Cayton (1945): 433–468. It was in the domain of insurance that the African American-owned businesses saw the most success; for small businesses, it was beauty salons and funeral homes. Frazier ([1949a]: 407) indicates that the same was true in other large cities, and that two-fifths of businesses owned by African Americans were established in the neighborhoods in which they lived.

29. Park, we recall, was one of the founders of the Chicago section of this association, of which he was briefly president.

30. The NAACP was founded in 1909, on the initiative of a minority of liberal whites critical of Booker T. Washington's moderate position, in a context marked by the strengthening of segregation in the South; see Meier, Rudwick (1976): 227.

31. See D. L. Lewis (1981): 34–45.

32. See Record (1951).

33. Randolph considered the NAACP to be an organization representing the perspective of the middle class, and he criticized its weak concern for the interests of the mass of workers. Despite some success, like the organization of the Pullman porters' union, its own positions were more familiar to the middle classes than to the working classes.

34. On Johnson, see the testimony of Burgess (1956); Valien (1958); Gilpin (1973); Robbins (1974); Stanfield (1985): 119–138; and the biography by Robbins (1996).

35. This book, published in 1920, was written by Emmett Scott. Scott, who was African American, was the former secretary of Booker T. Washington during the period in which Park worked at Tuskegee. Johnson was, with the historian Monroe Work (the first African American to receive an MA in Sociology at Chicago, in 1903), one of the two main authors of this largely descriptive book, but in which certain themes suggest the influence of Park, who is also quoted in the preface.

36. Johnson notably wrote a report on housing for the Conference on Building and Home Ownership of the Hoover administration and a report for the Committee on Farm Tenancy of the Roosevelt administration.

37. Valien (1958): 247.

38. D. L. Lewis (1981): 90–91, 125.

39. A book was then adapted from this issue of *Survey Graphic*: A. Locke (1925).

40. Frazier (1949a): 444–449, 467–491. In the South some progress also took place in instruction; for Alabama and regarding the role of foundations, see Bond (1939): 256–258, 262–286.

41. The CIO was born, between 1936 and 1938, from a schism in the American Federation of Labor dominated by skilled workers; its principal leader wished to create unions of industries (and not of occupations, the principle underlying the AFL); see Leuchtenburg (1963): 109–111.

42. Rumors concerning preparations for a revolt of African Americans—gathered in what were designated "Eleanor clubs" (an allusion to Eleanor Roosevelt)—were one sign among others of the intensity of race relations; these rumors were studied in Odum (1943).

43. See the report written in 1935 by Frazier, who was research director for the research commission: *The Complete Report of Mayor LaGuardia's Commission* (1969). Some whites participated in the riot alongside African Americans, and the report, consequently, was not characterized as a race riot. The difference in behavior with respect to the Chicago riot of 1919—in 1935 it was African Americans who instigated it—is evidently suggestive of the scale of transformations going on in the black community.

44. See McKee (1993): 258–260. Louis Wirth, who was very active in associations opposed to racial discrimination starting in the 1940s, participated for a time in the administrative council of the National Association of Intergroup Relations Officials.

45. Hirsch (1983): 17.

46. Yinger (1968): 135; see also Wright (1967).
47. *Report of the National Advisory Commission on Civil Disorders*: 112.
48. Hughes (1963b).
49. Stanfield (1985): 61–96; D. Fisher (1993): 53–54. A quick presentation of the involvement of foundations in issues of relations between racial and ethnic groups can be found in Nielsen (1972): 332–344.
50. Stanfield (1985): 76.
51. *Proceedings of the Staff Meeting of the Laura Spelman Rockefeller Foundation*, August 24–27, 1927, quoted ibid.
52. The level of funding gave a measure of real, but limited, importance accorded to Fisk by the Laura Spelman Rockefeller Foundation: before 1929 Fisk University received less than half the support accorded to the University of North Carolina, which itself received less than a seventh of the funding attributed to the University of Chicago; the basic data can be found in Bulmer (1982).
53. Stanfield (1985): 100.
54. Ibid.: 124–126.
55. Ibid.: 87–90. Some studies on agriculture gave rise to what were then well-known works of sociology: Vance (1932); Raper (1936). Studies on industry were centered on the hiring of black workers in the metallurgical and meat industries, and on their relations with unions; see Cayton, Mitchell (1939).
56. C. Johnson (1941).
57. Frazier (1940a).
58. A. Davis, Dollard (1940). One study focused on Chicago youths: Warner, Junker, Adams (1941). A later study was entrusted to another black sociologist, Ira De Augustine Reid (1940).
59. See Flack (1969).
60. Lagemann (1989): 123. I quote here the first formulation of the project, in 1935.
61. Stanfield (1985): 161–184; see also Frazier (1944b), which gives a public version of Frazier's judgment. Several reports written for Myrdal were later published. Various sociologists were involved in different ways in this research, including Richard Sterner, a Swedish statistician, and Arnold Rose, a young American sociologist. Samuel Stouffer replaced Myrdal during his voyage to Sweden during the war. Detailed analyses of the conditions of the production of Myrdal's research can be found in Lagemann (1989): 123–146; Jackson (1990). Southern (1987) examines the interpretations of these analyses.
62. Stanfield (1985): 108.
63. Stanfield (1984): 132–133.
64. Adorno, Frenkel-Brunswick, Levinson, Sanford (1950). This study was funded by the American Jewish Committee. The Rockefeller Foundation funded other studies in this domain starting in 1946, but their results were not published until the end of the period taken into account here. The events of the early 1960s sparked a new wave of studies, partly funded by official commissions and the government.
65. Shore (1987): 256–260.
66. The Works Progress Administration directly supported different groups of intellectual workers and thus contributed to the (at least supplementary) funding of studies.
67. Some of Stouffer's research on African Americans in the army was funded by the army and by the Rockefeller Foundation; see D. Fisher (1993): 187–189.
68. While Park evokes the case of American Indians in only one of his later articles, the notes for his courses attest that he was not ignorant of it.
69. I have not made use of another available source: Park's papers—especially his course notes—that have been preserved at Chicago and at Fisk University.

70. Among the fairly specific analyses of Park's essays, see Lyman (1972); Matthews (1997); Lal (1990). Park's articles prior to his recruitment into sociology have a clearly very different character than his later texts, but nothing indicates that they were read by social science researchers. One of the changes sometimes noted in Park's analyses concerns his increasing insistence upon race conflicts and their effects.

71. On the characterization of the regime of segregation in the South, see Woodward (1974). The notion of folk society—which Redfield developed—was honed by Park in a 1931 essay: in it, Park opposes societies marked by change—those of the cities—with those that were immobile (folk societies). In these latter, "All the activities of life tend to be controlled by custom and to conform to the normal expectation of the community. In an immobile society, personal and social relations tend to assume a formula and ceremonial character. Social status is fixed by tradition, social distances are maintained by social ritual and etiquette" (Park [1931b] [in *Race and Culture*: 11]).

72. Park (1913b) (in *Race and Culture*: 204–220).

73. In a 1918 article, Park, however, still half-substantifies the idea of race by using a formula for which he would later be reproached, that of a "racial temperament" acquired through experience that had made the black race "the lady among the races" (*Race and Culture*: 280)—a claim that would later shock not only black intellectuals, perhaps above all, as Fred Matthews suggests, because of the connotation of gender; see also on this point Drake (1984): lvl. This claim was certainly less shocking to Frazier, since he employed it in one of his later books, restricting it to the middle class (Frazier [1957a]: 221). It is also necessary to recall that similar phrases can be found in Du Bois (see Meier [1963]: 194). Olivier Cox (1901–1974), a radical black sociologist who spent time at the University of Chicago in the 1930s, interprets Park's position as implicitly marked by an only partial emancipation from ambient racism: "I have become convinced, from my personal association with and study of these men [Ellsworth Faris, William Ogburn, and Robert Park], that they were profound liberals in the sense in which that term is currently defined by direct-action leaders. They were men possessed of praiseworthy attitudes towards Negroes, but still strongly opposed to any definition of them as fully equal to whites; they were willing to do many things *for* Negroes but sternly opposed to Negroes taking such initiative as would move them along faster than a *proper* space" (Cox [1965]: 11).

74. *Encyclopedia Britannica* (11th edition) 19 (1911): 344–345; this article was written by an assistant at the British Museum.

75. Odum completely abandoned this point of view after 1918 and was, in the 1930s, one of the spokespeople of the liberals of the South.

76. Park (1913b) (in *Race and Culture*: 207).

77. Ibid.: 208–209.

78. Quoted in Strickland (1966): 40.

79. Park (1913b) (in *Race and Culture*: 213).

80. Ibid.: 215–218.

81. Park (1939b) (in *Race and Culture*: 81–116).

82. Ibid.: (in *Race and Culture*: 81).

83. Ibid.: 83.

84. Ibid.: 101.

85. Park (1944).

86. Here I paraphrase the formulation found in an article by Park (1926a) (in *Race and Culture*: 254).

87. Park (1939b) (in *Race and Culture*: 106). The insecurity of African Americans struck Park early. An autobiographical fragment contains the following remark: "the thing that impressed me most, however, was the tragic insecurity—as it seemed to me then under which colored people lived" (AREPA, file 1: 3).

88. Park (1928a) (in *Race and Culture*: 243).

89. Park (1937a) (in *Race and Culture*: 186).

90. Park (1943) (in *Race and Culture*: 311).

91. See especially Park, Burgess (1924): 722. The religious dimension present in the later use of Indianists is absent from Park and Warner's definitions.

92. The first formulation of this type of analyses is found in Warner (1936); see also B. Gardner, M. Gardner, Davis (1941).

93. This point is explicit in Warner, Junker, Adams ([1941]: 10–12), as well as a short time later in the methodological note of Warner for *Black Metropolis* by Drake and Cayton ([1945]: 781).

94. Park (1939b) (in *Race and Culture*: 114, 116).

95. Letter reproduced by Cayton in his obituary for Park published in the *Pittsburgh Courier*, February 26, 1944.

96. See the preface to Pierson's book (1942) resulting from a 1937 dissertation (Park [1942]). On Pierson's lasting influence on Brazilian sociology, see Brochier (2016): 42–61.

97. See the preface to the book by R. Adams (1937) on intermarriage in Hawaii (Park [1937b]).

98. Park (1923a). Park wrote other reviews over the course of the 1920s on books by authors linked to the Harlem Renaissance, particularly for the *American Journal of Sociology*.

99. Park wrote a preface for the book by Gosnell (1935) on this subject: see Park (1935).

100. Park (1926a) (in *Race and Culture*: 249).

101. By here reading Park's analyses in reference to later historical studies, I obviously do not postulate that they depend less than Park's analyses on the society and the circumstances that gave rise to them.

102. However, the MA thesis of Guy Johnson in 1922 focused on the reappearance of the Ku Klux Klan in the South (see also G. Johnson [1923]); this reappearance was followed two or three years later by the establishment of the Ku Klux Klan in the North that does not seem to have been studied by the Chicago sociologists.

103. The only allusion to these types of factors of transformation of race relations can be found in a remark in the preface to the book by R. Adams; see Park (1937b) (in *Race and Culture*: 195).

104. For a description centered on this aspect of slavery, see Elkins (1959).

105. Park (1926b) (in *Race and Culture*: 149–151). For presentations of Park's sociology of relations between races centered on this cycle, see Lyman (1972); Matthews (1977); Steinberg (1981). Among the rare exceptions figure Wacker (1975), perhaps more explicit than Wacker (1983); Lal (1986; 1990); Kivisto (2004).

106. The indeterminate character of the timetable is one of Lyman's arguments supporting that the race relations cycle is not a theory that could be subjected to verification, which is obviously true.

107. Park (1930b): 281.

108. Ibid.: 283.

109. Ibid.: 282.

110. The meaning of the term "assimilation" was no more fixed fifteen years later, as evinced by the fact that a major journal like *Social Forces* could still accept an article (Woolston [1945]) culminating in its definition. The terminology was not fixed, if it ever was, before the publication of the book by Gordon ([1964]: 60–83), which relies on the historical experience acquired over the course of a longer period.

111. Park (1926b) (in *Race and Culture*: 151). The importance for Park of the model of the Hawaiian Islands is, to my knowledge, clearly recognized only by Smith, Killian (1974): 199.

112. Park, undated manuscript (between 1930 and 1944), AREPA, file 5: 2.

113. Frazier (1950): 414. Frazier criticizes the tendency of Park's students, contrary to what he himself saw as Park's intentions, to transform the propositions he had advanced into revealed truths rather than verifying them. I am unaware which specific student he has in mind. When Frazier picked up

the idea of a cycle in one of his books, he also chose the version proposed by Bogardus and not that of Park; see Frazier (1949a): 692.

114. Myrdal was also one of the first to insist upon the criticism of the race relations cycle; see Myrdal, Sterner, Rose (1944): 1025–1064.

115. Vander Zanden (1973): 44.

116. I leave to the side another important theme of Park's essays: that of personality type induced by migrations and the resulting cultural conflicts, which is to say the theme, borrowed from Simmel, of the marginal man, "the first cosmopolite and citizen of the world" (Park [1928b] [in *Race and Culture*: 354]).

117. Park (1917).

118. Ibid. (in *Race and Culture*: 227).

119. Park (1925) (in *Human Communities*: 176).

120. AECH, file 20: 10.

121. Frazier (1940b): 785.

122. One of the rare utilizations of the term "caste" can be found regarding the difference between slaves working in agriculture and domestic slaves, comparing whose status was higher: see Doyle (1937): 74.

123. Ibid.: 169.

124. One of the first studies to insist upon these conflicts came out just after Doyle's book: Aptheker (1943).

125. The author of the preface to the 1971 edition of Doyle's book, Artur Sheps, argues (p. vii) that the study had been set aside as "a study in Uncle Tomism." No reviews that I have consulted—in the *American Sociological Review*, in *Social Forces*, in the *Journal of Negro History*, and in *Opportunity*—directly confirm this interpretation. It is, however, completely possible that this reaction was not expressed publicly.

126. Doyle does not seem to have benefited from financial support other than the indirect support of a scholarship accorded by one of the Rockefeller foundations.

127. Johnson (1934): 103.

128. Ibid.: 209.

129. Ibid.: 104.

130. Ibid.: 104.

131. Ibid.: 128.

132. Ibid.: 150.

133. Ibid.: 151.

134. Ibid.: 179.

135. This report—Johnson, Embree, Alexander (1935)—is presented as the synthesis of ongoing research, funded principally and in secret by the Rockefeller Foundation, according to Stanfield (1985): 128.

136. Johnson (1934): 212.

137. A letter from Park to Johnson suggests that the former was not familiar with the book until it had been completed.

138. Johnson (1941): 71–78.

139. Ibid.: 327.

140. *Growing Up in the Black Belt* also includes an appendix written by the psychoanalyst Harry Stack Sullivan, who played an advisory role for the study, alongside the anthropologist Hortense Powdermaker.

141. Du Bois (1899).

142. Ibid.: 309–321 (see especially p. 311). It was regarding the leisure activities of African Americans that Du Bois developed this picture of social classes, while also seeking to rectify it with the ordinary perception of the period, which did not see the black population as anything but an undifferentiated mass. In a later study in 1902, Du Bois categorized the black population by professional group.

143. In their generation, aside from Johnson and Frazier, only Ira De Augustine Reid (1901–1968), Johnson's successor as the secretary of the Urban League who had obtained a PhD at Columbia and was chair of the Department of Sociology at the University of Atlanta in the 1930s, also gained a national reputation in sociology. Two other black sociologists would later hold prominent, but less academic, positions: Horace Cayton for his book with Saint Clair Drake on the black community of Chicago—Cayton did not make a career in sociology, although he participated in the community of sociologist—and Olivier Cox, a sociologist of Jamaican origin, who in 1938 obtained a PhD at the University of Chicago and gained some visibility through his vehement critiques of the works of Park, Warner, and Ruth Benedict.

Biographical elements concerning Frazier can be found in the dissertation of Grace Harris (1975), in the testimonies of Arthur Davis (1962) and Horace Cayton (1964), as well as in the book by Anthony Platt (1991). Platt, however, adopted an interpretation of Frazier's work that somewhat minimized his relationship with the sociologists of the Chicago tradition. This interpretation accorded poorly with Frazier's research themes—such as the study of the family and the church in his last book—as well as with his address as president of the American Sociological Society: see Frazier (1949b).

144. Cayton (1964); A. P. Davis (1962). The social futures of Frazier's siblings, who went on to careers that included a lawyer, a doctor, and a nurse, confirms the well-groundedness of this interpretation.

145. On Frazier's political opinions and his reactions to practices of racial discrimination, see Harris (1975): 26–27, 40–41; A. Platt (1991): 29–30, 53–56, 181–186.

146. Frazier's MA thesis was titled *New Currents of Thoughts among the Colored People of America*.

147. During the period in which Frazier was at Howard, this university was host to a notable portion of the principle black intellectuals of his generation: the economist Abram Harris, who along with the anthropologist Allison Davis was one of the first African Americans to be hired by the University of Chicago as a full professor, the philosopher Alain Locke, the historians Rayford Logan and John Hope Franklin, the critic Sterling Brown, the political scientist Ralph Bunche, etc.

148. Frazier (1939; 1949a).

149. Bahr, Johnson, Setz (1971).

150. Frazier (1925). This article, which appears in Alain Locke's volume on the "new Negro" who led the Harlem Renaissance, is not based on systematic evidence. One might doubt that it aroused much interest among the broad audience for which it was intended.

151. Frazier (1929). The comparison of this article with the preceding one also suggests that the politico-moral critique of the black bourgeoisie that was the subject of one of Frazier's last books, in 1955, was not the result of a momentary mood.

152. Frazier (1944a): 314 [© University of Chicago Press].

153. Frazier (1932): 178.

154. Ibid.

155. Frazier (1930).

156. Ibid.: 737.

157. Frazier (1932): 32.

158. Ibid.: 45.

159. Ibid.: 47.

160. On the list of books quoted in the principal American journals between 1944 and 1968 assembled by Bahr, Johnson, Setz (1971), this book figures in eighth place, accompanied by another book by Frazier, *The Negro in the United States* (1949a).

161. Burgess (1939): ix.

162. Even in the mid-1960s, historians did not always follow a very different approach: see for example the description of the community (and the families) of African Americans in South Carolina in Williamson (1965): 300–325.

163. Frazier (1939): 41.

164. Ibid.: 170.

165. Ibid.: 172.

166. Frazier (1949a): 680. This is also what Hughes claimed in an essay written in 1955 but published in 1961 (SE: 171).

167. For a well-argued criticism of the interpretations given by Frazier and Johnson on the place of women in the black family as being the legacy of slavery and not African heritage, see Herskovits (1941): 167–182. On the reception of Herskovits's book, especially among Boasian anthropologists, see Jackson (1990): 120–124.

168. A. Platt (1991): 136.

169. See Blassingame (1972); Levine (1977); Stuckey (1977); Raboteau (1978): 48–60, which proposes a nuanced assessment of the respective limits of Frazier and Herskovits's interpretations in terms of religion; Sobel (1987).

170. The principal argument concerning Frazier's evidence on the matrifocal family can be found in Gutman (1976): 633–634.

171. Frazier (1939): 96.

172. Gutman (1976): 461–475.

173. Moynihan (1965).

174. A. Platt (1991): 111–120.

175. Valentine (1968).

176. Frazier (1939): 374.

177. Frazier (ibid.: 394) evokes the changes that had been ongoing since 1914, remarking that there then existed a small minority of old families (different through their skin color, the age of their genealogy, their culture) and the immense minority of the black population.

178. Frazier (1949b).

179. This criticism was developed by Blumer (1958). The studies of two of Blumer's students, Lohman and Reitzes (1952; 1954), offer empirical justifications in support of Blumer's criticisms.

180. Frazier (1949b): 6.

181. See Lopata (1954), as well as the two books that later resulted from this dissertation, in 1976 and 1996.

182. Vlasek's (1982) interpretation of Frazier's essays distinguishes two conceptions of assimilation different from what he would later adopt over the course of his career.

183. Frazier (1949a): 693.

184. Ibid.: 696.

185. Ibid.: 695.

186. Frazier (1957a). This book, published in French before English (Frazier [1955]), was perceived as engaged and bitter. Chapter 10 offers an excellent testament, in which we see the shadow of Charles Johnson, to the experience of the connection of black intellectuals of the period to the white world.

187. Frazier (1955b): 370.

188. Frazier (1962): 139.

189. Wirth (1945).

190. Matthews (1987) analyzes Wirth's position as that of an assimilationist, and as such explains the rapid decline of his reputation after 1952. This interpretation seems to me to be too exclusively attentive to the sympathies Wirth displayed by Wirth, as well as overestimating the coherence of his positions.

191. See Hughes (1963a)—an article written in 1952—as well as Hughes (1948). The version given by Hughes of having received funding is confirmed by Shore (1987): 198.

192. Miner (1939).

193. The list of pertinent cases evoked a posteriori by Hughes is longer and more subtle: Hughes (1963a) (SE: 538) also wonders if it would not have been more worthwhile to begin by studying one of the cities in northern Quebec in which new industries were being established and that lacked a Francophone middle class.

194. For purposes of comparison, Hughes went to study the place of contacts between Catholic workers and Protestant business executives of the Rhine; see Hughes (1935).

195. Persons ([1987]: 145–146) considers this questioning of Park's sociology as radical, and consequently interprets Hughes's return to Chicago as the end of the Chicago sociology of ethnic relations in its previous definition.

196. The evolution of Drummondville until the present day has been very different from that which seemed to be emerging on the eve of 1940: the Anglophones, textile industry executives who had contributed to the evolution of the linguistic frontier, would almost completely abandon the region before 1970, according to evidence that I collected during a short visit in 1998.

197. See Hughes (1946a; 1946b; 1949); E. Hughes, H. Hughes (1952).

198. AECH, file 98: 10.

199. Hughes (1946a).

200. J. Williams (1949); Hale (1949); G. Edwards (1952).

201. Blumer (1965).

202. Ibid.: 253.

203. Blumer (1958) proposes an overall panorama of studies in the domain of race relations, which includes the subdomains that Blumer designated as "prejudice" and "discrimination," which were conducted by social psychologists.

204. Myrdal (1944): 1009.

205. One of Park's last articles (*Race and Culture* [1943]: 310–311) expressed, to the contrary, great skepticism that the knowledge of social science could contribute to the resolution of racial conflicts. This corresponded to Park's experience, as we have seen, but not to that of many of his students, such as Charles Johnson.

206. See Higham (1975): 218–219.

207. Blumer (1958): 438.

208. The interest sparked shortly thereafter by the book of Adorno, Frenkel-Brunswick, Levinson, Sanford (1950) on the authoritarian personality also contributed to this orientation, although it did not focus on the case of black Americans.

209. See Frazier (1949a): 1, 11; Blumer (1958). Blumer was, during this period, the most radical and constant critic of studies of attitudes. An initial challenge, on an empirical basis, of this field of study can be found in the article by Richard LaPiere (1934), which later became famous.

210. Rossi (1964); Blauner (1970); Metzger (1971); Lyman (1972). The term "failure" is repeated in the recent book by McKee (1993).

211. The essay by Singer (1962) was published almost simultaneously with that of Hughes. It went unnoticed at first, but its orientation seemed premonitory due to its call for African Americans to claim an ethnic identity, as well as the essay by Back (1963).

212. Hughes (1963b). According to his correspondence (1961 letter to Herbert Gans, in AECH, file 124: 11), Hughes had previously envisaged devoting his presidential address to a completely different subject: professional careers. One might think that his final choice was influenced by current events.

213. Ibid. (SE: 478).

214. Hughes here alludes to his opposition to the symbolic name change of the American Sociological Society, which expressed his hostility toward demands for the recognition of sociologists as collectively forming a profession, with the pretense correlated to controlling a sector of activity.

215. Ibid.: 494 [© Transaction Books, 1984].

216. Ibid.: 492.

217. Hughes (1967). This text remains unpublished in accordance with its author's wishes.
218. Glazer (1963).
219. The correspondence of Hughes gives examples of the ignorance, at the end of the 1960s, of Park's analyses among sociologists who specialized in the subject and were then in the middle of their careers (such as Tumin, Bressler, or Glock); see AECH, file 96: 9.
220. Steinberg (1995): 62.

9. ON THE MARGINS OF THE CHICAGO TRADITION: NELS ANDERSON AND DONALD ROY

1. Iverson (1977).
2. Thompson (1970).
3. On Frank Tannenbaum, see chapter 7. Taking this case account allows for a demonstration of the contribution of Pragmatism to the point of view of the Chicago sociologists on the empirical investigation of the social world.
4. Kincheloe (1972: 1989).
5. There is no information available to me regarding all sociologists trained at the University of Chicago exhaustive enough to support the claim that none of them had a social origin and experience comparable to those of Anderson and Roy. However, they were the only ones of their generation always cited by those who knew them to belong to a separate world.
6. Some of the evidence concerning Anderson was accessible to me thanks to Allan McDonell, to whom I owe the initial information that drove me to study this example in greater detail. Through his intervention, I gathered, in May 1993, the testimonies of several friends of Nels Anderson at the University of New Brunswick—Hugh Lautard, Noel Iverson, David Rehorick, Brent McKeown, and Frank Wilson—for which I thank him. An early version of this analysis, different on many points on account of it predating my perusal of Anderson's notes that were preserved in the Burgess archives, can be found in Chapoulie (1998).
7. In 1993, when the book's French translation was published, it was treated as a typical monograph.
8. Anderson (1961; 1972; 1980–1981; 1982; 1983). I have also made use of a letter from Anderson to B. Y. Card of Brigham Young University, preserved in the Department of Sociology of the University of New Brunswick.
9. See the introduction to the papers Nels Anderson left the library archives of the University of Utah, which give a rather precise chronology (although it includes at least one error) of the movements and the jobs of Nels Anderson. I here mention only a small portion of them.
10. Compared with the anecdotes Anderson recounted to his friends, his biographical essays seem to have somewhat understated the difficulty of his living conditions over the course of these years.
11. Anderson (1972).
12. See Carey (1975): 47. The classmate with the social background least different from Anderson's was probably Guy Brown. Anderson later claimed that Brown had a certain familiarity with the hobos who worked in the countryside, and together they collected and published the biography of a migrant worker reliant on social services.
13. Testimony of Guy Johnson in IJTC. According to what he later told his colleagues at the University of New Brunswick (although it seems not very believable), during a "down and out" period Anderson lived for one winter in a Chicago prison, thanks to the benevolence of a judge. Some of his classmates would be surprised to discover him incarcerated during a visit to the prison led by one of their professors.
14. Anderson (1975): 164–165 [© E. J. Brill, Leiden, 1975].

15. See the testimony of Harriet and Ernest Mowrer in IJTC. Robert Faris ([1970]: 66) reports that some years later another student of sociology at the University of Chicago was unsuccessful in collecting biographies of hobos using a religious mission as intermediary.

16. Anderson (1961 [1923]): 173. On the biography of Reitman, see Bruns (1987).

17. Reitman (1937).

18. I doubt, but have not been able to formally establish, that this was a common name for this neighborhood at the time. Zorbaugh (1929), who studied it in part, does not use it, and the term appears neither in the index of the book by Bruns (1987) nor in that of the history of the development of the city of Chicago by Mayer, Wade (1969). The term was perhaps introduced in 1917 in an article by a journalist, of which an excerpt appeared, on Park's suggestion, as an epigraph to *The Hobo*.

19. Anderson (1961): xii.

20. Anderson collected approximately four hundred questionnaires during a stay in the region of Salt Lake City and around sixty biographies in Chicago. A significant amount of the evidence from which he wrote his book has been preserved in AEWB, file 126: 11, and file 127: 1 and 2. I have found no indication of the reasons for the absence of certain originals of the documents that appear in the book. Two of these documents were published in Anderson (1998).

21. Anderson (1972). The point is confirmed by a 1967 letter from Anderson to Hughes (AECH, folder 24) and another to Raushenbush (AREPA, folder 6: 6).

22. In 1923, there was still only one project in the series. Various testimonies suggest that Park, perhaps the only leader approached for the series, was expecting Thrasher's book on youth gangs. It was in 1926 that another book explicitly mentions *The Hobo* as belonging to this series, according to what I have been able to discern from examining the available original editions.

23. Anderson (1975): 169.

24. The category "homeless" is imprecisely defined, as revealed by the later evolutions of the phenomenon and the usage of the term in the United States. In 1922, the homeless in Chicago lived in hotels when they had the means, in different shelters and asylums organized by charitable associations, in makeshift housing, or, in the summer, in camps on the shores of Lake Michigan.

25. Anderson (1961): xii. Small's reaction does not surprise me: in opposition to many of sociology's founders, and also to what the speculative character of his own publications suggests, many testimonies insist that he was convinced of the necessity of empirical investigation.

26. *Ninth New Collegiate Dictionary*, 1983.

27. Montgomery (1987): 78.

28. Montgomery (1987) makes only one allusion to hobos, as do Rodgers ([1974]: 227) and Dubofsky ([1969]: 438). This last book focuses on the Industrial Workers of the World (IWW), one of the major attempts to organize workers of the period 1905–1925. The IWW is briefly mentioned by Anderson in his book and analyzes the unsuccessful attempts of organizing the types of workers typically included in the category of hobos, especially agricultural workers and butchers, see Anderson (1961) [1923]: 174–175; 292–293; 313–315; 446–448. In Spence (1971) can be found a description of the category of hobos, the unspecified sources of which include Anderson's three books on the subject.

29. Rodgers (1974): 285.

30. See Bruns (1987): 22. Anderson himself cites an example of this deprecatory usage (which he does not remark upon) of the term hobo in an excerpt of an official report: "their ambitions and hopes go to pieces, and they gradually sink into the ranks of migratory and casual workers. Continuing their existence in these ranks they begin to lose self-respect and become 'hobos'" (Anderson [1961] [1923]: 65).

31. James Eads How (1874–c. 1930) belonged to a family of railroad and public works industrialists. He studied theology and then attended Harvard and Oxford before coming into contact with the Fabian Society. He left some of his inheritance to "those who had earned it" (in his own phrasing) and spearheaded various social justice activities.

32. Bruns ([1987]: 44–45) indicates neither the date nor the precise reference, but this is evidently a document preserved in the Reitman papers. Jacob Coxey (1854–1942), a public works contractor from Ohio, had earned the title of "General" in 1894 by organizing a march on Washington of workers demanding a policy of funding road construction with the goal of providing jobs to unemployed migrant workers during the economic depression of 1893–1894.

33. Anderson (1975): 163.

34. Anderson (1961) [1923]: 87.

35. AEWB, folder 126, documents 150, 46, 75.

36. Anderson (1975): 167.

37. AEWB, folder 126, document 73.

38. This was a photocopied print run of a small number of copies of the 1930 book accompanied by a short preface, intended for some friends of the University of New Brunswick.

39. Anderson (1975): 167 [© E. J. Brill, Leiden, 1975].

40. Park (1929): 8 (in *Human Communities*: 78; Grafmeyer, Joseph [1979]: 170).

41. Anderson (1961) [1923]: 95.

42. Two of the documents that he wrote are based on his own recollections of the conditions in which he himself, following his elder brother, had left the family home. (His three other brothers would later do the same.) Summarized and revised, these documents (36, pp. 80–81; 40, pp. 83–84) figure in *The Hobo*. Anderson modified the length of his absence—three years instead of two months— according to his handwritten notes. He partly attributes his departure to his fascination with the letters his elder brother wrote to their parents, in which he painted a rosy picture of his poor living conditions.

43. On this point see Anderson (1940): 9–12.

44. According to Anderson's correspondence with Louis Wirth, in ALW, folder 1: 2.

45. Anderson (1940): 17–24. Much later, the book by Douglas Harper (1982)—revised from the last dissertation supervised by Hughes at Brandeis—recalled the continued, but certainly less numerous, existence of vagrant manual laborers in the United States.

46. Park (1921) (in *Society*: 197). This text also appears in *Introduction to the Science of Sociology*.

47. Even in Cressey's case, the model of reference was provided by "The Stranger," an essay by Simmel (1908), more so than by the situation of anthropologists, as shown by an article discovered by Martin Bulmer in the Burgess archives: see P. G. Cressey (1983).

48. Anderson (1961): xxvii–xxix.

49. Even earlier, Anderson had undoubtedly maintained a certain distance with respect to hobos: he wrote in the preface to the 1978 edition of *The Milk and Honey Route*: "But while I lived the migratory life of hobos, who constituted the work force of the frontier, I avoided being identified in any way with hobo culture."

50. Anderson (1983): 403.

51. Shortly thereafter, Anderson considered studying another delicate subject: prostitution. Reitman advised against it, suggesting, "Your sociology friends will not be proud of acquaintance with one who is an expert in vice problems. It is safer to be an expert on poverty, if you don't get too close to the poor" (Anderson [1975]: 173 [© E. J. Brill, Leiden, 1975]).

52. AEWB, folder 127, document 80. The notes on Anderson's visit to gambling halls are not further reproduced in his book.

53. The only allusions to this survey can be found in the documents upon which chapter 1 and pp. 127–128 are based, but Anderson did not reproduce the document, however instructive, that he had written: AEWB, folder 126, documents 37 and 115. Anderson's autobiographical documents make no reference to the collection of this material, which seems to have preceded the collection of the rest of the evidence on the Chicago hobos preserved in the Burgess archives by at least six months.

54. Solenberger (1911).

55. Anderson (1975): 169.
56. Interview with Guy Johnson in IJTC.
57. Anderson (1983): 405.
58. The only allusion appears in the quotation of an excerpt from Park, Miller (1921): Anderson (1961): 82.
59. By contrast, this type of questioning can be found a little later in P. G. Cressey's (1932) monograph on the "taxi-dance halls," which contains among the finest ethnographic analyses published at this time.
60. Anderson (1983): 404.
61. This dissertation, supervised by Harvey Zorbaugh at New York University, focused on the history of a slum neighborhood in Manhattan (Anderson [1975]: 180); its title was *The Migration of the Slum in Manhattan*, according to Pullman (1972).
62. Anderson, Bain, Lundberg (1929).
63. Anderson (1975): 170 [© E. J. Brill, Leiden, 1975; see also Anderson (1982): 14. It seems, however, that Anderson refused an employment offer from the University of Utah, since he wanted to settle in New York.
64. Anderson (1940): 1.
65. Anderson (1975): 171–177.
66. Thanks to William Thomas, Anderson first taught for a time at the New School for Social Research. A little later, he taught at Columbia University.
67. Anderson (1942).
68. I have borrowed the essence of these biographical indications from Pullman (1982) and testimonies that I collected at the University of New Brunswick.
69. Anderson (1975): 183 [© E. J. Brill, Leiden, 1975]. On many occasions in his correspondence, Anderson expressed regret at not having found an academic position; see, for example, a letter to Louis Wirth from 1945, in ALW, folder 1: 2.
70. Anderson's prolific output contrasts with the meager production of a substantial number of sociologists trained at Chicago, who, like Zorbaugh and Thrasher, hardly wrote after 1930.
71. For the collection of evidence upon which these analyses are based, I owe a particular debt to Howard S. Becker, who alerted me to the existence of these archives. I have also benefited from the generous assistance of Thomas Harkins, archivist at Duke University.
72. See ADR, folder M, at Duke University, where Roy spent almost all of his career as a sociologist. This folder notably includes a memorandum from Roy's second wife (presenting herself as his cousin), which seems to me to contain several minor inaccuracies, some testimonies of Roy's childhood friends that she solicited, and some of Roy's letters that contained autobiographical content. The folder also contains a summary of Roy's activities and publications established by Huw Beynon, an English sociologist who was his friend and who collaborated in the initial classification of Roy's archives. This material can be complemented by a close reading of Roy's dissertation, his articles, and some of his lectures. I have also made use of Roy's correspondence with Hughes, in AECH, folder 53, especially a letter by Roy from July 1, 1946, as well as the testimonies of Howard Becker and Edward Tiryakan. The differences between these diverse sources are limited.
73. A confirmation of this obsession can also be found in Roy (1959): he reports that the workers with whom he worked joked about his farm.
74. ADR, folder G. There were about fifty-five thousand homeless in Seattle at the time. Roy had himself registered as homeless. I have found no trace of any direct contact between Roy and Anderson. I have, however, mentioned, without insisting one way or another, some points of coincidence between their lives.
75. Lundberg and Queen were two of the leaders of the operationalist current in sociology, and Hayner was a former student of Park whose research related to urban ecology. In 1937, the University of Wisconsin counted another of Park's students, Edgar Thompson, as visiting professor.
76. An article was adapted from this thesis: Roy (1939).

77. Like Anderson, Roy envisaged undertaking a literary career: on two occasions, he wrote novels, one of which was inspired by the study of Hooverville.
78. Letter to Hughes of July 1, 1946, in AECH, folder 53: 6–7.
79. Whyte ([1994]: 116–119) describes this training without mentioning Roy (or any other sociology students who participated in it).
80. ADR, folder L, lecture from April 1956 titled "Suggestions on Non-Academic Training for Industrial Research."
81. Roy left his job as a machine operator during a staff reduction, although the company had offered to transfer him to another workshop; see Roy (1952a): 53.
82. Roy was not the only sociologist of this generation of Chicago graduates to have worked as a factory worker: this was also the case for Orvis Collins—who, as we have seen, wrote at least one article on blue-collar labor—and probably for Robert Habenstein as well.
83. Roy (1959; 1974).
84. Roy (1950), in ADR, folder L.
85. An article resulted from this collective reflection: Collins, Dalton, Roy (1946); and some of the analyses of Whyte (1955).
86. In a letter to Thompson, April 29, 1950 (in ADR, folder M), Hughes displayed unusual enthusiasm in his assessment of Roy's characteristics: "I don't think you will be disappointed in Don Roy. I have been through his thesis mss again, and it verges on genius. As to being cocky, I can understand this as an impression from some of his manners. The odd thing is that, in fact, he is quite timid."
87. See, for example, Goffman (1959) or Becker (1963).
88. ADR, folder M.
89. Gilman (1956).
90. ADR, folder L.
91. Roy (1952a): 3.
92. In the preface to the second edition of Mathewson's book on the same subject—the limitation of production by laborers—initially published in 1931, Roy indicates the two knew each other in 1945. However, neither his dissertation nor his articles from the 1950s include any reference to this book.
93. In a summary of his dissertation (ADR, folder G), Roy evokes, without distancing himself, an interpretation of the relations between employers and laborers in terms of social disorganization "in the sense of Sutherland." This confirms what I previously suggested as to Roy's influence on the analyses of sociologists of the Chicago tradition.
94. Roy (1952a): 36.
95. P. Young (1939).
96. Roy (1952a): 40.
97. The only precise explication of this point is found in Roy (1952a): 80.
98. See H. Harris (1982).
99. Roy (1952a): 99.
100. Ibid.: 311, 339, 208, 224–227.
101. Roy (1953): 508.
102. Roy (1954).
103. Roy (1952a): 23 [rights reserved].
104. Roy (2006b); I found this article, written in 1954 in ADR, folder L. Its translation into French, published in Roy (2006a), led to its publication in English thanks to Howard Becker.
105. See Burawoy (1979), as well as the critical review published by Roy (1980) in which he compares his results with those of Burawoy.
106. Roy cites two other articles on the stereotypical perception of "inferior" groups by "superior" groups on multiple occasions: an article by Copeland (1939) on the relationship between blacks and whites, and an article by Weinberg (1942) on the relationship between prisoners and guards.

107. Notes preserved in his archives confirm Roy's attention and sensitivity to class differences. In his field notes, he criticizes Warner for being primarily interested in forms of social participation and neglecting the study of access to the basic tools that assured the survival of the working class, as well as the domain of class interactions (ADR, folder F).

108. Roy (1970): 220.

109. Letter to Hughes, March 5, 1956, in AECH, folder 53 (the phrase in italics was underlined by Roy).

110. Letter to Hughes, January 13, 1956, in AECH, folder 53. (the phrase in italics was underlined by Roy). Roy's interest in the working class sometimes seems to have been accompanied by an interest in the upper classes, as evidenced by various details, beginning with the thesis of a student on the upper classes of Philadelphia, which is preserved in Roy's archives.

111. Gouldner (1962).

112. Roy's references in this matter always remained the same, notably including Mary Parker Follett, as well as the social experiments organized by the ex-union leader Joe Scanlon (who had, thanks to active labor participation, brought about a substantial increase in productivity in a steel mill threatened by closure) and by James Lincoln, the president of a company that produced electrical equipment.

113. Roy (1962) (in ADR, folder L).

114. Roy (1978) (in ADR, folder G).

115. ADR, folder F.

CONCLUSION

1. Hughes (1952) (SE: 299).

2. Burke (1935): 49.

3. Wittgenstein (1991): 26–28.

4. The term "Chicago tradition," such as it is used by those who recognize themselves as part of it—see for example Fisher, Strauss (1978)—seems to me less likely to encourage a rigid characterization in abstract terms: in sociology, as in other domains, there was more than one way in which one could be affiliated with a tradition. There also exist more flexible use of the concept of a school, such as that resulting from the analyses of Abbott (1999). However, their subtlety risks being lost in later borrowings.

5. Goffman (1983): 16–17.

6. It would be possible here to compare sociological works and the publications of various journalists or essayists, who often had a background in the world that they studied. I doubt that many cases can be found in which researchers specializing in a domain in sociology were frontrunners in noticing new phenomena and publishing books or articles on these subjects that reached a relatively wide audience.

7. I have demonstrated a comparable phenomenon in the new beginnings of French sociology after 1945; see Chapoulie (1991).

8. For an archetypal example of this type of characterization, see Faught (1980).

9. As Howard S. Becker once suggested to me during a conversation, if one wishes to use the term "school" for the Chicago sociologists, the characterization of a "school of activities," as defined by Gilmore (1988) regarding the musical world, certainly works the best.

10. Veyne (1971).

11. Gusfield (1984): 48 [© Ablex Publishing Corp., Norwood, NJ, 1984].

12. I have expanded more broadly upon the question of the relationship of the Chicago tradition to French sociology in Chapoulie (2008).

13. The first translation of a book by William James into French was published in 1903, followed by several others before 1914, but their reception was unenthusiastic. The first translation of a book by Dewey did not appear until 1922. Peirce was neglected in France for even longer.

14. For a later example, see the difficulty encountered by a Belgian researcher in obtaining characterizations using principles that he deemed satisfactory from several researchers trained at Chicago in the 1940s and 1950s: Verhoeven (1995): 100–148.

15. Blumer (1969a). There were more references in Blumer's (1928) dissertation, but it was not published. There are surely other exceptions to sociologists' indifference to the Chicago tradition with respect to the abstract formulation of their approach. Anselm Strauss, starting in the 1970s, attempted to explain the connection to pragmatism in several essays; see Strauss (1964); Fisher, Strauss (1978); and especially Strauss (1996b). As his personal papers and course plans demonstrate, Donald Roy was also very conscientious of the formulation of the philosophical foundation of his approach.

16. I have some hesitations in using the label "Marxist" to encapsulate fundamentally heterogeneous orientations whose point of commonality resides much more in the political and intellectual context of a period than in texts—i.e., the works of Marx—that would serve as guideposts. It seems to me, and has seemed to me for thirty years, that if circumstances had been different the intellectual dispositions of the majority of French philosophers would have found elsewhere than with Marxism a line of argument to challenge any approach to social phenomena that gave a central place to empirical investigation. Marxism such as it has been interpreted is not an immediately available justification for a perspective that had other reasons for existing. I briefly examine this point in Chapoulie (1991).

17. On the relationship between Halbwachs and the Chicago tradition, see Topalov (2015).

18. On the contacts of Hughes with Friedmann and his circle, see the appendix to the English version, published in 1987, of Chapoulie (1984): 283–286.

19. See, for example, Herpin (1973) and Chapoulie (1973)—these two publications focus on works dating from the 1940s to the 1960s—as well as Bertaux (1976). The latter text is an unpublished research report, but it probably contributed more than any other to the spread of interest in the Chicago tradition in France).

20. This was the case for Chombart de Lauwe (1952), and later for Castells (1972), Duchac (1974), and Grafmeyer, Joseph (1979).

21. Lind (1938).

AFTERWORD TO THE ENGLISH TRANSLATION OF *LA TRADITION SOCIOLOGIQUE DE CHICAGO*: HOW SHOULD THE HISTORY OF THE SOCIAL SCIENCES BE WRITTEN?

I thank Jacques Siracusa for his notes on an early version of this afterword.

1. Collini (1999): 387.

2. Hughes (1971): 54.

3. My first reflections on the history of the social sciences can be found in a 2003 text paying homage to Jennifer Platt, later published in an Italian digital journal (Chapoulie 2009) as a precursor to a discussion of the social sciences by Jennifer Platt, Alan Sica, Johan Heilbron, and Daniel Geary. A later reflection can be found in Chapoulie (2005).

4. See Chapoulie (2000; 2001; 2003a; 2003b; 2008a; 2008b; 2017).

5. Throughout the following I set aside the history of the discipline of history, a more frequently discussed domain distinct from the history of the other social science disciplines.

6.   *Les étapes de la pensée sociologique* by Raymond Aron (1967) and *Masters of Sociological Thought* by Lewis Coser (1971) are two frequently read examples of this type of book, issuing from introductory courses. See also, for the United States, Schwendinger & Schwendinger (1974).

7.   For examples, see the contributions on Australian sociology by Dianne J. Austin-Broos and on American sociology by Jonathan H. Turner in the collection edited by Genoy (1989), as well as most of the contributions in the more recent book edited by Calhoun (2007). A superficial critical assessment of the state of the history of sociology before 1980 can be found in Szacki (1981).

8.   For arguments in favor of this type of history, see Seidman (1985); Boudon (1992).

9.   See for example Furner (1975); Haskell (1977), and the judicious critique by Kuklick (1980) of the conceptual scheme underlying books that reintroduce a form of presentism. Biographies of some of those connected to the social sciences, for example Karl (1974), also figure among the first monographs to break free from the conventional narrative. The research conducted by P. F. Lazarsfeld at Columbia University on research methods represents another type of exception: Oberschall (1972).

10. For the case of the history of the natural sciences in the United States, see the reflections of Thomas Kuhn (1971). I omit mention here of the United States's tradition of history of ideas according to Arthur Lovejoy's definition, and the consequences that held for the history of the social sciences. This is presented and discussed in Kelley (1991) following the near-extinction of its initial form.

11. Hollinger (1973: 378). The term "behavioral science" (which generally includes psychology and linguistics) is as common in English as "social science," perhaps because it figures in the title of the principal journal in the field of sociology, the *Journal of the History of Behavioral Sciences*. Here I prefer "social sciences" because my remarks do not pertain to the history of psychology or linguistics. It should be understood that this usage does not exclude those specializations that did not become their own academic disciplines in some national sense, but remained attached to various others, as for example social psychology in France (see Apfelbaum, 1993). To simplify phrasing, the principal reference is made here generally only in the case of sociology.

12. This perspective, adopted in my first article on the history of the ethnographic approach in sociology, was shared by two British sociologists, Martin Bulmer and Jennifer Platt.

13. The expression "history in its own right" is the title given by Fernand Braudel to the last collection of essays by Lucien Febvre (*Pour une histoire à part entière* [Paris: Éditions de l'EHESS, 1982/1962]).

14. To my knowledge, the only critique of the usage of the notion of influence (omnipresent in research of the history of social sciences) regarding painting can be found in Baxandall (1991: 106–111).

15. The critique of the orientation termed "presentist" in historical studies was initially formulated in the context of political history in an essay by the English historian Herbert Butterfield (1931). In the case of sociology, histories of its progress coexisted with a smaller number complaining of its regrettable degradation in the wake of some major work: the logic of questioning is the same.

16. Stocking (1965). The quotations below can be found on pages 215 and 217. The second issue of *Journal of the History of Behavioral Sciences* contains an article on French psychology by a future professor at the Sorbonne, Maurice Reuchlin, which follows the model of the conventional narrative: "The historical background for national trends in psychology: France." Fifteen years later, revivals of Stocking's critique of sociology appeared in the United States thanks to the historian Henrietta Kuklick (1980) and the sociologist Robert Alun Jones (1983). Critiques of the presentist manner of writing history of the social sciences were based on Thomas Kuhn and reflections on the history of the natural sciences, but they may also have relied on the reflections of Lucien Febvre throughout his critical notes, reproduced in *Combats pour l'histoire*: see especially pages 324 and 333 in a 1927 essay, in Febvre (1992: 318–336).

17. An analysis of the obstacles to a historical perspective on the natural sciences in the Anglo-Saxon world can be found in an essay by Stephen Toulmin (1977).

18. On the significance of Kuhn's book for historians, see Hollinger (1973).

19.   Skinner (1969).

20.   The second point is expanded in Chapoulie (2017), chapter 2.

21.   Jacques Roger, "Pour une histoire historienne des sciences" (1984) in Roger (1995: 45–73) (see p. 66 and 57 for the three following quotations). Roger's essay, unique in French scholarship for a long time, describes the state of the history of science before the 1980s. See Pestre (1995) for a more recent treatment of the program of a "history on its own terms" of the sciences, and for an overview of this history since the mid-1980s in a collection edited by Pestre (2015).

22.   I was, however, aware of, without having participated in, the collective undertaking of reflecting upon the history of the social sciences organized in France by Claude Blanckaert, Roger's associate. A preliminary meeting of the researchers took place in 1987. Some of their communications, which concern almost all of the prehistory of the disciplines, were published in issue 54 of *Communications*, in 1992. For a quick history of this collective undertaking, see Blanckaert (1993). See also the contributions to issues 3 and 4 of the fourth series of the *Revue de synthèse* (1988), some of which develop criticisms of the strictly disciplinary frame of the history of social science and its presentism. An overview of the publications issuing from these meetings can be found in Blanckaert (1999). Sociology is not represented among them.

23.   The historical approach has encountered similar obstacles in other areas of history—including education, religion, and medicine—that were also initially the realm of elite members of the fields, frequently in the later stages of their careers. These proposed analyses limited to certain subjects directly linked to a presentist program connected to their position and the professional ideology associated with it.

24.   On the *trade* associated with research activities, see Polanyi (1966), which uses the expression "tacit knowledge."

25.   On this point, see Chapoulie (2017), chapter 2. The conception of science to which the social sciences refer is only a lay version, for which logical empiricism provides the most systematic elaboration. The principal reference for sociologists is an article on the explication by Carl Hempel, also discussed by philosophers of history (reprinted in Hempel [1965]: 331–496).

26.   For an illustration of this difficulty, see the justifications presented by Boudon (1992) in favor of a presentist conception: he sustains that the works of the pantheon of founding fathers that he himself organized constitute a bastion of "solid theories," "robust hypotheses," and "incontestable discoveries"—these two latter expressions seem to apply to the analyses of *Formes élémentaires de la vie religieuse*. Should one recall that from the time of its publication the book's documentary base did not seem very solid to specialists in Australian anthropology (including the Durkheimian Radcliffe-Brown), and that totemism is a long-abandoned category? The enduring interest aroused by this book suggests simply that knowledge—that which can be transmitted—is of a completely different nature in the social sciences than that offered by the natural science disciplines.

27.   The situation of historians who focus on the subject of sociology is somewhat different, and arguably more favorable than that of sociologists. To the list of the achievements of the historical profession should be added a greater degree of distance from sociology as a subject as well as, notably, the absence of engagement within it. By contrast, the frequency with which sociologists borrow historical concepts is not necessarily beneficial, as illustrated by Kuklick's criticism of how the conceptual scheme of professionalization was borrowed to analyze the evolution of sociology in the United States (Kuklick [1980]).

28.   As far as I am concerned, the fortuitous discovery in the 1970s of just how unconvincing the explanations were of the development of education in France on the part of sociologists led me to archival work, and then to publication in history journals, and finally to an enduring relationship with historians. Thus, I discovered a writing style and more broadly a trade in which I had received no training, and ultimately I came to epistemological and methodological reflections on historical work.

29. In the preface to *The Essential Tension* (1990: xii–xiii), Thomas Kuhn recalls an excellent piece of advice he gave to his students: "When reading the works of an important thinkers, look first to the apparent absurdities in the text and ask yourself how a sensible person could have written them. When you find an answer . . . when those passages make sense, then you may find more central passages, ones you previously thought you understand, have changed their meaning."

30. Fred Davis (1973).

31. For an overview of the utilization of the history of social science in American sociology and anthropology at the end of the twentieth century, see Kuklick (1999).

32. We can limit ourselves here to citing the well-known example of *The Social System* (1951) by Talcott Parsons, and in France the multiple attempts to reappropriate and reinterpret the work of Durkheim and Mauss. The labels associated with research or its authors, claimed or imputed ("Marxist," "interactionist," "Durkheimian," "functionalist," etc.) are also important elements in the professional ideologies of researchers performing similar functions, which should shed a critical light on their use in historical analyses.

33. To cite Jacques Siracusa, according to the perspective that I adopt the conventional narrative is a sort of institutional appendage, a subdomain engendered by the normal functioning (or, rather, malfunctioning) of the discipline concerned.

34. This last point is systematically discussed in *Enquête sur la connaissance du monde social*.

35. See, for one example, Gillespie (1993).

36. Roger (1995: 66) reports that "the historian departs from [the text] to see the problems it poses and must return to it in order to explain them." For the social sciences—in contrast, for example, with physics after 1850—there is no translation of texts into a formalized language. Starting with texts implies paying attention to language in the context of the period—an important distinction from the history of ideas in the tradition of Lovejoy, for which the "concepts" are the point of departure.

37. In lieu of more or less systematic presentations of theories in the manner of philosophical analyses, sociology substitutes a presentation in the form of a corpus of definitions and propositions. One of the first examples of this can be found in an article by Robert K. Merton (1945) regarding *Suicide* by Durkheim. The influence of logical empiricism is evident here.

38. Before the important (and underappreciated) book by Ricca Edmonson (1984), and more indirectly the publication of an article by Joseph Gusfield (1976), little attention was accorded in the field of sociology to the rhetorical dimension of social science texts and its relationship with the audiences of these disciplines.

39. Passeron (2006): 130–133; Blumer (1969): 140–152.

40. We find here the minimum characterization of their production generally accepted by historians, according to the formula of Pomian (1999: 34): "a narrative shows itself to be historical when it demonstrates the intention to submit itself to scrutiny in terms of its adequacy for the extra-textual reality of the past that it concerns."

41. These different points are presented in detail in *Enquête sur la connaissance du monde social* regarding ethnographic, historical, and statistical methods of research.

42. Carey (1975). The question is developed further in Chapoulie (2017).

43. This essential idea itself is never substantially developed by Hughes. The most explicitly exemplified development can be found in an essay, "Going Concerns: The Study of American Institutions" (1962).

44. On missionaries and American anthropology, see for example Salamone (1977). The importance of informants is barely apparent before the 1960s: the collection by Casagrande (1960) and the later publications by Victor Turner.

45. Rose (1962). This collection notably includes essays by E. Burgess, H. Blumer, E. Hughes, F. Frazier, A. Strauss, E. Goffman, H. S. Becker, E. Freidson, H. Gans, G. Stone, and T. Shibutani, but also by several sociologists who are not generally connected to the so-called Chicago school, like Sheldon Stryker, Manford Kuhn, and Irwin Deutscher.

46. Obviously, it is possible to distinguish another period and generation of actors (that of Albion Small and Charles Henderson) who institutionalized sociology as a discipline of instruction and research at the University of Chicago and in the Midwest without producing research that served as a model for the following generation.

47. It is clearly possible to treat the period in which Park's influence over PhD students was fully exercised as separate from the period 1934–1945. This transitional period is marked by the simultaneous weakening of the institutional position of the Chicago sociologists (with the creation of the *American Sociological Review* and the departure and semi-retirement of Robert Park), and by an increasing interest in a statistical approach and development, by former students of William Ogburn, of a sociology based on such—an evolution mentioned only in *La tradition sociologique de Chicago*.

48. The book by James Bennett (1981) about criminologists' usage of criminals' autobiographies to obtain public support is, to my knowledge, the first to draw attention to this dimension of research in the social sciences. The author, in the acknowledgments section of the book, highlights Helen MacGill Hughes for the historical documents that she provided, as well as Richard McKeon, a philosopher, historian, and former student of Dewey who was a professor of philosophy at the University of Chicago and one of the first to pay attention to the importance of rhetoric.

49. The fact that no book ever resulted from William Lawton's PhD dissertation on the activities of Du Pont and Nemours, despite the author's efforts, is here an example of note.

50. One can see why the notion of field, originally introduced by Bourdieu (1976) for the study of literary production in France, was not appropriated for the study of an undertaking like that of the Chicago sociologists. It was practically the same case for a the discipline of sociology, which depends on close but variable relationships with diverse sectors of activities in which only half the same criteria of legitimacy are frequently imposed.

51. Notably in two essays: "The Improper Study of Man" (1956) and "The Dual Mandate of Social Science" (1959), reprinted in Everett C. Hughes, (1971).

52. Fine (1995).

53. Febvre (1982): 69.

APPENDIX: REMARKS ON RESEARCH METHODS

1. Baxandall (1985): 58–62.
2. See especially Camic (1992); Maines, Bridger, Ulmer (1996).
3. See Briand, Chapoulie (1992).
4. See Chapoulie (2018).
5. See descriptions of this experience: Chapoulie (2000b).

References

For this second edition, the bibliography has been updated, particularly for historical studies concerning the context in which sociology developed. In the case where there exist more recent editions presenting significant differences, I have indicated in brackets the date of the original edition when I have referred to a later edition.

Abbott, Anfolderf the Second Chicago School," in Fine (1995: 221–272).

Abbott, Andrew (1999): *Department and Discipline. Chicago Sociology at One Hundred.* Chicago, University of Chicago Press.

Abbott, Andrew; Gaziano, Emanuel (1995): "Transition and Tradition: Departmental Faculty in the Era of the Second Chicago School," in Fine (1995: 221–272).

Abbott, Andrew; Egloff, Rainer (2008): "The Polish Peasant in Oberlin and Chicago. The Intellectual Trajectory of W. I. Thomas," *The American Sociologist*, 39 (4): 217–258.

Abbott, Edith (1924): *Immigration: Select Documents and Case Records*, Chicago, University of Chicago Press.

—— (1926): *Historical Aspects of the Immigration Problem: Select Documents*, Chicago, University of Chicago Press: 881.

Adams, Romanzo (1937): *Interracial Marriage in Hawaii*, New York, Macmillan Publishers.

Adams, Richard N.; Preiss, Joseph J. (eds.) (1960): *Human Organization Research*, Homewood (IL), Dorsey Press.

Adorno, Theodor W.; Frenkel-Brunswik, Else; Levinson, Daniel J.; Sanford, R. Nevitt: (1950): *The Authoritarian Personality*, New York, Harper and Row.

Agnew, Elizabeth N. (2003): *From Charity to Social Work. Mary E. Richmond and the Creation of an American Profession*, Champaign, University of Illinois Press.

Alinsky, Saul (1972): "Candid Conversation," *Playboy*, March: 59–68, 150, 169, 178.

Allport, Gordon W. (1935): "Attitudes," in C. M. Murchison (ed.): *A Handbook of Social Psychology*, Worcester (MA), Clark University Press: 798–844.

Alpert, Harry (1954): "The National Science Foundation and Social Science Research," *American Sociological Review*, 19 (2): 208–211.

—— (1960): "The Government's Growing Recognition of Social Science," *The Annals of the American Academy of Political and Social Science*, 327: 59–67.

Anderson, Elijah (1990): *Streetwise. Race, Class and Change in an Urban Community*, Chicago, University of Chicago Press.

Anderson, Margo J. (1988): *The American Census. A Social History*, New Haven (CT), Yale University Press.

Anderson, Nels (1961) [1923]: *The Hobo: The Sociology of the Homeless Man*, Chicago, University of Chicago Press.

—— (1930): "The Migration of the Slum in Manhattan," PhD in Sociology, New York University.

—— (1930): [under the pseudonym Dean Stiff] *The Milk and the Honey Route. A Handbook for Hobos*, New York, Vanguard Press.

—— (1934): "Vagrancy," *Encyclopædia of the Social Sciences*, vol. XV, New York, Macmillan 205–208.

—— (1940): *Men on the Move*, Chicago, University of Chicago Press.

—— (1942): *Desert Saints: The Mormon Frontier in Utah*, Chicago, University of Chicago Press.

—— (1961): Introduction to the second edition of *The Hobo*, Chicago, Phoenix Books, University of Chicago Press: v–xxi.

—— (1972): "Recollections of Nels Anderson," Conférence à l'Université du Nouveau Brunswick, January 12: 13.

—— (1975): *The American Hobo*, Leiden (Netherlands), E. J. Brill.

—— (1980–1981): "Sociology Has Many Faces, Part I," *Journal of the History of Sociology*, 3 (1): 1–25.

—— (1982): "Sociology Has Many Faces, Part II," *Journal of the History of Sociology*, 3 (2): 1–19.

—— (1983): "A Stranger at the Gate. Reflections on the Chicago School of Sociology," *Urban Life*, 11 (4): 396–406.

—— (1998): *On Hobos and Homelessness*, Chicago, University of Chicago Press.

Anderson, Nels; Bain, Read; Lundberg, George (1929): *Trends in American Sociology*, New York, Harper.

Apfelbaum, Erika (1993): "Quelques leçons d'une histoire de la psychologie sociale," *Sociétés contemporaines*, 13: 13–24.

Aptheker, Herbert (1943): *American Negro Slave Revolts*, New York, Columbia University Press.

Archdeacon, Thomas J. (1983): *Becoming American. An Ethnic History*, New York, Free Press.

Aron, Raymond (1967): *Les étapes de la pensée sociologique*, Paris, Gallimard.

Aubert, Vilhelm (1952): "White Collar Crime and Social Structure," *American Journal of Sociology*, 58 (3): 263–271.

Back, Kurt W. (1963): "Sociology Encounters the Protest Movement for Desegregation," *Phylon*, 24 (3): 232–239.

Bahr, Howard M.; Johnson, Theodore J.; Seitz, M. Ray (1971): "Influential Scholars and Works in the Sociology of Race and Minority Relations, 1944–1968," *The American Sociologist*, 6 (4): 296–298.

Baker, Paul J. (1973): "The Life Histories of William I. Thomas and Robert E. Park," *American Journal of Sociology*, 79 (2): 243–260.

Bannister, Robert C. (1966): *Ray Stannard Baker: The Mind and Thought of a Progressive*, New Haven (CT), Yale University Press.

—— (1979): *Social Darwinism. Science and Myth in Anglo-American Social Thought*, Philadelphia, Temple University Press.

—— (1987): *Sociology and Scientism. The American Quest for Objectivity (1880–1940)*, Chapel Hill, University of North Carolina Press.

—— (1992): "American Sociologists and Fascism, 1930–1950," in Stephen P. Turner, Dirk Käsler (eds.): *Sociology Responds to Fascism*, London, Routledge: 172–213.

—— (1998): "Dorothy Swain Thomas: Soziologischer Objectivismus: Der harte Weg in die Profession," in Claudia Honegger, Teresa Wobbe (ed.): *Frauen in der Soziologie*, Munich (Germany), Oscar Beck: 226–257.

Barkan, Elazar (1992): *The Retreat of Scientific Racism. Changing Concepts of Race in Britain and the United States Between the World Wars*, Cambridge (UK), Cambridge University Press.

Barnard, John (1969): *From Evangelicalism to Progressivism at Oberlin College, 1866–1917*, Columbus, Ohio State University Press.

Barnes, Henry E. (1948): *An Introduction to the History of Sociology*, Chicago, University of Chicago Press.

Barton, Allen H.; Lazarsfeld, Paul F. (1955): "Some Functions of Qualitative Analysis in Social Research," *Frankfurter Beiträge zur Soziologie*, 1: 321–361.

Bash, Harry H. (1979): *Sociology, Race and Ethnicity. A Critique of American Ideological Intrusions upon Sociological Theory*, New York, Gordon and Breach.

Baxandall, Michael (1985): *Patterns of Intention*, New Haven (CT), Yale University Press.

Becker, Howard S. (1951a): "Role and Career Problems of the Chicago Public School-Teacher," PhD in Sociology, University of Chicago (published in facsimile in 1980, New York, Arno Press).

—— (1951b): "The Professional Dance Musician and His Audience," *American Journal of Sociology*, 57 (2): 136–144, in Becker (1963): 79–100.

—— (1952a): "The Career of the Chicago Public School Teacher," *American Journal of Sociology*, 57 (5): 470–477, in Becker (1970): 165–175.

—— (1952b): "Social-Class Variations in the Teacher-Pupil Relationship," *Journal of Educational Sociology*, 25 (8): 451–465, in Becker (1970): 137–150.

—— (1953a): "The Teacher in the Authority System of the Public School," *Journal of Educational Sociology*, 27 (3): 128–141, in Becker (1970): 151–163.

—— (1953b): "Some Contingencies of the Professional Dance Musician's Career," *Human Organization*, 12 (1): 22–26, in Becker (1963): 101–119.

—— (1954): "Deviant Behavior: A Research Memorandum," unpublished manuscript.

—— (1958): "Problems of Inference and Proof in Participant Observation," *American Sociological Review*, 23 (6): 652–659, in Becker (1970): 25–138.

—— (1962): "The Nature of a Profession" in *Education for the Professions*, part 2, Chicago, University of Chicago Press: 27–46, in Becker (1970): 87–103.

—— (1963): *Outsiders. Studies in the Sociology of Deviance*, New York, Free Press of Glencoe (French translation: [1985] *Outsiders, Études de sociologie de la déviance*, Paris, A. M. Métailié).

—— (1970): *Sociological Work, Method and Substance*, Chicago, Aldine.

—— (1983): "Everett C. Hughes," Paper for the special session dedicated to Everett Hughes at the annual meeting of the American Sociological Association (ASA), Detroit (MI), September 30, forthcoming in French.

—— (1985): Afterword to the French translation of *Outsiders*: 238–244.

—— (1986): *Doing Things Together. Selected Papers*, Evanston (IL), Northwestern University Press.

—— (1988): "Herbert Blumer's Conceptual Impact," *Symbolic Interaction*, 11 (1): 13–21.

—— (1996): "À propos de *Outsiders*," interview conducted in 1985 with Jean-Michel Chapoulie and Jean-Pierre Briand, in *Hommages à Howard S. Becker*, texts collected by Jean-Pierre Briand and Henri Peretz, *Travaux et Documents*, 1, Saint-Denis (France), Presses de l'Université Paris 8: 63–78.

—— (1997): "Entretien" with Jean-Michel Chapoulie.

—— (1999): "The Chicago School, So-Called," *Qualitative Sociology*, 22 (1): 1–7.

—— (2006): "Introductory Note to Donald Roy's Article on Cooperation and Conflict in the Factory," *Qualitative Sociology*, 29 (1): 55–57.

Becker, Howard S.; Carper, James (1956): "The Development of Identification with an Occupation," *American Journal of Sociology*, 61 (4): 289–298, in Becker (1970 Interview): 189–201.

Becker, Howard S.; Geer, Blanche (1957): "Participant Observation and Interviewing: A Comparison," *Human Organization*, 16 (1): 28–32.

—— (1960): "Participant Observation: The Analysis of Qualitative Field Data," in Adams, Preiss (1960): 267–289.

Becker, Howard S.; Geer, Blanche; Hughes, Everett C.; Strauss, Anselm L. (1961): *Boys in White, Student Culture in Medical School*, Chicago, University of Chicago Press.

Becker, Howard S.; Geer, Blanche; Hughes, Everett C. (1968): *Making the Grade. The Academic Side of College Life*, New York, John Wiley.

Becker, Howard S.; Geer, Blanche; Riesman, David; Weiss, Robert S. (eds.) (1968): *Institutions and the Person. Essays Presented to Everett C. Hughes*, Chicago, Aldine.

Becker, Howard S.; Debro, Julius (1970): "Dialogue," *Issues in Criminology*, 5 (2): 159–179, in Becker (1986): 25–46.

Beckmire, Regena M. (1932): "The Study of Highland Park as a Residential Suburb," MA in Sociology, University of Chicago.

Bedford, Scott (1927): *Readings in Urban Sociology*, New York, Appleton and Co.

Beers, Clifford (1908): *A Mind That Found Itself*, New York, Longmans, Green and Co.

Bennett, James (1981): *Oral History and Delinquency. The Rhetoric of Criminology*, Chicago, University of Chicago Press.

Berger, Bennett M. (ed.) (1990): *Authors of Their Own Lives, Intellectual Autobiographies by Twenty American Sociologists*, Berkeley, University of California Press.

Bernard, Luther L. (1909): "The Teaching of Sociology in the United States," *American Journal of Sociology*, 15 (2) on the Polish peasants in (1960) *A History of American Workers, 1920–1933. The Lean Years*, New York, Houghton Mifflin.

—— (s.d.): "William Isaac Thomas," from an unpublished book preserved in the Luther Bernard archives at Pennsylvania State University.

Bernstein, Irving (1960): *The Lean Years: Workers in an Unbalanced Society*, Boston, Houghton Mifflin.

Bertaux, Daniel (1976): *Histoire de vie ou récits de pratiques? Méthodologie de l'approche biographique en sociologie*, Paris, mimeographed report for CORDES.

Besnard, Philippe (1987): *L'anomie, ses usages et ses fonctions dans la discipline sociologique*, Paris, Presses Universitaires de France.

Blackwell, James E.; Janowitz, Morris (eds.) (1974): *Black Sociologists. Historical and Contemporary Perspectives*, Chicago, University of Chicago Press.

Blanckaert, Claude (1993): "La société française pour l'histoire des sciences de l'homme," *Genèses*, 10: 124–135.

—— (ed.) (1999): *L'histoire des sciences de l'homme. Trajectoires, enjeux et questions vives*, Paris, L'Harmattan.

Blassingame, John W. (1972): *The Slave Community. Plantation Life in the Antebellum South*, New York, Oxford University Press.

Blau, Peter M.; Duncan, Otis D. (1967): *The American Occupational Structure*, New York, John Wiley.

Blauner, Robert (1970): "Black Culture: Myth or Reality," in Norman E. Whitten Jr.; John F. Szwed (eds.), *Afro-American Anthropology. Contemporary Perspectives on Theory and Research*, New York, Free Press: 347–366.

—— (1972): *Racial Oppression in America*, New York, Harper and Row.

Blumenthal, Albert (1932): *Small-Town Stuff*, Chicago, University of Chicago Press.

Blumer, Herbert (1928): "Method in Social Psychology," PhD in Sociology, University of Chicago.

—— (1933): *Movies and Conduct*, New York, Macmillan.

—— (1937): "Social Psychology" in Emerson P. Schmidt (ed.): *Man and Society*, New York, Prentice Hall: 144–198.

—— (1939): *Critiques of Research in the Social Sciences. An Appraisal of Thomas and Znaniecki's "The Polish Peasant in Europe and America,"* New York, Social Science Research Council.

—— (1939): "The Nature of Race Prejudice," *Social Process in Hawaii*, vol. V (June): 16–20, in Lyman, Vidich (1988): 183–195.

—— (1947): "Sociological Theory in Industrial Relations," *American Sociological Review*, 12 (3): 271–278, in Lyman, Vidich (1988): 297–308.

—— (1948): "Public Opinion and Public Opinion Polling," *American Sociological Review*, 13 (5): 542–554, in Blumer (1969a): 195–208.

—— (1954): "What Is Wrong With Social Theory?" *American Sociological Review*, 19 (1): 3–10, in Blumer (1969a): 140–152.

—— (1955): "Reflections on Theory of Race Relations," in Lind (ed.): 3–21.

—— (1956): "Sociological Analysis and the 'Variable,' " *American Sociological Review*, 22 (6): 683–690, in Blumer (1969a): 127–139.

—— (1958): "Research on Racial Relations, United States of America," *International Social Science Bulletin*, 10 (3): 403–447.

—— (1965): "Industrialisation and Race Relations," in Guy Hunter (ed.): *Industrialisation and Race Relations: A Symposium*, London, Oxford University Press: 220–253.

—— (1966): "Foreword," in Severyn T. Bruyn: *The Human Perspective in Sociology*, Englewood Cliffs (NJ), Prentice Hall: iii–xvi.

—— (1968): "In Memoriam Joseph D. Lohman," *American Sociologist*, 3 (3): 255–256.

—— (1969a): *Symbolic Interactionism. Perspective and Method*, Englewood Cliffs (NJ), Prentice Hall.

—— (1969b): "Fashion: From Class Differentiation to Collective Selection," *Sociological Quarterly*, 10 (3): 275–291.

—— (1971): "Social Problems as Collective Behavior," *Social Problems*, 18 (3): 298–306.

—— (1975): "Symbolic Interaction and the Idea of Social System," *Revue Internationale de Sociologie*, série II, 11 (1–2): 3–12.

—— (1990): *Industrialization as an Agent of Social Change. A Critical Analysis*, New York, Aldine De Gruyter.

—— (2004): *George Herbert Mead and Human Conduct*, Walnut Creek (CA), Altamira Press.

Blumer, Herbert; Hauser, Philip M. (1933): *Movies, Delinquency and Crime*, New York, Macmillan.

Bodnar, John (1985): *The Transplanted. A History of Immigrants in Urban America*, Bloomington, Indiana University Press.

Bogardus, Emory S. (1911): "The Relation of Fatigue to Industrial Accidents," PhD in Sociology, University of Chicago.

—— (1926): *The New Social Research*, Los Angeles, J. R. Miller.

—— (1928): *Immigration and Race Attitudes*, Boston, Heath Social Relations Series.

—— (1949): "The Sociology of William I. Thomas," *Sociology and Social Research*, 34 (1): 34–48.

—— (1959): "W. I. Thomas and Social Origins," *Sociology and Social Research*, 43 (5): 365–369.

—— (1962): "Some Pioneer American Sociologists," *Sociology and Social Research*, 47 (1): 25–33.

Bond, Horace Mann (1939): *Negro Education in Alabama. A Study in Cotton and Steel*, Washington, D.C., Associated Publishers.

Booth, Charles (ed.) (1889–1891): *Life and Labour of the People of London*, London, Williams and Norgate.

—— (1902–1903): *Life and Labour of the People of London*, London, Macmillan, 17 vols.

Boudon, Raymond (1992): "Comment écrire l'histoire des sciences sociales," *Communications*, 1992, 54: 299–317.

Bourdieu, Pierre (1976): "Le champ scientifique," *Actes de la recherche en sciences sociales*, 2–3: 88–104.

Boyer, Paul (1978): *Urban Masses and Moral Order in America, 1820–1920*, Cambridge (MA), Harvard University Press.

Breckinridge, Sophonisba; Abbott, Edith (1910): "Chicago Housing Conditions," *American Journal of Sociology*, 16 (3): 289–308.

—— (1911): "Chicago Housing Conditions," *American Journal of Sociology*, 16 (4): 433–468.

—— (1911): "Chicago Housing Conditions," *American Journal of Sociology*, 17 (1): 1–37.

—— (1912): *The Delinquent Child and the Home. A Study of the Delinquents Wards of the Juvenile Court of Chicago*, New York, Charities Publication Committee.

Bressler, Marvin (1952): "Selected Family Patterns in W. I. Thomas' Unfinished Study of The Bintle Brief," *American Sociological Review*, 17 (5): 563–571.

Briand, Jean-Pierre; Chapoulie, Jean-Michel (1991): "The Uses of Observation in French Sociology," *Symbolic Interaction*, 14 (4): 449–469.

—— (1992): *Les collèges du peuple. L'enseignement primaire supérieur et le développement de la scolarisation prolongée sous la Troisième République*, Editions du CNRS/ INRP/Presses de l'ENS.

Brochier, Christophe (2016): *La naissance de la sociologie au Brésil*, Rennes (France), Presses Universitaires de Rennes.

Brody, David (1980): *Workers in Industrial America. Essays on the Twentieth Century Struggle*, New York, Oxford University Press.

Brown, William O. (1930): "Race Prejudice: A Sociological Study," PhD in Sociology, University of Chicago.

—— (1931): "The Nature of Race Consciousness," *Social Forces*, 10 (1): 90–97.

Brunner, Edmund de Schwinitz (1957): *The Growth of a Science. A Half Century of Rural Sociological Research in the United States*, New York, Harper and Brothers.

Bruns, Roger A. (1987): *The Damndest Radical. The Life and World of Ben Reitman, Chicago's Celebrated Social Reformer, Hobo King, and Whorehouse Physician*, Urbana, University of Illinois Press.

Bruyn, Severyn T. (1966): *The Human Perspective in Sociology*, Englewood Cliffs (NJ), Prentice Hall.

Bucher, Rue; Fritz, Charles E.; Quarantelli, E. L. (1956): "Tape-Recorded Interviews and Social Research," *American Sociological Review*, 21 (3): 359–364.

Bucher, Rue; Strauss, Anselm L. (1961): "Professions in Process," *American Journal of Sociology*, 66 (4): 325–334.

Bulmer, Martin (1982): "Support for Sociology in the 1920s," *The American Sociologist*, 17 (4): 185–192.

—— (1983a): "The Society for Social Research," *Urban Life*, 11 (4): 421–439.

—— (1983b): "The Methodology of the Taxi-Dance Hall: An Early Account of Chicago Ethnography from the 1920s," *Urban Life*, 12 (1): 95–101.

—— (1984): *The Chicago School of Sociology. Institutionalization, Diversity, and the Rise of Sociological Research*, Chicago, University of Chicago Press.

Bulmer, Martin; Bulmer, Joan (1981): "Philanthropy and Social Science in the 1920s: Beardsley Ruml and the Laura Spelman Rockefeller Memorial, 1922–1929," *Minerva*, 19 (3): 347–407.

Bulmer, Martin; Bales, Kevin; Sklar, Kathryn Kish (1991): *The Social Survey in Historical Perspective, 1880–1940*, Cambridge, Cambridge University Press.

Burawoy, Michael (1979): *Manufacturing Consent*, Chicago, University of Chicago Press.

Burgess, Ernest W. (1916): "The Social Survey. A Field for Constructive Service by Departments of Sociology," *American Journal of Sociology*, 21 (4): 492–500.

—— (1923): "The Study of the Delinquent as a Person," *American Journal of Sociology*, 28 (6): 657–680.

—— (1924): "The Growth of the City: An Introduction to a Research Project," *Publications of the American Sociological Society*, 18: 85–97, in Park, Burgess (1925): 47–62; Grafmeyer, Joseph (1979): 127–143.

—— (1939): "Editor's Preface," in Frazier (1939): ix–xvii.

—— (1945a): "The Contribution of Robert E. Park," *Sociology and Social Research*, 29 (4): 255–61.

—— (1945b): "Sociological Research Methods," *American Journal of Sociology*, 50 (6): 474–482.

—— (1948): "William I. Thomas as a Teacher," *Sociology and Social Research*, 32 (4): 760–764.

—— (1955): "Our Dynamic Society and Social Research," *Midwest Sociologist*: 3–7, in Burgess (1974): 355–358.

—— (1956): "Charles Spurgeon Johnson: Social Scientist, Editor, and Educational Statesman," *Phylon*, 17 (4): 317–321.

—— (1961): "Social Planning and Race Relations," in Jitsuichi Masuoka; Preston Valien (eds.): *Race Relations, Problems and Theory*, Chapel Hill, University of North Carolina Press: 13–25.

—— (1973): *Ernest W. Burgess on Community, Family, and Delinquency* (ed. by Leonard S. Cottrell; Albert Hunter; James F. Short), Chicago, University of Chicago Press.

—— (1974): *The Basic Writings of E. W. Burgess* (ed. by Donald J. Bogue), Chicago, Community and Family Study Center.

Burgess, Ernest W.; Bogue, Donald J. (eds.) (1964): *Contributions to Urban Sociology*, Chicago, University of Chicago Press.

Burgess, Ernest W.; Bogue Donald J. (1964): "Research in Urban Society: A Long View," in Burgess, Bogue (1964: 1–14).

Burke, Kenneth (1935): *Permanence and Change*, New York, New Republic.

Butterfield, Herbert (1931): *The Whig Interpretation of History*, New York, Norton.

Buxton, William; Turner, Stephen, P. (1992): "From Education to Expertise: Sociology as a 'Profession,' " in Terence C. Halliday; Morris Janowitz (eds.): *Sociology and Its Publics. The Forms and Fates of Disciplinary Organization*, Chicago, University of Chicago Press: 373–407.

Cahnman, Werner J. (1978): "Robert E. Park at Fisk," *Journal of the History of the Behavorial Sciences*, 14 (4): 328–336.

Calhoun, Craig (ed.) (2007): *Sociology in America. A history*, Chicago, University of Chicago Press.

Camic, Charles (1986): "The Matter of Habit," *American Journal of Sociology*, 91 (5): 1039–1087.

—— (1992): "Reputation and Predecessors Selection: Parsons and the Institutionalists," *American Sociological Review*, 57 (4): 421–445.

—— (1994): "Reshaping the History of American Sociology," *Social Epistemology*, 8 (1): 9–18.

Carey, James T. (1958): "The Development of the University Evening School in Urban America: An Aspect of Institutionalization in Higher Education," PhD in Sociology, University of Chicago.

—— (1975): *Sociology and Public Affairs. The Chicago School*, Beverly Hills (CA), Sage Publications.

Carlin, Jerome E. (1959): "The Lawyer as Individual Practitioner," PhD in Sociology, University of Chicago.

—— (1962): *Lawyers on Their Own. A Study of Individual Practitioners in Chicago*, New Brunswick (NJ), Rutgers University Press.

Carr, Lowell Juilliard (1941): *Delinquency Control*, New York, Harper.

Carroll, Mollie R. (1920): "The Attitude of the American Federation of Labor toward Legislation and Politics," PhD in Sociology, University of Chicago.

Carson, Mina (1990): *Settlement Folk. Social Thought and the American Settlement Movement, 1885–1930*, Chicago, University of Chicago Press.

Carter, Wilmoth A. (1959): "The Negro Main Street of a Contemporary Urban Community," PhD in Sociology, University of Chicago.

—— (1962): *The Urban Negro in the South*, New York, Vantage Press.

Casagrande, Joseph B. (ed.) (1960): *In the Company of Man. Twenty Portraits of Anthropological Informants*, New York, Harper.

Castells, Manuel (1972): *La Question Urbaine*, Paris, Maspéro.

Cavan, Ruth Shonle (1928): *Suicide*, Chicago, University of Chicago Press.

—— (1983): "The Chicago School of Sociology," *Urban Life*, 11 (4), 407–420.

Cayton, Horace (1963): *Long Old Road*, New York, Trident Press.

—— (1964): "E. Franklin Frazier: A Tribute and Review," *Review of Religious Research*, 5 (3): 137–142.

Cayton, Horace R.; Mitchell George S. (1939): *Black Workers and the New Unions*, Chapel Hill, University of North Carolina Press.

Cefaï, Daniel (2002): "Faire du terrain à Chicago dans les années cinquante: L'expérience du Field Training Project," *Genèses*, 46: 122–137.

Chapin, Stuart F. (1936): "Social Theory and Social Action," *American Sociological Review*, 1 (1): 1–11.

Chapoulie, Jean-Michel (1973): "Sur l'analyse sociologique des professions," *Revue française de sociologie*, 14, (1): 86–114.

—— (1984): "E. C. Hughes et le développement du travail de terrain en France," *Revue française de sociologie*, 25 (4): 582–608 (English translation with an appendix in [1987] "Everett C. Hughes and the Development of Fieldwork in Sociology," *Urban Life*, 15 (3–4): 259–298).

—— (1985): "Introduction" to the French translation of *Outsiders* by H. S. Becker, Paris, Editions A. M. Métailié: 9–21.

—— (1991): "La seconde fondation de la sociologie française, les États-Unis et la classe ouvrière," *Revue française de sociologie*, 32 (3): 321–364.

—— (1996): "E. C. Hughes et la tradition de Chicago," introduction to the volume of translations of E. C. Hughes: *Le Regard Sociologique*, Presses de l'EHESS: 13–57 (English translation in "E. C. Hughes and the Chicago Tradition," *Sociological Theory*, 14 [1]: 3–29).

—— (1997a): "Remarques sur le style d'analyse des essais d'Everett C. Hughes," *Actes de la Recherche en Sciences Sociales*, 115: 97–99.

—— (1997b): "La conception de la sociologie empirique d'Everett Hughes," *Sociétés contemporaines*, 27: 97–109.

—— (1998): "Seventy Years of Fieldwork in Sociology: From Nels Anderson's *The Hobo* (1993) to Elijah Anderson's Streetwise (1991)," in L. Tomasi (ed.): *The Tradition of the Chicago School of Sociology*, Aldershot (UK), Ashgate: 105–127.

—— (1999): "Robert E. Park, la tradition de Chicago et l'étude des relations entre les races," *Sociétés contemporaines*, 33–34: 139–157.

—— (2000a): "L'étrange carrière de la notion de classe sociale dans la tradition de Chicago en sociologie," *Archives Européennes de sociologie*, 46 (1): 53–70.

—— (2000b): "Enseignemer le travail de terrain et l'observation: un témoignage sur une expérience (1970–1985)," *Genèses*, 39: 138–155.

—— (2001): "Sur un classique ignoré, *Le Paysan Polonais en Europe et en Amérique*, et l'histoire de la sociologie," *Revue d'histoire des sciences humaines*, 5: 143–169.

—— (2005): "Un cadre d'analyse pour l'histoire des sciences sociales," *Revue d'histoire des sciences humaines*, 13: 99–126.

—— (2003): "Ernest W. Burgess et les débuts d'une approche sociologique de la délinquance aux Etats-Unis," *Déviance et Société*, 27 (2): 103–110.

—— (2008a): "Une interprétation de la sociologie de Robert E. Park dans son contexte historique," in Suzie Guth (dir.), *Modernité de Robert Park*, Paris, L'Harmattan: 133–154.

—— (2008b): "Malentendus transatlantiques: la tradition de Chicago, Park et la sociologie française," *L'homme*, 187–188: 223–246.

—— (2009): "Rejoinder to Daniel Geary, Johan Heilbron, Jennifer Platt, and Alan Sica," *Sociologica*, 3 (2–3), DOI: 10.2383/31368.

—— (2017): *Enquête sur la connaissance du monde social. Anthropologie, histoire, sociologie. France-États-Unis 1950–2000*, Rennes (France), Presses Universitaires de Rennes.

Chapple, Elliot D. (1953): "Applied Anthropology in Industry," in Alfred Kroeber (ed.): *Anthropology Today, an Encyclopedic Inventory*, Chicago, University of Chicago Press: 819–831.

Chicago Commission on Race Relations (1922): *The Negro in Chicago. A Study of Race Relations and a Race Riot in 1919*, Chicago, University of Chicago Press.

Chombart de Lauwe, Paul-Henri (ed.) (1952): *Paris et l'agglomération parisienne*, Paris, Presses Universitaires de France.

Cloward, Richard A.; Ohlin, Lloyd E. (1960): *Delinquency and Opportunity. A Theory of Delinquent Gangs*, New York, Free Press.

Coben, Stanley (1964): "A Study in Nativism: The American Red Scare of 1919–20," *Political Science Quarterly*, 79 (1): 52–75.

Coghlan, Catherine L. (2005): "Please Don't Think of Me as a Sociologist": Sophonisba Preston Breckinridge and the Early Chicago School," *The American Sociologist*, 36 (1): 3–22.

Cohen, Albert K. (1955): *Delinquent Boys. The Culture of the Gang*, Glencoe, Free Press.

Cole, Stephen (1975): "The Growth of Scientific Knowledge: Theories of Deviance as a Case Study," in Lewis A. Coser (ed.): *The Idea of Social Structure. Papers in Honor of Robert K. Merton*, New York, Harcourt Brace Jovanovich: 175–220.

Collini, Stefan (1988): " 'Discipline History' and 'Intellectual History': Reflections on the Historiography of the Social Sciences in Britain and France," *Revue de Synthèse*, 4th series, 3–4: 387–399.

Collins, Orvis (1945): "Ethnic Behavior in Industry: Sponsorship and Rejection in a New England Factory," *American Journal of Sociology*, 51 (2): 293–298.

Collins, Orvis; Dalton, Melville; Roy, Donald (1946): "Restriction of Output and Social Cleavage in Industry," *Applied Anthropology*, 5 (3): 1–14.

Colyer, Corey J. (2014): "W. I. Thomas and the Forgotten 4 Wishes: A Case Study in the Sociology of Ideas," paper presented at the Annual Meeting of the American Sociological Association, San Francisco (CA), August 2014.

Connelly, Mark Thomas (1980): *The Response to Prostitution in the Progressive Era*, Chapel Hill, University of North Carolina Press.

Converse, Jean M. (1987): *Survey Research in the United States. Roots and Emergence 1890–1960*, Berkeley, University of California Press.

Cooley, Charles Horton (1909): *Social Organization. A Study of the Larger Mind*, New York, Charles Scribner's Sons.

—— (1922): *Social Process*, New York, Charles Scribner's Sons.

Copeland, Lewis C. (1939): "The Negro as a Contrast Conception," in Thompson (1939): 152–179.

Coser, Lewis A. (1971): *Masters of Sociological Thought. Ideas in Historical and Social Context*, New York, Harcourt Brace Jovanovich.

Cox, Oliver C. (1965): "Introduction," in Nathan Hare: *The Black Anglo-Saxons*, New York, Marzani & Munsell: 1–14.

Cravens, Hamilton (1978): *The Triumph of Evolution. American Scientists and the Heredity-Environment Controversy, 1900–1941*, Philadelphia, University of Pennsylvania Press.

Cressey, Paul F. (1938): "Population Succession in Chicago: 1898–1930," *American Journal of Sociology*, 44 (1): 59–69.

Cressey, Paul G. (1932): *The Taxi-Dance Hall, a Sociological Study in Commercialized Recreation and City Life*, Chicago, University of Chicago Press.

—— (1983): "A Comparison of the Roles of the 'Sociological Stranger' and the 'Anonymous Stranger' in Field Research," *Urban Life*, 12 (1): 102–120.

Curtis, Susan (1991): *A Consuming Faith. The Social Gospel and Modern American Culture*, Baltimore (MD), Johns Hopkins University Press.

Dalton, Melville O. (1949): "A Study of Informal Organization among the Managers of an Industrial Plant," PhD in Sociology, University of Chicago.

—— (1950a): "Conflicts between Staff and Line Managerial Officers," *American Sociological Review*, 15 (3): 342–351.

—— (1950b): "Unofficial Union-Management Relations," *American Sociological Review*, 15 (5): 611–619.

—— (1951): "Informal Factors in Career Achievement," *American Journal of Sociology*, 56 (5): 407–415.

—— (1959): *Men Who Manage*, New York, Wiley.

Daniels, John (1914): *In Freedom's Birthplace. A Study of Boston Negroes*, Boston, Houghton Mifflin.

Davis, Allen F. (1967): *Spearheads for Reform. The Social Settlements and the Progressive Movement, 1890–1914*, New Brunswick (NJ), Rutgers University Press.

Davis, Allison (1946): "The Motivation of the Underprivileged Worker," in Whyte (1946): 84–106.

Davis, Allison; Dollard, John (1940): *Children of Bondage. The Personality Development of Negro Youth in the Urban South*, Washington, D.C., American Council of Education.

Davis, Arthur P.: "E. Franklin Frazier (1894–1962): A Profile," *The Journal of Negro Education*, 31 (4): 429–435.

Davis, Fred (1958): "Polio in the Family, A Study of Crisis and Family Process," PhD in Sociology, University of Chicago.

—— (1959): "The Cabdriver and His Fare: Facets of a Fleeting Relationship," *American Journal of Sociology*, 65 (2): 158–165.

—— (1963): *Passage through Crisis. Polio Victims and Their Families*, New York, Bobbs-Merrill.

—— (1973): "The Martian and the Convert: Ontological Polarities in Social Research," *Urban Life and Culture*, 2 (3): 333–343.

—— (1974): "Stories and Sociology," *Urban Life and Culture*, 3 (3): 310–316.

—— (1991): "Herbert Blumer and the Study of Fashion: A Reminiscence and a Critique," *Symbolic Interaction*, 14 (1): 1–21.

Deegan, Mary Jo (1988): *Jane Addams and the Men of the Chicago School, 1892–1918*, New Brunswick (NJ), Transaction Publishers.

—— (2002): *Race, Hull-House and the University of Chicago. A New Conscience against Ancient Evils*, Westport (CT): Praeger.

—— (2005): "A Trouble behind the Gendered Division of Labor in Sociology: The Curious Marriage of Robert E. Park and Clara Cahill Park," in Anthony J. Blasi (ed.): *Diverse Histories of American Sociology*, Leiden (Netherlands), Brill: 18–39.

Deegan, Mary Jo; Burger, John S. (1981): "W. I. Thomas and Social Reform: His Work and Writings," *Journal of the History of the Behavorial Sciences*, 17 (1): 114–125.

Deutscher, Irving (1973): *What We Say/What We Do. Sentiments and Acts*, Glenview, Scott, Foresman and Co.

—— (1984): "Choosing Ancestors: Some Consequences of the Selection from the Intellectual Traditions," in R. M. Farr; S. Moscovici (eds.): *Social Representations*, Cambridge, Cambridge University Press: 71–100.

Devine, Edward T. (1909a): "Results of the Pittsburgh Survey," *American Journal of Sociology*, 14 (5): 660–667.

—— (1909b): *Misery and Its Causes*, New York, Macmillan.

Dibble, Vernon K. (1975): *The Legacy of Albion Small*, Chicago, University of Chicago Press.

Diner, Steven J. (1975): "Department and Discipline: The Department of Sociology at the University of Chicago, 1892–1920," *Minerva*, 13 (4): 514–553.

—— (1980): *A City and Its Universities. Public Policy in Chicago, 1892–1919*, Chapel Hill (NC), University of North Carolina Press.

Dollard, John (1937): *Caste and Class in a Southern Town*, New Haven (CT), Yale University Press.

Donovan, Frances R. (1929): *The Saleslady*, Chicago, University of Chicago Press.

Douglass, Harlan Paul (1925): *The Suburban Trend*, New York, The Century Co.

Doyle, Bertram W. (1937): *The Etiquette of Race Relations in the South*, Chicago, University of Chicago Press.

—— (1944): *A Study of Business Employment among Negroes in Louisville*, Louisville (KY), University of Louisville.

Drake, Saint Clair (1983): "The Tuskegee Connection: Booker T. Washington and Robert E. Park," *Society*, 20 (4): 82–92.

—— (1984): "Introduction," in Booker T. Washington: *The Man Farthest Down* [1912], New Brunswick (NJ), Transaction Publishers: v–lxiv.

Drake, Saint Clair; Cayton, Horace (1945): *Black Metropolis. A Study of Negro Life in a Northern City*, Chicago, University of Chicago Press.

Dubofsky, Melvyn (1969): *We Shall Be All. A History of the Industrial Workers of the World*, Chicago, Quadrangle.

—— (1994): *The State and Labor in Modern America*, Chapel Hill, University of North Carolina Press.

Du Bois, W. E. B. (1899): *The Philadelphia Negro. A Social Study*, Philadelphia, University of Pennsylvania Press.

Dulczewski, Zygmunt (1992): *Florian Znaniecki. Life and Work*, Poznán (Poland), Nakom.

Duneier, Mitchell (1992): *Slim's Table. Race, Respectability, and Masculinity*, Chicago, University of Chicago Press.

Duster, Troy (1983): "Discussion," organized by Troy Duster between Howard Becker, Aaron Cicourel, John Kitsuse, Edwin Lemert, David Matza, and Sheldon Messinger, Berkeley (CA), Institute for the Study of Social Change.

Dzuback, Mary Ann (1991): *Robert M. Hutchins. Portrait of an Educator*, Chicago, University of Chicago Press.

Edmondson, Ricca (1984): *Rhetoric in Sociology*, London, Macmillan.

Edwards, Lyford (1927): *The Natural History of Revolution*, Chicago, University of Chicago Press.

Edwards, Gilbert Frank (1952): "Occupational Mobility of a Selected Group of Negro Male Professionals," PhD in Sociology, University of Chicago.

Eggan, Fred (1974): "Amongst the Anthropologists," *Annual Review of Anthropology*, 3: 1–19.

Elkins, Stanley (1959): *Slavery: A Problem in American Institutional and Intellectual Life*, Chicago, University of Chicago Press.

Emerson, Robert (1997): "Le travail de terrain après Hughes: continuités et changements," *Sociétés Contemporaines*, 27: 39–48.

England, Ralph W. Jr. (1960): "A Theory of Middle Class Juvenile Delinquency," *Journal of Criminal Law and Criminology*, 50 (6): 535–540.

Eubank, Earle Edward (1915): "A Study of Family Desertion," PhD in Sociology, University of Chicago.

Evans, Richard (1986–1987): "Sociology Journals and the Decline of the Chicago School, 1929–1941," *History of Sociology*, 6–7: 109–130.

Farber, Bernard (1988): "The Human Element: Sociology at Chicago," *Sociological Perspectives*, 31 (3): 339–359.

Faris, Ellsworth (1921): "Are Instincts Data or Hypotheses?" *American Journal of Sociology*, 27 (2): 184–196.

—— (1937): *The Nature of Human Nature*, New York, McGraw Hill.

—— (1948): "W. I. Thomas (1863–1947)," *Sociology and Social Research*, 32 (4): 755–759.

Faris, Robert E. L. (1948): *Social Disorganization*, New York, Ronald Press.

—— (1970): *Chicago Sociology: 1920–1932*, University of Chicago Press (first edition [1967]: San Francisco, Chandler).

Faris, Robert E. L.; Dunham, H. Warren (1939): *Mental Disorders in Urban Areas. An Ecological Study of Schizophrenia and Other Psychoses*, Chicago, University of Chicago Press.

Faught, Jim (1980): "Presuppositions of the Chicago School in the Work of Everett Hughes," *American Sociologist*, 15 (2): 72–82.

Febvre, Lucien (1992) [1953]: *Combats pour l'histoire*, in the Armand Colin/Pocket edition.

—— (1982) [1962]: *Pour une histoire à part entière*, Paris, Éditions de l'EHESS.

Feffer, Andrew (1993): *The Chicago Pragmatists and American Progressivism*, Ithaca (NY), Cornell University Press.

Fine, Gary Alan; Ducharme, Lori J. (1995): "The Ethnographic Present: Images of Institutional Control in Second-School Research," in Fine (1995): 108–135.

Fine, Gary Alan (ed.) (1995): *A Second Chicago School? The Development of a Postwar American Sociology*, Chicago, University of Chicago Press.

Finestone, Harold (1976): *Victims of Change. Juvenile Delinquents in American Society*, Westport (CT), Greenwood.

Fish, Virginia K. (1985): "Hull House: Pioneer in Urban Research during its Creative Years," *History of Sociology*, 6 (1): 33–70.

Fisher, Berenice; Strauss, Anselm L. (1978): "The Chicago Tradition: Thomas, Park and Their Successors," *Symbolic Interaction*, 1 (1): 5–23.

Fisher, Donald (1993): *Fundamental Development of the Social Sciences. Rockefeller Philanthropy and the United States Social Science Research Council*, Ann Arbor (MI), University of Michigan Press.

Flack, Bruce Clayton (1969): "The Work of the American Youth Commission, 1935–1942," PhD diss., Ohio State University.

Fleming, Donald (1963): "Social Darwinism," in Arthur M. Schlesinger, Jr.; Morton White (eds.): *Paths to American Thought*, Boston, Houghton Mifflin: 123–146.

—— (1967): "Attitude: The History of a Concept," *Perspectives in American History*, 1: 287–365.

Floro, George K. (1954): "The City Manager in the State of Michigan: A Sociological Study of Manager Careers," PhD in Sociology, University of Chicago.

—— (1955): "Continuity in City-Manager Careers," *American Journal of Sociology*, 61 (3): 240–246.

Frazier, E. Franklin (1925): "Durham: Capital of the Black Middle Class," in Alain Locke (ed.): *The New Negro*, New York, A. and C. Boni: 333–340.

—— (1929): "Bourgeoisie Noire," in V. F. Calverton (ed.): *Anthology of the Negro Literature in America*, New York, The Modern Library: 329–388.

—— (1930): "Occupational Classes among Negroes in Cities," *American Journal of Sociology*, 35 (5): 718–738.

—— (1932): *The Negro Family in Chicago*, Chicago, University of Chicago Press.

—— (1939): *The Negro Family in the United States*, Chicago, University of Chicago Press.

—— (1940a): *Negro Youth at the Crossways. Their Personality Development in the Middle States*, Washington, D.C., American Council of Education.

—— (1940b): "Review of Bertram Doyle's 'The Etiquette of Race Relations in the South,' *American Sociological Review*, 5 (4): 785.

—— (1942): "The Negro's Cultural Past," *The Nation*, 154, February 14: 195–196.

—— (1944a): "Rejoinder to W. T. Fontaine's Social Determination in the Writings of Negro Scholars," *American Journal of Sociology*, 49 (4): 313–314.

—— (1944b): "Review of 'An American Dilemma. The Negro Problem and Modern Democracy,'" *American Sociological Review*, 9 (3): 326–330.

—— (1949a): *The Negro in the United States*, New York, Macmillan Publishers.

—— (1949b): "Race Contacts and the Social Structure," *American Sociological Review*, 14 (1): 1–11.

—— (1950): "Review of Robert Park's Race and Culture," *American Journal of Sociology*, 55 (4): 413–415.

—— (1953): "Theoretical Structure of Sociology and Sociological Research," *British Journal of Sociology*, 4 (4): 292–311.

—— (1955): *Bourgeoisie Noire*, Paris, Plon.

—— (1957): *Race and Culture Contacts in the Modern World*, New York, Knopf.

—— (1957a): *Black Bourgeoisie*, New York, Free Press (English translation of Frazier [1955]).

—— (1962): "Condition of Negroes in American Cities," *Transactions of the Fifth World Congress of Sociology*, Washington, D.C., September 2–8, vol. 3: 133–139.

—— (1969): *The Complete Report of Mayor La Guardia's Commission on the Harlem Riot, March 19, 1935*, New York, Arno Press.

Frazier, E. Franklin; Lincoln, C. Eric (1964): *The Negro Church in America*, New York, Schocken.

Freidson, Eliot (1960): "Client Control and Medical Practice," *American Journal of Sociology*, 65 (4): 374–382.

—— (1970): *Profession of Medicine. A Study in the Sociology of Applied Knowledge*. New York, Dodd, Mead and Co.

—— (1977): "The Development of Design by Accident," in R. H. Elling; M. Sokolowska (eds.): *Medical Sociologists at Work*, New Brunswick (NJ), Transaction: 115–133.

Furner, Mary (1975): *Advocacy and Objectivity. A Crisis in the Professionalization of American Social Science (1865–1905)*, Lexington, University of Kentucky Press.

Galliher, John F.: (1995): "Chicago's Two Worlds of Deviance Research: Whose Side Are They On?" in Fine (1995): 164–187.

Galpin, Charles J. (1915): *The Social Anatomy of an Agricultural Community*, Madison (WI), AES bulletin 34.

Gans, Herbert (1968): "The Participant-Observer as a Human Being: Observations on the Personal Aspects of Field Work," in Becker, Geer, Riesman, Weiss (1968): 300–317.

—— (1990): "Relativism, Equality, and Popular Culture," in B. Berger (1990): 432–451.

—— (1997): "Reply," *Contemporary Sociology*, 26 (6): 789–790.

Gardner, Burleigh (1977): "The Anthropologist in Business and Industry," *Anthropological Quarterly*, 50 (4): 171–173.

Gardner, Burleigh B.; Whyte, William F. (1946): "Methods for the Study of Human Relations in Industry," *American Sociological Review*, 11 (5): 506–512.

Gardner, Burleigh B.; Gardner, Mary R.; Davis, Allison (1941): *Deep South*, Chicago, University of Chicago Press.

Gaylord, Mark S.; Galliher, John F. (1988): *The Criminology of Edwin Sutherland*, New Brunswick (NJ), Transaction Publishers.

Gaziano, Emanuel (1996): "Ecological Metaphors as Scientific Boundary Work: Innovation and Authority in Interwar Sociology and Biology," *American Journal of Sociology*, 101 (4): 874–907.

Geiger, Roger L. (1988): "American Foundations and Academic Social Science, 1945–1960," *Minerva*, 26 (3): 315–341.

Genov, Nicolai (ed.) (1989): *National Traditions in Sociology*, London, Sage Publications.

Getis, Victoria (2000): *The Juvenile Court and the Progressives*, Chicago, University of Illinois Press.

Gibbons, Don C. (1979): *The Criminological Enterprise. Theories and Perspectives*, Englewood Cliffs (NJ), Prentice Hall.

Gilbert, James (1986): *A Cycle of Outrage. America's Reaction to the Juvenile Delinquent in the 1950s*, New York, Oxford University Press.

Gilkeson, John S. (1995): "American Social Scientists and the Domestication of 'Class' 1929–1955," *Journal of the History of the Behavorial Sciences*, 31 (4): 331–346.

Gillespie, Richard (1991): *Manufacturing Knowledge. A History of the Hawthorne Experiments*, New York, Cambridge University Press.

Gillin, John L. (1926): *Criminology and Penology*, New York, The Century Press.

Gilman, Glenn W. (1956): *Human Relations in the Industrial Southeast. A Study of the Textile Industry*, Chapel Hill, University of North Carolina Press.

Gilmore, Samuel (1988): "Schools of Activity and Innovation," *The Sociological Quarterly*, 29 (2): 203–219.

Gilpin, Patrick Joseph (1973): "Charles S. Johnson: An Intellectual Biography," PhD, Vanderbilt University.

Ginger, Ray (1986): *Altgeld's America. The Lincoln Ideal Versus Changing Realities. Chicago from 1892–1905*, New York, M. Wiener (republication of a 1958 book, with an introduction by Gary Gerstle).

Glaser, Barney G.; Strauss, Anselm L. (1965): *Awareness of Dying*, Chicago, Aldine.

Glazer, Nathan (1963): "Reality Comes to US Sociology," *New Society*, 49, September 5: 14–15.

Glick, Clarence E. (1928): "Winnetka: A Study of a Residential Suburban Community," MA in Sociology, University of Chicago.

Goffman, Erving (1953): "Communication Conduct in an Island Community," PhD in Sociology, University of Chicago.

—— (1959): *The Presentation of Self in Everyday Life*, Garden City (NY), Doubleday.

—— (1961): *Asylums. Essays on the Social Situation of Mental Patients and Other Inmates*, Garden City (NY), Doubleday.

—— (1963): *Stigma. Notes on the Management of Spoiled Identity*, Englewood Cliffs (NJ), Prentice Hall.

—— (1983): "The Interaction Order," *American Sociological Review*, 48 (1): 1–17.

—— (1988): *Les moments et leurs hommes*, Paris, Seuil/Éditions de Minuit: 186–230.

Gold, Ray (1952): "Janitor versus Tenants: A Status-Income Dilemma," *American Journal of Sociology*, 57 (5): 486–493.

—— (1954): "Toward a Social Interaction Methodology for Sociological Field Observation," PhD in Sociology, University of Chicago.

—— (1958): "Roles in Sociological Field Observations," *Social Forces*, 36 (3): 217–233.

—— (1964): "In the Basement: The Apartment-Building Janitor," in Peter Berger (ed.): *The Human Shape of Work. Studies in the Sociology of Occupations*, New York, Macmillan: 1–49.

Goldstein, Rhoda L. (1954): "The Professional Nurse in the Hospital Bureaucracy," PhD in Sociology, University of Chicago.

Goodspeed, Thomas Wakefield (1916): *A History of the University of Chicago. The First Quarter-Century*, Chicago, University of Chicago Press.

Gordon, Milton J. (1964): *Assimilation in American Life. The Role of Race, Religion and National Origins*, New York, Oxford University Press.

Gosnell, Harold (1927): *Getting out the Vote. An Experiment in the Stimulation of Voting*, Chicago, University of Chicago Press.

—— (1935): *Negro Politicians. The Rise of Negro Politics in Chicago*, Chicago, University of Chicago Press.

Gosnell, Harold; Merriam, Charles (1924): *Non-Voting. Causes and Methods of Control*, Chicago, University of Chicago Press.

Gould, Joseph E. (1961): *Chautauqua Movement. An Episode in the Continuing American Revolution*, Albany, State University of New York Press.

Gouldner, Alvin (1962): "Anti-Minotaur: The Myth of Value-Free Sociology," *Social Problems*, 9 (3): 209–217.

—— (1970): *The Coming Crisis of Western Sociology*, New York, Basic Books.

Grafmeyer, Yves; Joseph, Isaac (eds.) (1979): *L'École de Chicago. Naissance de l'écologie urbaine*, Paris, Editions du Champ Urbain.

Greene, Victor (1975): *For God and Country. The Rise of Polish and Lithuanian Ethnic Consciousness in America, 1860–1910*, Madison, The State Historical Society of Wisconsin.

Grossman, James R. (1989): *Land of Hope. Chicago, Black Southerners and the Great Migration*, Chicago, University of Chicago Press.

Gusfield, Joseph R. (1954): "Organizational Change: A Study of WCTU," PhD in Sociology, University of Chicago.

—— (1955): "Social Structure and Moral Reform: A Study of the Woman's Christian Temperance Union," *American Journal of Sociology*, 61 (3): 221–232.

—— (1963): *Symbolic Crusade. Status Politics and the American Temperance Movement*, Urbana, University of Illinois Press.

—— (1976): "The Literary Rhetoric of Science: Comedy and Pathos in Drinking Driver Research," *American Sociological Review*, 41 (1): 16–34.

—— (1984): "On the Side: Practical Action and Social Constructivism in Social Problem Theory," in Joseph W. Schneider; John I. Kitsuse (eds.): *Studies in the Sociology of Social Problems*, Norwood (NJ), Ablex Publishing Corporation: 31–51.

—— (1990): "My Life and Soft Times," in B. Berger: 104–129.

—— (1992): "The Scholarly Tension: Graduate Craft and Undergraduate Imagination," in J. MacAloon (1992): 167–177.

—— (1995): "Preface" in Fine (ed.) (1995): ix–xiv.

Guth, Suzie (2007): *Histoire de Molly fille de joie. San Francisco, 1912–1915*, Paris, L'Harmattan.

—— (dir.) (2008): *Modernité de Robert Park*, Paris, L'Harmattan.

—— (2012): *Robert E. Park. itinéraire sociologique de Red Wing à Chicago*, Paris, Harmattan.

Gutman, Herbert G. (1976): *Black Family in Slavery and Freedom, 1750–1925*, Cambridge, Basil Blackwell.

Habenstein, Robert W. (1962): "Sociology of Occupations: The Case of the American Funeral Director," in Rose (1962): 225–246.

—— (1963): "Critique of 'Profession' as a Sociological Category," *Sociological Quarterly*, 4 (3): 291–300.

—— (1968): "The Phoenix and the Ashes," in Becker; Geer; Riesman; Weiss (1968): 208–218.

Haerle, Rudolf K. (1991): "William Isaac Thomas and the Helen Culver Fund for Race Psychology: The Beginnings of Scientific Sociology at the University of Chicago, 1910–1913," *Journal of the History of the Behavorial Sciences*, 27 (1): 21–41.

Hale, William (1949): "The Career Development of the Negro Lawyer in Chicago," PhD in Sociology, University of Chicago.

—— (1952): "The Negro Lawyer and his Clients," *Phylon*, 13 (1): 57–63.

Hall, Oswald (1944): "The Informal Organization of the Medical Practice in an American City," PhD in Sociology, University of Chicago.

—— (1946): "The Informal Organization of the Medical Profession," *The Canadian Journal of Economics and Political Science*, 12 (1): 30–44.

—— (1948): "The Stages of Medical Career," *American Journal of Sociology*, 53 (5): 327–336.

—— (1949): "Types of Medical Careers," *American Journal of Sociology*, 55 (3): 243–253.

Halley, Lois K. (1924): "A Study of Motion Pictures in Chicago as a Medium of Communication," MA in Sociology, University of Chicago.

Hammersley, Martyn (1989): *The Dilemma of Qualitative Method. Herbert Blumer and the Chicago Tradition*, London, Routledge.

Hannerz, Ulf (1980): *Exploring the City. Inquiries toward an Urban Anthropology*, New York, Columbia University Press.

Hapgood, Hutchins (1903): *The Autobiography of a Thief*, New York, Fox, Duffield & Company.

—— (1939): *A Victorian in the Modern World*, New York: Harcourt, Brace.

Hare, Nathan (1962): "Rebels without a Name," *Phylon*, 32 (3): 271–277.

Harper, Douglas A. (1982): *Good Company*, Chicago, University of Chicago Press (French translation: *Les vagabonds du Nord-Ouest américain*, Paris, Harmattan, 1998).

Harris, Chauncy D. (1943): "Suburbs," *The American Journal of Sociology*, 49 (1): 1–13.

Harris, Grace E. (1975): "The Life and Work of E. Franklin Frazier," PhD, University of Virginia.

Harris, Howell J. (1982): *The Right to Manage. Industrial Relations Policies of American Business in the 1940s*, Madison (WI), University of Wisconsin Press.

Hartmann, Edward George (1948): *The Movement to Americanize the Immigrant*, New York, Columbia University Press.

Harvey, Lee (1986): "The Myths of the Chicago School," *Quality and Quantity*, 20: 191–217.

—— (1987): *Myths of the Chicago School of Sociology*, Aldershot (UK), Avebury.

Haskell, Martin R.; Yablonsky, Lewis (1974): *Juvenile Delinquency*, Chicago, Rand McNally.

Haskell, Thomas L. (1977): *The Emergence of Professional Social Science*, Urbana, University of Illinois Press.

Havighurst, Robert J.; Loeb, Martin B.; Warner, W. Loyd (1944): *Who Shall be Educated. The Challenge of Unequal Opportunities*, London, Kegan Paul.

Hawkins, Hugh (1979): "University Identity: The Teaching and Research Functions," in Alexandra Oleson; John Voss (eds.): *The Organization of Knowledge in Modern America, 1860–1920*, Baltimore, Johns Hopkins University Press: 285–312.

Hayner, Norman (1923): "The Sociology of Hotel Life," PhD in Sociology, University of Chicago.

—— (1936): *Hotel Life*, Chapel Hill, University of North Carolina Press.

Hays, Samuel P. (1957): *Response to Industrialism, 1885–1914*, Chicago, University of Chicago Press.

—— (1964): "The Politics of Reform in Municipal Government in the Progressive Era," *Pacific Northwest Quarterly*, 55 (October): 157–169.

Healy, William (1915): *The Individual Delinquent. A Text-Book of Diagnosis and Prognosis for All Concerned in Understanding Offenders*, Boston, Little Brown.

Helm-Hayes, Rick; Santoro, Marco (eds.) (2016): *The Anthem Companion to Everett Hughes*, London, Anthem Press.

Heap, Chad (2003): "The City as a Sexual Laboratory: The Queer Heritage of the Chicago School," *Qualitative Sociology*, 26 (4), 457–487.

Hegner, Herman F. (1897): "Scientific Value of The Social Settlement," *American Journal of Sociology*, 3 (2): 175–182.

Henderson, Charles (1893): *An Introduction to the Study of the Dependent, Defective and Delinquent Classes*, Boston, D. C. Heath and Co.

—— (1894): *Catechism for Social Observation and Analyses of Social Phenomena*, Boston, D. C. Heath and Co.

—— (1909): *Education with Reference to Sex*, Bloomington, Public School Pub. Co.

—— (1914): *The Cause and Cure of Crime*, Chicago, A. M. McClung.

Herpin, Nicolas (1973): *Les sociologues américains et le siècle*, Paris, Presses Universitaires de France.

Herskovits, Melville J. (1941): *The Myth of the Negro Past*, New York, Harper and Brothers.

Heyl, Barbara S. (1968): "The Harvard 'Pareto Circle,' " *Journal of the History of the Behavorial Sciences*, 4 (4): 316–333.

Higham, John (1975): *Send These to Me. Jews and Other Immigrants in Urban America*, New York, Atheneum.

Hill, Joseph A. (1936): "Composition of the American Population by Race and Country of Origin," *The Annals of the American Academy of Political and Social Science*, 188 (November): 177–184.

Hiller, Ernest T. (1928): *The Strike. A Study in Collective Action*, Chicago, University of Chicago Press.

Hinkle, Roscoe C. (1980): *Founding Theory of American Sociology, 1881–1915*, London, Routledge.

Hinkle, Roscoe C.; Hinkle, Gisela J. (1965) [1954]: *The Development of Modern Sociology, Its Nature and Growth in the United States* (8th edition), New York, Random House.

Hirsch, Arnold M. (1983): *Making the Second Ghetto. Race and Housing in Chicago, 1940–1960*, Cambridge, Cambridge University Press.

Hofstadter, Richard (1955): *The Age of Reform. From Bryan to F. D. R.*, New York, Knopf.

Hogan, David J. (1985): *Class and Reform. School and Society in Chicago, 1830–1930*, Philadelphia, University of Pennsylvania Press.

Hollinger, David A. (1973): "T. S. Kuhn's Theory of Science and Its Implications for History," *The American Historical Review*, 78 (2): 370–393.

Holt, Hamilton (ed.) (1906): *The Life Stories of Undistinguished Americans as Told by Themselves*, New York, James, Potter & Co. (republished in 2000).

Homans, George Caspar (1949): "The Strategy of Industrial Sociology," *American Journal of Sociology*, 54 (4): 330–337.

—— (1984): *Coming to my Senses. The Autobiography of a Sociologist*, New Brunswick (NJ), Transaction Publishers.

Horak, Jacob (1920): "The Assimilation of the Czechs in Chicago," PhD in Sociology, University of Chicago.

Horowitz, Helen Lefkowitz (1976): *Culture and the City. Cultural Philanthropy in Chicago from the 1880s to 1917*, Lexington, University Press of Kentucky.

Horowitz, Irving Louis (ed.) (1969): *Sociological Self-Images. A Collective Portrait*, Beverly Hills (CA), Sage Publications.

House, Floyd N. (1924): "Industrial Morale: An Essay in the Sociology of Industrial Control," PhD in Sociology, University of Chicago.

—— (1936): *The Development of Sociology*, New York, McGraw-Hill.

Howerth, Ira W. (1894): "Present Condition of Sociology in the United States," *The Annals of the American Academy of Political and Social Science*, 5 (September): 112–121.

Hoyt, Homer (1941): "Forces of Urban Centralization and Decentralization," *The American Journal of Sociology*, 46 (6): 843–852.

Hughes, Everett C. (1928): "A Study of Secular Institution: The Chicago Real Estate Board," PhD in Sociology, University of Chicago.

—— (1931): *The Chicago Real Estate Board. The Growth of an Institution*, The Society for Social Research of the University of Chicago, Series II, Monograph no. 1, Chicago (Abridged version of the dissertation, republished in 1979 by Arno Press, New York).

—— (1935): "The Industrial Revolution and the Catholic Movement in Germany," *Social Forces*, 14 (2): 286–292 (SE: 255–264).

—— (1937): "Institutional Office and the Person," *American Journal of Sociology*, 43 (3): 404–413 (SE: 132–140).

—— (1943): *French Canada in Transition*, Chicago, University of Chicago Press (French translation by Jean-Charles Falardeau [1945]: *Rencontre de deux mondes. La crise d'industrialisation du Canada Français*, Montreal, Parizeau).

—— (1946a): "The Knitting of Racial Groups in Industry," *American Sociological Review*, 11 (5): 512–19 (SE: 265–275).

—— (1946b): "Race Relations in Industry," in W. F. Whyte (ed.) (1946): 107–122.

—— (1948): "The Study of Ethnic Relations," *Dalhousie Review*, 27 (4): 477–482 (SE: 153–158).

—— (1949): "Queries Concerning Industry and Society Growing out of Study of Ethnic Relations in Industry," *American Sociological Review*, 14 (2): 211–20 (SE: 73–86).

—— (1951a): "Work and the Self," in J. N. Rohrer; M. Sherif (eds.): *Social Psychology at the Crossroads*, New York, Harper: 313–323 (SE: 338–347).

—— (1951b): "Studying the Nurse's Work," *American Journal of Nursing*, 1951, 51: 294–95 (SE: 311–345).

—— (1951c): "Bastard Institution," unpublished course, published in SE: 98–105.

—— (1952): "The Sociological Study of Work: An Editorial Foreword," *American Journal of Sociology*, 57 (5): 423–426 (SE: 298–303).

—— (1956): "Social Role and the Division of Labor," *Midwest Sociologist*, 17 (1): 3–7 (SE: 304–310).

—— (1958): *Men and Their Work*, Glencoe, The Free Press.

—— (1960): "The Place of Field Work in Social Science," in B. H. Junker (1960): iii–xiii (SE: 496–506).

—— (1961): "The Nature of Racial Frontiers," in J. Masuoka; P. Valien (eds.): *Race Relations: Problems and Theory. Essays in Honor of Robert E. Park*, Chapel Hill (NC), University of North Carolina Press (SE: 167–173).

—— (1962): "Going Concerns: The Study of American Institutions," presented at the annual meeting of the Southwestern Sociological Society (SE: 52–64).

—— (1963a): "The Natural History of a Research Project: French Canada," *Anthropologica*, 5 (2): 225–239 (SE: 530–542).

—— (1963b): "Race Relations and the Sociological Imagination," *American Sociological Review*, 28 (6): 897–90 (SE: 478–485).

—— (1964): "Founders of Social Science: Robert E. Park," *New Society*, December 31: 18–19 (SE 543–549).

—— (1967): "My Personal Experience of Race," Unpublished lecture to the meeting of the American Sociological Association of August 31, 1967.

—— (1970a): "Teaching as Field Work," *The American Sociologist*, 5 (1): 13–18 (SE: 566–576).

—— (1970b): "The Humble and the Proud: The Comparative Study of Occupations," *The Sociological Quarterly*, 11 (2): 147–156 (SE: 417–427).

—— (1971): *The Sociological Eye. Selected Papers*, Chicago, Aldine.

—— (1974): "Who Studies Whom?" *Human Organization*, 33 (4): 327–334.

—— (1976): "The Social Drama of Work," *Mid-American Review of Sociology*, 1 (1): 1–7.

—— (1994): *Everett C. Hughes on Work, Race, and the Sociological Imagination*, Chicago, University of Chicago Press.

—— (1996): *Le regard sociologique*, Paris, Éditions de l'EHESS (collection of essays translated into French with an introduction by J.-M. Chapoulie).

—— (1997): "Careers," *Qualitative Sociology*, 20 (3): 389–397.

Hughes, Everett C.; Hill, Mozell C. (1946): "The Negro Man and His Work. Social Differentiation among the Negro Male Workers," *The Southwest Journal*, 2 (2): 129–139.

Hughes, Everett C.; Hughes, Helen MacGill (1952): *Where Peoples Meet: Racial and Ethnic Frontiers*, Glencoe, The Free Press.

Hughes, Everett; Hughes, Helen MacGill; Deutscher, Irwin (1958): *Twenty Thousand Nurses Tell Their Story*, Philadelphia, Lippincott.

Hughes, Everett; Thorne, Barry; De Baggis, Agostini; Gurin Arnold; Williams, David (1973): *Education for the Professions of Medicine, Law, Theology and Social Welfare*, New York, MacGraw Hill.

Hughes, Helen MacGill (1940): *News and the Human Interest Story*, Chicago, University of Chicago Press.

—— (ed.) (1961): *The Fantastic Lodge. The Autobiography of a Girl Drug Addict*, Boston, Houghton Mifflin.

—— (1980): "Robert Ezra Park: The Philosopher, Newspaperman, Sociologist," in R. K. Merton; M. Riley (eds.): *Sociological Traditions from Generation to Generation. Glimpses of the American Experiences*, Norwood (NJ), Ablex Pub: 67–79.

—— (1980-1981): "On Becoming a Sociologist," *Journal of the History of Sociology*, 3 (1): 27–39.

—— (1895): *Hull House Maps and Papers, by Residents of Hull House, a Social Settlement. A Presentation of Nationalities and Wages in a Congested District of Chicago, Together with Comments and Essays on Problems Growing out of the Social Conditions*, New York, Crowell.

Hunter, Albert J. (1973): "Introduction," in Burgess (1973): 3–15.

—— (1980): "Why Chicago? The Rise of the Chicago School of Urban Social Science," *American Behavioral Scientist*, 24 (2): 215–27.

Hutchins, Robert M. (1936): *The Higher Learning in America*, New Haven (CT), Yale University Press.

Iverson, Noel (1977): "Homage to a Pioneer," Address in honor of Nels Anderson, Annual Conference of the Atlantic Association of Sociologists and Anthropologists, Acadia University, Wolfville, Nova Scotia.

Jackson, Walter A. (1990): *Gunnar Myrdal and America's Conscience. Social Engineering and Racial Liberalism, 1938–1987*, Chapel Hill, University of North Carolina Press.

James, William (1899): "On a Certain Blindness in Human Beings," in (1983) *The Works of William James*, vol. 10, *Talks to Teachers on Psychology and to Students on Some of Life's Ideals*, Cambridge (MA), Harvard University Press: 132–149.

—— (1902): *The Varieties of Religious Experience. A Study in Human Nature, Being the Gifford Lectures on Natural Religion Delivered at Edinburgh in 1901–1902*, New York, London [etc.], Longmans, Green, and Co.

Janowitz, Morris (1966): "Introduction," in Thomas (1966): vii–lviii.

Jaworski, Gary D. (2000): "Erving Goffman: The Reluctant Apprentice," *Symbolic Interaction*, 23 (3): 299–308.

Johnson, Charles S. (1934): *Shadow of the Plantation*, Chicago, University of Chicago Press.

—— (1936): "The Conflict of Caste and Class in an American Industry," *American Journal of Sociology*, 42 (1): 55–65.

—— (1938): *The Negro College Graduate*, Chapel Hill, University of North Carolina Press.

—— (1941): *Growing Up in the Black Belt*, Washington, D.C., American Council on Education.

—— (1944): "Robert E. Park," *Sociology and Social Research*, 28 (5): 354–58.

Johnson, Charles S.; Embree, Edwin R.; Alexander, Will (1935): *The Collapse of Cotton Tenancy*, Chapel Hill, University of North Carolina Press.

Johnson, Guy Benton (1923): "A Sociological Interpretation of the New Ku-Klux Movement," *Social Forces*, 1 (4): 440–445.

Johnson, Guy Benton; Johnson, Guion Griffis (1980): *Research in Service to Society. The Fifty Years of the Institute for Research in Social Sciences at the University of North Carolina*, Chapel Hill, University of North Carolina Press.

Jones, Robert Alun (1983): "The New History of Sociology," *Annual Review of Sociology*, 9, 447–469.

Junker, Buford H. (1960): *Field Work. An Introduction to the Social Sciences*, Chicago, University of Chicago Press.

Kaplan Daniels, Arlene (1972): "The Irreverent Eye," *Contemporary Sociology*, 1 (5): 402–409.

Karl, Barry D. (1974): *Charles E. Merriam and the Study of Politics*, Chicago, University of Chicago Press.

—— (1983): *The Uneasy State. The United States from 1915 to 1945*, Chicago, University of Chicago Press.

Karl, Barry D.; Katz, Stanley N. (1981): "The American Private Philanthropic Foundations and the Public Sphere, 1890–1930," *Minerva*, 19 (2): 236–270.

Karsh, Bernard (1955): "The Labor Strike in a Small Community," PhD in Sociology, University of Chicago.

—— (1968): "Human Relations versus Management," in Becker; Geer; Riesman; Weiss (1968): 35–48.

Kaufman, Bruce E. (1993): *The Origins and Evolution of the Field of Industrial Relations in the United States*, Ithaca (NY), ILR Press.

Kawabe, Kisaburo (1921): *The Press and Politics in Japan*, Chicago, University of Chicago Press.

Kawamura, Tadao (1928): "The Class Conflict in Japan as Affected by the Expansion of Japanese Industry and Trade," PhD in Sociology, University of Chicago.

Kelley, Donald R. (1990): "What Is Happening to the History of Ideas?" *Journal of the History of Ideas*, 51 (1), 3–25.

Killian, Lewis M. (1952): "The Effects of Southern White Workers on Race Relations in Northern Plants," *American Sociological Review*, 17 (3): 327–331.

—— (1994): *Black and White. Reflections of a White Southern Sociologist*, New York, General Hall.

Kincheloe, Samuel C. (1972): *The American City and Its Church*, New York, Friendship Press.

—— (1989): *The Church in the City. Samuel Kincheloe and the Sociology of the City Church* (ed. by Yoshio Fukuyama), Chicago, Exploration Press.

Kiniewicz, Stefan (dir.) (1969a): *Historia Polski 1795–1918*, vol. 3, Warszawa, Panstwowe Wydawnictwo.

—— (1969b): *The Emancipation of the Polish Peasantry*, Chicago, University of Chicago Press.

Klausner, Samuel Z.; Lidz, Victor M. (eds.) (1986): *The Nationalization of the Social Sciences*, Philadelphia, University of Pennsylvania Press.

Klautke, Egbert (2013): *The Mind of the Nation. Völkerpsychologie in Germany, 1851–1955*, New York, Bergahn Books.

Kobrin, Solomon (1959): "The Chicago Area Project: A Twenty-Five Years Assessment," *The Annals of the American Academy of Political and Social Science*, 322 (March): 20–32.

Kraditor, Aileen S. (1967): *The Ideas of the Women Suffrage Movement, 1890–1920*, New York, Columbia University Press.

Kreisberg, Louis (1952): "The Retail Furrier: Concepts of Security and Success," *American Journal of Sociology*, 57 (5): 478–485.

—— (1953): "Customer versus Colleague Ties among Retail Furriers," *Journal of Retailing*, 29: 173–176, 190–191.

Kuhn, Thomas S. (1962): *The Structure of Scientific Revolutions*, Chicago, University of Chicago Press.

—— (1977): *The Essential Tension. Selected Studies in Scientific Tradition and Change*, Chicago, University of Chicago Press.

Kuklick, Henrika (1973): "A Scientific Revolution: Sociological Theory in the United States, 1930–1945," *Sociological Inquiry*, 43 (1): 3–22.

—— (1980): "Restructuring the Past: Toward an Appreciation of the Social Context of Social Science," *The Sociological Quarterly*, 21 (1): 5–21.

—— (1984): "The Ecology of Sociology," *American Journal of Sociology*, 89 (6): 1433–1440.

—— (1999): "Assessing Research in the History of Sociology and Anthropology," *Journal of the History of the Behavioral Sciences*, 35(3), 227–237.

Kurtz, Lester R. (1982): "Robert E. Park's Notes on the Origins of the Society for Social Research," *Journal of the History of the Behavorial Sciences*, 18 (3): 332–340.

—— (1984): *Evaluating Chicago Sociology. A Guide to the Literature, with an Annotated Bibliography*, Chicago, University of Chicago Press.

Lagemann, Ellen Condliffe (1989): *The Politics of Knowledge. The Carnegie Corporation, Philanthropy, and Public Policy*, Middletown (CT), Wesleyan University Press.

Lal, Barbara Ballis (1986): "The Chicago School of American Sociology, Symbolic Interactionism and Race Relations Theory," in John Rex; David Mason (eds.): *Theories of Race and Ethnic Relations*, Cambridge, Cambridge University Press: 280–298.

—— (1990): *The Romance of Culture in an Urban Civilization. Robert E. Park and the Chicago School*, London, Routledge.

Landesco, John (1929): *Organized Crime in Chicago*, Chicago, Illinois Association for Criminal Justice.

Lannoy, Pierre (2004): "When Robert E. Park Was (Re) Writing 'the City': Biography, the Social Survey, and the Science of Sociology," *The American Sociologist*, 35 (1): 34–62.

—— (2008): "Park à l'école de Boston ou de l'américanisation de son anthropologie," in Suzie Guth (dir.): *Modernité de Robert Park*, Paris, L'Harmattan: 83–114.

Lannoy, Pierre; Ruwet, Coline (2004): "Autorité de chaire et modèle de chair," *Archives européennes de sociologie*, 45 (1): 81–112.

LaPiere, Richard T. (1934): "Attitudes vs. Actions," *Social Forces*, 13 (2): 230–237.

Larsen, Otto N. (1992): *Milestones and Millstones. Social Science at the National Science Foundation, 1945–1991*, New Brunswick (NJ), Transaction Publishers.

Laub, John H. (1983): *Criminology in the Making. An Oral History*, Boston, Northeastern University Press.

Lawson, Lawrence B. (1955): "The Protestant Minister in Chicago," PhD in Sociology, University of Chicago.

Lawton, William C. (1955): "The Du Ponts: A Case Study of Kinship in the Business Organization," PhD in Sociology, University of Chicago.

Lee, Raymond M. (2008): "Park, Bogardus et l'enquête sur les relations interaciales dans la région du Pacifique," in Suzie Guth (ed.): *Modernité de Robert Park*, Paris, L'Harmattan: 189–211.

Lemert, Edwin M. (1951): *Social Pathology*, New York, McGraw-Hill.

—— (1976): "Response to Critics: Feedback and Choice," in Lewis A. Coser; Otto N. Larsen (eds.): *The Uses of Controversy in Sociology*, New York, Free Press: 244–249.

Lengermann, Patricia Madoo (1979): "The Founding of American Sociological Review," *American Sociological Review*, 44 (2): 185–198.

—— (1988): "Robert E. Park and the Theoretical Content of Chicago Sociology: 1920–1940," *Sociological Inquiry*, 58 (4): 361–377.

Lengermann, Patricia Madoo; Niebrugge-Brantley, Jill (2002): "Back to the Future: Settlement Sociology, 1885–1930," *The American Sociologist*, 33 (3): 5–20.

Leuchtenburg, William E. (1963): *The Perils of Prosperity, 1914–1932*, Chicago, University of Chicago Press.

Levine, Lawrence W. (1977): *Black Culture and Black Consciousness. Afro-American Folk Thought from Slavery to Freedom*, New York, Oxford University Press.

Lewis, David J.; Smith, Richard L. (1981): *American Sociology and Pragmatism. Mead, Chicago Sociology and Symbolic Interaction*, Chicago, University of Chicago Press.

Lewis, David Levering (1981): *When Harlem Was in Vogue*, New York, Knopf.

Lichtenstein, Nelson (1982): *Labor's War at Home: The CIO in World War Two*, New York, Cambridge University Press.

—— (1989): "From Corporatism to Collective Bargaining: Organized Labor and the Eclipse of Social Democracy in the Postwar Era," in Steve Fraser; Gary Gerstle (eds.): *The Rise and Fall of the New Deal Order, 1930–1980*, Princeton (NJ), Princeton University Press: 122–152.

Liebow, Elliot (1967): *Tally's Corner*, Boston, Little Brown.

Lind, Andrew (1938): *An Island Community. Ecological Succession in Hawaii*, Chicago, University of Chicago Press.

—— (ed.) (1955): *Race Relations in World Perspective*, Honolulu, University of Hawaii Press.

Lindesmith, Alfred R. (1937): "The Nature of Opiate Addiction," PhD in Sociology, University of Chicago.

—— (1947): *Opiate Addiction*, Bloomington (IN), Principia Press.

—— (1968): *Addiction and Opiates*, Chicago, Aldine.

Lindner, Rolf (1996): *The Reportage of Urban Culture. Robert Park and the Chicago School*, New York, Cambridge University Press.

Lindstrom, Fred B.; Hardert, Ronald A. (eds.) (1988): "Kimball Young on Founders of the Chicago School," *Sociological Perspectives*, 31 (3): 269–297.

—— (1988): "Kimball Young on the Chicago School: Later Contacts," *Sociological Perspectives*, 31 (3): 298–314.

Lindstrom, Fred B.; Hardert, Ronald A.; Johnson, Laura L. (eds.) (1995): *Kimball Young on Sociology in Transition, 1912–1968*, Lanham (MD), University Press of America.

Link, Arthur S. (1959): "What Happened to the Progressive Movement in the 1920s," *American Historical Review*, 64 (4): 833–851.

Link, Arthur Stanley; McCormick, Richard L. (1983): *Progressivism*, Arlington Heights, Harlan Davidson.

Lipsitz, George (1981): *Class and Culture in Cold War America. A Rainbow at Midnight*, South Hadley (MA), J. F. Bergen.

Lissak, Riva Shpak (1989): *Pluralism and Progressives. Hull House and the New Immigrants, 1890–1919*, Chicago, Chicago University Press.

Locke, Alain (ed.) (1925): *The New Negro, An Interpretation*, New York, A. and C. Boni.

Locke, Harvey J. (1948): "Research Methods as Viewed by W. I. Thomas," *Sociology and Social Research*, 32 (6): 907–910.

Lofland, Lyn H. (ed.) (1980): "Reminiscences of Classic Chicago: The Blumer-Hughes Talk," *Urban Life*, 9 (3): 251–281.

Lohman, Joseph D. (1937): "The Participant Observer in Community Studies," *American Sociological Review*, 2 (6): 890–898.

—— (1958): "A Sociologist-Sheriff Speaks out about Juvenile Delinquency," *Phi Delta Kappan*, (February): 206–214.

Lohman, Joseph D.; Reitzes, Dietrich (1952): "Note on Race Relations in Mass Society," *American Journal of Sociology*, 58 (3): 240–246.

—— (1954): "Deliberately Organized Groups and Racial Behavior," *American Sociological Review*, 19 (3): 342–344.

Loomis, Charles P.; Loomis, Zona K. (1967): "Rural Sociology," in Paul F. Lazarsfeld; William Sewell; Harold Wilensky (eds.): *The Uses of Sociology*, New York, Basic Books: 655–691.

Lopata, Helena Znaniecka (1954): "The Functions of Voluntary Associations in an Ethnic Community: Polonia," PhD in Sociology, University of Chicago.

—— (1976a): *Polish Americans. Status Competition in an Ethnic Community*, Englewood Cliffs (NJ), Prentice Hall.

—— (1976b): "Florian Znaniecki: Creative Evolution of a Sociologist," *Journal of the History of the Behavioral Sciences*, 12: 203–215.

—— (1994): *Polish Americans*, New Brunswick (NJ), Transaction Publishers (second edition, but with different phrasing).

—— (1995): "Postscript," in Fine (1995: 365–386).

—— (1996): "Polonia and the Polish Peasant in Europe and America," *Journal of American Ethnic History*, 16 (1): 37–46.

Lortie, Dan Clement (1958): "The Striving Young Lawyer: A Study of Early Career Differentiation in the Chicago Bar," PhD in Sociology, University of Chicago.

Lubove, Roy (1962): "The Progressives and the Prostitute," *Historian*, 24: 308–330.

—— (1965): *The Professional Altruist. The Emergence of Social Work as a Career, 1880–1930*, Cambridge (MA), Harvard University Press.

Luker, Ralph (1998): *The Social Gospel in Black and White. American Racial Reform, 1885–1912*, Chapel Hill, University of North Carolina Press.

Lyman, Stanford M. (1972): *The Black American in Sociological Thought*, New York, G. P. Putnam's Sons.

—— (1990): "Robert E. Park Reconsidered: The Early Writings," *The American Sociologist*, 21 (4): 342–351.

—— (1992): *Militarism, Imperialism and Racial Accommodation. An Analysis and Interpretation of the Early Writings of Robert E. Park*, Fayetteville (AR), University of Arkansas Press (contains Park's articles previous to his being hired by the University of Chicago).

Lyman, Stanford M.; Vidich, Arthur J. (1988): *Social Order and the Public Philosophy. An Analysis and Interpretation of the Work of Herbert Blumer*, Fayetteville, University of Arkansas Press (contains about thirty articles by Blumer).

Lynd, Robert S.; Lynd, Helen Merrell (1929): *Middletown. A Study in Modern American Culture*, New York, Harcourt Brace.

—— (1937): *Middletown in Transition. A Study in Cultural Conflicts*, New York, Harcourt Brace.

MacAloon, John J. (ed.) (1992): *General Education in the Social Sciences. Centennial Reflections on the College of the University of Chicago*, Chicago, University of Chicago Press.

McCarthy, Kathleen D. (1982): *Noblesse Oblige. Charity and Cultural Philanthropy in Chicago, 1849–1929*, Chicago, University of Chicago Press.

McDowell, Harold (1954): "The Principal's Role in a Metropolitan School System: Its Functions and Variations," PhD in Sociology, University of Chicago.

McGovern, James R. (1968): "The American Woman's Pre-World War I Freedom in Manners and Morals," *The Journal of American History*, 55 (2): 315–333.

McKee, James B. (1993): *Sociology and the Race Problem. The Failure of a Perspective*, Urbana (IL), University of Illinois Press.

McKenzie, Roderick D. (1923): *The Neighborhood. A Study of Local Life in the City of Columbus, Ohio*, Chicago, University of Chicago Press (author's dissertation published in five issues of the *American Journal of Sociology* between September 1921 and May 1922).

McKinney, John C. (1966): *Constructive Typology and Social Theory*, New York, Irvington.

McNeill, William H. (1991): *Hutchins' University. A Memoir of the University of Chicago, 1929–1950*, Chicago, University of Chicago Press.

Madge, John (1962): *The Origins of Scientific Sociology*, New York, Free Press.

Magubane, Zine (2014): "Science, Reform, and the 'science of Reform': Booker T. Washington, Robert Park, and the Making of a 'Science of Society,' " *Current Sociology Monograph*, 62 (4): 568–583.

Maines, David; Bridger, Jeffrey C.; Ulmer, Jeffery T. (1996): "Mythic Facts and Park's Pragmatism: On Predecessor-Selection and Theorizing in Human Ecology," *Sociological Quarterly*, 37 (3): 521–549.

Malinowski, Bronislaw (1922): *The Argonauts of Western Pacific. An Account of Native Enterprise and Adventure in the Archipelagoes of Melanesian New Guinea*, London, Routledge.

—— (1926): *Crime and Custom in Savage Society*, London, Routledge.

Manis, Jerome G.; Meltzer, Bernard N. (1967): *Symbolic Interaction. A Reader in Social Psychology*, Boston, Allyn and Bacon.

Mannheim, Karl (1929): *Ideologie und Utopie*, Bonn (Germany), F. Cohen.

—— (1932): "Review of 'Methods in Social Science' ed. by Stuart A. Rice," *American Journal of Sociology*, 38 (2): 273–283.

—— (1953): *Essays in Sociology and Social Psychology*, London, Routledge.

Margold, Charles W. (1926): *Sex Freedom and Social Control*, Chicago, University of Chicago Press.

Martindale, Don (1960): *The Nature and Types of Sociological Theory*, Boston, Houghton Mifflin.

Masuoka, Jitsuichi; Valien, Preston (eds.) (1961): *Race Relations. Problems and Theory*, Chapel Hill (NC), University of North Carolina Press.

Mathewson, Stanley B. (1931): *Restriction of Output among Unorganized Workers*, New York, Viking Press.

Matthews, Fred H. (1977): *Quest for an American Sociology. Robert E. Park and the Chicago School*, Montréal (Canada), McGill-Queen's University Press.

—— (1987): "Louis Wirth and American Ethnic Studies. The Worldview of in Enlightened Assimilationism, 1925–1950," Moses Rischin (ed.): *The Jews of North America*, Detroit (MI), Wayne State University Press: 123–143.

—— (1989): "Social Scientists and the Culture Concept, 1930–1950. The Conflict between Processual and Structural Approaches," *Sociological Theory*, 7 (1): 106–120.

Matthews, Jean V. (2004): *The Rise of the New Woman. The Women's Movement in America, 1875–1930*, Chicago, Ivan R. Dee.

Matza, David (1969): *Becoming Deviant*, Englewood Cliffs (NJ), Prentice Hall.

Mayer, Harold; Wade, Richard (1969): *Chicago. Growth of a Metropolis*, Chicago, University of Chicago Press.

Mayo, Elton (1933): *The Human Problems of an Industrial Civilization*, New York, Macmillan.

Mead, George H. (1918): "The Psychology of Punitive Justice," *American Journal of Sociology*, 23 (5): 577–602.

—— (1934): *Mind, Self, and Society*, Chicago, University of Chicago Press.

Meier, August; Rudwick, Elliott (1976) [1966]: *From Plantation to Ghetto*, New York, Hill and Wang (third edition).

Meltzer, Bernard N.; Petras, John W.; Reynolds, Larry T. (1975): *Symbolic Interactionism. Genesis, Varieties and Criticism*, Boston, Routledge & Kegan Paul.

Mennel, Robert M. (1973): *Thorns and Thistles. Juvenile Delinquents in the United States, 1825–1940*, Hanover (NH), University Press of New Hampshire.

Merton, Robert K. (1938): "Social Structure and Anomie," *American Sociological Review*, 3 (5): 672–682.

—— (1947): "Selected Problems of Field Work in the Planned Community," *American Sociological Review*, 12 (3): 304–312.

—— (1969): "Social Problems and Sociological Theory," in R. K. Merton; R. A. Nisbet (eds.): *Contemporary Social Problems*, New York, Harcourt Brace: 697–737.

Merton, Robert K.; Reader George; Kendall, Patricia L. (1957): *The Student-Physician. Introductory Studies in the Sociology of Medical Education*, Cambridge (MA), Harvard University Press.

Metzger, L. Paul (1971): "American Sociology and Black Assimilation: Conflicting Perspectives," *American Journal of Sociology*, 76 (4): 627–647.

Michael, Jerome; Adler, Mortimer J. (1933): *Crime, Law and Social Science*, New York, Harcourt Brace & Co.

Miller, Herbert A. (1924): *Races, Nations and Classes*, Philadelphia, Lippincott.

Miller, Walter B. (1962): "The Impact of a 'Total-Community' Delinquency Control Project," *Social Problems*, 10 (2): 168–191.

Mills, C. Wright (1943): "The Professional Ideology of Social Pathologists," *American Journal of Sociology*, 49 (2): 165–180.

Miner, Horace (1939): *Saint-Denis. A French-Canadian Parish*, Chicago, University of Chicago Press.

Montgomery, David (1987): *The Fall of the House of Labor. The Workplace, the State and American Labor Activism, 1865–1925*, Cambridge, Cambridge University Press.

Moore, Wilbert E. (1947): "Current Issues in Industrial Sociology," *American Sociological Review*, 12 (3): 651–657.

Morgan, Graham J. (1982): "Preparation for the Advent: The Establishment of Sociology as a Discipline in American Universities in the Late Nineteenth Century," *Minerva*, 20 (1–2): 25–58.

Mowrer, Ernest R. (1927): *Family Disorganization. An Introduction to a Sociological Analysis*, Chicago, University of Chicago Press.

—— (1941): "Methodological Problems in Social Disorganization," *American Sociological Review*, 6 (6): 839–852.

Moynihan, Daniel P. (1965): *The Negro Family. The Case for National Action*, Washington, D.C., Office of Policy Planning and Research (reproduced *in extenso* in Lee Rainwater; William L. Yancey: [1967] *The Moynihan Report and the Politics of Controversy*, Cambridge [MA], MIT Press: 41–124).

Mueller, John H. (1928): "The Automobile. A Sociological Study," PhD in Sociology, University of Chicago.

Muller, Dorothea R. (1966): "Josiah Strong and American Nationalism," *Journal of American History*, 53 (3), 487–503.

Murray, Stephen O. (1986): "Edward Sapir in the "Chicago School" of Sociology," in W. Cowan; M. K. Foster; K. Koerner (eds.): *New Perspectives in Language, Culture and Personality*, Amsterdam (Netherlands), J. Benjamins: 241–287.

—— (1988): "W. I. Thomas, Behaviorist Ethnologist," *Journal of the History of the Behavorial Sciences*, 24 (3): 381–391.

Myrdal, Gunnar (with Richard Steiner and Arnold Rose). (1944): *An American Dilemma: The Negro Problem and Modern Democracy*, New York, Harper and Row.

National Advisory Commission on Civil Disorders. (1968): *Report of the National Advisory Commission on Civil Disorders*, New York, Gossett and Dunlap.

Nelson, Leona Bernice. (1953): "The Secularization of a Church-related College," Ph D. Sociology, University of Chicago.

Nielsen, Waldemar A. (1972): *The Big Foundations*, New York, Columbia University Press.

Oberschall, Anthony (1965): *Empirical Social Research in Germany, 1848–1914*, Paris, Mouton.

Odum, Howard (1910): *Social and Mental Traits of the Negro*, New York, Columbia College.

—— (1943): *Race and Rumors of Race*, Chapel Hill, University of North Carolina Press.

—— (1951): *American Sociology. The Story of Sociology in the United States*, New York, Longmans, Green & Co.

Ogburn William F. (1922): *Social Change With Respect to Culture and Original Nature*, New York, B. W. Heubsch.

—— (1930): "The Folk-Ways of a Scientific Sociology," *Scientific Monthly*, 30 (April): 300–306.

—— (1940): "Social Trends," in Louis Wirth (ed.): *Eleven Twenty-Six. A Decade of Social Science Research*, Chicago, University of Chicago Press: 64–77.

Orbach, Harold L. (1993): "Znaniecki's Contribution to the Polish Peasant," in Renzo Gubert; Luigi Tomasi (eds.): *The Contribution of Florian Znaniecki to Sociological Theory*, Milan (Italy), Franco Angeli: 142–158.

Owens, B. Robert (2012): "Mapping the City: Innovation and Continuity in the Chicago School of Sociology, 1920–1934," *The American Sociologist*, 43 (3): 264–293.

Pacyga, Dominic A. (1991): *Polish Immigrants and Industrial Chicago. Workers on the South Side, 1880–1922*, Columbus, Ohio State University Press.

Palmer, Vivien M. (1928): *Field Studies in Sociology. A Student's Manual*, Chicago, University of Chicago Press.

—— (1932): "The Primary Settlement Area as a Unit of Urban Growth and Organization," PhD in Sociology, University of Chicago.

Park, Robert E. (1904): *Masse und Publikum*, Bern, Lak and Grunau (Switzerland) (English translation: *The Crowd and the Public*, Chicago, The University of Chicago Press, 1972).

—— (1908): "Agricultural Extension Among the Negroes," *The World To-Day*, XV (August): 820–826, in Lyman (1992): 254–261.

—— (1913a): "Negro Home Life and Standards of Living," *The Annals of the American Academy of Political and Social Science*, 49 (September): 147–163, in Lyman (1992): 262–275.

—— (1913b): "Racial Assimilation in Secondary Groups with Particular Reference to the Negro," *Publication of the American Sociological Society*, VIII: 66–83 (*Race and Culture*: 204–220).

—— (1915): "The City: Suggestions for the Investigation of Human Behavior in the City Environment," *American Journal of Sociology*, 20 (5): 577–612.

—— (1917): "Race Prejudice and Japanese-American Relations," "Introduction" in Jesse Steiner (1917) (*Race and Culture*: 223–229).

—— (1918): "Education in Its Relation to the Conflict and Fusion of Cultures," *Publication of the American Sociological Society*, 13: 38–63 (*Race and Culture*: 261–283).

—— (1921): "Sociology and the Social Sciences," *American Journal of Sociology*, 26 (4): 401–424 (*Society*: 187–209).

—— (1922): *The Immigrant Press and Its Control*, New York, Harper and Row.

—— (1923a): "Negro Race Consciousness as Reflected in Race Literature," *American Review*, I (September–October): 505–516 (*Race and Culture*: 284–300).

—— (1923b): "A Race Relations Survey," *Journal of Applied Sociology*, 8: 195–205 (*Race and Culture*: 158–165).

—— (1923c): "National History of the Newspaper," (in *Society*: 89–104).

—— (1924): "Experience and Race Relations," *Journal of Applied Sociology*, 9: 18–24 (*Race and Culture*: 152–157).

—— (1925): "The Concept of Position in Sociology," *Publications of the American Sociological Society*, 20: 1–14 (with another title in *Human Communities*: 165–177).

—— (1926a): "Behind Our Masks," *Survey Graphic*, 56 (May): 135–139 (*Race and Culture*: 244–255).

—— (1926b): "Our Racial Frontier on the Pacific," *Survey Graphic*, 56 (May): 192–196 (*Race and Culture*: 138–151).

—— (1928a): "The Bases of Race Prejudice," *Annals of the American Academy of Political and Social Science*, 140 (November): 11–20 (*Race and Culture*: 230–243).

—— (1928b): "Human Migration and the Marginal Man," *American Journal of Sociology*, 37 (6): 881–893 (*Race and Culture*: 354–356).

—— (1929): "The City as a Social Laboratory," in T. V. Smith; Leonard D. White (ed.): *Chicago. An Experiment in Social Science Research*, Chicago, University of Chicago Press: 1–19 (*Human Communities*: 73–87).

—— (1930a): "Murder and the Case-Study Method," *American Journal of Sociology*, 36 (3): 447–454.

—— (1930b): "Social Assimilation," *International Encyclopedia of the Social Sciences*, vol 2: 281–283.

—— (1931a): "The Sociological Methods of William Graham Sumner and of William I. Thomas and Florian Znaniecki," in S. A. Rice (ed.): *Methods in Social Science. A Case Book*, Chicago, University of Chicago Press (*Society*: 243–266).

—— (1931b): "The Problem of Cultural Differences" (*Race and Culture*: 3–24).

—— (1934): "Industrial Fatigue and Group Morale," *American Journal of Sociology*, 40 (3): 349–356 (*Society*: 293: 300).

—— (1935): "Politics and the 'Man Farthest Down,'" in Gosnell (1935): xiii–xxv (*Race and Culture*: 166–176).

—— (1936): "Human Ecology," *American Journal of Sociology*, 42 (1): 1–15 (*Human Communities*: 145–158).

—— (1937a): "The Etiquette of Race Relations in the South," in B. Doyle (1937): xi–xxiv (*Race and Culture*: 177–188).

—— (1937b): "The Race Relations Cycle in Hawaii," in R. Adams (1937): vii–xiv (*Race and Culture*: 189–195).

—— (1939a): "Symbiosis and Socialization: A Frame of Reference for the Study of Society," *American Journal of Sociology*, 45 (1): 1–25 (*Human Communities*: 240–261).

—— (1939b): "The Nature of Race Relations," in Edgar T. Thompson (ed.): *Race Relations and the Race Problem*, Durham (NC), Duke University Press: 3–45 (*Race and Culture*: 81–116).

—— (1941): "Methods of Teaching. Impressions and a Verdict," *Social Forces*, 20 (1): 36–46.

—— (1942): "The Career of the Africans in Brazil," in Pierson (1942): xi–xxi (*Race and Culture*: 196–203).

—— (1943): "Race Ideologies," in W. F. Ogburn (ed.): *American Society in Wartime*, Chicago, University of Chicago Press: 165–183 (*Race and Culture*: 310–315).

—— (1944): "Missions and the Modern World," *American Journal of Sociology*, 50 (3): 177–183 (*Race and Culture*: 331–341).

—— (sd): "An Autobiographical Note," in *Race and Culture*: v–ix.

—— (1950–1955): *The Collected Papers of Robert Ezra Park*, Everett C. Hughes; Charles S. Johnson; Jitsuichi Masuoka; Robert Redfield; Louis Wirth (eds.), Glencoe (IL), Free Press: Vol. 1 (1950), *Race and Culture*; Vol. 2 (1952), *Human Communities. The City and Human Ecology*; Vol. 3 (1955), *Society. Collective Behavior, News and Opinion, Sociology and Modern Society*.

—— (2008): *Le sociologue et le journaliste*, Paris, Seuil/Presses de Sciences Po (French translation of essays on the press, presented by Géraldine Muhlman and Edwy Plenel).

Park, Robert E.; Burgess, Ernest W. (1924) [1921]: *Introduction to the Science of Sociology*, Chicago, University of Chicago Press.

Park, Robert E.; Burgess, Ernest W. (1925): *The City*, Chicago, University of Chicago Press.

Park, Robert E.; Miller, Herbert A. (1921): *Old World Traits Transplanted*, New York, Harper.

Parmelee, Maurice (1918): *Criminology*, New York, Macmillan.

Passeron, Jean-Claude (2006) [1991]: *Le raisonnement sociologique*, Paris, Albin Michel.

Parot, Joseph John (1981): *Polish Catholics in Chicago, 1850–1920*, DeKalb, Northern Illinois University Press.

Parsons, Talcott (1939): "The Professions and Social Structure," *Social Forces*, 17 (4): 457–467.

—— (1942): "Propaganda and Social Control," *Psychiatry*, 5: 551–572.

—— (1951): *The Social System*, New York, Free Press.

Parsons, Talcott; Barber, Bernard (1948): "Sociology, 1941–1946," *American Journal of Sociology*, 53 (4): 245–257.

Peneff, Jean (1990): *La méthode biographique. De l'École de Chicago à l'histoire orale*, Paris, Armand Colin.

Peretz, Henri (1996): "Preface," in Whyte (1996): 5–27.

Perlman, Richard I. (1959): "Delinquency Prevention: The Size of the Problem," *The Annals of the American Academy of Political and Social Science*, 322: 1–9.

Persons, Stow (1987): *Ethnic Studies at Chicago, 1905–1945*, Urbana, University of Illinois Press.

Pestre, Dominique (1995): "Pour une histoire culturelle des sciences," *Annales*, 50, 3, 487–522.

—— (ed.) (2015): *Histoire des sciences et des savoirs*, vol. 3, Paris, Éditions du Seuil, 2015.

Philpott, Thomas L. (1978): *The Slum and the Ghetto. Neighborhood Deterioration and Middle-Class Reform in Chicago, 1880–1930*, New York, Oxford University Press.

Pierson, Donald (1942): *Negroes in Brazil. A Study of Race Contact at Bahia*, Chicago, University of Chicago Press.

Piven, Frances F.; Cloward, Richard A. (1971): *Regulating the Poor. The Function of Public Welfare*, New York, Pantheon Books.

Platt, Anthony M. (1969): *The Child Savers*, Chicago, University of Chicago Press.

—— (1991): *E. Franklin Frazier Reconsidered*, New Brunswick (NJ), Rutgers University Press.

Platt, Jennifer (1983): "The Development of the 'Participant Observation' Method in Sociology: Origin Myth and History," *Journal of the History of the Behavorial Sciences*, 19 (4): 379–393.

—— (1993): "Networks of Scientism," unpublished lecture.

—— (1992): "Acting as a Switchboard. Mrs. Ethel Sturges Dummer's Role in Sociology," *American Sociologist*, 23 (3): 23–36.

—— (1996): *A History of Sociological Methods in America, 1920–1960*, Cambridge (UK), Cambridge University Press.

—— (1997): "Hughes et l'École de Chicago: Méthodes de recherches, réputations et réalités," *Sociétés Contemporaines*, 27: 13–27.

Polanyi, Michael (1966): *The Tacit Dimension*, London, Routledge.

Polsky, Ned (1969) [1967]: *Hustlers, Beats and Others*, Chicago, University of Chicago Press.

Pomian, Krystof (1999): *Sur l'histoire*, Paris, Gallimard.

Pullman, Douglas R. (1972): "Nels Anderson," lecture delivered on the occasion of Dr. Nels Anderson receiving the Honorary Doctor in Laws from the University of New Brunswick.

Queen, Stuart A. (1957): "Social Disorganization," *Sociology and Social Research*, 42 (3): 167–175.

Raboteau, Albert J. (1978): *Slave Religion. The Invisible Institution in the Antebellum South*, New York, Oxford University Press.

Rainwater, Lee (1969): "The Sociologist as Naturalist," in I. L. Horowitz (1969): 91–100.

Raper, Arthur F. (1936): *Preface to Peasantry. A Tale of Two Black Belt Counties*, Chapel Hill, University of North Carolina Press.

Raushenbush, Winifred (1979): *Robert Park. Biography of a Sociologist*, Durham (NC), Duke University Press.

Reckless, Walter C. (1933): *Vice in Chicago*, Chicago, University of Chicago Press.

Record, Wilson (1951): *The Negro and the Communist Party*, Chapel Hill, University of North Carolina Press.

Redfield, Robert (1941): *The Folk Culture of Yucatan*, Chicago, University of Chicago Press.

Reid, Ira De Augustine (1939): *The Negro Immigrant. His Background, Characteristics and Social Adjustment, 1899–1937*, New York, Columbia University Press.

—— (1940): *In a Minor Key. Negro Youth in Story and Fact*, Washington, D.C., American Council of Education.

Reitman, Ben L. (1937): *Sister of the Road. The Autobiography of Box-Car Bertha as Told to Dr. Ben L. Reitman*, New York, Sheridan House.

Reuter, Edward B. (1926): *The American Race Problem. A Study of the Negro*, New York, Thomas Y. Crowell.

—— (ed.) (1934): *Race and Culture Contacts*, New York, McGraw-Hill.

Reynolds, Marylee (1995): *From Gangs to Gangsters. How American Sociology Organized Crime, 1918–1934*, Guilderland (NY), Harrow and Weston.

Rice, Stuart (1931): "Hypotheses and Verification in Clifford R. Shaw's Studies of Juvenile Delinquency" in Rice (ed.): *Methods in Social Sciences. A Case Book*, Chicago, University of Chicago Press: 549–565.

Richmond, Mary (1899): *Friendly Visiting among the Poor, a Handbook for Charity Workers*, New York, Macmillan.

Roades, Mabel Carter (1906): "A Case Study of Delinquent Boys in the Juvenile Court in Chicago," PhD in Sociology, University of Chicago.

Robbins, Richard (1974): "Charles S. Johnson," in J. Blackwell, M. Janowitz (1974) (eds.): 56–84.

—— (1996): *Sidelines Activist. Charles Johnson and the Struggle for the Civil Rights*, Jackson, University Press of Mississippi.

Rock, Paul (1979): *The Making of Symbolic Interactionism*, Totowa (NJ), Rowman and Littlefield.

Rodgers, Daniel T. (1974): *The Work Ethic in Industrial America, 1850–1920*, Chicago, University of Chicago Press.

—— (1982): "In Search of Progressivism," *Reviews in American History*, 10 (4): 112–132.

Roethlisberger, Fritz J.; Dickson, William J. (1939): *Management and the Worker. An Account of a Research Program Conducted by the Western Electric Company, Hawthorne Works, Chicago*, Cambridge (MA), Harvard University Press.

Roger, Jacques (1995): *Pour une histoire des sciences à part entière*, Paris, Albin Michel.

Rose, Arnold M. (ed.) (1962): *Human Behavior and Social Processes. An Interactionist Approach*, London, Routledge & Kegan Paul.

Rose, Michael (1976): *Industrial Behaviour*, Harmondsworth (UK), Penguin, Macmillan.

Rosen, Ruth (1982): *The Lost Sisterhood. Prostitution in America, 1900–1918*, Baltimore, Johns Hopkins University Press.

Rosenberg, Rosalind (1982): *Beyond Separate Spheres. Intellectual Roots of Modern Feminism*, New Haven (CT), Yale University Press.

Ross, Dorothy (1991): *The Origins of American Social Science*, London, Cambridge University Press.

Rossi, Peter H. (1964): "New Directions for Race Relations Research in the Sixties," *Review of Religious Research*, 5 (3): 125–132.

Roth, Julius A. (1959): "Letter to the Editor," *American Sociological Review*, 24 (3): 398.

—— (1963): *Timetables. Structuring the Passage of Time in Hospital Treatment and Other Careers*, New York, Bobbs-Merrill.

—— (1965): "Hired Hand Research," *The American Sociologist*, 1 (1): 190–196.

Roy, Donald (1935): "Hooverville. A Study of a Community of Homeless Men in Seattle," MA Thesis, University of Washington.

—— (1939): "Hooverville. A Community of Homeless Men," *Studies in Sociology* (Southern Methodist University, Dallas [TX]), IV (1–2): 37–45.

—— (1950): "Participation, the Key to Cooperation," Conference at the University of North Carolina, in ADR, folder L.

—— (1952a): "Restriction of Output by Machine Operators in a Piecework Machine Shop," PhD in Sociology, University of Chicago.

—— (1952b): "Quota Restriction and Goldbricking in a Machine Shop," *American Journal of Sociology*, 57 (5): 425–442.

—— (1953): "Work Satisfaction and Social Reward in Quota Achievement," *American Sociological Review*, 18 (5): 507–514.

—— (1954): "Efficiency and the Fix: Informal Intergroup Relations in a Piecework Machine Shop," *American Journal of Sociology*, 60 (3): 255–266.

—— (sd) [1954]: "Cooperation and Conflict in the Factory: Some Observations and Questions Regarding Conceptualization of Intergroup Relations within Bureaucratic Social Structure," unpublished article, in ADR, folder L, Duke University (English translation (2006): "Cooperation and Conflict in the Factory: Some Observations and Questions Regarding Conceptualization of Intergroup Relations within Bureaucratic Social Structures," *Qualitative Sociology*, 29 (1): 55–57).

—— (1959): "Banana Time," *Human Organization*, 18 (4): 158–168.

—— (1962): "Deus ex Machina. Unresolved Problems of Industrial Relations and Their Pending Solution," Conference in Symposium Interpersonal Relations and Group Dynamics, University of North Carolina, Chapel Hill, March 11–13, in ADR, folder L.

—— (1969): "Introduction," in Stanley B. Mathewson: *Restriction of Output among Unorganized Workers*, Carbondale and Edwardsville, Southern Illinois University Press, Felter & Simons: xv–lii.

—— (1970): "The Study of Southern Labor Union Organizing Campaigns," in Robert W. Habenstein (ed.): *Pathways to Data. Field Methods for Studying Ongoing Social Organizations*, Chicago, Aldine: 216–244.

—— (1974): "Sex in the Factory: Informal Heterosexual Relations between Supervisors and Work Groups," in Clifton D. Bryant (ed.): *Deviant Behaviour. Occupational and Organizational Bases*, London, Rand McNally College Pub: 44–66.

—— (1978): "Human Labor and Humane Labor," Conference Freedom and Equality in the American Economy, Hilton Inn, Burlington (NC), March 9–11, in ADR, folder G.

—— (1980): "Book Review: *Manufacturing Consent* by Michael Burawoy," *Berkeley Journal of Sociology*, 24: 329–339.

—— (2006): *Un sociologue à l'usine*, Paris, La découverte (French translation of Roy, 1952b; 1953; 1954; 1954b; 1974; 1959; 1980; original publication of [1954]).

Rucker, Darnell (1969): *The Chicago Pragmatists*, Minneapolis, University of Minnesota Press.

Saint Arnaud, Pierre (2003): *L'invention de la sociologie noire aux États-Unis. Essai en sociologie de la connaissance scientifique*, Quebec City (Canada), Presses de l'université Laval/Syllepse.

Salerno, Roger A. (1987): *Louis Wirth. A Bio-Bibliography*, Westport (CT), Greenwood Press.

—— (2007): *Sociology Noir. Studies at the University of Chicago in Loneliness*, Jefferson (NC), McFarland.

Scott, Emmet J. (1920): *Negro Migration during the War*, New York, Oxford University Press.

Seidman, Steven (1985): "The Historicist Controversy: A Critical Review with a Defense of a Revised Presentism," *Sociological Theory*, 3 (1), 13–16.

Sellin, Thorsten (1938a): *Culture Conflict and Crime*, New York, Social Science Research Council.

—— (1938b): "Culture Conflict and Crime," *American Journal of Sociology*, 44 (1): 97–103.

Shaw, Clifford R. (1930): *The Jack-Roller. A Delinquent Boy's Own Story*, Chicago, University of Chicago Press.

Shaw, Clifford R.; McKay, Henry D. (1931): *Social Factors in Juvenile Delinquency, Report on the Causes of Crime, vol. 2, Report of the National Commission on Law Observance and Law Enforcement*, Washington, D.C., US Government Printing Office.

—— (1932): "Are Broken Homes a Causative Factor in Juvenile Delinquency?" *Social Forces*, 10 (4): 514–524.

—— (1942): *Juvenile Delinquency and Urban Areas*, Chicago, University of Chicago Press.

Shaw, Clifford R.; Zorbaugh, Frederick; McKay, Henry D.; Cottrell, Leonard S. (1929): *Delinquency Areas*, Chicago, University of Chicago Press.

Shaw, Clifford R.; Moore, Maurice E. (1931): *The Natural History of a Delinquent Career*, Chicago, University of Chicago Press.

Shaw, Clifford R.; McKay, Henry D.; McDonald, James F. (1938): *Brothers in Crime*, Chicago, University of Chicago Press.

Shibutani, Tamotsu (1966): *Improvised News. A Sociological Study of Rumor*, New York, Bobbs-Merrill.

—— (1970) (ed.): *Human Nature and Collective Behavior. Papers in Honor of Herbert Blumer*, New York, Prentice Hall.

Shibutani, Tamotsu; Kwan, Kian (1964): *Ethnic Stratification*, New York, Macmillan.

Shideler, Ernest H. (1925): "The Business Center as an Institution," *Journal of Applied Sociology*, 9 (4): 269–275.

—— (1927): "The Chain Store: A Study of the Ecological Organization of a Modern City," PhD in Sociology, University of Chicago.

Shils, Edward (1948): *The Present State of American Sociology*, Glencoe, Free Press.

—— (1980): *The Calling of Sociology and Other Essays on the Pursuit of Learning*, Chicago, University of Chicago Press.

—— (1990): "Robert Maynard Hutchins," *The American Scholar*, 59 (2): 211–235.

—— (1991a): "Robert E. Park, 1864–1944," *The American Scholar*, 60 (1): 120–27.

—— (1991b): "Ernest W. Burgess" in E. Shils (ed.): *Remembering the University of Chicago. Teachers, Scientists, and Scholars*, Chicago, University of Chicago Press: 3–14.

Shore, Marlene (1987): *The Science of Social Redemption. McGill, the Chicago School and the Origins of Social Research in Canada*, Toronto (Canada), University of Toronto Press.

Short, James F. (1969): "A Natural History of One Sociological Career," in I. L. Horowitz (1969): 117–132.

Schwendinger, Herman; Schwendinger, Julia R. (1974): *The Sociologists of the Chair. A Radical Analysis of the Formative Years of North American Sociology, 1883–1922*, New York, Basic Books.

Sibley, Elbridge (1963): *The Education of Sociologists in the United States*, New York, Russell Sage.

—— (1974): *Social Science Research Council. The First Fifty Years*, New York, SSRC.

Sica, Alan (1990): "A Question of Priority: Small at Chicago or Blackmar at Kansas?" *Mid-American Review of Sociology*, 14 (1–2): 1–12.

Simmel, Georg (1908): *Soziologie. Untersuchungen über die Formen der Vergesellschaftung*, Leipzig (Germany), Duncker & Humblot.

—— (1908): "Exkurs über den Fremden," in *Soziologie. Untersuchungen über die Formen der Vergesellschaftung*, Leipzig (Germany), Duncker & Humblot (Partial English translation: "The Sociological Significance of the 'Stranger,' " in Park, Burgess (1924): 322–327).

Simpson, Richard L. (1961): "Expanding and Declining Fields in American Sociology," *American Sociological Review*, 26 (3): 458–466.

Singer, L (1962): "Ethnogenesis and Negro-Americans Today," *Social Research*, 29 (4): 419–432.

Siu, Paul C. P. (1953): "The Chinese Laundryman: A Study in Social Isolation," PhD in Sociology, University of Chicago.

—— (1987): *The Chinese Laundryman. A Study in Social Isolation*, New York, New York University Press.

Skinner, Quentin (1969): "Meaning and Understanding in the History of Ideas," *History and Theory*, 8 (1): 3–53.

Small, Albion K. (1895): "The Era of Sociology," *American Journal of Sociology*, 1 (1): 1–15.

—— (1896): "Scholarship and Social Agitation," *American Journal of Sociology*, 1 (5): 564–582.

—— (1905): *General Sociology*, Chicago, University of Chicago Press.

—— (1912): "Socialism in the Light of Social Science," *American Journal of Sociology*, 17 (6): 804–819.

—— (1916): "Fifty Years of Sociology in the United States," *American Journal of Sociology*, 21 (6): 721–864.

Small, Albion K.; Vincent, George E. (1894): *An Introduction to the Study of Society*, New York, American Book.

Smelser, Neil J. (1986): "The Ogburn Vision Fifty Years Later," in N. J. Smelser; D. R. Gerstein (eds.): *Behavioral and Social Science. Fifty Years of Discovery*, Washington, D.C., National Academy Press: 21–35.

Smigel, Erwin O. (1954): "Trends in Occupational Sociology in the United States: A Survey of Postwar Research," *American Sociological Review*, 19 (4): 398–404.

Smith Charles U.; Killian, Lewis (1974): "Black Sociologists and Social Protest," in Blackwell; Janowitz (1974): 191–228.

Smith, Dennis (1988): *The Chicago School. A Liberal Critique of Capitalism*, London, Macmillan.

Smith, Harvey L. (1947): "The Sociology of Race in Industry," MA in Sociology, University of Chicago.

Smith, T. V.; White, Leonard D. (eds.) (1929): *Chicago. An Experiment in Social Science*. Chicago, University of Chicago Press.

Snodgrass, Jon (1976): "Clifford R. Shaw and Henry D. McKay: Chicago Criminologists," *The British Journal of Criminology*, 16 (1): 1–19.

—— (ed.) (1982): *The Jack-Roller at Seventy*, Lexington (MA), D. C. Heath and Co.

Snow, David A.; Davis, Philip W. (1995): "The Chicago Approach to Collective Behavior," in Fine (1995): 188–22.

Sobel, Mechal (1987): *The World They Made Together*, Princeton (NJ), Princeton University Press.

Solenberger, Alice W. (1911): *One Thousand Homeless Men*, New York, Russell Sage Foundation.

Solomon, David N. (1952): "Career Contingencies of the Chicago Physician," PhD in Sociology, University of Chicago.

Sorokin, Pitirim A. (1936): "Is Accurate Planning Possible?" *American Sociological Review*, 1 (1): 12–28.

—— (1963): *A Long Journey*, New Haven (CT), College and University Press.

Sorrentino, Anthony. (1972): *Organizing against Crime. Redeveloping the Neighborhood*, New York, Human Sciences Press.

Southern, David W. (1987): *Gunnar Myrdal and Black-White Relations. The Use and Abuse of "An American Dilemma," 1944–1969*, Baton Rouge, Louisiana State University Press.

Spear, Allan H. (1967): *Black Chicago. The Making of a Negro Ghetto, 1890–1920*, Chicago, University of Chicago Press.

Spence, Clark C. (1971): "Knights of the Tie and Rail—Tramps and Hoboes in the West," *Western Historical Quarterly*, 2 (January): 5–19.

Spero, Sterling D.; Harris, Abram L. (1931): *The Black Worker. The Negro and the Labor Movement*, New York, Columbia University Press.

Stanfield, John H. (1984): "Dollars for the Silent South," in Merle Back; John S. Reed (eds.): *Perspectives on the American South*, vol. 2, New York, Gordon and Breach: 117–138.

—— (1985): *Philanthropy and Jim Crow in American Social Science*, Westport (CT), Greenwood.

Steffens, Lincoln (1904): *The Shame of the Cities*, New York, McClure, Philips & Co.

Stephan, Frederick F. (1926): "Some Social Aspects of the Telephone," MA in Sociology, University of Chicago.

Steinberg, Stephen (1981): *The Ethnic Myth. Race, Ethnicity, and Class in America*, Boston, Beacon Press.

—— (1995): *Turning Back. The Retreat from Racial Justice in American Thought and Policy*, Boston, Beacon Press.

Steiner, Jesse (1917): *The Japanese Invasion*, Chicago, A. C. McClung & Co.

—— (1956): "Comments on Changes in American Sociology," *Sociology and Social Research*, 40 (6): 409–411.

Stocking George W. Jr. (1965): "On the Limits of 'Presentism' and 'Historicism' in the Historiography of the Behavorial Sciences," *Journal of the History of the Behavorial Sciences*, 1 (3): 211–218.

—— (1968): *Race, Culture and Evolution. Essays in the History of Anthropology*, Chicago, University of Chicago Press.

—— (1979): *Anthropology at Chicago*, Chicago, Joseph Regeinstein Library, University of Chicago.

—— (1985): "Philanthropoids and Vanishing Cultures," *History of Anthroplogy*, 3: 113–145.

Stonequist, Everett V. (1937): *The Marginal Man*, New York, Charles Scribner's Sons.

Storr, Richard J. (1966): *Harper's University. The Beginning*, Chicago, University of Chicago Press.

Stouffer, Samuel A.; Suchman Edward A.; De Vinney Leland C.; Williams, Robin J. Jr. (1949): *The American Soldier. Adjustment during Army Life* (Studies in Social Psychology in World War II, vol. I), New York, Wiley.

Stouffer, Samuel A.; Lumsdaine, Arthur A.; Lumdsdaine, Marion Harper; Williams, Robin M. (1949): *The American Soldier. Combat and its Aftermath* (Studies in Social Psychology in World War II, vol. II), Princeton (NJ), Princeton University Press.

Strauss, Anselm L. (1964): "Introduction," in Georges H. Mead (1956): *Georges H. Mead: On Social Psychology*, Chicago, University of Chicago Press: vii–xxv.

—— (1991): "The Chicago Tradition's Ongoing Theory of Action/Interaction," in A. L. Strauss: *Creating Sociological Awareness*, New Brunswick (NJ), Transaction Publishers: 3–32.

—— (1996a): "Everett Hughes: Sociology's Mission," *Symbolic Interaction*, 19 (4): 271–283.

—— (1996b): "A Partial Line of Descent: Blumer and I," *Studies in Symbolic Interaction*, 20: 3–22.

Strauss, Anselm L.; Schatzman, Leonard; Bucher, Rue; Ehrlich, Danuta; Sabshin, Melvin (1964): *Psychiatric Ideologies and Institutions*, New York, Free Press.

Strickland, Arvarh E. (1966): *History of the Chicago Urban League*, Urbana, University of Illinois Press.

Strong, Josiah (1885): *Our Country. Its Possible Future and Its Present Crisis*, New York, The American Home Mission society.

—— (1895): "Local Alliances," *American Journal of Sociology*, 1 (2): 170–181.

—— (1913): *Our World. The New World-Life*, Garden City (NY), Doubleday.

Stuckey, Sterling (1977): *Slave Culture. Naturalist Theory and the Foundations of Black America*, New York, Oxford University Press.

Sumner, William Graham (1906): *Folkways. A Study of the Sociological Importance of Usages, Manners, Customs, Mores and Morals*, New York, Ginn & Co.

Sutherland, Edwin H. (1934): *Principles of Criminology*, Philadelphia (PA), J. B. Lippincott (2nd edition under a new title).

—— (ed.) (1937):*The Professional Thief*, Chicago, University of Chicago Press.

—— (1940): "White-Collar Criminality," *American Sociological Review*, 5 (1): 1–12.

—— (1945): "Social Pathology," *American Journal of Sociology*, 50 (6): 429–435.

Szacki, Jerzy (1981): "Réflexions sur l'histoire de la sociologie", *Revue Internationale des Sciences Sociales*, 33 (2), 270–281.

Taft, Donald R. (1936): "Nationality and Crime," *American Sociological Review*, 1 (5): 724–736.

Tanenhaus, David (2004):*Juvenile Justice in the Making*, Oxford, Oxford University Press.

Tannenbaum, Frank (1938): *Crime and the Community*, New York, Ginn & Co.

—— (1969): *The Balance of Power in Society and Other Essays*, New York, Macmillan Publishers.

Taylor, Graham (1911): "The Story of the Chicago Vice Commission," *The Survey*, May 6: 239–247.

Taylor, Graham R. (1915): *Satellite Cities. A Study of Industrial Suburbs*, New York, D. Appleton and Co.

Thomas, Evan A. (1978): "Herbert Blumer's Critique of *The Polish Peasant*: A Post Mortem on the Life History Approach in Sociology," *Journal of the History of the Behavorial Sciences*, 14 (2): 124–131.

—— (1986): "The Sociology of William I. Thomas in Relation to 'The Polish Peasant,'" PhD, University of Iowa.

Thomas, John L. (1950): "Marriage Prediction in *The Polish Peasant*," *American Journal of Sociology*, 55 (6): 572–77.

Thomas, Wiliam I. (1896): "On a Difference of the Metabolism of the Sexes," PhD in Sociology, University of Chicago.

—— (1901): "The Gaming Instinct," *American Journal of Sociology*, 6 (6): 750–763.

—— (1905): "The Province of Social Psychology," *American Journal of Sociology*, 10 (4): 445–455.

—— (1906): "Review of *The Life Stories of Undistinguished Americans as Told by Themselves* by Hamilton Holt," *American Journal of Sociology*, 12 (2): 273–274.

—— (1906): "The Adventitious Character of Woman," *American Journal of Sociology*, 12 (1): 32–44.

—— (1907): "The Mind of Woman and the Lower Races," *American Journal of Sociology*, 12 (4): 435–469.

—— (1907): *Sex and Society. Studies in the Social Psychology of Sex*, Chicago, University of Chicago Press.

—— (1908): "The Significance of the Orient for the Occident," *American Journal of Sociology*, 13 (6): 729–742.

—— (1909): "Woman and the Occupations," *American Magazine*, 68 (September): 463–470.

—— (1909): *Sourcebook for Social Origins. Ethnological Materials, Psychological Standpoint, Classified and Annotated Bibliographies for the Interpretation of Savage Societies*, Chicago, University of Chicago Press.

—— (1912): "Race Psychology: Standpoint and Questionnaire, with Particular Reference to the Immigrant and the Negro," *American Journal of Sociology*, 17 (6): 725–773.

—— (1914): "The Prussian-Polish Situation: An Experiment in Assimilation," *American Journal of Sociology*, 19 (5): 624–639.

—— (1917): "The Persistence of Primary Group Norms in Present Day Society," in H. S. Jennings; J. B. Watson; A. Meyer; W. I. Thomas (eds.): *Suggestions of Modern Science Concerning Education*, New York, Macmillan: 171–197, in Thomas (1966): 168–181.

—— (1918): "The Professor's Views," *Chicago Tribune*, 22 April 1918: 15–16.

—— (1923): *The Unadjusted Girl. With Cases and Standpoint for Behavior Analysis*. Criminal science monograph, no. 4, Boston. Supplement to the *Journal of the American Institute of Criminal Law and Criminology*.

—— (1927): "The Configuration of Personality," in *The Unconscious. A Symposium*, Knopf: 143–177.

—— (1936): *Primitive Behavior: An Introduction to the Social Science*, New York, McGraw-Hill.

—— (1966): *W. I. Thomas on Social Organization and Personality*, Morris Janowitz (ed.), Chicago, University of Chicago Press.

Thomas, William I.; Znaniecki, Florian (1927) [1918–1920]: *The Polish Peasant in Europe and America*, New York, Knopf (first edition, vols. 1–2: Chicago, University of Chicago Press; vols. 3–5: Boston, Badger Press).

Thomas, William I., Thomas, Dorothy Swaine (1928): *The Child in America. Behavior Problems and Programs*, New York, Knopf.

Thomas, Dorothy Swaine (1970): "Contribution to the Herman Wold Festschrift," in Tore Dalenius; Georg Karlsson; Sten Malmquist (eds.), *Scientists at Work. Festschrift in Honour of Herman Wold*, Stockholm (Sweden): Almqvist and Wiksell, 213–227.

Thompson, Edgar T. (1932): "The Plantation," PhD in Sociology, University of Chicago.

—— (ed.) (1939): *Race Relations and the Race Problem. A Definition and an Analysis*, Durham (NC), Duke University Press.

—— (1945): "Sociology and Social Research in the South," *Social Forces*, 23 (3): 356–365.

—— (1970): "Sociology at Duke University," Department of Sociology, Duke University (handwritten, 26 pages).

—— (1975): *Plantation Societies, Race Relations and the South. The Regimentation of Populations*, Selected Papers, Durham (NC), Duke University Press.

Thompson, Helen Bradford (1903): *The Mental Traits of Sex. An Experimental Investigation of the Normal Mind in Men and Women*, Chicago, University of Chicago Press.

Topalov, Christian (2003): "La fin des communautés locales vue par un sociologue de Chicago, Harvey W. Zorbaugh," *Annales de la recherche urbaine*, 93: 159–167.

—— (2007): "Femmes du monde: un sociologue enquête à Chicago en 1924," *Genèses*, 66: 138–161.

—— (2008): "Sociologie d'un étiquetage scientifique: urban sociology (Chicago, 1925)," *Année sociologique*, 58, (1): 203–234.

—— (2014): "Le Local Community Research Committee, la recherche sur projet et l'âge d'or' de la sociologie de Chicago (1923–1930)," *Genèses*, 94: 81–113.

—— (2015): *Histoires d'enquêtes. Londres, Paris, Chicago (1880–1930)*, Paris, Éditions Garnier.

Thrasher, Frederic M. (1926): "The Gang as a Symptom of Community Disorganization," *Journal of Applied Sociology*, 11 (1): 3–20.

—— (1927): *The Gang. A Study of 1,313 Gangs in Chicago*, Chicago, University of Chicago Press.

Throop, Robert, and Lloyd Gordon Ward. (2007). "A Beautiful and Impressive Southern Woman of Decidedly Individualistic Outlook: Notes on the Life of Harriet Park Thomas." The Mead Project. https://brocku.ca/MeadProject/Scrapbooks/Holding/Harriet_Thomas2.html.

Toulmin, Stephen (1977): "From Form to Function: Philosophy and History of Science in the 1950s and Now," *Daedalus*, 106 (3): 143–162.

Turner, Ralph H. (1988): "Collective Behavior without Guile. Chicago in the Late 1940s," *Sociological Perspectives*, 31 (3): 315–324.

Turner, Stephen Park; Turner, Jonathan H. (1990): *The Impossible Science. An Institutional Analysis of American Sociology*, Beverly Hills (CA), Sage.

Valentine, Charles A. (1968): *Culture and Poverty, Critique and Counter Proposals*, Chicago, University of Chicago Press.

Valien, Preston: (1958): "Sociological Contributions of Charles Johnson," *Sociology and Social Research*, 42 (4): 243–248.

Vander Zanden, James W. (1973): "Sociological Studies of American Blacks," *Sociological Quarterly*, 13 (1): 32–52.

Van Kleek, Mary (1946): "Towards an Industrial Sociology," *American Sociological Review*, 11 (5): 501–505.

Verdet, Paule (1996): "Une Française à l'école de Hughes," *Sociétés Contemporaines*, 27: 59–66.

Verhoeven, Jef C. (1993): "An Interview with Erving Goffman," *Research on Language and Social Interaction*, 26 (3): 317–348.

—— (1995): *Methodological and Metascientific Problems in Symbolic Interactionism*, Katolieke Universiteit, Leuven, Belgium.

Veyne, Paul (1971): *Comment on écrit l'histoire. Essai d'épistémologie*, Paris, Éditions du Seuil.

Veysey, Laurence R. (1965): *Emergence of the American University*, Chicago, University of Chicago Press.

Vice Commission of Chicago (1911): *The Social Evil in Chicago. A Study of Existing Conditions with Recommendations*, Chicago, Illinois.

Vidich, Arthur J.; Lyman, Stanford M. (1985): *American Sociology. Worldly Rejections of Religion and Their Directions*, New Haven (CT), Yale University Press.

Vlasek, Dale R. (1982): "E. Franklin Frazier and the Problem of Assimilation," in Hamilton Cravens (ed.): *Ideas in America's Culture*, Ames, Iowa State University Press.

Volkart, Edmund H. (ed.) (1951): *Social Behaviour and Personality, Contributions of W. I. Thomas to Theory and Social Research*, New York, SSRC (republished by Greenwood [1981]).

Wacker, Fred R. (1975): "Race and Ethnicity in American Social Science, 1900–1950," PhD in History, University of Michigan.

—— (1983): *Ethnicity Pluralism and Race. Race Relations Theory in America before Myrdal*, Westport (CT), Greenwood.

—— (1995): "The Sociology of Race and Ethnicity in the Second Chicago School," in Fine (1995): 136–163.

Wade, Louise (1964): *Graham Taylor. A Pioneer for Social Justice, 1851–1938*, Chicago, University of Chicago Press.

Waite, Cally L. (2001): "The Segregation of Black Students at Oberlin College after Reconstruction," *History of Education Quarterly*, 4 (3): 344–364.

Wallace, Robert W. (1992): "Starting a Department and Getting under Way: Sociology at Columbia, 1891–1914," *Minerva*, 30 (4): 496–512.

Warner, W. Lloyd (1936): "American Caste and Class," *American Journal of Sociology*, 42 (2): 234–237.

Warner, W. Lloyd W.; Davis, Allison (1939): "A Comparative Study of American Caste," in Thompson (1939): 219–245.

Warner, W. Lloyd; Low, Josiah O. (1947): *The Social System of the Modern Factory. The Strike: A Social Analysis*, New Haven (CT), Yale University Press.

Warner, W. Lloyd; Junker, Buford H.; Adams, Walter A. (1941): *Color and Human Nature. Negro Personality Development in a Northern City*, Washington, D.C., American Council of Education.

Warner, Mildred (1988): *W. Lloyd Warner, Social Anthropologist*, New York, New York Publishing Center for Cultural Resources.

Washington, Booker (and Robert Park) (1912): *The Man Farthest Down*, Garden City (NY), Doubleday.

Waskow, Arthur I. (1966): *From Race Riot to Sit-In. 1919 and the 1960s*, Garden City (NY), Doubleday.

Watson, Walter T. (1930): "Division of Labor: A Study in the Sociology and Social Psychology of Work Satisfaction," PhD in Sociology, University of Chicago.

Wax, Murray L. (1972): "Tenting with Malinowski," *American Sociological Review*, 37 (1): 1–13.

—— (1997): "Chicago in the 1950s," conference organized by the Centre de recherches sociologiques et historiques sur l'éducation (CRSHE) at the École Normale Superieure Fonteney-Saint-Cloud, November 6.

Wax, Murray L.; Wax, Rosalie H.; Dumont, Robert V. (1964): *Formal Education in an American Community. Peer Society and the Failure of Minority Education*, Supplement to *Social Problems*, 11 (4) (2nd edition [1989]: Prospect Heights (IL), Waveland Press).

Weber, Marianne (1926): *Max Weber, ein Lebensbild*, Tübingen, J. C. B. Mohr.

Weinberg, Kirson S. (1942): "Aspects of the Prison's Social Structure," *American Journal of Sociology*, 47 (5): 717–726.

Weiss, Richard (1979): "Ethnicity and Reform: Minorities and the Ambiance of the Depression Years," *Journal of American History*, 66 (3): 566–585.

Weiss, Robert S. (1997): "Souvenirs sur Everett Hughes," *Sociétés Contemporaines*, 27: 79–87.

Westley, William A. (1951): "The Police: A Sociological Study of Law, Custom, and Morality," PhD in Sociology, University of Chicago.

—— (1953): "Violence and the Police," *American Journal of Sociology*, 59 (1): 34–41.

—— (1956): "Secrecy and the Police," *Social Forces*, 34 (3): 254–257.

—— (1970): *Violence and the Police: A Sociological Study of Law, Custom and Behavior*, Cambridge (MA), MIT Press.

White, Ronald C.; Hopkins, C. Howard (1976): *The Social Gospel. Religion and Reform in Changing America*, Philadelphia, Temple University Press.

Whitley, Richard (1984): *The Intellectual and Social Organization of the Sciences*, Oxford (UK), Clarendon Press.

Whyte, William Foote (1943a): *Street Corner Society*, Chicago, University of Chicago Press (2nd edition: 1955) (French translation under the same title [1996]: Paris, La Découverte).

—— (1943b): "Social Organization in the Slums," *American Sociological Review*, 8 (1): 34–39.

—— (ed.) (1946): *Industry and Society*, New York, McGraw-Hill.

—— (1948): *Human Relations in the Restaurant Industry*, New York, McGraw-Hill.

—— (1969): "Reflections on my Work," in Horowitz (1969): 44–49.

—— (1987): "From Human Relations to Organizational Behavior: Reflections on the Changing Scene," *Industrial and Labor Relations Review*, 40 (4): 487–500.

—— (1994): *Participant Observer. An Autobiography*, Ithaca (NY), ILR Press.

Wiebe, Robert H. (1967): *The Search for Order, 1877–1920*, New York, Hill and Wang.

Wildes, Henry Emerson (1927): *The Press and Social Currents in Japan*, Chicago, University of Chicago Press.

Wiley, Norbert (1979): "The Rise and Fall of Dominating Theories in American Sociology," in W. E. Snizek; E. R. Fuhrman; M. K. Miller (eds.): *Contemporary Issues in Theory and Research. A Metasociological Perspective*, London, Aldwych Press: 47–79.

—— (1986): "Early American Sociology and the Polish Peasant," *Sociological Theory*, 4 (1): 20–40.

Williams, Josephine (1949): "The Professional Status of Women Physicians," PhD in Sociology, University of Chicago.

Williams Joyce E.; MacLean, Vicky M. (2005): "Studying Ourselves: Sociology Discipline-Building in the United States," *American Sociologist*, 36 (1): 111–133.

Williams, Vernon J. (1989): *From a Caste to a Minority. Changing Attitudes of American Sociologists towards Afro-Americans, 1896–1945*, Westport (CT), Greenwood.

Williamson, Joel (1965): *After Slavery. The Negro in South Carolina During Reconstruction, 1861–1877*, Chapel Hill, University of North Carolina Press.

Wilner, Patricia (1985): "The Main Drift of Sociology between 1936 and 1982," *History of Sociology*, 5 (2): 1–20.

Winkin, Yves (1988): "Erving Goffman: Portrait du sociologue en jeune homme," in Goffman (1988): 13–92.

Wirth, Louis (1928): *The Ghetto*, Chicago, University of Chicago Press.

—— (1931): "Clinical Sociology," *American Journal of Sociology*, 37 (1): 49–66.

—— (1938): "Urbanism as a Way of Life," *American Journal of Sociology*, 44 (1): 1–24.

—— (ed.) (1940): *Eleven Twenty-Six. A Decade of Social Science Research*, Chicago, University of Chicago Press.

—— (1944): "Race and Public Policy," *Scientific Monthly*, 58 (April): 302–312, in Wirth (1964): 270–291.

—— (1945): "The Problems of Minority Group," in R. Linton (ed.): *The Science of Man in the World Crisis*, New York, Columbia University Press: 342–372, in Wirth (1964): 244–269.

—— (1964): *Louis Wirth on Cities and Social Life. Selected Papers*, A. J. Reiss Jr. (ed.), Chicago, University of Chicago Press.

Wirth Marvick, Elizabeth (1964): "Biographical Memorandum," in Wirth (1964): 333–340.

Wiseman, Jacqueline (1987): "In Memoriam Herbert Blumer," *Journal of Contemporary Ethnography*, 16 (3): 243–249.

Wittgenstein, Ludwig (1991): *Philosophical Investigations. The German Text, with a Revised English Translation*, 50th Anniversary Commemorative Edition, Hoboken (NJ), Wiley-Blackwell (English translation from the German *Philosophical Untersuchungen* [1953]).

Woods, Robert A. (ed.) (1898): *The City Wilderness, A Settlement Study by Residents and Associates of the South End House*, Boston, Houghton Mifflin.

Woodward, C. Vann (1974) [1955]: *The Strange Career of Jim Crow*, New York, Oxford University Press (3rd edition).

Woolbert, Richard L. (1930): "The Social Effect of the Radio," MA in Sociology, University of Chicago.

Woolston, Horace (1945): "The Process of Assimilation," *Social Forces*, 23 (4): 416–424.

Worcester, Kenton W. (2001): *Social Science Research Council, 1923–1998*, New York, SSRC (contains Sibley [1974] as an appendix).

Wright, Caroll D. (1899): *Outline of Practical Sociology*, New York, Longmans, Green and Co.

Wright, Nathan Jr. (1967): "The Economics of Race," *American Journal of Economics and Sociology*, 26 (1): 1–12.

Yinger, J. Milton (1968): "Recent Developments in Minority and Race Relations," *The Annals of the American Academy of Political and Social Science*, 378: 130–145.

Young, Erle F. (1925): "The Social Base Map," *Journal of Applied Sociology*, 9 (3): 202–206.

—— (1944): "A Sociological Explorer: Robert E. Park," *Sociology and Social Research*, 28 (6): 436–39.

Young, Kimball (1948): "William Isaac Thomas (1863–1947)," *American Sociological Review*, 13 (1): 102–104.

—— (1962–63): "Contributions of William Isaac Thomas to Sociology," *Sociology and Social Research*, 47 (1): 3–24; 47 (2): 123–137; 47 (3): 251–272; 47 (4): 381–397.

—— (1995): *Kimball Young on Sociology in Transition, 1912–1968. An Oral Account of the 35th President of the ASA*, Fred B. Lindstrom; Ronald A. Hardet; Laura L. Johnson (eds.), Boston, University Press of America.

Young, Pauline V. (1932): *The Pilgrims of Russian-Town*, Chicago, University of Chicago Press.

—— (1939): *Scientific Social Surveys and Research*, New York, Prentice-Hall.

Zaretsky, Eli (1984): "Editor's Introduction," in Thomas, Znanieki, *The Polish Peasant in Europe and America*, abridged edition, Champaign, University of Illinois Press: 1–53.

Znaniecki, Florian (1948): "William I. Thomas as a Collaborator," *Sociology and Social Research*, 32 (4): 765–767.

Zorbaugh, Harvey W. (1929): *The Gold Coast and the Slum. A Sociological Study of Chicago's Near North Side*, Chicago, University of Chicago Press.

Index